CHALLENGES OF EXPANDING INTERNET: E-COMMERCE, E-BUSINESS, AND E-GOVERNMENT

IFIP – The International Federation for Information Processing

IFIP was founded in 1960 under the auspices of UNESCO, following the First World Computer Congress held in Paris the previous year. An umbrella organization for societies working in information processing, IFIP's aim is two-fold: to support information processing within its member countries and to encourage technology transfer to developing nations. As its mission statement clearly states,

> IFIP's mission is to be the leading, truly international, apolitical organization which encourages and assists in the development, exploitation and application of information technology for the benefit of all people.

IFIP is a non-profitmaking organization, run almost solely by 2500 volunteers. It operates through a number of technical committees, which organize events and publications. IFIP's events range from an international congress to local seminars, but the most important are:

- The IFIP World Computer Congress, held every second year;
- Open conferences;
- Working conferences.

The flagship event is the IFIP World Computer Congress, at which both invited and contributed papers are presented. Contributed papers are rigorously refereed and the rejection rate is high.

As with the Congress, participation in the open conferences is open to all and papers may be invited or submitted. Again, submitted papers are stringently refereed.

The working conferences are structured differently. They are usually run by a working group and attendance is small and by invitation only. Their purpose is to create an atmosphere conducive to innovation and development. Refereeing is less rigorous and papers are subjected to extensive group discussion.

Publications arising from IFIP events vary. The papers presented at the IFIP World Computer Congress and at open conferences are published as conference proceedings, while the results of the working conferences are often published as collections of selected and edited papers.

Any national society whose primary activity is in information may apply to become a full member of IFIP, although full membership is restricted to one society per country. Full members are entitled to vote at the annual General Assembly, National societies preferring a less committed involvement may apply for associate or corresponding membership. Associate members enjoy the same benefits as full members, but without voting rights. Corresponding members are not represented in IFIP bodies. Affiliated membership is open to non-national societies, and individual and honorary membership schemes are also offered.

CHALLENGES OF EXPANDING INTERNET: E-COMMERCE, E-BUSINESS, AND E-GOVERNMENT

5th IFIP Conference e-Commerce, e-Business, and e-Government (I3E'2005), October 28-30, 2005, Poznan, Poland

Edited by

Matohisa Funabashi
Hitachi Ltd.
Japan

Adam Grzech
Wroclaw University of Technology
Poland

 Springer

Library of Congress Cataloging-in-Publication Data

A C.I.P. Catalogue record for this book is available from the Library of Congress.

Challenges of Expanding Internet: E-Commerce, E-Business, and E-Government
Edited by Matohisa Funabashi and Adam Grzech

   p. cm. (IFIP International Federation for Information Processing, a Springer Series in
Computer Science)

ISSN: 1571-5736 / 1861-2288 (Internet)
ISBN 978-1-4419-3952-4   e-ISBN 978-0-387-29773-6

Printed on acid-free paper

9 8 7 6 5 4 3 2 1
springeronline.com

Contents

General Chair's Message   xi

Program Co-Chairs' Message   xiii

Program Committee   xv

Organizing Committees   xvii

External Reviewers   xix

Keynotes

Innovations transforming e-Business   xxi
   Liba Svobodova

SAP and the age of logistics. How to meet tomorrows business challenges   xxiii
   Kurt Weiss

Innovative Business Models

Value process and business process in e-Business modeling   1
  Mohammed Dewan, Baolin Wu, Yun Yang

V A3: Governance selection in value webs   17
  Jaap Gordijn, Jasper Soetendal, Edwin Paalvast

From an e-Business revenue model to its software reference architecture   33
  Volker Gruhn, Thorsten Weber

e-Collaboration and e-Services

Selecting supply partners for e-Collaboration   49
  Sung Ho Ha, Gye Hang Hong

e-Collaboration architecture for customer-driven business processes
in inter-organizational scenarios   63
  Otmar Adam, Pavlina Chikova, Anja Hofer, Sven Zang,
  Dominik Vanderhaeghen

Monitoring middleware for service level agreements in
heterogeneous environments   79
  Graham Morgan, Simon Parkin, Carlos Molina-Jimenez, James Skene

G2G, G2B, and G2C Models

Using software agents to personalize access to e-Offices   95
  Jarogniew Rykowski

Evaluating e-Government : a process oriented approach   111
  Christian Seel, Oliver Thomas, Bettina Kaffai, Thomas Matheis

A knowledge-sharing framework for public administrations   125
  Olivier Glassey

One-Stop Government – Service Integration

Configuring e-Government services using ontologies   141
  Dimitris Apostolou, Ljiljana Stojanovic, Tomas Periente Lobo,
  Jofre Casas Miro, Andreas Papadakis

A business rule engine applied to e-Government services integration   157
Aqueo Kamada, Manuel Mendes

Towards dynamic composition of e-Government services:
a policy-based approach   173
Ivo Santos, Edmundo Madeira, Volker Tschammer

e-Government - Trust and Security

Employing ontologies for the development of security critical
applications: the secure e-poll paradigm   187
*Lazaros Gymnopoulos, Maria Karyda, Stelios Dritsas,
Theodoros Balopoulos, Stefanos Gritzalis, S. Kokalakis, C. Lambrinoudakis*

Development and evaluation of a system for checking
for improper sending of personal information in encrypted e-mail   203
*Kenji Yasu, Yasuhiko Akahane, Masami Ozaki,
Koji Semoto, Ryoichi Sasaki*

HYPR&A - a security model for the support of processes
in e-Government   219
Tatyana Podgayetskaya, Wolffried Stucky

e-Health and e-Democracy

Policy-rich multi-agent support for e-Health applications   235
*Lars Braubach, Winfried Lamersdorf, Zoran Milosevic,
Alexander Pokahr*

Pursuing electronic health: a UK primary health care perspective   251
Mkwana Ndeti, George Carlisle

e-Petitioning: enabling ground-up participation   265
Nicholas Adams, Ann Macintosh, Jim Johnston

Architecture of multi channel multi database voting system   281
Annapareddy Vasudhara Reddy, S.V. Raghavan

Public e-Services for Citizens and Enterprises

Practitioner buy-in and resistance to e-enabled information
sharing across agencies   297
Susan Baines, Pat Gannon-Leary, Rob Wilson

LegalURN: a framework for organizing and surfing
legal documents on the web   313
    Caterina Lupo, Luca De Santis, Carlo Batini

A web service approach to geographical data distribution among public
administrations   329
    Lorenzino Vaccari, Alexander Ivanyukovich, Maurizio Marchese

Digital Goods and Products

Second generation micropayment systems: lessons learned   345
    Robert Parhonyi, Lambert J.M. Nieuwenhuis, Aiko Pras

Value analysis of retail electronic payments market   361
    George Rigopoulos, John Psarras, Dimitrios Askounis

Personalized discount – a fuzzy logic approach   375
    Nicolas Werro, Henrik Stormer, Andreas Meier

B2B, B2C, and C2C Models

Dynamic model harmonization between unknown e-Business systems   389
    Makoto Oya, Masumi Ito

Active advertisement in supermarkets using personal agents   405
    Jarogniew Rykowski

A smart HTTP communicator: SMACH   421
    Yosuke Murakami, Yusuke Takada, Makoto Oya

e-Marketplaces, e-Hubs, and Portals

Mobile portal implementation strategy: a theoretical exploration   435
    Ping Gao, Jan Damsgaard

Cross-organizational workflows: a classification of design decisions   449
    Pascal van Eck, Rieko Yamamoto, Jaap Gordijn, Roel Wieringa

BIOVAULT: solving the problem of replay in biometrics
- an electronic commerce example   465
    Basie von Solms, Bobby Tait

Computing for e-Commerce

Integration of XML data in peer-to-peer e-Commerce applications 481
   Tadeusz Pankowski

Using ebXML for supply chain traceability 497
   Alessio Bechini, Mario Giovanni C. A. Cimino, Andrea Tomasi

An XML-based data model for vulnerability assessment reports 513
   George Valvis, Despina Polemi

User Behavior Modeling

Admission control for the customers over the vendor's VPN 527
   Narendra Kumar, Pallapa Venkataram, Satyanaga Kumar

Role of the customer value in the software as a service concept 543
   Markku Sääksjärvi, Aki Lassila

ROBALO: A Risk-Oriented Job Dispatching Mechanism for workforce
management system 559
   Shi-Cho Cha, Hung-Wen Tung, Han-Chao Lee,
   Tse-Ming Tsai, Raymund Lin, Chih Hao Hsu

Pervasive Technologies for e-Commerce

Discovery and query: two semantic processes for web services 571
   Po Zhang, Juanzi Li, Kehong Wang

DynG: a multi-protocol collaborative system 591
   Thomas Huriaux, Willy Picard

Development concept for and trial application
of a "Multiplex Risk Communicator" 607
   Ryoichi Sasaki, Saneyuki Ishii, Yuu Hidaka,
   Hiroshi Yajima, Hiroshi Yoshiura, Yuuku Murayama

Index of Authors **623**

GENERAL CHAIR'S MESSAGE

Welcome to the 5th IFIP Conference on e-Commerce, e-Business and e-Government, I3E'2005, sponsored by three IFIP Technical Committees: TC6, TC8, and TC11. I3E'2005 continues the tradition that evolved out of the inaugural conference held in 2001 in Zurich (Switzerland) and since made its journey through the world: 2002 Lisbon (Portugal), 2003 Sao Paulo (Brazil), 2004 Toulouse (France).

This year we are happy to hold the event in Poznan, a city of 600,000 inhabitants in western Poland. Poznan is the capital of the most affluent province of the country – Wielkopolska – which means the "Greater Poland". For more than one thousand years, Poznan's geographical location has predestined the city to be a significant scientific, cultural and economic center with more than just regional influence. The city is situated on the strategic cross-roads from Paris and Berlin in the west, to Warsaw and Moscow in the east, and from Scandinavia through the Baltic Sea in the north to the Balkans in the south. Poznan is a great research and university center with a dynamic potential. 120 000 students are enrolled in 19 state run and private institutions of higher education here, among which the Poznan University of Economics with its 18,000 students is one of the biggest.

The I3E'2005 Conference provides a forum for users, engineers, and scientists in academia, industry, and government to present their latest findings in e-commerce, e-business, or e-government applications and the underlying technology to support those applications. The submitted contributions address challenging issues of innovative business models, digital goods, products and services, user behavior, pervasive technologies, portals, trust and security, and public e-services for citizens and enterprises.

This conference has been made possible through the efforts of many people. I wish to thank everyone involved, including those who worked diligently behind the scenes and without formal recognition. First, I would like to thank the Program Chairs: Motohisa Funabashi from Hitachi Ltd., Japan, and Adam Grzech from the Technical University of Wroclaw, Poland, together with the Liaison Chairs representing different continents: Europe: R. Suomi, TuKKK, Finland; North America: J. Urban, Arizona State University, USA; South America: M. J. Mendes, Unisantos, Brazil; and

Asia-Pacific: Y. Zhang, Victoria University, Australia, for putting together an excellent technical program.

I would like to thank the Program Committee members and reviewers for a very rigorous and outstanding reviewing process. Almost all papers were reviewed by three members of the Program Committee or by external reviewers. I believe that such reviewing process guaranteed and assured high quality papers that are interesting and of timely importance for the attendees.

We are honored that the I3E Steering Committee, chaired by Dr. Volker Tschammer from the Fraunhofer Institute for Open Communication Systems FOKUS, Berlin, Germany, had confidence in us to manage the conference in Poznan. I take an opportunity of the jubilee fifth I3E conference to acknowledge Dr. Volker Tschammer for his initiative and engagement in running the whole series of I3E conferences.

I wish to thank Dr. Liba Svobodova form IBM Zurich Research Laboratory, and Dr. Kurt Weiss from Betreuer Hochschulen, SAP-Switzerland, for accepting our invitations to serve as keynote speakers.

Many thanks to my co-workers from the Poznan University of Economics – Dr. Jarogniew Rykowski and Jacek Chmielewski – who solved many technical problems, maintained online submission systems and supported editing of the Conference Proceedings.

I wish to thank organizers of special tracks: Dr. Anna Grabowska from the Technical University of Gdansk, Poland, who organized a special track of e-learning, Prof. Irene Krebs from the Brandenburg University of Technology, Cottbus, Germany, who organized a special track "Innovative Education Technologies using SAP", and Dr. Waclaw Iszkowski from the Polish Chamber of Information Technology and Telecommunications who contributed to the organization of the industrial track.

Special thanks to local governments: Marshal's Office of the Wielkopolska Region, and City Hall of Poznan, co-organizers of the Conference, for financial and logistic support. Thanks also to the Ministry of Science and Information Society Technologies and companies presenting their achievements at the industrial track for their financial support making this Conference more available to the audience.

Thank you – attendees – for your participation in I3E'2005, and welcome to Poznan, Poland. I hope you enjoy the Conference and grow professionally and personally.

Wojciech Cellary
I3E'2005 General Chair
The Poznan University of Economics, Poland

Program Co-Chairs' Message

Within the last decade several new developments have contributed to many new opportunities, as well as to a need for intensive research and development. New applications are driven by the desire for ubiquitous high-quality access to offered and available services at reasonable cost.

A considerable amount of research and development activities are currently going on world wide in order to adopt Internet services to the particular needs of users working in various environments and having an access to a great amount of information provided by commerce, business and public institutions. Expanding understanding and usage of Internet rise different technological problems and societal impacts. The emergence of the new societal environment created by Internet is a historical necessity; digitization becomes a correlate of most human activities nowadays including e-economy, e-medicine, e-government, etc.

As a medium of communication the Internet reached a relative maturity, whilst as a new societal environment it is still in the making. The Internet produces an enormous and huge e-environment society requiring intermediaries who guide, search, integrate and authenticate knowledge and information. The are many open questions such as Internet usage and services models, information and knowledge distribution, access to services, contents design and maintenance, security, etc.

These questions were intensively discussed at the past four editions of IFIP Conference on e-Commerce, e-Business and e-Government, and are going to be discussed at the 5th edition of the event. Organizers of the I3E'2005 Conference in Poznan have obtained 130 submissions for possible consideration for publication. The submitted papers originated from 34 countries from all over the world; in the decreasing order of submissions: Brazil, Germany, Japan, United Kingdom, Greece, China, Italy, Poland,

Australia, South Africa, India, Netherlands, Spain, South Korea, Taiwan, The Netherlands, Bulgaria, Canada, Lithuania, Luxembourg, Switzerland, USA, Finland, China, Singapore, Austria, Bangladesh, Belgium, Denmark, France, Jordan, Pakistan, Portugal, and Sweden. After thorough reviewing process, 40 research papers has been selected for presentation at the I3E'2005 and publication by Springer Science & Business Media within the IFIP series. The acceptance rate was 30%.

The 5th IFIP I3E'2005 proceedings contains a selection of 40 research contributions, which were extended to incorporate the numerous suggestions made by the international reviewers. All accepted papers addressed problems located into three main categories: e-commerce, e-business and e-government. Some of them are interdisciplinary and addressed to problems common for the three mentioned areas.

The editors are convinced that this book provides the most relevant and highly up-to-date summary of problems, and of suitable solutions in area of applications supporting commerce, business and government activities. We believe that the papers will be found as high quality, interesting and of timely importance.

The quality and success of IFIP I3E'2005 are due to all participants, but we have no doubts the success relies on the hard work of organizing committee members and volunteers from the Poznan University of Economics.

We would like to thank all members of the Program Committee and reviewers for their hard work in reviewing the manuscripts.

Thanks to all the Local Arrangements and Liaison Chairs as well as Steering Committee members for their excellent cooperation.

Many thanks to Dr Jarogniew Rykowski and Mr Jacek Chmielewski who provided and maintained online submission system for their helpful support.

Special thanks to Prof. Wojciech Cellary who took care of all activities necessary to prepare and provide the event.

Motohisa Funabashi
Hitachi Ltd., Japan

Adam Grzech
Wroclaw University of Technology, Poland

Program Co-Chairs

Program Committee

Witold Abramowicz, *Poznan University of Economics, Poland*
Stephane Amarger, *Hitachi Europe, France*
Kazuo Asakawa, *Fujitsu Laboratories, Japan*
Reza Barkhi, *Virginia Tech, USA*
Stephane Bressan, *National University of Singapore, Singapore*
Fred Cummins, *EDS, USA*
Bogdan D. Czejdo, *Loyola University N. O., USA*
Dirk Deschoolmester, *University of Gent, Belgium*
Steve Elliot, *University of Sydney, Australia*
Ayako Hiramatsu, *University of Osaka Sangyo, Japan*
Shinichi Honiden, *National Institute of Informatics, Japan*
Rei Itsuki, *University of Hiroshima International, Japan*
Arun Iyengar, *IBM Research, USA*
Farouk Kamoun, *University of Tunis, Tunisia*
Tej Kaul, *Western Illinois University, USA*
Mitch Kokar, *Northeastern University, USA*
Norihisa Komoda, *University of Osaka, Japan*
Irene Krebs, Brandenburg *University of Technology, Germany*
Winfried Lamersdorf, *University of Hamburg, Germany*
Yi-chen Lan, *University of Western Sydney, Australia*
Ronald M. Lee, *Florida International University, USA*
Feng Li, *University of Newcastle, United Kingdom*
Oscar Mayora, *Create-Net, Italy*

Organizing Committees

General Chair

Wojciech Cellary, *Poznan University of Economics, Poland*

Program Co-Chairs

Motohisa Funabashi, *Hitachi Ltd., Japan*
Adam Grzech, *Wroclaw University of Technology, Poland*

Liaison Chairs

Europe: Reima Suomi, *TuKKK, Finland*
North America: Joseph Urban, *Arizona State University, USA*
South America: Manuel J. Mendes, *Unisantos, Brazil*
Asia-Pacific: Yinhuo Zhang, *Victoria University, Australia*

Local Arrangements Co-Chairs

Jarogniew Rykowski, *Poznan University of Economics, Poland*
Jacek Chmielewski, *Poznan University of Economics, Poland*

Steering Committee

Steve Elliot, *Australia*
Ake Groenlund, *Sweden*
Dipak Khakhar, *Sweden*
Kai Rannenberg, *Germany*
Stephanie Teufel, *Switzerland*
Volker Tschammer, *Ger1many*

External Reviewers

INNOVATIONS TRANSFORMING E-BUSINESS

Liba Svobodova
IBM Research GmbH
Zurich Research Laboratory
CH-8803 Rüschlikon, Switzerland
svo@zurich.ibm.com

Driven by business innovation, competitive pressures and technical feasibility, e-business has evolved from its early manifestations embracing the Internet to advanced models emphasizing flexibility and adaptability and enabling complex and dynamic value networks. New business services and service delivery models are emerging.

Software development supports these trends by shifting towards a flexible, standards-based, service-oriented solution assembly approach. Scientific and technological advancements in various disciplines such as speech technology, sensor networks, and exploitation of unstructured information are enabling new applications and services and increased productivity. Breakthroughs in algorithms combined with the availability of extensive data and computational power are dramatically increasing the capabilities of analytics and optimization tools to address complex business problems and interactions in the on demand world.

Where is further innovation needed? What kind of research is needed to establish the foundation for the future? What professional skills will be needed in the increasingly dynamic on demand business world?

While the paths of technological innovations resulting in hardware and software products and solutions are well established, more scientific rigor and interdisciplinary approach is needed to foster the transition of services into an innovative discipline, encompassing and combining business, technology, and organizational aspects (www.research.ibm.com/ssme).

Liba Svobodova was born in Prague, Czech Republic, where she studied electrical engineering at the Czech Technical University (CVUT). She received the MS (1970) and PhD (1974) degrees in EE/CS from Stanford University in California. She held faculty positions at the Columbia University in New York and the Massachusetts Institute of Technology / Laboratory for Computer Science, where she did pioneering work in the area of resilient distributed systems. In 1982, she joined the IBM Zurich Research Laboratory in Rüschlikon, Switzerland. Over many years she managed research projects in the areas of computer networks and distributed systems, security, and network services and applications. Her current responsibilities focus on technical strategy and development of research directions, in particular in the Services area. She engages in the IBM Industry Solutions Lab (ISL) in Zurich, where customers and researchers come together to discuss emerging technologies and solutions and their potential impact on business. She is also responsible for University Relations programs at the IBM Zurich Research Lab.

SAP AND THE AGE OF LOGISTICS
How to Meet Tomorrows
Business Challenges

Kurt Weiss
Betreuer Hochschulen
SAP (Schweiz) AG
Althardstrasse 80
CH-8105 Regensdorf
e-mail:kurt.weiss@sap.com

We all have heard about the industrial revolution. Starting in 1750 with the invention of the steam engine, manual work was gradually replaced by machines. The consequences for industry and business were dramatic and partly painful. However, when it ended about 150 years later almost everybody in the industrial world was far better off.

Today things are happening again. This time mental work is replaced by machines. Not gradually but rapidly. The consequences for business are even more dramatic than they were 250 years ago. And they will continue to be dramatic, at an accelerated pace, during the next few years.

How to cope with the situation? One of the main challenges for most companies (and of course also for the public sector) will be to improve the efficiency and structure of their business processes. Streamlining logistics is the call of the day. Only if this is thoroughly pursued there will be room for profit with innovations. We are in the age of logistics.

SAP is fully prepared to meet this challenge. And, sure enough, everybody in a few years will be better off once more.

Kurt Weiss is a physicist (University of Zurich). He started his career as a scientist in basic research with Philips Research in Eindhoven (Netherlands) and as a guest professor at UC Los Angeles and the Johann-Wolfgang-Goethe-Universität Frankfurt (Germany). He then focused his interests on applied work. First as head of research at HILTI AG (Liechtenstein) and later as director at the ETH Lausanne for a Swiss-wide coordinated research effort in applied optics (IOT). Realizing an old dream he then served for five years as director of the Theater am Kirchplatz in Schaan before accepting from SAP (Switzerland) AG the responsibility to conceive and run SAPCollege (a new training program for SAP consultants). To day he runs for SAP a program to establish the art of mapping business processes onto software as a new academic discipline at the Swiss Higher Learning institutions. In addition he presents seminars about the ever more important necessity to think and act in processes and teaches MBA courses on Business, Vision, and Strategy.

VALUE PROCESS AND BUSINESS PROCESS IN E-BUSINESS MODELLING[1]

Mohammed N. Dewan, Baolin Wu and Yun Yang
CICEC - Centre for Internet Computing and E-Commerce, Faculty of Information and Communication Technologies, Swinburne University of Technology, Melbourne, Australia 3122, e-mail: {mdewan,bwu,yyang}@it.swin.edu.au

Abstract: When almost anyone in business can answer what their value proposition is, not all of them will be able to answer what their value process is. The number will even vary of who can answer what their business process is. But it is necessary to know the 'value processes' of the proposed value based on which 'business processes' are derived. The ability to incorporate between the value processes and the business processes is one of the crucial factors that play for the companies very significant roles to be competitive in today's challenging market. A number of research works can be found on value creation and value supply but none of them clearly explains the complex relationships between the value process and the business process or the importance of incorporation between these two in e-business modelling. In this paper we clearly define the value process and the business process and show the depth of relationships and the importance of relationships between them in e-business modelling with an illustration.

Key words: E-business model, Value, Value proposition, Value process, Business process.

1.   INTRODUCTION

Business modelling is already a widespread term though it is considered that only some views of business have been investigated. The ability to utilise advanced technology for modelling, analysis and simulation of various aspects of ever-changing businesses has made a significant

[1] This work is partly supported by Swinburne Vice Chancellor's Strategic Research Initiative Fund 2002-2004.

contribution to the way businesses are planned and operated these days. It is believed that at this stage unambiguous and well-defined models exist only for several narrow business areas, but wide and comprehensive models are still very informal and generic. Moreover, most of the modelling ideas of e-business are hardly understood by the stakeholders when articulated just by words. It is important for effective business decision making to have clear and concise modelling that allows the extraction of critical values from business processes and specifies the rules to be enforced accurately. Therefore, it is necessary to have clear ideas about value and value proposition for each and every business. Traditionally a business has been viewed as "the processes composed of value-adding activities", and the output of organisations' activities are considered the "value to the customer" [29]. But we argue that the value to a customer should be everything including products and services that relates to the satisfaction of customer's needs. It can be a 'content value' or 'context value' [32] or can be a combination of both. Before, values were mainly offered to the customers as the forms of product or service [27]. But now values to the customers do not simply mean providing product or service rather something that satisfies what customers want with product or service though product or service is the main tool for providing value to the customers. Similarly, different researchers have defined value proposition in different ways, such as, Keeney [19], Kambil et.al. [18], Petrovic & Kittl [25]. Value propositions define the relationship between what a supplier offers and what a customer purchases, by identifying how the supplier fulfils the customer's needs across different customer roles [18]. It describes the benefits and therefore the value a customer or a value partner gains from the business. We define value proposition as the description of the value that a product, service or process will provide a customer with.

Along with the value, the value process and the business process perform very important and significant roles to the successfulness in the competitive market. A value process means exactly how the value was processed by one actor that was required by the other to fulfil the demand. A value process includes the process of anything that contributes as part of the satisfaction of the customer whereas a business process means the processing of each value unit which is the detailed total number of activities and resources required to deliver a specific value. Devenport [9] defined business process as "a structured, measured set of activities designed to produce a specified output for a particular customer or market". In other words, a business process is a collection of related structural activities that produce a specific outcome for a particular customer; or a business process is a set of logically related business activities that combine to deliver something of a value (e.g. products, goods, services or information) to a customer. Both the value process and the business process are important in the sense that the value process guides the business process and the business process supports the value process. The efforts of a company that focus on the value to the customer can be the appropriate strategic alternative in that it can capitalise on opportunities and mitigate threats of an e-business environment, as well as preserve strengths and offset weaknesses of organisation's value creating capabilities [15]. But it is still not clear from the previous research how the value process is related to the business process and what the importance of relationship between these two processes is in e-business modelling.

In the following section we discuss previous research works in this area. Section 3 analyses the requirements. In Section 4, we clearly define and explain the value process, the business process, their complex relationships and the importance of relationships in e-business modelling. Section 5 illustrates the realisation of our arguments via an example. Finally, we conclude and point out future work in Section 6.

2.   RELATED WORKS

There is still no common understanding of various aspects of business models, such as, how a business model is defined, or how to develop a business model, or what the principles of modelling are. But based on the work of the key researchers in this area it has been found that there are some common elements that they consider in their modelling approach. Although none of the approaches demonstrates clearly the importance of the value process and its relationships with the business process in e-business modelling, most of them provide with one or many of the following common elements in their modelling: (i) definition, (ii) main components, (iii) taxonomy, (iv) designing tool, (v) changing methodology, and (vi) evaluation framework.

Timmers [35] was the first who defined the business model with respect to its architecture for the product, service and information flows, the benefits of the various business actors, and the sources of revenues. Weill & Vitale [36], being influenced by Timmers, suggest a subdivision into so called atomic e-business models, which are analysed according to its strategic objectives and value proposition, sources of revenue, critical success factors and core competencies. According to Rappa [31], the business model spells-out how a company makes money by specifying where it is positioned in the value chain. The modelling approaches by Petrovic et al. [26] and Auer & Follack [6] are very similar, who view a business model as a model that "describes the logic of a 'business system' for creating value that lies behind the actual processes". Tapscott, Ticoll and Lowy [34] provide a typology of business models that they call b-webs. They identify five generic b-webs, which are classified according to their degree of value integration and their degree of control of the value creation process. In the methodology proposed by Afuah and Tucci [1], one can find a list of business model components, from the scope over pricing and the revenue source to connected activities and capabilities in this approach; but it is less clear how the value is delivered to the customer. The proposed business model by Gordijn and Akkermans [13] is based on *e³-value* methodology, which consists of building blocks that can be used to represent an e-business idea and a modelling process to model, analyse, and evaluate such an idea. Osterwalder & Pigneur [23] conceive the business model as "description of the value a company offers to one or several segments of customers and the architecture of the firm and its network of partners." They propose e-business ontology based on four pillars: product innovation, infrastructure management, customer relationship, and financial aspects. There are some more researchers who have worked in this area. Among them the research works of Amit and Zott's [4], Hawkins' [16], Stabell and Fjeldstad [33], Linder and Cantrell [20], Applegate [5], Hamel [14], Papakiriakopoulos et al. [24] are worth mentioning.

From the previous researches, what we notice is that different approaches on e-business modelling by different researchers are based on different constituents. Some approaches have considered product, service, and information flow as the major element whereas some of them have considered value or value proposition as the minor element of the modelling. But interestingly, some of the approaches even do not consider 'value' as one of the elements of the e-business modelling. Although some of the approaches considered 'value' as a minor aspect of their modelling but none of them clearly describe the significance of the value process and its relationship with the business process in modelling. We, in this paper, show the importance of the value process and the business process with their comprehensive explanation and the importance of their interrelationship in e-business modelling. As this paper mainly discusses the 'value process' and the 'business process' in e-business modelling, we believe it is necessary to refer to our published work [10] as background without addressing the details here due to the space limit.

3.   REQUIREMENTS ANALYSIS

We argue that a competitive value should be considered as one of the most effective elements to be successful in the challenging market. It is considered that each act or activity (transaction) between the actors within a business is driven by value. The activity might be between two actors within one organisation, or might be between two organisations, or might be between an organisation and a customer. In addition, the value can help companies to attract new customers, increase customers' switching costs and lock-in them in much more efficient and effective ways in e-business, making possible for sustainable strategic competitiveness. That is why we argue that the value plays one of the most significant roles to be successful and it should be considered as a major aspect for modelling. We believe that the supply of value by one actor is based on the value requirements of another actor. Although IS/IT and e-business have a very strong relationship as IS/IT capabilities support e-business processes a great deal and IS/IT is viewed as more than an automating or mechanising force to fundamentally reshape the way a business is conducted nowadays but the thoughts of both the value process and the business process do not differ much between traditional businesses and modern e-businesses except the differences in the business process activities.

The nature and types differ from business to business. Therefore, information for each business varies too. To obtain the value process, value propositions need to be clearly defined by the company. Moreover, each company must be able to provide some attribute information regarding its business strategy, such as, type of revenue, source of revenue, number of actors involved, product or service types the company sells, etc. All operational information of the business also must be made available by the company to derive the business processes of each value unit.

4. ROLES OF TWO PROCESSES IN MODELLING

To analyse the particular activities through which companies can generate competitive advantages it is useful to identify the chain of value creation activities of the business. But before processing the value, the organisation needs to decide what value is to be processed which means the value proposition needs to be decided before value processing. Figure 1 shows the logical positions of value proposition, value process, and business process. We believe that the value proposition sits on top of the value process, that is, the value proposition is required to derive the value process, and similarly, the value process sits on top of the business process, which means, the value process is required to derive the business process.

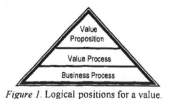

Figure 1. Logical positions for a value.

Albrecht [2] provides a useful classification to map customers' needs that we think should be considered when deciding value proposition. It is not always easy to decide about the value propositions as sometimes potential customers even do not know what exactly they want. Therefore, strategic managers may have to go through the process of questionnaires and interviews, and if necessary, any other innovative ideas to find out about the customers' needs. Even if the customers' needs are known the organisation needs to investigate how successfully that product or service is going to contribute to the customers' total satisfaction and how preferably the customers are accepting their value compared to the competitors'. Once the value proposition is identified the next step is to get the value processes followed by the business processes.

4.1 Value process

4.1.1 Background

Behind the value proposition, there is a process of how to fulfil and support the proposition in the sense that the value is created. The process is not the business process that describes how the business operates physically; it rather depicts a value process required for the value completion. Porter [28] introduces the value chain as a tool for developing competitive advantages. Stabel and Fjeldstad [33] extend the idea of 'value chain framework' of Porter and Millar [29]. They extend the idea with the 'value shop' and 'value network'. The 'value shop' depicts the process of value creation of service providers and the 'value network' specifies the brokerage and other intermediary activities. But it is always crucial on how to process the value that is to be delivered to the customer.

According to our approach, there are two elements in the value process - value addition activities and value creation activities. Value addition activities are activities that are required to add some value to the final value indirectly whereas value creation activities are the activities that are required to create some value to be added to the final value directly. A set of such value activities are performed to form the value process. The process of materialisation of each value proposition is divided into units based on the number of activities of value creation and value addition required to create the value completely. The number of units will vary from value proposition to value proposition, product to product, organisation to organisation. The relationships of these units vary too. Some of the units might be related in a very simple way whereas some others might be related in a very complex manner. The above two types of activities are classified into two groups:

external activities and internal activities. External activities include value addition activities and value creation activities that are carried out outside the organisation's environment; and internal activities include value addition activities and value creation activities that are carried out inside the organisation's environment. Figure 2 symbolises the value process and the business process by showing the relationships between value creation and value addition units.

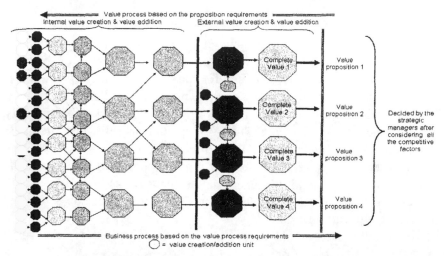

Figure 2. Value creation and value addition processes.

4.1.2 Why value process in modelling?

There are number of reasons why we need to consider the processing of the organisation's value in business modelling although reasons will differ from value type to value type, business activity to business activity, organisation to organisation, and depending on organisational focus and requirements. But we believe that commonly the main reasons or the drivers behind the value process inclusion in modelling are a combination of the following:

- The need to evaluate the customer satisfaction;
- The need to evaluate the business process efficiency;
- The need to evaluate the efficiency of the human resources; and
- The need to evaluate business practice as part of the overall development of the business.

The evaluation of the customer satisfaction, the business process efficiency, and the human resources efficiency is extremely important to measure the overall development of the business. The results from these evaluations in combination indicate the success rate of the overall business.

The success rate of the business helps managers to take measures for the development of the overall business.

4.2   Business process

4.2.1   Background

According to Davenport and Short [8] business processes have two important characteristics: (i) they have customers, internal or external, (ii) they cross organisational boundaries, i.e., they occur across or between organisational subunits. One technique for identifying business processes in an organisation is the value chain method proposed by Porter and Millar [29]. Processes are generally identified in terms of beginning and end points, interfaces, and organisation units involved, particularly the customer unit. Processes may be defined based on three dimensions [8]:

- *Entities*: Processes take place between organisational entities. They could be Inter-organisational, Inter-functional or Inter-personal.
- *Objects*: Processes result in manipulation of objects. These objects could be Physical or Informational.
- *Activities*: Processes could involve two types of activities: Managerial and Operational.

In relation to our approach a business process means the processing of each value unit which is the detailed total number of activities and resources required to deliver a specific value. These activities are normally performed by business actors who are involved in the business. To be competitive in the market, the following types of questions should be answered once the value is delivered to find out the efficiency of the business process:

- Did the supplied value fulfil the demand completely?
- Did the supplier use full capability to supply the value?
- Was the value supplied equal to the value proposed?

4.2.2   Why business process in modelling?

The need for the inclusion of the business process in business modelling is quite obvious as it delivers the required value generally proposed by the companies in their value proposition. Moreover, a business process not only processes the value for the customer but also represents real-time integration of the processes of a company with those of its suppliers, business partners, and customers. There are vital reasons why business process should be considered as one of the most important factors in business modelling.

Cousins & Srewart [7] identify five common drivers or needs behind the business process designing. They are, the need:

- To Increase efficiency;
- To evaluate business practice as part of an organisational development;
- To evaluate potential new business ventures or business offerings;
- To manage the organisation's knowledge resources; and
- To manage human resources.

Although the above needs are crucial in business process designing, we believe that they are also the main reasons why the business process should be included in modelling. We also believe that in addition to the four drivers of the value process (Section 4.1.2), the above five drivers are the main reasons why an organisation should analyse its business process carefully based on the requirements of the value process.

4.3 Relationships between two processes

For the completion of each value unit a value process is identified and then based on the value process, the business process is identified. After the value propositions are decided by the managers strategically, the company needs to look into the process of how the proposed value can be created. Similar to the value process, the process of creation of each value unit is divided into business process units based on the number of activities and resources required to create the value completely. The number of business process units varies from value unit to value unit, product to product, business to business.

As the companies exchange nothing but the value with the customers we believe that a business process is guided by the value process of an organisation as the processing of value provides the guidelines for the business process. A value process is how the total 'value' is completed whereas a business process is what resources and activities are required to create and deliver the value. A unit of value is created and supplied by one or more business process units. The business process is required for the value process. A value process cannot deliver a value without a business process and a business process does not know what to process without a value process. We also believe that wherever there is a value process, there is a business process. That is why it can be said that the value process and the business process are sometimes the two sides of the same coin. A value process is called in terms of the requirements of the value, whereas a business process is called in terms of the supply of the value. The total business process including resources and activities required is considered as the input, whereas the total value process that completes the 'value' is considered as the output. Figure 3 shows the relationships between value process and business process.

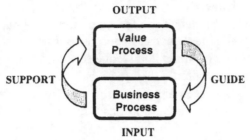

Figure 3. Relationships between processes.

A company produces the value based on the value offered to its customer. To produce and supply the value, the company needs value processes. Processing of values is only possible if there are business processes. Business processes can be completed without the proper guidance of value processes, but they will be inefficient and sometimes useless for the company. If there is no integrated relationship between the value process and the business process, and the business process is not guided and directed by the value process, the company will not be able to evaluate the customer satisfaction as well as the efficiency rate of the business process and the human resources. As a result, it will be difficult for the company to evaluate business practice as part of the overall development of the business.

So, what we see is that the value process and the business process are interdependent one on another. At the same time, one is inseparable from another. To get the desired output, we need to know the input. To provide with the proper input, we need to evaluate the output. Therefore, it is very important to understand the coordination and the relationships between these two processes to run a successful business.

5.   EXAMPLE

We, in this section, provide an example of value processes and business processes of a company that sells more than one value to its consumers through the Web. Though the company sells multiple values to the customers, we, here, only show the process of a part of the specific value that contributes to the completion of a full value. Because the demonstration of the complex value processes and business processes of the whole value would be very space consuming. Moreover, we are not permitted to show the complex value processes and business processes of the company because of commercial in confidence. We only use the information made available by the company intentionally. Please note that some of the information of the company has been modified here to simplify our example.

The company is one of the leading multi-brand online car purchasing service, providing new and pre-owned automobiles and related products and services. Customers can research, price, order, purchase, and insure a vehicle online through their service via Website that offers product information for nearly every make, model and style of automobile available in that country. The company gives customers all the tools needed to make an informed purchasing decision, including vehicle reviews, ratings, safety features and specifications. The company offers customers the choice of three distinctive options for car purchasing as value propositions: (a) purchasing a new car online through the company's award-winning Direct Channel; (b) being matched with a top-quality new car dealer of their choice via the company's Connect Channel; or (c) locating and purchasing a used vehicle through the company's Used Channel.

5.1   Value process

In this section we look at the company's offered values step-by-step and see how each of those values is processed. In other words, we look at the parts of the values that contribute to the completion of the values which we call 'sub-values' to see how each of the value is completed to be delivered to the customers. This company offers four main values to the customers of which one or many can be consumed. They are facilities to buy a car, sell a car, finance a car, and insure a car. In this example, we only focus on the processes of one value offered by the company which is the 'facility to buy a car'. If we look from the value process point of view we find that each of these four values is composed of one or many sub-values. Each of the sub-values is then considered as a value which is again composed of sub-values.

For example, in Figure 4, value *Buy a new car* is composed of four sub-values which are *Choose the car, Place the order, Complete the purchase with the dealer or with the Internet representative,* and *Pick up the car.* In the next stage, the sub-value *Choose the car* is considered as a value which is again composed of sub-values such as, *Research and compare the car* and *Select options and see prices.* Similarly, other sub-values are also considered as values which are constructed of some sub-values at a certain level till the bottom level of the value process. Please note that for the simplicity of the demonstration in this example we narrowed down our selection to just one sub-value to be considered as value in each level of the value process although in the same level sub-values for other values exist that are to be considered as values, too.

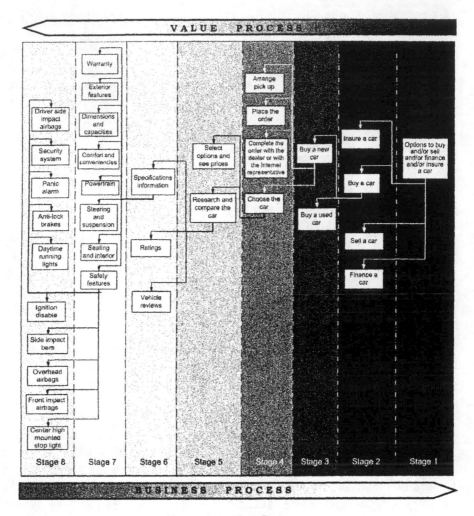

Figure 4. Process flow.

5.2   Business process

In the business process we look at the total resources and activities required to complete a specific value. Because a value cannot be created without business process and a business process does not know what to do without a planned value that needs to be created, there must be a business process for every value process and there is value process behind every value completion. Now in Figure 4, if we look at the value *Facility to research and compare the car,* we find that including some other business processes, the following main business processes are required to complete and deliver the value:

- Collect and store all the information about the features of the cars that consumers are concerned about such as, Price, Engine Specifications, Transmission, Fuel Economy, Warranty, Resale value, Safety, etc.
- Collect and store the information about vehicle reviews.
- Collect and store the information about vehicle ratings.
- Sort the information about the features according to the make and the model of the cars.
- Provide the online mechanism for the consumers to compare the cars based on features, reviews, ratings, etc.

Similarly, other values or sub-values also need business processes which are the value addition and value creation activities and resources required to complete and deliver the value. So the business process to complete and deliver the value *Facility to research and compare the car* would be the total resources and activities required to complete the processes mentioned in the above paragraph with bulleted points. Furthermore, the collection and storage of information about vehicle specifications involve internal and external value addition and value creation activities. To collect and store the information about vehicle reviews and ratings more external activities are required than internal activities whereas sorting of information involves more internal activities than external activities. In Figure 4, we only demonstrate seven levels of business process activities in brief by narrowed down our selection to just one sub-value to be considered as value in each level of the value process although in the same level sub-values for other values exist that are to be considered as values which involve internal and external business process activities, too.

5.3 Relationships between two processes

What we see in the above example is that none of the values or sub-values in Figure 4 can be delivered without value processes as well as business processes. Section 5.1 shows the value process of the *Buy a new car* value and Section 5.2 explains briefly the business processes for the *Facility to research and compare the car* value. We cannot show the detailed relationships of the business process units and the value process here because of commercial in confidence and the space limit but in brief we can see that the *Facility to research and compare the car* value cannot be delivered without the business processes mentioned in Section 5.2 while those business processes would not be there if there was no value and value process already decided. Therefore, we can say that the value process and the business process are interdependent and interrelated. They are also integrated parts of the business modelling and wherever there is a value process there is at least a business process and vice-versa.

6.   CONCLUSION AND FUTURE WORK

We believe that the value process and the business process are the major elements of e-business modelling. We have mentioned a number of reasons in the paper to support this argument. As mentioned in this paper, a number of research works can be found on value creation and value supply but the complex relationships between the value process and the business process or the importance of integration between these two in e-business modelling are not clear from any of the existing approaches. We have, in this paper, with comprehensive literature review clearly defined the value process and the business process and demonstrated the importance of the value process and the business process in e-business modelling. We also discussed the complex relationships and the importance of relationships between these two processes and provided an example to illustrate how our arguments can be realised. Our further research will include the evaluation of value processes and business processes based on simulation.

7.   REFERENCES

[1] Afua, A., and C. Tucci. 2001. *Internet Business Models and Strategies*. International Editions. New York: McGraw-Hill.

[2] Albrecht, K. 1993. *Total Quality Service Das einzige,was zählt*. Düsseldorf: Econ-Verlag.

[3] Alt, R., and H. Zimmerman. 2001. Introduction to Special Section - Business Models. *Electronic Markets* 11, no. 1: 3-9.

[4] Amit, R., and C. Zott. 2001. Value creation in e-business. *Startegic Management Journal* 22: 493-520.

[5] Applegate, L. M. 2001. Emerging e-business models: lessons learned from the field. *Harvard Business Review*.

[6] Auer, C., and M. Follack. 2002. Using Action Research for Gaining Competitive Advantage out of the Internet's Impact on Existing Business Models. *Proc. of the 15th Bled E- Commerce Conference- eReality: Constructing the Economy*. Bled, Slovenia.

[7] Cousins, J. and T. Stewart. 2002. "What is Business Process Design and Why Should I Care? " Web page, [accessed 4 July 2005]. Available at
http://uk.builder.com/whitepapers/0,39026692,60088578p-39001068q,00.htm

[8] Davenport, T. H., and J. E. Short. 1990. The New Industrial Engineering: Information Technology and Business Process Redesign. *Sloan Management Review*.

[9] Devenport, T. H. 1993. *Process Innovation*. Boston: Harvard Business School Press.

[10] Dewan, M., B. Wu, and Y. Yang. 2004. An Approach to Value Based E-Business Modelling. *Proc. of the 5th International WE-B Conference (WEB' 04)*. Perth, Australia.

[11] Giaglis, G. M., R. J. Paul, and D. I. Doukidis. 1999. Dynamic Modeling to Assess the Business Value of E-Commerce. *Int'l Journal of Electronic Commerce* 3, no. 3: 35-51.

[12] Gordijn, J., and H. Akkermans. 2001. e³ Value: A Conceptual Value Modeling Approach for e-Business Development. *First International Conference on Knowledge Capture, Workshop Knowledge in e-Business*.

[13] ———. 2001. Designing and Evaluating E-Business Models. *IEEE Intellegent Systems,* 16, no. 4: 11-17.

[14] Hamel, G. 2000. *Leading the Revolution.* Boston: Harvard Business School Press.

[15] Han, D., and J. Han. 2001. Value-based Strategy for Internet Business. MIT Working Paper.

[16] Hawkins, R. 2001. "The Business Model as a Research Problem in Electric Commerce." *STAR (Socio-economic Trends Assessment for the digital Revolution) IST Project,* Issue Report No. 4. SPRU - Science and Technology Policy Research.

[17] Hunt, K. L., G. A. Hansen, E. F. Madigan, and R. A. Phelps . 1997. Simulation Success Stories: Business Process Reengineering. *Proc. of the 1997 Winter Simulation Conference*ed. S. Healy K. J. Withers D. H. and Nelson B. L. Andradottir, Atlanta, GA.

[18] Kambil, A., Ginsberg A., and M. Bloch. 1997. Re-Inventing Value Propositions. *Working Paper,* Stern School of Business, New York University.

[19] Keeney, R. L. 1999. The Value of Internet Commerce to the Customer. *Management Science,* 45, no. 4: 533-44.

[20] Linder, J. C., and S. Cantrell. 2001. Changing Business Models: Surveying the Landscape . Institute for Strategic Change, Accenture.

[21] Ninios, P., K. Vlahos, and D. W. Bunn. 1995. Industry Simulation: System Modelling With an Object Oriented / DEVS Technology. *European Journal of Operational Research* 81: 521-34.

[22] Osterwalder, A., S. B. Lagha, and Y. Pigneur. 2002. An Ontology for Developing e-Business Models. *DSIage.*

[23] Osterwalder, A., and Y. Pigneur. 2002. An e-Business Model Ontology for Modeling e-Business. *Proc. of the 15th Bled E- Commerce Conference.* Bled, Slovenia.

[24] Papakiriakopoulos, D., A. Poulymenakou, and G. Doukidis. 2001. Building e-Business Models: An Analytical Framework and Development Guidelines. *Proc. of 14th Bled Electronic Commerce Conference.* Bled, Slovenia.

[25] Petrovic, O., and C. Kittl. 2003. Capturing the value proposition of a product or service. *Position paper for the international Workshop on Business Models.* Lausanne, Switzerland.

[26] Petrovic, O., C. Kittl, and R. D. Teksten. 2001. Developing Business Models for eBusiness. *Proc. of the International Conference on Electronic Commerce 2001.*

[27] Porter, M. 1985. *Competitive Advantage.* New York: Free Press.

[28] ———. 1980. *Competitive Strategy.* New York: Free Press.

[29] Porter, M., and V. E. Millar. 1985. How information gives you competitive advantage. *Harvard Business Review.* 63, no. 4: 149-60.

[30] ———. 2001. Strategy and the Internet. *Harvard Business Review* 79, no. 3: 62-78.

[31] Rappa, M. 2004. "Managing the digital enterprise - Business models on the web." Web page, [accessed 4 April 2004]. Available at http://digitalenterprise.org/models/models.html

[32] Rayport, F. J., and J. J. Sviokla. 1995. Exploiting the Virtual Value Chain. *Harvard Business Review:* 75-85.

[33] Stabell, C. B., and O. D. Fjeldstad. 1998. Configuring value for competitive advantage: on chains, shops, and networks. *Strategic Management Journal* 19: 413-37.

[34] Tapscott, D., D. Ticoll, and A. Lowy. 2000. *Digital Capital - Harnessing the power of business webs .* Boston: Harvard Business School Press.

[35] Timmers, P. 1998. Business Models for E-Markets. *Electronic Markets* 8, no. 2: 3-8.

[36] Weill, P., and M. Vitale. 2001. *Place to Space: Migrating to eBusiness Models.* Boston: Harvard Business School Press.

VA^3: GOVERNANCE SELECTION IN VALUE WEBS

Jaap Gordijn,[1] Jasper Soetendal,[2] and Edwin Paalvast[3]

[1] *Vrije Universiteit Amsterdam*
The Netherlands
gordijn@cs.vu.nl

[2] *Currently employed at Accenture*
The Netherlands
jasper@soetendal.nl

[3] *Cisco Systems,*
The Netherlands
epaalvas@cisco.com

Abstract   To deal with complex customer needs, enterprises increasingly form constellations, rather than just operate on their own. Cisco Systems and Dell are good examples of organizers of such constellations in their own industries. An important problem while designing these constellations is the selection of a performing enterprise for each value adding activity in the constellation. In this paper, we propose a *model*-based approach to do so. We use the existing e^3-*value* methodology to represent a value constellation formally, and extend e^3-*value* with VA3; a step-wise approach that assists in selecting enterprises for performing value activities. How VA3 practically works, is illustrated using a case study on Cisco Systems.

Keywords: Value webs, governance structures, e^3-*value*

1.   Introduction

Today, end-customers more and more buy products from *value webs*. Such webs are constellations of companies that offer jointly a good, service, or a combination of these to a customer. Well known examples include Cisco Systems and Dell, but many other small constellations exist.

To design and model a value web, we have developed in earlier work (Gordijn and Akkermans, 2003) the e^3-*value* methodology, addressing the creation, exchange and consumption of economic value in a network of enterprises (see also Sec. 2). The e^3-*value* approach models value webs using pre-defined and formalized constructs, e.g. actor, market segment, value activity and value exchange. There are a number of reasons for *modeling* value webs, such as: (1) a better, and shared, understanding of the web by the stakeholders involved compared to an ambigious textual outline of the value web, (2) the possibility to use software tools for the design and analysis of value webs (see e.g. http://www.cs.vu.nl/~gordijn/tools.htm), and (3) a precise statement of the value web, usable for software engineers to do software requirement analysis.

So, the e^3-*value* methodology produces a *value model* showing enterprises (actors), exchanging things of economic value with each other, and performing value adding activities. Execution of these activities leads to profit (and need satisfaction in case of end-customers). An important issue in value webs, and thus in e^3-*value* , is the *assignment* of value adding activities to *performing* enterprises. On the one extreme, a *single* enterprise may perform *all* value adding activities by itself; on the other extreme, *each* value adding activity can be executed by a *different* company. Significant work has been done on this value activity assignment problem, including strategy decision making (e.g. (Porter, 1985; Porter, 2001)) and transaction economics (e.g. (Williamson, 1985; Williamson, 1998)). However, this work has not been integrated into a *model*-based approach, such as e^3-*value* , yet. So, the key contribution of this paper it that we propose a stepwise, model-based approach, called VA^3 to select performing actors for value activities, based on the forementioned contributions. Ultimately, VA^3 should support the designer of value models and thus should be seen as prescriptive. In this paper, we have a more modest goal: to assess whether VA^3 can be used to describe a case study adequately.

This paper is structured as follows. Sec. 2 articulated the aforementioned value activity assignment problem. In Sec. 3 we propose the VA^3 approach for dealing with the assignment problem. Then we illustrate VA^3 using a case study in Sec. 4. Finally, in Sec. 5 we present our conclusions.

2.   The value activity assignment problem

The e^3-*value* methodology

As Fig. 1 shows, an e^3-*value* model can be represented graphically . Experiences with business users in various research projects have shown that this is a particular useful feature of e^3-*value* . Following, we discuss the e^3-*value* constructs only briefly (more information can be found in (Gordijn and Akkermans, 2003)).

First, Fig. 1 (a) contains a series of **actors**. An actor is entity that is perceived by its environment as an independent economic (and often legal) entity. An actor makes a profit or increases its utility. In a sound, sustainable, value model each actor should be capable of making profit. In the example *buyer*, *seller* and *producer* are all actors.

An actor may have a need. This need is expressed by means of a **start stimulus** that triggers exchanges of goods and services between actors. Here, the need is *watch DVD*. In order to satisfy the need, an actor exchanges objects of economic value with other actors. The **value objects** are services, products, money, or even consumer experiences. The important point here is that a value object is of value for one or more actors. In the example at hand, *DVD*, *fee*, and *transport* are all examples of a value object. These value objects are offered/requested via value ports of an actor. The concept of **port** enables to abstract away from the internal business processes, and to focus only on how external actors and other components of the business model can be 'plugged in'. Ports are grouped into a **value interface**, expressing that the objects via *all* ports in the interface should be exchanged or *none at all*. This models economic recicprocity and bundling. So, *buyer* can only obtain a *DVD* if he pays a *fee* for it, and vice versa. The start stimulus and the value interface of *buyer* are connected by means of a **connection element**, representing that in order to satisfy a need, a *buyer* should exchange value objects via that specific interface. A **value exchange** is used to connect two value ports with each other. It represents one or more potential trades of value objects between value ports. As a result of the semantics of a value interface (all its ports should exchange values or none at all), value exchanges occur in combinations. E.g., a *fee* and a *DVD* should both be exchanged between buyer and seller. Such a combination is called a **value transaction**.

Additionally, actors can perform value activities. Such a **value activity** is an operation with which an actor *creates profit*. In this case, *seller* earns money with *selling DVD's*. Since value activities create profit, the assignment of value activities to performing actors is an important problem while designing e^3-*value* models. Providing guidelines how to do so is the key contribution of this paper.

Connection elements and exchanges form a **dependency path** (with on the path the value exchanges). This path is used to count the number of value exchanges as a start stimulus occurs. These counts are the basis for net cash flow calculations, to assess whether the business value model is profitable for every actor involved. The end stimulus represents the end of the path, and signals that counting of the number of exchanges can be stopped.

Actors perform value activities

An important decision during the design of value models is the assignment of activities to performing actors. This decision influences *how* enterprises are creating profit and thus is seen as important. To exemplify the decision, consider Fig. 1 (b). There is one important difference with Fig. 1 (a): whereas in (a) *seller* performs transportation of DVD's itself, in (b) there is a *logistic*

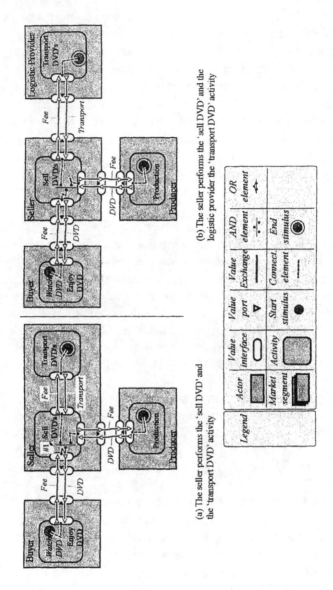

Figure 1.   An e^3-*value* model.

provider for DVD transportation. In other words, the value activity *transport DVD* has been assigned to a different enterprise. As a result, *logistic provider* creates now profit with the *transport DVD* activity, and not *seller*.

The decision to assign an activity to another actor can be represented by an e^3-*value* model, but how to take such a decision? This paper proposes a multi-perspective, step-wise approach called VA^3 to make such a decision.

Obviously, the VA^3 approach is closely connected to the existing e^3-*value* method.

3. VA^3: A stepwise approach for assigning value activities to actors

Governance structures

An e^3-*value* model can be seen as a set of value activities, connected by means of value exchanges. At the one extreme, all value activities can be performed by one large enterprise; At the other extreme, each value activity can be assigned to a different enterprise. We consider the assignment of activities to performing actors as a governance structure selection problem. A **governance structure** describes the organisational form of value exchanges between activities, specifically which actors are involved and which coordination mechanism is used. Various goverance structures can be characterized by the following properties (see e.g. (Malone et al., 1987; Williamson, 1985; Pyke and Johnson, 2003)):

Scope of the supplier-buyer relation. A supplier and buyer may select each other *per business transaction*, they may have *medium/long term contracts* that are used for more than one transaction, or supplier and buyer may be in the same company and have a *hierarchical* relationship.

Coordination costs. According to (Malone et al., 1987), coordination costs include the transaction costs of all the information processing necessary to co-ordinate the work of people and machines that perform the primary processes.

Production costs. Production costs include costs for primary processes to create goods and services (Malone et al., 1987).

Product adaptability. Adaptability is the ability to adapt the product or service to the needs of buyer and the agility too react on uncertainties.

Information sharing. Information sharing quantifies the amount of information sharing between supplier and buyer.

Asset specific investments. Asset specific investments are those investments that a firm needs to invest to be able to perform the value activity under consideration.

Business with competitors. Business with competitors refers to the amount of business the supplier will do with the competitors of the buyer.

Based on these characteristics, we sketch four different governance structures, using (Williamson, 1985) and (Pyke and Johnson, 2003) as a starting point. For explanatory purposes, we assume a situation with two value activities, va_1 and va_2 and activity va_1 wants to buy a good or service from va_2 and pays for that in return (see Fig. 2). Using the goverance structures below, these activities can be assigned to actors in different ways.

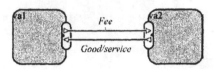

Figure 2.   Value activities exchanging objects of value.

Market governance. In case of market governance, va_1 and va_2 are assigned to different actors, and this assignment may change on a per *transaction* basis. *Coordination* costs are high because for each transacion, the best supplier has to be found. However, *production* costs are low because for the supplier economies of scale apply. The possibility to *adapt* the final product is low because in order to obtain the parts (half-products) from someone else, standardization of these parts is important. *Information sharing* is not so easy, since for each transaction, a new infrastructure to do so needs to be created. The actor performing va_1 has no asset specific investments; these are all done by the actor performing va_2. Obviously, the actor performing va_2 does also business with the competitors of the actor performing va_1.

Hierarchical goverance. In the situation of hierarchical governance, va_1 and va_2 are done by the same actor. There is a single point of decision authority rather than various actors in a market. *Coordination* costs are low because no other enterprise has to be found and managed to perform va_2. *Production* costs of half-products are high because the enterprise produces only for itself and as a consequence, economies of scale are difficult to reach. The possibility to *adapt* the final product is high because there are no contractual restrictions regarding the half-products and va_2 is directly controlled. *Information sharing* between both activities can be exploited at a maximum extent. Asset specific investments are high, because the enterprise can not use others to do these investments. Finally, because both activities are performed by the same enterprise, there are no competition issues.

Relational and joint governance. Relational goverance and joint governance are both structures that suppose that va_1 and va_2 are performed by different enterprises, but these enterprises have a closer relationship compared to market governance. In the case of relational governance, contracts are set up that are used for a series of transactions between enterprises. These contracts can agree on design, quality, quantity and delivery schedules of products. It lowers coordination somewhat (because not for every transaction a new enterprise has to be found), and information sharing may be useful.

Joint governance is about a strategic partnership between two firms. Not only a series of transactions is governed, rather the entire cooperation between enterprises. This creates opportunities for low coordination costs, high adaptability of the end product to customer needs, intensive information sharing, and half-products which are only limited available to competitors.

Governance structures can be represented by e^3-*value* models. Fig. 3 (a) shows that activity a_2 is performed by an actor, part of a market segment. The actor has to be selected on a per transaction basis from the market segment. A **market segment** is an e^3-*value* construct, denoting a set of actors that assign economic value to objects in the same way. Relational governance is presented in Fig. 3 (b). Two opions are available: If an actor has contracted many other actors for the performance of activity a_2, the leftmost part is selected, modelling that a selection is made from a pre-defined set of actors. In case there is a contract with only one actor, the rightmost part applies. In Fig. 3 (c) joint governance is shown. Here, two enterprises form a partnership. Each enterprise performs its own activity (activity a_1 and a_2 respectively), but there is an additional activity, performed by the partnership, to model that both partners need coordination. Finally, in case of hierarchical governance, Fig. 3 (d) can be used. Here, both activities a_1 and a_2 are performed by the same enterprise.

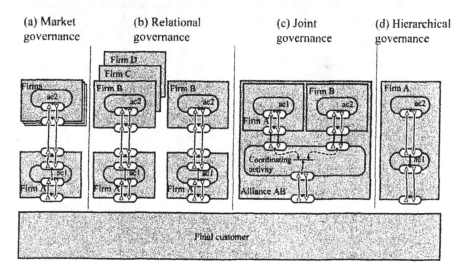

Figure 3.   Four governance structures in e^3-*value* .

A multi-perspective approach

How to assign value activities to performing actors? In this paper, we reduce this question to finding an appropriate governance structure for each value activity. A series of factors influence the choice for a particular governance structure (see e.g. (Ghosh and John, 1999) and (Hamilton and Wada, 2001)). In this paper, we consider a company's strategy, transaction costs, possession of information, and available resources.

Strategy. In (Porter, 2001) it is stated that strategy, and strategy alone, determines governance structure, in favour of hierarchical governance. This is a bit one-sided, biased view on the disadvantages of market, relational, or joint governance (see e.g the discussion in (Porter, 2001), and reactions (Ticoll, 2001)). Companies employing other forms than hierarchical governance (Dell, Cisco Systems, American Airlines, Citybank, Dow Chemical, Siebel) have proven to be very successful. Therefore, we will not regard hierarchy as the most preferred governance structure on beforehand. However, we will not disregard Porters opinion. We suppose that least one value activity should be governed internally, to sustain competitive advantage and to reach the necessary distinction from competitors.

Transaction costs. Williamson (Williamson, 1998) shares a similar one-sided, biased view on the expected influence of his theory on make-or-buy decisions. Transaction costs, and transaction costs alone, determine governance structure. Although, in time, Williamsons view on this matter changes more and more towards a more multi-perspective approach. Aspects like strategic positioning and available resources are also likely to influence the governance decision.

Possession of information. It is widely accepted that possession of information can be of commercial interest and may be lead to competitive advantage. Therefore, while deciding on a goverance structure, possession of information should be taken into account.

Available resources. Apart from strategy, transactional costs and possesion of information, the resources of a firm are believed to play a role in the value activity assignment problem. Resources can be defined as the scarce and imperfectly mobile skills, assets or capabilities owned by a firm for the purpose of performing one or more activities. These resources are by definition a competitive advantage to a firm; they cause positive performance differences. In their research on governance value, (Ghosh and John, 1999) distinguish marketing resources, technological resources, and channel resources, based on earlier research (including (Day and Wensley, 1988)). Possession of these resources by a specific value activity may result in choosing hierarchical governance, to exploit competitive advantage.

Steps in selecting a governance structure

How do we use strategy and transaction costs issues, as well as available information and resources of an enterprise to arrive at a governance structure?

Starting point for the governance structure selection is the *preference of market governance*. *Hierarchical governance*, the other extreme of the governance spectrum, is the least preferred governance structure. Only with sound motivations, hierarchical governance is chosen. This assumption follows transaction cost theory and is in contradiction with Porters opinion, as he states that for strategic reasons, hierarchical governance is preferred to market governance. We assume that these strategic reasons exist for a *limited* amount of value activities only. Therefore, we regard market governance, based on Williamson's arguments, as the default governance.

Starting point is a value model consisting of *only value activities*, exchanging value objects (e.g. Fig. 1 (a) but then *without* actors). For a value model, an enterprise considers each activity, in order to select a specific governance model, following a series of steps that are illustrated in Fig. 4 and presented below.

Step 1: Is the value activity under consideration mission critical? For each value activity, the first question is whether the value activity is mission critical for an enterprise. In other words, if this value activity will not be performed, is it still possible for an enterprise to offer its core value object(s) to its customers? A *core* value object is offered by an enterprise to its customers and is seen as crucial for profit generation and sustainability for that enterprise. If a value activity is not mission critical, market governance is a suitable governance structure, otherwise we proceed to step 2.

Step 2: Are transaction costs high? If a value activity is considered as mission critical, next step is to research the transaction costs for the value activity. Important aspects to determine transaction costs are asset specificity, uncertainty and frequency. To determine whether transaction costs are high, these three aspects need to be evaluated: Asset specificity, Uncertainty, and Frequency. The assignment of these values should be done on basis of the transaction cost theory (see (Williamson, 1985) for more details). If asset specificity is high, uncertainty is medium or high and frequency is recurrent, the transaction costs are high. This is the case if highly asset specific investments need to be done to perform a value activity. In addition, the uncertainty is high, so adaptability, agility is very important, so direct control and extensive information sharing is needed. We then continue with step 4. If asset specificity is low or medium, uncertainty is low or frequency is occasional, transaction costs are low or medium. In these cases transaction costs give no reasons for joint or hierarchical governance , and we continue with step 3.

Step 3: Does the value activity under consideration provide useful information? If a value activity is mission critical and the transaction costs are low or medium, question is whether this value activity provides useful information. We will define information useful if the possession of information increases competitive advantage significantly. By enabling better performance, more efficient business processes or useful client information, information increases competitive advantage. If a value activity provides this sort of information, this information should be governed internally or shared by the supplier, so the governance structure should be hierarchical or joint governance, to be decided upon in step 4. This only applies if the useful information can not be acquired in case other governance structures are deployed. Otherwise, relational governance is selected.

Step 4: Are resources available for the value activity under consideration?
If a value activity is decided to be mission critical, and involves high transaction costs or provides useful information, the last question is whether the value activity should be performed internally, or outsourced to a joint venture. Both joint governance and hierarchical governance result in comparable advantages on information exchange, adaptability and co-ordination costs. The question is then whether investments in resources to perform the value activity in case of hierarchical governance are justified in relation to expenses for joint governance. If the needed resources for a value activity are available internally already, the decision for hierarchical governance can be taken without any doubt. If available resources conflict with a value activity, joint governance should be chosen. If resources are not available internally and no conflicts occur, a serious consideration is needed.

Earlier, we defined hierarchical governance the less preferred governance structure. Unless resources are internally available, joint governance is preferred to hierarchical governance. One exception on this principle exists: If contracting and co-ordinating costs for joint governance are expected to be significantly higher than needed investments for hierarchical governance, then the latter governance structure should be chosen. Obviously, it is difficult or impossible to calculate all contracting and co-ordinating costs involved by joint governance, as difficult as it is to forecast the exact amount of needed investments to acquire resources for hierarchical governance. Nevertheless, it is important to do this as conscientious as possible.

4.   A case study: Cisco Systems

We have used VA^3 in two case studies: Dell and Cisco Systems (?). Here we concentrate on Cisco Systems, a leading company on computer networking equipment and software. The goal of the case study is to assess whether, by following the VA^3 approach, reasonable explanations can be found for the current structure of Cisco Systems. So, the goal is *not* to test whether the VA^3 approach arrives at the same structure as Cisco Systems has in real life. We have information from three sources: (1) one of the co-authors has been working for Cisco's International Internet Business Solution Group; this group advises Cisco and its main customers about their e-business strategy, (2) literature on Cisco Systems (Slywotzky and Morrison, 2001; Hartman et al., 2000), and (3) one of the co-authors is operations director of Cisco Systems.

Based on our internal knowledge of Cisco Systems, we have constructed an e^3-*value* model (see Fig. 5) consisting of value activities connected by means of value exchanges (note that the diagram does also contain enterprises; these enterprises are not part of the starting point rather show the result of the coming steps). The activity *Consuming Networking Power* models that a consumer needs networking power (meaning a solution for datacommunication needs; not equipment in the first place) for this business. The *Providing Networking Power* activity bundles networking equipment, and online and on-site services. Activities, such as *Providing Equipment* require hardware, software, assemblies of these and quality control, and so result in new value activities.

Step 1: Mission criticality. Initially, we assume that all value activities are needed to offer Cisco System's core product namely *networking power*. So all listed value activities are mission critical.

Step 2: Transaction costs. Most value activities have low or medium transaction costs. Only the value activities developing software, quality control and providing networking power need asset specific investments. Most of Cisco's activities require no asset specific investments. None of Cisco's hardware suppliers is allowed to supply more than 25% of its production to Cisco. Cisco values the independence of their suppliers, requiring that the production lines of their suppliers can be used or redeployed for the production of non-Cisco products. If asset specific investments need to be done, Cisco supports the supplier with both financials and expertise. Developing software for Cisco equipment is highly idiosyncratic, in other words, this software needs to be developed especially to the characteristics of Cisco equipment. The expertise that is needed for this activity can hardly be redeployed for other activities. Quality control requires asset specific investments, because test cells need to be developed, to test Cisco's product. The test cells test whether a product meets all Cisco quality norms, and whether it is compatible with other Cisco equipment. Such Cisco-specific test hardware can not be redeployed for any other use. Providing networking power requires asset specific investments. An actor that wants to be a reseller of Cisco's products, needs to follow courses, obtain certificates and meet quality requirements. These investments, needed to be acknowledged as a reseller by Cisco, can not be redeployed for any other value activity or partner. Since all needed investments for all other value activities could be redeployed for other buyers, asset specificity is low or medium. Neither are these value activities subject to high uncertainty or occasional frequency. Therefore, the transaction costs for these value activities are low or medium, are considered in step 3 for relational governance. The activities with high transactional const are considered in step 4 for hierarchical or joint governance.

Step 3: Useful information. Six out of the eleven value activities provide useful information to Cisco. Quality control provides valuable information on the quality of a product, and the outcomes of a production line. Consulting provides useful information on the needs and wishes of customers. Providing equipment and providing networking power offers direct contact with customers, providing useful information on their needs and interests. In addition, the sales history of customers is known; this can be used for customer relationship management. Providing services, whether on-line or on-site, provide useful information on what customer needs what support for what equipment. Based on this knowledge, both production and support can be improved. Consequently, these activities are considered for joint or hierarchical governance in step 4. For all other activities, relational governance is selected, meaning that they are outsourced.

Step 4: Resources. Cisco Systems possesses resources for four value activities.

Developing software. The expertise Cisco has on network software is immense. The Internet Operating System (IOS), developed by Cisco Systems, has become the industry-wide standard for moving data among connected computer systems (Slywotzky and Morrison, 2001). IOS is licensed to all big actors in the industry, so it is a revenue source for Cisco. Being the company that created the standard is essential to the success of Cisco. This resource should be used to perform the value activity software development.

Quality control. With the Autotest quality control, Cisco is able to guarantee the quality of each produced piece of equipment, without the need of physical presence of dedicated personnel. An Autotest test cell is a sealed 'black box' placed on the location of the product manufacturer. If a product leaves the product line, it is plugged into the test cell and tested on performance and compatibility with other Cisco products. Only if a product passes the test, it may be labelled a Cisco product. This resource can be used for the value activity quality control.

Providing network power. Cisco's Supply Chain Management is one of the worlds most advanced. It enables Cisco to tightly co-ordinate the production, supply and assembly of equipment. To assure the quality and delivery times of the produced goods, Cisco has access to the Enterprise Resource Planning systems of all its partners. This high level of transparency and control enables Cisco to deliver high-quality, build-to-order equipment right on time. These resources should be used to perform the value activity providing equipment.

Providing online services. Finally, with Cisco Connection Online (CCO), Cisco offers millions of web pages to resellers and customers, providing product information, support and updates.

Because Cisco Systems already possesses the resources for the above activities, these activities are considered for hierarchical governance.

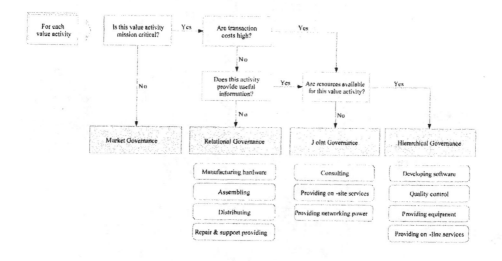

Figure 4. Governance spectrum for Cisco.

In sum, following the steps in Sec. 3 , we decide on the assignment of value activities to performing actors (see Fig. 4). This decision diagram shows that relational governance is advised for the value activities manufacturing hardware, developing software, assembling, distributing and repair & support providing. For consulting, providing on-site services and providing networking power joint governance is advised. The value activities quality control, providing equipment and providing on-line services should be performed internally. Based on these conclusions, an e^3-*value* model can be constructed (see Fig.5). For the relational governed value activities, the names of Cisco's partners are used if applicable. In all other cases, a descriptive name, like 'hardware supplier', is used. The value activities consulting, providing on-site services and providing networking power are joined with Cisco's internal activities in the strategic alliance Cisco Reseller Network.

5. Conclusion

Is the Cisco value model produced by the $V A^3$ steps different from the real situation? The most important difference concerns the activity *providing networking power*; $V A^3$ selects joint governance while in reality, Cisco Systems

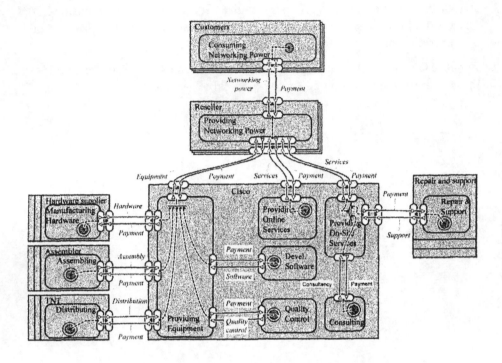

Figure 5.   Value activities assigned to actors in the Cisco value web.

handles this value activity differently for different clients. For ISP's (Internet Service Providers), the *providing networking power* activity is governed hierarchically. The consideration for doing so is that ISP's require very specific knowledge concerning Cisco's products, which can only be delivered by own staff. For all other clients, Cisco maintains a network of direct sellers and value-added resellers (Slywotzky and Morrison, 2001). Such a large amount of partners would usually suggest market or relational governance. However, some characteristics of joint governance are present. Long-time relationships exist, because resellers need to invest in Cisco certifications and knowledge. Therefore, we would characterise the governance structure for the non-ISP clients as joint governance. In conclusion, selection of an appropriate governance structure depends also on the type of customer and therefore, governance selection can not be seen in isolation.

Are the VA^3 steps useful to understand and explain Cisco's value model? Sec. 4 provides numerous considerations and explanations for the current value model of Cisco Systems. For example, reasons to keep *autotesting* under hierarchical control are the asset specific investments, the information on production lines, and the already available resources for testing. Additionally, *developing software* is highly idiosyncratic and uses already existing resources (IOS). So, we experienced that the main value of using VA^3 for an existing company as Cisco Sytems is explaining, in a structured way, the value web of Cisco Systems. In future research, we will model more case studies using VA^3, to assess its descriptive value.

Currently, the VA^3 approach takes a *single enterprise* perspective on selecting a performing actor for a value activity. However, in real life many enterprises will *compete* for the execution of a specific value activity. This will specifically occur if the activity at hand is of strong commercial interest. Consequently, extending the VA^3 approach with support for *negotiating* the assignment of an activity to a performing actor, is an additional topic for further research.

Acknowledgements. This work has been partially supported by the Dutch Ministry of Economic Affairs, as the FrUX project (Freeband User eXperience).

References

Day, G. and Wensley, R. (1988). Assessing advantage: A framework for diagnosing competitive superiority. *Journal of Marketing*, (52):1–20.

Ghosh, M. and John, G. (1999). Governance value analysis and marketing strategy. *Journal of Marketing*, (63):131–145.

Gordijn, J. and Akkermans, J. (2003). Value-based requirements engineering: Exploring innovative e-commerce ideas. *Requirements Engineering Journal*, 8(2):114–134.

Hamilton, B. and Wada, T. (2001). Market position, resource profile, and governance: Linking porter and williamson in the context of international courier and small package services in japan. *Strategic Management Journal*, 22(3):251–273.

Hartman, A., Sifonis, J., and Kador, J. (2000). *Net Ready - Strategies for Success in the E-conomy*. McGraw-Hill, New York, NY.

Malone, T., Yates, J., and Benjamin, R. (1987). Electronic markets and electronic hierarchies. *Communications of the ACM*, 30(6):484–497.

Porter, M. E. (1985). *Competitive Advantage - Creating and Sustaining Superior Performance*. Free Press, New York, NY.

Porter, M. E. (2001). Strategy and the Internet. *Harvard Business Review*, (march):63–78.

Pyke, D. and Johnson, M. (2003). Sourcing strategy and supplier relationships: Alliances vs. eprocurement. In Billington, C., Lee, H., Neale, J., and Harrison, T., editors, *The Practice of Supply Chain Management*. Kluwer Publishers.

Slywotzky, A. and Morrison, D. (2001). *How Digital is your business?* Crown Business, New York, NY.

Ticoll, D. (2001). Reaction on strategy and the internet. *Harvard Business Review*, pages 137–140.

Williamson, O. (1985). *The Economic Instituations of Capitalism*. Free Press, New York, NY.

Williamson, O. (1998). Transaction cost economics: How it works, where it is headed. *De Economist*, 146(1):23–58.

FROM AN E-BUSINESS REVENUE MODEL TO ITS SOFTWARE REFERENCE ARCHITECTURE

Volker Gruhn, Thorsten Weber
Chair of Applied Telematics/e-Business, Department of Computer Science, University of Leipzig

Abstract: Revenue models define *how* a company creates their revenues and hence they are an integral part of business models. While a lot of research on business models and revenue models of the e-Business already exists, there is a shortfall of a concept to derive appropriate software architectures for the underlying software system directly from these models. This is interesting since a software system for companies of the e-Business is the fundamental basis to operate this business in practice. In this paper a concept is introduced to derive an important part of the overall software architecture for business models based on a characterization of its revenue model. For that purpose, a 'classification cycle' is defined including a set of criteria which enables you to conclude technical decisions for the design of a software architecture. Using this classification cycle, a variety of revenue models can be identified. Within this paper we focus on the specific revenue model subscription of services as one example. The derived architecture serves as a software reference architecture for all business models which are based on this type of revenue model. It means that in case a software system has to be developed for a business model using this revenue model, the software architecture presented in this paper can be used as a sample solution to refer to. Thus, it helps architects to derive a fundamental part of the overall software architecture in an easy and efficient way.

Key words: business model, revenue model, software reference architecture, e-Business

2.   RELATED WORK

Zerdick et al. (1999) define the revenue model as the 'determination of the sources of revenue'. They investigate revenue models for the e-Business isolated from business models. This approach is also pursued by Skiera and Lambrecht (2000). However, they classify possible revenue models within e-Business but do not analyze the relation of these models to the underlying software architecture.

Other authors use a different approach by defining revenue models as a part of the encompassing business model. One of the first definitions of a business model in e-Business is given by Timmers (1998, 1999). According to him, 'a business model is defined as the organization (or 'architecture') of product, service and information flows, and the sources of revenues and benefits for supplier and customer'. It becomes obvious that the revenue model that Timmers calls 'sources of revenue' is an integral part of a business model. Buchholz (2001) defines a business model as a 'brace of four constitutive components', where the revenue model is one of them. Also Wirtz (2001) and Doubosson-Torbay, Osterwalder and Pigneur (2001) see revenue models as a part of business models.

However, we could not identify any research that analyzes the dependency of business models and its related software architecture in depth. Only a few authors deal with this relation at all. One approach in this area is delivered by Bartelt and Lamersdorf (2000). They define four methods for the designing of business models. One of these methods are so called 'modules of functionality' like product-catalogues and search engines. They are identified within business models and can be used independently from a precise case and thus can be reused in other business models. However, this approach does not deliver a set of such functionality modules and identifies only some examples which cannot be used in general. Furthermore, they do not investigate these modules of functionality for the domain of the revenue generation.

Due to this shortfall we chose an alternative approach that is described in the next chapters to derive a software reference architecture on the basis of a characterization of a revenue model. A software reference architecture can be interpreted as 'a collection of computational components [...] together with a description of the interactions between these components – the connectors' (Gerlan and Shaw, 1993). Thereby, multiple descriptions can be given depending on different aspects one wants to focus on. We describe in this article our software reference architecture using UML class diagrams (OMG, 2005) to place emphasis on static aspects, and sequence diagrams to place emphasis on dynamic aspects of the system.

1.   MOTIVATION

e-Business is characterized and influenced both by the usage of information technology for business purposes and by the occurrence of adapted or completely new generated business models. To lead a company successfully, there has to be a clear understanding of how the revenues can be generated. The offered value a customer is willing to pay for as well as the related processes of revenue generation are defined in the revenue model. Thus, a revenue model is one of the core elements in planning and realizing a company. Analyzing the literature, it becomes obvious that there is a common understanding that a revenue model is an integral part of a business model.

To realize a business model in the e-Business, there is a special focus on the software architecture of its underlying software system, because, like the 'e' suggests already, the processes are supposed to be performed mostly electronically. Thus, the business model and its underlying software architecture are tightly connected. Since the revenue model is a very important element of the business model, the software architecture also has to be designed according to the requirements which have to be satisfied to generate revenues. There are other elements of a business model like its procurement or distribution model that influence the overall software architecture of the complete software system, but we focus on this fundamental aspect.

The purpose of this article is to develop a software reference architecture to support the application of one revenue model within its encompassing business model. Thus, the reference architecture helps architects to derive an important part of the overall software architecture which is necessary to realize a business model. Within this article it will be focused on the subscription revenue model as one possible revenue model in e-Business. It can be applied to different business models like Internet-Service-Provider, online magazines or even e-shops which offer an ongoing claim of their products using a subscription.

Therefore, the revenue model has to be characterized in a way which enables a company to derive technical decisions for the design of this software architecture. Because of the mutual dependency between the revenue and the business model, the criteria for this characterization have to be based on the business model itself. This article shows a way of deriving a software architecture on this background. Using the resulting software reference architecture for the subscription revenue model in practice, the planning, (re-)designing and implementing of new applications for business models becomes more reliable and effective.

Since we claim to derive a reference architecture, this term yet has to be defined. More generally than an architecture, a reference model is according to Bass, Clements and Kazman (1997) 'a standard decomposition of a known problem into parts that cooperatively solve the problem'. Then, a (software) reference architecture is 'a reference model mapped onto software components [...] and the data flow between these components'. Related to our article, the known problem is represented by the revenue models. This domain is decomposed into functional parts which can be implemented as components and their relations. Thus, a sample solution is given that can be used as a reference during the development of a software architecture related to this domain.

3.   CLASSIFICATION OF THE SUBSCRIPTION REVENUE MODEL

Subscription is taken as the relevant e-Business revenue model for this article. Other examples of revenue models are transaction fees, advertising or profiling, but here we focus on the subscription revenue model. In general, a subscription represents a contract between a supplier of an offer and its customer (the subscriber) about the claim of a specific amount of a specific offer within a specific period for a specific price.

The agreed amount represents the maximum the customer is allowed to obtain during the period. In the case that this amount is exceeded, additional entities are charged separately. In the majority of the cases, the subscriptions are extended automatically and the price is paid per period.

In this section, the revenue model subscription and its variations are characterized. Therefore, some key criteria are identified with regard to the purpose of reasoning design decisions of an appropriate software architecture. Using these criteria the classification of the revenue model enables two things:

- to identify different variations (or subtypes) of the revenue model and
- to be able to derive decisions for the software architecture of the underlying software system which enables the application of this revenue model.

For the classification of the revenue model, the 'classification cycle' is used. The following paragraph introduces this tool.

3.1   The classification cycle

Related to the elements of the definition of a business model the classification criteria to characterize a revenue model are grouped into four sections: actor-related, offer-related, benefit-related and revenue-related criteria. The close dependencies between the revenue model and its business model are considered via this approach. The characterization of the revenue model is based on criteria that are linked to its encompassing business model. Nine criteria were collected as a result of related work research and own considerations. In the following, the criteria are introduced in brief.

3.1.1   Actor-related criteria

The actor-related criteria are the customer role and the customer relation. The customer role may obtain one of the parameters informant, buyer, seller, or value integrator (actors within communities where the customer itself generates the value). This criterion limits the possible ways of receiving money from the customer. It is not limited that a customer only acts in one role. For example, a customer on a market platform may sell his own products and buy products from other participants. The important question from a software architecture point of view is whether a customer role has to be supported or not. The customer relation might be anonymous, identified or identified and authenticated. An online bank for example has to be sure that the customer is the person he claims to be. Therefore, special authentication procedures have to be supported in this case. In general, depending on this criteria the design of customer profile management and access control is influenced.

3.1.2   Offer-related criteria

Offer-related criteria are consistency, pricelevel and origin of the products or services. The consistency is one of the most important criteria since it provides information about the ways the company has to manage their products internally and how the shipment can be handled. Possible values are services, digital goods, physical goods, or information. The pricelevel ranges from nano via micro and medium to macro[1] and gives information about possible payment methods. The origin of the offer may either be self-determined or over-directed. This differentiation is important

---

[1]   According to Reif (2001), the ranges are (in €) nano (0,001 to 0,1), micro (>0,1 to 5), medium (>5 to 1000) and macro (>1000).

for devices which the product management component has to maintain and to control.

3.1.3 Revenue-related criteria

The revenue-related criteria comprise the payment method and the revenue origin. The origin of the revenues can be direct or indirect and is addressing either the end-consumer (direct) or third parties like other companies (indirect). The latter parameter occurs for example in advertisement-based revenue models. As we mentioned earlier already, payment methods are influenced among others by the pricelevel of the offering. A company has to decide whether its customers are claimed using invoices, direct debits, credit cards, or external payment providers which offer for example a method to transfer prices also on a nano or micro level.

3.1.4 Benefit-related criteria

The last section is the benefit related criteria. Two criteria can be found here: the primary benefit and the additional benefit for a customer. The primary benefit does not have static values but answers the question 'what is the customer willing to pay for?' This criterion can thus be interpreted as the revenue model in a nutshell and contains the most important value from a customer point of view. The additional benefit can be e-Business-inherent, personalization or anonymity. In the case that one of the last two values is selected, the design of the software architecture has to consider this fact strongly. Otherwise, the e-Business-inherent means nothing but benefits that are encompassed anyway by using the e-Business technology like time savings due to independency of physical distances or convenience by ordering products simply using a PC. In this case, nothing has to be considered in particular.

This total of nine criteria, grouped in their sections and arranged in the classification cycle are used to characterize a revenue model. This classification cycle, which can be seen in Figure 1, is a general tool to describe revenue models of the e-Business. However, within this article, it is only applied to classify the subscription revenue model. Thus, only a limited set of all parameter values will be used.

As it will be classified in the following, we concentrate only on one variation of the subscription revenue model: subscription of services. Other variations like subscription of digital products or subscription of physical products are not within the scope of this article. Nevertheless, it becomes obvious that the product consistency is the most relevant criterion of subtypes of the subscription revenue model.

3.2 Classifying the subscription of services revenue model

The classification cycle in figure 1 shows the characteristics of the subscription of services revenue model.

Figure 1. Classification cycle of the revenue model subscription of services

A typical example for a business model which offers services to subscribe is an Internet Service Provider who offers web-access to its customer. Based on this example, the following considerations are explained.

4. FROM REVENUE MODEL TO SOFTWARE REFERENCE ARCHITECTURE

Based on this characterization of the subscription of services revenue model by using the classification cycle, technical decisions for a software reference architecture are derived within this section.

The company offers services (criteria consistency). The primary benefit for the customer is the ongoing supply of these services. Therefore, he subscribes to this service by concluding a contract. These criteria obviously affect the way how the offers have to be maintained by a software system. In addition, the origin of the offer is self-determined. This leads to the requirement that the company has to create, change and maintain its services by itself. For the given example of an Internet Service Provider, the company has to offer a variety of different tariffs for its customers to meet a wide range of different whishes depending on the personal behavior of each customer. The tariff determines the kind of service the customer subscribes and is volume or time related. The maximum available amount of units for each kind has to be fixed by the tariff plus the time period in which these units have to be consumed. Furthermore, the tariff defines the price for this package and the costs of additionally claimed units within one period. All these parameters have to be fixed within a tariff. While the contract itself contains personal information about the customer and maybe determines general issues like e.g. the payment method, the tariffs contain the detailed description of the service. Therefore, contract and tariffs belong to one component but will be realized in separate classes. A selected tariff is then aligned to a contract.

To be able to distinguish various statuses of a customer this is a relevant information that has also to be stored in the contract. By providing a status, it is possible to lock out users from using any services if it is required, for example if they did not pay their last bill correctly. Thus, the risk of betrayal can be reduced for the company.

It also became obvious, that depending on the tariff different reference values (volume or time) have to be charged and therefore have to be logged. Since the customer relationship is identified, each customer session has to be investigated separately regarding the activities of the user. At the end of a session, a logging mechanism must determine the relevant reference value and the consumed entities and save it persistently. For revision purposes and to create itemized bills, each session has to be saved separately. Therefore, an appropriate usage account has to be realized in a separate component. This component performs the central processes to charge the customer in accordance to the use of the subscription revenue model.

Obviously, customer profiles have to be supported as well. That the origin of the revenue is direct can be seen at the criteria. This means that the end-customer transfers the revenues. They act as identified buyer who pay their bills by using invoices or direct debits. In addition, there is no need for any anonymity assumed to be an additional benefit[2]. Thus, the customer disposes of a customer profile. Access data like login and password and private address data have to be saved there. Furthermore, a debit account, saving all financial transactions, is necessary within the customer profile.

---

[2] In case the customer relation is classified as identified, it is hardly possible in practice that there the additional benefit might be anonymity.

This account will be periodically charged with the amount of the invoice (therefore debit account) and in return will be credited on the event of incoming financial transactions. Since a history of all transactions has to be available, each transaction has to be stored in an own data record. Thus, the account will be realized by two classes where one class (better: the instances of one class) contains the data records. The complete customer profile will be realized by a further component which contains cooperative classes.

The invoice was mentioned already. The invoice has to determine and sum up the consumed entities and compare this value with the customer's chosen tariff at the end of a period. In case the summed up value extends the maximum count of entities, the difference has to be calculated separately based on the defined price. Otherwise, the invoice will show the defined price for the subscription. The final amount will be charged and added as a new data record of the customer's debit account and a physical version of the invoice has to be created and send to the customer. An own component will implement the invoice. This component will gather the relevant information from the customer profile component, the contract and tariff component, and the usage account component. Therefore, references between these components have to be considered in the reference architecture.

To summarize: the following components were derived based on the classification of the revenue model:

- a contract and tariff component which separates both elements in own classes
- a usage account component which is responsible for the logging of the user activities depending on the tariff; this is the central component to charge the customer using this revenue model
- a customer profile component which comprises classes for personal data and for debit account data
- a invoice component

These considerations are picked up again in the next chapter where a detailed appropriate software reference architecture is represented.

5. A SOFTWARE REFERENCE ARCHITECTURE FOR THE SUBSCRIPTION REVENUE MODEL

According to the views defined by Gruhn and Thiel (2000), the software architectures are described on a software-technical level in the following. Since it is a goal of the represented reference architectures to identify relevant components which realize necessary functionality to implement the revenue model, these components are identified within the software-technical architecture by encompassing their belonging classes.

The following figure 2 shows the class diagram of the reference architecture. The grey boxes encompass the classes to their related components.

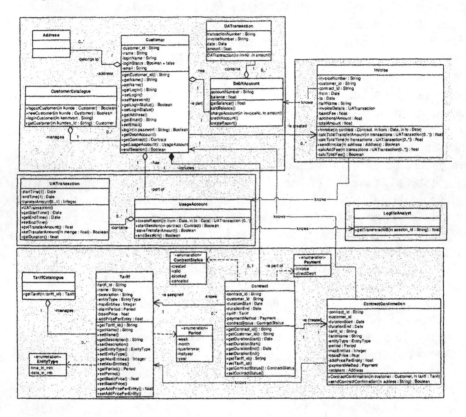

Figure 2. Class diagram of the software reference architecture

As it can be seen, five components are defined, while in the previous section only four main components were derived from the classification cycle of the revenue model. The reason for this is that the UsageAccount component needs additional services from another component called *LogfileAnalyst*. Before we analyze its role in more detail, we look at the other components.

The *CustomerProfile* component contains five classes which should be largely self-explaining. A user can have multiple addresses that lead to the creation of an own class. The *DebitAccount* contains header information like the current balance. The transactions are stored as instances of *DATransactions*. Therefore, the constructor of this class is activated by the

DebitAccount, handing over the relevant information which it received earlier by the invoking component, e.g. the *Invoice*. In addition, a *CustomerCatalogue* is necessary to create new instances of *Customer* or to deliver a reference of a customer object to an invoking class.

The *ContractAndTariff* component contains the separated classes *Contract* and *Tariff* as required, while an instance of *Tariff* is assigned to an instance of *Contract*. A class *TarifCatalogue* is similar to a *CustomerCatalogue* and delivers a reference to a *Tariff* object. A further class of this component is the *ContractConfirmation* which will be generated by the time the customer places the contract. It contains contract-relevant data and will be sent to the customer.

As mentioned earlier, the central component related to the core process of this revenue model is the *UsageAccount* component. With the input of the *LogfileAnalyst* component this component reports the activities within a session and stores them persistently into a separate data record. Figure 3 shows this component.

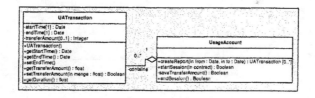

Figure 3. UsageAccount component

The process of the logging and the roles of the participating classes is shown in detail in the sequence diagram in figure 4. By the time a customer logs in and a new session is started, the method *startSession* of the class *UsageAccount* is called. It controls at first the status of the contract to ensure the customer is allowed to consume the services. Assuming a positive response, the *UsageAccount* initiates a new instance of the class *UATransactions*.

The data which have to be logged depend on the tariff the related customer had chosen. Either the transferred data volume or the connected time is relevant. In either case, by the time the customer logs out and ends the session, the relevant information has to be determined and saved within the *UATransactions* data record. Therefore, the method *endSession* of *UsageAccount* is invoked. In case the transferred data volume has to be recorded, this information has to be determined at first. Therefore, the component *LogfileAnalyst* can be used, which gathers the information by parsing the log file. This information can be saved afterwards within the created instance of *UATransaction*. The duration of the session is always saved in the data record independently of the tariff for reporting reasons.

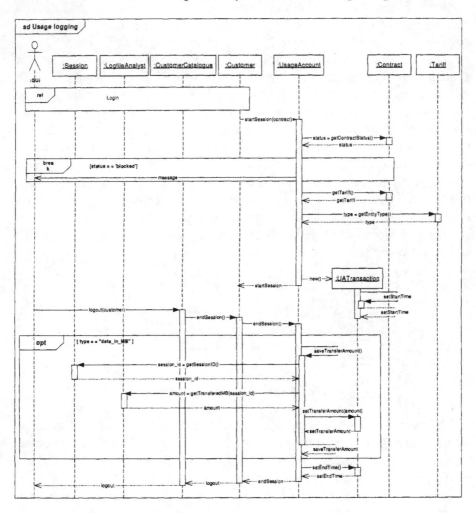

Figure 4. Sequence diagram of the usage logging

The last component to be discussed is the *Invoice* which comprises one equally named class. The constructor of this class is called at the end of each subscription period from a controller of the complete system which is not described here in any detail. The constructor receives the relevant parameters to calculate the chargeable amount which are a reference to the relevant customer, its contract, and the invoice period. Figure 5 shows the interaction of the participating components during the invoicing.

For the calculation, the tariff chosen by the customer has to be compared with the used entities during this expired period.

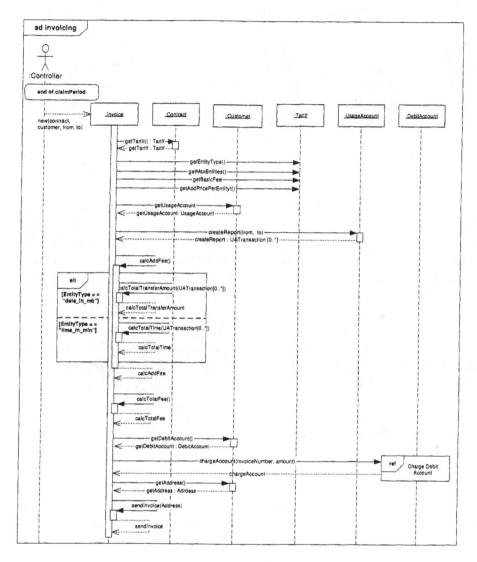

Figure 5. Sequence diagram of the invoicing

The tariff is received from the *ContractAndTariff* component, the used entities from the *UsageAccount* component. If the amount of consumed units is not higher than the maximum amount according to the tariff, only the agreed subscription fee has to be charged to the *DebitAccount* of the customer. In case the used entities exceeded this maximum, an additional price has to be calculated by the invoicing and charged to the account. At the end, a physical invoice has to be sent to the customer.

6.   VALIDATION

A German Lottery company was rebuilding its internet platform recently. One of the offered games on the platform can be played in a subscription mode, so that the customer automatically takes part on the draws according to his configured parameters like draw days, predictions, and bet amounts. To ensure the participation, the stake has to be available on the customers account in advance. This virtual account is part of the customers profile. By the time the bets are placed into the system, the stake is withdrawn automatically from this account. To agree on the conditions of the contract, the customer has to sign on to the platform and configure his subscription.

The design of the platforms software architecture was derived from the reference architecture presented in the previous section. Because of the divergent specification of bets, some components had to be adapted slightly. The *ContractAndTariff* component had to be changed in a way to treat the individually configured bets as tariffs. Thus, a bet was assigned to a contract rather than a tariff. Furthermore, the *UsageAccount* and the *Invoice* components were adapted, because each participation on a draw had to be logged and the regarding bet amount had to be withdrawn from the customers account immediately. Nevertheless, the usage of the software reference architecture was helpful to design the required architecture with reduced effort and in reduced time.

7.   CONCLUSIONS

This paper focused on the creation of a software reference architecture for a revenue model of the e-Business based on a business model related characterization of this revenue model. Therefore, we introduced a classification cycle including relevant classification criteria. The parameters of these criteria, selected in accordance with a specific revenue model, enabled us to derive requirements and conclusions for the design of an appropriate software architecture. Because we focused on the domain of the subscription of services revenue model, the software architecture can be considered as a reference architecture. The benefit of this software reference architecture was proven already during its application within a practical software development project.

At this point, wee see the need of further research in order to extend the usage of the classification cycle to further revenue models and to derive more appropriate software reference architectures. It is our aim to get a comprehensive set of reference architectures which can be used to a large variety of business models within the e-Business.

ACKNOWLEDGEMENT

The Chair of Applied Telematics/e-Business is endowed by Deutsche Telekom AG.

The authors can be contacted at {gruhn, weber}@ebus.informatik.uni-leipzig.de

REFERENCES

Bass, L., Clements P.C., and Kazman, R., 1997, *Software Architecture in Practice*, Addison Wesley

Bartelt, A., and Lamersdorf, W., 2000, Business Models of Electronic Commerce: Modeling and Classification (German: Geschäftsmodelle des Electronic Commerce: Modellbildung und Klassifikation), in: *Verbundtagung Wirtschaftsinformatik 2000*, pp. 17-29, Shaker

Buchholz, W., 2001, Netsourcing Business Models – Business Models for purchasing platforms (German: Netsourcing Business Models - Geschäftsmodelle für Einkaufsplattformen), in: Dangelmaier, W., Pape, U., and Rüther, M., ed., *Die Supply Chain im Zeitalter von E-Business und Global Sourcing*, pp. 37-52

Dubosson-Torbay, M., Osterwalter, A., and Pigneur, Y., 2001, eBusiness model desing, classification and mesurement, (October 5, 2004) http://citeseer.ist.psu.edu/dubosson.torbay01ebusiness.html

Garlan, D., Shaw, M., 1993, An Introduction to Software Architecture, in: *Advances in Software Engineering and Knowledge Engineering*, pp. 1-39, World Scientic Publishing Company

Gruhn, V., and Thiel, A., 2000, *Componentmodels - DCOM, JavaBeans, EnterpriseJavaBeans, CORBA* (German: *Komponentenmodelle - DCOM, JavaBeans, EnterpriseJavaBeans, CORBA*), Addison-Wesley

Object Management Group: OMG Unified Modeling Language Specification, March 2005, Version 2.0.

Reif, W., 2001, What is E-Commerce? (German: Was ist E-Commerce?), University of Augsburg, (May 5, 2003) http://www.uni-augsburg.de/lehrstuehle/info1/lehre/ss01/e-ommerce/folien/Definition.pdf

Skiera, B., and Lambrecht, A., 2000, Revenue Models for the Internet (German: Erlösmodelle im Internet), (December 13, 2003) http://www.ecommerce.wiwi.uni-frankfurt.de/skiera/publications/Erloesmodell.pdf

Timmers, P., 1998, Business Models for Electronic Markets, in: Gadient, Y., Schmidt, B., Selz, D., ed., *EM – Electronic Commerce in Europe. EM – Electronic Markets*, Vol.8. No. 2, 07/98, (May 10, 2005) http://www.electronicmarkets.org/modules/pub/view.php/electronicmarkets-183

Timmers, P., 1999, *Electronic Commerce – Strategies and Models for Business-to-Business Trading*, John Wiley & Sons Ltd. England

Wirtz, B.W., 2001, *Electronic Business*, 2. Auflage, Gabler

Zerdick, A., et al., 1999, The Internet Economy – Strategies for Digital Business (German: Die Internet-Ökonomie - Strategien für die digitale Wirtschaft), Springer

SELECTING SUPPLY PARTNERS FOR E-COLLABORATION IN SUPPLY CHAINS

Sung Ho Ha, Gye Hang Hong
School of Business Administration, Kyungpook National University, Korea; Korea University, Korea

Abstract: The system we propose supports a partner selection process in an e-business environment. The system evaluates partners' supply capabilities and market conditions changed over time with multi-criteria, including quantitative and qualitative criteria. It helps selecting the optimal partners for maximizing revenue under a level of supply risk. The proposed system has been applied to partner selection problem under the supply chain of an agriculture industry.

Key words: Supply chain; e-collaboration; supplier selection; e-business.

1.   INTRODUCTION

In industrial companies, as procurement activities account for the 50-90% of the whole business activities, the direct and indirect consequences of poor partner selection become more severe, making decisions of purchasing strategies and operations primary determinants of profitability.

Companies have more chances for selecting more effective partners due to the globalization of trade and the prevalence of the Internet. They can purchase better quality goods at a cheaper price and with better delivery conditions. However, there exist complicated issues, including the increasing number of available suppliers and the market conditions which have changed over time.

The research fields of partner selection are divided into four parts: problem definition, formulation of criteria, pre-qualification, and final selection (Boer et al., 2001). Especially, pre-qualification and final choice parts are currently being actively pursued. We have come up with the following conclusions by examining the existing research results: When selecting supply partners, we should consider changes of supply capabilities and supply market conditions over time; Partners should be evaluated with both quantitative and qualitative criteria (e.g. price, quality, or delivery performance); We must select suppliers which maximize the revenue of a purchasing company and satisfy the procurement conditions as well which the purchasing company wants to impose.

2.   SUPPLY PARTNER SELECTION METHODS

2.1   Existing literature review

In a review of supplier selection methods by Boer et al. (2001), the authors divided the supplier selection process into two steps of pre-qualification and final choice. The pre-qualification step can be defined as the process of reducing the set of all suppliers to a smaller set of acceptable suppliers. They pinpointed four categories of methods: Categorical methods, data envelopment analysis (DEA), clustering analysis (CA), and case-based reasoning (CBR).

Holt (1998) reviewed and compared several decisional methods (CA, bespoke approaches, multi-attribute analysis, multiple regressions, and multivariate discriminant analysis) which have been applied in supplier selection. He suggested that CA offers the greatest potential for pre-qualifying all suppliers. CA reduces the probability of rejecting a good supplier too early in the process via subjective reduction of the often large original set. CA can enlarge the scope for rationalization of the selection process by identifying the criteria involved. Because of these merits, we use a CA method for evaluating all available suppliers in the pre-qualification stage.

Methods suggested in final choice step are categorized into linear weighting, total cost of ownership, mathematical programming, statistical, and artificial intelligence models. Most methods belong to linear weighting and mathematical programming models (MP). MP allows a decision-maker to formulate a decision problem in terms of a mathematical objective function that subsequently needs to be maximized or minimized by varying the values of variables in the objective function. Weber and Desai (1996) illustrated how parallel axis analysis can be used to identify alternative paths in which inefficient vendors can become efficient providers of a product. Weber et al. (1998) expanded their models to negotiate with suppliers selected by multi-objective programming models under non-cooperative negotiation strategy. Especially, they showed that the values of supplier selection change according to the number of suppliers.

In linear weighting models, weights are given to the criteria, and the biggest weight indicates the highest importance. Ratings of the criteria are multiplied by their weights and summed in order to obtain a single figure for each supplier. The supplier with the highest overall rating can then be selected. Lee et al. (2001) suggested a supplier selection and management system (SSMS) which uses the linear weighting model to calculate the weights of tangible and intangible criteria and to rank the supplier's performance. Characteristic of the system resides in the process which identifies the weak criteria of selected suppliers by comparison with alternative suppliers. The SSMS informs us of the directions improving supplier performance.

2.2　Problems to solve

The static assessment for partner selection in the current research results does not cope with changes in supply capabilities and supply market conditions over time. It can be difficult for a supplier to maintain the same capability conditions during all supply periods depending on types of industries. Especially, it is very serious when we select a partner for agriculture products which have seasonal availabilities and have a wide fluctuation of capability over time. All partners can not maintain the same capabilities during all analysis periods because of changes in the delivery condition, inventory level, and market environments. Even if a partner maintains a constant supply capability, the risk level of the supply market can change over time. We can not evaluate these capability condition changes if we use the average values of criteria during the total periods of analysis. We can lose a chance to find the better solution. Thus, it is important that we divide all periods of analysis into several meaningful period units, evaluate supply conditions of each period unit, and put the results together (Talluri and Sarkis, 2002).

We consider multi-criteria (quantitative and qualitative criteria) to evaluate suppliers' capability conditions. In an early study on partner selection criteria, Dickson (1966) identified 23 criteria that have been considered by purchasing managers in various partner selection problems. Since the Dickson's study, many researchers have identified important criteria varied by industry and buying situation, and have suggested multi-criteria models. In his portfolio approach, Kraljic (1983) identified the purchasing situation in terms of two factors: profit impact and supply risk. Profit impact includes such elements as the expected monetary volume involved with the goods or services to be purchased and the impact on future product quality. Indicators of supply risk may include the availability of goods or services under consideration and the number of potential suppliers. Therefore we decide to consider such criteria as price, delivery, quality, quantity, reputation and position, warranties and claim, and information share together. By applying these criteria, we can identify several groups of partners who have low supply risk and above the needed profit. Then, we select the optimal partners, which maximize the revenue within the groups.

3.   DYNAMIC PARTNER SELECTION IN A SUPPLY CHAIN

The dynamic partner selection system consists of five major modules, as shown in Figure 1: *Prediction Module, Segmentation Module, Pre-Qualification Module, Optimization Module,* and *Update Module.* After building a long-term purchasing plan, a purchaser company searches for partners who can deliver a product or a service, assesses them, and selects the optimal ones. As described in the previous sections, the supply market conditions and the capabilities of partners change over time. Therefore, the selection system must be able to predict changes of the supply market conditions by period of time and segment the total purchasing period into several meaningful periods according to the changes. The system must select optimal partners who can not only deliver their products or services stably, but also maximize the revenues under changed market conditions within each meaningful period. We will describe the system's modules in detail in the following subsections.

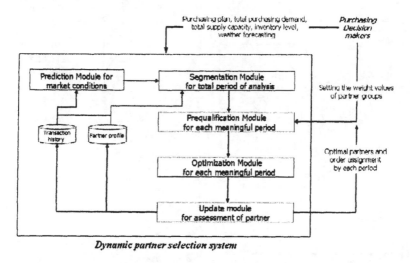

Figure 1. The architecture of dynamic partner selection system.

3.1 Prediction Module (PM)

The Prediction Module (PM) predicts the total size of a supply market during the total purchasing period and the market size by period. The total supply capacity of all partners, total inventory level, and operation rate (e.g. weather in an agriculture industry) are used as prediction factors. A purchaser investigates values of the prediction factors and inputs these values to the selection system. The PM retrieves, then, the most similar cases from past cases. A case is defined as a record which consists of the supply condition fields (total supply capacity, total inventory level, and operation rate) and supply market fields (total size, size by period) in a transaction history database. For finding the cases which are most similar with values of the prediction factors, we use a hybrid approach of Memory And Neural Network-based learning (MANN) (Shin et al., 2000). The MANN method is one of the feature weighting methods for overcoming weakness of k-NN method, meaning that all features of k-NN have the same weight.

As shown in Figure 2, the PM calculates the weight of each prediction factor from the neural network. Because an important factor has a greater effect on prediction than others, we give it a higher weight when finding a similar case.

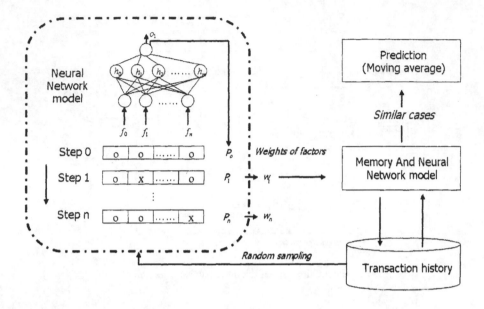

Figure 2. The procedure for calculating the weight of each factor.

The process for calculating the weight of each factor is as follows: First, we build a neural network having an input layer (total supply capacity of all partners, total inventory level, and operation rate), an output layer (total size of supply market), and one hidden layer with m nodes. Then, we train the neural network with a training set of k cases which are randomly sampled from the transaction history database.

Second, we use a sensitivity method to calculate the degree of importance of each factor: 1) A factor is selected and removed from the trained neural network, as shown in step 1 of Figure 2; 2) The weights of all nodes are set at zero and a new result is predicted from the modified neural network model; 3) The new result is compared with the initial result obtained from step 0. For comparison, we use the following sensitivity function:

$$w_i = \frac{(\sum_L \frac{|p^o - p^i|}{p^0})}{n} \tag{1}$$

where p^o is an initial result and p^i is the new result calculated when ith factor is removed. L is a set of all n cases used for calculating the sensitivity of each factor. The new result is compared with the initial result obtained from step 0; 4) The degree of importance of all factors is calculated.

Third, we calculate the similarity between each case (x) and the query (q), the expected values for predicting a coming supply market condition with the weights of the prediction factors. The similarity is obtained by using the weighted Euclidean distance equation.

$$D(x,q) = \sqrt{\sum_{f=1}^{n} w_f \times difference(x_f, q_f)^2} \qquad (2)$$

where w_f is the weight value assigned to factor f, and $difference(x_f, q_f)$ is calculated from $|x_f - q_f|$. The higher the similarity of a case, the greater weight the case has.

After calculating the similarity values of all cases, we finally select K cases having higher similarity of all cases and calculate the total size of the supply market and the market size by period by averaging out K cases.

3.2 Segmentation Module (SM)

After predicting the total size of the supply market and the market size by period, we compare those with a predicted purchasing demand (how much quantity competitor companies of the purchaser will purchase). The supply and the demand change over time. The difference between supply and demand may become smaller in any period and the difference may become larger in another period. The former is a case having a low risk because the purchaser can find alternatives easily and pay a low switching cost even if a partner does not deliver products or services to him. The latter is, however, a case having a high risk.

Therefore, we consider a supply risk of the market to assess partners effectively under these market conditions, and divide the total purchasing period into several meaningful periods according to the supply risk. Park and Park (2003) suggested a method for dividing the whole period into several meaningful period units. They segmented sales records for the total period with a genetic algorithm and a linear regression model. We adopt this method in our system to divide the total period, as shown in Figure 3.

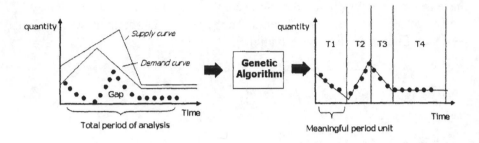

Figure 3. Dividing total analyzing period into several meaningful period units

We calculate the difference (gap) between supply and demand in each period to measure a level of risk and plot the differences in the graph. The plotting points are represented by binary codes, such as (1,0,0,0,1,0,0,0,0,1,0,0,1,0,0,0,0,0,0). The starting point of each period is 1; otherwise, it is 0. We find the best segmentation of periods by using a genetic algorithm with the following fitness function and binary representation.

$$Fitness\ function = \alpha \sum_{i=1}^{N} R_i^2 w_i + \beta F(N), \tag{3}$$

Where N is the number of intervals, w_i is the ratio of periods in the ith interval to the whole periods, R_i^2 is the residual error of the ith interval, $0 \le \alpha \le 1$, $0 \le \beta \le 1$, and $\alpha + \beta = 1$.

We can obtain four meaningful periods, as shown on the right of Figure 3. When the total purchasing period is defined as one year, the risk level of the market in the first and second meaningful periods is relatively lower than that in other periods because the gap is increased or decreased slowly. However, the risk level of the market in the third and fourth periods is very dangerous if a purchaser manages his partner loosely.

3.3 Pre-Qualification Module (PQM)

In the previous sections, we described the importance of an assessment model considering both quantitative criteria and qualitative criteria. The proposed system implements this assessment by aid of two modules, pre-qualification and optimization.

After dividing the total period into several meaningful period units, in the pre-qualification phase we segment partners into several groups which have similar supply conditions in each meaningful period. We use Self-Organizing Map (SOM), a clustering tool using an unsupervised learning scheme, to train the neural network. Unsupervised learning comprises those techniques for which the resulting actions or desired outputs for the training sequences are unknown. The network is only given the input vectors, and then self-organizes these inputs into categories (Ha and Park, 1998).

The SOM is designed as follows: 1) Normalization: we normalize values of supply conditions into 0 ~ 1; 2) Clustering: we design a SOM which has 7 inputs and 9 outputs. The inputs include quantitative criteria (quality, frequency, price, and quantity) and qualitative criteria (reputation and position, warranties and claim, and information share). Outputs are the number of clusters to which a supply partner belongs. The SOM segments the partners into several groups with similar characteristics; 3) Pre-qualification: The system compares the characteristics of each group with the purchaser's needs in each meaningful period. For comparison, the system measures the distance between partner groups and needs of the purchaser, and selects groups which are close to the needs.

$$Distance\ (G, I) = \sqrt{w_d \times x_d + w_p \times x_p + w_q \times x_q + w_{qty} \times x_{qty} + \ldots\ldots} \qquad (4)$$

In the case of a high risk level, we assign higher weights to the criteria such as frequency, quantity, reputation and position, and warranties and claim. In the case of a low risk level, however, we assign higher weights to the criteria such as price, quality. Weights difference among criteria changes according to the gradient of gaps between demand and supply within each period (see Figure 4).

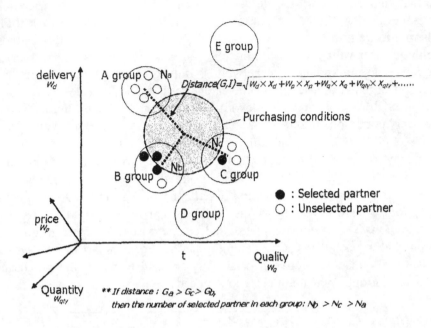

Figure 4. Selecting suppliers which maximize revenues under supply risks.

3.4   Optimization Module (OM)

After the pre-qualification stage, we decide on a final partner who can maximize revenue and satisfy the procurement conditions which the purchasing company wants. The following mixed integer model is designed to satisfy the procurement conditions.

$$Max \ Z = \sum_{i=1}^{I}\sum_{k=1}^{K}\sum_{t=1}^{T} R_{ikt} \times x_{ikt} \tag{5}$$

subject to

$$\sum_{i=1}^{I}\sum_{k=1}^{K} x_{ikt} \leq D_{t}, \ for \ all \ t \tag{6}$$

$$x_{ikt} \leq min(S_{it}^{u}, L_{it}^{u})Y_{ikt}, \ for \ all \ i,k,t \tag{7}$$

$$x_{ikt} \geq \max(S_{it}^l, L_{it}^l)Y_{ikt}, \text{ for all } i,k,t \tag{8}$$

$$\sum_{i=1}^{I} \sum_{k=1}^{K} y_{ikt} \leq N_t, \text{ for all } t \tag{9}$$

$$\sum_{i=1}^{I} y_{ikt} \geq \rho_{k+1,t} \sum_{i=1}^{I} y_{i(k+1)t} \geq \cdots \geq \rho_{k+K,t} \sum_{i=1}^{I} y_{i(k+K)t}, \text{ for all } t \tag{10}$$

$$x_{ikt} \geq 0, \text{ for all } i,k,t \tag{11}$$

$$y_{ikt} \in (0,1), \text{ for all } i,k,t \tag{12}$$

where x_{ikt} is quantity ordered from the supplier i who belong to cluster k in period t, R_{ikt} is revenue per unit made from the supplier i who belongs to cluster k in period t, D_t is purchasing demand in period t, S_{it}^u is maximum order quantity available from supplier i in period t, S_{it}^l is minimum order quantity available from supplier i in period t, L_{it}^u is maximum amount of business to be given to supplier i in period t, L_{it}^l is minimum amount of business to be given to supplier i in period t, N_t is the number of supplier to be selected in period t, $\rho_{k+n,t}$ is ratio of number of supplier selected in cluster $k+n$ to number of supplier selected in cluster k in period t, y_{ikt} is 1 if supplier i of cluster k is selected in period t; 0, otherwise.

Objective function (5) shows the maximization of revenue during total planning periods under following constraints: Constraint (6) shows a purchasing demand in period t. Total order quantity of all suppliers cannot exceed the purchasing demand in period t. Constraints (7) and (8) show potential constraints of suppliers and policy constraints of a purchaser.

Constraint (9) is a limitation of the number of suppliers who are selected in period t. It can be a policy of purchaser. As the number of suppliers increases, the management cost increases and supply risk decreases. Constraint (10) shows a limitation for selecting suppliers in terms of the supply risk of cluster. If cluster 7 is superior to cluster 1, for example, the number of cluster 7 is ρ times as large as the number of cluster 1. The suppliers who have a low supply risk are finally selected more than other suppliers as maximizing the revenue. We choose the final suppliers and their supply quantities by using the mathematical model and determine other supply conditions from the cluster features.

3.5   Update Module (UM)

After selecting the optimal partners and collaborating with them during
the total purchasing period, the dynamic supplier selection system assesses
the transaction history of the partners. The occurrence of the back-order,
troubles of information share, and changes in warranty and claim strategy
are reevaluated and the result of assessing a partner is updated in the partner
profile database. The updated results are applied to the partner selection for
the next purchase.

4.   APPLICATION

The dynamic supplier selection system has been applied to the partner
selection under a supply chain of the agriculture industry. Agricultural
products which farmers' associations produce are supplied for purchasers
such as wholesalers and manufacturers. Purchasers process or package the
produces and deliver them to customers. Because agricultural products are
apt to be decomposed and because suppliers have different delivery intervals,
harvest quantities and level of inventory facility, and changes of supply
conditions by period are larger than other industries. Purchasers are not
supplied enough quantities on time and they paid much money for being
supplied from other suppliers. It is a very important issue how purchasers
select suppliers in this supply environment.

We analyzed the data of the past one year with the proposed model. For
comparison, we also applied the revised Weber method (Weber et al., 1998)
to the same experimental data. Suppliers could be selected and the order
quantities could be assigned to selected suppliers for the next year. The
results from two models were compared in terms of revenue, shortages of
order, and the number of managing suppliers, as shown in Figure 5.

The findings were: first, the proposed model can manage fewer suppliers
than the revised Weber method and the supply risk (i.e., shortage of order) of
our model is lower than the revised Weber method. When both models select
three suppliers respectively, the suppliers who are selected by our model can
fulfill order quantities on time without shortages of order. The revised
Weber method, however, produces many shortages of order in all
meaningful periods (especially, T2 in which sales are high). The revised
Weber method should increase the number of suppliers to resolve the
shortages and should pay more cost than our method.

Second, our model creates more revenue than the revised Weber during
all periods. The revised Weber method increases the number of suppliers in
order to increase revenue. However, revenue in the revised model can not

increase more than that of our model since maximum order quantities assigned to the best supplier are limited by distributing order quantities to other suppliers.

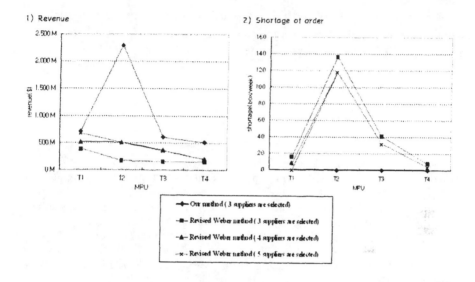

Figure 5. Comparing the proposed method to the revised Weber method

5.   CONCLUSIONS

A dynamic partner selection system was proposed for supporting a partner selection in an e-business environment. Three problems caused from current selection process were identified and a method was proposed to solve them.

1) Evaluating suppliers' capabilities and market conditions over time,
2) Considering multi-criteria for evaluating suppliers' capabilities conditions,
3) Selecting suppliers to maximize revenue and to satisfy the procurement conditions.

The method was applied to the case of the agriculture industry and was compared to the revised Weber model in terms of the revenue, the shortage of order, and the number of managing suppliers. No shortage of order occurred in the proposed method, while shortages of order occurred except during the first meaningful period in the revised Weber model. Because of such shortages, the number of managing suppliers is increased and the order amount of each supplier is decreased in the revised Weber model. As a result, the revenue of the revised Weber model was less than that in the proposed method.

Further works can extend the range of application to other industries in which supply conditions change according to time. In addition, because many supplied products are aggregated to one final product in several industries, it is very difficult to measure the profit of final product as an effect each supplied product has.

References

Boer, L., Labro, E., and Morlacchi, P., 2001, A Review of Methods Supporting Supplier Selection, *European Journal of Purchasing and Supply Management.* 7:75-89.

Dickson, G. W., 1966, An Analysis of Vendor Selection Systems and Decisions, *Journal of Purchasing.* 2(1):5-17.

Ha, S. H., and Park, S. C., 1998, Application of Data Mining Tools to Hotel Data Mart on the Intranet for Database Marketing, *Expert System With Applications.* 15:1-31.

Holt, G. D., 1998, Which Contractor Selection Methodology?, *International Journal of Project Management.* 16(3):153-164.

Kraljic, P., 1983, Purchasing must become Supply Management, *Harvard Business Review.* 61(5):109-117.

Lee, E.-K., Ha, S., and Kim, S.-K., 2001, Supplier Selection and Management System Considering Relationships in Supply Chain Management, *IEEE Transactions on Engineering Management.* 48(3):307-318.

Park, J. H., and Park, S. C., 2003, Agent-based Merchandise Management in Business-to-Business Electronic Commerce, *Decision Support System.* 35:311-333.

Shin, C. K., Yun, U. T., Kim, H. K., and Park, S. C., 2000, A Hybrid Approach of Neural Network and Memory-Based Learning to Data Mining. *Int J IEEE Trans. on Neural Networks.* 11(3):637-646.

Talluri, S., and Sarkis, J., 2002, A Model for Performance Monitoring of Suppliers, *International Journal of Production Research.* 40(16):4257-4269.

Weber, C. A., and Desai, A., 1996, Determination of Path to Vendor Market Efficiency using Parallel Coordinates Representation: A Negotiation Tool for Buyers, *European Journal of Operational Research.* 90:142-155.

Weber, C. A., Current, J. R., and Desai, A., 1998, Non-cooperative Negotiation Strategies for Vendor Selection, *European Journal of Operational Research.* 108:208-223.

E-COLLABORATION ARCHITECTURE FOR CUSTOMER-DRIVEN BUSINESS PROCESSES IN INTER-ORGANIZATIONAL SCENARIOS

Otmar Adam, Pavlina Chikova, Anja Hofer, Dominik Vanderhaeghen and Sven Zang
Institute for Information Systems (IWi) at the German Research Center for Artificial Intelligence (DFKI), Saarbruecken, Germany

Abstract: Heterogeneous customer requirements in combination with technological improvements enable new or improved customer-driven business processes. The management of such processes requires a deep but flexible integration of enterprises. In this context new forms of cooperation like E-Collaboration, describing the efficient and effective collaboration of participants in a value-added network, arise. In order to manage customer-driven business processes across such networks, existing concepts for business process management need to be adapted and extended. In this paper an E-Collaboration architecture is presented, that shows how cross-enterprise, customer-driven processes can be planned, implemented and controlled. The architecture is based on the differentiation of global and local knowledge in the widely used Architecture for Integrated Information Systems (ARIS), developed at the IWi. Another important building block is the life-cycle-model that serves as a guideline for the process-oriented creation and operation of collaborations towards a common customer-driven production and bundling of goods and services.

Key words: E-Collaboration, Customer-Driven Process Management, Inter-Organizational Business Processes, Architecture, Process-Oriented Life-Cycle

1.   INTRODUCTION

The growing importance of cooperation is a result of globalization in combination with the disappearance of political borders, technological advances caused mainly by the Internet as well as the alignment of business processes with customer needs (Naisbitt, 1986). Today the customer's position has significantly changed. Differentiation features as innovation level and additional benefits determine increasingly the purchase decision. As a consequence the markets have been turned into customer markets, on which products and services are aligned according to customer needs. Customers are being actively involved in business processes and have strong influence on which products, at which time, for which price and in which quality are produced. In this context customer-driven business processes realize the so called end-to-end-business. That means that customers do not have to combine anymore the offers of different enterprises, but that relevant enterprises rather cooperate in order to meet customer demands by providing a complete solution (Scheer, Grieble and Zang, 2003; Röhricht and Schlögel, 2001).

The borderless enterprise has been the subject of scientific discussion for years, as an organizational structure able to fulfill end-to-end requirements (Kanter, 1991; Mertens and Faisst, 1995; Picot, Wigand and Reichwald, 1997). Today new technologies based on public networks and open standards serve as enablers for effective cooperation. Therefore enterprises have the opportunity to build up new forms of cooperation characterized by a flexible and low-cost infrastructure in order to be permanently successful in largely saturated markets. The collaborative production of goods and services has been established as a crucial factor in the consciousness of economic entities. The opening of an organization's borders is no longer regarded as a necessary evil, but rather as an opportunity with strategic importance (Kanter, 1991).

Current approaches addressing solutions to specific problems of dynamically interacting organizations are summarized under the term "Business Integration"; the field of investigation is referred to as "Electronic Collaboration (E-Collaboration)" (Scheer et al., 2002). E-Collaboration describes the Internet-based collaboration of all participants in a value-added network (Scheer, Grieble and Zang, 2003). It allows a comprehensive information exchange not only between employees but also between departments and even between enterprises and encourages creative cooperation at all levels. As first case-studies show, the increase in added-value is out of proportion to the amount of participants in the network (Schubert, Wölfle and Dettling, 2003). Unlike former concepts, as e.g. E-Procurement, which focused only on small parts of the value chain, E-Collaboration incorporates all stages of added value and customer-driven business processes. While the technological implementation (Linthicum, 2003) on the one hand and the life-cycle of cooperation (Liebhart, 2002) on the other hand have already been intensively researched, too little consideration has been given to interconnecting business management and technological concepts. A rethinking from the pure technology driven implementation or profit-driven business model discussion to an integrated view that spans from the conceptual level to the system blueprint is needed.

For a detailed and systematic analysis and redesign of inter-organizational processes enterprises need an architecture that offers a set of integrated methods from the business concept level up to the implementation into ICT-systems. The appropriate graphic representation of these contents and user-friendly, intuitive tools that ensure the flawless connection of the different levels is of great importance in order to support the exchange of ideas and the reconciliation of interests between the different recipients within the network.

For these purposes a proposal for Architecture for E-Collaboration enabling customer-driven business processes in value-added networks is developed in this article.

2.   E-COLLABORATION ARCHITECTURE

Compared to traditional business processes the complexity of inter-organizational customer-driven processes has raised considerably as a result of the changing customer requirements, the numerous possibilities of interactions as well as the strategic, structural and cultural differences between partners and customers. Coordinating business partners turns out to be more difficult, especially because of the differing objectives and the lack of inherent organizational arrangements and behavior regulations as they exist within an enterprise (Scheer, Beinhauer and Habermann, 2000). The allocation of resources of the business partners, the determination of responsibilities for material and financial exchange relationships, as well as the information and data exchange over interfaces have to be planned, arranged and "lived" together. Thus the demands imposed to Customer-Driven Process Management concepts increase.

Existing Business Process Management methods and phase models are used as a foundation in the architecture presented here, which are adapted to the specifications of collaborative scenarios related to customer-centric business processes. Especially because of its completeness of vision and its proven practicability both in the scientific and the economic context the "ARIS House" (Scheer, 2002) is accepted as a generic framework for business process management and serves as a basis for further considerations. The ARIS House describes a business process, assigning equal importance to the questions of organization, functions, outputs and the required data. First, it isolates these questions for separate treatment, in order to reduce the complexity of the field of description, but then all the relationships are reintegrated using the Control View introduced for this purpose.

The E-Collaboration Architecture is presented here in a three-tier framework that is connected through control loops, following the concept of business process excellence of Scheer (Scheer and Borowsky, 1999), which consists of a model to track a complete life-cycle of business process management, including modelling, real-time control and monitoring of business processes. The first layer focuses on the E-Collaboration strategy. At the centre of the second layer, the "E-Collaboration Process Engineering", there are design, optimization and controlling of both enterprise spanning and internal customer-driven processes. The third layer, "E-Collaboration Process Execution", deals with the (operational) implementation of customer-driven business processes in value-added networks as well as their support through information and communication technologies. The structure of the layer model is shown in Figure 1.

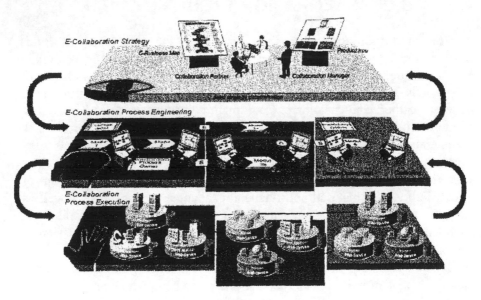

Figure 1. E-Collaboration architecture

2.1   Views on business process models

As described above, the framework is based on the ARIS House and divides it into a vertical axis of global knowledge of all collaboration partners and a horizontal axis of local knowledge of the single participants (cf. Figure 2). The organization view and the output view are global knowledge because a goal-oriented collaboration is impossible without them.

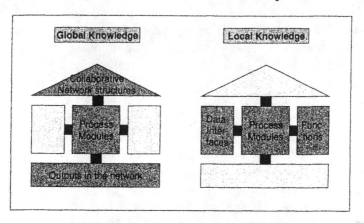

Figure 2. Global and local knowledge in value-added networks

At the time the interaction occurs between two partners, local knowledge is shared (bilaterally) between the partners, i.e. additional information, like data structures and semantics, are exchanged. Updates of the local knowledge do not influence the network as network knowledge has to be available for all partners. Changes in the global network knowledge and as a consequence changes in the output and organization view have to be accessible to all partners immediately, for example if a company leaves the network or if a product or service is no longer available within the network.

Global and local knowledge merge gradually in the step-by-step development of E-Collaboration process engineering. Following the distinction between global and local knowledge, a language is needed for the exchange of these knowledge fragments. Because the necessary detail functions and data schemes of the respective enterprise are determined in the data and the function view, these are treated from a micro perspective. They are characterized by an intensive internal interdependence, whereas externally a standardized encapsulation has to be provided. Interfaces of the data and function views to other network participants become visible in the process view in form of attribute correlations to process modules and concern the technological field of the cooperation during the realization much more intensely than the conceptual one.

This technique enables the generation of public (visible to network partners) and private (enterprise-internal) views and levels of detail for management, process owner and IT-experts out of an E-Collaboration model.

2.2   E-Collaboration Strategy

Before using the architecture there is an awareness of one or more enterprises that they can profit by collaboration with complementary core competence partners. Afterwards, in the formation phase, mostly referred to initiation and agreement of the enterprise network, the collaboration partners are determined by the shared goals of the collaboration and the aspired win-win situation of all partners. The decision if and with which enterprises an E-Collaboration scenario should be implemented is taken by every single enterprise individually and rationally; for this reason it depends highly on the expected economical profit of the individual partner. In the next step, the joint aims of the collaboration have to be defined as synthesis of the individual aims.

Enterprise spanning business processes are not planned in detail at the strategic level but designed as concentrated, high-level process modules related primarily to customer needs and requirements. Thus, they combine the public knowledge about the collaborative processes that is shared by all participants. Business process models for e-collaborative scenarios at the strategic level no longer act on the assumption of a chronological view of the process alone, but more on a role-based, customer-driven process model to discover new value-added potentials. To facilitate the collaborative customer service or product delivery, graphical methods, like product models, are also used at this stage for the determination of a common service or product bundle. They simplify and put the often implicit objectives into concrete terms. In addition to the characteristic features of a customer service or a product over its entire life-cycle, the organizational units participating in the production are contained in a product model (Genderka, 1995). By means of product trees enterprises can conceal detailed service descriptions in an internal view that puts special focus on the organizational aspects of the product offered by the partners. In an external view they just provide the information required for the configuration of the common service bundle in the form of product bundle models (Scheer, Herrmann and Klein, 2004). Regarding customer services, the strategic layer has to be extended, whereas there will be initialized not only service models but also directives and phases for providing services, in which the customer himself is involved.

The question about the core competences in the enterprises is directly associated with the question which customer-driven processes remain in the enterprise and which are supposed to be assigned to partner enterprises or collaboratively operated (Jost and Scheer, 2002). This decision again has direct effects on the IT-systems used, e.g. whether a portal is supposed to be implemented or the participation in an electronic marketplace is sought. E-

Collaboration strategic and technical problems cannot be considered independently from each other; therefore the IT-architecture is already initialized.

As the basic parameters of the collaboration are determined on the first layer the procedures and the interactions are planned in more detail at the engineering layer.

2.3   E-Collaboration Process Engineering

On this layer each partner considers their part in the inter-enterprise customer-driven process. Each party models its own internal processes. The event-driven process chain (EPC) (Keller, Nüttgens and Scheer, 1992) - as a widely accepted method for process modelling in research and in practice (Davis, 2001) is used for the design of the process flow within an enterprise (local view).

The global view on the collaborative customer-driven process is generated in order to manage the common processes and to reduce the complexity of integrating the participating organizational units into one virtual unit. In doing so it is important that the partners provide access to all relevant information described as global knowledge beforehand and at the same time are able to hide their business secret. Both aims are achieved by enhancing the EPC with a new construct, the process module (Grieble, Klein and Scheer, 2002). It serves as an abstraction for more detailed sub-processes that contain the local knowledge and thus encapsulates crucial process information.

To generate a public view the ARIS House was expanded respectively the EPC had to be enhanced by a new construct "interface", that stands for the interfaces that link private process models within the collaborative customer-oriented scenario.

For the collaborating partners only the data at the interfaces, that is the input respectively output data of the single process modules (resp. EPC), are relevant for the realization of the collaboration. Thus it is guaranteed that the enterprise-owned EPC is only visible internally. Fuelled by the global need for organizational and output information, parts of the local business process models can then be visualized by an appropriate graphical method in order to gain knowledge of the common customer-driven processes and to reduce the complexity of integrating the participating organizational units into one virtual unit.

The collaboration partners have to continuously compare the result of the implementation with their customer-oriented goals and adjust deviations. Hitherto the management has obtained its knowledge about the company's success from figures of the past, e.g. cash-flow, trading volume or profit made. The causes for fluctuations, requiring immediate counter measures, are not discernible. Until the problem is recognized, valuable time has elapsed. Therefore new measurement categories which allow a reliable and contemporary evaluation of the process efficiency are required. The information needed cannot be extracted from the record and transaction oriented applications alone. Key performance-indicators must be defined based on records, log-files, time stamps etc. These can be measured and analyzed by means of intelligent tools (Jost and Scheer, 2002).

The controlling function is a must when there is a high degree of uncertainty as with E-Collaboration projects. The management can permanently control the implementation of the strategic collaboration configuration and promptly evaluate whether the expected value-added potentials and customer-oriented aims have been reached.

2.4   E-Collaboration Process Execution

Instead of closed systems that have been used so far, E-Collaboration requires the integration of different applications. Component based architectures that are process-driven and rely on fully developed standards and interfaces can be seen as a state-of-the-art approach to overcome these problems (McMichael, 2003).

The term "process-driven" emphasizes the importance of the process models created on the preliminary layer. At the execution layer these models are used for process orchestration. Orchestration in this context describes the composition of business objects in a process flow. In detail it defines the complex interaction between business objects, including the business logic and execution order of the interactions. Without orchestrating business objects the overall context between the single process steps would be lost.

Collaboration partners must access data and applications in an easy and secure way. Standardized mark-up languages for exchanged documents like the Extensible Markup Language (XML) are designed for this purpose. But the meaning of mark-up tags, e.g. data fields in orders and bills, varies from one enterprise to another. There are a lot of promising efforts for standardization, but there is not one common standard.

With the use of XML the technological basis for interoperability has been established, the interoperability between the semantic business process definitions is however still missing. Efforts like BPMI's Business Process Modelling Language (BPML) promise standardization for the management of inter-organizational business processes that involve different applications, departments and business partners (Smith and Fingar, 2003). This standard, which is based on XML, complements existing B2B protocols like RosettaNet, Biz-Talk and ebXML. On the one hand, BPML acts as an intermediary between business process modelling tools and IT. On the other hand, BPML enables the interoperability between modelling tools. Furthermore, a wide acceptance of the Business Process Execution Language for Web Services (BPEL4WS) by BEA, IBM, and Microsoft as well as the newly finalized specification of the Web Services Choreography Interface (WSCI) mainly driven by BEA, Intalio, SAP and Sun show the importance of such standardization efforts for interoperability (Shapiro, 2001). While BPML is seen as more conceptually-oriented, the latter two focus on the transformation into the system-level by orchestrating web services.

For the computer supported activity coordination in enterprise networks an information system is required that supports this two step coordination. In a repository, which is logically centralized but can be physically distributed across the enterprise network, the global knowledge is stored. Especially data about the possible participants of coordinated or orchestrated output delivery, characteristics of their products and collaborative processes are stored there. The repository is similar to the idea of an UDDI repository for the retrieval of web services (Homan, Kalavagunta and Klima, 2002), but enriched with business logic and information about the conduct of business processes.

3.   E-COLLABORATION LIFE-CYCLE

The life-cycle-model presented in this section serves as a manual for the process-oriented setting-up and operation of enterprise collaborations towards a common customer-driven production and bundling of goods and services. Using a consistent phase model and standardized modelling methods increases transparency and structuring of collaborations and creates a basis for communication between participants, including management that lays down strategies, process-owners in the departments and IT-experts that integrate the different application systems. Despite the increased complexity of a network process in comparison to internal processes, those involved have to adapt to constantly occurring changes in a fast and flexible way.

The presented life-cycle-model is a fusion of classic phase-models of business process transformation into IT with life-cycle-models of virtual enterprises. The resulting dynamic model is consistent with the structure-oriented architecture for E-Collaboration and follows the represented classification of the view concept into global and local knowledge. It is aimed to support E-Collaboration through the appropriate use of IT with the simultaneous improvement of inter-organizational and customer-driven processes.

Protecting internal know-how is of paramount importance to the network participants, even though the business process knowledge has to be used jointly. Following the view concept presented in paragraph 2.1, this implies that the life-cycle alternates between phases that focus on global and on local issues in order to reach a coherent solution (cf. Figure 3). In comparison to classical knowledge management models, like the one of Nonaka, the E-Collaboration life-cycle considers only explicit knowledge that is already formalized (implicit knowledge is already transformed to explicit) (Nonaka and Takeuchi, 1995).

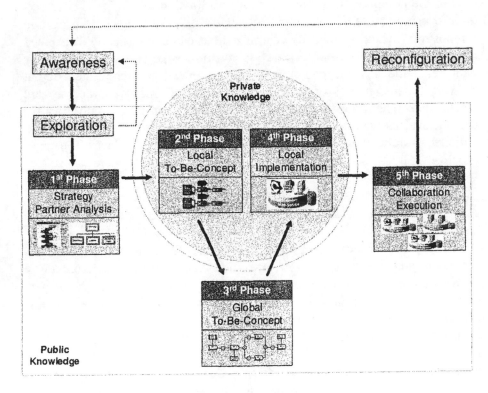

Figure 3. E-Collaboration life-cycle

Awareness for a value-added collaboration by plugging complementary core competencies has to be established in the mind of enterprises from the very beginning of the focused core-phase-model. This awareness can be initiated by a special demand, e.g. an enterprise might be confronted by a consumer order which cannot be fulfilled by the enterprise itself.

After partner-choice has succeeded, the first phase of the collaboration, the so-called „Strategy Partner Analysis", can start. Collaboration is initiated for all participants under the special consideration of common aims and a strived win-win situation. Thus individual aims are integrated into a common strategy – for instance by creating a common service tree, in which creation the customer is also involved. The next step is the as-is analysis concerning collaboration partners and possible value-added modules. At this strategic level the question "who delivers what?" but not "how?" is answered. Partner analysis provides models of the organization view. The structure of new collaborative products is used, for instance, for the design of e-collaboration scenario diagrams. The second phase, so called "Local To-Be-Concept", concerns the comparison of an existing or a new (local) as-is model and the (global) to-be concepts. According to predefined values about collective service creation, intra-organizational business processes can be derived. From process modelling and optimization over process controlling to execution affected processes were aligned to requirements of the collaborative customer-centric scenario predefined on the strategic layer. Every participant models his own internal processes by the use of standardized methods of business process management, e.g. the EPC. Every partner declares the process parts as public or private by defining particular attributes to model units. A process management software tool has to be extended to the particular attributes and the possibility to illustrate internal and external views. In the third phase "Global To-Be-Concept" coordinated public parts are spread over the network, establishing a common to-be concept. Every partner is able to connect his own private model with every other public process models. A virtual customer-driven process chain of the whole collaboration is designed. Therefore a common representation of process models is necessary. The Business Process Modelling Language (BPML) can be seen as an appropriate tool to enable such a data exchange. Furthermore the semantic combination of models is necessary. As long as ontology-based approaches do not reach a productive state, this process remains a manual one. During the second and third phase methods and tools from the collaborative, technical layer of the framework are used. The integrated collaborative business process model enables all partners to configure their application systems locally in a fourth phase called "Local Implementation". Reference systems for interfaces are made available by interface definitions of the common to-be concept. Now every partner is prepared for the execution of interactions within the collaborative framework. That is the transition to the fifth phase called "Collaboration Execution". Based on a bilateral base, interacting information systems are able to communicate by using the standardized protocols and interfaces. The concrete transaction is arranged and executed. The aim of this phase is to support collaboration through the appropriate use of ICT. That requires primarily the configuration of interfaces and the implementation of inter-organizational workflows; at the same time the permanent monitoring and adoption of the collaboration, based on business ratio defined in the conception phase, must be guaranteed (Scheer, Grieble and Zang, 2003). After the transaction completion of a cooperation project, the consortium can be redesigned and reconfigured by demand regarding newly developed or modified customer requirements. The life-cycle goes back to its initial point called "Awareness", this time for a change within the collaboration instead of a new establishment.

In order to automate inter-organizational processes, the conceptual models are transformed into formal models that are used as configuration data for the orchestration of business objects. The applications of the partners have to communicate bilaterally to negotiate the interface specifications based on the formal models defined in the repository. Local knowledge is generated by this negotiation for a certain situation. After this collaboration task has ended no updates of configuration changes etc. are reported to any other party except at the time when a new direct interaction occurs. In this context multi-agent systems offer a solution to achieve an automated or at least semi-automated interface-configuration (Blake, 2003; Denti, Ricci and Rubino, 2003).

4.   CONCLUSIONS AND REALIZATION IN RESEARCH PROJECTS

The vision of this paper is to develop an architecture and a life-cycle-model that provides a generic solution concept, which transfers business recommendations into ICT-solutions based on a holistic customer-driven process management approach. The foundation stone is laid as the varied methods presented in the paper clearly show.

The described conceptual design of inter-enterprise and customer-driven business processes is currently elaborated in the research project "Architecture for Collaborative Scenarios (ArKoS)", funded by the German Federal Ministry of Education and Research (BMBF). As a proof of concept the presented architecture and methods will be implemented in a software prototype and will be used in real-life showcases (Zang, Hofer and Adam, 2004).

ArKoS is one of the projects in a research effort conducted by the Institute for Information Systems to improve inter-organizational business process management. In doing so the project reverts e.g. to the results of the successfully accomplished project InfoCitizen (Adam, Werth and Zangl, 2003). This project, funded by the European Commission under the 5th Research Framework Program, aimed at creating a pan-European Information Architecture for European Public Administrations (EPA) as well as at developing specific information technology that supports this architecture and ensures a seamless information exchange between public administrations on a pan-European level. Moreover, with this solution the EPAs have been enabled to provide transparent and integrated public services for their customers, i.e. citizens and businesses. Eleven organizations within five different EU-countries (Germany, Greece, Italy, Portugal, and Spain) worked together for two years to succeed in the challenge of pan-European interoperability. A prototype of an agent-based interoperability platform with a service repository was developed. The business processes are stored in an XML-representation and the agent platform dynamically invokes the service offers which are implemented as distributed web services.

On this basis a broad and intense dissemination and deployment impact is conducted. The generic methods developed will enable enterprises in the construction industry to seamlessly integrate partners, building owners and subcontractors in collaboration scenarios on the technology but especially on the conceptual level. Each user will experience intuitively understandable business process design, planning and control so that cooperation procedures will be very clear. User-specific views on business process models will enable new user groups to use business process models. Moreover ICT can actively support customer-driven process management by checking, verifying or even automatically negotiating consistency and interoperability of models.

5.   REFERENCES

Adam, O., Werth, D., and Zangl, F., 2003, Conceiving and Implementing Pan-European Integrated Public Services, in: *Electronic Government, Second International Conference, EGOV 2003, Prague, Czech Republic, September 1-5, 2003, Proceedings*, R. Traunmüller, ed., Springer, Berlin, pp. 135-138.

Blake, M. B., 2003, Coordinating Multiple Agents for Workflow-oriented Process Orchestration (June 29, 2004); http://www.cs.georgetown.edu/~blakeb/pubs/blake_ISEB 2003.pdf.

Davis, R., 2001, *Business Process Modelling with ARIS: A Practical Guide*, Springer, London et al.

Denti, E., Ricci, A., and Rubino, R., 2003, Integrating and Orchestrating Services upon a MAS Coordination Infrastructure, (June 3, 2004); http://www.ai.univie.ac.at/~paolo/conf/ESAW03/preproc/E0011.pdf.

Genderka, M., 1995, *Objektorientierte Methode zur Entwicklung von Produktmodellen als Basis integrierter Ingenieursysteme*, Shaker, Aachen.

Grieble, O., Klein, R., and Scheer, A.-W., 2002, Modellbasiertes Dienstleistungsmanagement, in: *Veröffentlichungen des Instituts für Wirtschaftsinformatik*, A.-W. Scheer, ed., No. 171, Universität des Saarlandes, Saarbrücken.

Homan, D., Kalavagunta, S., and Klima, C., 2002, Web Services and Integration, *InformationWeek*, (911):65-70.

Jost, W., and Scheer, A.-W., 2002, Geschäftsprozessmanagement: Kernaufgabe einer jeden Unternehmensorganisation, in: *ARIS in der Praxis: Gestaltung, Implementierung und Optimierung von Geschäftsprozessen*, W. Jost, and A.-W. Scheer, ed., Springer, Berlin et al., pp. 33-44.

Kanter, R. M., 1991, Transcending Business Boundaries: 12,000 World Managers View Change, *Harvard Business Review* 69(3):151-164.

Keller, G., Nüttgens, M., and Scheer, A.-W., 1992, Semantische Prozessmodellierung auf Grundlage „Ereignisgesteuerter Prozessketten (EPK)", in: *Veröffentlichungen des Instituts für Wirtschaftsinformatik*, A.-W. Scheer, ed., No. 89, Universität des Saarlandes, Saarbrücken.

Liebhart, U. E., 2002, *Strategische Kooperationsnetzwerke: Entwicklung, Gestaltung und Steuerung*, Dt. Univ.-Verl., Wiesbaden.

Linthicum, D. S., 2003, *Enterprise Application Integration*, 4th ed., Addison-Wesley, Boston et al.

McMichael, C., 2003, Business Process Integration May Eclipse EDI, EAI, *HP Chronicle* 17(6):1, 6.

Mertens, P., and Faisst, W., 1995, Virtuelle Unternehmen – eine Organisationsstruktur für die Zukunft?, *technologie & management* 44(2):61-68.

Naisbitt, J., 1986, *Megatrends: Ten New Directions Transforming Our Lives*, 6th ed., Warner Books, New York.

Nonaka, I., Takeuchi, H., 1995, *The knowledge-creating company - How Japanese companies create the dynamics of innovation*, Oxford University Press, New York.

Picot, A., Wigand, R. T., and Reichwald, R., 1997, *Information, Organization and Management: Expanding Markets and Corporate Boundaries*, Wiley, Chichester et al.

Röhricht, J., and Schlögel, C., 2001, *cBusiness: Erfolgreiche Internetstrategien durch Collaborative Business am Beispiel my-SAP.com®*, Addison-Wesley, München et al.

Scheer, A.-W., 2002, *ARIS – Vom Geschäftsprozess zum Anwendungssystem*, 4th ed., Springer, Berlin et al.

Scheer, A.-W. et al., 2002, Geschäftsprozessmanagement – The 2nd wave, *IM Information Management & Consulting*, 17(Sonderausgabe):9-15.

Scheer, A.-W., Beinhauer, M., and Habermann, F., 2000, Integrierte E-Prozessmodellierung, *Industrie Management* 16(3):19-26.

Scheer, A.-W., and Borowsky, R., 1999, Supply Chain Management – die Antwort auf neue Logistikanforderungen, in: *Logistik Management – Intelligente I+K Technologien*, H. Kopfer, and C. Bierwirth, ed., Springer, Berlin et al., pp. 3-14.

Scheer, A.-W., Grieble, O., and Zang, S., 2003, Collaborative Business Management, in: *E-Collaboration - Prozessoptimierung in der Wertschöpfungskette*, W. Kersten, ed., Dt. Univ.-Verl., Wiesbaden, pp. 29-57.

Scheer, A.-W., Herrmann, K., and Klein, R., 2004, Modellgestütztes Service Engineering – Entwicklung und Design neuer Dienstleistungen, in: *Dienstleistungsinnovationen: Dienstleistungsmanagement Jahrbuch 2004*, M. Bruhn, and B. Stauss, ed., Gabler, Wiesbaden.

Schubert, P., Wölfle, R., and Dettling, W., 2003, *E-Business-Integration: Fallstudien zur Optimierung elektronischer Geschäftsprozesse*, Hanser, München et al.

Shapiro, R., 2001, *A Comparison of XPDL, BPML and BPEL4WS*, Cape Visions, Rough Draft, pp. 1-17.

Smith, H., and Fingar, P., 2003, *Business Process Management: The Third Wave*, Meghan-Kiffer Press, Tampa.

Zang, S., Hofer, A., and Adam, O., 2004, Cross-Enterprise Business Process Management Architecture - Methods and Tools for Flexible Collaboration, in: *On the Move to Meaningful Internet Systems 2004: OTM 2004 Workshops, International Workshop on Modeling Inter-Organizational Systems (MIOS) of OTM'04, Larnaca, Cyprus*, R. Meersmann et al., ed., Springer, Berlin, pp. 483-494.

MONITORING MIDDLEWARE FOR SERVICE LEVEL AGREEMENTS IN HETEROGENEOUS ENVIRONMENTS

Graham Morgan[1], Simon Parkin[1], Carlos Molina-Jimenez[1], James Skene[2]

[1]*School of Computing Science, University of Newcastle upon Tyne, UK;* [2]*Department of Computer Science, University College London, UK*

Abstract: Monitoring of Service Level Agreements (SLAs) is required to determine if the Quality of Service (QoS) provided by a service provider satisfies the expectations of a service consumer. Although tools exist that can generate the software required to evaluate SLAs from the SLA specifications themselves, the code required to gather metric data is still predominantly coded by hand: a time consuming task. In this paper we describe an SLA monitoring implementation that can generate metric data gathering software directly from machine readable SLAs. Assuming that an organisation specialising in SLA monitoring and evaluation may not wish to be tied to any one particular middleware platform and/or SLA language, we aim to provide generic monitoring services that may be suitable for use in heterogeneous environments. We demonstrate the flexibility of our approach by providing monitoring solutions for observed systems implemented using Web Services and Enterprise Java Bean (EJB) middleware using a third party SLA language.

Key words: monitoring, service level agreements, middleware

1.   INTRODUCTION

Service Level Agreements (SLAs) specify the Quality of Service (QoS) associated with the interaction between the provider of a service and a service consumer. SLAs are gaining in importance as increasing numbers of companies conduct business over the Internet (e.g., banking, auctions), requiring the positioning of SLAs at organisational boundaries to provide a basis on which to emulate the electronic equivalents of contract based business management practices.

Monitoring is required to collect statistical metrics about the performance of a service to determine if the QoS agreed upon between provider and consumer is realised. Third parties may assume responsibility for monitoring SLAs to ensure the results of the evaluation process are trusted by both the provider and consumer [2].

Our previous work on the monitoring of SLAs [13] presented an architecture that covers the fundamental issues of SLA monitoring: SLA specification, separation of the computation and communication infrastructure of the provider, service points of presence, metric collection approaches, measurement service and evaluation & detection service. As a next step, we now turn our attention to the implementation of our architecture. As in our previous work on design, we assume the viewpoint of an organisation that is concerned with the provisioning of third party monitoring for participants of SLAs. If such an organisation is to support SLA monitoring for many different types of clients then an assumption that only a single SLA language will suffice and all technologies are enabled via a single middleware standard may not be realistic.

To facilitate the process of SLA evaluation, metric data must be gathered by software components, possibly within the service provider domain, as specified by an SLA. Hand coding such software on a per SLA basis is a time consuming task, especially if an organisation specialising in SLA monitoring must deal with many thousands of SLAs. The automated parsing of machine readable SLAs by an SLA violation and detection tool-kit can derive the software components required for SLA violation detection [14]. However, deriving the software components required for the monitoring of metric data in a similar manner has not yet been addressed.

Building on our previous work on the design of an SLA monitoring architecture, this paper presents an approach to SLA monitoring that requires minor tailoring to work with different SLA languages and middleware platforms. Our system is capable of deriving the appropriate metric gathering software directly from machine readable SLAs. We demonstrate the suitability of our approach by tailoring our system to work with an application providing services across the Internet, governed by SLAs described using an existing SLA language, deployed over Enterprise Java Beans (EJB) and Web Service middleware.

This paper is organised as follows. Section 2 describes background and related work, section 3 describes our implementation and section 4 provides conclusions and future work.

2. BACKGROUND & RELATED WORK

For completeness, and to clarify our approach to SLA monitoring, this section continues with a description of our previous work on the development of an SLA monitoring architecture. Via this description we identify when it may be possible to ease the development of metric gathering middleware via software automatically generated directly from SLAs. We then present a discussion in which we determine the suitability of other works in providing a general purpose SLA monitoring service for heterogeneous environments (existence of different SLA languages and middleware platforms).

2.1 SLA Monitoring Architecture

The architecture we proposed [13] for monitoring SLAs is shown in Fig. 1. For sake of simplicity, we assume that the provision of the service is unilateral, that is, the service flows only from the provider to the service consumer, as opposed to bilateral provisioning where the two interacting parties provide services to each other; bilateral provisioning is a more general scenario and may be represented by two complimentary unilateral deployments. With unilateral service provisioning we need to monitor the observance of only two contractual obligations: (i) the provider's obligations, dictating that the service must satisfy certain QoS requirements; and (ii) the service consumer's obligations, which dictate how the service consumer is expected to use the service.

We assume that calculations relating to QoS are specified explicitly (e.g., maximum latency) in a computer readable format, allowing automated SLA evaluation and violation detection.

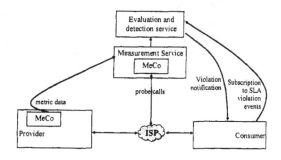

Fig. 1. Architecture for unilateral monitoring of QoS

The components shown in Fig. 1 assume responsibility for SLA monitoring and evaluation:

- *Metric collector (MeCo)* – Gathers metric data associated with the performance and usage of the observed system.
- *Measurement service* – Measures a given list of metrics at specified intervals.
- *Evaluation and violation detection service* – Inspects gathered metric data to determine if SLA violation has occurred and informs provider/consumer of such violations.

The MeCos shown in the Fig. 1 gather metric data relating to the provider's obligations (MeCo in measurement service) and the consumer's obligations (MeCo in service provider). This scenario assumes a probing style approach to service monitoring. That is, synthetic load is generated by a simulated client (provided by measurement service) to determine if the provider is satisfying SLAs [3] [9]. An alternative to probing would be to have a MeCo co-located with the consumer and gather metric data associated with actual client calls. We consider only the probing approach in this paper as it may not be possible to deploy monitoring at the consumer side (as consumers may not always agree to accept metric collection responsibilities).

To ease the development costs of monitoring middleware solutions, the automated production of MeCos from SLAs for use over a variety of middleware platforms would be welcome. This is analogous to the production of client/server stubs for easing the implementation of *remote procedure call* (RPC) code: an interface specification is parsed to produce the required code to enact communications across process space (possibly between nodes on a network).

Once metric data has been received by the measurement service, the data must be prepared in a suitable format for handling by the evaluation and detection service. This should be straightforward as the SLA specifies exactly what data is required and in what form. However, an organisation specialising in SLA monitoring may utilise a number of SLA languages for satisfying the different requirements found in a variety of application domains. In this situation the measurement service must be capable of interfacing with the evaluation and detection service via a number of different SLA language standards, even though the measurement service's basic functionality remains unaltered. Therefore, an appropriate approach to implementation would be to allow the measurement service to work with arbitrary SLA languages with only the minimum of tailoring. As the SLA identifies the types of metric data to be evaluated, the ability to automatically generate code that provides translation of metric data to a format suitable for processing by an SLA evaluation tool (which is SLA language dependent) is required.

We may summarise opportunities for automated code generation to ease implementation in the following ways:

1. Ease the development of a MeCo using SLAs to automatically derive metric gathering software for a number of varying middleware platforms.
2. Ease the development of software for enabling SLA language integration into the measurement service by automatically deriving such software from the SLAs themselves.

2.2   Implementation/Deployment Issues & Related Work

An approach to MeCo deployment is via the use of middleware interceptors (e.g., [8]). Interceptors are middleware components that can be placed between application components to provide additional functionality (e.g., security, redirection). Interceptors provide an opportunity to implement SLA monitoring with the minimum of modification to an observed system. Popular implementations of middleware standards (i.e., CORBA, EJBs, Web Services) provide interceptor type mechanisms. Therefore, the use of interceptors is widely advocated as the appropriate way of providing SLA monitoring for distributed applications. However, existing implementations of MeCo type interceptors are middleware dependent (e.g., CORBA [5] [7], Web Services [1] [4] [6]), making a single implementation unfit for deployment over a number of middleware platforms. This homogeneous approach makes existing metric data gathering solutions difficult to use in heterogeneous environments (requiring a single implementation to be substantially modified or combining different implementations).

There are a number of SLA languages proposed by the literature (e.g., Web Service Level Agreements (WSLA) [4], Quality Description Languages (CDL) [5], Service Level Agreement Language (SLAng) [11]). Unfortunately, no existing implementation allows the use of multiple SLA languages.

The process of automated code generation from SLAs for the purposes of SLA evaluation has been demonstrated (e.g., [6] [11]). However, using an SLA to generate a MeCo (or equivalent) for gathering appropriate metric data has not yet been realised. The related work that comes closest to automated MeCo generation from SLAs is [6]. Via the use of *business management platform* (BMP) agents the work presented in [6] concentrates on the automation of SLA monitoring for Web Services. The distributed nature of the approach described in [6] provides an opportunity to manage metric data collection at observed systems with the minimum of human involvement. However, this peer-to-peer approach is not suitable for all application types, and not suitable for an organisation delivering SLA monitoring services using our architecture.

As demonstrated by [7] (QoS monitoring associated with network traffic engineering), scalability may be a requirement for a practical deployment of SLA monitoring. When delivering SLA monitoring services (even in an e-commerce environment) scalability of message dissemination is desirable (especially to a third party monitoring service that may have hundreds, or thousands, of clients). [7] highlights the usefulness of *message oriented middleware* (MOM) as an appropriate message dissemination medium for metric data. An alternative to MOM would be to use a client/server approach (e.g, RPC).

The client/server model requires clients and servers to record references to each other to enable the initiation of bi-directional information flow. The scalability of such a model is difficult to maintain when the number of interconnected clients and servers may be appropriately measured in hundreds or thousands. Furthermore, when using RPC the processing of messages must be handled as and when messages are received by clients and servers. The MOM model is considered suitable for large-scale data dissemination as it tackles these two problems by presenting a weakly coupled message passing environment. In the MOM model, information flow is not based on the referencing of the sender and receiver, as in client/server, instead information flow is based on the properties of a message. Evidence provided by [7] indicates that propagation of metric data and SLA violation notifications can be best served via the use of MOM technologies.

In summary, the monitoring of SLAs in an environment consisting of different SLA languages and different middleware platforms is not possible using existing approaches. Furthermore, the automated generation of code specifically for metric data gathering, although desirable and progressed by [6] [7], is not realised. In addition, providing a messaging infrastructure using MOM technologies is shown to be beneficial [7] when developing a scalable metric gathering solution. However, this scalability issue appears only to have been addressed in traffic engineering (as opposed to inter-organisational middleware) solutions.

In the remainder of the paper we describe the implementation of our monitoring architecture. The primary focus of the paper is the easing of the development of SLA monitoring and evaluation software for heterogeneous environments. A description of how we use MOM as a basis for our messaging services to allow for scalability is provided for completeness.

3.   IMPLEMENTATION

As already mentioned in Section 2, our approach to SLA monitoring is based on our earlier work described in [13], culminating in the architecture shown in Fig. 1. For our SLA language we use SLAng [11]. SLAng represents the product of work carried out at University College London (UCL).

SLAng meets the needs of an SLA language to support the construction of distributed systems and applications with reliable QoS characteristics. The *Unified Modeling Language* (UML) is used to model the language, producing an abstract syntax. This language model is embedded with an object-oriented model of services, service consumers and their behaviour. Constraints are defined formally using the *Object Constraint Language* (OCL), providing the semantics. This approach permits natural and economical modeling of design and analysis domains and the relationships between them, supporting both manual and automatic analysis.

The monitoring system we have constructed uses metric collection as defined in SLAng and uses the SLAng engine for automating SLA evaluation. From an SLA defined using SLAng it is possible to automate the production of the appropriate software components needed for SLA evaluation (incorporated into the SLAng engine). It is worth noting that the SLAng engine only checks a limited number of system performance metrics, notably those related to request latency, service availability and percentage of service usage (i.e., how many requests service consumers are issuing over a period of time). We have developed a formal notation for describing conventional contracts by means of Finite State Machines (FSMs) for representing more application dependent QoS [17]. However, for brevity and to demonstrate our work we only consider metrics as described using SLAng.

We assume that the communications that are required to be monitored are enacted over middleware technologies that support message interception. This is a valid assumption as all major middleware vendors provide a mechanism for message interception in their technologies (e.g., interceptors in CORBA, handlers in SOAP, interceptors in EJB containers).

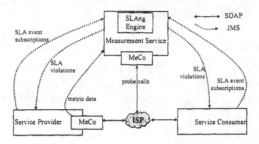

Fig. 2. SLAs monitoring architecture with message oriented middleware

The architecture shown in Fig. 2 alters the architecture shown in Fig. 1 to accommodate our approach to implementation. For completeness (some of the descriptions deviate little to those presented in section 2) we provide descriptions of the components in Fig. 2:

- *Service provider MeCo* - Intercepts service consumer requests (and associated outgoing responses) and records measurements based upon a service consumer's usage of the service provider's platform. These measurements aid in determining if a service consumer is violating an SLA by using a service inappropriately (excessively in our case study).
- *Measurement service MeCo* – Observes the performance of a service provider by assuming the role of a service consumer. Periodic probing of the service provider is enacted by the measurement service MeCo to gain measurements relating to the performance of a service provider as viewed by a service consumer. These measurements aid in determining if a service provider is satisfying service consumers as specified in an SLA.
- *Measurement service* – Responsible for collecting the measurements gathered from MeCos and informing SLA participants of SLA violations.
- *SLAng engine* – A sub-system of the measurement service that is responsible for detecting SLA violations given metric data supplied by the measurement service.
- *Messaging service* – Provides communication platform across which metric data and SLA violation notifications are propagated.

The measurement service is within the domain of a trusted third party, ensuring that service provider and consumer may abide by the decisions on SLA violations generated by the SLAng engine.

In the following sections we describe the implementation of each component and how different components collaborate to provide SLA monitoring and SLA violation notification. Our implementation is based on SLAng, EJB and Web Services. We state the type of tailoring that may be required to enable other SLA languages, including SLA engines, and middleware platforms to work with our Java implementation.

3.1   Metric Collectors (MeCos)

MeCos are responsible for gathering metric data and propagating such data to the measurement service for evaluation. Service providers have a MeCo within their organisational domain for monitoring service consumer usage. MeCos are suitable for use with arbitrary middleware platforms (and associated protocols). Different middleware platforms may be supported with the use of *MeCo hooks*. Irrelevant of middleware platform, MeCo hooks determine what metric data to gather from loading classes (*metric data classes*) from the class repository (classes generated directly from SLAs). A wrapper class (*platform wrapper*) is required to allow integration of the metric data classes into a specific platform (a MeCo hook is the combination of platform wrapper classes and metric data classes).

A MeCo hook (specifically the platform wrapper component) is middleware dependent and is responsible for the interception of consumer request/reply messages and passing such messages through the MeCo. So far, we have demonstrated the use of MeCo hooks for supporting Web Services using SOAP and Enterprise Java Beans (EJBs) using Java Remote Method Invocation (Java RMI). This combination was chosen as these two approaches are combined in many vendor middleware products that provide implementations of *Java 2 Enterprise Edition* (J2EE), a well known architecture designed to ease the development of enterprise computing solutions.

The specification of J2EE defines a platform for developing Web-enabled applications using Java Server Pages (JSPs), Servlets and EJBs. Application servers for Java components (also called J2EE servers) are expected to provide a complete implementation of J2EE. Web Services provide a presentation of services for inter-organisational communications with the back end application logic implemented using EJBs. We used the JBOSS application server [10] for our J2EE implementation.

Our SOAP MeCo hook implementation is based on *Apache eXtensible Interaction System* (Axis) [15]. Axis provides handlers (*Axis Handlers*) that may be chained together to provide a mechanism for interception, and possible alteration of a SOAP message (e.g., add/remove headers, manipulate the body), at different points during traversal of the protocol stack (i.e., before request is processed by server side logic or before reply is received by a client). Axis handlers provide an appropriate opportunity to redirect SOAP messages to a MeCo (via MeCo hooks) for metric gathering. The addition of Axis handlers does not require alterations to the application logic, therefore the introduction of monitoring at the service provider may be achieved in a transparent manner. We use JBoss interceptors to implement MeCo hooks suitable for interception of Java RMI invocations.

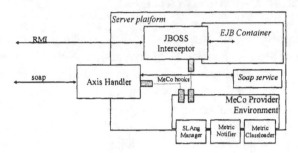

Fig. 3. Service Provider use of MeCos

Fig. 3 shows the architecture of MeCo deployment in the service provider. The MeCo provider environment contains a number of components that cumulatively satisfy the metric collection and dissemination (back to the measurement service) requirements of our monitoring system (Fig. 2):

- *SLAng Manager* – Examines an SLA (as used by SLAng engine) to determine the metric data that the MeCo is to observe. The product of parsing an SLA is a Java class (*metric data class*) that may be used for gathering the appropriate metric data. This metric data class is stored in a class repository for later use. As there may be many SLAs that a MeCo is responsible for monitoring at any one observed site, streamlining of the monitoring may occur by avoiding duplicate monitoring requests. For example, if SLA_1 and SLA_2 describe the upper bound latency for a client invocation C_1, then the message interception associated with C_1 by a single MeCo hook may satisfy the monitoring requirements of both SLA_1 and SLA_2.
- *Metric Notifier* – Based on the deduction of what to monitor made by the SLAng manager, the metric notifier assumes responsibility for managing the appropriate message passing between MeCo and measurement service. This requires the lifecycle management of message channels over which metric data will travel.
- *Metric Classloader* – Loads the metric data classes for implementing the monitoring of the required data as specified by the SLAng manager. Metric data classes are loaded from the class repository. Each class represents a metric type as specified by an SLA used by the SLAng engine (e.g., response time).

The MeCo provider environment was developed in a modular fashion so the minimum of tailoring is required to make a MeCo work with different middleware platforms, and different SLA languages. The MeCo hooks, as already discussed, allow different protocols and associated middleware platforms to be supported (only the platform wrapper parts of the MeCo hooks require tailoring on a per-middleware/protocol basis). For each SLA language a different SLAng manager and class repository is required as SLA parsing (by the SLAng manager) and different mechanisms for metric data monitoring are required. This approach has the benefit of allowing SLA language extensions to be incorporated into a MeCo as and when required.

The MeCo in the measurement service differs from the MeCo located in the service provider in that the measurement service MeCo is employed to periodically probe the service provider. Probing in this manner is carried out to gain metric data relating to how service providers appear to be performing as viewed by a service consumer (e.g., response time of service provider). A tool suitable for producing synthetic load may be used (e.g., JMeter [16]), to simulate the clients and implement the desired probing strategy. Alternatively, a basic probing strategy may be created and enacted automatically by the MeCo by parsing the appropriate SLAs. The probing strategy enacted by the MeCo is sufficient for determining SLA violations. Configuration relating to the probing of a service provider is located in a Web Service Descriptor Language (WSDL) file. WSDL files are used to describe how to communicate with a Web Service, and as such can be used to configure the probe to send messages to the target server. The (Java) classes required to enact probing are created via the parsing of additional extensibility elements defined in the given WSDL file. These elements also provide a realistic set of parameters to supplement this approach to probing. As with the platform wrapper class in the service provider MeCo, a platform wrapper class is used for implementing the probing for a specific middleware platform (EJB/RMI or Web Services/SOAP).

Once requests have been created and sent as part of a probing strategy, they are intercepted by the measurement service MeCo in the manner described previously (via MeCo hooks) with metric data passed from the MeCo to the measurement service.

3.2 Messaging Service

The messaging service is responsible for passing metric data from the service provider MeCo to the measurement service and passing SLA violation detection messages from the measurement service to interested parties of an SLA. The *Java Messaging Service* (JMS) [12] was chosen as the message platform.

The JMS specification does not indicate how the underlying system implementation is achieved, resulting in a number of varying solutions available from different vendors. A number of solutions that attempt to provide scalability have been proposed (e.g., [18]). Therefore, our scalability concerns are related to the way we use the standard JMS API (not the underlying messaging implementation itself).

JMS supports point-to-point and publish/subscribe models of interaction. Point-to-point is based on the notion of queues, with a queue identified as an asynchronous mechanism for passing messages from suppliers to consumers. Publish/subscribe is based on topics, with clients publishing and subscribing to well defined topics. The topic acts as a mechanism for gathering and distributing related messages (as perceived by an application) to clients and allows subscribers and publishers to be unaware of each other's existence.

The topic approach was chosen with the measurement service creating a topic on a per operation basis (e.g., the name of a method associated with an operation). We call such topics *metric topics* (in our approach each metric topic relates to a clause in an SLA).

A MeCo disseminates metric data by publishing such data on a metric topic. We found that this approach provided an opportunity to allow multiple SLA engines (checkers) to be employed. A problem with existing SLA engines is their lack of scalability when faced with checking increasing numbers of SLAs [14]. Therefore, employing additional engines (via additional measurement services) and so provide an opportunity to improve scalability is desirable in an SLA monitoring implementation. Via this method we may also allow different SLA languages to be used. The introduction of additional measurement services (and associated SLA engines) in this manner is straightforward: a measurement service registers as a consumer for the metric data they are interested in (to enable SLA violation detection). Additional measurement services may be added with minimum disruption to the overall function of the monitoring infrastructure (via subscription to appropriate metric topics). This approach may support multiple third party measurement services: a service provider may provide services to multiple consumers, with such consumers requiring different third parties to govern their SLA violation detection mechanisms (requiring different measurement services).

Propagating an SLA violation to SLA participants is achieved via a JMS topic (SLA topics). Such topics are created on a per SLA basis, with organisations assuming responsibility for registering as subscribers on the SLAs they participate in. An SLA topic message consists of a metric ID (associated with the metric that was violated) and the value that caused such a violation.

3.3 Measurement Service

The measurement service evaluates metric messages received from metric topics and notifies organisations, via SLA topics, of SLA violations. The measurement service contains a number of components (Fig. 4):

- *SLAng Message Manager* – Examines an SLA and determines which metric and SLA topics are required. Metric and SLA topics are created when required by the SLAng message manager. In addition, when an SLA is withdrawn from use the SLAng message manager deletes the appropriate SLA and metric topics (after determining that the metric topics flagged for deletion are no longer required by other, active, SLAs).
- *Metric Listener* – Subscribes to the appropriate metric topics as instructed by the SLAng message manager and assumes responsibility for consuming metric topic messages and translating such messages to a format suitable for acceptance by the SLAng engine.
- *SLAng Engine* – Receives messages from the metric listener and issues SLA violation notification messages.
- *Violation Notifier* – Subscribes to the appropriate SLA topics as instructed by the SLAng message manager and assumes responsibility for translating violation notification messages received from the SLAng engine to JMS messages and issuing such messages on SLA topics.
- *Metric Manager* – Generates appropriate Java classes for implementing SLA language specific functions (e.g., providing metric data in suitable format for evaluation by SLAng engine).

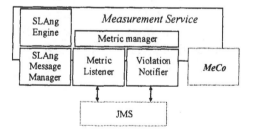

Fig. 4. Measurement service

The metric listener must translate the metric data it receives from metric topics into a suitable format for submission to the SLAng engine. This requires a service usage message to be created. A service usage message is a description of how a service was used and relates to the SLA clauses governing service/consumer interaction. The SLAng engine examines service usage messages to determine if SLA violation has occurred or if service usage has been enacted within acceptable bounds. The violation notifier includes in the violation message details relating to what caused the SLA violation in the message issued to the appropriate SLA topic.

The service usage message is SLA language/engine dependent. However, a class repository is used (in a manner similar to how a MeCo realises what metric data to gather), to maintain a collection of Java classes that produce service usage messages as and when required. Therefore, as the metric manager is responsible for creating such classes, then a metric manager must be developed on a per SLA-language basis. In addition to creating service usage messages, there exists classes in the class repository that provide the appropriate interface code required to communicate with an SLA engine.

4.   CONCLUSION

We have described an implementation of SLA monitoring that, with tailoring, provides an opportunity to monitor service provision over a number of different middleware platforms with the possibility of using different SLA languages. The software components required to gather metric data may be automatically derived from SLAs, reducing the need to hand code such components on a per-SLA basis from scratch. We have demonstrated our implementation using a third party SLA language and evaluation tool and gathered metric data from EJB and Web Service components. The way in which MOM may be used as a basis on which to create scalable SLA monitoring implementations is described.

Our future work, in the short term, is concerned with engineering tasks: extending our system to cover additional middleware platforms (e.g., CORBA, .NET) and the inclusion of a variety of SLA languages. In the long term we are seeking to extend our scope of applications to cover interactive media (e.g., online games).

Acknowledgements

This work is part-funded by the UK EPSRC Grant GR/S63199: "Trusted Coordination in Dynamic Virtual Organisations" and by the European Union under Project IST-2001-34069: "TAPAS (Trusted and QoS-Aware Provision of Application Services)".

5. REFERENCES

1. M. Debusmann, A. Keller, "SLA-Driven Management of Distributed Systems Using the Common Information Model", in Proceedings of the 8th IFIP/IEEE IM, 2003
2. C. Overton, "On the Theory and Practice of Internet SLAs", Journal of Computer Resource Measurement 106, 32-45, Computer Measurement Group, 2002
3. A. Habib, S. Fahmy, S. R. Avasarala, V. Prabhakar, B. Bhargava, "On Detecting Service Violations and Bandwidth Theft in QoS Network Domains", Computer Communications, Elsevier, Vol. 26 Issue 8, Pages 861-871, 2003
4. A. Keller, H. Ludwig, "The WSLA Framework: Specifying and Monitoring Service Level Agreements for Web Services", IBM Research Report, 2002
5. R. Schantz, J. Zinky, D. Karr, D. Bakken, J. Megquier, J. Loyall, "An Object-Level Gateway Supporting Integrated-Property Quality of Service", ISORC '99, 1999
6. A. Sahai, V. Machiraju, M. Sayal, L. J. Jin, F. Casati, "Automated SLA Monitoring for Web Services", HP-Labs Report HPL-2002-191, 2002
7. A. Asgari, P. Trimintzios, M. Irons, R. Egan, G. Pavlou, "Building Quality-of-Service Monitoring Systems for Traffic Engineering and Service Management", Journal of Network and Systems Management, Vol. 11, No. 4, 2003
8. J. Pruyne, "Enabling QoS via Interception in Middleware", HP-Labs Report HPL-2000-29, February 2000
9. Keynote Systems, http://www.keynote.com, as viewed November 2004
10. JBoss project, http://www.jboss.org, as viewed September 2004
11. J. Skene, D. Lamanna, W. Emmerich, "Precise Service Level Agreements", Proceedings of the 26th International Conference on Software Engineering, Pg. 179 – 188, 2004
12. Sun Microsystems, Java Message Service (JMS) Specification, http://java.sun.com/products/jms, Version 1.1, 2002
13. C. Molina-Jimenez, S. Shrivastava, J. Crowcroft, and P. Gevros, "On the Monitoring of Contractual Service Level Agreements", In Proceedings of the IEEE Conference on Electronic Commerce CEC\04, San Diego, 2004
14. J. Skene and W. Emmerich, "Model Driven Performance Analysis of Enterprise Information Systems", Electronic Notes in Theoretical Computer Science, 82(6), 2003
15. R. Irani, S. J. Basha, "AXIS: Next Generation Java SOAP", Peer Information; 1st edition, 2002.
16. K. H. Hanse, "Load Testing your Applications with Apache JMeter", Java Boutique Internet, http://javaboutique.internet.com/tutorials/JMeter/, as viewed November 2004
17. C. Molina-Jimenez, S. K. Shrivastava, E.Solaiman, J. P.Warne, "Contract Representation for Run-time Monitoring and Enforcement", In Proceedings of the IEEE International Conference on E-Commerce (CEC 2003), California, USA, 24-27 June 2003
18. Arjuna Technologies, "Arjuna Messaging Service", http://www.arjuna.com/products/arjunams/index.html, as viewed November 2004.

USING SOFTWARE AGENTS TO PERSONALIZE ACCESS TO E-OFFICES

Jarogniew Rykowski

The Poznan University of Economics, Mansfelda 4, 60-854 Poznan, Poland
e-mail:rykowski@kti.ae.poznan.pl

Abstract: In this paper, we propose a framework capable of personalization of both the access and the behavior of an e-office. Our solution is based on ACE software agents, partially prepared by (and for) office supplicants, executed in both user personal devices and the e-office network. The main goal of our framework is to provide a universal system for monitoring and notifying about information changes, on one hand, and user-defined customization of e-office services, on the other hand. The framework enables service personalization, user-defined combining and "pipelining" of services, individual brokerage among services and supplicants, and personalization of information delivery. The framework makes it possible to adjust fixed, closed software environment of an e-office to individual requirements and expectations of different users.

Key words: Software agents, personalization, monitoring, e-administration, e-government

1.   INTRODUCTION

Recently, a progress in telecommunication (mainly mobile) and mass and personal computing creates many new interesting areas for tele-informatics [4, 13]. Among others, e-administration seems to be one of the most promising [5]. Recently, many countries stressed on wide introduction of e-administration utilities to citizens [3, 20, 24]. However, comparing with traditional administration, usually what is really changed is a way of access (internet- and telecommunication-based) only. A centralized core of an (e-)office usually remains unchanged, being stable and common (i.e., behaving in the same way) for all the users [6, 7]. Moreover, several "back office" activities are performed in the traditional manner, i.e., manually or at least with the help of a local (inaccessible by supplicants) computer system.

Similar to the "traditional" internal organization of an e-office, a typical way of access to an e-office is realized in the "traditional" (however, this time from an Internet user point of view) manner, as a Web interface. Such access, quite easy for advanced, educated users, may be a great obstacle for some people. Moreover, in contrast to classical mass computer systems (as databases, Web data sources, bank systems, etc.), each access to an e-office is different, due to wide differences in user expectations and requirements, restrictions of an environment, places of interest, etc. Thus, a natural need arises to personalize an access to an e-office by (or at least for) end-users. Soon, this need is extended to the personalization of the behavior of an e-office, monitoring information changes, further combining different e-offices into a consistent, complex, however individual e-service, etc.

So far, little work has been devoted to such personalization of access and behavior of an e-office. In this paper, we propose a single framework capable of solving these problems. Our solution is based on software agents, partially prepared by (and for) office supplicants, executed in both user personal devices and the e-office network. The proposed agent-based framework may be used for (1) mass personalization of e-office information systems, both: a way of access and office behavior, (2) combining e-office services and activities to create "virtual e-services", (3) monitoring different office activities and notifying users about "interesting" facts, (4) formatting and sending information to the users via different communication channels (SMS/MMS, e-mail, WAP/WWW, etc.), and (5) taking special profits of mobile devices and mobile communication. Due to special techniques used for preparing, storing, and executing agents, the proposed framework may be used even in closed highly secured e-administration systems.

The remainder of the paper is organized as follows. In Section 2, main rationale for using software agents to contact e-offices is presented. In Section 3, the ACE framework is described being a basis for our proposal. In Section 4, overall system architecture is presented, and basic agent classes are described. In Section 5, typical scenario is given of creating and using ACE agents for contacting an e-office. Section 6 concludes the paper.

2.   MAIN RATIONALE FOR USING AGENTS TO CONTACT E-OFFICES

In the traditional approach, the supplicants have to accommodate themselves to the organization of an office (time, place, form, etc.). Even if modern technologies offer several new possibilities to access an e-office, such restriction is still a must. A supplicant is forced to use certain communication channels, fixed forms and documents, given authorization schema (login, password, PKI keys), etc. However, user expectations are growing. As possibilities of computer and telecom networks grow, a need arises to incorporate new technologies in our everyday work, including efficient, modern ways of contacts with e-administration. A natural trend is to *personalize the access* to an e-office, to adjust to the possibilities of the end-user device, on one side, and user individual requirements and restrictions, on the other side (personal data, national language, etc.).

Users tend to communicate with an e-office in the same manner as for the traditional human staff. In today's systems, however, due to automatization and fixed organization, methods of access to an e-office are quite restricted. Usually, a specialized Web page is used as the main tool for access to an e-office. From a user point of view, however, it is not efficient and comfortable. First, information and forms from the page are fixed, even if generated dynamically from some templates, fixing the way of access to the e-office. Second, there are serious limitations while trying to personalize Web-based access, both technical and economical [18]. Third, a Web page is usually devoted to an on-line access – the results of a user demand are accessible immediately, and may be immediately displayed. However, manual "back office" and essential clerks' activities introduce temporary or longer delays that force the access to be changed to the off-line form. To this goal, such tools as e-mail (and even SMS/MMS) seems to be a better choice. However, users cannot send requests by e-mails, mainly due to the lack of formatting and automatic reception of natural-language-based information by the e-office computer system. As a result, a user is forced to use a Web page for registering a request, and e-mail or similar tool for getting the results. The meantime correspondence is also performed in this mixed style.

The above WWW/e-mail mixed interface is quite tiresome. Besides, it is quite natural that people tend *to use modern communication technologies*, as IM, SMS/MMS, and voice gateways (like PTT), previously devoted to human-human communication, as basic communication channels to e-administration, in both directions – to and from an e-office. However, as stated above, it is quite difficult to provide automatic syntax/semantic analysis for natural-language messages [2, 19], unformatted and with fuzzy meaning. This task is traditionally performed by the human staff of an office. In general, Thus, such simplified solutions as chatterbots [10, 23] are used. However, a chatterbot should be pre-programmed with several keywords to be extracted from a message and further processed. Both the keywords and the algorithm for the extraction should be individualized for particular users, and this is not a trivial task. Thus, so far the chatterbot interfaces are used quite rarely, mainly as generic interfaces to information systems, such as company's front-end, help desk, etc. [11], with limited support for e-office applications.

The trend for individualizing the way of access to an e-office may be broadened to the *personalization of the behavior of the e-office* (to some extent, of course). This covers mainly processing individual cases, and pipelining of several e-services. Even if for a single e-office most of the user cases are similar, there are always some cases that need special attention. However, it is not economically and technically justified to provide a very complex system with large functionality, to deal with any case. Moreover, as one cannot foresee all the possible expectations and demands of all the potential users – it is not possible to satisfy all the users (and the clerks). Instead, a system should be open, with a possibility of incorporating a new functionality once an individual need arises. This also concerns a need for *combining several e-offices into a consistent, single "pipeline"*, when a result created by an e-office is used as an input to another office. So far, such service combining has to be performed manually by the users.

When a user case is processed for a longer time, a supplicant needs to be informed about current state of such process. Thus, a need for *continuous monitoring of the request* arises. Usually, it is needed to contact the office to get the latest info, in a manual, on-line manner. From the user point of view, a phone is the best tool for performing such fast checks. However, from a clerk point of view, unexpected phone calls are serious disruptions of his/her work. A automatic tool capable of getting the "phone-like" natural-language requests and sending the latest info would be very appreciated by both sides.

Last but not least, the *user identification, directly adopted from classical distributed systems, is not efficient enough*. First, the classical approach – user name/password – is easy to crack, especially for non-secured channels as e-mail and SMS/MMS. Traditional PKI cryptography is available mainly from the stationary computers or specialized hardware devices (at least a tokenizer or a specialized mobile phone, so far quite expensive and thus not very popular), and mainly for WWW/WAP connections. However, hardware IDs of end-user devices (e.g., IMEI or subscriber number of a mobile phone) and PKI-based digital signatures may be applied to fix a context (basic user/call identification), to determine both contents and formatting of the messages. Regrettable, so far hardware IDs are not widely used for automatic identification and context detection, especially in e-administration.

We propose to resolve all the above problems by the use of a set of individual, system- and user-defined programs – software agents. These agents are to be executed both at the server-side (i.e., in the internal e-office network), and at the client-side (personal mobile devices of supplicants and private stationary computers). In the next sections we describe our framework based on imperative, user-defined software agents and Agent Computing Environment. We propose specialized architecture of a system capable of performing a brokerage among e-offices and office supplicants.

3. SOFTWARE AGENTS TECHNOLOGY

In our approach, we used a classical definition of a software agent, as presented in [8, 14, 25]. A software agent is a program, executed at a given place, characterized by: (1) autonomy – agents process their work independently without the need for human management, (2) communication – agents are able to communicate with one another, as well as with humans, and (3) learning – agents are able to learn as they react with their environment and other agents or humans. As follows from the above definition, an agent may be programmed by its owner, thus allowing unrestricted personalization of behavior of this agent [2]. Agents may be executed in different places, according to owners' needs and possibilities of the end-user hardware [12].

The ACE framework is based on a set of distributed Agent Servers [15, 16], each of them capable of storing and executing software agents. The agents may be moved among Agent Servers. There are "light" Agent Servers with limited functionality to be executed in a "thin" hardware/software environment (e.g., mobile phones), and "thick", massively used Agent Servers located in stationary network hosts. The "light" servers are mainly used for executing individual agents of an owner of a mobile device, while the "thick" ones are used by many users in parallel, usually to access certain services, external software systems, and public communication channels.

There are two basic classes of ACE agents: public System Agents, and Private Agents. Public *System Agents* SAs are created by trusted users (usually system designers), to be used in a mass manner by many users, providing information in a standardized form and with optimum effort. As overall efficiency is of primary concern, SAs are programmed in Java. A way of usage of a given SA cannot be changed by an ordinary user, however, it may be parameterized during the invocation [17].

The *Private Agents* PAs are created and controlled by their human owners. Unless directly ordered by its owner, the agent cannot be accessed by any other agent. For private agents, the main problem is to achieve a reasonable trade-off between overall system security and a need for remote (i.e., server-side) execution of user-defined, thus „untrusted" (from the local administrator point of view) code. Several restrictions and limitations must be applied to user-defined code, protecting the system from (intentional or accidental) damages. Thus, a specialized language is proposed to program agent behavior, based on XML and equipped with several non-standard mechanisms like run-time monitoring of CPU time and memory allocation [15]. The language is of imperative type, thus allowing much wider personalization of the agent code in comparison with the classical declarative approach. XML-programmed private agents may invoke huge library of on-site, residential, Java-based system agents: communicators, services, brokers to external software systems, tools and utilities, etc. Usually, a small private agent, being a "light" mobile entity, is able to use (i.e., execute) several system agents, to achieve different goals. From the user point of view, the system is effective and powerful, and even small private agents are "intelligent" enough to fulfill complex requirements. From the system point of view, private agents executed at server-side do not pose a threat to local environment and other agents.

A typical Agent Server is equipped with several specialized system agents, so called input/output gateways, able to communicate with an external world (including other Agent Servers, local and remote software, and humans) via communication channels of different type and purpose. In general, two basic types of human-agent communication gateways are available: textual and Web-based. A *textual gateway* is able to exchange flat text messages among humans and agents. Textual gateways may use such means as an e-mail SMTP/POP3 connection, SMS/MMS connection, a voice gateway, etc. Once sent by a textual message, an ACE agent may act as a chatterbot, analyzing the message via keyword extraction and analysis [19].

Web-based gateways are used to access an agent via a WWW/WAP page, and from specialized ACE applications. For semi-automatic formatting of both contents and presentation of the data to be sent, XSL-T technology was adopted with XSL transformations defined in a personal manner and stored in private agent variables [18]. To improve data presentation, automatic detection of a technical characteristics of the end-user device is applied.

Gateways to external data sources are mainly used for automatic monitoring of information changes. As a change is reported by an external data source, a gateway invokes a selected agent. The agent may next pass the notification about "interesting" changes to user(s), via certain tele-communication gateways. What is "interesting" for the user is programmed by him/her in the code of the private agents [15, 17]. Thus, a set of user's agents is an "intelligent", personalized filter of changes of monitored data.

To facilitate monitoring, so called subscriptions may be used. A *subscription* is a request of automatic execution of (a part of) agent code after introducing certain change(s) in agent's internal variables. A resulting message (subscription alert) is asynchronously (i.e., at a time that cannot be predicted in advance) sent to a subscriber – either agent owner (a human), or another agent. A subscription is set by the agent owner, and at any time may be revoked or changed. The executed agent code is usually responsible for filtering changes towards detecting "critical" updates. The subscriptions permit efficient monitoring of data changes. Once a change is detected, is it checked and eventually reported as an alert. However, as long as there is no change in monitoring information, the agent code is not activated.

4. OVERALL SYSTEM ARCHITECTURE

The ACE framework, described in Section 3, is a generic agent-based environment. As such, this framework should be adjusted to given applications. The adjustment covers building specialized SA agents – gateways and drivers to external systems included – and proposing some prototypes (patterns, skeletons) for PA agents, to be further personalized by the end-users. The SAs are responsible for assuring communication with an e-office (WAP/WWW, e-mail, SMS/MMS, voice gateways, XML-based external applications and systems, etc.), standardization of input/output messages, basic brokerage with services from the internal e-office network, caching and synchronizing the access to the services, etc. There are as well some specialized SAs being system-defined utilities, as for example natural-language parser (programmable chatterbot), national-language detector, XML, HTML and WML formatters, etc. A detailed list of SAs depends on given application, thus here we cannot provide a fixed description. This also concerns user-defined PAs. We describe here a generic system architecture only, assuming that this is a starting point for user-specific applications.

Note that fixing the architecture levels to a mixture of the private and the public layer is not a significant restriction to the personalization of the system behaviour. A set of specialized SAs and user-defined PAs may be changed and extended at any time, both from the system, and from a particular user points of view. Different users observe different behaviour of their individual agents, and the whole system is efficient and scalable.

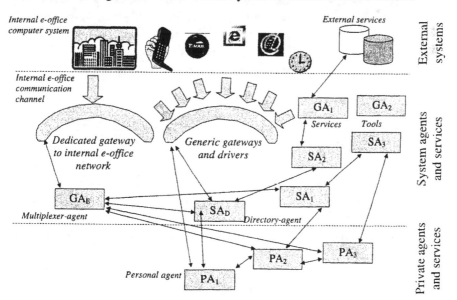

Figure 1. Layered architecture of an ACE-based access to an e-office

The layered system architecture is presented in Fig. 1. There are three basic system layers: (1) connections with external systems and communication channels, (2) basic, predefined system services of an e-office, and (3) private, user-defined agents and services. The presented architecture comprises only logical connections among agents and external systems. The agents may be distributed in the network, in particular, some (private) agents may be executed in end-user device (a palmtop, a notebook, a private stationary host), while some agents (both system and private) – in the local area network of an e-office. Physical connections among distributed agents are realized via specialized agent-agent gateways of distributed Agent Servers, with a possibility of encryption, tunnelling, firewalling, etc. Thus, agent-agent communication is safe, even if the communicating agents are distributed across the network.

Beside typical gateways for basic communication channels (e-mail, WAP/WWW, SMS/MMS, PTT/voice gateway) there are five basic classes of ACE agents: a broker-agent capable of contacting local area network of an e-office, system tools and services, catalogue-agents capable of informing about capabilities of system-defined agents (mainly the above-mentioned system tools and services), user tools and services, and user personal agent.

In general it is not possible to determine detailed characteristics and functionality of a typical agent belonging to one of these classes – this is application- and user-dependent. However, it is possible to describe a general strategy of providing and using agents belonging to all these classes. Such description is given in the next sections of this paper. Note that fixing agent classes and thus (somehow) agent functionality does not restrict introducing new agents and agent classes, in particular monitoring agents, other directory-agents, agent-brokers to/from Web Services and other software systems, agents-gateways for new communication channels, etc.

5.   AGENTS CONNECTED WITH INTERNAL E-OFFICE NETWORK

For obvious security reasons, user agents should not access directly services from a local area network of an e-office. Instead, one or more broker-agents should be provided, to act as a firewall/proxy between ACE agents (both system and private) and back-office services and databases. Basic functionality of such agent(s) is the following:

● *Multiplexing and synchronizing requests* generated asynchronously by the population of ACE agents (a proxy for back-office systems).
● *Access standardization* – providing one single standardized way of accessing all the back-office data sources. To this goal, XML should be

used as a basic communication and data storage tool. Agent-broker may be specialized for communication with different data sources accessible by different communication standards and with different data format. Note that a new back-office data source/service may be added at any time, and such modification requires no changes in existing agents.

- *Continuous control over connections* to/from back-office systems, including billing for using the services/information, storing logs of user and system activities, verifying access rights, generating security and missing-information alerts, etc.

- *Caching frequently accessed information* – for slowly-changed information (as most of the information provided by e-offices) for a mass user, an information-cache may substantially reduce network traffic to and from massively accessed back-office systems. For example, such information as law regulations and office rules may be distributed efficiently in a mass manner.

- *Generating user- and source-specific alerts* the ACE agents are waiting for. Important changes in the information provided by back-office data sources may be quickly reported to the agents. To this goal, user-defined subscriptions (cf. Section 3) may be used, to free agents from continuous monitoring and comparison of information changes.

Using broker-agents permits personalized access to back-office data sources with no decrease in the overall security level. In extreme cases, a broker-agent may be linked with a restricted part of the local area network of an e-office by a dedicated hardware and office-specific protocol (e.g., a serial-cable connection capable of sending only text files at request). Note that the details about an implementation of a safe connection between broker-agents and back-office data sources are usually hidden for the ordinary users. Note also that the broker-agent may be able to filter the whole information flow, including blocking given users (user agents), addresses, specific requests, messages containing specific words, etc.

5.1 System defined tools and services

The system defined tools and services are implemented by system agents, usually prepared by e-office staff to be massively used by the population of users. It is not possible to provide here a description of the agents of this layer, as detailed functionality of the agents depend on given application area. Some examples of commonly used system tools and services are the following: wrappers, formatters, cache utilities, data analysers, etc.

Usually, as the ACE framework is mainly used for brokerage rather for implementation of end-user services, the agents of this layer are used as drivers and gateways to some external systems. These are tasks similar to the broker-agent mentioned in previous section, however, addressed to the systems independent of an e-office. For example, there may be an agent capable of collecting last law regulations from an official government site, some agents providing links with other e-offices, etc. Moreover, one may imagine a situation when a single agent implements an idea of a "virtual office", combining functionality of several branches of an e-office into a single, consistent service. Note that "virtual services" may be personalized by user private agents as well.

An example of an idea of a "virtual service" is given in [17], however, for the domain of Web Services [9, 21]. This idea may be extended to non-standardized Internet services as well, including Semantic Web and its extensions [1, 22] and proprietary solutions of particular e-offices. "Virtual services" permit efficient distribution of component services, as well as information exchange among different e-offices and e-office branches.

Even if system tools and services cannot be programmed by ordinary users, wide usage of subscriptions (cf. Section 3) makes is possible to effectively distribute personalized information about data changes. Once subscribed to a given system service, user private agents are immediately informed about „interesting" changes of the information provided by an e-office. What is "interesting" is programmed in both a subscription (i.e., as a variable of a system agent) and in the way of accepting a subscription alert (i.e., as a code/variable of a private agent).

5.2   Catalogue-agents

Usually, a potential functionality/organization of an e-office is reach enough to be too complicated to an ordinary user. Thus, a catalogue of e-office services would be appreciated. The main goal of such catalogue, being a specialized system agent, is twofold. First, human users may contact the catalogue to collect useful information about services and law/organizational restrictions on using these services. Second, user agents are able to get some formal information about contacting system agents (services) – lists of functions provided, function parameters, etc. Thus, private agents have a possibility of (semi-)automatically adjust to a specificity of a given e-office.

Catalogue-agent is able to generate user-understandable help messages and machine-understandable interface descriptions (meaning and types of invocation parameters) at request. The latter may be used to automatically adjust PAs to the specificity of an e-office. It's obvious that reacting to serious differences in the interfaces to system agents belonging to different e-offices cannot be fully automated, however, critical differences in interfaces may be immediately reported to user agents (mainly the personal agent) to notify "fatal" errors in communication with an e-office. It is up to the user to react to such notifications.

Similar to the system tools and services, the catalogue-agent may be implemented as a broker to an external WS Directory Server, LDAP or a similar service, including proprietary solutions for given e-offices.

5.3   User-defined tools and services

The role of this group of agents is similar to the layer composed of system defined tools and services (Section 4.2) except that this layer is composed of users' private agents. These agents may be executed either at client-side (i.e., in client's mobile devices and stationary PCs), and at server-side (i.e., in the Internet and in an internal local area network of an e-office, depending on application area). Usually, private agents executed at client side are related with data formatting and displaying, while the agents executed at server-side are related with monitoring of changes and user-defined brokerage. Client-side agents are related with (automatic) adjustment of both contents and format of the information to user personal needs and expectations, time, date and place of information delivery, restrictions for end-user hardware and software, characteristics of a communication link, etc. Note that client-side agents may be chosen automatically depending on current user's situation. For example, a user visiting a real office is able to use his/her mobile equipment only, with limited screen&keyboard possibilities, just to receiving very basic alerts and messages. The same user, while back home, is going to use wide screen of his/her stationary PC to get more details about reported e-office activities.

On the contrary, monitoring agents cannot be executed at client-side, as the permanent communication costs would be too high [12]. Thus, such agents should be migrated to a network server, possibly as close to the data source (i.e., e-office local area network) as possible. Working autonomously, user-defined monitors detect "critical" data changes (e.g., by the use of the above-mentioned subscriptions defined in system agents), filtering incoming information and informing owners about "interesting" facts. Note that (1) monitoring agents are strongly personalized, and (2) such agents must be executed at server-side, thus a trade-off arises between security and efficiency. From the system point of view, this trade-off is satisfied with the use of a mixture of ACE private and public agents.

5.4   User personal agent

A personal agent is a main entry point for a particular user, synchronizing all the incoming and outcoming messages, storing user preferences (with reference to preferred communication links, data formats, presentation interfaces, etc.). The agent is used as a main broker/synchronizer for all the traffic between a user (agent owner) and all the other agents working for this user (both system and private agents). Usually, the main task if this agent is to collect user request via a certain communication channel (i.e., from a certain agent-gateway), standardize this request (usually to the form of an XML message), choose the most adequate private/system agent to serve this request, and finally collect the response and send it back to the user.

The personal agent is also used for sending alerts generated by the user-defined subscriptions. According to current user preferences, an alert is formatted and sent via a certain communication channel – an SMS/MMS, e-mail, IM or a similar chat-based system, a notification waiting in a WWW server, etc. The "best" (at the moment) communication channel may be chosen automatically, taking into account current position of a user (reported by a specialized agent), user's last login (place and time), independent restrictions (e.g., user's availability, scheduled meetings and travels, etc.).

A special interest is taken to assure efficient communication with the use of "handicapped" devices as for example mobile phones. To this goal, a natural-language interface is provided, aiming in a personalized chatterbot conversation [19]. Note that such simplified NL interface may be adjusted to given user(s), thus allowing efficient conversation with automated services of an e-office in a human-to-human manner. This limits a necessity of learning different, fixed, complicated interfaces for different e-offices (to some extent). This also greatly improves an effectiveness of communicating via limited mobile channels, as for example popular SMS messaging, by incorporating user-defined abbreviations and user-specific vocabularies.

6.   TYPICAL SCENARIO OF USING ACE AGENTS FOR CONTACTING AN E-OFFICE

In the real life, we must adjust the way of contacting an office to the internal organization of this office: business hours, staff availability, clerk specialization, information workflow, etc. A specificity of an office case / supplicant should be taken into consideration as well. Generic strategy of using ACE agents to facilitate these goals is the following.

1) A supplicant addresses given branch(es) of an e-office, presenting details of his/her office case. In addition, the supplicant determines some personal preferences: mobile and stationary devices used, identifiers (e.g., a phone subscriber number, IMEI device number, PKI signature, IP/DNS address, e-mail account, etc.), preferable communication channels, etc.

2) The office branch proposes a set of predefined SAs and PAs to be installed for the supplicant in the Agent Servers located in the local area network of the office. This set of agents is capable of serving supplicant's case in a predefined way that is common for all the users.

3) The office branch proposes a set of PAs to be installed at client-side by the supplicant, to facilitate contacts with the e-office. It is up to the user to accept this set of agents or not. In the latter case, only the PAs executed in the office network are used. However, once a supplicant accepts PAs agents in his/her private hardware/software environment, he/she may profit in faster notifications (e.g., SMS messages sent to mobile phones), better adjustment to end-user devices, more personalized formatting and presentation methods, and other functionality related with client-side information processing (cf. Sections 4.4 and 4.5). Note that, as the supplicant may inform the office about detailed characteristics of the devices used and preferable communication channels, the generated client-side PAs may be customized, even if the server-side PAs are quite standardized (at the beginning, however, cf. Point 6 below).

4) The SAs and PAs installed are equipped with a set of predefined variables and subscriptions, to deal with the office case of the supplicant. The subscriptions are parameterized by case-dependent information, e.g., office case number, supplicant personal data, etc.

5) The set of accepted agents is installed and activated each time the change of information is detected related with any active subscription. The detected changes are filtered and eventually sent to the supplicant (usually, to the personal agent, and further via given communication channel directly to the end-user device, e.g., a mobile phone).

6) Once the supplicant is not satisfied with a subscription or PA behaviour, he/she has rights to redefine both data and code of his/her agents. For advanced users it is possible to fully personalize the behaviour of the system, both at server-, and at the client-side. For non-advanced users, it is still a possibility to define preferable communication channel, ways and timings of sending alerts, formats and contents of messages generated by the office agents (e.g., small SMS alerting vs. formatted HTML e-mails). Such changes are easily introduced by the office staff (at supplicant's request) or by the users, with the use of specialized agents.

Note that even if the users change the behaviour (i.e., the code) of their private agents executed at the server-side, the overall system security is not reduced due to continuous run-time inspection of "untrusted" (user-defined) agents (cf. Section 3). Note also that private agents are executed only in two "trusted" (from a user point of view) environments – an e-office local area network and private "network" of the user, usually composed of a mobile phone and a stationary home PC. Sending messaging among user agents may be encrypted (e.g., using PKI cryptography), increasing overall confidence level of contacts with the e-office (for particular users).

7.   CONCLUSIONS

In this paper, we propose a framework capable of personalization of access and behavior of an e-office. Our solution is based on ACE software agents, partially prepared by (and for) supplicants, executed in both user personal devices and the e-office network. The main goal of our framework is to provide a universal system for monitoring and notifying about information changes, on one hand, and user-defined customization of e-office services, on the other hand. The framework implements an idea of individual "virtual" service, enabling: (1) personalization of behavior of the service, (2) user-defined linking and "pipelining" of services, including services of different e-offices, (3) individual brokerage among services and supplicants, and (4) personalization of information delivery (time, place, form, communication channel, etc.).

The framework makes it possible to adjust fixed, closed software environment of an e-office to individual requirements and expectations of different users. To this goal, one does not need to interfere in e-office internal organization and software systems. Instead, user- and system-defined ACE agents are used as brokers among supplicants and the services offered by an e-office. The agents may be executed both at the client-side (mainly in personal mobile devices), and at the server-side (i.e., in the local area network of an e-office), with no decrease in overall system safety and security. Efficient distribution of agents improves system scalability, and restrict traditional bottlenecks of today's centralized offices.

The whole system is scalable and open for new users and services, including such non-standard functionality as reporting the less-busy business hours, current case state and missing documents, predicted timings, etc. The system is also open for new communication standards and growing functionality of end-user devices, mainly mobile equipment (for example voice gateways, IM and chat communication, etc.). Several natural-language interfaces makes it possible to communicate with the ACE agents as if they were humans, facilitating the usage of the system by non-advanced users.

Although the ACE framework is fully implemented and industry-tested [15÷19], we could not test the proposed application in a real (e-)office. Thus, we developed a simulator, being a set of ACE agents, to model a behavior of a sample e-office and different office supplicants. Even this simplified simulator showed that the system would be very useful, both for the supplicants, and for office staff. The initial implementation costs are quite low (a PDA/PC with Java environment installed, and an SQL-database for storing agents), in comparison with other parts of a local area network of a typical office. We are looking now for an office ready to implement and test our approach with real supplicants and services.

REFERENCES

[1] Benjamins, R., Agents and Semantic Web: a Business Perspective, http://www.agentlink.org/agents-barcelona/presentations/3_RichardBenjamins_final.pdf

[2] Bonett, M., Personalization of Web Services: Opportunities and Challenges, 2001, Ariadne Issue 28, http://www.ariadne.ac.uk /issue28/personalization/intro.html

[3] E-government - Electronic Government, EurActiv: homepage, http://www.euractiv.com/Article?tcmuri=tcm:29-117473-16&type= LinksDossier

[4] E-Government in developing countries, http://www1.worldbank.org/publicsector/egov/

[5] eGovernment leadership: High Performance, Maximum Value, The Government Executive Series, http://a456.g.akamai.net/7/456/1701/5e33f326cdecd2/ www.accenture.com/ xdoc/en/industries/government/gove_egov_value.pdf

[6] eOffice homepage: Virtual Office Management that Transforms Any Traditional Office, http://www.greatshop.com/eoffice20.html

[7] eOffice Services homepage, http://www.eofficeservices.biz/

[8] Franklin S., Graesser A. Is it an Agent, or just a Program? A Taxonomy for Autonomous Agents, 3rd Int. ATA Workshop, Springer-Verlag, 1996

[9] Lombardi, V., Designing for Web Services, April 2002, http://www.newarchitectmag.com/documents/s=2452/new1015627350101/index.html

[10] Marcus P. Zillman's chatterbot resources and sites, http://chatterbots.blogspot.com/

[11] Microsoft Agent home page, http://www.microsoft.com/msagent/default.asp

[12] Milojicic D., Trend Wars – mobile agent applications, IEEE Concurr., 1999, pp. 80-90

[13] Moriuchu, Y., Private Sector Recommendations to government on realization of e-government, in e-Government, http://www.gbde.org/egovernment/

[14] Nwana, H., Software Agents: an overview, Knowl. Eng. Rev. 11-1996-3, pp. 205-244

[15] Rykowski J., Agent Technology for Secure Personalized Web Services, 24th Int. Scientific School ISAT 2003, Szklarska Poreba (Poland), 2003, pp. 185-193

[16] Rykowski, J., Databases as repositories for software agents, in Emerging Database Research in East Europe eds. B. Thalheim and G. Fiedler, Pre-conference Workshop joined with the 29th VLDB Conference, Berlin, Germany, 2003, pp 117-123

[17] Rykowski J., Cellary W., Virtual Web Services - Application of Software Agents to Personalization of Web Services, 6th International Conference on Electronic Commerce ICEC 2004, Delft (The Netherlands), 2004, ACM Publishers; pp. 409-418

[18] Rykowski, J., Juszkiewicz, A., Personalization of Information Delivery by the Use of Agents, IADIS Int. Conf. WWW/Internet 2003, Algarve, Portugal, 2003, pp. 1056-1059

[19] Rykowski, J., Using software agents to personalize natural-language access to Internet services in a chatterbot manner, 2nd Int. Conf. L&T'05, Poznan, Poland, April 2005

[20] US President's Expanding Electronic Government initiative, http://www.whitehouse.gov/omb/egov/

[21] Web Services Activity home page, http://www.w3.org/2002/ws/

[22] Web Ontology Language (OWL), http://www.w3.org/2004/OWL

[23] Weizenbaum, Joseph: Computer power and human reason. From Judgment to Calculation. S.Francisco, 1976

[24] Westholm, H., Aichholzer, G. The impact of eEurope Initiative on public administration in Europe, http://www.prisma-eu.net/deliverables/SG1administration.pdf

[25] Wooldridge, M., Jennings, N.R., Intelligent agents: theory and practice, Knowledge Engineering Review 10-1995-2, pp. 115-152

EVALUATING E-GOVERNMENT
A Process-oriented Approach

Christian Seel, Oliver Thomas, Bettina Kaffai, Thomas Matheis
Institute for Information Systems (IWi) at the German Research Center for Artificial Intelligence (DFKI), Saarbruecken (Germany), iwi@iwi.uni-sb.de, http://www.iwi.uni-sb.de

Abstract: After the initial phase of E-Government and the exaggerated expectations for the new internet-based technologies, a pragmatic state of mind has evolved during the last few years. Thereby, it is especially the evaluation of the related financial benefits that has become a crucial aspect. The paper presented outlines a process-driven approach for the analysis of technology-driven performance impacts based on performance indicators. From a German perspective, existing evaluation concepts were concretized for the case scenario of German Plan Approval Procedures.[1]

Key words: Business Process Management, Process Performance, Public Administration, E-Government

1.   MOTIVATION

With the rise of Electronic or E-Government, public administrations (PAs) all over the world are forcing the usage of modern information and communication technologies (ICT). Aiming at an increase in efficiency, cost-effectiveness and transparency, the highest objective is to achieve the transaction-oriented and seamless integration of all parties involved. This requires well-defined approaches considering the organizational, as well as the technical perspective. In this context, process models constitute a well-proven and widely accepted instrument for merging technological and organizational aspects. In general, they can help PAs to revise their process struc-

---

[1] The results are based on the research project "RAfEG – Reference Architecture for E-Government", funded by the German Ministry for Education and Research.

tures, support change management and enable technical customizing and implementation.

In this context, the concepts from the area of the New Public Management (NPM), which aim e.g. at the creation of "lean" structures, constitute a precious enabler for the successful implementation of technical solutions and their usage [14] [15] and provide well-proven concepts. Since the late 1960's initial reform attempts were undertaken, but did not obtain the anticipated effect [1]. In the 1980's, the NPM initiated a reform process that continues even today and was introduced worldwide in PAs. It comprises administrative reform strategies led by an economical interpretation of administrative processes [18]. The core elements contain the setup of a decentralized management and organizational structure, the control of outputs, as well as competition and customer orientation [11]. Additionally, the NPM's basic principle of target-oriented management offers concepts and principles for controlling the efficiency and effectiveness-impact of E-Government solutions.

As to the last-mentioned aspect, adequate and approved performance indicators which complement the E-Government process structures should be incorporated into the models. By doing so, the control of process efficiency according to the PA's strategic goals is facilitated. In addition, benchmarking among various PAs can be easily conducted if their E-Government processes are based on common indicators and corresponding indicators. The indicators may as well be benchmarked with the same indicators in conventional processes that don't use ICT, thus showing the potentials of E-Government and justifying further efforts.

The presented paper outlines an approach for the setup of performance indicators as an integrated part of process models. In the first part, basic aspects of Process Performance Measurement within PAs are described. A case scenario from the German ministerial administration demonstrates the concrete realization.

2.   FRAMEWORK AND APPROACHES

2.1   The House of Business Process Management

Experience in the area of business engineering show the need for a comprehensive, methodological framework in order to consider all the relevant factors for effective and efficient ICT usage. With the ARIS – House of Business Process Management (HOBE) shown in Figure 1, a widely accepted approach is available. Even if the concept was originally invented for the business area, its basic logic is of common validity and can also be used in the field of PA [4].

Figure 1. HOBE – House of Business Process Management [16]

Level one – the Strategy Level – builds the foundation for process-related activities. Aspects such as the identification of E-Government-relevant processes, corresponding process architecture or necessary applications are defined here. The overall administrative mission and strategy define the limits for the definition of process-related aspects. On level two – the Design and Optimization Level – the concrete appearance of E-Government processes according to the preferences defined at level one is fixed. Existing structures must be analyzed and – if necessary – revised. New processes for areas non-existent in the past are defined according to optimization principles. In this context, the usage of reference processes allows the consideration of best practices and leads to time and cost advantages in designing process structures. The realization of these processes by selecting and using adequate technological concepts such as Enterprise Resource Planning or workflow or document management systems is part of the Execution Level. During their daily operations, the systems deliver a variety of data indicating the actual performance of the supported process structures. The performance information is transferred to the Controlling Level, which assures the analysis of the as-is performance. Here, the availability of process models that provide a set of performance indicators and basic principles for the measurement's realization is of crucial interest.

The ongoing comparison of the actual performance indicator's value with their performance goals allows a systematic and planned revision of the processes. These feedback-mechanisms support continuous process management based on exact and valid data. At the same time, the process performance shows the impact of the E-Government solutions and their effectiveness. Thus, the evaluation of the cost and efficiency-related measures, such as the average cycle time, calculation of the resulting cost structures and their comparison to the Return-on-Investment-related target values support the monitoring of the E-Government solution's profitability.

The aspects of the Process Performance Measurement as outlined above show the basic principle of comparing as-is measures to target values in order to define the degree of goal fulfillment. Starting with the aspects set on the first level of HOBE, the strategic goals must be "translated" into concrete measures and targets for operative process monitoring.

Reference Models can support this initiation of Process Performance Measurement by providing various sets of performance indicators and operational definitions for the measurement. According to the basic idea of reference modeling – the creation and application of common-type models valid for a class of application scenarios – the model's user selects the measures and then uses them as a basis for "customizing", according to the framework conditions of "his" administrational unit. Because of the actual lack of adequate reference models which meet the requirements of E-Government [12] [7] [19], integrated systems of reference processes, metrics and measuring procedures are missing. Additionally, the fields of NPM and E-Government are often strictly separated in administrational practice without using the complementary possibilities. Nevertheless, the design of best-practice measurement scenarios, their link to the identified E-Government processes, as well as concepts for the ongoing, system-based measurement are of crucial importance for controlling E-Government success. Various concepts are already available in the area of NPM which support the development of measurement approaches as part of reference models for E-Government. Focusing on the strategy and controlling levels, the following sections outline the development of measurement scenarios and demonstrate the potential of NPM-driven concepts for dealing with E-Government challenges.

2.2   Evaluating E-Government – Implications on the Strategy Level

As mentioned above, the first step on the strategy level is the identification of the relevant E-Government processes, as well as the definition of the corresponding process architecture. The aspect mentioned last is realized in a top-down approach that systematically specifies the various relevant procedures from a high to a detailed level. The relevant specifications are deduced from the E-Government strategy, which should e.g. contain the ranking of administrative outputs according to their E-Government impact. Considering the services' specific target groups, the main success factors, such as cycle times, quality of service or cost efficiency, can be evaluated as a basis for the definition of target values indicating the performance of the E-Government processes.

Here, the Balanced Scorecard [9] concept could be useful in realizing the systematic link between E-Government strategy, process strategy and strategic targets. The Balanced Scorecard is a multi-perspective approach aiming, on the one hand, at the "balance" of a strategy by considering various perspectives and on the other, on the operationalization of the corresponding strategic goals and their "translation" into a set of measurable targets. Originally, the concept was developed for the business area and contained the financial, customer, business process and learning perspective. The perspectives are interrelated through cause and effect relationships showing the ability to realize the strategy and to monitor this relationship.

In the meantime, the benefits of this instrument of strategic management have become widely accepted – also within the sphere of the PA. Various examples demonstrate the successful usage, such as in US city administrations [8], the Austrian federal government [6] or various federal ministries in Germany [17]. In the context of E-Government, the Balanced Scorecard concept helps to operationalize the administration's E-Government strategy. In a first step, the high-level strategic goals are extracted or formulated and assigned to the perspectives, which must be explicated in advance (e.g. financial, process, technical and recipient's perspective). The verification of the interdependencies between the targets enables the proof of the strategy's completeness. Subsequently, a set of performance indicators covering the various perspectives is developed for each strategic goal in a top-down approach.

2.3 Evaluating E-Government – Implications on the Design Level

The design of the E-Government process on the design level is based on the specifications from the strategic level. From the areas of process and quality management, a wide set of procedure models is available which support the concrete project procedure. Referring to the usage of performance indicators, two areas of use are possible. First, an initial measurement of the as-is processes focuses the process outputs and leads to the evaluation of the actual process performance. Its comparison to the performance goals shows the necessity and potentials of the process optimization. Second, the data analysis based on the process specifics and its inputs helps to find the so called "root causes", meaning the concrete aspects that are responsible for the performance gaps and that have to be re-designed in order to optimize the process structures. The result consists of adequate and E-Government-strategy conform process structures.

The definition of the measurement scenarios is tied closely to the activities on the controlling level of HOBE, because the ongoing performance measurement which monitors the new processes after the completion of the process design and the technical implementation is based on the specifications done during the optimization projects. Approaches which help to define the indicators are presented in the following section.

2.4   Evaluating E-Government – Implications on the Controlling Level

On the Controlling Level, the process-oriented measurement scenario is developed and implemented based on the findings of the design level. As mentioned above, the process output represents the object of consideration for the process performance's evaluation. Accordingly, the performance indicators represent so-called "output measures". Their target values are based on the – internal or external – requirements. The comparison to the as-is values shows the overall process quality and performance.

For the development of the measurement scenarios, possible indicators are collected in a first step, with regard to the strategic objectives, in order to build a basic pool. The most appropriate ones are selected according to their potential for indicating the performance and impacts of process adjustments. Thus, it is crucial to focus the "key"-indicators, concentrating on the relevant and easy collectible data [13]. Operational definitions, such as the description of the measure's characteristics, the availability and source of data, the measurement period or those responsible for the data collection are defined in the second step. Finally, the target values for each indicator are concretized on the basis of as-is values [6]. The ongoing comparison to these performance goals allows the evaluation of process performance. In addition, the as-is performance before implementing an E-Government solution – e.g. evaluated in the early process design phase – can be used as a so-called "baseline". The gap between this baseline and the as-is performance values after the E-Government implementation shows efficiency improvements or lacks and also allows the evaluation of the (financial) benefits.

The comparison of the as-is performance to the target values corresponds to the concept of benchmarking, which is a well-proven management instrument. The general intention consists in the analysis and improvement of organizational performance and the ability to execute. Based on performance indicators, a comparison with "Best in class"-results enables the evaluation of improvement potentials [3]. The development of performance indicators and the corresponding measurement specifics for the benchmarking in PAs is subject to a variety of approaches especially on the municipal level. They provide "ready-to-use" measurement scenarios and can support the evaluation of relevant indicators. From the German perspective, the performance indicators provided by the German "IKO Net", initiated and coordinated by the KGSt, a public consulting agency for municipal administrations, represent a widely accepted approach. More than 1,600 municipal administrations are members of the IKO Net. The aim of this network is to provide a basis for municipal administrations which allows them to benchmark their performance in selected areas on a regular basis. The KGSt serves as a "catalyst" and provides a total of 56 sets of performance indicators and the corresponding operational definitions for 35 fields of administrative activities, such as human resource or waste management. The participating municipalities' measurement results are stored in a central database which is maintained by the KGSt and is used for interorganizational performance comparisons [10]. Because of its extent and usability, this concept was chosen to inspire the design of performance indicators as part of a process model which is the subject of the case study presented in section 3.

Additionally, concepts of quality management help to structure measurement scenarios and support the definition of adequate metrics. The Common Assessment Framework (CAF) shown in Figure 2, provides nine dimensions and the corresponding sets of criteria which enable the self-assessment and evaluation of strengths and improvement potentials for PAs. The CAF was initiated by the ministers of the EU in 2000 and is based on the model of the European Foundation for Quality Management and the performance ratios of the Speyer Quality Contest. The nine rating categories, assigned to the categories "Enablers" and "Results", focus on aspects of organizational development and contain criteria for performance ranking. The definition of the categories follows the basic logic as outlined in section 2.3: The evaluation of the results leads to the as-is performance ("Measurement"), whereas the analysis of the enablers shows the causes for the actual performance level ("Analysis"). The criteria used for the evaluation of the actual performance per category are explained within the CAF as questions and come with rating scales. During the self-assessment, the parties involved must answer these questions by using the scales [2]. As a consequence, the measurement of performance aspects, e.g. based on the indicators of the IKO Net, facilitate this process.

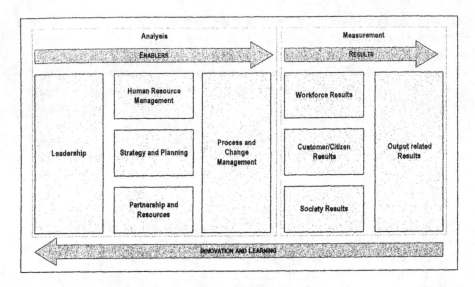

Figure 2. CAF – Common Assessment Framework [2]

The second part of the activities at the controlling level is the ongoing measurement and analysis of process performance according to the specified metrics and measuring principles. The collection of data can be realized in different ways depending on the PA's individual requirements. Accordingly, manual data collection and analysis can be carried out using questionnaires or scoring lists and spreadsheets as for example, provided by Excel. In order to use the automation potentials in deducing the relevant data from the executive systems according to the basic idea of HOBE, the usage of professional performance management tools is crucial.

The following case scenario demonstrates the development of a measurement scenario based on the outlined approaches for the domain of the Plan Approval Procedure within the traffic environment. The goal of the corresponding research project "RAFEG – Reference Architecture for E-Government" is the design of a comprehensive reference process model, as well as the implementation of a prototype which covers the corresponding technical components for the process execution. The reference model will – in addition to reference process structures – provide typical performance indicators and measurement concepts in order to allow a coherent process performance measurement.

3.   CASE SCENARIO

The first step of the RAFEG project was the development of a process model for the case scenario of Plan Approval Procedures. These specific administrative procedures take place for all public construction efforts, such as the construction of streets, airports or railways and legitimate building projects as far as public interests are concerned [5]. In order to construct the process model for Plan Approval Procedures, three main steps were carried out as shown in Figure 3. First, the legal framework was analyzed in order to get an overview of the specific regulations affecting the processes. Based on this, in a second step, the development of an initial, component-based process scenario was realized which served as a basis for the as-is evaluation of "real life" procedures in various administrations on the German federal state level. Last but not least, the additional information gained here was integrated into the models in order to complete them.

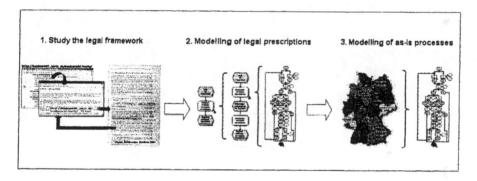

Figure 3. Project procedure – A detailed overview of the procedure for the development of the process model is documented in [19]

Figure 4 gives an overview of the process module "gather statements" which serves as an example for the development of the measurement scenario. Here, stakeholders such as for example, nature conservation organizations and public agencies, are invited to give their feedback based on planning documents specifying the construction project. The plan approval agency collects and stores the incoming statements as a basis for subsequent negotiations on project modifications. The collection and documentation of the involved organization's declarations represent one of the module's outputs and serves as input for the following module "handle objections and statements".

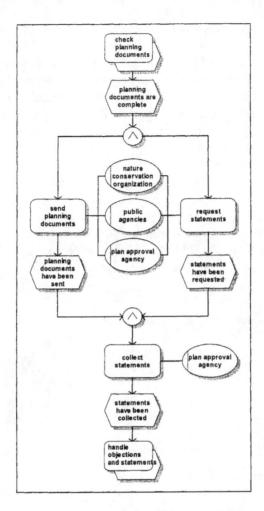

Figure 4. Process module "Gather statements"

For the identification of performance indicators and measures, the monitoring of process quality, process costs and the cycle time were named as the partner administration's target dimensions. In order to operationalize them for the entire process, the CAF-result dimensions and their accompanying criteria provided an initial point. The usage of the European concept covers the requirement of common validity for the process model-related performance indicators. Table 1 demonstrates the selected aspects and their assignment to the target dimensions.

In the next step, the evaluation criteria were operationalized for the various process modules in order to enable concrete measurement and performance evaluation. Hereby, the performance indicators of the IKO Net, covering the areas of "environmental conservation" and "construction planning", provided precious input. Table 2 shows the measures and their operational definitions. According to the principle of output orientation, the indicators are tied to the process module's results. The displayed output measures characterize the process output "sent planning documents".

Table 1. Evaluation criteria

Rating Category	Evaluation Criteria	Addressed Targets
Output related Results	Cost effectiveness	Process costs
	Efficiency·	Cycle time
	Involvement of the internal stakeholders	Process quality
	Ability to satisfy the stakeholder's requirements	Process quality
		Process costs
	Budget fulfillment·	Process costs, quality
	Fulfillment of financial targets	Process quality
	Ability to satisfy the stakeholder's financial requirements·	Process costs
	Effective use of resources	
Customer/Citizen Results	Number of complaints	Process costs, quality
	Cycle time of the complaint processing	Cycle time
	Involvement of Stakeholders	Cycle time
	Received and documented proposals	Process quality
	Customer Relationship Management	Process quality
	Number of returned files containing defects	Process costs, quality
Workforce Results	Number of sick leaves	Cycle Time
	Fluctuation rate	Process quality
	Productivity	Cycle time
		Process costs
Society Results	Consideration of environmental aspects in decision processes	Process quality

Beyond those shown, a set of performance indicators and measurement specifications was developed for each of the process modules. The link to the relevant CAF "Result" dimensions and the corresponding evaluation criteria ensured the completeness of the measurement scenarios. The experience gained has shown, that the consideration of process structures on a high level is sufficient and ensures concentration on crucial indicators. Additionally, the definition of measurement scenarios per process module ensures the ability of the staff responsible to monitor "their" process modules. The accumulation of the collected data leads to the performance evaluation of the overall process "Plan Approval Procedure". Based on the specifics defined within the measurement scenario, those in charge within the PAs can select and customize measurement specifics. The setup of a process performance measurement is facilitated and time and cost advantages are realized.

Christian Seel, Oliver Thomas, Bettina Kaffai, Thomas Matheis

Table 2. Output measures process module "Gather statements"

Process module	Output	Performance indicator	Explication	Unit
	Output 3.2: Sent planning documents	3.2.1 Total of sendouts	Number of planning documents sent to the recipients	pcs.
		3.2.2 Number of defective units	Number of documents that contain a defect: formal defects as e.g. missing recipients; content related defects as e.g. missing documents	pcs.
		3.2.3 Average cycle time	Period between the reception of the planning documents and their sendout compared to the total of sendouts	dys.
		3.2.4 Number of corrections	Number of process cycles (re-work) that have to be performed to eliminate defects	pcs.
		3.2.5 Average correction time	Period between the approval of a defect and its elimination compared to the number of defective units	dys. /unit
		3.2.6 Percentage of rework related costs	Process cost for reworks including staff and other resource cost compared to the total costs	%
		3.2.7 Total process costs per unit	Costs per sent document	€
		3.2.8 Percentage of efforts	Plan approval agency's efforts caused by the sendout compared to the total efforts	%

4. CONCLUSION

This paper outlined the development of process performance indicators and measurement scenarios which enable the implementation of a Performance Measurement for E-Government processes. Based on approaches developed in the field of NPM, the indicators and their operational definitions have been explicated and linked to process modules which cover the case scenario of German Plan Approval Procedures. At present the project is still in progress and first as-is measurements are realized at the PAs involved in RAFEG in order to achieve a baseline for the actual process performance and to find realistic target values considering the requirements of the stakeholders involved. The data already available, such as total cycle times, is collected and new data, such as the number of defective outputs, is evaluated. In a later phase, the prototypically developed system-components for the execution of the Plan Approval Procedures will be implemented and provide the required data. At this stage, the implementation of the indicators in a professional tool for process performance management providing interfaces to the prototype is intended. The comparison to the actual baseline will show the impact of ICT usage and display the benefits of the E-Government approach within the field of Plan Approval Procedures.

5. REFERENCES

[1] Lothar Beyer; Hans Brinckmann: Kommunalverwaltung im Umbruch: Verwaltungsreform im Interesse von Bürgern und Beschäftigten, Bund-Verlag, Cologne, 1990, pp. 14–20.

[2] Deutsches CAF-Zentrum: Common Assessment Framework (CAF) : Ein gemeinsames Europäisches Qualitätsbewertungssystem. German Ministry of internal affaires, Berlin, 2003, p. 6.

[3] Oliver Grieble: Modellgestütztes Dienstleistungsbenchmarking – Methoden, Implementierung, Anwendung, Eul, Lohmar, 2004, p. 24–30.

[4] Ralf Heib: Effiziente Verwaltungsprozesse durch E-Government, in: Scheer et al. (Eds.): Innovation durch Geschäftsprozessmanagement : Jahrbuch Business Process Excellence 2004/2005, Springer, Berlin, 2004, pp. 385–394.

[5] Werner Hoppe; Hans Schlarmann; Reimar Buchner: Rechtsschutz bei der Planung von Straßen und anderen Verkehrsanlagen (3. compl. rev. ed.). Beck, Munich, 2001.

[6] Christian Horak; Franz Schwarenthorer: Die Balanced Scorecard in der öffentlichen Verwaltung, Ministry for public services and sports, Vienna, 2002.

[7] Erika Horn; Thomas Off: eGovernment-Architekturen auf Basis der eLoGo-Referenzmodelle, in: Nierhaus (Ed.): KWI-Projektberichte, Nr. 9, University of Potsdam, Potsdam, 2004, p. 4.

[8] Robert S. Kaplan: City of Charlotte, Harvard Business Review, Boston, 3/1999.

[9]   Robert S. Kaplan; David P. Norton: The balanced scorecard – translating strategy into action, Harvard Business School Press, Boston, 1996.

[10]   KGSt: Arbeit mit Kennzahlen, Teil 1: Grundlagen, KGSt, Cologne, 2001.

[11]   Ralf Klischewski; Klaus Lenk: Understanding and Modelling Flexibility in Administrative Processes, in: Traunmüller; Lenk (Eds.): Electronic Government. Proceedings of the first International Conference, EGOV 2002, Aix-en-Provence, France. Springer, Berlin, 2002, pp. 129–136.

[12]   Klaus Lenk: Prozessmodelle für eGovernment, in: Kubicek et al. (Eds.): Innovation@Infrastruktur : Informations- und Dienstleistungsstrukturen der Zukunft. Jahrbuch Telekommunikation und Gesellschaft 2002, Hüthig, Heidelberg, 2002, pp. 199–205.

[13]   Udo Rienaß: Die wirkungsorientierte Steuerung im Landeseinwohneramt Berlin – Kennzahlen und Leistungsvergleiche, in: Kuhlmann; Bogumil; Wollmann (Eds.): Leistungsmessung und -vergleich in Politik und Verwaltung : Konzepte und Praxis, VS Verlag für Sozialwissenschaften, Wiesbaden, 2004, pp. 186–203.

[14]   Kuno Schedler: eGovernment und neue Servicequalität der Verwaltung? in: Gisler; Spahni (Eds.): eGovernment: Eine Standortbestimmung (2. ed.), Paul Haupt, Berne, 2001, pp. 33–51.

[15]   Kuno Schedler; Isabella Proeller: New Public Management (2. ed). Paul Haupt, Berne, 2003, p. 83.

[16]   August-Wilhelm Scheer: ARIS – House of Business Engineering, in: Becker; Rosemann; Schütte (Ed.): Referenzmodellierung : State-of-the-Art und Entwicklungsperspektiven, Physica, Heidelberg, 1999, pp. 2–21.

[17]   Andreas G. Scherer; Jens-Michael Alt: Strategische Steuerung und Balanced Scorecard. Bundesverwaltungsamt, Berlin, 2002.

[18]   Eckhard Schroeter; Hellmut Wollmann: New Public Management, in: Bandemer; Blanke; Wewer (Eds.): Handbuch zur Verwaltungsreform, Leske + Budrich, Opladen, 1998, pp. 59–70.

[19]   Oliver Thomas et al.: EPK-Referenzmodelle für Verwaltungsverfahren, in: Nuettgens; Rump (Eds.): EPK 2004 : Geschäftsprozessmanagement mit Ereignisgesteuerten Prozessketten. Gesellschaft für Informatik (GI), Bonn, 2004, pp. 39–54.

A KNOWLEDGE-SHARING FRAMEWORK FOR PUBLIC ADMINISTRATIONS

Olivier Glassey
Fraunhofer FOKUS, Kaiserin-Augusta-Allee 31, 10589 Berlin,
olivier.glassey@idheap.unil.ch

Abstract: This paper describes a framework that supports knowledge modeling and sharing within public administrations, and a prototype of such a knowledge-sharing system. We will first give a brief theoretical introduction on processes of knowledge creation, transfer and application, and then we will present our framework and discuss how it relates to these processes. We will furthermore illustrate this with a case study and show the architecture of the prototype we developed in this context.

Key words: knowledge models, process models, public administration, methodology, knowledge sharing, prototype, RSS

1. INTRODUCTION

The goal of this paper is to describe a framework we developed in order to model and share knowledge within public administrations. This framework is based on a formal methodology, on eight different models for graphical representation and on a knowledge-sharing system.

To define our methodology we used the knowledge management life-cycle proposed by Nissen, Kamel & Sengupta (2000). They studied four life-cycle representations and created an amalgamated model consisting of 6 phases: *create, organize, formalize, distribute, apply* and *evolve* knowledge. They made a review on what tools, technologies and practices were available for each of these phases. Likewise we propose a set of instruments for each phase, which we will describe in section 2.

The focus of our framework is on graphical representation: Eppler & Burkhard (2004) define knowledge visualization as all graphic means that can be used to construct and convey complex insights. They propose several visualization types:

- *Heuristic sketches* or ad-hoc drawings
- *conceptual diagrams*: abstract, schematic representations of structural relationships
- *visual metaphors*: used to structure information and convey normative knowledge through the connotations of the metaphor
- *animations*: interactive descriptions of procedural knowledge
- *knowledge maps*: they do not represent knowledge but rather reference it
- *scientific charts*: based on computational algorithms

In their review of conceptual foundations for knowledge management and in the section dedicated to knowledge transfer, Alavi & Leidner (2001) classify knowledge transfer channels as *informal* or *formal*, *personal* or *impersonal*. They mention a few examples: coffee break meetings are typically informal, personnel transfers within departments during a training period are formal and personal, knowledge repositories are formal and impersonal, and so on. For their analysis framework, Alavi & Leidner (2001) rely on the four processes of knowledge creation defined by Nonaka & Takeuchi (1995):

- From implicit to implicit knowledge: *socialization*
- From implicit to explicit knowledge: *externalization*
- From explicit to explicit knowledge: *combination*
- From explicit to implicit knowledge: *internalization*

Using our framework we made a feasibility study for a knowledge management system in a German public administration, which we will briefly explain in section 3. One of the focuses of this study was knowledge sharing amongst the domain workers: was there any, and if so, how did the clerks share knowledge and what were the potential problems? As we found out that there was no systematic and formalized knowledge sharing processes, we proposed an architecture for such a system and developed a small prototype (section 4). This architecture was not only technical, but also organizational, as McLure Wasko & Faraj (2005) explain that the availability of electronic communication technologies is no guarantee that knowledge sharing will actually take place and examine why people voluntarily contribute knowledge. They identified the main problems that sharing knowledge could arise in what they call networks of practice, i.e. loosely knit groups of individuals who are engaged in a shared practice but who do not necessarily know each other:

- Knowledge seekers have no control over the *respondents* and the *quality of the responses*.
- Knowledge contributors have no assurances that those they are helping will ever help them in return (*reciprocity*).

From their detailed survey on knowledge sharing, McLure Wasko & Faraj (2005) conclude that contributors care about their personal/professional reputation within the network of practice and that reputation is a sufficient mean to guarantee the quality of responses in most cases. Furthermore they found out that contributors do not expect direct reciprocity but rather third-party reciprocity, given that there is a critical mass of active participants within the network of practice.

2.   KNOWLEDGE MODELLING

In previous work (Glassey 2005), we developed a framework called MIMIK (Method and Instruments to Model Integrated Knowledge). We will not explain this framework in detail here, although we will provide several examples. MIMIK supports the 6 phases developed by Nissen & al. (2000): *create*, *organize*, *formalize*, *distribute*, *apply* and *evolve* knowledge. However we considered that creating and evolving knowledge belonged to the same phase: in most cases organizations do no create knowledge ex-nihilo and then evolve it; we would rather consider it as a continuous creation cycle. The goals of MIMIK are to identify:
- Strategic goals of an organization
- Actors and roles
- Knowledge resources
- Processes
- Interactions between these elements.

As the main goal of our work was to represent knowledge graphically, we needed a formalism to do so and we analyzed what was being done in process methodologies. One basic way to represent knowledge in organizations is the use of business rules (Ross 1997). They can be found in all sectors of activity and do not have to be linked to an information system. Some of them are implicit, meaning that they are not written anywhere but they belong nevertheless to the "business culture". However the basic formalism proposed by Ross (1997) is not sufficient in all cases to model the "know-why". Indeed, a "knowledge unit" is anything worth storing that may help things to be done better in the future: help, best practices guidelines, examples, stories, lessons learned, troubleshooting advice or training material (Fraser & al. 2003) and business rules cannot model all of these types of knowledge. A different approach is described by authors such as Gamper & al. (1999) and Gruber (1993) that use ontologies (explicit specification of a conceptualization, the latter consisting of identified concepts and relationships assumed to exist and to be relevant) in order to model knowledge. We prefer this method as we previously used RDF to build a data-model for e-Government (Glassey 2004) and found it more powerful and flexible than classical data models such as Entity-Relationship-Model used in ARIS (Scheer 2001) or than business rules. RDF (Resource Description Framework) is a W3C standard for defining metadata and encoding machine-readable semantics (Noy & al. 2000). It is based on XML and uses graph theory to represent knowledge. It is also a suitable format for specific domain ontology modeling.

However ontologies still cannot represent complex knowledge such as storytelling or human advice. As Samuel Johnson put it in the 18th century already: "Knowledge is of two kinds. We know a subject ourselves or we know where we can find information upon it". The goal of the component-based architecture we propose is to model "the information upon knowledge" and to describe this knowledge. We identified several attributes that allowed us to do so, beginning with the type of knowledge. Capurro (2004) compares the knowledge typology proposed by Zahn & al. (2000) with the classical Aristotelian one. Here we will only summarize the main points of Capurro's knowledge typology:

- *Know-how*: knowledge about how to make things (technical knowledge) and knowledge acquired through experience and remembrance (empirical knowledge).
- *Know-why*: logical reasoning (scientific knowledge).
- *Know-what*: knowledge about the best means to achieve given goals, usually a combination of know-how and know-why (practical knowledge).

Capurro (2004) furthermore states that what can be managed is information or explicit knowledge and that implicit knowledge can only be "enabled". In this context, explicit means that it can be clearly observed and expressed (and also digitalized), as opposed to implicit knowledge that can not be directly formulated (skills, experiences, insight, intuition, judgment, etc.) When knowledge is explicit, it can be represented as declarative or procedural knowledge. We are aware that in the domain of cognitive sciences, the distinction between procedural and declarative models is related to the brain memory system (see for example Ullman, 2001), but here we used these terms here in a limited sense, as defined in computer science:

- *Declarative* knowledge components represent domain knowledge (facts, events, etc.) in terms of concepts and relations.
- *Procedural* knowledge components describe actions to be taken in order to solve a problem step by step.

For cases where knowledge is implicit and cannot be formalized, we introduced the concept of distribution: knowledge can be individual or collective, and in both cases components identify who has this knowledge or where it can be found. Finally we added a set of metadata (know-where, know-when, know-who, etc.) describing these knowledge-components and making it possible to manage them. Fig. 1 shows the complete component-based architecture under the form of a class diagram, but it can also be formalized in RDF.

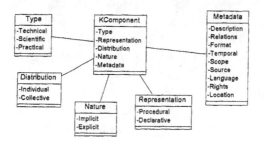

Figure 1. Knowledge component.

The goal of MIMIK is to provide meta-knowledge on the organization and to model goals, actors, roles, processes and organizational knowledge. We based our work on the model theory approach developed by Wyssusek & al. (2001) to integrate process modeling and knowledge management. They provide an epistemological foundation to justify their approach, but they do not offer any practical methodology or examples. That is why we created a conceptual framework that aimed at the integration of both these approaches.

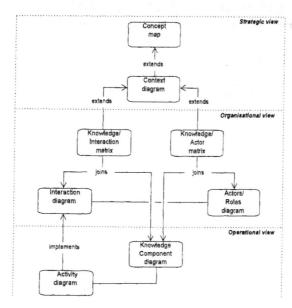

Figure 2. Metamodel showing formal relations between the different types of diagrams proposed by the MIMIK framework.

MIMIK consists of 8 types of diagrams, most of them being inspired or directly taken from existing modeling techniques, mostly UML. As in UML or other modeling languages, it is not necessary to use all of them in order to provide a good representation of reality. Users should rather select the diagrams that suit their needs and goals in terms of modeling. We will provide examples for most of these diagrams, but more explanations can be found in Glassey (2005).

Concept maps (*Cmap*) are the top-level diagrams and show the strategic goals of an organization in terms of functions or processes (Fig. 3). Let us mention that the metamodel of our framework is in itself a concept map. These concept maps can be decomposed in several levels, a terminal node of this type of diagram is implemented by a context diagram (*Cdiag*).

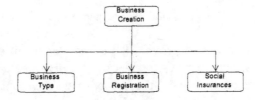

Figure 3. Concept Map.

Context diagrams (Fig. 4) are almost exactly the same as use cases in UML, but we added the concept of knowledge packet. A knowledge packet is an abstract representation of a set of knowledge components. These components encapsulate documents, databases, files, implicit knowledge and so on. They provide metadescriptions for "knowledge units", thus allowing us to show what type of knowledge is necessary in order to complete a process and which knowledge is relevant in a given context. Context diagrams provide an abstract view of the "know-what".

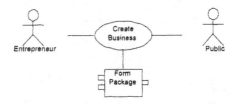

Figure 4. Context Diagrams.

To model organizational structure we used actor-role diagrams, which allowed us to add formal distinction between actors and roles, which does not exist in UML. These actor-role diagrams can be either classical organizational charts or matrices that formally link actors and roles in cases where the organization is too complex to be shown graphically in an intelligible way. We will not show that here, but let use mention that the abstract actors represented in context diagrams can be linked to these actor-role diagrams. Moreover the actors described in such diagrams are used in the knowledge-actor matrices (see further on).

Fig. 5 shows a knowledge-interaction matrix, formally linking knowledge components to the interactions that implement a use case. In UML an interaction is the specification of how messages are sent between objects or other instances and interaction diagrams (sequence or collaboration diagrams) emphasize object interactions. We comply with this definition and use collaboration or sequence diagrams to specifically describe each interaction shown in this matrix. By matching the "know-why" (knowledge components) and the "know-how" (interaction diagrams), this matrix shows the "know-what" at the operational level.

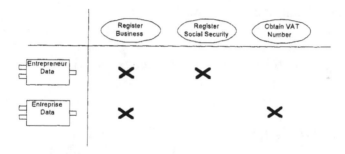

Figure 5. Knowledge-Interaction Matrix.

Exactly as knowledge-interaction matrices link knowledge components and interactions, the concept of knowledge-actor matrices (Fig. 6) create a formal relation between knowledge components and real actors within an organization. They provide an organizational view of the "know-what" or more precisely they show the "who-knows-what". That proves very useful in order to introduce implicit knowledge in a graphical model: it might not be possible to transform it into explicit knowledge but at least we know who has this knowledge within an organization. Knowledge-interaction matrices can also link actors and interaction diagrams provided a small constraint: within interaction diagrams modelers should only use roles that were defined in actor-role diagrams.

The concept of knowledge matrix (*Kmax*) provides a formal link between the strategic and operational models: it describes the interactions between strategic goals, actors, knowledge and processes such as explained at the beginning of section 2.

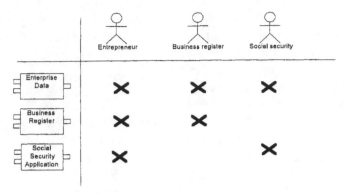

Figure 6. Knowledge-Actor Matrix

At the operational level MIMIK uses standard UML collaboration and sequence diagrams, grouped under the name of interaction diagrams (*Idiag*), as well as UML activity diagrams. The knowledge components (*Kcomp*) are integrated as objects (or instances of the Kcomp class) in interaction and activity diagrams.

3.   CASE STUDY

Between October 2004 and January 2005 we made a feasibility study in the German County of Herford in Nordrhein-Westfalen in order to assess the potential of a knowledge-based system in the domain of family law (Glassey, Gordon & Pattberg 2005). This system should allow clerks to manage more efficiently the recovering of social benefits paid to elderly persons. In short, the state supports elderly persons that are without financial resources and, under given conditions, it has a right to ask some of this money back from the relatives (mostly the children) of these elderly people. The offices we worked with were to decide whether a child has to support financially his/her parents, and if so, how much money is to be paid. The goals of this feasibility study were:
- To describe the actual work processes
- To evaluate the consistency and the quality of the actual work processes
- To propose optimized work processes
- To develop a prototype for a legal knowledge-based system.

Our team[1] created a model of the relevant laws and regulations used in order to make such parent support decisions. We also led interviews with the

---

[1] This feasibility study was a collaboration between Fraunhofer FOKUS, Herford County and Fachhochschule für öffentliche Verwaltung Nordrhein-Westfalen (FhöV). Thomas

clerks in order to identify their work processes and to describe how they acquire and share knowledge, as the regulations in that domain change quite often and the workers have to rely on up-to-date legal sources. Furthermore, two test cases were submitted to ten clerks. Finally we created an online questionnaire in order to find out how they solved the test cases, what information and knowledge they needed and where they found them if they had to specifically research it. This was a very interesting experimentation field as the work processes were weakly formalized and the knowledge was completely decentralized and disseminated, and not directly explicit in many cases. Indeed, the clerks have to interpret regulations in order to make a decision, and formalizing this process can be quite difficult.

Using the MIMIK framework we identified the three strategic missions of "Elternunterhalt" (parent support): *monitoring* the changes in *law and regulations*, *integrating these changes* into the daily work of the organization and *handling the actual* parent support *cases*.

For the first strategic mission (*monitoring*) we found out that the clerks who answered the online questionnaire used legal texts and databases extensively, including case law:

- The majority of the clerks (75%) use legal texts weekly or several times monthly, the other 25% use them once a month or less.
- They all read various specialized publications in the domain of social welfare. 65% of the respondents read these several times per month.
- They all (except one) take part in training seminars about once a year.
- 40% of their work time is dedicated to doing legal research for particular cases, reading legal journals and publications and calculating the amounts of money the relatives have to pay.

However, each clerk is doing it his/her own way and using different sources (up to 20 different legal sources). Furthermore, there was absolutely *no structured or formalized sharing and integration of this knowledge* (no process corresponding to the second strategic mission). If we refer to the Nonaka & Takeuchi model (1995) presented in the introduction, the only knowledge creation process we identified was *socialization*, and *externalization* and *combination* were almost non-existent. For example, different units at commune and county levels developed their own forms and spreadsheets tables in order to acquire data from the potential social beneficiaries and to calculate the amounts of money their relatives might have to pay. In some cases, clerks would only share knowledge with their colleagues during informal discussions on the phone or at the coffee break and only a handful of them use email to share their specific domain

Gordon, Dirk Arendt, Olivier Glassey and Jonas Pattberg constituted the FOKUS team, Monika Müller represented the FhöV and Paul Bischof, Michael Borgstedt and Marion Ziemens the Herford County. Rainer Fischer served as legal expert.

knowledge. The only "formal" knowledge acquisition activity consists of an annual continuing education seminar.

On the other hand the *actual work processes* describing how the cases are treated and decisions are made were *rather formal, although implicit*. With the help of clerks we were able to define how they conducted interviews and we developed detailed interaction and activity diagrams, which we will not show here. As mentioned in the introduction, one of the goals of this feasibility study was to evaluate the quality and the consistency of the work processes, thus the test cases. We will not present the detailed results here, only a few key points:

- Between 75% and 79% of the respondents found that the cases were clear, well formulated and realistic; they said they understood what they were expected to do and they believed they had all the necessary information in order to solve the cases; finally they agreed that they had enough knowledge and support tools to solve the cases.
- However 44% of them said they had problems to solve the cases; in case 1, 20% of the solutions were not defensible and the respondents needed an average of 152 minutes to solve it; in case 2, 33% of the solutions were not defensible and the respondents needed an average of 162 minutes to solve it.

We expected that these tasks could be optimized with the use of knowledge management technology: a knowledge-sharing system would support the first two strategic missions (monitoring and integrating the changes) and a legal rule-based system should help optimize the consistency and the quality of processes for the third strategic goal. Furthermore the IT infrastructure is already in place: all workers use word processing tools and email, and most of them also have Internet access. Very briefly put, our proposition for process optimization was to select one or several clerks that would have the formal responsibility to monitor the changes in the legal sources and to publish these changes using the prototype that we will present in the next section.

4.   PROTOTYPE

The prototype was based on two different tools: a legal rule-based system to support the resolution of the cases and a knowledge-sharing system. The rule-based system will be presented in another publication, but let us mention a few key facts: it is accessible through a simple web-browser, it integrates more than 200 rules and it solved both test cases correctly.

Here we will concentrate on the prototype of a knowledge-sharing system (KnowS). Its architecture is based on RSS (Really Simple Syndication). RSS is a family of XML file formats for web syndication. The XML files (or RSS feeds) provide "items" containing short descriptions of web content together with a link to the full version of the content. In order to access these feeds, users rely on applications called feed readers that check RSS-enabled Web pages and retrieve any updated content that it finds. Websites featuring RSS feeds include The New York Times, The Wall Street Journal, BBC, news.com, Liberation, etc. RSS is widely implemented in the weblog community in order to share the latest weblog entries. According to a Pew Internet and American Life Project survey (Rainie 2005), there were 8 millions bloggers in the United States at the beginning of 2005 and 27% of Internet users say they read blogs. Furthermore, Gordon (2003) showed that RSS can be used for public participation platforms, for example to facilitate public consultation, deliberation, and participation or "engagement" in policy-making processes such as urban planning. For more on RSS we recommend (Winer 2005) or wikipedia.org.

Using blog platforms, end users can publish new knowledge via a Web interface, a simple email sent to a special address or a dedicated feed publishing client. This requires no specific knowledge (other than being able to send an email, at the most basic level of use), the input text is automatically transformed in an RSS feed by the system. A "moderator" should validate this new content before it is available to anyone, but it is not required. In our Herford example, clerks would be notified when colleagues have found new pieces of knowledge in legal databases, online law commentaries, or when they have themselves implemented a new form or a new calculation formula. A moderator could then validate or complete this knowledge published by a clerk. All clerks could then rely on this knowledge in their daily work, as it would have been validated by a "domain expert". Furthermore, specific thematic RSS feeds can be defined: users can then choose precisely what knowledge they want to receive.

Once new knowledge has been published, it can be used in very flexible ways. Users can simply visit the Web page of the blog, but they can also use Web aggregators such as Bloglines.com, their own email client or a specialized feed-reader that provides more advances functionalities. However, the Internet and American Life Project survey on blogs (Rainie 2005) stated that only 5% of Internet users rely on dedicated aggregators to get RSS feeds. RSS aggregators and, to some extend, email clients offer powerful content management capabilities, such as filters to limit access to only relevant content: a user can for example subscribe only to feeds that aggregate content on social welfare issues and limit this to parent support, they can furthermore implement filters stating that all feed elements not concerning the Land of Nordrhein-Westfalen are to be deleted. This is very useful to avoid information overflow, that is to limit the risk that the users will not read the feeds anymore because they receive to much irrelevant information.

RSS feeds support "enclosures", which allow the addition of any type of multimedia files, similar to an attachment in an email. Thus we added this functionality to our prototype: it can be used to share automatically new documents, files or any piece of digitalized information. With an advanced RSS reader, it becomes possible to check periodically (once a day, every week, etc.) selected feeds and to download relevant documents automatically.

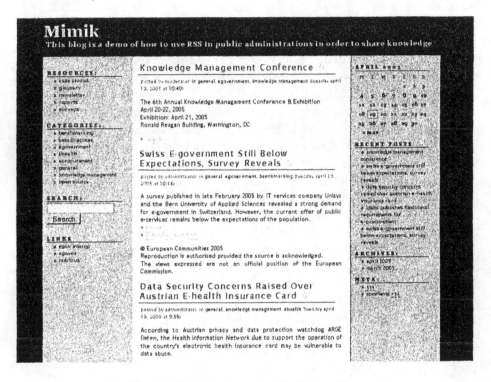

Figure 7. Web interface to the Mimik demo blog.

The KnowS prototype comes in three "flavors", that is three technical architectures corresponding to different needs. The first one is based on existing services: Blogger.com, a weblog platform owned by Google, and Feedburner.com, a free post-processing service that allows publishers to enhance their feeds. It allowed us to create a simple proof of concept[2] for what was presented in the previous paragraphs, without any material acquisition or software installation. However Blogger does not support categories for blog entries: we believed that this could prove very useful to

---

[2] It can be seen at mimik-demo.blogspot.com

organize and personalize knowledge. Indeed by matching categories and interactions such as defined in the knowledge-interaction matrices, we could implement a system corresponding to the knowledge models created with MIMIK. Moreover Blogger's user rights management is very limited. For these reasons, we built a second KnowS prototype (Fig. 7) operating on a dedicated blogging platform: WordPress[3] offers good categories' management tools and 10 levels of users' rights (read, write, edit, validate, publish...). We consider this type of blog publishing platform, powerful and simple to use, would be sufficient in most cases in order to implement a knowledge-sharing system for public administrations. In some complex cases however, a complete content management system supporting RSS could be necessary. In order to illustrate such a technical architecture, we created a third prototype based on Agora[4], a specialized Web content platform developed on top of the SPIP[5] system at the initiative of the French government. To summarize the advantages of this system, it allowed us to integrate categories and keywords, thus to have a finer knowledge organization, and to assign the control over the content of single categories and keywords to given users. With these functionalities we were able to match not only the knowledge-interaction matrices in the system, but also the knowledge-actor matrices. Finally, let us mention that the two more complex versions[6] of KnowS integrate directly most metadata defined for the knowledge components. RSS provides a *description* for content and integrates various tags (author/*source* of an RSS element,. *publication date*, *language*). The KnowS prototype supports several *temporal markers* (published, updated, validity), it has advanced *rights* management functions and supports embedded files with MIME type description (*format*). Moreover it is possible to use permalinks (a type of URL designed to refer to a specific information item and to remain unchanged permanently) to identify the *location* of a knowledge element and to show *relations* between these knowledge elements with track-backs (system allowing bloggers to see who has written another entry concerning a given post).

5.   CONCLUSIONS

As we mentioned in the introduction, the MIMIK framework is focused on knowledge visualization and in this paper we have shown several types of

---

[3] WordPress is based on PHP/MySQL, available under GPL licence at www.wordpress.org
[4] www.agora.gouv.fr
[5] Spip is a popular Web publishing system written in PHP/MySQL, available under GPL licence at www.spip.net
[6] Both run on a local server and cannot be accessed because they are behind a firewall.

visualization: concept maps (*Cmap*) can be used to create heuristic sketches; context diagrams (*Cdiag*), interaction diagrams (*Idiag*) and knowledge components diagrams (*Kcomp*) are typical conceptual diagrams; knowledge matrices (*Kmax*) provide basic knowledge maps. In the introduction we also defined fundamental concepts of knowledge creation and transfer: Fig. 8 shows how we think the different MIMIK models and tools support the knowledge creation life-cycle and what main knowledge creation processes they facilitate.

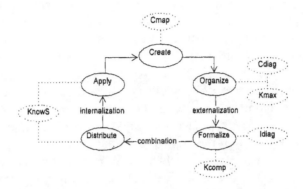

Figure 8. Knowledge creation cycle and MIMIK models.

Finally we showed with the knowledge-sharing system (*KnowS*) prototype that it was possible to define a technical architecture supporting knowledge creation and transfer. On the other hand we have not been able to test it in a real situation and thus could not investigate the issues of quality of responses, reciprocity and reputation linked with knowledge sharing over networks of practices.

6.   REFERENCES

Alavi, M. & Leidner, D. E. (2001). Review: Knowledge management and knowledge management systems: Conceptual foundations and research issues. *MIS Quarterly* 25(1), 107-136.

Capurro, R. (2004). Skeptical Knowledge Management. In H. C. Hobohm (Ed.), *Knowledge Management: Libraries and Librarians Taking Up The Challenge* (pp. 47-57). Munich: Saur.

Eppler, M. J. & Burkhard, R. A. (2004). Knowledge Visualization. Retrieved 21.04.2005, from http://www.knowledgemedia.org/modules/pub/view.php/knowledgemedia-67.

Fraser, J., Adams, N., Macintosh, A., McKay-Hubbard, A., Pariente Lobo, T. & Fernandez Pardo, P., et al. (2003,). Knowledge Management Applied to E-government Services: The Use of an Ontology. *Proceedings 4th International Working Conference KMGov 2003*, Heidelberg: Springer Verlag.

Gamper, J., Nejdl, W. & Wolpers, M. (1999,). Combining Ontologies and Terminologies in Information Systems. Paper presented at the *5th International Congress on Terminology and Knowledge Engineering*, Innsbruck, Austria.

Glassey, O. (2004). Developing a one-stop government data model. *Government Information Quarterly* 21(2), 156-169.

Glassey, O. (2005). Knowledge Component-based Architecture for Process Modelling. Paper presented at the eGOV INTEROP'05 Conference, Geneva, Switzerland, February 23-24, 2005.

Glassey, O., Gordon, T. & Pattberg, J. (2005). Machbarkeitsstudie eines wissensbasierten Rechtsberatungssystems im Kreis Herford. In E. Schweighofer, Liebwald, D., Menzel, T. & S. Augeneder (Eds.), *Aktuelle Fragen der Rechtsinformatik 2005*, Boorberg Verlag.

Gordon, T. (2003). An Open, Scalable and Distributed Platform for Public Discourse, Informatik 2003. *Informatik 2003*, Vol. 2, 232-234.

Gruber, T. (1993). Towards principles for the design of ontologies used for knowledge sharing. *International Journal of Human-Computer Studies* 43(5-6), 907-928.

McLure Wasko, M. & Faraj, S. (2005). Why should I share? Examining Social Capital and Knowledge Contribution in Electronic Networks of Practice. *MIS Quarterly* 29(1), 35-57.

Nissen, M. E., Kamel, M. N. & Sengupta, K. C. (2000). A Framework for Integrating Knowledge Process and System Design. *Information Strategy: The Executive's Journal* 16(4), 17-26.

Nonaka, I. & Takeuchi, H. (1995). *The Knowledge Creating Company: How Japanese Companies Create the Dynamics of Evolution*. Oxford University Press.

Noy, F., Fergerson, R.W. & Musen, M. (2000). The Knowledge Model of Protégé-2000: combining interoperability and flexibility. Retrieved 12.01.2003, from http://www.smi.stanford.edu/projects/protege/.

Rainie, L. (2005). The State of Blogging, Pew Internet & American Life Project, February 2, 2005. Retrieved 10.03.2005, from http://www.pewinternet.org/.

Ross, R. (1997). *The Business Rule Book: Classifying, Defining and Modelling Rules, Version 4.0*. Houston, TX: Business Rules Solutions.

Scheer, A. W. (2001). *ARIS - Modellierungsmethoden, Metamodelle, Anwendungen*. Berlin Heidelberg: Springer-Verlag.

Ullman, M. T. (2001). A Neurocognitive Perspective on Language: The Declarative/Procedural Model. *Nature Reviews - Neuroscience* 2(10), 717-726.

Winer, D. (2005). RSS 2.0 Specification, RSS at Harvard Law. Retrieved March 10, 2005, from http://blogs.law.harvard.edu/tech/rss.

Zahn, E., Foschiani, S. & Tilebein, M. (2000). Nachhaltige Wettbewerbsvorteile durch Wissensmanagement. In: *Wettbewerbsvorteile durch Wissensmanagement* (pp. 239-270). Stuttgart: Methodik und Anwendungen des Knowledge Management.

CONFIGURING E-GOVERNMENT SERVICES USING ONTOLOGIES

Dimitris Apostolou[1]*, Ljiljana Stojanovic[2], Tomas Pariente Lobo[3], Jofre Casas Miró[4], Andreas Papadakis[5]

*Author to whom correspondence should be addressed; [1]PLANET S.A., Louise Riencourt 64, 11523, Greece, dapost@planet.gr, +302106905000; [2]Forschungszentrum Informatik, Haid-und-Neu-Str. 10-14, 76131 Karlsruhe, Germany; [3]INDRA, Avda. De Brusselas, 35, 28108 Alcobendas, Spain; [4]Institut Municipal d'Informàtica, Ajuntament de Barcelona, Ajuntament de Barcelona,Av. Diagonal, 220 4a. 08018. Barcelona; [5]Archetypon S.A., 236 Sygrou Av., 176 72 Athens, Greece

Abstract: The increasing complexity of e-Government services demands a correspondingly larger effort for management. Today, many system management tasks, such as service verification and re-configuration due to changes in the law, are often performed manually. This can be time consuming and error-prone. The main objective of the OntoGov (IST-2002-507237) project is to overcome the above mentioned problems by developing a semantically-enriched platform that will facilitate the consistent configuration and re-configuration of e-Government services. This paper outlines the overall OntoGov platform and demonstrates how the Service Modeller can be used to consistently model e-Government Services.

Key words: semantic technologies, e-Government services, ontologies.

1. INTRODUCTION

In order to fully realise the e-Government potential for productivity growth (Liikanen, 2003), it is not sufficient to modernise the front office by offering public services over the Internet through e-Government portals. Problems arise from the wide gap and inconsistencies that exist between the perspective of policy makers and public administrations' managers on the one hand and the technical realization of e-Government on the other hand. For instance, a change in policy or legislation that affects a particular Public

Administration (PA) business process does not propagate seamlessly into the corresponding e-Government service provided via the portal. Furthermore, problems arise from the loss of critical knowledge about the service configuration. Hence, for e-Government initiatives to succeed, in addition to modernising the front office by offering public services via Internet portals, attention should be also paid to streamlining, re-organising and supporting the back-office processes of public administrations that provide services to citizens. Furthermore, actions should be taken to limit the loss of critical knowledge assets during the life cycle of e-Government services.

The main objective of the OntoGov (IST-2002-507237) project is to develop a semantically-enriched platform that will facilitate the consistent configuration and re-configuration of e-Government services. This paper outlines the overall OntoGov platform and demonstrates how the Service Modeller, an intermediary project result, can be used to consistently configure an e-Government Service. The remaining of this paper is organised as follows: In Section 2, state of the art and related projects are reviewed. In Section 3, the project's software platform is outlined. In Section 4, an overview of the service modelling approach is presented while in Section 5, service configuration is illustrated using a real-life scenario. Finally, the benefits of our approach are outlined in Section 6.

2.   STATE OF THE ART AND RELATED PROJECTS

State of the art in e-Government includes realising the concept of one-stop e-Government (Hagen and Kubicek, 2000), especially together with the idea of service portals with life-situation navigation (Tambouris and Wimmer, 2004). The basic ideas of one-stop e-Government are already well-developed and their technical realisation on top of state-of-the-art Web Service technology. What is not solved sufficiently, are the methodological and technological prerequisites as well as the back-office processes, which help turning one-shot investments into one-stop approaches into sustainable, long-term endeavours which can be maintained effectively and consistently over a longer period of time. This idea requires on one hand a higher level of re-configurability and on-the-fly changes of services – which is not provided by today's web service technology; and on the other hand a well-understood and technically supported knowledge logistics along the horizontal dimension (many implementing sites) and vertical dimension (several levels of decision-making).

To deal on the one hand with re-configurability and changes of e-Government services and on the other hand with knowledge-enhanced back-office processes for configuring eGov services, we need tools based on robust conceptual models. In OntoGov, we are using Semantic Web technologies for constructing ontologies, which represent the meaning of processed data and resources and provided functionality of e-Government services. Ontologies have been employed by other projects in the e-Government domain, each with a primary objective: The e-POWER project (van Engers et al., 2002) has employed knowledge modelling techniques for e.g. consistency checks, harmonisation or consistency enforcement in legislation. The SmartGov project (Adams et al., 2003) developed a knowledge-based platform for assisting public sector employees to generate online transaction services by simplifying their integration with already installed IT systems. Similarly, the ICTE-PAN project (Loukis et al., 2003) developed a methodology for modelling PA operations, and tools to transform these models into design specifications for an e-Government system. Further, there are a number of ongoing projects e.g. Terregov (Benamou, 2004), Qualeg (Tatsiopoulos, 2004), that make use of semantic technologies for achieving semantic interoperability and integration between e-Government systems.

3. ONTOGOV PLATFORM OVERVIEW

In principal, the lifecycle of an e-Government service starts when PA Managers trigger the generation or the change of a service. In order to accomplish this task, PA Managers need to have a high-level view of the service model, links to related laws, resources involved and inter-relations with other services. Such a high-level view is provided by the service models developed through OntoGov's Ontology Management System (see Figure 1).

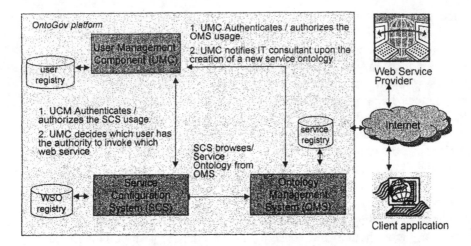

Figure 1. Bird's eye view of the OntoGov platform

The **Ontology Management System (OMS)** is used for creating, modifying, querying, and storing ontology-based descriptions of e-Government services. It focuses on the service lifecycle management, which includes service modelling, service reuse, service discovery, service composition as well as service reconfiguration. The OMS comprises: (i) The *Service Modeller*, an editor for the semantic description of e-Government services. It has a graphical user interface that enables domain experts to create and maintain service ontologies. (ii) The *KAON2 OIModeller*, a graphical tool for general-purpose ontology creation and maintenance. (iii) The *Service Registry* that enables the registration and searching for ontologies.(iv) The *Service API* that provides capabilities for the automatic identification of problems (i.e. inconsistencies) in the description of the e-Government services that can arise during the modelling or changes in relevant data (e.g. in the law). When such problems arise, it assists the domain experts in identifying the sources of the problem, in analysing and defining solutions for resolving them. Finally, it helps in determining the ways for applying the proposed solutions.

The role of the **Service Configuration System (SCS)** is to bridge the gap between the service definition provided by the OMS, and the generation, deployment and execution of the e-Government service. Configuration, generation and deployment of the e-Government service is handled by the SCS Configuration Framework (Figure 2), while execution of services is handled by the SCS Runtime Framework (Figure 3).

The result of the OMS is a set of ontologies that defines among other things the service model and the domain information needed to provide a service. The service model is defined through the process ontology and becomes the main source of information for the Configuration Framework. This information is transformed to a machine-readable service description allowing its execution on a server. This task is performed through the *SCS Builder* component.

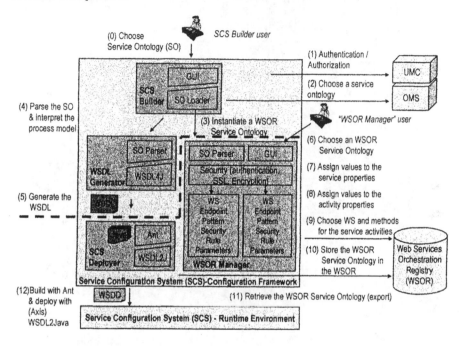

Figure 2. Functional Architecture of the Service Configuration Framework – Configuration Framework

The *Web Service Orchestration Registry (WSOR)* is an ontology-based repository where the mapping among activities of the service model and their implementation (Web services) is performed.

The SCS Runtime Framework, allows the execution of the service. Within the SCS Runtime Framework the end point derives the request to the *Process Engine* component, which is a workflow tool that is in charge of querying the Service Ontology (process model information) and selecting the first activity described in the process model. The Process Engine sends control to the *WS Manager*. The WS Manager looks up in the WSOR ontology the implementation that, according to the data provided by the consumer or derived from the process, should be invoked to accomplish the activity selected. The *Synchronization Manager* hides the complexity of dealing with synchronous/asynchronous calls. Execution and monitoring (logging) of the service is done by the *SCS Audit and Tracking component.*

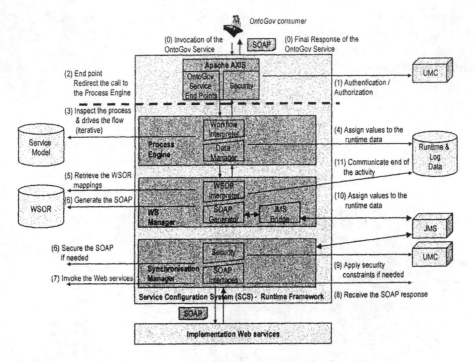

Figure 3. Functional Architecture of the Service Configuration Framework – Runtime Framework

The acceptance of the OntoGov approach poses strict security and management requirements. In order to leverage the OntoGov functionality the PAs are expected to expose some of their resources and to allow access to their procedures in an IT environment. Such an open and flexible approach can only be built on a reliable platform of trusted relationships. The **User Management Component (UMC)** supports the areas of User and Group management, Authentication, Access control and Messaging – extending over the security considerations. It is an auxiliary component of the platform, supporting a personalized working environment, the co-existence of the components and the shielding of sensitive resources.

4.   SERVICE MODELLING IN ONTOGOV

Based on the analysis of the existing standard for Semantic Web Services (i.e. OWL-S and WSMO) and by taking into account the e-Government specific requirements (Stojanovic et al., 2004), we have defined a *meta ontology cluster* that contains general ontologies that may be used for describing e-Government services and do not change from one deployment to another. It consists of following ontologies:

- the *Legal Ontology* defines the structure of the legal documents, which includes paragraphs, sections, amendments, etc.;
- the *Organisational Ontology* models an organisation by defining its organisational units, roles, persons, resources etc.
- the *Lifecycle Ontology* comprising instances of all (design) decisions relevant for the new service (e.g. technical or process immanent reasons), including instances of the legal and organizational ontologies;
- the *Domain Ontology* contains domain specific knowledge;
- the *Service Ontology* describes the elements for modelling the service flow. It includes the *Domain Ontology* for defining inputs and outputs as well as the *Lifecycle Ontology* for explaining reasons that motivate the decisions;
- the *LifeEvent Ontology* models the categorization of the e-Government services;
- the *Profile Ontology* contains metadata about e-Government services and includes all previously mentioned ontologies.

The *Profile Ontology* and the *Service Ontology* are defined based on the corresponding OWL-S ontologies by taking into account the e-Government specificities such as a reference to the law that is modelled through the *Legal Ontology*. The *Domain Ontology* defines the "terminology" used in the e-Government domain (e.g. type of documents such as passport). The *Organisation Ontology* is defined to take into account experiences from the business process modelling and reengineering, since changes in the organizational structure can cause changes in the process model. The *LifeEvent Ontology* is specific for the e-Government domain and it is defined to support better searching for E-Government services.

The *Lifecycle Ontology* is defined to help the domain expert introduce the changes in the service description and to document the reasons for these changes (Apostolou et al. 2005). This means that in the OntoGov project we use ontologies not only for describing and composing services provided by public administrations, but also for modelling dependencies between decisions of the different stakeholders (e.g. politicians, public managers and software developers) in order to make services easier to develop and maintain.

5. ILLUSTRATION OF THE USE OF THE ONTOLOGY MANAGEMENT SYSTEM

In this section we illustrate how an e-Government service is modelled using the Ontology Management System on the basis of an example. In the example we use the real service "Minor Building Work License" as this is being offered by the municipality of Barcelona. In the past, there were two kind of licenses; the citizen had to bring the documentation to the Citizens Attention Office and the municipal architects had to study it. It could take from 1 to 4 months, due to the large amount of licenses requested. Currently, the municipality of Barcelona is involved in an e-Government process reengineering to simplify the service. In order to achieve this goal, two main steps are followed:

1. Change in the legal municipal normative in order to simplify the procedure. Moreover, a new type of building licence is being introduced.
2. Use of OntoGov platform and other tools so that time and human action in the procedure is reduced as much as possible.

Essentially the new service will be able to detect the kind of building construction the citizen wants to perform and act accordingly. For instance, if a citizen wants to change the structure of a building, s/he will be asked to provide documents related to the security of the works, a project signed by an architect, etc. However, if s/he only wants to change colour of the façade, he may get the license immediately. But what happens if the citizen wants to change the façade's colour of the building placed in the 401st of Mallorca Street? The service will be able to notice the difference: in that number there is the Sagrada Família temple. Therefore, there are many variables to take into account when a citizen requests a minor building construction. This automation is provided in a number of service steps as these are described in Table 1.

Table 1. "Minor Building Work License" service steps

No	Service Activity
1	Ask the citizen about the address and the kind of the works
2	Decide if they are major or minor works (the service is just offered for the minor works case)
3	In case of being minor works, perform more concrete questions about the works
4	Decide which one of the 3 different licenses includes this kind of minor works
5a	If it is an "Assabentat" (informed regime): - store the data related to the works - grant the license to the citizen.
5b	If it is a "Comunicat" (prior notification regime): - store the data related to the works - store the citizen data

No	Service Activity
	- display the list of documents the citizen must provide before receiving the license.
	- display the payments he must perform before receiving the license.
5c	If it is a "Llicència" (standard license):
	- store the data related to the works
	- store the citizen data
	- display the list of documents the citizen must provide
	- warn the municipal architects about the procedure so that they can study it in depth.

The development of this service with ONTOGOV's OMS will be as follows:

The domain expert extends and creates instances of the meta-ontologies for the following ontologies:

- Domain ontology, comprising concepts like data (e.g. kind of highway, name of the highway, number, boolean answers to questions related to the works, etc.) and documents (e.g. application form, informed regime license, etc.)
- Legal ontology, comprising instances of process relevant law or regulations, e.g. basis of this service is the new municipality's ordinance governing minor works (1-1-2005). Then several instances will be initiated in the legal ontology indicating the related law[1] ('Ordenança reguladora d'obres menors'), the title ('Títol 2: Règim d'assabentat') and article ('Article 13: Abast i presentació del règim d'assabentat').
- Organisational ontology, comprising instances of process relevant organizational units, e.g. involved in the service are the organizational units 'I.M.I.', 'Municipality of Barcelona', and 'Town-planning department' with its roles and personnel.

---

[1] Note: example is taken from the Catalan legislation

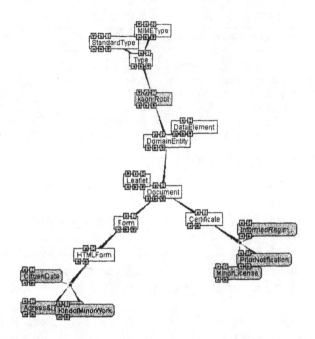

Figure 4. Parts of the Domain Ontology

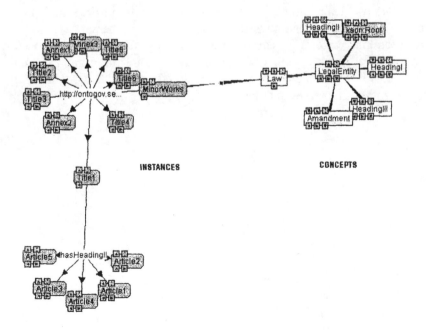

Figure 5. Parts of the Legal Ontology

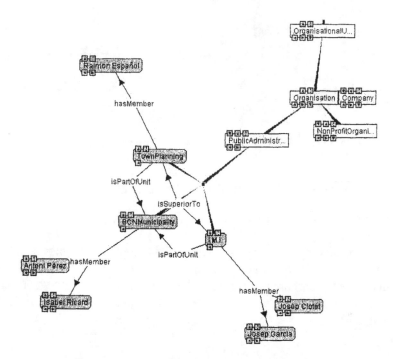

Figure 6. Parts of the Organisational Ontology

Furthermore, the Domain Expert designs the service using the Service Modeller. First of all s/he creates the service model by naming it and including the ontologies related to it (already modelled with the OI-Modeller from the meta-ontologies). Then s/he must think about the process workflow and perform four main actions during the modelling process:

- To decide which atomic services he will need and place them into the graph.
- To establish the relationships between these atomic services by using the different options available in the OntoGov's Service Modeller (split, join, switch, etc.).
- To keep the consistency between the outputs and the inputs of every atomic service and its following ones.
- To establish at least one first service and one last service so that the workflow may be understandable by the Ontogov's Service Modeller.

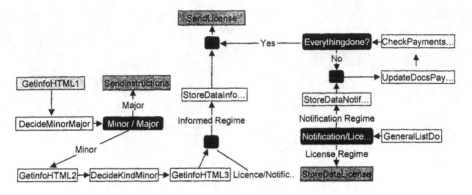

Figure 7. "Minor Building Work License" service

After the design process is completed, it is the task of the Service Configuration System to generate the definition of the new service while the User Management Component will notify the IT consultant that a service model has been created and is ready to be implemented and deployed (not described herein).

6.   CONCLUSIONS

In this article, we highlighted a novel application of semantic technologies in the e-Government domain: utilising semantics to support the consistent configuration and change management of e-Government services. The benefits of utilising ontologies in the configuration of e-Government services include the ability to perform consistency checks. The following consistency checks are currently being performed by the Service Modeller:

(C1) Each service has to have a reference to at least one business rule (law). E.g. The Minor Building Work License service has reference to the municipality's ordinance governing minor works (1-1-2005). C1 enables to find the corresponding service if a law is changed

(C2) Each service has to have at least one resource that controls its execution. E.g. The Minor Building Work License service has reference to the 'Town-planning department' with its roles and personnel.

(C3) Each service has to have at least one software component attached to it that implements it. E.g. The Minor Building Work License service has reference to the 'Building Database' (containing information about city buildings as well as list of the documents the citizen must provide for every kind of construction works) and to the HOST database (containing the current state of the payments).

(C4) Each service has to have at least one input. E.g. the kind of construction works to be performed.

(C5) Each service has to have at least one output. E.g. which of the 3 different types of licenses apply (if work is classified under 'minor works').

(C6) Each service input has to be either output of some other service or is specified by the end-user. C6 ensures that a change in an output of an activity is propagated to the inputs of successor activities and vice versa

(C7) If the input of a service is the output of another service, then it has to be subsumed by this output.

(C8) If the input of a service subsumes the input of the next service, then its preconditions have to subsume the preconditions of the next one. C8 prohibits the changes which lead to non-optimal service reconfiguration. For example, if the preconditions for 'Decide Kind Minor' include a constraint that the building has not to be preservable, the preconditions of the next activity cannot be that the building is historical.

(C9) If two services are subsumed by the same service, then their preconditions have to be disjoint.

(C10) If a service specialises another service, one of its parameters (i.e. inputs, outputs, pre- or post-conditions) has to be different. The difference can be achieved either through the subsumption relation with the corresponding counterpart or by introducing a new one.

(C11) Inputs, outputs, pre- and post-conditions have to be from the domain ontology.

(C12) Any specialization of the activity A1 must always be a predecessor of any specialization of the activity A2, where A1 and A2 are two activities defined in the Meta Ontology and their order is given in advance (i.e. A1 precedes A2).

Further benefits of our semantics-based approach include the support for conflict resolution and change propagation. Based on the consistency checks described above, the system, by providing an inconsistencies discovery mechanism, will notify the domain experts about logical conflicts. Moreover, it will provide enough information to analyse the sources of conflicts. Its role will be to inform a domain expert about the necessity for updating an e-Government service, and to allow the application of the service changes, enabling an easy spotting of potential problems. Finally, the system will propagate changes from the changes in business rules (e.g. laws) to the changes in the semantic web services and within services. This will guarantee the transfer of all dependent service ontologies into another consistent state.

Finally, in case of a change of a law the OntoGov system can be queried to retrieve affected service activities. In our example, "GenerateListDocs" (displays the list of documents the citizen should have provided before receiving the license) and "DecideKindMinor" (decides which kind of license must be granted) are based on various decisions. The different documents to be provided before starting the works are defined by law, depending on each kind of works. The heritage catalogue level of a certain building or the affectations of the street where this building is placed (they are both necessary in order to decide the kind of the license) are located in the town-planning department databases, whereas the citizen data and the state of the payments must be stored in the Municipality HOST. If a new government is stricter in the security within the building works and modifies the existing law affecting it, the list of documents the citizen must provide will change. The OntoGov system will search for all service implementation decisions based on this legal reason and, as a result, all affected services and activities will be listed and proposed for modification. In the example, this is the service "Minor Works License" with its activity "GenerateListDocs". Similarly, if some building loses its heritage catalogue level, the activity "DecideKindMinor" will be affected.

ACKNOWLEDGEMENT

The research presented in this paper was financed by the EC in the project "IST PROJECT 507237 - OntoGov".

REFERENCES

Adams, N., S. Haston, A. Macintosh, J. Fraser, A. McKay-Hubbard, and A. Unsworth, (2003) SmartGov: A Knowledge-Based Design Approach to Online Social Service Creation, in Bramer, M., Ellis, R., Macintosh, A; (eds.). 'Applications and Innovations in Knowledge-Based Systems and Applied Artificial Intelligence XI'; Proceedings of AI-2003 the 23rd Annual International Conference of the British Computer Society's Specialist Group on Artificial Intelligence ; Peterhouse College, Cambridge, UK, 16th-17th December, 2003.

Apostolou, D., L. Stojanovic, T. Pariente Lobo, B. Thoenssen, (2005) Towards a Semantically-Driven Software Engineering Environment for eGovernment, TCGOV 2005, pp. 157-168, 2005.

Benamou, N. (2004) "Terregov project overview", IANOS conference, Budapest, 2004.

Hagen M., Kubicek H. (2000) One-Stop-Government in Europe: Results of 11 national surveys, University of Bremen, Bremen, Available at http://infosoc2.informatik.uni-bremen.de/egovernment/cost/one-stop-government/home.html, 2000.

Liikanen, E., (2003) e-Government and the European Union, speech by Mr Erkki Liikanen (Member of the European Commission, responsible for Enterprise and the Information Society) at the Internet and the City Conference "Local eGovernment in the Information Society" Barcelona - 21 March 2003.

Loukis, E., S. Kokolakis, (2003) Computer supported collaboration in the Public Sector: the ICTE-PAN Project, in preceedings of eGOV 2003 / DEXA 2003.

Stojanovic, L. et al.,(2004a) available as Deliverable D2, http://www.ontogov.com, 2004.

Tambouris E., Wimmer M. (2004) Online one-stop government: a single point of access to public, in *Digital Government: Strategies and Implementations in Developed and Developing Countries*, Wayne Huang, ed., Idea Publishing Group, 2004.

Tatsiopoulos, C., (2004) "QUALEG approach to intra-government interoperability", in Workshop on Technological and architectural challenges, eGOV04 Conference, Zaragoza Spain, 1st September 2004.

van Engers, T., J. M. Patries, J. Kordelaar, J. den Hartog, E. Glasséee, (2002). Available at http://lri.jur.uva.nl/~epower/ (March 2005)

A BUSINESS RULE ENGINE APPLIED TO EGOVERNMENT SERVICES INTEGRATION

Aqueo Kamada[1,2] and Manuel Mendes[2,3]

[1]CenPRA, Rod. Dom Pedro I, km 143.6, 13082-120, Campinas, SP, Brazil; [2]Unicamp, Cidade Universitária "Zeferino Vaz", 13083-970, Campinas, SP, Brazil; [3]Unisantos, Rua Dr. Carvalho de Mendonça, 144, 11070-906 Santos, SP, Brazil

Abstract: A great part of applications is increasingly based on the Internet and the needs for changes in these applications happen in shorter and shorter periods. Companies, governments and people who wait for almost instantaneous implementations of those changes stimulate this scenario of high demand for changes. In the context of these fast changes, the approaches based on business rules are aiming for an implementation of solutions that are more flexible to changes and that are in a language easily understandable to business people in a business perspective. This article presents a proposal of a Business Rule Engine customized for e-Government applications, considering the componentization and/or Web "servicification" of life event applications with access to several legacy back office systems. The proposed Business Rule Engine is in conformance with the Business Semantics of Business Rules (BSBR) meta-model, which is in its final phase of specification by OMG.

Key words: Business Rule, Business Rule Engine, e-Government, Web Services and business component.

1. INTRODUCTION

Modern companies are increasingly adopting new models of business processes to improve the competitiveness in a market that expects a fast reaction to changes according to customers' demands. These modern companies have noticed the inherent conflict between the fluidity and agility they want their businesses to accomplish and the rigidity and control in which their systems operate. The incompatibility among agile businesses and rigid systems annuls the efforts indeed to change the business and quickly to capitalize in business opportunities[1]. It is thus verified, that, whether a company is aggressive or conservative in the adoption of changes, the changes are inevitable and they happen in a continuous and relentless way. Therefore, companies that don't get to answer with agility to the changes of the business rules lose in competitiveness.

Business rules technologies are becoming very popular in many groups of companies, such as, financial and insurance groups, which are using some form of rule engine. According to a Gartner study[2], the average ROI for a rules implementation across all industries is a conservative 10% to 15%. Another prominent factor are BPM tools (Business Process Management), most of which are based on rules. Many rules based process initiatives are user driven rather than technology driven. Users are initiating projects to define business vocabularies and business rule definition rather than these initiatives being forced upon them by the IT groups[3].

Another issue strongly related to business rules is knowledge management (KM). Successful initiatives in KM can be found in call centers and help desks and new applications with high potential to benefit of KM systems are Web applications and self-service systems. These applications should have well-structured dialogues, presupposing environment where the human intervention needs to be minimum and everything is subject to fast changes[4]. All the dialogue characteristics could be easily treated as business rules, once they represent the knowledge of a company that can be codified. Therefore, there is a great opportunity to do the connection between business rules and KM.

The main challenges in business rules management can be summarized in the following topics:

1. It is difficult to capture and formalize business rules that were "lost" in the specifications of requirements, use cases. For example this happens in the extraction of business rules starting from UML notations, such as pre-conditions, pos-conditions, basic and alternative flows (operation rules) of use cases; OCL restrictions (restriction rules); and data and derived attributes (derivation rules),

2. Business rules may be related with several use cases. For example, a rule that says "any transaction with value higher than $ 10.000,00 must be reported to the government" can be related with several use cases, such as "doing a deposit", "doing a withdrawal", etc.

3. Weakness in the combined execution of business rules that contemplate the control and relationships aspects among rules, and considering the components that implement specific logics of business. It is necessary to create mechanisms that take into account the existence of many legacy applications, with quite stable portions and that it is possible the use of

these legacy applications through the componentization or "servicification" of them.

There are several business rules products[5,6,7] that are well established and demonstrate the effectiveness of their use, but there is not a definitive guide, up to now, for an effective management of Business Rules. Ron Ross[8], who is considered the father of the theory of Business Rules, asserts that changes in the businesses constantly happen, in small or large scale, and it is rare to find a software product that can be changed easily once implemented. He also affirms that the lack of ability and flexibility to change increases significantly business' costs. He concludes that the "software needs to be the agent of the change, not the enemy of the change." Thus, it seems that, without an approach to identify the rules in the terminology of businesses and a way to translate these rules in computerized systems, with a minimum or no programming effort, it may be impossible to reach the goal, of being at the same time more precise, faster and cheaper.

The Business Rules can bring the benefits of the agility, but their effective use requires urgently supporting architectures. One of the solutions for this challenge is the development of business rules interpreters (Business Rules Engine, BRE) based on the variability of rules that, in its turn, has implications in the architecture of the rules.

In this paper, a business rule engine is proposed, one which makes the combination of control aspects of business rules with the execution of Web services or components that implement specific applications already developed in the context of governments. Therefore this proposal considers the existence of business rules, representing portions that are dynamic and sensitive to the market changes, requiring quick answer to these changes. It also takes into account the existence of a large number of government applications, with quite stable portions and, usually, of difficult maintenance, which have to be combined with other portions that are pretty volatile. The chosen scenario to exercise the ideas behind the proposed business rules engine is the same one used in the context of the eGOIA project[9], which is the civil identification public scenery from São Paulo State, Brazil. eGOIA is a 3 years project partially funded by the European Union through the @LIS program[10].

This paper is organized as follows. Section 2 presents some issues related to business rules, types, processes, standards and tools. Section 3 presents an e-Government scenario to exercise the combined execution of business rules and Web services. In section 4 we introduce the execution and architecture of integrating business rule engine and the business vocabulary and rules repository complemented by Web services infrastructure. Section 5 presents the conclusion of the paper.

2.   BUSINESS RULES CONCEPTS AND STANDARDIZATION

This section presents some discussion on business rules concepts, types, and considerations for separating rules from processes, standards and tools.

2.1   Business Rule Definitions

There are several business rule definitions, many of them very similar and using almost the same keywords in its definition. We present here an adapted one from the Business Rules Group, which considers two definitions for business rules[11]: one that represents the business perspective and another that represents the perspective of Information Technology (IT).

From the business perspective, a business rule is a premise that guides the business' behavior, in defense of a business policy that was formulated with regard to an opportunity, a threat, a force, or a weakness.

From the IT perspective, a business rule is a declaration that defines or restricts an aspect of the business or, in other words, defines the structure of the business and controls the behavior of the business.

In the context of our proposal we define a business rule as "an enterprise statement that defines or constrains some aspects of the business, according to the enterprise's policies and, therefore, influences the behavior of the business".

2.2   Basic Types of Business Rules

Business rules can be classified in several ways[12], among which the following seem the most relevant[11]:

- Structural business rules prescribe criteria for how the business chooses to organize (i.e., structure) the things it deals with by expressing a necessity or a possibility. Such rules express criteria for correct decisions, derivations or business computations. For example, the following rule expresses a necessity: The Customer has at least one of the following: a Rental Reservation, an in-progress Rental or a Rental completed in the past 5 years.
- Operative business rules are those that govern the conduct of business activities by expressing an obligation or prohibition. In contrast to structural rules, operative rules are ones that can be directly violated by people involved in the affairs of the business. For example, the following rule expresses a prohibition: "A Customer who appears intoxicated must not be given possession of a Rental Car".

2.3   Rules and Process

There is a lot of discussion concerning to the nature of a process and of a rule. In part, this is due to the division of the market around rules driven by BPM applications (Business Process Management) and pure rules engines. One way to look at it is that it potentially removes all the decision diamonds of the process' flows and replaces them with declarative, sharable business rules definitions[13]. Yet Zachman[14] considered that, in the past, the reason for separating data and process was that data definitions changed more slowly than processes, and that the same argument can be applied for processes and rules, making another interesting observation. Thus, the idea is that the business processes are relatively static and only the rules are dynamic. Sinur's study[15] showed that, in practice, close to 65% of business rules were actually relatively static, while 35% were very volatile. Of these volatile rules, only half were typically satisfactory to be updated directly by the business users.

2.4   Business Rules Standards and Tools

A lot of research and standardization in Business Rules are being developed. OMG is specifying the Business Semantics of Business Rules (BSBR)[11,16]. BRG created the BR Manifesto[17] and W3C is specifying the Semantic Web Rule Language (SWRL)[18].

Figure 1 display the evolution of standards that can be used to represent business rules or that are converging to represent them.

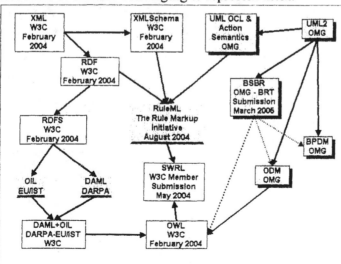

Figure 1. XML Standards towards Business Rules

2.4.1   The BSBR Meta-model

Due to the lack of a consensus to define business rules, OMG published a request for proposal (RFP)[16] requesting proposals to present solutions to allow business people to define the policies and the rules that run their businesses in their own language, in terms of the artifacts with which they accomplish their businesses. Besides that the other objective is to capture those rules in a clear way, not ambiguous and quickly transformable in other representations, such as the representations for the business people, for the software engineers, and for the automated systems of business rules execution. This RFP requested proposals for (i) a MOF metamodel for the specification of business rules for business people; (ii) a metamodel for the capture of vocabularies and definitions of the conditions used in business rules; (iii) an XML representation of business rules and vocabularies based on XMI in order to allow rules and vocabulary interoperability among software tools that manage business rules.

The resulting BSBR Metamodel is intended not for business people but for software engineers that build tools for business people.

In this paper, the following convention is used, adapted from BSBR[11], for the representation of facts and business rules:

- *italics - key words of the rule or fact*
- **bold - verbs or actions**
- **underlined bold** – **community vocabulary terms**

Following there are some examples of structural and operative business rules defined according to this metamodel.

- structural business rule: *A* **rental** *always* **has** *exactly one* **return branch**.
- operative business rule: *Each* **driver** *of a* **rental** *must* **be** *a* **qualified driver**.

2.4.2   Business Rules Tools

The main commercial tools for business rules execution are Blaze Advisor[5], CleverPath Aion[6], BRS RuleTrack[7], Haley[19], Jrules[20], VALENS[21], Corticon Decision Management[22] and Jess[23]. The main open source business rules engines are OFBiz Rule Engine[24], Mandarax[25], Drools[26] and Jena 2[27].

3.   BUSINESS RULES USAGE SCENARIO

This section presents an e-Government scenario to exercise the execution of business rules. This scenario is inserted in the context of a Brazilian e-Government applications environment, in the São Paulo State[9]. To simplify, the scenario considers only some services related to the civil identification community and the specific life event of a citizen that had his/her identification card (Id Card) lost or stolen..

3.1   Scenario Description

When a citizen has his/her Id Card stolen or lost he/she will go to a Government Portal in order to register the incident in an official form called BO (Bulletin of Occurrence) provided by a government agency through a back office system called BO System. Then, the Id Card Cancellation service provided by another back office system called Civil Identification System is accomplished to avoid the improper use of the Id Card. After that, the citizen can request for an Id Card replacement (new issue), provided by these two legacy systems plus a set of complimentary legacy systems. The issuing of new replacement cards may also be necessary for people who are getting older or when people may not be recognized because of the old document's photograph, or even due to name change by marriage or even signature change.

3.2   Business Rules for Civil Identification Community

Adherent to the concept of rule set as a "collection of business rules grouped together for some purpose", included in the proposed BSBR metamodel[11], are the defined rule sets related to the Civil Identification Community.

In some of the business rules the actions *(italics parenthesized texts)* that could be executed by the components or Web services are included. The execution of the business rules associated with the Id Card Cancellation service bases on the following facts (understood as atomic units that communicates something) stored in the Business Vocabulary and Rule Repository (BVRR, proposed in this paper and detailed in the next section).

- An **Identification Card** **identifies** a **Citizen**.
- An **Id Card** is an **Identification Card**.
- An **Incident Report** **registers** an **Incident**.
- A **BO** is an **Incident Report**.

The rule sets, contained in the Repository, related to the Id Card Cancellation service could be formalized like these:

Rule Set 1 - Rules to Id Card Cancellation
- **Rule 1.1** - An **Id Card** must be **cancelled** *(Update_Id_Card_Status)* only if one of the following facts is true:

- The **citizen** lost his/her **Id Card** and the **citizen** registered a **BO** and the **Id Card is registered**
- The **citizen** lost his/her **Id Card** and the **citizen** registered a **BO** and the **Id Card is pre-registered**

Rule Set 2 - Rules to register BO
- **Rule 2.1** - A **citizen** must **register** a **BO** *(BO_Register)* only if one of the following facts is true:
  - The **citizen** lost his/her **Id Card**
  - The **citizen has** his/her **Id Card stolen**
- **Rule 2.2** - A **BO** is registered if a **BO Data exists** electronically *(ReceiveBO)*.

Rule Set 3 - Rules to register or pre-register Id Card
- **Rule 3.1** - An **Id Card** is registered if the **Id Card Data** exists electronically *(Retrieve_Id_Card_Data)*.
- **Rule 3.2** - An **Id Card** must **be pre-registered** electronically using a **BO Data** *(PreRegister_Id_Card)* only if the **Id Card** is not **registered**.

Rule Set 4 - Rules to log information
- **Rule 4.1** - A **lost Id Card** with a **registered BO** whose **BO Data** is different from **Id Card Data** must **have** this **information** (differences) logged *(Log_CancellationService_Result)*.
- **Rule 4.2** - All **service actions** must **have** their **information** logged *(Log_CancellationService_Result)*.

The rule set for requesting an Id Card Replacement Issue service is:
Rule Set 5- Rules to request Id Card Replacement
- **Rule 5.1** - A **Citizen** should **request** an **Id Card replacement issue** *(Request_IdCard_Replacement)* only if at least one of the following facts is true:
  - The **Citizen** lost his/her **Id Card** and the **Citizen** registered a **BO** and the **Id Card** has been **cancelled**
  - The **Citizen** wants to change his/her **photograph**
  - The **Citizen** wants to change his/her **name**
  - The **Citizen** wants to change his/her **signature**

3.3   Discovering the user's desires

Imagine a Web Portal that is based on life events that begins to treat the citizen's desires with orientations, such as **(orientation 1) - "Please, enter a short sentence indicating what happened to you or what do you want to do."**

Assuming that the citizen enters: **"I lost my identification card"**, the system can then provide a new orientation, such as **(orientation 2) - "Please, enter the number of your identification card:............. "**. Thus, with the provided Id Card number and a few interactions the system discovers that the citizen's **desire and reason** can be resumed to "the **request for a new issue of an identification card, due to the loss** of the citizen's Id card".

Although the strategies to discover user's desire are very interesting, they are outside the scope of this article.

3.4   Discovering the facts and the business rules

After the citizen's desires have been discovered the Business Rule Engine **(BRE) generates the fact "citizen lost Id Card"** in the Repository. The BRE begins its job by searching for facts and business rules. It discovers that the main rule **(Rule 5.1)** related to the citizen's desire is included in the rule set **"Rules to request Id Card Replacement"**. As it can be seen in this main rule, the dispatching of the action *(Request_IdCard_Replacement)* has as pre-condition the facts "<u>**Citizen** lost</u> <u>**Id Card**</u>" and "<u>**Citizen** registered **BO**</u>" and "<u>**Id Card** is cancelled</u>". To simplify, it is assumed that the Citizen does not want to change anything, although he/she could change the photograph, name and signature.

All the facts and business rules that have direct or indirect relationship with the reason **"loss of the identification card"** must be considered, which means all the facts and rule sets listed in the subsection 3.2.

3.5   Executing Business Rules combined with legacy components

This section intends to show how actions should be dispatched when a business rule is in execution. In general these actions are implemented as Web services and/or components wrapping accesses to legacy applications.

When searching the BVRR, the BRE discovers that it is necessary to execute actions in order to generate the facts "The <u>**citizen** registered a **BO**</u>" and "The <u>**Id Card** is cancelled</u>".

Based on the **Rule 2.1**, an action *(BO_Register)* should be dispatched, since the condition "The <u>**citizen** lost</u> his/her <u>**Id Card**</u>" was satisfied. Assuming that the citizen accepted and supplied the necessary data to register a BO, the BO data begins to exist electronically and the fact "The <u>**citizen** registered a **BO**</u> " is generated.

As it can be seen in **Rule 1.1,** to cancel an Id Card it is necessary to have one of the conditions "The <u>**Id Card** is registered</u>" or "The <u>**Id Card** is</u>

pre-registered" satisfied. Thus, if the action *(Retrieve_Id_Card_Data)* of **Rule 3.1** returns with success, i.e., The Id Card is electronically registered; the fact "The **Id Card is registered**" is generated. On the other hand, if the action *(Retrieve_Id_Card_Data)* returns unsuccessfully, i.e., Id Card is not electronically registered, it is assumed, by **Rule 3.2** of the same rule set, that the Id Card needs to be pre-registered. The action *(PreRegister_Id_Card)* executed successfully generates the fact "The **Id Card is pre-registered**".

At this point, the successful execution of the action *(Update_Id_Card_Status)* generates the fact "The **Id Card is cancelled**".

Returning to **Rule 5.1**, once all of the pre-conditions are satisfied the action *(Request_IdCard_Replacement)* is dispatched to begin the process of requesting an Id Card replacement issue.

At the end of the accomplishment of the business service, the action *(Log_CancellationService_Result)* will be dispatched by **Rule 4.2,** to register all of the executed actions.

4. BUSINESS RULES EXECUTION ARCHITECTURE

This section introduces the architecture of execution of business rules, showing some details of how the difficulties and weaknesses in business rules are treated.

4.1 The Architecture Modules

Figure 2 presents the Business Rule Server composed by the Business Rule Engine (BRE) and by the Business Vocabulary and Rule Repository (BVRR).

The BRE gets from Service Scope Bounder the service profile and from BVRR all the rule sets associated to the service, then it executes the business rules found and finally returns the result to the service.

These modules are basic parts common to many of the proposals of business rules execution architectures[28]. As it is proposed in the Figure, to execute the business rules, BRE cooperates with Web Services Infrastructure (WSI), leaning on specific Web Service (WS) or components stored in the BCR. These WS or components implement specific logics and procedures of the business that are less susceptible of changes then the rules. Therefore, BRE makes the combination of the business rules execution control aspects with the execution of WS or component that implement specific logics of business. This approach, with the support of WSI or BCR, takes into account the existence of applications already developed (legacy), with quite stable portions and, usually, of difficult maintenance. Thus, it takes into account the possible use of these legacy applications through its Web "servicification" or "componentization" to facilitate the integration process in the phases of design and execution of business rules. From the BRE viewpoint, given a description of the WS or component, it is considered that WSI or BCR will return the URL of the WS or component. From now on we will only refer to WSI even though the same can be applied to BCR.

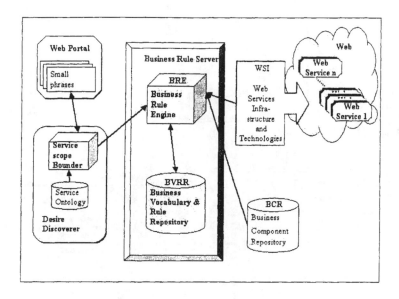

Figure 2. Business Rule Execution Architecture

4.2   The Interaction between Modules

The sequence diagram in the Figure 3 shows the interaction among the modules of the architecture. The context of the Civil Identification community is considered to show this interaction. Thus, the service could be a "request for a replacement issue of an identification card 123".

The Service Scope Bounder calls the BRE passing as a parameter to the Service profile. The Service profile contains all the properties needed to execute the service, such as, service identifier, citizen data, Id Card number, reason, etc. The BRE gets from the BVRR the rule sets associated with the service. For each business rule in the rule sets, the BRE also gets from the WSI all the WS URLs needed by the business rules. These WS will be dispatched by the business rule during its execution. The first business rule that will be considered for execution is the one that has the citizen's desire as an action, which is the **Rule 5.1.** Considering that, before dispatching the action *(Request_IdCard_Replacement),* the pre-conditions of that rule have to be satisfied, the rule is stacked, and other rules are executed. One of these rules could be **Rule 2.1,** whose execution could generate the fact "The **citizen registered** a **BO**". And, thus, successively the BRE will execute the rules in order to satisfy all the pre-conditions.

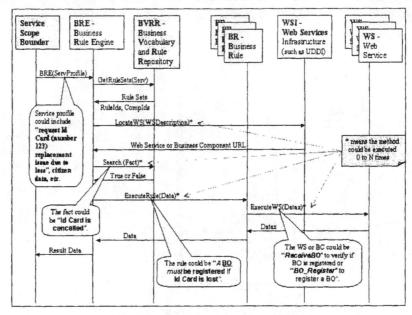

Figure 3 Sequence Diagram for Business Rules Execution.

4.3   The Architecture Repositories

This section describes the repositories of the proposed architecture.

4.3.1   BVRR - Business Vocabulary and Rule Repository

BVRR is a repository that defines terms, facts and business rules of specific application domains or that make sense for a community's user. It also defines the relationships and existent associations among these elements. Examples of business terms related to the civil identification application domain that could be stored in BVRR, are: Identification Card, Id Card, Id Card loss, Id Card replacement issue, Cancellation of Id Card, BO, Bulletin of Occurrence, Service Tax Payment, etc. Examples of facts in BVRR are: the BO is registered, the Id Card is cancelled, the Id Card is registered, etc. Examples of business questions/decisions and their respective business rules expressed in business people language and their possible formalizations are listed in Table 1.

Table 1. Examples of Business Rules associated to the Id Card cancellation.

Business Decisions	Business Rules for business people	Possible formalization
Is the BO registered?	When an Id Card is lost it is necessary to register a BO.	*A* **BO** *must* **be registered** *if an* **Id Card is lost**
Is the Id Card canceled?	A lost Id Card must be canceled.	*An* **Id Card** *must* **be cancelled** *if the* **Id Card is lost**
Is the Id Card pre-registered electronically?	An Id Card not electronically registered should be pre-registered electronically with BO data.	*An* **Id Card** *must* **be pre-registered** *electronically with* **BO Data**
Does anybody need to be notified about the system's faults?	All system failure should be notified to a supervisor by e-mail	*All* **system failure** must **have** the **information sent** *to the* **supervisor** *by* **e-mail**

4.3.2   WSI – Web Services Infrastructure (or BCR - Business Component Repository)

WSI is an infrastructure that provides functionalities, among other things, to locate WSs and return its URLs. BCR is a repository of basic software components. These WSs and basic components are in most of the cases encapsulation of application portions or services provided by legacy applications. Descriptions of some government's components that could be stored in BCR or wrapped as WSs are listed in Table 2.

Table 2. Government Web Services (or Business Component) examples

Web Service	Description
BORegister	Register a BO
IdCardStatusUpdate	Update the Id Card Status in the Civil Identification system.
IdCardStatusQuery	Query Id Card Status in the Civil Identification system database.
BODataGet	Get BO Data from BO legacy system database.
IdDataGet	Get Id Card Data from Civil Identification legacy system database.
IdPreRegister	Accomplish the Id Card pre-registration on the Civil Identification system.
GuideGet	Get service guide data from Service Guide System.

5.   CONCLUSION

Nowadays, the companies are confronted with all types of business rules. Regulatory institutions, business units, customers, competitors and the conditions of the market generate business rule changes all the time, which are translated in more business rules. The companies need fast reaction to the changes of the customers' demands. Businesses try to support quite individualized relationships with growing numbers of customers and partners for products and services with growing complexity.

In the context of public administrations, there are portions of business logic that are very static, normally supported by legacy systems, with severe constraints in terms of laws, policies and procedures. On the other hand there are portions of business logic that should be dynamic to improve the effectiveness of the public administration. Unfortunately, many of the government applications are rigid because their business rules are totally "lost" in the generated code and it is difficult to maintain them. The consequence is that the governments have difficulties in being agile on answering to changes demanded by citizens, enterprises and the government itself. The proposed business rule engine aims to contribute to the resolution of this problem. It considers that the business rules must be structured, classified and properly related with well-defined parts of the generated code, which, in this case, are defined as Web services or business components.

This proposal manages successfully, at least partially, the three main challenges related to the business rules engines initiatives. The first challenge, the difficulty in the capture and formalization of business rules, which are "lost" in the specifications of requirements is minimized once the pre-conditions, pos-conditions are directly structured in the business rule statement. The obligation and prohibition restrictions are managed by the Jess backward-chaining mechanism, once the action will be dispatched only if the pre-conditions are satisfied. The second challenge, the relationship of business rules with several use cases can be structured through the use of rule set concept, where for each use case is associated the necessary rule sets to deal with that specific use case. Finally, the third challenge, which is the weakness in the combined execution of business rules and Web services is successfully accomplished. The first prototype of this BRE, designed as an extension of the Jess rule engine, is indicating that the proposed approach really annuls that weakness.

Further research is needed in order to formalize the relationship structure of business rules and use cases. Also is needed to focus on other formalization aspects of business rules "lost" in the specifications, such as UML alternative flows, OCL restrictions and derived attributes. Another issue that has to considered is to turn this proposal adherent to other standardization efforts, such as SWRL.

REFERENCES

1. Standard based Framework, Cuecent BPMS, http://www.bahwancybertek.com/cuecentBpms.html, accessed in 12/05/2005.
2. Sinur, James, VP Gartner - The Rules Resurrection Is Upon Us, The Business Rules Forum, Semantic Arts Inc., 2003
3. Chapin, Donald - Capturing the Language of Business, Business Semantics Limited, 2002
4. Ross, Ronald G. - Serving Up Knowledge in: Principles of Business Rule Approach, Addison-Wesley, 2003
5. Blaze Advisor, Fair Isaac, http://www.fairisaac.com/Fairisaac/Solutions/Product+Index/Blaze+Advisor/, 15/05/05
6. CleverPath Aion, Business Rules Expert, Computer Associates, http://www3.ca.com/Solutions/Product.asp?ID=250, accessed in 15/05/05
7. BRS RuleTrack, Business Rule Solutions LLC, http://www.brsolutions.com/prod_support.php, accessed in 15/05/05
8. Ross, Ronald G., The Business Rule Book: Classifying, Defining and Modeling Rules, Version 4.0, Business Rule Solutions, 1997
9. eGOIA - Electronic Government Innovation and Access, http://www.egoia.info/, accessed in 14/05/2005.
10. @LIS : Alliance for the Information Society, http://europa.eu.int/comm/europeaid/projects/alis/index_en.htm, accessed in 14/05/2005.
11. BSBR - bei/2005-03-01, Version: 7.0, 2005
12. Ross, Ronald G., Principles of Business Rule Approach, 77-80, Addison-Wesley, 2003
13. Burlton, Roger - From Strategic Intent to Requirements Definition, Business Rules Forum, 2004
14. Zachman, John, Business Rules and the Framework, http://semarts.com.decisivenet.com/DesktopModules/ViewArticle.aspx?ArticleID=723&mid=3476, 2003
15. Sinur, J. - Gartner, WITH-19-9972, Notices of Research, 2003.
16. Business Semantics of Business Rules RFP - br/2003-06-03, 2003
17. BRG, The Business Rules Manifesto, http://www.businessrulesgroup.org/brmanifesto.htm, accessed in 15/05/2005
18. W3C, Semantic Web Rule Language (SWRL), 2005
19. Haley, Haley Enterprise, http://www.haley.com/0424686433342466/THE.html,
20. Jrules, ILOG, http://www.ilog.com, accessed in 14/05/2005
21. VALENS, LibRT, www.LibRT.com, accessed in 14/05/2005
22. Corticon Decision Management, Corticon, http://www.avoka.com/bpm/corticon.shtml, accessed in 14/05/2005
23. Friedman-Hill, Ernest, Jess in Action, Manning Publication Co., 2003
24. OFBiz Rule Engine, Open For Business Project, http://www.ofbiz.org/, accessed in 15/05/2005
25. Mandarax, The Mandarax Project, http://mandarax.sourceforge.net/, accessed in 15/05/2005
26. Drools, Implementation of Forgy's Rete algorithm, http://drools.org/, accessed in 15/05/2005
27. Jena 2, A Semantic Web Framework, http://www.hpl.hp.com/semweb/jena2.htm, accessed in 15/05/2005
28. Chisholm, Malcolm, How to Build a Business Rules Engine, Elsevier, Morgan Kauhfmann Publishers, 2004

TOWARDS DYNAMIC COMPOSITION OF E-GOVERNMENT SERVICES
A Policy-based Approach

Ivo J. G. dos Santos[1], Edmundo R. M. Madeira[1] and Volker Tschammer[2]

[1]*Institute of Computing, University of Campinas, PO Box 6176, 13083-970, Campinas, SP, Brazil;* [2]*Fraunhofer FOKUS, Kaiserin-Augusta-Alle 31, 10589 Berlin, Germany*

Abstract: The use of Information and Communication Technologies in governmental process and services, often known as e-Government, has gained momentum over the last decade. The demands for the on-line delivery of each time more complex and citizen-centric services and also the need for enabling citizen participation in governmental processes and decisions have created a series of technological challenges. If, on one hand, Service Oriented Architecture (SOA) appears as a natural and direct solution for problems like heterogeneity, on the other, issues like how to deal with the dynamism of the processes, the autonomy of the different entities involved and the privacy of data being exchanged still must be treated. We present in this article the first steps towards an effective solution to dynamically compose e-government services. These compositions are mediated through policies which provide different levels of autonomy and privacy in the involved interactions. Semantics are used to help building up the compositions, which are made effective through techniques like Orchestration, Choreography or a combination of both.

Key words: e-Government; Collaboration; Web Services; Dynamic Composition; Autonomy and Privacy Policies.

1. INTRODUCTION

The Information and Communication Technologies (ICTs) are being applied vigorously by governmental offices at national, regional and local levels around the world[1], a phenomenon often named Electronic Government (e-Government). The Online Service Delivery is perhaps the most common manifestation of this phenomenon. Nevertheless, citizen participation in government decisions through electronic means (e-Democracy) is also gaining momentum.

When it comes to delivering more complex services (which involve more than one entity) a series of problems arise. The first one is the implicit heterogeneity of the information systems in each one of those entities and therefore a challenge is to find a way to integrate them (or compose the services they provide to deliver a new one) without the need of doing big changes in the already running systems. Besides that, issues like the autonomy of the entities involved in the service provision and the privacy of the information being exchanged among different partners play important roles to make the integration a reality.

The SOA (Service Oriented Architecture) appears as a powerful choice to solve the integration problems mentioned before. Its concept of applications based on (Web) services and their compositions, regardless of how those services are implemented, helps breaking the first integration barrier: the technological heterogeneity. But it also creates new challenges, like finding effective ways to describe those services, to compose them dynamically and also to mediate (or not) their interactions.

We show in this article the first steps towards an effective solution to dynamically compose e-Government services. We rely on SOA as a technological base and propose the use of policies to mediate the compositions. These policies are intended to provide different levels of autonomy and privacy inside the composite services. The contribution we present in this work is in the context of the development project of a Collaborative e-Government Platform (*CoGPlat*), a middleware which intends to offer a set of services and facilities based on e-Governance and e-Democracy premises.

This article is organized as follows: in Section 2 we present as background an overview of the main concepts and technologies related to our work; in Section 3 a brief discussion on the state-of-the-art of e-Government projects and also on Cross-organizational Systems Collaboration research is shown; in Section 4 we introduce and discuss our proposal for the transparent composition of e-Government services; in Section 5 we present the final considerations, future steps of our project and also suggest extensions to our work.

2. BACKGROUND

2.1 E-Government: e-Governance and e-Democracy

The term Electronic Government (*e-Government*), as an expression, was coined after the example of Electronic Commerce. In spite of being a relatively recent expression, *e-Government* designates a field of activity that has been with us for several decades and which has attained a high level of penetration in many countries[2].

What has been observed over the recent years is a shift on the broadness of the *e-Government* concept. The ideas inside *e-Governance* and *e-Democracy* are to some extent promising big changes in public administration. The demand now is not only simply delivering a service on-line. It is to deliver complex and new services, which are all citizen-centric. Another important demand is related to the improvement of citizen's participation in governmental processes and decisions so that the governments' transparency and legitimacy are enforced. In order to fulfill these new demands, a lot of research has been done over the recent years (see Section 3) but many challenges are still to be faced, not only in the technological field, but also in the political and social aspects.

2.2 Service-oriented Architecture

Service-oriented Architecture (SOA) is a component model that inter-relates the different functional units of an application (called *services*) through well-defined interfaces and contracts between these services. These interfaces are defined in a neutral manner that should be independent of the hardware platform, the operating system, and the programming language the service is implemented in. This allows services, built on a variety of such systems, to interact with each other in a uniform and universal manner [3,4].

On the Internet, the *Web Services* technology represents a manifestation of the SOA. A *Web Service* can be defined as an application which is made public through the publication of an interface (or a port) - note that the way the application is implemented is not important at all to a service client. The service interface is described and accessed through a set of Internet standards and protocols, like XML (eXtended Markup Language), HTTP (HyperText Transfer Protocol), SOAP (Simple Object Access Protocol) and WSDL (Web Services Description Language) [5].

2.2.1   Service Compositions

There are some scenarios (in fact most of them) in which the access to a single service is not enough to fulfill a goal. In order, for instance, to implement a business process or to solve a scientific problem using a SOA approach, it is usually necessary to compose various services. The fact that these compositions may themselves become new services makes composition in SOA a recursive operation[6].

There are two composition techniques usually considered when composing *Web Services*: orchestration and choreography. There isn't yet a common sense regarding these concepts, but to the context of our work, we will adopt the following definitions[7]:

– *Orchestration*: A service composition described as an *orchestration* describes all interactions that are part of a process in terms of sequence of activities, conditional events, etc. It is very similar to a workflow description on a traditional workflow system. The viewpoint is often centralized and the description is executed by an orchestration engine;

– *Choreography*: A service composition described as *choreography* is more collaborative and less centralized in nature. Only the public message exchanges are considered relevant. Differently from Orchestration, there is not an entity that has a global view/control of the composition. The *choreography* definitions are used usually as guidelines/protocols during the composition development time. They may also be used as validation rules during the composition execution time.

In "real world" scenarios usually both approaches must be considered. In terms of specifications, the most relevant to the context of our work are BPEL4WS[8] and WS-CDL[9]. The BPEL4WS (Business Process Execution Language for Web Services), or simply BPEL, defines a language based on XML that describes the control logic required to coordinate the participant services on a process flow - BPEL is, essentially, a layer over WSDL. BPEL defines both Abstract and Executable business processes. The WS-CDL, or simply CDL, represents an on-going effort being held by the W3C (World Wide Web Consortium) to establish a choreography standard language. CDL is also XML-based and describes peer-to-peer collaborations of Web Services by defining their common and complementary observable behavior. WS-CDL does not treat executable processes, but only the choreography aspects of a composition, and therefore can be used as a compliment to BPEL and other composition specifications.

2.2.2 Semantic Web and Services

A series of efforts towards the creation of the Semantic Web are gaining momentum[10]. From a high-level perspective, one of the major goals of the Semantic Web is to shape information in an unambiguous, machine-processable way, thus enabling a better exchange of information both between humans and computers and among computers[11]. The major effort of the Semantic Web community has been the release of expressive languages and formalisms to describe information, such as OWL[12] (Web Ontology Language) and RDF[13] (Resource Description Framework). In terms of Web services, a computer-interpretable description of the service (and the means by which it is accessed) must be provided. OWL-S[14] is a language that tries to define the ontology necessary to provide such descriptions of services on the Semantic Web, promising to enable the automatic Web service discovery, invocation, composition and also execution monitoring.

3. RELATED WORK

3.1 E-Government

Next we briefly present some projects in the e-Government area which, as our work, study ways to enhance the provision of e-Government services, and therefore complement our proposal.

EU-Projects. The European Union (EU) has over the recent years paid a lot of attention to the challenges of e-Government and a series of research projects have been sponsored by its commissions. Some of these projects are briefly presented next.

The *TerreGov* (*Impact of e-Government on Territorial Government Service*) is an on-going project which addresses the issue of interoperability of e-Government services[15]. Its first results include a series of studies on the state-of-the-art in e-Government, on the requirements for new e-Government applications and also on the technological alternatives that could be used to implement the desired interoperability (where *Web Services* and also *semantics* play an important role).

The *eMayor* is a collaboration project between municipalities of four countries of the EU, several universities and firms providing technology[16]. It is supported by the European Commission's Research and Development Department. It promises to develop and implement an open, secure, and affordable e-Government platform for small and medium European public organizations. It intends to support the secure communication of municipalities amongst themselves, businesses and citizens.

Another relevant on-going project, *eGOIA* (*Electronic Government Innovation and Access*), aims to implement a demonstration system supporting the access of citizens, through the Internet, to integrated public e-Government services[17]. Technically the project is based on two main paradigms – back-office and front-office integration. The first concentrates on a unified approach to access already existing and newly emerging government services. The second focus on providing an intuitive user-interface integrating the diverse e-Government services available.

Some important results were also presented by the already finished *PRISMA* project[18], especially in terms of providing a systematic analysis and synthesis of current and future impacts of new ICTs on government services in Europe. Within the context of e-Government and e-Democracy, six major service fields have been examined in detail: administrations; health; persons with special needs: the disabled and elderly environment; transport; and tourism.

3.2   Cross-organizational System Collaboration

The problem of cross-organizational system integration appeared first in e-Business workflow systems and is also present in the e-Government field. Schulz[19] proposes a classification of business processes into private and shared. The private processes expose interaction points where the shared processes connect to, in such a way that a business process can be part of two or more organizations. A framework to support these two categories of processes, BPFA (Business Process Framework Architecture) is also introduced. BPFA consists of a set of components that execute instances of an inter-organizational process model, extending a company's workflow infrastructure and allowing process-oriented communication among partners and customers.

Santos and Madeira[20] extended Schulz model proposing a set of policies to regulate the interactions and applied it with Dynamic Virtual Enterprises. The interaction policies adopted in our work (Section 4.3) extend these two proposals and adapt them to a Collaborative e-Government environment.

Dijkman and Dumas[21] propose a multi-viewpoint approach, based on a control-flow perspective in terms of *Petri nets*[22], to design composite services. They identify four viewpoints from which it is possible to describe the control-flow aspect of Web Services: the choreography viewpoint, the interface behavior viewpoint, the provider behavior viewpoint and the orchestration viewpoint.

4. TRANSPARENT COMPOSITION OF E-GOVERNMENT SERVICES

4.1 CoGPlat: A Collaborative e-Government platform

The proposal for transparent composition of e-Government services we present next in this section is part of the development project of a Collaborative e-Government platform called *CoGPlat*[23]. *CoGPlat*'s main goal is to support the interaction and the collaboration of governmental entities, organizations (public, private and nonprofit) and citizens in different public administration scenarios, ranging from the electronic delivery of integrated services to the support for citizen participation in government decisions. *CoGPlat* is being developed as a service-oriented middleware (not as an end-user application) in order to provide a set of general services and facilities to be used by specific applications and tools. In this article we are going to focus in one of these facilities, the *Transparent Services Unit*, which is responsible for the dynamic integration and management of public services.

4.2 The Transparent Services Unit

The *Transparent Services Unit* (*TSU*) is the *CoGPlat*'s facility responsible for composing multiple (Web) services into new ones in a transparent manner. These new services are then delivered to citizens and/or entities through applications that run over the platform. Besides composing the services, the TSU is also responsible for managing their execution, which is regulated by a set of interaction policies (Section 4.3).

In order to dynamically realize those compositions, the TSU matches the semantic descriptions of the available services to the desired functionalities of the new e-Government service. It then builds up an execution plan, which can be an orchestration, choreography or a combination of both.

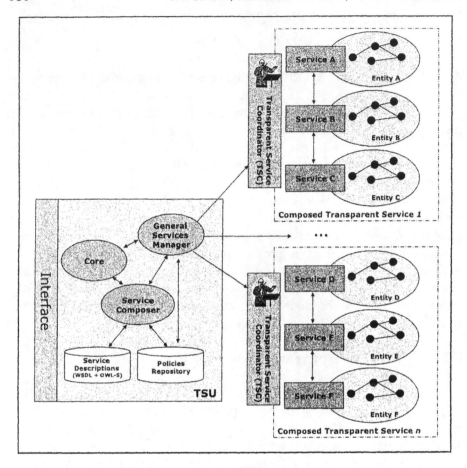

Figure 1. Transparent Services Unit

Figure 1 presents an overview of the TSU infrastructure, composed of the following elements:
- *Interface*: provides communication with the other platform units and to the client applications;
- *Core*: executes the coordination among the other TSU elements. It is also responsible for non-functional requisites such as persistency, transaction support etc;
- *Service Composer*: dynamically builds the execution plans (service compositions) by matching new service demands with the available service descriptions (WSDL + OWL-S) and also according to the existing policies;
- *General Services Manager*: coordinates the various TSCs;
- *Transparent Service Coordinator* (TSC): the TSC is responsible for managing a Transparent Service instance, coordinating the composition

and guaranteeing its correct execution, either through orchestration, choreography or their combination. There is one TSC associated with each new Transparent Service.

- *Service:* a service is considered to be an application which has a well-known interface and which provides some functionality that can be used by applications over the platform. A service in our context is always linked to an entity and can be itself a composition of services internal to this entity.
- *Entities:* are real organizations, usually representing an administrative domain. Can be government unities, private companies, NGOs etc.

4.3 Policies

When composing e-Government services, the issues of autonomy of the entities involved and of the privacy of the date being exchanged is always present. In order to enable compositions which fulfill these demands and provide different levels of autonomy and privacy among the entities participating in a Transparent Service, *CoGPlat* implements a set of Interaction Policies. These policies were previously proposed and successfully applied in a *Virtual Enterprise* scenario[20], being now adapted to the context of e-Government applications.

The Interaction Policies are classified into two categories: *Entity Autonomy Policies* (CoGPlat x Entity) and *Entity Cooperation Policies* (Entity x Entity).

Entity Autonomy Policies. Determine the level of control the platform (and therefore the applications running over it) will have over the internal stages of a service. At the moment an entity service is selected to participate in a Transparent Service, a negotiation takes place to define what level of interaction this entity wishes to have with the platform. According to the chosen level, the TSC can act in one of the following manners:

1. *Supervisor*: The TSC does not have any action on the entity inside domain. A *Supervisor* policy is sub-divided into:
   - *Consulting-only*: the TSC can only ask for status information about a service running on the entity's internal domain;
   - *Selective*: the TSC and the entity negotiate in which points of the execution plan interactions will be allowed;
   - *Participative*: the TSC can interact with all activities of the execution plan
2. *Executor*: the TSC has total control over the tasks running on the entity's internal workflow, being the responsible for composing also these tasks.

Entity Cooperation Policies. Determine the collaboration levels on the interactions between two entities that participate on the same Transparent Service instance. The following policies are available:

1. *Total Cooperation*: the two entities fully trust each other, and therefore can communicate in a decentralized peer-to-peer manner;
2. *Controlled Cooperation*: there is a pre-established set of information that should be passed to the next entity and another set that should be hidden by the TSC;
3. *Total Privacy*: there is no interaction between the entities. All information is returned to the TSC, which has access to the service execution plan and then decides what to do next, hiding from the following entity the activities and data from the previous one.

Policies and Composition. An entity is allowed to select different policies when participating on different dynamic services. In addition, a dynamic service is usually composed of multiple entities and therefore can have multiple policies. So, policies are fundamental to the dynamic construction of the execution plan and also to the correct selection of the service composition mechanisms to be used (Orchestration and/or Choreography).

As already mentioned, the TSC is the entity responsible for implementing the correct execution of the plan on the entities and for applying the interaction policies. When, for example, the composition is made up by services of an entity that controls others, an orchestration approach is more appropriate. On the other hand, when there is only collaboration among the entities (no administrative links or hierarchy and fully decentralized control), choreography is the most appropriate choice. Table 1 presents some examples of the behavior of the TSC (type of composition) according to the selected Entity Autonomy Policy.

Table 1. Examples: Autonomy Policies x Composition

	Autonomy Policy	*Composition*	*Service Control*
(a)	Supervisor :: Consulting-only	Choreography	Decentralized
(b)	Supervisor :: Selective	Orchestration + Choreography	Partially Decentralized
(c)	Supervisor :: Participative	Orchestration	Centralized on TSC
(d)	Executor	Orchestration	Centralized on TSC

In Table 1: (a) According to the Consulting-only Supervisor policy, the TSC has no intervention on the entities' services and can only participate on a choreography to validate the messages exchanged; (b) The policy here allows the TSC to interact with some of the internal services, performing a partial orchestration; (c)Here, the TSC has total control over the internal activities, and performs a full orchestration of the internal services; (d) This last policy allows the TSC to access the internal resources of the entity's workflow system. Here it can either use orchestration or even dispatch objects (mobile agents, for instance), which will have control over the local activities.

4.4 An Example

An interesting example of where a *Transparent Service* could be used is the process of obtaining an authorization to build a house near the coast, emitted by the municipality in conjunction with other authorities. Suppose that, to get this hypothetic authorization, different entities must be contacted, on a specific and pre-determined chronological sequence: (1) City Hall, (2) Civil Engineering Department, (3) Navy, (4) Fire Department and again the (5) City Hall (and suppose that steps 2 and 3 are independent and could be done in parallel). This process is usually slow because it consists basically of the transportation of documents from one entity to the other. Inside each one of the entities, an internal process is performed when the request arrives in order to make it available for the next entity. This is a typical scenario where a Composite Service could be created to handle all this process flow for the citizen. Besides the transparency offered, the process could also gain speed because each of the participating entities would have its services integrated in a seamless manner to the platform (according to the chosen autonomy and cooperation policies).

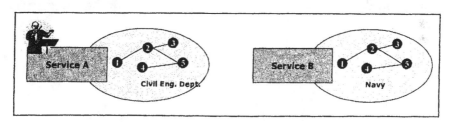

Figure 2. The Authorization Example

As seen in Figure 2, the Civil Eng. Department (administered by the City Hall, the owner of the *CoGPlat* infrastructure in this example) could select, for instance, to have a *Supervisor Participative* relationship with the TSC, letting the platform orchestrate the internal steps involved in the process. The Navy, on the other hand (and for obvious reasons), could choose the most autonomous policy (*Supervisor Consulting-Only*) so that no interference from the platform is allowed in its internal processes, preserving the privacy and integrity of its internal data.

5.   FINAL CONSIDERATIONS

We present in this article the first steps towards an effective way to dynamically compose e-Government services. The contribution we present is in the context of an on-going project which intends to model and develop a Collaborative e-Government Platform (*CoGPlat*). The focus of this article is to describe and discuss one of the facilities of this platform, the *Transparent Services Units*.

Service-Oriented Architecture, Orchestration, Choreography and *Semantics* are applied to facilitate the dynamic integration of heterogeneous services delivered by different governmental and private entities.

Besides the completion of the TSU prototype, the next steps of our project include the adoption of the WS-CDL specification as a standard for the choreography of services in the whole CoGPlat platform (as BPEL already is for orchestration) and also the development of a series of other example applications (starting with Municipalities and Metropolitan Regions) to show the potentials of the infrastructure. We are also studying the possibility of adopting some formalism (like Petri-Nets or Pi-Calculus[24]) to be a standard way to describe the service compositions.

ACKNOWLEDGEMENTS

The authors would like to thank CAPES, CNPq and the WebMaps project for financial support. Additional thanks to the Fraunhofer FOKUS Institute and its ELAN Competence Center.

REFERENCES

1.   G. Marchionini, H. Samet, and L. Brandt. Digital government. *Communications of the ACM*, 46(1):25-27, January 2003.
2.   K. Lenk and R. Traunmüller. Electronic government: Where are we heading? In *EGOV 2002 - LNCS*, vol. 2456, pp 1-9, Springer-Verlag, 2002.
3.   M.P. Papazoglou and D. Georgakopoulos. Service-oriented Computing. *Communications of the ACM*, 46(10):25-28, October 2003.
4.   IBM.   New   to   SOA   and   Web   services. *http://www-128.ibm.com/developerworks/webservices/newto/*, July 2005
5.   World Wide Web Consortium (W3C). Web Services Description Language (WSDL) Version 2.0, W3C Working Draft, *http://www.w3.org/TR/wsdl20/*, 2004.
6.   F. Curbera, R. Khalaf, N. Mukhi, S. Tai, and S. Weerawarana. The next step in Web Services. *Communications of the ACM*, 46(10):29-34, October 2003.
7.   C. Peltz. Web Services Orchestration and Choreography. *IEEE Computer*, 36(10):46-52, 2003.

8. BEA Systems, IBM, Microsoft, SAP AG, and Siebel Systems. Business Process Execution Language for Web Services (BPEL4WS) - Version 1.1. *http://www-128.ibm.com/developerworks/library/specification/ws-bpel/*, 2003.

9. World Wide Web Consortium (W3C). Web Services Choreography Description Language Version 1.0 (WS-CDL). *http://www.w3.org/TR/ws-cdl-10/*, Working Draft, 17 Dec 2004.

10. T. Berners-Lee, J. Hendler, and O. Lassila. The Semantic Web. *Scientific American*, 284(5):34-43, 2001.

11. J. Barthès and C. Moulin. TERREGOV Technological State of the Art - v1, version 2, *http://www.terregov.eupm.net*, December 2004.

12. D. L. McGuinness and F. van Harmelen. OWL Web Ontology Language Overview. *http://www.w3.org/TR/owl-features/*, W3C Candidate Recommendation, August 2003.

13. World Wide Web Consortium (W3C). Resource Description Framework Primer. *http://www.w3.org/TR/rdf-primer/*, W3C Recommendation, February 2004.

14. The OWL Services Coalition. OWL-S: Semantic Markup for Web Services. White paper. *http://www.daml.org/services*, July 2004.

15. TERREGOV Project Web Site, *http://www.terregov.eupm.net*, in May 2005.

16. eMayor Project Web Site, *http://www.emayor.org*, in May 2005.

17. eGOIA - Electronic GOvernment Innovation and Access, Technical Report n. 01, *http://www.egoia.sp.gov.br/pub/Annual-Technical-Report-eGOIA-2004-Delivered.pdf*, 2004

18. PRISMA Project Web Site, *http://www.prisma-eu.net*, in May 2005.

19. K. Schulz and M. Orlowska. Architectural issues for cross-organizational b2b interactions. In *ICDCSW '01: Proceedings of the 21st International Conference on Distributed Computing Systems*, page 79, USA, IEEE Computer Society, 2001.

20. I.J.G. Santos and E.R.M. Madeira. Vm-Flow: Using web services orchestration and choreography to implement a policy-based virtual marketplace. In *Proceedings of the World Computer Congress 2004 - 4th IFIP Conference on e-Commerce, e-Business, and e-Government*, vol. 9, pp. 265-285, Toulouse, France, Kluwer Academic Publishers, August 2004.

21. R. Dijkman and M. Dumas. Service-oriented design: A multi-viewpoint approach. *International Journal of Cooperative Information Systems (IJCIS)*, 13(4):337-368, 2004.

22. W.M.P. van der Aalst. The application of Petri nets to workflow management. *The Journal of Circuits, Systems and Computers*, 8(1):21-66, 1998.

23. I.J.G. Santos and E.R.M. Madeira. Cogplat: Using composition to enable collaborative e-government services. In *EU-LAT Workshop on e-Government and e-Democracy, Vol. 8 of e-Government and e-Democracy: Progress and Challenges*, pp. 17-27, Santiago, Chile, May 2004.

24. R. Milner. Communicating and Mobile Systems: The pi-Calculus. Cambridge University Press, 1999.

EMPLOYING ONTOLOGIES FOR THE DEVELOPMENT OF SECURITY CRITICAL APPLICATIONS
The Secure e-Poll Paradigm

DRITSAS S.[1], GYMNOPOULOS L.[2], KARYDA M.[2], BALOPOULOS T.[2], KOKOLAKIS S.[2], LAMBRINOUDAKIS C.[2], GRITZALIS S.[2]

[1]*Department of Informatics, Athens University of Economics and Business, GR-10434, Greece*

[2]*Laboratory of Information and Communication Systems Security (Info-Sec-Lab, Department of Information and Communication Systems Engineering, University of the Aegean, Samos, GR-83200, Greece*

Abstract: Incorporating security in the application development process is a fundamental requirement for building secure applications, especially with regard to security sensitive domains, such as e-government. In this paper we follow a novel approach to demonstrate how the process of developing an e-poll application can be substantially facilitated by employing a specialized security ontology. To accomplish this, we describe the security ontology we have developed, and provide a set of indicative questions that developers might face, together with the solutions that ontology deployment provides.

Key words: Security Ontology, Application Development, Internet Voting, e-Poll

1.   INTRODUCTION

Elections constitute a fundamental function of democracy, not only by providing a means for the orderly transfer of power, but also by promoting citizens' confidence in the government through their participation. Within the last years, there has been a strong interest in voting over the Internet as a means to provide a convenient way of voting, and thus increase participation in elections. Election systems, however, need to meet demands concerning security, and especially confidentiality, among others. Security features are most important in the case of *remote Internet voting*, which poses increased security requirements with respect to other Internet voting types, such as *poll site Internet voting*, or *kiosk voting*.

In this paper we address the issue of developing a secure e-poll application, employing a specialized security ontology. Since developing electronic government and especially electronic voting applications requires meeting a wide range of security requirements, we have developed a security ontology that facilitates the development of secure applications by assisting the design and development process.

In the next section we give an overview of the connection between ontologies and software development, emphasizing on the role ontologies can play for building secure applications. In section three we describe the security ontology we have developed and its specific context. Section four demonstrates how this ontology can substantially facilitate the process of developing a secure e-poll application. Finally, section five discusses the advantages and limitations of the proposed use of ontologies in secure application development, and the last section presents our overall conclusions and directions for further research.

2.   ONTOLOGIES AND SOFTWARE ENGINEERING

An ontology is a formal, explicit way for modelling and describing a segment of the world for which we agree to recognize the existence of a set of objects and their interrelations. They constitute an "*[e]xplicit specification of a conceptualization*" [25]. Thus, an ontology is the attempt to express an exhaustive conceptual scheme within a given domain, typically a hierarchical data structure containing all the relevant entities, their relations and the rules within that domain.

In computer science, ontologies are mainly used as a means for modelling information and for providing inference and reasoning techniques. For example, ontologies enable computers to go beyond the mere layout of documents by capturing their semantics and enabling computers to process them in a meaningful way.

2.1   Ontology based software engineering

Ontologies could play an important role in software engineering, as they do in other contexts, where they: (a) provide a source of precisely defined terms that can be exchanged between people, organizations and applications, (b) provide a shared understanding concerning the domain of study, and (c) represent all hidden assumptions concerning the objects related to a certain domain. Although there are many research efforts to develop ontologies, software engineering still does not have a detailed ontology, which describes the concepts, that domain experts agree upon, as well as their terms, definitions and meanings.

Nowadays it is well understood that ontologies provide a useful theoretical and methodological tool for facilitating the software engineering process. In addition, it has been argued that security issues should be taken into consideration in all the stages of the software development process. Unfortunately, security features are typically built into an application in an ad hoc manner or are only integrated later during the system lifetime. In this context, it is obvious that we need methodologies, which can support the integration of security throughout the development life cycle, since it is generally accepted that security should be *"built in"* rather than *"added on"* applications.

Currently, a number of software engineering methodologies have been proposed for handling security issues at the design level: NFR [9, 10], Tropos [11], i* [12], RBAC [13], M-N framework [14], GBRAM [15,16]. Most of these methodologies consider the specification and validation of security requirements from the business goals, but do not refer to how these requirements can be translated into system components, nor do they offer any specific suggestion for related and applicable implementation techniques. Additionally, most of the above approaches are rather close to the technical aspects of security and particularly of specific application domains. As such, they do not provide a generic model of security and thus cannot be used for specifying security patterns. Such patterns could be used in order to incorporate security requirements and techniques into the software development process.

Therefore, we believe that the development of a security ontology that describes the basic security-related concepts would be very useful.

2.2 Security ontologies

Today, software developers lack a common approach that would bridge the desirable security requirements with the techniques that can be adopted in order to design and implement secure applications. A first step towards this could be the development of an ontology that will support the modelling of the basic security concepts and their integration into a model-driven software development process. The advantages of deploying such an ontology are: (a) express the most important security concepts, (b) realize the relations among the above concepts, (c) provide a common understanding and vocabulary of security issues among application developers, and (d) facilitate the development of secure applications.

However, to the best of our knowledge, today there is not a shared body of practice for the development of a security ontology that will be used as a common base for the development of secure applications. Loosely related work focuses only on access control issues [24]. Standards discussed include XML Signatures [3] and integration with Security Assertions Markup Language (SAML) [4, 5]. Furthermore, work on KAON [6] focuses mostly on the managing infrastructure of generic ontologies and metadata, whereas in [7] authors present a policy-ontology.

Raskin et al. presented an ontology-driven approach to information security [8]. They argue that a security ontology could organize and systematize security concepts (e.g. attacks). Furthermore, the inherent ontology modularity could support the reaction to attacks by relating certain controls with specific attack characteristics, as well as attack prediction.

The KAoS Policy and Domain Services is another approach based on ontologies for the representation of security related concepts [17]. Specifically, while the approach was primarily oriented to the dynamic requirements of software agent applications, it has been used in general-purpose environments as well [18]. The KAoS framework proposes a detailed Ontology for Security Policies along with other notions (such as Actors, Entities, etc.) [19].

3.   RESEARCH METHODOLOGY

It is widely accepted that no general and robust methodology exists for developing ontologies. However, several guidelines exist for dealing with the development of an ontology. According to [1], the two first steps towards the development of an ontology are: (a) determining its domain and scope, and (b) considering the use of existing ontologies.

3.1   Building a Secure Application Ontology

First of all, we decided that the e-poll domain of our developed ontology should have the following characteristics:

- Voter authentication is a mandatory requirement. Voters are issued credentials to authenticate themselves.

- There is a specific list of authorized voters (not everyone is allowed to vote).
- Voters are not allowed to vote more than once.
- Voters vote from any computer connected to the Internet.
- The ballot is constructed by the election officials or organizers and voters are presented with predefined multiple choices or/and with alternative ways of expressing opinion (to accommodate asset and range voting).

Our approach during the development of the ontology was heavily influenced by the related work presented in section 2, and was focused on the context of electronic voting. In order to produce an instantiated ontology, we used in a fair extent databases like the CRAMM database of countermeasures [2].

Besides choosing the basic concepts and instantiating our ontology, we also came up with subclasses. It should be noted however that our efforts were focused in the high level design of the ontology, and not on trying to include every possible subclass or instance we could think of. Details about the actual ontology are given in section 4.2.

3.2   Methods and Tools

Finding and reusing existing material was only one step towards the development of our ontology. We generally followed the steps provided in [1]; giving emphasis in the iterative procedure they propose. Every cycle in this procedure had roughly four phases: determining competency questions, enumerating important terms, defining classes and class hierarchy, and instantiating.

Competency questions are loosely structured questions that a knowledge base built on the ontology should be able to answer. Setting and elaborating on competency questions is an efficient way to identify and then focus on the desired area. Next, we give an example of a competency question and the respective answer given during the ontology construction:

```
Q: Are voters stakeholders of the system?
A: Yes.
```

Enumerating important terms within the scope set by competency questions and the respective answers is a prerequisite for defining ontology classes. We gathered approximately one hundred related terms. Some of them formed ontology classes; other formed properties of classes and some were not used at all.

In the next phase, classes and the class hierarchy were developed. In Figure 1, we depict the full ontology hierarchy, together with class slots and their facets. After that, the relations between classes and also the domain and range of each slot were elaborated.

Figure 1. The ontology hierarchy.

The last phase in each cycle is that of instantiation; each class was given specific instances. The number of instances is depicted in parentheses in Figure 1.

The four phases described above were repeated several times. The ontology was queried after each iteration (please refer to section 4.3), and iterations ended only when the results obtained were considered satisfactory.

The tools used for developing and validating the ontology were Protégé and Racer. Protégé [21] is a software tool used by system developers and domain experts to construct domain ontologies. Protégé itself provides only core functionality; to develop our ontology, we used the Protégé plug-in, which facilitates the development of OWL [26] and RDF [27] ontologies.

Racer [22] is an inference engine that can be used for query answering over RDF documents. We used Racer in order to check our developed ontology (see section 4.2) for inconsistencies, and for submitting queries to the ontology in order to verify its validity (see section 4.3). The queries were expressed in the new Racer Query Language (nRQL).

nRQL is a description logic query language for retrieving individuals from an A-box (a set of assertions about individuals) according to specific conditions. It allows the use of variables within queries which are bound against those A-box individuals that satisfy these conditions. The language is substantially more expressive than traditional concept-based retrieval languages offered by previous description logic reasoning systems. A description of nRQL's syntax is beyond the scope of this paper, but the interested reader is referred to [23].

The integration between Protégé and Racer was achieved through the RQL Tab plug-in, which allows the OWL plug-in of Protégé to send queries to Racer and receive back the results.

4.   DEVELOPING A SECURE APPLICATION FOR E-POLLS

4.1   The e-Poll Application

Remote Internet voting is an attractive solution, especially for the disabled, since it allows voting from home or work; at the same time however, such systems face significantly higher risks with regards to the confidentiality and integrity of the voting process. Developing applications that support Internet voting is therefore a security critical task, since application designers and developers make critical decisions about issues concerning the confidentiality and integrity of the data, as well as about the availability of the voting system.

To validate the usability of the ontology we developed, we employed it to the design and development of a secure e-poll application. The application we worked on supports Internet voting for organizations as well as for other bodies (e.g. local authorities) wanting to organize an e-poll. It is a distributed application, requiring that people participating in the e-poll have Internet access and can visit the web site that is hosting the e-poll. Organizers, on the other hand, use the back-office application, that can help them manage all necessary voting processes, such as voter registration, vote tallying, ballot design and so forth.

Generally, the voter registration process is considered one of the weakest links in the electoral process. Secure and reliable Internet-based voter registration relies on appropriate authentication infrastructure. Since an adequately secure authentication infrastructure is not yet available, initial registration for the e-poll system is conducted offline. After being registered, voters are provided with a password and/or a digital signature from the election organizers. They can use this authentication means for voting from their home, work, or any other place having Internet access.

For the Internet poll application to be used in a trustworthy manner, a list of requirements must be satisfied: voter authentication, ballot confidentiality, ballot integrity, reliable vote communication, storage and tallying, prevention of multiple voting, protection against attacks on the server as well as the application side. To address these security critical issues during the design of the e-poll application, we used the security ontology we developed, as described in the following paragraphs.

4.2   Secure e-Poll Ontology

Based on the above scenario, we used the methods and tools presented in section 3.2.1 to develop a security ontology that corresponds to the specific context. We will now present the basic concepts of the ontology along with their relationships in triplets of directly connected concepts.

The basic concepts of the proposed ontology are: objective, countermeasure, stakeholder, threat, asset, attacker, and deliberate attack. *Objectives* are the desired properties of the system (e.g. vote anonymity). A *countermeasure* is an action taken to protect an asset against threats (e.g. investigation of incidents). *Stakeholders* are the people that place value on the system (e.g. voter). A *threat* is a potential for a damage of an asset (e.g. fire). *Assets* are pieces of information or resources upon which stakeholders place value (e.g. e-poll application server). An *attacker* is a person, which deliberately damages an asset (e.g. hacker). *Deliberate Attack* is a deliberate human action that damages an asset (e.g. vote corruption).

In Figure 2, we depict the direct relations of the "Objective" concept. Objectives are *defined* by Stakeholders, and they are *threatened* by threats.

Figure 2. Relations of the class "Objective".

Countermeasure's and Asset's direct relations are depicted in Figure 3. We place those two concepts together because they are related with the same two concepts: Threat and Stakeholder. Of course the relations are different: Stakeholders *implement* Countermeasures while they *use* Assets, and Countermeasures *address* Threats while Threats *damage* Assets.

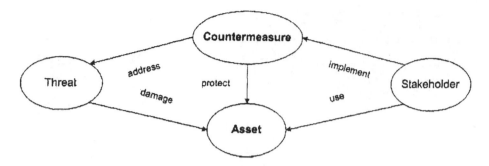

Figure 3. Relations of the classes "Countermeasure" and "Asset".

In Figure 4, we depict the direct relations of the "Threat" notion. Countermeasures *address* Threats and thus *protect* Assets while Threats *threaten* Objectives and *damage* Assets.

This dual "*behaviour*" of the Threat concept can be explained by the rest of Figure 4. As one can see in Figure 4 a Deliberate Attack is a *subclass of* the Threat class and is *realized* by an Attacker.

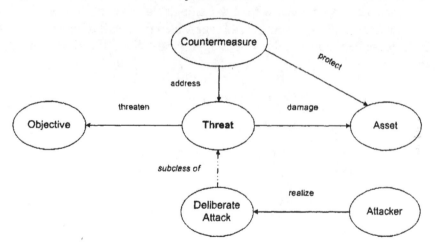

Figure 4. Relations of the class "Threat".

Stakeholder's direct relations are depicted in Figure 5. A Stakeholder *defines* Objectives, *implements* Countermeasures and *uses* Assets (e.g. a voter uses the e-poll system to vote etc.). As stated before, Countermeasures protect Assets.

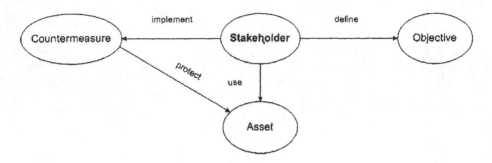

Figure 5. Relations of the class "Stakeholder".

4.3   nRQL Queries and Results

An ontology gains practical value when it is able to give consistent answers to real-world questions. This section lists a number of questions a software developer faced with an e-poll software project is likely to come up with. These questions should not be regarded as exhaustive, but as indicative of what the ontology can deal with and reason about. Each of the questions is firstly expressed formally as an nRQL query, then the result of executing this query is presented, and finally, where appropriate, the rationale behind the result is explained.

Q1.   Which are the typical objectives of an e-poll system?

nRQL Query:
```
(retrieve (?obj) (?obj |Objective|))
```

nRQL Result:
```
(((?OBJ |Vote_Anonymity|))
 ((?OBJ |Confidentiality|))
 ((?OBJ |Availability|))
 ((?OBJ |Integrity|))
 ((?OBJ |Voter_Eligibility|))
 ((?OBJ |Accountability|))
 ((?OBJ |Accuracy|)))
```

Q2.   Which threats might compromise the vote anonymity objective?

nRQL Query:
```
(retrieve (?threat)
(|Vote_Anonymity| ?threat is_threatened_by|))
```

nRQL Result:
```
(((?THREAT |Impersonation|))
 ((?THREAT |Malicious_Code|))
 ((?THREAT |User_Error|))
 ((?THREAT |OS_Bugs|))
 ((?THREAT |Application_Bugs|))
 ((?THREAT |Attack_On_Voter_Terminal|)))
```

Q3. Which countermeasures protect a voter's personal data?

nRQL Query:
```
(retrieve (?cm)
  (|Voter_Data| ?cm |protected_by|))
```
nRQL Result:
```
(((?CM |Encryption|))
 ((?CM |Access_Control|))
 ((?CM |Certificates|))
 ((?CM |Intrusion_Detection_SW|))
 ((?CM |Malicious_SW_Detection|)))
```

Q4. Which countermeasures can prevent vote replay?

nRQL Query:
```
(retrieve (?cm)
  (?cm |Vote_Replay| |address|))
```
nRQL Result:
```
(((?CM |Identification|))
 ((?CM |Authentication|))
 ((?CM |Auditing|)))
```
Using identification and authentication we can audit the persons that have voted. To prevent them from voting again, we need to check the audit before accepting any vote.

Q5. Should the e-poll organizer be regarded as a threat to vote anonymity?

nRQL Query:
```
(retrieve () (|ePoll_Organizer|
  |Compromise_Anonymity| |realizes|))
```
nRQL Result: `T(rue)`

The e-poll organizer should not be trusted more than is necessary, especially since she is in a privileged position. Therefore, he should be regarded as a threat to vote anonymity.

Q6. Which assets are confidential?

nRQL Query:
```
(retrieve (?asset) (and (|Confidentiality|
  ?threat |is_threatened_by|) (?asset ?threat
  |damaged_by|)))
```
nRQL Result:
```
(((?ASSET |Ballot|))
 ((?ASSET |Voter_List|))
 ((?ASSET |Voter_Data|))
 ((?ASSET |Voter_Credentials|))
 ((?ASSET |Vote|))
 ((?ASSET |Cryptographic_Keys|)))
```
To answer this question, we first have to find the possible threats to the confidentiality objective and then list the assets that may be damaged by these threats. For example, confidentiality is threatened by user errors; and a user error may disclose the user's vote.

Q7.   Which countermeasures can prevent a hacker but not a vandal?

nRQL Query:
```
(retrieve (?cm) (and (and (|Hacker| ?threat
|realizes|) (not (|Vandal| ?threat |realizes|)))
(?cm ?threat |address|)))
```

nRQL Result: `((((?CM |OS_Permissions|))))`

Operating system permissions are likely to be more effective against a hacker's objectives than against a vandal's, since the vandal's main intention is to irrevocably destroy the system than to just alter its functionality.

Q8.   Which threats are not present in an homomorphic encryption voting scheme, but are present in other voting schemes?

nRQL Query:
```
(retrieve (?threat) (and (?schemes
|Voting_Schemes|) (and (?schemes ?threat
|damaged_by|) (not (|Homomorphic_Encryption|
?threat |damaged_by|)))))
```

nRQL Result:
```
(((?THREAT |Vote_Selling|))
((?THREAT |DoS_Attack|))
((?THREAT |Compromise_Anonymity|)))
```

Most e-voting schemes are based on homomorphic encryption, mixnets or secret sharing among several mutually distrustful election authorities [20]. The stated question aims to illustrate the threat environment in which homomorphic encryption has advantages compared to the other approaches. The justification of the answer is the following:

- In mixnet schemes, when the domain of the possible votes is sufficiently large, a voter may effectively uniquify his/her vote (e.g. by altering the vote's low-significance bits) and sell it to a buyer who had pre-chosen it. This is much harder to do in homomorphic encryption, as only an aggregate (sum) of the votes is disclosed and not the votes themselves.
- As mixnet schemes operate, they necessarily perform a massive amount of communication between the different parties. This makes them much more vulnerable to a denial-of-service attach than other schemes.
- Election schemes based on secret sharing among several mutually distrustful election authorities suffer from the vulnerability that, if a sufficient number of these authorities cooperate, they can link votes to voters. The security of the other schemes is not based on trust among authorities, and hence this vulnerability does not apply to them.

We believe we have demonstrated that the developed ontology is able to give useful answers to the questions a software developer faced with an e-poll software project is likely to come up with.

5. DISCUSSION

Questions similar to the ones presented in the previous section are very likely to come up in any design and development process concerning electronic voting, or electronic government applications. In these cases, designers and developers need to make critical decisions for security related issues. We believe that by employing a specialized ontology, such as the one presented in section three of this paper, all involved parties, including the people that will use the application to organize an electronic voting, as well as the developers, can have a common frame of reference and thus build a common understanding on security related issues.

A security ontology, in particular, such as the one presented in this paper, can be an aid to security critical issues, such as identifying the possible threats to the application that is being developed and deciding on the designated countermeasures to be incorporated at the early stages of designing and developing the application.

It should not go without mention, however, that to address the issue of secure applications effectively and thoroughly, developers need fully developed, specialized ontologies. In this paper we have presented an ontology that can be further developed and enhanced, so as to support the development of other security critical applications.

6. CONCLUSIONS AND FURTHER RESEARCH

In this paper we established that the process of developing a security critical application can be substantially facilitated by employing a specialized security ontology. To do this, we developed such an ontology for the domain of e-poll and demonstrated how software developers working in related software projects can use the ontology to get useful answers for a wide range of security questions. Furthermore, we argued that developing and using similar ontologies brings additional benefits, such as the formation of a common understanding among designers and developers.

We intend to further investigate the possibilities offered by employing security ontologies in this and other security critical contexts.

7. REFERENCES

1. Noy, N.F. and Mc Guinness, D.L. "Ontology Development 101: A Guide to Creating Your First Ontology", Stanford Knowledge Systems Laboratory Technical Report KSL-01-05. (2001)

2. CCTA, CRAMM User Manuals, ver. 5.0, United Kingdom, (2002)
3. IETF and W3C XML Signature Working Group. http://www.w3.org/Signature/
4. OASIS Security Service TC. Security Assertion Markup Language (SAML)
5. http://www.oasis-open.org/committees/security/ (accessed September 2004)
6. Bozsak, E., Ehrig, M., Handschub, S., Hotho: KAON - Towards a Large Scale Semantic Web. In: Bauknecht, K.; Min Tjoa, A.; Quirch¬ma¬yr, G. (Eds.): Proc. of the 3rd International Conference on E-Commerce and Web Technologies, (2002), pp. 304-313
7. Kagal, L., Finin, T., Joshi, A.: "A policy language for a pervasive computing en¬vironment". In IEEE 4th International Workshop on Policies for Dis¬tributed Systems and Networks, (2003)
8. Raskin, V., Hempelmann, C., Triezenberg, K., and Nirenburg, S.: Ontology in Information Security: A Useful Theoretical Foundation and Methodological Tool. In Viktor Raskin and Christian F. Hempelmann, editors, Proceedings of the New Security Paradigms Workshop, New York. ACM, (2001)
9. Chung, L.: Dealing with Security Requirements during the development of Information Systems. CaiSE '93. The 5th Int. Conf of Advanced Info. Systems Engineering. Paris, France, (1993)
10. Mylopoulos, J., Chung L., Nixon, B.: Representing and Using Non-Functional Requirements A Process Oriented Approach. IEEE Trans. Soft Eng., vol. 18. pp. 483-497 (1992)
11. Mouratidis, H., Giorgini, P., Manson, G.: An Ontology for Modelling Security: The Tropos Project. Proceedings of the KES 2003 Invited Session Ontology and Multi-Agent Systems Design (OMASD'03), United Kingdom, University of Oxford, (2003)
12. Liu, L., Yu, E., Mylopoulos, J.: Analyzing Security Requirements as Relationships among Strategic Actors. (SREIS'02), Raleigh, North Carolina, (2002)
13. He, Q., Antón, I., A.: A Framework for modeling Privacy Requirements in Role Engineering. Int'l Workshop on Requirements Engineering for Software Quality (REFSQ) Austria Klagenfurt / Velden (2003)
14. Moffett, D., J., Nuseibeh, A., B.: A Framework for Security Requirements Engineering. Report YCS 368, Department of Computer Science, University of York, (2003)
15. Antón, I., A.: Goal-Based Requirements Analysis. ICRE '96 IEEE Colorado Springs Colorado USA pp.136-144 , (1996)
16. Antón, I., A., Earp, B., J.: Strategies for Developing Policies and Requirements for Secure Electronic Commerce Systems. 1st ACM Workshop on Security and Privacy in E-Commerce (2000)
17. Uszok, A., Bradshaw, J., Jeffers, R., Suri, N., Hayes, P., Breedy, M., Bunch, L., Johnson, M., Kulkarni, S. and Lott, J. KAoS Policy and Domain Services: Toward a Description-Logic Approach to Policy Representation, Deconfliction and Enforcement. In Proceedings of the IEEE Workshop on Policy (2003)
18. Uszok, A., Bradshaw, J., Jeffers, R. (2004). KAoS: A Policy and Domain Services Framework for Grid Computing and Semantic Web Services. In Proceedings of the Second International Conference on Trust Management (iTrust 2004), Springer-Verlag
19. http://ontology.ihmc.us/ontology.html
20. Smith, W.: Cryptography Meets Voting, http://www.math.temple.edu/~wds/homepage/cryptovot.pdf
21. Protégé, http://protege.stanford.edu/
22. Racer Inference Engine, http://www.sts.tu-harburg.de/~r.f.moeller/racer/
23. The New Racer Query Language, http://www.cs.concordia.ca/~haarslev/racer/racer-queries.pdf

24. Denker, G., Access Control and Data Integrity for DAML+OIL and DAML-S, SRI International, USA, (2002)
25. Gruber T. Toward principles for the design of ontologies used for knowledge sharing, in Formal Ontology in Conceptual Analysis and Knowledge Representation, Kluwer (1993).
26. Web Ontology Language (OWL), http://www.w3.org/2001/sw/WebOnt/
27. O. Lassila, Ralph Swick (eds).: Resource Description Framework (RDF) Model and Syntax Specification, W3C Recommendation 22 February 1999, http://www.w3.org/TR/REC-rdf-syntax/

DEVELOPMENT AND EVALUATION OF A SYSTEM FOR CHECKING FOR IMPROPER SENDING OF PERSONAL INFORMATION IN ENCRYPTED E-MAIL

Kenji Yasu[1], Yasuhiko Akahane[2], Masami Ozaki[1], Koji Semoto[1], Ryoichi Sasaki[1]

[1]*Tokyo Denki University 2-2, Kanda-Nishiki-Cho, Chiyoda-Ku Tokyo, 101-8457 Japan;*
[2]*Nippon System Development Co.,Ltd. 3-3-7, Koraibashi, Chuo-Ku Osaka, 541-0043 Japan*

Abstract: There have been cases, in recent years, where customer information or other personal information has been leaked, and protective measures for personal information have become important. Corporations and other organizations have increasingly adopted software with e-mail monitoring capability to prevent leakage of personal information to the outside through e-mail. However, if the e-mail is encrypted, it is completely impossible to check whether personal information is being improperly sent. The authors have designed and implemented a system for solving such problems. Experiments to detect personal information were conducted using the implemented system, and we were able to confirm the basic effectiveness of the system. This paper reports on those results.

Key words: personal information, encrypted e-mail, check system, privacy, security, network

1.   INTRODUCTION

Problems such as the leakage of customer and employee information have become more serious due to the dissemination of the Internet, and measures for protecting personal information have become very important. On the other hand, encrypted e-mail (using protocols such as S/MIME to protect the confidentiality of e-mail from 3rd parties) is becoming more common.

However, if encrypted e-mail is allowed, there is a problem in that managers cannot check for leakage of personal information, and yet no studies have previously been done on checking for personal information in encrypted e-mail. The authors attempted to solve this problem by improving the S/MIME system which is widely used for encrypted e-mail, and thereby resolve these conflicting needs.

When Alice sends Bob an encrypted e-mail using the conventional S/MIME system, the encrypted e-mail can be decoded only by Bob, not by e-mail servers en route. So we designed an S/MIME system extended to enable conversion to plain text by a check system installed in the e-mail server. The message can be restored to the conventional S/MIME format by deleting the extension part of the data (created using the extended S/MIME system) before sending the message to the destination from the e-mail server.

Therefore, this system has the distinguishing feature that no special software to support extended S/MIME is needed on the side which receives the encrypted e-mail, and reception can be done with conventional e-mail software supporting S/MIME.

In this system for checking for improper sending of personal information, the message is first restored to plain text at the e-mail server, and then the system checks for personal information using pattern matching. However, checking for personal information only works for plain text, and one potential problem is that violators who wish to evade checking for personal information can do so by using some additional system besides encrypting with S/MIME to encrypt the main text or file attachments.

A check system for personal information is already commercially available, but problems like this have not been previously studied.

The authors' system aims to realize a system which can handle cases like this.

Section 2 describes the designed check system and the checking concept, and explains each check system. Section 3 describes implementation of the designed check system, and Section 4 describes the results of experiments conducted to evaluate the effectiveness of each checking technique using the implemented check system. Section 5 summarizes the paper and describes future issues and directions.

2. SYSTEM CONFIGURATION AND FUNCTION

2.1 System configuration

This paper considers a network configuration inside a small company, as indicated in Fig. 1. As the minimal set of users, it is assumed that there is an employee named Alice, and a manager above Alice. Before explaining the check system, we first describe the necessary preconditions.

a) Alice and Bob can send and receive encrypted e-mail.

b) Alice sends e-mail to Bob via the e-mail server T.

c) The system developed by the authors to check for improper sending of personal information is installed at the e-mail server T, and checks all e-mail which passes through.

d) As a person supervising subordinates, the manager does not engage in improper behavior.

The system will be explained assuming that these preconditions are satisfied. The following symbols are used in this paper in the explanation of encrypted e-mail given below.

P_B : Public key to Bob
P_T : Public key to mail server T
K : Common key
M : Mail message

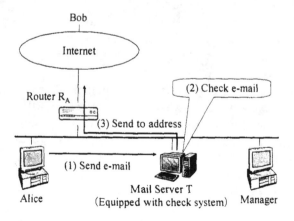

Figure 1. Network configuration

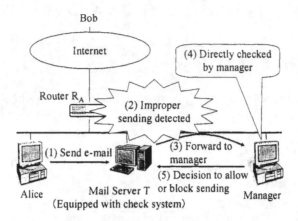

Figure 2. Flow when system discovers improper sending

When the check system detects e-mail suspected of being improper sending of personal information, a decision must be made based on things such as company policy. Here the e-mail is stopped so that it is not sent to the outside. The e-mail is also sent to the manager, who carefully examines the content of the e-mail, checks whether it is in fact improper sending of personal information, and makes a decision based on factors like company policy. If the manager carefully examines the detected e-mail, and determines there is no problem, then the manager can allow the check system to send the e-mail to the outside.

Installing the check system makes it possible for the manager to check only e-mail which is suspected of being improper sending of personal information. That reduces the manager's burden by reducing the number of e-mails which need to be checked.

In order for the check system to check encrypted mail, it is necessary to decrypt into plain text e-mail. However, conventional S/MIME uses the existing system indicated in Table 1, and is an encrypted e-mail format in which basically only the receiver Bob can decrypt the message. Therefore encrypting to plain text e-mail is impossible with the check system.

Thus the authors used the public key P_T for the e-mail server T to add an encrypted shared key for e-mail encryption to the conventional encrypted e-mail format, and thereby attempted to resolve the problem by adopting the system proposed in Table 1.

Table 1. Encrypted e-mail format

Method in the past	$P_B(K), K(M)$
Design method	$P_B(K), K(M), P_T(K)$

In the proposed system in Table 1, the check system can obtain a plain text e-mail message, according to the following procedure, when an encrypted e-mail is sent.

1) The check system obtains the shared key K by decrypting $P_T(K)$ using the secret key S_T of the e-mail server T.
2) The e-mail message M is obtained by decrypting $K(M)$ using the shared key K.

If the e-mail message decrypted in this way is found to have no problems after completion of the e-mail check described in Section 2.2, it is erased to protect confidentiality. By removing the $P_T(K)$ part from the encrypted mail prior to decryption, the message is converted to an encrypted e-mail format the same as the conventional format in Table 1, and then the message is sent. However, if the check system sends the message to the Manager due to suspicions of improper sending, the message is sent by adding the encryption of the shared key K using the Manager's public key to the conventional system.

The plain text mail only appears at the e-mail server T. Therefore, compared with the system where the sender sends plain text e-mail and encryption is done after checking at the server, this system enables protection of confidentiality on the in-house network, and thus has a higher degree of safety.

When the checked encrypted e-mail is sent to the outside, $P_T(K)$ is deleted, and thus the format is the same as the conventional S/MIME encrypted e-mail format. Therefore, this system has the advantage that the receiver can use e-mail software supporting S/MIME, just as before.

In-company users such as Alice must go through the trouble of installing a plug-in to extend the functionality of the e-mail software. However, encrypted e-mail is sent by automatically adding the public key P_T of the e-mail server T on the e-mail software side, so there is almost no extra burden.

2.2 Processing flow at the e-mail server

Section 2.1 described how the check system is installed in the e-mail server T, and how the system checks whether personal information is contained in any e-mail which passes through the e-mail server T. The authors believe that there is a problem in e-mail checking due to the fact that the check can be evaded by using improper encryption techniques. The following describes the concept underlying measures to counter this problem, and the flow of checking using those measures.

It is conceivable that legitimate users may send legitimate encrypted e-mail using the ordinary S/MIME system. However, if a user attempts to improperly smuggle out personal information via e-mail, knowing that each and every e-mail is checked, it is hard to imagine that the message will be sent as is in plain text. In other words, there is a possibility that the offender will attempt to smuggle out the information by using some technique for improper encryption (where their own encryption is applied to the e-mail body or attachment files) prior to encrypting with ordinary S/MIME.

Encryption techniques can be roughly divided into two categories: strong encryption which has randomness, and weak encryption which does not have randomness. The authors believe that check methods suited to each type should be applied to these two encryption techniques. It is likely possible to handle the majority of improperly encrypted e-mail by introducing a "strong encryption check" part to check for strong encryption techniques, and a "weak encryption check" part to check for weak encryption techniques. The aim here is to check for improperly encrypted e-mail before checking for personal information. If encrypted text is detected with these two checks, it is assumed that the e-mail is sent to the manager, not the outside, and handled based on the manager's discretion or in-house policy.

As pre-processing for these procedures, it was decided to check addresses, and thereby reduce the number of e-mails to be checked. In address checking, the system looks at the address and checks whether sending is prohibited (black address) or whether the address requires no checking (white address). If the check results indicate no problem, the e-mail is sent to the outside.

Fig. 3 shows the flowchart of e-mail check processing performed by the check system for improper sending of personal information, based on the above concept. Checking for personal information is done in the "personal information check" part in Fig. 3. The four check parts, including the "personal information check" part are described in detail in Section 2.3.

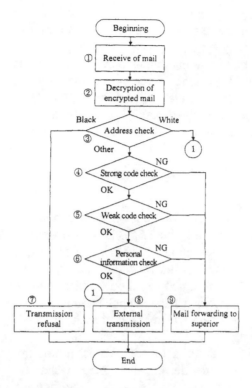

Figure 3. Processing flow at e-mail server

2.3 Each check system

The following describes the results of studying what sort of techniques to use for checking for each check system.

1) Address check

Two lists are created beforehand -- a black list to which sending of mail is prohibited, and a white list for which e-mail checking is unnecessary -- and during address checking, the system checks whether the address belongs on either of these lists. If either list applies, the result is "white" or "black", and if neither applies, the result is "other". The processing flow is as indicated in Fig. 3.

2) Strong encryption check

As explained above, if the e-mail is encrypted with ordinary S/MIME, but the data is encrypted beforehand (intentionally) with a system other than S/MIME, personal information checking cannot be done. Therefore, for strong encryption, it was decided to determine whether the encrypted text is random or not by using the randomized character of data produced by encryption.

For the method of determining randomness, we referred to the NIST[1] and chose three systems of testing randomness: the serial test, the linear complexity test, and the cumulative sum test. In order to improve the detection precision for encrypted text, it was decided to perform strong encryption checking using these 3 test systems. When these tests are performed, a value P is obtained as the result, and a determination of whether the text is encrypted or not is made by comparing with a threshold value.

3) Weak encryption check

Strong encryption checking was done for encryption techniques using strong encryption such as AES and Triple DES. However, with encryption techniques using weak encryption -- such as letter substitution codes or replacement codes -- the text is not random, so randomness will not work. Thus a check system was designed based on frequency of letter occurrence, where a message is suspicious if letters which shouldn't appear frequently do appear frequently, or if letters which should appear frequently don't appear frequently enough.

Here, it was decided to check for key words, in addition to characters. This makes it possible to detect encryption techniques using weak encryption which cannot be detected with a strong encryption check. However, encryption techniques employing weak encryption can be used to produce an infinite number of patterns, by just varying the technique, or the scope over which encryption is applied (ranging from the entire text to one part). Thus there is still a question whether all methods can be countered. Therefore, we also studied check systems which can handle other weak encryption systems.

As a new detection system, the authors developed a system for more efficiently detecting weak encryption by using the POPFile[2], spam filtering system which employs Bayes theory and in recent years has attracted attention as a countermeasure for spam e-mail due to its filtering precision.

4) Personal information check

As explained in Section 1, addresses, phone numbers and e-mail addresses appear with high probability in leaked personal information. Therefore, the authors performed personal information checking by detecting whether or not this type of information is contained in the message.

To detect personal information, the system extracts personal information from data using pattern matching, and finds the number of occurrences of each. If the number of occurrences for one type is 10 or higher, the system determines that it is possible that the data contains personal information. The reason that "10 of more" is used as the judgment criterion for personal information is that the number was decided by surveying reply mails not used for this experiment, from among past mail received by the authors themselves.

Table 2 shows the key words for extracting personal information. In general, it can be said that each type of personal information has the following characteristics.

a) Address

These are written using the geographical names of the prefecture, city, ward, town, and the numbers indicating things like blocks ("chome"). In some cases the prefecture name is omitted due to use of the postal code, but otherwise, it is always included.

b) Telephone numbers

Domestic telephone numbers always start with "0". In general, they are written by using a hyphen to separate different parts of the number, such as the area code and subscriber number.

c) E-mail addresses

These are written in half-size characters, using "@" to separate the account name and domain name.

The above features were described using regular expressions, and used as keywords to detect each type of personal information.

Table 2. Keywords using regular expressions

Item	Regular expression
Address	(\w+(City|Ward|Town|Village|County))+(\w| |)*?\d
Telephone number	[\((]{0,1}[0 0]\d{1,5}[\-———) (\)\(]{\d{1,4}[\-———) \)])\d{4}
Mail address	[0-9a-zA-Z \-\.]+@[0-9a-zA-Z \-\.]+

3.   IMPLEMENTATION

The authors developed: (1) a mail check program, implemented on an e-mail server, to check for improper sending of personal information, and (2) a plug-in to enable transmission of e-mail, encrypted using the system proposed in Table 1, with conventional mailers.

However, although the encryption system of the S/MIME compatible software needs to be modified so that things like $P_T(K)$ can be added, we were not able to obtain software supporting S/MIME which can be easily modified, and thus an implementation supporting the system proposed in

Table 1 was achieved by adding the minimum necessary function to a base of MIME system software.

As was described in Section 2.3, systems for weak encryption checking are currently being developed, so part (5) "Weak encryption check" in Fig. 3 (which shows the processing flow of the e-mail check program in (1)) has not been implemented. All other processing functions have been implemented.

The e-mail check program was implemented by using XMail[3] operating under Windows for the mail server, and the mail filtering capabilities of that software. The number of program steps is about 3000.

Also, AL-Mail32 (which enables functional extensions using plug-ins) was used for the client. However, encrypted e-mail is not supported by the standard version, so implementation was done by developing a plug-in equipped with a feature to automatically add the public key P_T of the mail server, and to enable sending and receiving of encrypted e-mail. The number of program steps was about 2800.

Table 3. Development Environment

Operating System	Windows XP
Development language	Microsoft Visual C++ 6.0

4. EVALUATION

4.1 Strong encryption check

Experiments were conducted to validate the effectiveness of the proposed strong encryption check system. To improve the precision of strong encryption checking, it was decided to detect encrypted text using 3 test systems[2]: the serial test, the linear complexity test, and the cumulative sum test.

P values were obtained from each test system as the analysis results, and these were compared with a preset threshold value (0.001). If the value was larger than the threshold, the text was determined to be encrypted. However, when multiple test systems are used, there is the problem of which P value to evaluate. Thus, the authors devised two methods of evaluating the P values obtained from the three test systems.

a) Minimum value evaluation method

Method of evaluation using the minimum of the P values obtained from each test system.

b) Maximum value evaluation method

The reverse of the method in a), where the maximum value is used.

In order to properly evaluate the detection accuracy of the minimum evaluation method and the maximum evaluation method, we compared detection accuracy using "precision rate" as defined by Eq. (1) and "recall rate" as defined by Eq. (2). Precision rate indicates the percentage of correct detections in the detection results, and recall rate is an index indicating the percentage of correct detections in detection results relative to all correct detections.

$$\text{Precision rate} = \frac{\text{Correct detections}}{\text{Correct detections} + \text{False positives}} \qquad (1)$$

$$\text{Recall rate} = \frac{\text{Correct detections}}{\text{Correct detections} + \text{False negatives}} \qquad (2)$$

Correct detections, false positives and false negatives (appearing in Eq. (1) and Eq. (2)) are defined as follows.

1) Correct detection

When encrypted text is judged to be "encrypted text"

When plain text is judged to be "non-encrypted text"

2) False positive

When plain text is judged to be "encrypted text"

3) False negative

When encrypted text is judged to be "non-encrypted text"

The reason that the case where plain text is judged to be "non-encrypted text" is included in 1) is that, if a certain plain text is checked and it is determined to be "non-encrypted text" this can be regarded as the correct detection of plain text which is not encrypted. Thus, the case where plain text is judged to be "non-encrypted text" can be defined as correct detection.

In 3), encrypted text is judged to be "non-encrypted text", so this can be regarded as missing encrypted text which should have been detected, and thus is defined as a false negative.

With the evaluation index now defined, experiments were conducted to evaluate which of the methods a) or b) was better. The data used in the experiment were 60 examples randomly selected from past e-mails received by the author himself. Text was extracted from these examples, and used as plain text. Encryptions of the plain text with Triple DES were used as the encrypted text.

In order to evaluate the maximum value evaluation method and the minimum value evaluation method, the precision rate and recall rate of each method were found, and these are indicated in Table 4. As explained in Section 1, the purpose of this research was to prevent the improper sending to the outside of personal information. Thus, to minimize the occurrence of the worst case where encrypted personal information is improperly sent to the outside, it is necessary to improve recall rate and minimize false negatives in strong encryption checking, even if there is some drop in precision rate.

Table 4. False positive rate for each evaluation method [%]

	Recall rate	Precision rate
Minimum value evaluation method	100	70.0
Maximum value evaluation method	98.3	97.5

When the two evaluation methods are compared using Table 4, the maximum value evaluation method has the highest recall rate, although the precision rate is somewhat low. Thus, it was concluded that using the maximum value evaluation method would be best.

Also the false negative rate for the maximum value evaluation method was 2.5%, but the data used was small in size (300 bytes or less), and 2.5% is thought to be a small amount for personal data which can be released at one time. Thus the system has safety as good or better than the numerical values.

4.2 Weak encryption check

For this system, we used an enhanced version of POPFile. Its effectiveness was studied by conducting various experiments on how to correctly differentiate between ordinary plain text and encrypted text which has been encrypted using a weak encryption system.

Due to space limitations, detailed results will be presented at another time, but it appears that a correctness rate of 80% may be possible if iterative learning is applied.

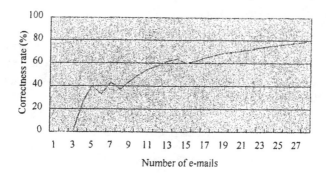

Figure 4. Experimental results for weak encryption check

In the future, we hope to raise the correctness rate, and reduce processing time.

4.3   Personal information check

A performance evaluation using the detection method described in Section 3.2 was conducted by detecting (respectively) addresses, telephone numbers and e-mail addresses, and finding their precision rate and recall rate, indicated by Eq. (1) and Eq. (2). For the experiment data, we used 4 data files in name-list format, containing a large amount of personal information. For this experiment, correct detection, false positives and false negatives were defined as follows.

1) Correct detection

When the correct information which should be detected is detected using pattern matching

2) False positive

When incorrect information which should not be detected is detected using pattern matching

3) False negative

When correct information which should be detected cannot be detected using pattern matching

If false positives are too frequent in detection of personal information, the system will mistakenly judge unrelated, normal e-mails to be cases of improper sending. If this happens, the number of e-mails to be checked by the manager will increase, and there is a risk that this will conflict with the goal of reducing work load. If there are too many false negatives, there will be an increase in misses, where e-mails involved in improper sending (which should be detected) are not detected, and there is a risk that it will be impossible to do proper checking for improper sending.

As a result of conducting experiments to detect personal information, it was possible to obtain results where the average precision rate and recall rate were each at least 95% (as shown in Table 5), and thus it was possible to show the effectiveness of the proposed system.

Table 5. Results of personal information detection [%]

Data Name	Address		Telephone number		E-mail address	
	Precision rate	Recall rate	Precision rate	Recall rate	Precision rate	Recall rate
A	99.5	99.6	100	95.3	100	99.4
B	100	100	100	100	-	-
C	100	99.2	98.9	98.2	100	98.3
D	99.0	99.5	97.5	96.8	100	98.6
Average	99.6	99.6	99.1	97.6	100	98.8

4.4 Evaluation of processing time

For this Section, experiments were conducted using three types of data: plain text e-mail, e-mail encrypted with strong encryption, and e-mail encrypted with weak encryption, and the processing time for each check was measured and evaluated using a Pentium4 2.4GHz PC. The results are as shown in Fig. 5.

Average processing times [sec]

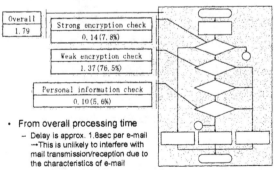

Figure 5. Evaluation of processing time

The average processing time per e-mail, averaged over all processing times, was approximately 1.8 seconds. Compared with the case where this check system is not installed, the system causes a delay of approximately 1.8 seconds per e-mail. However, the character of e-mail is such that a certain degree of delay is permissible, and thus it is thought that the delay is not a problem on the whole. However, it will be desirable to increase speed further in the future.

5. CONCLUSION

This paper: (1) proposed a system enabling checking for personal information at an e-mail server by enhancing S/MIME, and (2) presented a system to check for the outflow of specific personal information. A check system for improper sending of personal information was completed, and the various check functions were experimentally evaluated. In experiments on the function of personal information checking, the system was effective in detecting personal information using pattern matching. In experiments on the function of strong encryption checking, the system was effective for detecting encrypted text using the randomness test method. In evaluating the function of the overall system, the results showed it is possible to properly detect e-mail which may possibly be the improper sending of personal information, and that, for the most part, the evaluation of processing time revealed no problems.

Studies like the following will be needed in the future:
1) Improving detection precision, and reducing processing time, for weak encryption
2) Improving experiment precision for achieving practical application

6. REFERENCES

1. NIST Special Publication 800-22, A Statistical Test Suite for Random and Pseudorandom Number Generators for Cryptographic Applications, 2001.
2. POPFile, (last visit 20 April 2005); http://popfile.sourceforge.net/.
3. XMail, (last visit 20 April 2005); http://www.xmailserver.org/.

HYPR&A - A SECURITY MODEL FOR THE SUPPORT PROCESSES IN EGOVERNMENT

Tatyana Podgayetskaya, Wolffried Stucky
University of Karlsruhe, D-76128 Karlsruhe, Germany, {tpo,wst}@aifb.uni-karlsruhe.de

Abstract: During eGovernment processes often sensitive data are worked on. The authorization to work on or pass data on should not only of security policy certainly, but also by the technology and/or Business Process support systems (BPS Systems) to be supported. HyPR&A, hybrid process-oriented role and task security model, is a model for eGovernment organizations, which support eGovernment processes. In this article HyPR&A is developed and adapted on basis of architecture for Workflow Enactment services for BPS System

Key words: security model, workflow, information system, eGovernment.

1. INTRODUCTION

1.1 Problem definition. Output situation.

In eGovernment organizations process mostly follows the exact rules, i.e. they are already pre-defined, so that it often lacks flexibility and speed of the process execution. Causes for this can be endangered treatment of different process-referred tasks. This situation knows bureaucratic completion of existing data or missing support of exceptional cases due to e.g. absence of the partner, by the existing information system, as well as incorrect or missing allocation access rights of the responsible persons coworkers to necessary documents for the treatment of tasks.

1.2   Administrative processes in eGovernment

Processes in the eGovernment surrounding field, which support functions of the administration, are called administrative processes. The administrative coworkers (internal user) are to guarantee safe handling sensitive data and the use only for process purposes. During the information transfer in administrative organizations one can define two important aspects: on the one hand certain coworkers of the organization of the administration may work on only certain data of customer (external user), on the other hand some administrative processes are lokations spreading; thus the information flow concerns different fields, which are cared for by coworkers from different departments.

The conversion of administrative processes to eGovernment structures requires detail knowledge of the very different kinds of administrative operational sequence in such organizations eGovernment business process therefore exhibits - just like within other ranges like the free economy or the science - different complexity degrees.

The process modelling in the public organizations differs however from that one in enterprises particularly by legal aspects, if as by legal defaults no flexibility is possible and process modelling as well as Process Reengineering close borders are put. Therefore one speaks with the administration of a static sequence organisation contrary to the flexible process cycles with business enterprises. In addition comes still the hierarchical structuring of the public administration, which makes a fast adjustment more difficult to new conditions.

Thus now the organizations and ranges can be identified, within which is eGovernment possible. On the basis of the national administration interfaces result to the citizens (G2C), to here the second sector so mentioned, the economy, and not least to here the third sector so mentioned (von Lucke and Reinermann, 2000). This covers beside non-commercial and non-government organizations used ranges such as universities and hospitals.

1.3   Characteristic of eGovernment process

The eGovernment processes exhibit a set of characteristic characteristics, which differentiate them from other processes. These characteristics must be supported by a IT system:
- Each process is defined, implemented and controlled by an organization. This meant, an institution has such a process

- Special sensitivity because of the execution of sovereign document for natural or legal entities
- High safety requirements with pronounced data security (authentifizierte and encrypted data communication; clear defined access rights; examination and keeping of the user data)
- Constantly available service for the users (24/7)

Thus the next necessary step is the definition of the kinds of role, which are included into eGovernment -processes; these are the external users, i.e. those persons, who take eGovernment processes up and beneficiaries of their results are, as well as internal users, thus the woman employees and coworkers of those institutions, which implement these processes. An external user is a person, who takes a service up, which is implemented by means of a eGovernment process. In the predominant majority of all cases this person does not belong to the implementing organization, however also coworkers of the organizations can request these achievements. This clash of interest is solved by a dynamic division of tasks in the BPS System on architectural level. (Podgayetskaya et al., 2003; Podgayetskaya and Stucky, 2004).

1.4   Solution

In this article is introduced a hybrid process-orientated role and task security model in an Workflow environment (HyPR&A), suitably for eGovernment organizations. The HyPR&A model is based on the RBAC model (NIST, 2002, Sandhu et al., 1996) as well as the model of task and role (Schier, 1999) the characteristic consists of the fact that in this model a relationship from roles, objects and tasks to processes, which are supported by theBPS System is embedded. The HyPR&A concept is based on the consideration that one can control the information flows within a system by the allocation of the roles to tasks as well as the categorization of the roles and objects.

2.   SECURITY IN INFORMATION SYSTEMS

With respect to view to IT security with respect to information systems one can differentiate two aspects in the last years for the support from business process cycles with respect to systems: the development of roll-based access control models (RBAC), which are very well for the organization administrative structures in the enterprise and authorities suitable (Eckert, 2003), and process-oriented security models, which are specific for the business process completion in Workflow systems (Weiner et al., 2003; Hung and Karlapalem, 2003; Botha, 2001).

2.1   Access control in information systems

Access control system can be based on three principles, on DAC (discretionary access control), MAC (mandatory access control) and RBAC (role based access control).

The most important concept from DAC is that the user, who possesses the data is able, the entrance to these data to control. DAC steers the entrance to information based on the identity of the user as well as rules, who specify, which user entrance to which parts of information has DAC functioned only for the controlling of system-oriented resources such as data bases (Pernul, 1992), file systems etc. DAC cannot steer, when access rights can be given or extracted to subjects to objects.

MAC be based on hierarchical security level and assigns its own security stage to each user and each information part or each application. With MAC it can will prevent that a program (in form of a Trojan horse) releases a user file, however cannot not be prevented that a user releases independently his files. With RBAC access rights are bound not directly to a user, but at roles. Roles serve as template for the description of fields. Access rights are assigned to users indirectly by their role affiliation. It is differentiated according to four reference models for RBAC (Sandhu et al., 1996; NIST, 2002): basic RBAC; hierarchical RBAC; constrained RBAC; symmetric RBAC. RBAC supports several well-known security principles: information hiding, leases privilege, separation from tasks as well as data abstraction. However RBAC cannot be used directly to model in order to force security policy, since it was not developed, in order purpose and tasks from data to. (Fischer-Hübner, 2001; He, 2003).

2.2   Security models for Workflow environment

In the past ten years several security models for Workflow environments were developed, among them WAM (Workflow Authoriziation Model), which however only a static beginning for the treatment of the authorization river in the Workflow and data layer support, (Atluri and Huang, 1996) and MLS (Multilevel Security Workflow), which does not know a clear separation between fundamental workflow system components (Atluri et al. 1997).

With the help of roll and were based security model (R&A model) and the CoSAWoE model can the fundamental security requirements be fulfilled as far as possible, however the administration of resources and communication partners is not regarded here (Schier 1999).

W-RBAC (Weiner et al., 2003) the model contains controlled overwriting of restrictions and places a pair of roll-based entrance control models well-known for workflow systems forwards, generally as W-RBAC-models. In this work it is permitted, a clean separation of the tasks between authorization and workflow aspects of the system for the definition from preferences in the selection of the users, who implement tasks to accomplish.

The Secure Workflow Model of Hung and Karlapalem (2003) concerns itself with problems in heterogeneous environment, in which business processes run, and associated security requirements. In this work an authorizing model with invariants for Workflow in view to agents, events and data is presented and proven that the Workflow execution is safe. Unfortunately this model can be supported only heavily by existing techniques and systems.

The work of Weiner, Bartelmess and Kumar looks similar with their idea. The difference consists of it that by Weiner et al.(2003) as reason for authorizing the RBAC model of Sandhu is used, the control of workflow happens already on access control level. The difference between data flow and supervisory data flow as well as the level of workflow is by Weiner et al. (2003) in the model level missing, the control of workflow effected however because of the use of RBAC.

2.3 Architecture for eGovernment with security requirements

In principle all security models for workflow systems, regarded so far, refer to cross-organizational workflow. The use of RBAC techniques found increasing application within the eGovernment-range (Dridie et al., 2003). In the context of the project Webocracy service architecture CSAP was developed, in which a RBAC system was developed and implemented based on the core RBAC model. In CSAP the administrative requirements for the administration of roles, users and authorizations are implemented (Dridie, 2004). The use of RBAC models in information systems leads to the natural development of security models for workflow systems. Rutgers University's digitally Government Project develops at present in 'Model for dezentralized Workflow change management' (Atluri and Chun, 2003). Software producer Fabasoft offers the product to eGov Suite, the one roll-based organizational model with ACL (access control list) used, the structured and unstructured Workflows for eGovernment supported.

By Podgayetskaya and Stucky (2004) was suggested an IT architecture for eGovernment organizations. This architecture is based on the consideration, the existing technologies such as Workflow systems or Business Process Support (BPS) systems to use data base systems and web services for typical processes in organizations of the administration. The hierarchical structure of the public administrations is illustrated in the Workflow Enactment service of this model by components, so that the basic requirement of this service is fulfilled: To increase security of the data communication in open systems (Podgayetskaya et al., 2003) One of the most important aspects in this architecture is to cover security. Authentifizierung takes place via a central Registration server. Kerberos protocol are used for thies.

3. HYPR&A – HYBRID PROCESS-ORIENTATED SECURITY MODEL OF ROLE AND TASK

HyPR&A (hybrid process orientated security model of role and task) is a model for organizations of the administration, which support eGovernment - processes, those on the RBAC model (Sandhu et al., 1996; Fischer-Hübner, 2001) as well as are based to the model of task of role (Schier, 1999). In this model a relationship from objects and tasks to processes, which are supported by the BPS System, is embedded. The HyPR&A concept is based on the consideration that one can control the information flows within a system by the allocation of the roles to tasks as well as the categorization of the roles and objects.

3.1 HyPR&A Description

A basic idea of the HyPR&A Sicherheitsmodells lies in the allocation from roles and tasks to processes. The fundamental elements of HyPR&A are processes (P), tasks (A), roles (R), access rights (Z) as well as subjects (s) and objects (O). These elements stand in certain relations to each other.

A subject is called active element of a system. Such an element kannn a change in status cause. The subjects form the subject set of S. An object is called passive element of a system. An object can contain also personal data, e.g. of patient data or student data. The objects do not form the object set of O an element at the same time can actively and passive be.

Resources in the BPS System are all subjects and objects. Resources form a resources set of Ress, which consist of all subjects and objects.

Each system supports certain processes. Each process consists of a set of tasks, which are subject according to the possible processing sequences a partial order.

If the same tasks during different processes or during a process occur several times, they are regarded as different tasks. One can reach this if necessary by name additive and is thus no restriction of the public.

Certain objects are assigned to each process. An object can several processes be assigned at the same time and/or can in different tasks be at the same time worked on. The subjects (e.g. a person or a program), which similar knowledge and abilities have, form certain groups. These groups are called roles.

Roles are partitioned according to the activities by subjects, which fill out these roles, hierarchically. In this kind a role hierarchy is formed. In the information system. In our case we regard suggested architecture for BPS System (Podgayetskaya and Stucky, 2004).

Roles are all subjects, which are grouped after certain abilities for the treatment of the tasks, i.e. certain roles have certain rights to objects. Roles and access rights form in each case the role role of R and the access rights set of Z.

A subject is authorized by the BPS System to exercise certain roles or process tasks. The roles and tasks, which can be filled out and/or settled by subjects, are called authorized roles and authorized tasks.

The roles and tasks, which are filled out in each case and/or settled by subjects at this time, are called actuell roles and actuell tasks.

All data and/or objects during administrative processes, with which during these processes one works, can be differentiated according to five categories (internal_confidential, internal_open, internal_private, external_private, external_open).

Into the HyPR&A concerning role administration in the BPS System in four categories are divided. Within a category the roll-hierarchical structure is maintained. These categories correspond to structures in organizations of the administration (administrator, process_owner, process_manager, external_user).

The allocation of the categories of objects and roles is represented in table.

Table 1. Interaction of object and role categories

Categorie of objects and roles	internal_conf idential	internal_ open	internal_private	external_ private	external_open
administrator	x	x		x	x
process_owner	x	x	x	x	x
process_manager		x			x
external_user				x	x

Here x means entrance from (categorie of) roles to objects (of objects).

3.2   HyPR&A in Entity Relationship notation

The subjects, objects, tasks, process, roles already and access rights are introduced form in each case the subject set of S, object set of O, task set of A, process set of P, role role of R and access right set of Z. These sets are represented as entity types S, O, A, P, R and Z for the he modelling.

The connections between these entity types are now following-measured as relations represent (whereby some characteristics lead to possible statements across the cardinality (1:n and n:m)).

The relations AP (allocation from tasks to processes) exists, RH (role hierarchy is represented as relationship between arbitrary roles), SR (a relationship between subjects and roles), AR (the role task-dependentness), SA (all possible authorized tasks for subject), SAR (role dependence of task of subject), ZR (relationship from access rights to roles), and OP (relationship from objects to processes).

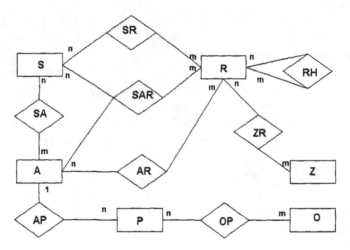

Figure 1. HyPR&A in ERM notation

3.3   Security characteristics

The security characteristics of the model was developed as being certain rules for the security model. These should remain unchanged, so that the model ensures its robustness.

1. Validation

The relations in HyPR&A support only permitted respectively valid pairs. If the arising pairs in one do not seem to the relationship described above, they are rejected immediately by the security modeland the further execution of the process is broken off.

2. Object categorization and allocation.
   The objects are first categorized and assigned afterwards to processes.

3. Role categorization and allocation.
   The categorization of the roles applies to each role. Within a category incomparable pairs can be. It is to be stressed that this rule does not stand in the contradiction for hereditary relationship with the right assignment, because this follows the roll-hierarchical principle.

Table 2. Example

category	hierachy	role	subject
external_user	1	graduate students	Mr. Studentmann
	0	undergraduate students	
	1	tutor	

Possible roll-hierarchical structures within this category
{graduate students(subject), undergraduate students(subject)}, so that undergraduate students(subject) < graduate students(subject) – {0 < 1} ;
{tutor(subject), undergraduate students(subject), so that undergraduate students(subject) < tutor(subject) – {0 < 1}.
- Determined pairs, e.g. {tutor(subject), graduate student(subject)} one can regard as incomparable pairs for subject.

4. Task-Role-Subject
   A subject can select several tasks as well as several roles within a process, if these tasks for it are authorized (definition, relation SA) and if the subject is assigned to an authorized role (definition, relation SR). A subject may update these tasks (to settle), if it is justified due to the task(s)-role(s) relationship to it (relation SAR).

5. Subject Object Relationship
   A subject can access the objects within the process, if the authorized role as well as the tasks (relations SA, SR) are categorized valid and the role(s).
   A subject may access several objects within the process, if a combination of role(s) – task(s) pair(s) valid for it, exists (relation SAR) and the allocation object role category is correct (table 1). This means that certain conditions must be fulfilled. A subject may accept several roles, which are not mutually exclusive. Further the subject in this role or one of these roles must be allowed to settle the assigned tasks.

Finally it must be examined whether the intended role(s) – task(s) combination is valid. Only if these conditions are fulfilled, the possibility that this subject in these roles may access this object exists, in order to settle the tasks within this process.

3.4   HyPR&A model as RBAC and Workflow Unit

We plot HyPR&A. Here (Figure 2) the two ranges workflow unit and role-based beginning are shown as RBAC for the conversion in an information or a BPS system. The connection between Rbac and Workflow architecture consists of the roles and objects, which the information or BPS system contains.

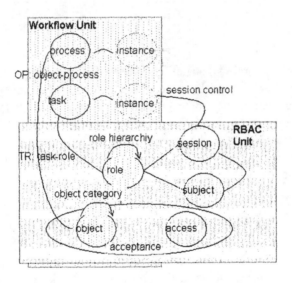

Figure 2. HyPR&A as workflow and RBAC units

The structure of HyPR&A is adapted to the architecture of the Workflow Enactment service and/or to the architecture of the Workflow engines (Podgayetskaya and Stucky, 2004). The HyPR&A structure is two-dimensional: the vertical level consists the Workflow unit, horizontal has the RBAC unit. The Workflow represents the control and data flow, thus on the one hand the respective tasks and their processes as well as on the other hand in and to outgoing data each the tasks. In HyPR&A the supervisory data flow marks the allocation from objects to processes as well as from tasks to processes. Data flow clarifies the allocation of roles and objects as well as of tasks and roles.

3.5   HyPR&A during the registration process

The expiration of registration is a ordinary process in numerous organizations of the administration such as hospitals (patient admission), citizen office or universities (seminar -, examination registration). This process is identified-drawn due to the active participation of external users as external process. For the expiration of registration the following steps are characteristic:

1. The user selects exactly one process, which he/she needs with the announcing procedure[1]
2. Afterwards he/they registers the necessary data e.g. in the form and
3. sends or hands this to the registration office over for further treatment

Here a process in a university one regards. We represent only registration for an examination. A subject is assoziert in this case with a studying. The role designated student for this role category (external user). In Figure 3 (left) is sketched this external announcing process in Petri Net notation. Figure 3 (right) points the HyPR&A support of this announcing process, thus the assignment of objects to roles and tasks as well as the expiration of assignment of appropriate access rights to a subject.

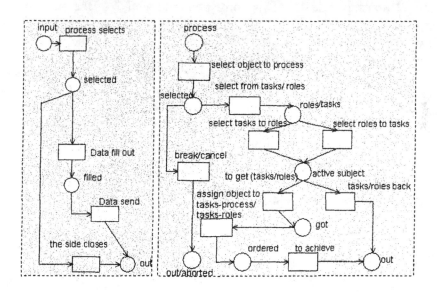

Figure 3. Cutout from external processes: on the left of expiration of announcing, on the access rights assignment in HyPR&A

---

[1] Within a process one can differentiate several process procedures, e.g. as registration with respect to the citizen office can only registration to the examination with respect to a university.

In the first step of the announcing procedure the objects are assigned to processes. But the necessary pairs from the relationship OP (object-process) are selected by the BPS system. According to the rules 2 and 3 is already categorized the roles as well as the assigned objects.

If the external user breaks the announcing procedure off and/or closes the side, the support of the process is broken off in accordance with HyPR&A by the BPS system. Also in the case the fact that the role selected task and/or the task of the roles enspricht (corresponds), e.g. the task may not do only by external user is implemented, the arrangement to objects refused and further not accomplished (Figure right; rule 1).

If an external user wants to resume the announcing procedure, certain tasks are assigned to the process (relationship task-process AP) and thus makes possible for the subject to exercise it.

HyPR&A ensures for the fact that these tasks of roles are assigned, which settle this role (can) to be able or that turned around this role for this assigned task during the process for the practice of the tasks responsibly is (relationship of task-roles AR).

The subject will update the role and/or tasks (relationship SA, SR) and only for it permitted role tasks - combinations during this process exercise (SAR relationship, rule 4). This corresponds to step 2 of the announcing procedure 'filling out the form'.

For execution of the third step 'delivery of the form to the registration office' rule 5(subject object relationship) is used over the assigned rights for the subject (relationship RZ). This means: the subject updates the role and tasks and has the possibility of exercising this role and of implementing the tasks. The data of the subject in an object of the category are external_private stored and passed on from the system to the treatment.

So only one role can be assigned as external users and only with the ensprechenden tasks, which are intended for this process and this role, during this process. The objects are assigned to the process in the system, so that according to categorization the respective process one makes.

The external as well as internal processes can contain confidential data. These data will be categorized in our model as well as in the system as internal_confidential, internal_private or external_private objects. The available case concerns only external_private objects.

For the treatment of the process in rule or several staff member of the organization is responsible. Therefore it is meaningful to assign to tasks of working on certain roles. Certain roles are responsible for certain tasks, therefore the sequence of the role tasks is not relevant - or task role arrangement.

The following allocation is made by the BPS system (table 3):

Table 3. HyPR&A allocation by BPS system

process	registration
category of object	external_private
object	person_date
category of role	external_user
role	student
	fill data
task	send data
	close site
subject	M. Mustermann

The execution of HyPR&A is independent of the process procedure, i.e. the HyPR&A rules apply to all processes, which are supported by the information and/or BPS system. Reason for it is the choice of the process as the first step, afterwards follows the independent allocation of tasks, roles and objects, which belong to this process.

4. SUMMARY

In this article a security model HyPR&A is suggested, which can be adapted to safety requirements in organizations of the administration. HyPR&A combines the conception of roles and objects in both concepts: Workflow and RBAC. This has the consequence that in accordance with the allocation to roles and tasks as well as from objects to processes access rights are assigned to the subjects

The structure of HyPR&A is adapted to the architecture of the Workflow Enactment service and/or to the architecture of the Workflow engines. The supervisory data flow runs in both directions: vertically and horizontal. Roles and objects are connected with the expiration component, which represents the processes in the information or BPS system.

A impotant aspect in the interaction of the architecture BPS system and the security model is the analysis and modelling of the Workflow models for applications. The safety requirements in the Workflow models presented here concern the data security. Due to its structure consisting of two units HyPR&A is well suitable for the support of these requirements. The structure of the Workflow unit corresponds to the expirations, objects and roles of the Workflow models; the RBAC unit exercises according to access supervision the roles. For the implementation of HyPR&A these Workflow models are thus in ancestor leaning to the suggested architecture BPS system respectively the Workflow engine developed.

At present exists no universal safety model, which fits for each system ideally and can cover all security requirements 100%. Therefore its own security model should be developed just like the processes themselves running in the system for each system on the basis of existing classical security models. HyPR&A, hybrid process-oriented security model of role and tasks, functioned in Workflow environments and is geeiget only for organizations of the administration, whose tasks, roles and data are connected with processes and their process cycles are more or less vordefinert. For this reason accurate categorization comes of objects and roles.

5.   REFERENCES

Atluri, V. and Chun, S.A., 2003, Handling Dynamic Changes in Decentralized Workflow Execution Environments, *DEXA 2003 Proceedings*: P. 813 - 825.

Atluri, V. and Huang W.-K. , 1996, An Authorization Model for Workflows, Proceedings of the 4th European Symposium on Research in Computer Security: *Computer Security*: P. 44 – 64.

Atluri, V., Huang W.-K. and Bertino, E., 1997, An Execution Model for Multilevel Seccure Workflows, *Proceedings of the IFIP TC11 WG11.3*: P. 151 – 165.

Botha, R.A.., 2001, CoSAWoE - A Model for Context-sensitive Access Control in Workflow Environments. *Dissertation, Rand Afrikaans University* i.Br.

Dridi, F., Muschall, B., Pernul, G., 2003, An Administration Console for the CSAP System. In: *Short Paper Proceedings of the 15th Conference on Advanced Information Systems Engineering (CAiSE 2003)*: P.345-350.

Dridi, F., Muschall, B.and Pernul, G., 2004., Administration of an RBAC System. Proc.of the 37th Hawaiian International Conference on System Sciences (HICSS 2004):P. 1014-1026

Eckert, C., 2003, IT-Sicherheit. Oldenburg.

Fischer-Hübner, S., 2001, IT-Security and Privacy: Springer Berlin et al.

He,Q., 2003, Privacy Enforcement with an Extended Role-Based Access Control Model NCSU *Computer Science Technical Report TR-2003-09*.

Hung, P. C. K., Karlapalem K.: A secure workflow. Proceedings of the Australasian information security workshop conference on ACSW, 2003, V21: P. 33 – 41.

Pernul, G.,1992, Security Constraint Processing During Multilevel Secure Database Design, in *Proceedings of Eighth Annual IEEE Computer Security Applications Conference*,: P. 229-247.

NIST, 2002, The Economic Impact of Role Based Access Control. Research Triangle Institute. *NIST Planning Report 02-01*..

Podgayetskaya, T., Ratz, D. and Stucky, W., 2003, Modell eines Workflow-Systems zur Erhöhung der Sicherheit von Web Services, Proceedings E. Otner (Hrsg.) in Symposium Entwicklung Web-Services basierter Anwendungen. In Rahmen der 33. Jahrestagung der GI: P. 37-52.

Podgayetskaya, T., Stucky, W., 2004, A Model of Business Process Support System for E-Government. DEXA 2004 *Proceedings. Published by the IEEE Computer Society*, P2195: P.1007-1015.

Sandhu, R.S., Coyne, E. J., Feinstein, H.L. and Youman, C.E., 1996, Role-Based Access Control Models, *IEEE Computer* 29(2): P. 38- 47.

Sandhu, R.S., Ferraiolo, D. F., Kuhn, D. R., 200, The NIST Model for Role Based Access Control: Towards a Unified Standard, Proceedings, 5th ACM Workshop on Role Based Access Control, P.26-37.

Schier, K., 1999, Vertraurenswürdige Kommunikation im elektronischen Zahlungsverkehr. *Dissertation*, Universität Hamburg i.Br.

Wainer, J., Barthelmess, P., and Kumar, A, 2003, W-RBAC - A Workflow Security Model *Incorporating Controlled Overriding of Constraints. J of Coop. Inf. Sys.4,*: P. 455-48.

POLICY-RICH MULTI-AGENT SUPPORT FOR E-HEALTH APPLICATIONS [1]

Lars Braubach[1], Winfried Lamersdorf[1], Zoran Milosevic[2], Alexander Pokahr[1]

[1] *Hamburg University, Department of Informatics, Distributed and Information Systems (VSIS), Vogt-Kölln-STr. 30, D-22527 Hamburg, Germany*

[2] *CRC for Enterprise Distributed Systems Technology (DSTC), c/o The University of Queensland, Level 7, General Purpose Building South, Q 4072 Brisbane, Australia*

Abstract: Modern hospital environments represent complex, distributed, and cross-organisational enterprises with a variety of complex and distributed systems applications. They include a multitude of resources at different places, they have to accommodate real-time requirements, and they have to support rather complicated and, in many cases, unforeseeable business processes. Many processes must strictly follow certain sets of rules, and both process and resource usage have to be dynamically optimized to guarantee the best service to all patients at all times. This paper discusses how state-of-the art agent technology, enriched with expressive policy constraints, can be used to support provision of better quality care for patients and more efficient health service delivery to health professionals. We apply results of our research in multi-agent systems and policy modelling to a set of requirements in the e-health domain.

Key words: Health applications, scheduling, distributed systems, (multi-) agent technology, event based policy monitoring.

[1] This work has been funded, in part, by the Co-operative Research Centre for Enterprise Distributed Systems Technology (DSTC) through the Australian Federal Government's CRC Programme (Department of Education, Science, and Training) and by the Deutsche Forschungsgemeinschaft (DFG) through the priority research programme (SPP) 1083 "Intelligent Agents in Real-World Business Applications".

1.   INTRODUCTION

Modern health care environments represent fairly complex examples of distributed enterprises and distributed applications. They provide a variety of rather complex and heterogeneous resources at different places, they have to accommodate requirements of quite complicated and – in many cases – unforeseeable workflow ("business") processes, which again have to strictly follow certain sets of rules and restrictions. Hospital environments today and health jurisdictions in general are faced with a rather high amount of complexity due to their inherent dynamics of the processes and distributed organization structure.

In this paper we consider new features of health care systems and identify some emerging technologies as enablers to deliver better quality care to citizens and more efficient service delivery to health professionals. We investigate a broader set of issues and a broader set of solutions based on distributed agent technology than the resource scheduling aspects as presented in (Paulussen et al. 2003). We consider other health areas where this technology could be applied, particularly in cases where agents could be used to monitor activities and policies of various actors in the system.

Section 2 highlights new features of health systems and possible technologies that could help deliver more effective and efficient services. Sections 3 and 4 outline distributed agent technology and a specific policy language respectively. These two solutions are to be integrated to support the features identified, as presented in section 5. Section 6 summarises key observations from the paper and outlines possible future research directions.

2.   NEW FEATURES OF HEALTH CARE DELIVERY

The nature of health care is changing because of a number of societal factors including the increasing pressure on health professionals and more educated population at large. This section summarises some of the new features and requirements related to the service delivery in the health domain. We provide several ideas how some information and communication technology (ICT) systems could be applied to support these new features.

2.1   Continuity of care and a patient-centric focus

There is an increasing pressure on health providers to deliver better and more effective care to consumers while ensuring economic efficiency of service provision. This requires seamless interoperability between business processes crossing organisational and jurisdictional boundaries and thus better integration and interoperability between the underlying ICT systems of various service providers. Consider, for example, the *care continuum* principle which denotes consumer care that spans public services, community services and acute services of public health providers but also, general practitioners and other non-government organisations. The main premise of this principle is that care of citizens (i.e. population) should start from early preventions, increasingly involving community services and that the acute services of hospitals should be utilised only when necessary. Another similar principle, the *continuity of care*, is oriented towards a single consumer going through an episodic session. This principle aims at ensuring smooth continuity of service delivery to the consumer while being discharged from one and assigned to one or more other health providers.

These two principles require a uniform view of a consumer (from both the individual and population perspectives) across all service providers and possibly all health jurisdictions with an implication for unique and reliable information about customers. This will ensure smoother delivery of care to consumers on their clinical path, and more efficient service delivery to service providers. For example, various *electronic health records (EHR)* initiatives form significant steps towards providing smoother delivery of care to citizens in their lifetime and also at the episodic level – in particular taking into account cross-organisational nature of service delivery. One example is Australian Health*Connect* initiative where current trials focus is on keeping standardised summary information about health events (e.g. health consultations and diagnostic test results) and recording EHR data such as patient's current medications and principal diagnoses (Health*Connect*).

2.2 Integration of health applications

Many existing systems in the health industry have been developed over many years using various generations of ICT technology, often adopting solutions of various vendors in an ad hoc manner. As a result, a typical health application system consists of many independently developed silos, frequently resulting in redundancy and duplication of information leading to inadequate and delayed treatment to consumers, e.g. unnecessary repetition of previous tests or examinations. This also adds unnecessary costs to the already stretched public funding of health jurisdictions.

In order to address this problem, many public health organisations are going through a transformation of their systems and processes, with an increasing focus on producing *enterprise architectures* for consolidating existing and delivering more interoperable future ICT systems. Examples are recent efforts in the UK, where there is a requirement that enterprise architectures for health also need to be aligned with UK's e-Government Interoperability Framework (eGif). Similar initiatives, but with a less cross-government alignment are in the US (eGov) and in Australia (NEHTA).

2.3 Sensitivity and privacy issues

While the emerging ICT systems will provide facilities for better recording of patients' health information as in case of electronic health record, there are many new challenges such as making sure that information about patients is exchanged and accessed according to patients' consents. For example, a patient may demand that only certain health professionals are allowed, while others are not, to view their EHR – and this consents need to be enforced. This is of particular importance in the environment of independent cooperating healthcare facilities and raises issues of defining the consent rules and monitoring the access and information exchange between independently governed health providers.

One solution for a privacy-preserving transfer protocol which ensures that access to the health information at the receiving facility continues to be governed by the patient's consent is discussed in (O'Keefe et al.).

2.4 Coordination of health-care delivery

The increasingly collaborative nature of health delivery, involving various health service providers, coupled with best-care practice guidelines and care plans for individual patients, requires a systematic approach to describing steps involved in episodic treatment of consumers. Some of the steps can be applied sequentially while others could apply concurrently and there is often information exchange between these steps. All these aspects require a way of describing collaborative service delivery, in a way similar to business processes in many industries, but also with more flexibility to reflect urgent or unexpected occurrences that need to be dealt with.

Possible ways of supporting such a collaborative environment is through the event-based coordination and choreography technologies as discussed in (Berry and Milosevic, 2005) or by utilising a distributed agent technology to support distributed and autonomous decision making.

2.5 Scheduling of resources

In many countries, the aging population and increasing mobility of people place significant pressure on medical staff and on the resources in hospitals, clinics and other health organisations. This requires sophisticated facilities for scheduling of resources. Although this area has been subject of previous research, the new health environment requires increasingly dynamic allocation of resources. Decentralized coordination among all involved parties (e.g. a local practitioner and a hospital) assures timely treatment of patients, and better utilization of scarce medical resources.

Solutions based on agent technology, e.g. as described in (Paulussen et al., 2003, and Paulussen et al., 2004) are well suited to address both the dynamics and uncertainty of the domain, as well as the inherently distributed and decentralized decision making in the context of resource scheduling.

2.6 Monitoring and public accountability

The size and complexity of health systems, and involvement of many actors in service delivery, require better monitoring of services. The large number of significant events that may require urgent attention introduces the need for a powerful notification mechanism to ensure safety of health delivery. To this end, event-based monitoring engines could be deployed to support run-time detection of sub-optimal or inadequate service delivery and generation of reminders to the staff for timely delivery of health services.

Further, a more collaborative and patient-centric delivery of health services will rely on standardised electronic health records (EHRs), and will also increasingly require more transparent access to key policies and best practice guidelines. This is also to support new philosophy in health delivery towards evidence-based treatment. While some policies refer to security and privacy as described above, other policies will also apply to the public accountability of health professionals. They will need to express duties and responsibilities of doctors, nurses and other service providers. One approach to describing enterprise policies that could be refined for the health domain is described in (Linington et al., 2004, Milosevic et al., 2004a, 2004b).

3. SUPPORTING E-HEALTH APPLICATIONS WITH AGENT TECHNOLOGIES

The previous section has introduced application characteristics of the health domain that put forth new demands on the technical infrastructure used to build ICT systems supporting health service delivery. *Agent technology* (see, e.g., Jennings and Wooldridge, 1998) provides a modelling paradigm and software infrastructure to support treating relevant subsystems of health service providers as autonomous self-dependent actors. The agent paradigm provides a natural means for communication with domain experts, as there is a direct mapping of organizational structures to technology. Moreover, software agents allow for system integration by wrapping ('agentifying') legacy code respecting the decentralized heterogeneous IT structure, existing in the health care sector (Nealon and Moreno, 2003).

3.1   The general BDI agent model

To support e-health applications, software agents could be designed and implemented to work on behalf of patients to ensure that care goals are satisfied or care plans are satisfactorily executed. They can be also implemented to support health professionals or health regulators to ensure that respective policies and guidelines are met. In general, the agent model is well suited for such applications because it is capable to capture the anthropomorphic aspects of patients or health providers in a quite natural way, through the so called "Belief-Desire-Intention" (BDI) model and theory which is based on mentalistic notions. The inner structure of such agents can be subdivided into beliefs, goals, and plans (Rao and Georgeff, 1995):

Beliefs represent what this agent knows/assumes about its environment. Beliefs are created through actions such as getting current state of environmental parameters including measuring their values, observing events of change or time passing, getting information about agents such as their location behaviour, progress of their processes and so on. *Goals* describe what is expected of agents to perform, what kind of state is to be achieved, or maintained or what policy should hold. *Plans* are concrete courses of action, performed by the agent to achieve its objectives; for example what are acceptable options for scheduling a patient with cardiac problems through various health departments to minimise her waiting time.

In addition to these mentalistic notions, BDI also offers a mechanism that allows deducing the agent actions in a rational manner from the current context. Thereby, goals can be seen as one motivational source for generating actions, as for a goal being pursued the BDI mechanism selects applicable plans under consideration of the current situation represented by the beliefs. These plans will subsequently get executed until the goal is reached or becomes unreachable (Braubach et al., 2004).

3.2   The multi-agent platform Jadex

The BDI model as briefly sketched above is implemented in the newly developed multi agent platform *Jadex*, which enhances the traditional BDI architectures in several aspects (Pokahr et al. 2005). Most notably, Jadex supports explicit goal representation and has built-in deliberation support for possibly conflicting goals.

In Jadex we distinguish between four goal types that address fundamentally different behaviour: perform, achieve, query and maintain. A *perform* goal is directly associated with actions that should be performed. An example could be "perform ward round". An *achieve* goal describes a world state that should be brought about, e.g. "achieve x-ray examination for patient Miller". *Query* goals are a means for an agent to retrieve information, for example "query charge nurse of the children's unit". Finally, *maintain* goals can be used to monitor a certain world state and re-establish this state whenever it gets violated, e.g. a "maintain antibiotics available" could be used to automatically reorder urgently needed medicaments.

Figure 1 depicts the Jadex architecture. At an abstract level, an agent can be seen as a black-box receiving and sending messages. Incoming messages, internal events and goal expressions are input for the agent's reaction and deliberation mechanism. Deliberation is thereby performed on two levels.

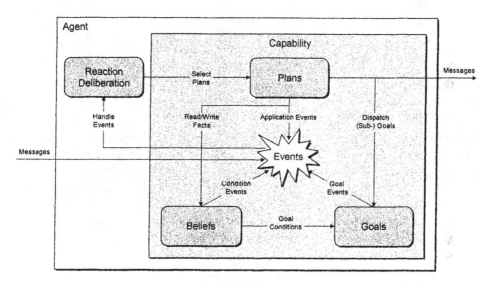

Fig. 1 Jadex architecture

On the goal level the component is responsible for deciding which goals currently need to be pursued. On the plan level, the traditional BDI mechanism as outlined in (Rao and Georgeff, 1995), is applied to select an option to bring about a given goal. To this end, all plan candidates applicable in the current context will be searched from the library of plans that contains the complete procedural knowledge set of an agent. From this set the agent will select the most acceptable by performing meta-level reasoning and will attempt to carry this plan out. If the plan fails the plan selection process starts over again, meaning that the agent can recover from plan failures by searching for alternative ways of achieving a goal.

When the agent processes incoming messages or internal events its behavior is more reactive as only deliberation on plan level is performed. At runtime plans can access the full range of BDI specific and general purpose actions, such as accessing the belief base, creating new top-level or sub-goals, and sending messages to other agents.

A Jadex agent consists of two kinds of specifications. On the one hand the static structure of an agent type is defined in an agent definition file (ADF), including the specification of its initial beliefs, plans and goals. The ADF is an XML file, which complies with the Jadex language as defined in a BDI meta-model within XML Schema. This structure specification is augmented by a declarative expression language for all elements such as goals and beliefs, which follows the Java syntax. The plan code, on the other hand, is written in Java and can access the BDI specific agent characteristics through an API.

4.   EVENT-BASED POLICY MONITORING

The combination of event-based technology capabilities and business pressures towards better governance, more accountability and better compliance, have placed more emphasis on *event-based monitoring* of enterprise systems. In the past, monitoring aimed at providing dashboard-like information about the status of the system and generation of appropriate alarms and notifications to signify undesired states of the system.

However, the current regulatory and legal policies require more proactive and real-time detection of policies or best practice violations of key actors involved in enterprise systems. This is true for both commercial and government environments. In addition, some inadequate medical treatments and health service delivery in a number of countries have identified a need for similar approaches to the public accountability in health domain. The situation is however more difficult in this domain, considering the complex nature of services and resource pressures in many health jurisdictions.

To partly address these issues, we believe that it is valuable to consider how some of the benefits of the agent technology discussed above could be augmented with policy-based constraints associated with agent's behaviour. This in turn would facilitate support for the event-based monitoring of selected activities of patients and health professionals.

In health applications, there is a wide range of policies that apply, with different measures to be taken in case of violations. These range from those that do not have significant risk on patients to those that have high risks and are not allowed to be violated at all. Accordingly, there are various measures that could apply such as preventative enforcement for the policies whose violations would have life-critical consequences to more discretionary enforcement in cases where failures to satisfy policies do not have so severe consequences. Below, we provide some examples of policies which may apply in the health domain. For example:

"A nurse is obliged to report to the doctor at least one day after the patient's examination".

"A doctor must not reveal the results of an examination before the patient gives permission for that".

"A doctor is allowed to prescribe (only) medicine which costs less than $ 1000".

"The waiting time for any patient before being assigned to a resource shall not exceed 2 hours".

In our previous work we have developed a generic policy language that is inspired by a deontic logic formalism. This language was used as part of a broader business contract language (BCL), as presented in (Milosevic et al., 2004a, 2004b). The language provides a declarative way of expressing key policies such as permissions, prohibitions and obligations similar to the natural language expressions. In brief, the key concepts of the language are:

* Behavioural constraints, expressed in terms of *event patterns*; an event pattern describes the relationship between events that reflect one or more actions of actors, or other occurrences such as changes in states of environmental variables; event patterns specify some combination of events of relevance for a policy; a singleton event type is used when listening for occurrences of a single event
* The organisational *role* to which the policy (i.e. the corresponding event pattern) applies
* The *modality*, i.e. obligation, permission or prohibition;

By applying this policy language, the policies as introduced in natural language introduced above could be expressed as follows.

```
Policy:     NurseReporting
Role:       Nurse
Modality:   Obliged
Condition:  AdviseDoctor after (PatientExamination) and before (PatientExamination add 1 day)
```

In this obligation policy above, the *AdviseDoctor*, *PatientExamination*, and *PatientExamination* are event types and their relationship is expressed as an event pattern. In this example we use *after*, *before*, *and* and *add* relationship operators. For a more detailed description of event operators available in the language see (Milosevic et al., 2004a, 2004b).

```
Policy:     PrivacyRespect
Role:       Doctor
Modality:   Not Permitted
Condition:  RevealExaminationResult before PatientGivesPermission
```

The example above is for a prohibition policy while a permission policy is:

```
Policy:     Doctor
Role:       DoctorGradeA
Modality:   Permitted
Condition:  PrescribeMedicine (PrescribeMedicine.cost < $1000)
```

This last example also shows the use of a singleton event pattern and how this event pattern exploits information from the *cost* parameter of the event *PrescribeMedicine* to check the satisfaction of this policy.

```
Policy:      PatientWaitingTime
Role:        resourceAgent
Modality:    Obliged
Condition:   PatientAssignmentToResourceTime before (PatientArrivalTime add 2 hrs)
```

Note that in the first and last policy, the *add* operator is used to describe a relative time point.

It is worth mentioning that this policy language was developed based on the consideration of a number of formalisms for the expression of deontic modalities and normative concepts and on a more pragmatic analysis of various business situations, in particular in the e-contracting area. Thus, this is an example of a domain specific language for the purpose of expressing enterprise policies. Our experience so far suggests a high expressive power of the language, for the expression of both the behavioural and the structural aspects of enterprise systems. Further description of the language is beyond the scope of this paper; more details could be found, e.g., in (Linington et al, 2004 and Milosevic et al., 2004a, 2004b).

5.   POLICY-ENRICHED AGENT SOCIETIES

This section investigates options for incorporating key aspects of the policy language described above. This is to add further capabilities to the software agents developed as part of Jadex system so that it is also possible to support policy-constrained applications. The aim here is to consider how options for applying policy-enriched agents could be applied to a wide variety of problems in e-health applications.

5.1   General implementation considerations

Policies and constraints as presented above are high level, abstract descriptions of behaviour expected from people (e.g. nurses or doctors) or agents (e.g. representing hospital resources). The abstract descriptions do not specify how these policies are handled by an underlying software system. Policy constraints could be just monitored (taking certain actions when they are violated) or directly enforced (i.e. prohibiting all actions that are not permitted). Mapping these policies to concrete agent implementations has to make these design decisions explicit.

Direct enforcement of policies is only possible, when users and agents perform all actions through the system. For example, when a request for an action is issued to the system, the system can check if proper permissions are available, before actually performing that action. Actions directly performed or required by persons thus cannot be enforced by the system, but could be monitored. A special type of agents, *monitoring agents* can be designed and implemented to observe the behaviour of people and other software agents, and possibly to take appropriate steps when certain events occur, e.g. the detection of existing or possibly arising policy violations. Depending on the criticality of policies, monitoring agents might just log violations for later evaluation, or initiate complex emergency procedures.

5.2   Applying policy agents to the hospital domain

In order to support observation of behavioural constraints and reaction to policy violations in the hospital domain, we introduce another type of agents, namely *policy agents*. They act according to their goals which expressed in terms of pre-defined policies and the plan options associated with each of the policies. Each plan would thus express specific actions through which the corresponding policy is to be satisfied. One style of expression could be by using business process concepts. Note that we assume that policy rules are typically defined as part of the environment in which software agents or people are located but, in this context, we are not concerned with the process of arriving at these policies.

In general, the task of a policy agent would be to detect existing or possibly forthcoming policy violations (such as in the execution of care plans) and to cooperate with other software agents for various purposes. One such purpose would be to notify other agents about possible problems so that these second group of agents, namely *notification agents*, can then send notifications, reminders or warnings to health professionals, patients etc.

So, a policy agent can, for example, recognize if some correlation of events or alarms (e.g. as a result of patient reaction to a medical treatment or as a result of a surgery) may signify a potential adverse effect of serious health consequences. If so, the policy agent could be further involved in monitoring subsequent escalation procedures. The procedures could involve different measures to be taken in cases of progressively higher levels of priorities for the actions to be undertaken by health professionals.

In terms of agents that monitor patients, i.e. *patient monitoring agents*, they can, e.g., monitor the state of patients or elderly people at home and if necessary either 'decide' whether to send reminders to the patients themselves or directly trigger some other agents in hospitals etc. Note that these software agents could also run on various mobile devices.

In summary, agents augmented by the policy constraints, could be used in a collaborative care delivery in order to help doctors and clinical professionals and also the patients in making sure that agreed processes, best practices, and regulatory policies are satisfied.

5.3 Implementing BCL with BDI agents

We now present a way to implement BCL constraints by incorporating policy expressions as part of agents into Jadex and, thus, deriving concrete agent implementations for policy constraint applications. In order to do so, we propose a design where the system *monitors* all obligations, but *enforces* permissions. In other words, an agent would have to monitor policies with the "obliged" modality but should not allow its principal to execute actions that are "not permitted". A natural way to represent such policies in BDI agents is to map obligations to *maintain goals* and map permissions to *preconditions of plans* (i.e. actions), as described below.

Monitoring Obligations

First, we use 'maintain' type of goals in BDI agents for monitoring obligations. For this, such goals should be created and dropped in accordance to certain events in the domain. In terms of the example above, whenever a nurse agent is informed about a performed examination on a patient, it will create a maintain goal to keep track whether the nurse has advised a doctor about the patient's state within one day after the examination. In a similar way, the agent can be also programmed to remind the nurse, e.g. say one hour, before the day has expired.

Along the same line, the examples as presented in section 4.3, e.g. the NurseReporting and the PatientAssignmentToResourceTime policies which are modelled as obligations, can be mapped to the following corresponding Jadex maintain goal specifications:

```
<!-- "A nurse is obliged to report to the doctor at least one day
after the patient's examination" -->
<maintaingoal name="NurseReporting">
   <maintaincondition>
     AdviseDoctor after (PatientExamination)
     and before (PatientExamination add 1 day)
   </maintaincondition>
   <creationcondition>PatientExamination</creationcondition>
</maintaingoal>

<!-- "The waiting time for any patient before being assigned to a
resource shall not exceed 2 hours" -->
<maintaingoal name="PatientAssignmentToResourceTime">
   <maintaincondition>
     PatientAssignmentToResourceTime before
     (PatientArrivalTime add 2 hrs)
   </maintaincondition>
   <creationcondition>NewTeatmentAdministered</creationcondition>
</maintaingoal>
```

The examples present how policies could be mapped to Jadex agents, if the agent would be able to parse and interpret the BCL statements. As this is a topic of ongoing work, currently the policy statements as shown above would have to be mapped to Java expressions. In principle, for each obligation considered a corresponding maintain goal type has to be defined. Moreover, it is necessary to individualize the general policies and obligations by introducing variables for important aspects. This means, instead of a global policy enforcement component, the agent has one goal template for each policy, which will be instantiated when the context demands it, e.g. a nurse reporting goal is created whenever a new patient examination has been done (cf. the creation condition). This goal is parameterised by the concrete patient examination for which the monitoring has to be done. Similarly, in the second example a new goal is created whenever a new treatment is administered.

Enforcing permissions

The policy agent serves as a mediator between the system and its principal. When the principal requests certain actions, the policy agent can check for permissions of the respective action, as long as these are issued through the system. In BDI agents, these permission checks are naturally represented in plan preconditions, which specify the context required to perform a certain action. When the agent is currently unable to perform the requested action (due to insufficient permissions of the principal) a failure message can be generated, providing information to the user.

```
<!-- "A doctor is must not reveal the results of an examinations
before the patient gives permission for that" -->
<plan name="RevealExaminationResultPlan">
    <body><!-- plan actions go here... --></body>
    <trigger><goal ref="RevealExaminationResult"/></trigger>
    <precondition>Not before PatientGivesPermission</precondition>
</plan>

<!-- "A doctor is allowed to prescribe (only) medicine which costs
less than $ 1000" -->
<plan name="PrescribeMedicinePlan">
    <body><!-- plan actions go here... --></body>
    <trigger><goal ref="PrescribeMedicine"/></trigger>
    <precondition>(PrescribeMedicine.cost &lt; $1000)</precondition>
</plan>
```

Typically, a doctor could use his computer to reveal examination results by sending them by email to another doctor. As part of this process its personal agent will be requested from the user interface to perform this action for him by creating a new goal, e.g. "RevealExaminationResult". The corresponding plan, "RevealExaminationResultPlan", requires a precondition that the patient has given permission. When the doctor is not allowed to reveal the results, the plan is not applicable, and as no other applicable plan can be found, the goal fails. This is reflected in the user interface by showing an adequate error message to the doctor. The usage of BDI plans for detecting and avoiding constraint violations additionally supports context dependent actions. By specifying more than one plan for a given goal preconditions can be used to choose among alternatives in the current context. For example, for the "PrescribeMedicine" goal, a second plan with the precondition cost of greater than or equal to $1000 could be introduced. This plan could automatically request permission for the subscription by the head of department.

6.   CONCLUSIONS AND FUTURE WORK

In this paper we presented several current problems in the e-health domain. We highlighted the difficulties and complexities of the domain, arising from the size, distributed nature of health care (both physically and organisationally), and from possible uncertainty associated with patients' reaction to treatments. We have then outlined one initial solution for dealing with an important class of complexities in this domain, namely the problems associated with ensuring that the actions of actors in the system are in accordance with the predefined set of rules that apply to the actors. These rules could correspond to the treatment procedures with which patients need to comply with or to the best care practices and evidence-based medicine with which health professionals need to comply. Thus, these rules have a lot of in common with the policies that apply in human societal organisations.

The solution proposed is developed to support those applications that require explicit dealing with the policies. This solution is based on the use of agent technology enriched with the expressions of policy constraints developed in our respective research organisations We found that the BDI agent model in general quite nicely reflects the key policy principle of specifying a set of behaviour choices over basic behaviour. This enables us to model e-health application problems in a direct and natural way involving relatively straightforward mapping from our policy language to BDI and Jadex goals and plans in particular.

In future, we plan to complete the mapping of the policy language to the Jadex BDI based agent system. We also plan to test the policy-enriched agent system using several real e-health applications. A particularly complex, but also one of the most important emerging e-health applications is chronic disease management, such as coronary artery disease, diabetes, and asthma. This segment incorporate all key features discussed in the paper and requires the tracking of patients over time and over various locations (including in their home) to monitor progression of the disease, compliance with the treatment and preventative care.

7.   REFERENCES

Berry, A., Milosevic, Z., 2005; Extending executable choreography with business contract constraints, with A. Berry, submitted to the International Journal of Cooperative Information Systems (IJCIS), to appear, in Vol 14, Nos. 2 & 3, Jun & Sep 2005

Braubach, L., Pokahr, A., Lamersdorf, W., Moldt, D., 2004, Goal representation for BDI agent systems, Proc. Second International Workshop on Programming Multiagent Systems: Languages and Tools, R.H. Bordini, M. Dastani, J. Dix, A. El Fallah-Seghrouchni (Eds.), pp. 9-20

e-GIF, http://www.govtalk.gov.uk/egif/specifications.asp

e-Gov, http://www.whitehouse.gov/omb/egov/c-3-6-chi.html

Health-Connect, http://www.healthconnect.gov.au

Jennings, N., Wooldridge, M., (eds.), 1998, Agent Technology: Foundations, Applications and Markets, Springer Verlag

O'Keefe, C., Greenfield, P., Goodchild, A., 2005, A Decentralised Approach to Electronic Consent and Health Information Access Control, Journal of Research and Practice in Information Technology, Vol. 37, Number 2, Australian Computer Soceiety.

Linington, P., Milosevic, Z., Cole, J., Gibson, S., Kulkarni, S., and Neal, S., 2004, *A Unified Behavioural Model and a Contract Language for Extended Enterprise* Data Knowledge and Engineering Journal 51, p. 5-29, Special issue on contract-driven coordination, October 2004

Milosevic, Z., Gibson, S., Linington, P. F., Cole, J., Kulkarni, S., 2004a, On design and implementation of a contract monitoring facility, IEEE Conference on Electronic Commerce, the 1st IEEE Workshop on Electronic Contracting, San Diego, July 2004

Milosevic, Z., Linington, P. F., Gibson, S., Kulkarni, S., Cole, J., 2004b, Inter-organisational collaborations supported by e-contracts, Proc. 4th IFIP conference on E-commerce, E-Business, E-Government, Toulouse, France

Nealon, J. Moreno, A., 2003, *Agent-based health care systems.* In *Applications of Software Agents Technology in the Health Care Domain,* J.Nealon and A.Moreno Eds., Whitestein series in software agent technology, Birkhäuser

NEHTA, http://www.nehta.gov.au/

Paulussen, T. O., Jennings, N. R., Decker, K. S. , Heinzl, A., 2003, Distributed patient scheduling in hospitals, Proc. *International Joint Conference on Artificial Intelligence,* Acapulco, Mexico

Paulussen, T. O., Zöller, A., Heinzl, A., Braubach, L., Pokahr, A., Lamersdorf, W., 2004, Patient scheduling under uncertainty, H. M. Haddad, *Proceedings of the 2004 ACM Symposium on Applied Computing* (SAC2004), A. Omicini, R.L. Wainwright, L.M. Liebrock (Eds.), Nicosia, Cyprus, ACM Press, pp. 309-310

Pokahr, A., Braubach, L., Lamersdorf, W., 2005, *Jadex: A BDI Reasoning Engine,* in R. Bordini, M. Dastani, J. Dix and A. Seghrouchni, (eds.), Multi-Agent Programming, Kluwer (to appear in 2005)

Rao, A., Georgeff, M., 1995, BDI Agents: From Theory to Practice, Lesser, V. (Eds.) Proceedings of the First International Conference on Multi-Agent Systems (ICMAS'95), MIT Press: Cambridge, MA, pp. 312-319

PURSUING ELECTRONIC HEALTH

A UK PRIMARY HEALTH CARE PERSPECTIVE

Mkwama Ndeti and Carlisle George
Middlesex University, School of Computing Science, The Burroughs, London NW4 4BT, UK

Abstract: This paper focuses on factors affecting the use of Information and communication technologies within a primary health care environment. A case study was carried out to investigate opinions and views of Primary Health Care staff on the provision of electronic health in the UK. The study found that in addition to anticipated concerns such as cost, clinician attitudes to IT, and organisational culture, staff also had concerns such as security and psychological aspects of implementing electronic health among others. The paper discusses the findings of the study and makes recommendations for best practice to ensure success in the pursuit of electronic health in the UK.

Key words: Electronic Health, Healthcare, Primary Care, NHS.

1.   INTRODUCTION

Very few studies, have investigated the impact of the UK National Health Service (NHS) Electronic Health[1] Agenda on clinicians and staff, and how its adoption will help pave the way for electronic health (e-Health). While many different factors (discussed later) could affect the pursuit of e-Health

---

[1] Electronic Health is defined as: *"an emerging field in the intersection of medical informatics, public health and business, referring to health services and information delivered or enhanced through the Internet and related technologies..... also a state-of-mind, a way of thinking, an attitude, and a commitment for networked, global thinking, to improve health care locally, regionally, and worldwide by using information and communication technology"* (Eysenbach , JMIR 2001)

within the NHS, this paper seeks to investigate how the UK National Program for IT (NPFIT)[2] agenda impacts on the different stakeholders in primary health care, and how this will affect the pursuit of e-Health within the NHS. The paper takes a case study approach with the following two objectives: (i) to establish whether the stakeholders in the provision of primary healthcare feel prepared for electronic healthcare and to look at the factors affecting the pursuit of electronic healthcare in Primary Care[3]; (ii) to determine the agenda that stakeholders in the provision of primary healthcare think should be given priority in the pursuit of electronic healthcare and whether this agenda ties in with the National Agenda.

2.   GOVERNMENT AND HEALTH SERVICES

The health sector is one of the most complex and information intensive public sector organizations in the UK. The need to have this wealth of information organized and structured is imperative for the health sector to achieve better outcomes. Currently the NHS is the body charged with the provision of health services in the UK and it continues to experience many problems. Many patients have complained of long waiting times to receive medical attention, inconsistent records, bureaucratic processes, discrimination and health inequalities among others (UK National Statistics, 2005). Furthermore, the situation is heightened by the changing and increasing expectations of patients. A major challenge is for the government (and NHS) to solve these problems and meet their obligation to provide quality healthcare to citizens.

In a response to the changing expectation and needs of patients the NHS produced a modernization agenda which culminated in an Information Strategy, 1998-2005 (NHSIA, 2004) that sought to provide: lifelong electronic health records for every person in the country; round the clock online access to patient records and information about best clinical practice for all NHS clinicians; genuinely seamless care for patients through General Practitioners (GPs), hospitals and community service sharing information across the NHS Information highway; fast and convenient public access to information and care through online information services and telemedicine; and a reduction of health inequalities. In attempting to meet these ambitious objectives the NHS and government hope to provide a platform for e-Health in the UK.

---

[2] NPFIT see: http://www.connectingforhealth.nhs.uk/. It includes: care record system; electronic booking service; electronic prescriptions; and national network infrastructure.

[3] Primary care refers to the basic or general level of care usually given by doctors and other healthcare professionals.

3.   THE CHALLENGE

The success of any initiative, especially one that is technologically inclined relies on the adoption and appreciation i.e. the benefits derived from the initiative. Among some of the obvious benefits anticipated are: reduction in waiting times; a lifetime patient record that will travel with you everywhere; easy access to the patient data and information; and increased efficiency. While the perceived benefits of the NHS modernisation agenda are obvious, the success of it lies in the adoption and acceptance by those for whom it is intended. The following are the some of the issues that have shaped the perceptions and adoption of ICTs in the Health Sector.

3.1   Medical Culture Vs Technology Culture

There is a big problem in implementing change in a culture where power and decision making is left in the hands of a few individuals. The health sector for instance, has a lot of authority vested in one person with a wide range of responsibility for patient care. Beaver (2003) describes this as the "horizontal" nature of the medical culture. The technology culture however is very structured in its own right and Beaver (2003) goes further to describe this as the "vertical" nature of technology. Finding a middle ground for the two may prove to be an uphill task in that while the horizontal nature of the medical culture believes in sharing information, the restrictive nature of technology is guided by providing access to only those who should have access to the information.

3.2   The Role Of Information In HealthCare

The health sector has very complicated and rich information needs for each department. The relevance of information shared between departments is relative. The information that one department may consider important may not be important to another department. Sheaf & Peel (1995) suggest *"What information is 'true' and 'valid' becomes a contested issue prone to different interpretations more heavily influenced by organisational culture, internal politics and individuals perceptions than any objective rationale"*.

The amalgamation of these complex information needs could prove to be a challenge in the pursuit of e-Health. For example, the Primary Care department may consider information about a patient's ethnicity crucial whereas it may not be of relevance to the Pharmacy department. Lack of proper information in the health sector could have adverse effects on the population (Eysenbach and Jadad, 2001).

3.3   Cost

Another factor that may not favour the pursuit of electronic health is that in the technology culture, technology is always changing and unfortunately these changes are industry instigated and more often than not have great cost implications. Furthermore, while the NHS assesses its priorities, other more justifiably urgent needs take precedence over IT. Benson and Neame (1994) cite an example where the cost of a new hospital such as the Chelsea and Westminster Hospital was estimated to be £300 million while investments in healthcare computing systems during the year 1992-93 came to £220 Million. From a pragmatic perspective, it appears more sensible to invest in a building a new hospital.

Cost has always been an inhibiting factor in determining the path taken by an organisation. In Great Britain much of the cost of health care is borne by the citizens through taxation. There is intensive pressure on the government to spend the taxpayers' money in ways that produce tangible benefits. A problem arises here as the benefits of ICTS may not be readily appreciated by taxpayers. However with the changing needs and expectations of the more informed and knowledgeable, citizens are slowly beginning to see the importance of ICTs in Health Care.

3.4   Clinician Attitudes towards the Internet

Increasingly, healthcare professionals have to deal with patients who have access to many information resources. Using the Internet, patients can easily acquire information about conditions that they perceive to have and use this information to challenge the decisions or recommendations of healthcare professionals. This has created some form of cynicism amongst healthcare professionals especially since information available on the Internet may sometimes lack integrity. Hence healthcare professionals may develop a hostile attitude towards the Internet as a resource. This may be consequential in the current hostilities towards adoption of information and communication technologies.

3.5   Organisational Culture

Organisational culture plays a big role in the adoption of ICTs. Bangert and Doktor (2003) argue that healthcare organisations today are designed and structured to promote efficiencies and effectiveness of a past era characterised by formal authoritarian rule and a "one best way" mentality. They argue that most implementation problems of clinical e-Health systems stem from organisational culture. Smith (2000) identifies characteristics of health organisations such as professional bureaucracy, individual perceptions, adhocracy and divisionalisation that could impede on the success of IT in the health sector. Benson and Neame (1994) further emphasize that the present organisational arrangements within the health care are seen as problems in their own right and thus business reengineering can help provide better goals for the health service, while keeping the needs of patients in mind.

4.   CASE STUDY METHODOLOGY

A case study based on a Primary Care Trust (PCT)[4], located in London UK, was carried out to investigate staff perceptions towards electronic healthcare in light of the study objectives (see Section 1). The PCT was assumed to be a model representation of a PCT within the specified Strategic Health Authority. The study consisted of a series of in-depth interviews (using semi structured questionnaires) conducted to gain a full understanding of the staff perceptions (attitudes and views) on e-Health.

Theoretical Sampling (Silverman 2000) was used to select some interviewees. Also, using a snowball approach one group identified and contacted other groups they felt would give important incite to the study. The groups identified for this study within the PCT stemmed from the following departments: (i) Primary Care, Information Services; (ii) Patient Advice and Liaison Services (PALS); and (iii) Complaints and Booking Services. Each of these groups was representative of the three categories identified for the study. Those involved in interacting directly with the patients (PALs, Complaints), those involved in service provision and commissioning (Primary Care) and those involved in actual information systems and Projects for primary care. (Information Services and E-Booking)

Six participants were interviewed from five departments and are identified as follows: Participant (IS) -Information Services; Participants (PAL1 and PAL2) - Patient Advice and Liaison Services; Participant (Com) – Complaints; Participant (PC)- Primary Care; and Participant (EB)- E-Booking. The analysis of research findings involved: transcription of the recorded interview tapes; detailed interpretation of the transcription; categorisation of the interpretation into the themes adopted for the research; and identifying whether the interview objectives were met through the information collected.

---

[4] In the UK, a Primary Care Trust provides a range of community health services and may oversee the management of several hospitals. For reasons of confidentiality the name of the Primary Care Trust where the study was carried out is withheld.

4.1   Interviews

The interviews were conducted in two stages.

Stage one concentrated on the background of the specific department. Interview questions focused: the history of the department; the role of the department within the PCT; the goals of the department; what the department hoped to accomplish; and information about the key players in the department.

Stage two focused on electronic health, examining the following themes: preparedness and concern assessment; priority assessment; benefit and appeal assessment; and assessment of success factors for E-Health. This paper reports on two of the themes namely: preparedness and concern assessment, and priority assessment.

5.   RESEARCH FINDINGS

5.1   Preparedness and Concerns for Electronic Health

5.1.1   Patient Confidentiality and Security

The biggest concern for all participants was the issue of patient confidentiality and security for electronic records. For example Participant (PALs1) remarked: *"Who decides who has access to what data about the patient and how do they decide that"*. All participants mentioned the Data Protection Act. The majority of the participants felt that having central systems like those pledged by the NPFIT would make the NHS vulnerable to hacker attacks. Further they were not sure whether the NHS had proper secure systems in place to prevent this.

5.1.2   Staff and Primary Care E-Health Attitudes

The majority of participants thought it important that the staff were informed and educated on the organisational and process changes anticipated with the e-Health agenda of NPFIT.

It is of interest to note that all of the participants felt that GPs would be the hardest group to convince of the benefits of e-Health. One participant cited the example of GPs taking part in a patient profiling exercise which required them to collect all relevant information (e.g. ethnicity and religion) about the patient. The participant pointed out that the GPs had no motivation and lacked the time and resources to collect this information, since they did not see what benefit they would derive from the exercise.

The participants also noted that another aspect of GPs attitudes towards IT initiatives was the feeling that they (GPs) were being monitored and would therefore require them to be accountable for some of their actions. Participant (PALs2) notes: *"A good example is monitoring of registration of Patients with GPs... Some feel that GPs are discriminating towards some patients so having an electronic form that would allow a patient to register himself online "anonymously " would mean that the GP would need to explain why for instance he did not accept a certain registration of a patient. It would provide a mechanism for monitoring their actions. However acceptance of these mechanisms will prove to be the greatest challenge for the NPFIT".*

The majority of participants felt that many members of staff had no idea about some of the ongoing initiatives or projects and that communication was vital to the success of the NPFIT agenda. This lack of information could lead to duplication of services and impede upon the adoption of "best practises" from previous projects. Participant (IS) noted: *"how do we accept a program or initiative we know nothing about?"*

On staff attitudes and skills, all participants felt that the majority of the staff were adequately trained, however some cited that there still seemed to be a feeling of technophobia amongst some of their colleagues. Participant (COM) noted: *"... staff needs to be informed that IT is not the enemy".*

5.1.3   History of Projects undertaken by the NHS and Government

It was important to note that there were some participants who were cynical of the success of the NPFIT agenda. The negative attitudes towards the NPFIT agenda were attributed to the history of previous failed projects undertaken by the NHS and government. Though they were sceptical about the success of the NPFIT initiative, they seemed somehow more hopeful about the present agenda since it appeared to have sought contributions from some of the stakeholders involved. This they felt was a different approach more likely to succeed.

5.1.4   High Expectations of NPFIT

The majority of the participants felt that the NPFIT had set very high expectations and questioned whether they would be able to meet these objectives given the time frames presented. Participant (PALs2) noted: *"...mapping of processes to patient needs and to Information technology is a Herculean task and needs to be well thought out"*

Similar observations noted that change is never painless and that there were always going to be people who would not like the changes anticipated with the NPFIT agenda, however, the participants agreed that these changes were inevitable for a more functional NHS.

5.1.5   Other Concerns

An interesting perspective presented by one of the participants was that NPFIT may have in some way neglected the psychological issues relating to e-Health. The participant felt that having efficient systems could possibly mean sacrificing the empathy and human emotional interaction associated with the provision of health care services. One of the words used to describe this was "impersonal". Another participant (PALs1) remarked: *"How would you present or relay information relating to one who has terminal illness and make this information available to the patient"*

5.2   Priority Assessment For Electronic Health

Upon presentation of the NPFIT agenda for e-Health all the participants felt that the Electronic Record System was most needed at the moment. To reach this decision it was important to note that the participants reflected on their own experiences not only as staff of the NHS but also as patients. They were familiar with some of the experiences that other patients encountered in light of inaccurate data or inconsistent records. The idea of having a patients' records available anywhere in the country was very appealing to all.

Regarding other priorities that participants felt were important, it was interesting to note all the participants had varied responses and had a bias towards their own departments. They cited examples of processes within their own environments which they felt should have been given priority over all other agenda items presented by the NPFIT.

The Primary Care participant, for example, felt that the department would benefit from an electronic process that would help them monitor and audit the services of the GPs in order to help them with the commissioning[5] exercise. For example, if there was a baby boom they would know to commission more pre-natal or post natal services within that particular region based on the data provided through the monitoring process.

One of the participants from Information Services felt that the monitoring of inequality and diversity was important for primary care. This is currently being facilitated by a process called "patient profiling". The system is not fully functional even though it has an online presence. The participant felt it

---

[5] Commissioning refers to the process of allocation of resources and services based on need and requirement of the health population.

should be given priority because if a patient had an appointment and required a translator or disability support, this could be arranged beforehand and the patient would be provided with these services at the time of the appointment.

The participant from Complaints felt that an online document archival system integrated with the complaints logging system would be important because currently all the complaints are stored in paper format. This would also be able to keep track of resolve times and send alerts/reminders to relevant parties required to action complaints. This kind of system would be able to study patterns and monitor trends on the nature of complaints and help the department resolve complaints quickly. The participant also believed that a system could help reduce the number of claims. The participant felt that it should be given priority because it would make the Complaints Department more efficient and pro-active compared to the reactive nature currently characteristic of the NHS.

The participants from PALS felt priority should be given to educating the public and the staff on the services available online and the different modes of access to these services. Participant (PALs2): *"It's all about behavioural change and Marketing and making the patients feel that irrespective of access method the response and times of response to their queries will be the same"*

The participant from E-Booking felt that offering patients choice regarding where and when they received their treatment was very important and should be given priority. It was perceived that offering patients a choice of appointment would reduce the waiting times, and Did-Not-Attends (DNAs). Participant (EB) noted: *"...this means that the patient is generally happy because the patient is more in control of their health, they choose when they are coming in. For example if they have to work or have dependents they can make their choice of where to go depending on their own schedules more. It also means that patients are more likely to turn up for their appointments"*.

6. DISCUSSION AND RECOMMENDATIONS

Every patient interaction begins in Primary Care. Much of the modernisation proposed will affect the providers of Primary Health Care the most. With over 300 Million consultations in Primary Health Care annually, the importance and contribution of Primary Care in the provision of health care cannot in anyway be underestimated. The NPFIT agenda will impact on the provision of primary care services directly. The following are some recommendations for successful implementation of the NPFIT agenda.

6.1   Education of Staff and Knowledge Management

A key observation made is that very few of the participants had an in-depth knowledge about the NPFIT agenda. While the NPFIT agenda includes a lot of re-organisational changes, training and educating the staff on the perceived benefit of the entire agenda is crucial in its adoption and acceptance. Furthermore training can more adequately prepare users of ICT systems for the anticipated organisational and environmental changes. Training can also stimulate discussions on issues and problems that users may encounter thus increasing their knowledge and appreciation of the systems proposed. However, training alone is not enough. A knowledge management environment needs to be created such that users with deficiencies in some areas know where to obtain information, support and help from those who are well versed in the area. A knowledge base documenting 'best practice', previous problems and information on how to resolve these problems within the environment, can help increase efficiency and productivity. It would also reduce the time spent in finding a resolution to pertinent issues. Staff and users should be encouraged to disseminate information crucial to the NHS success. While saying this, the NHS should be commended on the efforts it has placed so far in the training of its staff.

6.2   Changing Attitudes and Involvement of All

In order to successfully implement their agenda, the NPFIT should include all stakeholders in every stage of its progression. This would provide a sense of ownership and encourage collective responsibility by all involved. In documenting the findings of the research participants, one of the key observations made was that the staff appeared to be somewhat disjointed. There were several incidences of "passing the buck": participants feeling that some of the eminent problems arising from a dysfunctional process had nothing to do with them; and participants feeling that they were not at fault for problems encountered. No one wanted to take responsibility for issues that went beyond their department. The system or NHS organisational process was blamed. It was difficult to determine whether this was indicative and reflective of the NHS organisation as a whole or was merely an issue specific to the PCT. This, however, was beyond the scope of this research. However this observation may impinge on the success of the NPFIT as a whole. For it to be successful, a collective responsibility and ownership is required. While there is a significant benefit derived in having a national infrastructure and centralization, it is important to assess the local needs and verify whether these national objectives tie in with the local agenda. More significantly, both objectives should culminate into better health outcomes for the patient. It would be important not to loose site of the patient at any level.

While clinician involvement is important, the NPFIT needs to look at the adoption and acceptance of the systems it is proposing. Several research studies have been done to assess the attitudes apparent in the adoption of health information systems (Morris, 2003; Lapointe et al, 2002; Gardner and Luunsgarde, 1994). While these studies have presented many findings the salient issue discussed by all is that barriers built in acceptance of new systems can only be broken through continued use of the system.

In assessing changing attitudes towards ICTs in the health sector, Chismar and Wiley-Patton (2003) in their work on applying the Technology Acceptance Model (TAM) to physicians, found that organisations needed to emphasize the usefulness of the technology to physicians while focusing on the importance and utility of technology in performing daily tasks. A study by Hu et al (1999) concluded that the TAM could provide a rational representation of physicians' intention to use technologies. The study also found that perceived usefulness was a key determinant in establishing the attitudes that physicians would have towards the technology while strangely perceived ease of use was not. It is recommended that the NPFIT could use the TAM to help increase the adoption and acceptance of ICTs within the NHS

6.3   Encourage Research and Development

While collective responsibility and ownership is extremely crucial, a mechanism needs to be put into place where some of the recommendations and ideas given about improvement in service delivery within the NHS (especially in Primary Care) can be voiced or collected. Clinician involvement is very crucial for the success of the NPFIT agenda as clinicians generally interact with the patients and have grounded experience. This means that they can provide a useful insight in the development of the NPFIT agenda on how to improve the systems. Some of the suggestions made by the participants about what issues needed to be given priority (discussed earlier) were very valuable. Furthermore, these recommendations stemmed from the experiences of the staff on the ground.   If such a mechanism were put in place it would facilitate a culture of innovation and knowledge sharing. It would further provide a resource of information at both local and national level that could aide in the formulation of a strategic health policy. Building information systems based on strategic health policy is the first step towards success in e-Health.

6.4   Security Recommendations

The provision of secure and safe systems by the NHS should be paramount in their agenda. Following an NHS research study on the public's view of electronic records, the biggest concern expressed by the public was the possibility of unauthorised access to medical records (NHS, 2003). The participants interviewed in this study also reiterated this point. Not much was said about how this could be achieved or what the NPFIT proposes. A solid information and security policy needs to be put in place to address these concerns. This can help avoid errors such as when the Sheffield Hospital giving 50,000 confidential gynecological records to a data processing firm that hired people off the street to transcribe unprotected data (Beaver, 2003). It must be recognised, however, that putting in place a security policy in an organisation like the NHS that has varied information access needs is indeed a complex task.

The NPFIT agenda needs to take into account the "horizontal nature" of the health sector and those involved in administering health care. One crucial aspect of security that the NHS needs to note is that in most cases unauthorised access does not necessarily stem from outside the organisation. Usually the greatest unauthorised access threats stem from within an organisation. The NPFIT needs to find a way to address this. In its security policy, the NPFIT should guarantee that whatever action an individual takes while using the systems could be traced through provision of access. Hence one can tangibly monitor access by denying or allowing a user the right to access the processes relevant to him/her duties. However this in its own right does not stop users who are granted access from misusing or divulging information about patients to others. Generally, the challenge is a grave one and the onus is upon the NPFIT to look and find ways to resolve these pertinent issues.

6.5   Staffing Issues

The NPFIT agenda presents new opportunities for those within the NHS to pursue careers with the Local Service Providers and National Service Providers commissioned to implement the new e-Health systems. Staff retention can be very difficult even in an organisation like the NHS that invests large sums of money in training its staff. This means that if a member of staff who is involved in a project leaves then the project may be stopped until a new person is hired. This new person will need to be trained and given an orientation period to enable him/her to start working on the project. Unfortunately organisations have little control over staff who may want to leave. However, a proper mechanism should be put in place for a smooth handover from one worker to the next. This issue only goes further to reiterate the importance of having a knowledge management environment.

Another approach is to ensure that the members of staff involved in projects work in teams. Consequently if one team member leaves then there will be some form of continuity in his/her absence.

7.   CONCLUSION

In this study, participants felt that the adoption ICTs in their daily tasks could definitely improve their work performance and productivity. The NPFIT with all its teething problems is perhaps a good start. While participants' priorities showed biases towards their own departments, the interests of the entire population should be held paramount. However, it is important that the NHS look to its staff for ideas on improvements and involve all stakeholders in its planning, as this would lead to better health outcomes. Further a cohesive relationship needs to exist between all the parties involved to ensure the success of any initiative.

The study also found that with any modernisation agenda the core elements lie in realigning the organisational processes and the use of ICT to enhance the new and existent processes. ICTs within the NHS should be used as a means to the end and not an end itself.

Access to information and effective communication within the organisation will ensure participation and eventually ownership and involvement of all. The staff are an untapped resource of information for the NHS. A knowledge management environment can serve many purposes within the NHS. It can encourage innovation and lead to research and key developments within the NHS.

Should the research findings of this study be indicative of the views of the entire staff within the NHS then the NPFIT will have several difficulties in ensuring the success of its e-Health agenda if these issues and concerns are not addressed.

REFERENCES

Bangert D and Doktor R(2003) *The Role of Organizational Culture in the Management of Clinical e-health Systems* Proceedings of the 36th Hawaii International Conference on System Sciences (HICSS'03) 2003 IEEE The Computer Society

Beaver K (2003). *Healthcare Information Systems* 2nd Edition, New York, Auerbach Publications

Benson T and Neame R (1994). *Healthcare Computing* Essex, Longman Group Ltd.

Chismar W G and Wiley-Patton S(2003). *Does the Extended Technology Acceptance Model Apply to Physicians* Proceedings of the 36th Hawaii International Conference on System Sciences (HICSS'03) IEEE-The Computer Society

Eysenbach G, Jadad AR. (2001) *Consumer health informatics in the internet age. In: Evidence-based patient choice* (Editors: Adrian Edwards & Glyn Elwyn). Oxford University Press,

Eysenbach G. (2001) *What is e-health?* [editorial].Journal of Medical Internet Research 2001;3(2):e20 URL: http://www.jmir.org/2001/2/e20/ Accessed 12th March 2004

Gardner R M and Luunsgarde H P (1994) *Evaluation of User Acceptance of a Clinical Expert System*, The Journal of American Medical Informatics J Am Med Inform Assoc. Nov/Dec 1994;1:428-438.

Hu P J et al,(1999) *Examining the Technology Acceptance Model Using Physician Acceptance of Telemedicine Technology* Journal of Management Information Systems Vol. 16 No. 2, Fall 1999 pp. 91 - 112

Lapointe L, Lamothe L and Fortin J P, *The Dynamics of IT Adoption in a Major Change Process in Healthcare Delivery* Proceedings of the 35th Annual Hawaii International Conference on System Sciences (HICSS-35'02) 2002, IEEE

Morris L A (2003). *A survey of computer use in Scottish primary care: general practitioners are no longer techno phobic but other primary care staff need better computer access* Journal of Informatics in Primary Care (2003) 11: 5–11

NHS (2003). *"The Public view of Electronic Health Records"* http://www.dh.gov.uk/assetRoot/04/05/50/46/04055046.pdf. Accessed 10th March 2004

NHSIA (2004). National Health Service Information Authority, (1998-2005) *"Information for Health"*, http://www.nhsia.nhs.uk/def/pages/info4health/1.asp#Notes Accessed 16th March 2004

Sheaf, R & Peel V.(1995) *Managing Health Service Information Systems*. OU Press,

Silverman D (2000). *Doing Qualitative Research A Practical Handbook*. London Sage Publications, pp 105

Smith J(2000). *Health Management Information Systems: A handbook for Decision Makers*, Philadelphia, Open University Press pp 40

UK National Statistics (2005).http://www.performance.doh.gov.uk/nhscomplaints/index.html. Accessed 28th May 2005

E-PETITIONING: ENABLING GROUND-UP PARTICIPATION

Nicholas J. Adams[1], Ann Macintosh[1] and Jim Johnston[2]

[1]*International Teledemocracy Centre (ITC), Napier University, 10 Colinton Road, Edinburgh EH10 5DT, Scotland, UK;* [2]*The Scottish Parliament, Edinburgh, Scotland, UK.*

Abstract: This paper takes as background voter apathy and the emergence of petitions as a mechanism for political activity and considers the role of e-petitioning. It describes how an e-Petitioning System is being used to support the Scottish Parliament's four key principles of: sharing power; accountability; access and participation; and equal opportunities. It highlights the increasing uptake of e-petitions and the gradual understanding of how the integrated discussion forum can be used to facilitate dialogue on issues raised.

We briefly describe the Scottish Parliament Petitions processes and outline the key features of the e-Petitioner System, before showing how the e-Petitioner supports these Parliamentary processes. With a wealth of experience gained through operating the e-Petitioner System successfully at a national level, we then describe how this facilitated the re-engineering of the System for the specific needs of two Local Authorities in England.

Key words: e-Petitioning, e-Government, Public Authority, Parliament, Local Government

1.   PROBLEM ADDRESSED

In October 2004, 78 delegates from the parliaments of 22 EU member countries attended the European Conference of Members of National Parliaments in Information and Communication Technologies (*http://www.epri.org/epriweb/contents/introseite.php*).   The aim was to discuss how ICT could strengthen the importance of parliamentarians and parliaments.   One of the main issues to emerge was the need to strengthen parliamentary democracy with better involvement of citizens in political and democratic processes.   The conference also highlighted the decline in voter turnout at elections and general trends in increasing political apathy.

To counter political apathy and to re-engage the public the OECD report Citizens as Partners (2001) describes the urgent need for transparency, accountability and participation in political decision-making. It goes on to suggest three types of engagement strategies by which governments might meet this public demand. It states:

> "Citizens can make an active and original contributions to policy-making, when their relationship with government is founded on the principle of partnership. Active participation represents a new frontier in government-citizen relations for all OECD Member countries." (p. 41)

Petitioning is one way to achieve active participation and indeed in many countries around the world, citizens have long used petitions to make their feelings known about issues that concern them. Simply, a petition is a formal request to a higher authority, e.g. parliament or other authority, signed by one or a number of citizens. However, the format of petitions and the way petitions are submitted and subsequently considered by parliaments varies greatly from country to country. It is therefore interesting to note that recent research conducted on behalf of the Electoral Commission in the UK (2005) found that apart from voting in elections, signing petitions is the most frequently undertaken political activity in the UK. MORI undertook the survey which involved interviews with a representative sample of 2,065 adults aged 18+ across the UK. It reports that:

> "The past 12 months have seen a statistically significant increase in the number who say they have signed a petition over the past two or three years (from 39% in December 2003 to 44% in December 2004)." (p. 17)

As such this paper takes as background voter apathy and the emergence of petitions as a mechanism for political activity and considers the role of e-petitioning. It describes the increasing use of e-petitioning within the Scottish Parliament, which has accepted e-petitions since March 2000, and shows how the same e-Petitioner System is now in use in public authorities in England with only minor modifications to system functionality and associated political processes.

2.   PETITIONING AND THE SCOTTISH PARLIAMENT

In July 1999 the Scottish Parliament was officially opened. This gave devolved power for specific areas of government from the Westminster Parliament in London to a new Scottish Parliament. One of the main documents setting out how the new Parliament should work was The Consultative Steering Group (CSG) report, Shaping Scotland's Parliament (HMSO 1999). This identified 4 key principles as the basis for the way which the Parliament should conduct its work and these were unanimously agreed by the Parliament in 1999:

- Sharing the Power
- Accountability
- Access and Participation
- Equal Opportunities.

In relation to access and participation the CSG in its final report states that: 'it will also be important to develop a culture of genuine consultation and participation if people in Scotland, particularly those who do not currently engage in the political process, are to be encouraged to participate.'

Integral to developing this culture was the establishment of a Public Petitions Committee (PPC) whose remit consists solely of the consideration of petitions. As such, in its final Report the CSG states that:

"It is important to enable groups and individuals to influence the Parliament's agenda. We looked at a number of models in other Parliaments for handling petitions and concluded that the best of these encouraged petitions; had clear and simple rules as to form and content; and specified clear expectations of how petitions would be handled... We propose the establishment of a dedicated Petitions Committee."

The CSG also set up an Expert Panel on Information and Communications Technologies (ICT) whose remit included considering: 'how can ICT assist the realization of the Parliament's aim of promoting democratic participation, including community governance and citizen participation?' While e-petitioning was not considered by the CSG it should nevertheless be viewed as a direct response to the overall aims of the CSG especially within the context of encouraging democratic participation. This is a view shared by Coleman et al (2002) who argue:

"If technology is regarded as possessing autonomous qualities that can remedy the ills of democracy, it is bound to let us down; but if it can be utilised in the service of creative politics to make democratic politics more accessible, accountable and inclusive, there is real scope for the reinvigoration of governance."

The partnership between the Scottish Parliament and the ITC at Napier University began in December 1999 when the PPC agreed to allow an internet-based petition from the Centre's web site sponsored by the World Wide Fund for Nature to be the first electronic petition to collect names and addresses over the internet, eventually attracting 309 signatures and 9 comments. The PPC subsequently agreed to allow groups and individuals to submit e-petitions, and on the 14 March 2000 the Committee accepted its first e-petition.   This was a historical event as the Scottish Parliament became the first statutory body to formally accept e-petitions. Indeed, the Scottish Parliament is a recognised world leader in e-participation and:

> "Few countries have used technology to enable electronic petitioning to the extent of the Scottish Parliament." (OECD, 2004)

The PPC primarily provides an opportunity for individual members of the public to participate fully in the democratic process in Scotland by raising issues of public concern with the Parliament. However, there are no restrictions on who can submit a petition or the number of signatures required for a petition to be considered. The Committee has in its first six years considered over 800 petitions on a bewildering range of topics from every corner of Scotland.

The Committee is widely regarded as being relatively successful in enhancing participation in the political process. For example, the Scottish Civic Forum state that the Committee:

> "Has scored notable successes in allowing people from all over Scotland to participate, and in stimulating legislation on issues that are important to certain communities but might find it difficult to get attention in the normal sweep of executive policy making."

This success is also reflected in the feedback which the Committee has received from petitioners themselves. For example, as stated by a petitioner in the recent Health Committee public debate in the Parliament:

> "The people of Scotland should be well proud of this institution and of the fact that when ordinary people sign a piece of paper on the street and ask me whether it will make a difference, I can look them in the eye and say, "Yes, this can make and is making a difference."

This petitioner lodged an e-petition on the provision of consultant-led acute services in rural communities which attracted 1906 signatures on the website and 89 comments on the discussion forum.   The petition was subsequently referred to the Health Committee for its consideration.

The PPC is keen to promote the public petitions system including e-petitioning especially among groups traditionally marginalized from the political process. Therefore it has agreed a rolling programme of committee events aimed at providing practical advice and guidance to local community organizations across Scotland on petitioning and e-petitioning.

The PPC's role is to ensure that appropriate action is taken in respect of each admissible petition submitted and, in fulfilling this function, the

Committee takes responsibility for the initial consideration of the issues raised. It is not for the Committee to make recommendations in relation to the substantive issues arising from petitions but rather to assess whether a petition raises issues which would merit further consideration by the Parliament. If so, the Committee would generally formally refer a petition to the relevant subject committee. This generally involves hearing evidence from many petitioners in support of their petitions, conducting background research and seeking comments from key stakeholders on the issues raised in the petition. Ministers and public body representatives may also be called to appear before the Committee to supplement the information provided in their written responses.

3. THE E-PETITIONER SYSTEM

The e-Petitioner System comprises 2 sections:
- **The Front-End** – the publicly accessible web pages where the citizens interact with the system;
- **The Back-End** – the private Administrative Section which comprises password protected web pages for all administrative functions.

3.1 The Front-End

The Front-End provides citizens with 10 basic e-petition functions:
1. **About e-Petitions:** provides an overview of how to e-petition the Parliament and gives guidance on petitioning.
2. **Download e-Petition Template:** provides a downloadable template for construction of an e-petition. E-petitions must be submitted using this.
3. **List All e-Petitions:** lists the e-petitions along with the name of the individual or organisations who originally raised the petition and the current status of the petition.
4. **View/Sign Petition:** this is the main e-petition page. It contains the name of the person who originally raised the petition, 'the petition text', and the 'sign petition' facility. Here a user who agrees with the petition issue can add their name and address to the petition. The user is requested to provide a full postal address including postcode and country. The postcodes and countries are summarised and used in the brief to the Parliament. There is also a data protection statement detailing how the gathered information will be used, and there is a summary of the petition details, including how many people who have signed by that date, how many comments have been posted in the discussion forum, and a list of the 5 most recent signatures.

5. **Post Signing Questionnaire:** is an online evaluation questionnaire to monitor what users think of the system. It provides a way for the Parliament to assess user reaction.
6. **View Signatures:** lists the names, along with their countries, of all those who have signed the e-petition. Giving any further details of signatories would breach the Data Protection Act.
7. **Background Information:** this shows additional information, provided by the principle petitioner, which supports the petition and allows the users to be better informed about the petition issue.
8. **Discussion:** provides users with the opportunity to comment further on the petition and to generally discuss issues raised by the petition.
9. **Tell a Friend:** is an emailing facility for users to inform others about the petition.
10. **Progress in Parliament:** links to the Parliament's main petitions page, giving the number of the submitted petition so as to allow tracking of the petition through its life in the Parliament.

3.2 The Back-End

The Back-End provides 5 high-level commands through which either the parliamentary staff or members of the ITC can support and maintain the e-petitioning processes. These are:
1. **Edit e-Petition:** allows the petition details, such as closing date and status to be easily amended.
2. **Create e-Petition:** this is where a new petition is created on the website from a submitted e-petition template.
3. **Discussion:** houses all of the moderation facilities for the integrated discussion forum, including: adding any moderation comments; pulling together all the comments to produce an overall report; and viewing statistics – such as the number of times a comment has been viewed.
4. **Questionnaire:** displays the results of the evaluation questionnaire.
5. **Signatures:** displays the full address details of those who have signed the e-petition. It allows a mailing list to be created of those who said they were willing to have their email contact details added to this, and also allows administrators to remove invalid signatures from the public site.

Given that accessibility is a key aspect of the system, recent advances in web accessibility technologies are integrated wherever possible, and the current release of the e-Petitioner System is consistent with the Web Access Initiative's (WAI) Level 2 compliance specifications.

The signatures on an e-petition are simply the name and location given by a citizen who wishes to support a petition. While it would be technically possible to require citizens to provide digital signatures, that would be inconsistent with the objective of maximising accessibility since it would add to the technical competences required of citizens.

Duplicate names and addresses can occur, either through accidentally submitting the sign petition form more than once, or a person may sign a petition on multiple occasions. These are monitored and automatically marked as duplicates by the software.

Bogus signature or address detection could be automated, but experience of operating the e-Petitioner System over a number of years has shown it to be very difficult to do reliably – for example the most obvious mechanism of blocking multiple signatures from the same IP address can preclude legitimate signatures from different people within a single organisation (which may post only a single IP address), and can also be easily defeated by someone repeatedly using a dialup connection, where IP addresses are usually dynamically assigned – so developing facilities to enable manual moderation of signatures from within the administration section assisted by metrics has been preferred. These help identify any possible discrepancies, that could occur, but it is pertinent to note that Scottish Parliament set no minimum signatures requirement for a petition to be considered, thus there is little incentive for lobbying groups to fake e-petition signatures.

The e-Petitioner System is a dynamic website implemented in Active Server Pages. VBScripts generate the HTML, access and update the petition data. This data is maintained in a SQL Server relational database, with the exception of petition background information, which is stored to disk.

4. THE E-PETITIONER PARLIAMETNARY PROCESSES

The e-Petitions System within the Scottish Parliament should not be viewed as separate to the traditional paper method of petitioning but as an alternative method or supplementary method of gathering support for the aims of a petition through ICTs. The e-Petitioner System allows a petition to be hosted on the Parliament's website for an agreed period providing an opportunity to attract a wide audience and gather names in support of the petition. The petitioner may wish to use this method solely in gaining support or may wish to use it in addition to traditional face to face gathering of signatures. There is space for supporting information so that the issue can be placed in context, and each e-petition also has its own discussion forum where visitors and signatories can discuss the petition and surrounding issues online. The forum gives everyone the opportunity to comment further on the petition. They can make comments either for or against the petition and everyone can read their comments and reply to them. Having an integrated discussion forum as part of the petitioning process is important as it makes the process much more interactive and allows a constructive debate to occur on the issue. Those in favour have opportunity to provide further detail as to why they support the issue, and those against have an important opportunity to say why the petition should not go ahead or how it should be modified.

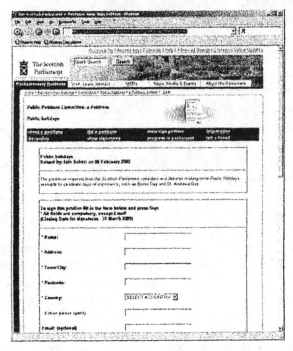

Figure 1. An example of an e-petition on the Scottish Parliament e-Petitioner System.

Unlike the e-petitions process introduced by the legislative Assembly of Queensland there is no requirement for an e-petition to be sponsored by a Member of the Scottish Parliament. Ordinarily a person (or organisation) wishing to raise a petition would contact the PPC clerking team and agree with them the text for the petition. This is necessary to ensure the petition is admissible within the Guidance on the Submission of Public Petitions[1].

While petitions are generally driven by a specific local issue such as a planning matter or closure of a school, the Committee has no remit to be involved in such issues which are essentially matters for the relevant local authority. Rather, the primary locus of the Committee is to hold the Scottish Executive to account and, therefore, petitions are required to identify which action they would like the Scottish Executive to take. This will generally take the form of calling for a review or change to Scottish Executive policy

---

[1] *htttp://www.scottish.parliament.uk/business/petitions/guidance/index.htm*

at the national level. This process supports both paper and electronic petitions, but as our interest is in the latter we shall only consider it here.

Once the text of the e-petition has been agreed, it is then entered into the e-Petitioner System through a form in the online administration section. In addition to the petition text, supporting information and further details on the Principal Petitioner can be added. This process also adds the petitioner's name as the first signature on the e-petition, and submits their supplied comment to the discussion forum for the petition to initiate debate.

The petition is then live and run for the prescribed period (usually 4–6 weeks), during which the signature list is regularly checked for spurious signatures, and the discussion forum moderated daily by the PPC clerking team. In particular, comments are checked to ensure that they are relevant to the aims of the petition and not potentially defamatory or inflammatory.

At the completion of this period the petition is closed, and a briefing paper is generated providing some analysis of the geographical breakdown of signatories and a summary of the discussion comments, and passed along with the list of signatures to the Principal Petitioner. They then decide whether they wish the petition to go further, and if they do then it is formally lodged by the PPC clerking team and published in the Business Bulletin and on the Parliament's website with a petition number, for example, PE100.

Such a petition is then considered at a meeting of the Public Petitions Committee where the petitioner may be invited to give evidence to the Committee. The Committee's annual report for the year ending 6 May 2005 indicated that the Committee considered 110 new petitions (of which 29 were e-petitions) and heard from 51 petitioners, so around half of all petitioners are invited to give evidence to the Committee.

An important aspect of the public petitions system in line with the CSG's emphasis on openness and transparency is that petitioners are advised of the progress of their petition at all stages of its journey through the system and that other interested parties may monitor this progress through each petition's feedback page on the website. The link between each e-petition and the relevant feedback page allows anyone to easily find out any subsequent action which occurred in relation to a petition. This completes the petitioning process.

5.   CURRENT STATUS IN THE SCOTTISH PARLIAMENT

In the current session of the Scottish Parliament (from September 2003 to date) 45 e-petitions have been raised on a number of issues ranging from 'supporting an investigation into Scottish football', 'Broadband for all of

Scotland by 2005' and 'support for a global campaign for education'. See *http://epetitions.scottish.parliament.uk/list_petitions.asp*. The majority of the e-petitions have been raised by individuals or community groups who have come together specifically to support the petition issue.

In this respect it is clear that the e-Petitions System has contributed to the aims of the CSG in enabling 'groups and individuals to influence the Parliament's agenda'. While there will inevitably be some debate as to whether this amounts to 'sharing the power' there is no doubt that it does encourage a more participatory role for Scottish citizens and lend some credibility to the notion that it is their Parliament. In this context the PPC has also taken steps to address equalities issues in its work with the aim of increasing awareness among all sections of Scottish society of the petitions processes. For example, the PPC has endorsed the Equal Opportunities Committee guidelines on mainstreaming equality in the work of parliamentary committees, introducing an equal opportunities monitoring form. They have also published guidance on the submission of petitions in: English, Arabic, Bengali, Cantonese, Gaelic, Punjabi and Urdu and Braille, with audio versions also available.

Petitions can be lodged in any language and the Parliament accepted its first non-English e-petition on 16 April 2004. This petition calling for the standardisation of school holidays in Scotland was lodged in Gaelic with an English translation. The representative nature of the e-Petitions System is also reflected in the range of issues which have been raised as e-petitions. For example, in relation to local transport for Scotland's disabled people, speech and language therapy services and calling for a public inquiry into the increase in autism.

A total of 20,812 signatures have been added to the petitions and 639 discussion comments have been posted. The most successful in terms of signatories is an e-petition calling for an investigation into the 'Upgrade of the A90 trunk road in Aberdeenshire' which collected 2606 signatures and 47 comments.

The e-Petitions System also provides the opportunity for petitioners to gather support for their petition globally. For example, the e-petition 'Culture and tourism policies regarding Robert Burns' ran over a 6 week period and collected a total of 1810 signatures. Although the majority, 1000, were from Scotland; 260 were from the United States; 144 from Canada; 142 from England; and the remainder from a further 35 countries ranging from Poland to Brazil. This information is provided in a briefing pack to the PPC and is useful in demonstrating the breadth of support for a specific issue.

When the e-Petitioner System was first launched, few citizens appreciated how the discussion forum could be used to support their cause. These early e-petitions typically received 1 or 2 comments. That situation has gradually changed and now users see the discussion forum as a means to tell their own story of how they have been affected by policy (or lack of it). For example, a petition raised in July 2004 requesting "that the Scottish Parliament urge the Scottish Executive to ensure the provision of acute 24hr a day all year round consultant-led services across Scotland, including rural communities" received 89 comments from 1906 signatories. Comments such as the following were received:

"Our Grandmother lives in Fort William and we visit Fort William a lot, and we have heard everyone talking about how important it is to have consultancy services in the Belford. We also know what is happening in PRI in Perth and think it is awful."

and

"My wife underwent major surgery at the Belford recently and we have only praise for the care, skill and dedication of the staff. The Belford is a major asset of the West Highlands and it is important that the expertise it offers remains accessible to the locality."

The discussion forum is helping to further the aims of the CSG in developing a 'culture of genuine consultation and participation' and encouraging communities who were previously excluded from the political process to participate in the work of the Parliament.

In increasing the level of participation, the e-Petitions System is also enhancing the accountability of MSPs. The CSG states that: 'The Scottish Executive should be accountable to the Scottish Parliament and the Parliament and Executive should be accountable to the people of Scotland' (HMSO, 1999:7). Here petitions allow the public to raise issues which otherwise might not be addressed by the politicians or encourages them to return to issues which have been considered previously, and the PPC in pursuing petitions on behalf of petitioners may then ensure the relevant Minister is held to account in relation to the policy issues addressed by it.

6. MONITORING THE E-PETITIONER SYSTEM

Visitors to the e-Petitioner site who choose to add their name to a petition are presented with an 'exit questionnaire'. This facilitates a degree of monitoring of what users think of the system, and is a way to assess user reaction. As the exit questionnaire is voluntary it has been completed by only 1,214 of the 20,812 e-petition signers – just under 6%. The table gives an overview of some of the responses to a few of the questions.

The final question asked is "Is there anything you think we should change about e-Petitioner?" Here there were a large number of open responses, the majority of which indicated there were no serious problems.

Question	Highest response	Percent	Second highest	Percent
Where have you been using this website today?	From home	67.92%	From work	24.63%
Did you require help with this website?	No	96.48%	Yes	2.78%
Did you find that signing the petition was ...	Easy enough	97.71%	Not sure	0.98%
Did you find reading the info provided was ...	Easy enough	95.74%	Didn't look at it	1.72%
Could you see yourself using this website again for other petitions?	Yes	81.34%	Not sure	16.28%

The results will not include any site users who visited but found e-Petitioner either uninteresting or too difficult to use, since they will not have signed an e-petition, so cannot be solely used as a basis for comprehensive evaluation, but the results make a valuable contribution, and were helpful for the process of deploying e-Petitioner in other arenas. An in-depth evaluation[2] of e-Petitioner took place in March 2001. This involved semi-structured interviews and participant observations. Petitioners indicated that they viewed e-Petitioner as a useful tool in influencing politicians. The ability to access at a convenient time and reach wider sections of society made possible by e-Petitioner were considered inherently more democratic.

In terms of access to the system, e-Petitioner is a widely used resource with some 30,594 visitors to the site staying 147 seconds and viewing 3.55 pages on average, during the 6 month period up until 30th April 2005.

7.   TRANSFERABILITY

In Spring 2004, Office of the Deputy Prime Minister (ODPM) of the UK Government initiated a National Project for Local e-Democracy to explore how ICT can change the way in which public authorities engage and work with Citizens (*http://www.edemocracy.gov.uk/default.htm*). As part of the initiative the ITC was invited to develop and evaluate a version of e-Petitioner to run in two local authorities. The project aimed to explore e-petitioning as a way for citizens to raise their own concerns within the formal processes of the local authority. E-petitioning was implemented and

---

[2] http://itc.napier.ac.uk/ITC_Home/Documents/e-petitioner_Rowntree_evaluation.doc

piloted by the *Royal Borough of Kingston upon Thames* who led the project, and *Bristol City Council*. The development of e-petitioning in the National Project stemmed from the experience of the Scottish Parliament and both Councils acknowledge how their use of the system has been derived from the Scottish Parliament's guidelines.

The ITC worked alongside the Councils' e-Democracy project managers to localise the e-Petitioner tool and embed it in their processes for handling petitions, while ensuring it remained sufficiently generic to be easily adapted to the needs of other Councils. In Kingston this work was coordinated through the IT Department, and in Bristol through the Corporate Consultation team. As well as deploying the system and developing procedures to handle e-petitions, the Councils' role included promoting the system internally (to Councillors) and externally (to members of the public).

Local authorities, by contrast, are much smaller entities than a Parliament, and have far fewer resources. So, frequently, in carrying out their core responsibilities of outworking the legislation created by the national Parliaments at a local level they find little left over to resource a formal petitions procedure. Consequently the petitions processes at Local Authority level tend to be less well defined. Often petitions cluster around a small number of departments in the Council, of which Planning is usually the most popular. Over time such departments would have devised their own processes for dealing with petitions, while many less frequently petitioned departments may have no processes at all.

Thus the first task in establishing the e-Petitioning System within a Local Authority is to formally define a petitions process that it suitable to their context. In Kingston, developing the e-petitioning process entailed a need to publish guidelines for the first time, and to put in place a mechanism for managing new e-petitions, as well as updating the site and publishing the Council's formal response to each petition. The addition of a new 'channel' for petitioning and the associated need to guide website visitors on how they might use it, established the case for publishing guidelines on petitioning in general. The Kingston e-Petitioner System[3] is shown in Figure 2.

As can be seen the e-Petitioner site is a 'localised' version of the system already operational on the website of the Scottish Parliament. The main effort in transferring the system lay in meeting the need for easy to use administration functions, in meeting accessibility requirements (Web Accessibility Initiative, 2004) which are now mandatory, and in providing a more modular architecture suited to the need for the software to be tailored to the varying needs of local authorities. The Scottish Parliament e-Petitioner System is maintained by ITC as a 'managed service', an

---

[3] See *http://e-petitions.kingston.gov.uk/*. The Bristol City Council e-Petitioner is available at: *http://www.bristol-city.gov.uk/item/epetition.html*

arrangement that could not meet the needs of the National Project tools to be sustainable beyond the life of the project. Kingston and Bristol required facilities for their own officers to administer their respective systems.

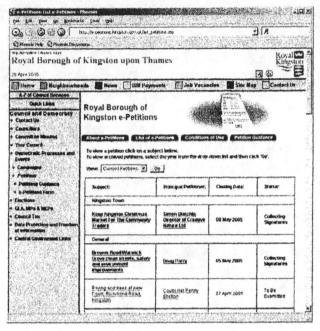

Figure 2. Listing Petitions in the Royal Borough of Kingston e-Petitioner System.

At the end of the pilot period (17 March 2005) an evaluation was undertaken (Whyte *et al.*, 2005). Over the period of the pilot there were 7 e-petitions for Kingston, and 9 paper petitions were presented to the Council in the same period. In Bristol there were 9 e-petitions and 22 on paper. The total number of e-petition signatures was 173 in Kingston and 890 in Bristol.

Citizens, Officers and Members who took part in the evaluation were almost unanimously in favour of e-petitioning. It has enjoyed strong support from Councillors in both Kingston and Bristol, particularly Kingston, and from the departments who are directly involved in the day-to-day servicing of representative government. The issues raised through e-petitioning are unarguably issues that are important to citizens, and are evidently addressed through local authority decision-making. E-petitions were raised on, for example, road crossings, telecoms masts, and Post Office closures. The e-Petitioning pilot has increased transparency in part by formalising the process for handling petitions for the first time. The publication of the site and its associated guidelines on petitioning makes both the process and the petition outcomes more visible. The added visibility applies to paper as well as e-petitions, since paper petitions that are presented at Council meetings are also listed on the e-Petitioner page. The evaluation states:

"The evaluation found much had been accomplished in both Councils. Over the one year project lifetime staff were recruited, the supplier contracted, e-Petitioner implemented, working practices and processes examined and the tool launched to be used by the public. E-Petitioner was used by hundreds of citizens in each Council area, and showed early signs of impacting on decision-making."

8. CONCLUSION

The Scottish Parliament's e-Petitions System has led the way in offering citizens the possibility of a more active interaction with the political process which is readily accessible and transparent and provides a direct means of holding elected politicians to account other than through the ballot box.

We have seen how the System has attracted growing interest from the Public to the point that to date in the current Session there have been a total of 20,812 signatures and 639 discussion comments made through the System, and perhaps its most telling selling point is that there are increasing signs that it is having an impact on the policy process within the Parliament.

The wealth of experience gained through operating the e-Petitioner System successfully at a national level has been seen to have facilitated the re-engineering of the System for the needs of Local Authorities, and through case studies on two English Local Authorities where e-Petitioner was deployed, are seeing early signs that e-Petitioner is a useful tool in enabling citizens to better engage with political processes at a local level also.

REFERENCES

Coleman, S., with Hall, N., and Howell, M. (2002), *Hearing Voices: The Experience of Online Public Consultations and Discussions in UK Governance*, Hansard Society.

HMSO (1999), *Shaping Scotland's Parliament*, Report of the Consultative Steering Group.

Macintosh, A., Malina, A., and Farrell, S. (Scottish Parliament) (2002), *Digital Democracy through Electronic Petitioning*; In McIver, W., and Elmagarmid, A.K. (eds). Advances in Digital Government: Technology, Human Factors, and Policy, Boston/Dordrecht/London, Kluwer Academic Publishers, pp 137-148.

OECD (2001), *Citizens as Partners: Information, Consultation and Public Participation in Policy-Making*, OECD, Paris.

OECD (2004), *Promises and Problems of e-Democracy; Challenges of Citizen on-line Engagement*, OECD, Paris.

The Electoral Commission (2005), *An Audit of Political Engagement 2*, Research Report March 2005. ISBN: 1-904363-60-1.

Web Accessibility Initiative (2004), *Web Content Accessibility Guidelines 2.0*, World Wide Web Consortium. Available at: http://www.w3.org/WAI/.

Whyte, A., Renton, A., and Macintosh, A. (2005), *e-Petitioning in Kingston and Bristol: Evaluation of e-Petitioning in the Local e-Democracy National Project*, Improvement and Development Authority, London. (Forthcoming)

Architecture of Multi Channel Multi Database Voting System

A.Vasudhara Reddy and S.V.Raghavan
Network Systems Laboratory, Department of Computer Science and Engineering, Indian Institute of Technology Madras, India. E-mail:{vasu,svr}@cs.iitm.ernet.in.

Abstract: Voting technology has seen various changes over the time, starting from traditional ballot voting system to the latest e-voting system. But technology couldn't affect the popularity of ballot voting system though it doesn't provide desirable blend of accessibility and efficiency. We believe that an architecture that combines the efficiency of current day technology and the ease of ballot voting system will revolutionize voting. We propose a novel architecture for voting system that uses multiple channels (ATM, Internet, cellular phone, telephone and ballot) and multiple databases to show that it is ideal in achieving accessibility, efficiency, feasibility and flexibility. We show through simulations that the proposed multi channel voting system is suitable for several countries. We compare the cost of this voting system with the traditional one in different scenarios with the help of a new metric.

Key words: Traditional voting, Online voting, Offline voting, Database synchronization, Voter anonymity, Voter authentication, Vote uniqueness.

1.   INTRODUCTION

Advances in technologies have changed nearly every facet of our lives. One of the exceptions to this trend has been in the area of the voting system. In the past, several attempts have been made for replacing traditional voting system with modern equipments. But none of them could see successful implementation all over. At present, traditional, mechanical and electronic voting systems are being used. But these systems are not efficient with respect to the overall voting time and cost. Hand-marked and hand-counted traditional voting process increases the time required for elections. In March

2000 the Arizona Democratic Party allowed for the first time remote Internet voting in its presidential preference primary [1]. In the 2001 general elections in Washington State, 69% of the votes were cast by mail [2]. Internet voting may offer a cloak for vote theft, voter coercion, and lost public confidence in the outcome. Remote Internet voting assumes a secure infrastructure of voter terminals that does not exist. Trustworthy elections are essential to democracy and achieving them requires a balance among security, convenience and cost. Due to the digital divide and current technological limitations, e-voting cannot be proposed as a universal means of voting but rather as an alternative option, supplemental to traditional voting [3]. In order to reduce voting time we need to adopt modern technologies such as Automated Teller Machine (ATM), Internet, telephone and cellular phones. In this work, we propose the Multi Channel Multi Database (MCMD) voting architecture which combines all the available modern technologies. It supports the use of existing voting systems and adds on new features with a few modifications in traditional voting process. Users of all classes benefit from this architecture as it has provision for multiple channels. The complexity of a system can be understood by the challenges that we discuss later in this paper for designing architecture. Presence of multiple channels should not give scope for voter to transfer their right to vote. Strong voter authentication is needed. A voter should be able to cast only single vote. Synchronization in multiple databases is needed.

The remainder of this paper is organized as follows. In Section 2, we describe design issues of MCMD voting system. The MCMD voting system architecture and voting process explained in Section 3 and Section 4 respectively. Simulation results are presented in Section 5. Section 6 concludes the paper and provides links to some future work.

2.   MULTI CHANNEL MULTI DATABASE VOTING SYSTEM

Every voting system must possess an easily accessible and friendly interface so that all eligible voters either educated or uneducated can easily cast their vote. Current offline voting systems take more time for casting vote and creates bottleneck at authentication, counting stages of voting process due to its rigidness. To eradicate this, some modern online voting technologies have been adopted in several places like Canada and Europe. But poor and uneducated peoples cannot use these modern technologies. So for reducing voting time and increasing accessibility, the MCMD architecture will adopt offline voting technologies and online technologies such as ATM, Internet, cellular phone and telephone. We assume that all servers, databases and communication lines in MCMD voting architecture work properly.

2.1 Design Issues of MCMD Voting System

2.1.1 Voter Authentication

Voter identification card is sufficient for perfect voter authentication in offline voting system. But in online voting system, voters cast their votes from remote places without any identification authority checking them in person. Though some authentications based on Personal Identification Number (PIN) and Transaction Number (TAN) are implemented in *Vote here gold* and *election.com* systems respectively, but anonymity cannot be guaranteed [7]. In public key and visual cryptography authentication methods, others have a chance to modify or break the information [8]. Partial authentication can be achieved in online voting system with the help of biometrics [6]. Face or voice recognition in Internet, face or fingerprint recognition in ATM and voice recognition in telephone or cellular phones can be used as biometrics. The above mentioned set of single metrics for authentication is not entirely reliable because, they can be stolen or twins may have same face characteristics and voice can be mimicked. Better authentication can be achieved by combining one or more biometrics with password or PIN. The authentication metrics for MCMD system have been tabulated in *Table 1*.

Table 1. Authentication metrics in MCMD voting system

S.No	Technology	Authentication Metric
1	ATM	Face + PIN
2	Internet	Face + Voice + Password
3	Cellular phone	Voice + Password
4	Land-line phone	Voice + Password
5	Offline voting	Identification card

2.1.2 Maintaining Uniqueness

Due to availability of multiple channels and databases in MCMD voting system, single user has the possibility to use different channels at a time and vote more than once. This violates the *uniqueness* principle of voting system [14, 15] and further, synchronization cannot be achieved in multiple databases. These drawbacks can be curbed with the help of database synchronization. For building synchronization any one of the methods can be considered:

- *Serialization:* It means serial usage of multiple channels by a single voter. Time between successive usage of channels by a single voter is greater than or equal to consistent time (time required to modify all the databases). Maintaining serialization practically is difficult because with multiple technologies, a single voter can cast multiple votes within consistent time.
- *Restriction on channel registration:* A single voter has eligibility to register for only one channel, others are discarded. Every voter has a chance to use one registered channel from which he can cast his vote. This restriction changes multi channel voting system to single channel voting system and sometimes, voter is unable to cast his vote because of unavailability of that channel.
- *Dependency and read-only channel databases:* If we conduct voting through multiple channels in independent way database synchronization and uniqueness cannot be achieved properly. Hence it must be made in a dependent way and also maintain the read-only property of all channel databases that are connected to a read-write global database. This MCMD system accepts single vote from a voter in first-come-first-serve priority basis even though multiple channels are used by him at the same time.

2.1.3   Maintaining Anonymity

Voter anonymity in MCMD system can be gained by maintaining anonymity in offline and online voting system. In offline voting system, voter is checked by proper authority and valid voter can cast his vote without revealing his identity. In online voting system, voter sends his information and vote through either wired or wireless channels. One special server (i.e. *Data Server*) separates the vote casted by the voter from his identity and records the vote. This simple voting protocol [10] is scalable, flexible, mobile and convenient but no way to ensure anonymity and correctness because of absence of crypto techniques. In simple cryptographic protocol [10], if servers team up then anonymity and correctness will not ensure and voters can prove how they voted. The problems in MIX net approach are, at least one of the MIX servers has to be honest and if number of servers is increased then protocol becomes slower [11]. FOO voting protocol uses the concept of blind signature and problems concerning voter anonymity and fake votes for non-voters can be introduced by the administration [12]. The combination of MIX net and FOO voting protocol are given in [13], it will ensure anonymity, scales well and also disallow fake votes, so we will use this in MCMD voting system.

2.2   Design of MCMD Voting System

2.2.1   Voting System

The entire MCMD voting system is classified into offline voting system and online voting system as shown in *Figure 1*.

- *Offline voting system:* In this, physical presence of voter must be needed along with his identification at voting station. Offline voting system is broadly divided into paper based offline voting system and paperless offline voting system. Traditional ballot voting system, machine readable ballot system and optical scan voting system are examples of paper based offline voting system [4]. Lever pull machine system and Direct Recording Electronic (DRE) voting system are examples of paperless offline voting system [5].

- *Online voting system:* In this, voter can vote from anywhere without going to voting station. Previously Internet voting was classified as poll-site Internet voting, kiosk voting and remote Internet voting [9]. Here we classify online voting system into stationary online voting system and mobile online voting system. Stationary communication devices such as Telephone, personal computer with Internet and ATM are examples of stationary online voting system. Mobile devices such as laptop with Internet and cellular phones are examples of mobile online voting system.

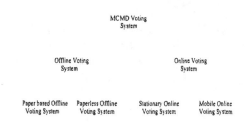

Figure 1. Classification of MCMD voting system

2.2.2   Voter Identification Card Design

Voter identification card should have complete and consistent voter information to authenticate voter across the multiple channels in MCMD voting system without any ambiguity. Single information of a voter may not be sufficient for authentication over different channels. This requirement calls for a sensitive design of voter identification card. So, it should contain information about the voter such as name, sex, date of birth, address, a unique voter identification number (*Vid*), photo and bar-code. Photo and bar-code with *Vid* is sufficient information for voter authentication in offline voting system. Password or PIN are provided for each voter along with his biometrics at registration phase of voting process, which are asked and checked for authentication in online voting system. This does not guarantee against proxy voting but eliminates bogus voting.

2.2.3   Databases Design

In MCMD voting system, each constituency has separate global database and set of channel databases one for each online channel. Global database contains complete voter information about the constituency voters and channel database contains the information of all voters who registered for that channel. Global database is a union of all station databases in a constituency. Station database contains complete voter information about the station voters or part of constituency voters. The set of rules to be satisfied while designing databases are: (1) Global database is union of all station databases that belong to a constituency. (2) No two station databases that belong to a constituency have the common data. (3) Union of all channel databases that belong to a station is subset of that station database. (4) Any two channel databases that belong to a station may or may not have the common data.

3.   MCMD VOTING SYSTEM ARCHITECTURE

MCMD voting architecture is designed to support multiple channels and distributed voter information databases seamlessly. The architecture of MCMD voting system for a constituency is shown in *Figure 2*. To describe the distributed architecture we introduce different kinds of servers and databases.

3.1   Functions of Different Servers

Each constituency has separate Offline Server (*OS*), Election commissioner Server (*EcS*), set of Data Servers (*DS*) and set of Portal Servers (*PS*). The communication between the servers is done through Acknowledgment (*Ack*) signal, which is either Positive Acknowledgment (*PAck*) signal or Negative Acknowledgment (*NAck*) signal depending on success or failure of operation. The functions of each server are given below:

- *Offline Server: OS* scans bar-code and *Vid* on the voter identification card and send *Vid* to the *EcS* for further validations and also receives *Ack* signal from *EcS*. If it is *PAck* signal then, ballot paper is issued to the voter or allow voter for further process in paperless offline voting system by the proper authority, else, it rejects the voter.

- *Portal Server: PS* is interface between voter and *DS* and it does two functions. Firstly, it forwards authentication information from voter to *DS* and also accepts *Ack* signal from *DS*. If it is *PAck* then, send electronic ballot paper to the voter else send *"incorrect_voter _authentication"* message to voter. Secondly, it forwards filled electronic ballot paper to *DS* and also receive *Ack* signal from *DS*. If it is *PAck* signal then, send *"successful_vote_acceptance"* message to voter, else, send *"duplicate_vote"* message to voter.

- *Data Server: DS* does two functions. Firstly, voter authentication is done after acceptance of authentication information from *PS* and send either *PAck* or *NAck* signal to *PS* depending on successful or unsuccessful voter authentication respectively. Secondly, it sends *Vid* to *EcS* after acceptance of filled electronic ballot from *PS* and receive *Ack* signal from *EcS*. If it is *PAck* signal then place voter's vote in electronic ballot box and send *"successful_vote_acceptance"* message to *PS*, else send *"duplicate_vote"* message to *PS*.

- *Election commissioner Server: EcS* is an important sever in MCMD voting system which has whole responsibility for checking status of voter (whether voter already voted or not) and also modify global database. It accepts *Vid* from *DS* or *OS* and check status flag of *Vid* record in global database for validity, if flag is set then, send *NAck* signal to either *DS* or *OS* to indicate duplicate vote else, set the flag and send *PAck* signal to either *DS* or *OS* to indicate valid vote.

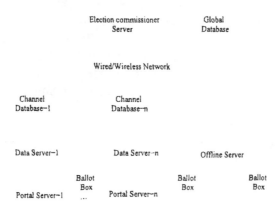

Figure 2. Architecture for MCMD voting system

3.2   Purpose of Different Databases

Databases store complete information about each eligible voter and also status information. In the proposed architecture, databases are distributed across the network. Each constituency has separate global database, set of channel databases and set of ballot boxes one for each online channel. The purpose of each database is given below:

● *Global database*: This read-write database contains a record for each eligible voter of a constituency. Each record has voter details and status flag which represents whether the voter has casted the vote or not. Initially all status flags are reset.

● *Channel database*: It is read only, projection of global database and constructed by taking subset of global database based on voter's online channel registration. This is used for checking voter authentication.

● *Ballot box*: Ballot box store votes, its abstraction can be realized as different kind of database based on specific channel and the technology used to realize that channel. For paper-based offline voting system ballot box is the database but, for paperless offline voting and online voting system electronic devices can be used as ballot box.

4.   MCMD VOTING PROCESS

Entire voting process in MCMD system contains set of steps which are represented as a precedence graph as shown in *Figure 3*. It contains set of nodes and set of arrows. Each node represents a step in voting process and each arrow shows the order of execution among those steps.

1. *Creation of Voter Information Database*: Election authority should maintain uniform, centralized and interactive voter information. The first step for conducting any election is to update voter information database that will add new voter information, update existing voter information and delete passed away voter information.

2. *Issuing Voter Identification Card*: Election authority distributes voter identification card to the voter before election process starts. It contains voter details and photo as per the latest voter database.

Figure 3. Precedence graph for MCMD voting process

3. *Registration for Online Channels*: This is an additional process to the current voting system. In this phase, voter can register for any number of online channels and at the same time he can store required authentication information for those registered channels based on technology available to him. The authentication information for ATM is combination of face, fingerprint and PIN; for Internet is combination of face, voice and password; for telephone and cellular phone combination of voice and password are used.

4. *Agreement with Service Providers*: The election authority has to take permission from service providers such as Internet Service Providers (ISP) for Internet service, banks for ATM service and telecommunication service providers for telephone and cellular phone service and has to pay money to them for providing services.

5. *Infrastructure Setup*: Election authority has to setup offline and online voting infrastructure based on the voters registration. These registration values are directly proportional to technology development in that voting place. If technology development is high then lesser number of offline voting stations are required or else more number of offline voting stations are required.

6. *Offline Voting Steps*:
   - Voter authentication is done manually by proper authority member.
   - If authentication is successful then *OS* sends *Vid* to *EcS* for checking the global database or else voter is trying to cast others' vote. So it doesn't allow him for further process.
   - *EcS* checks status of *Vid* record in global database, if flag is set then *EcS* sends *NAck* signal to *OS* else *EcS* sets the flag and sends *PAck* signal to *OS*.
   - If *OS* receives *PAck* signal from *EcS* then authority issues ballot paper to the voter to vote in paper-based offline voting system or allow voter to vote in paperless offline voting system or else voter's trying for duplicate vote and so reject that vote.
   - Store votes in ballot box. In paper based offline voting system voter stores vote in ballot box otherwise voter stores vote in electronic ballot box.

7. *Online Voting Steps*:
   - Voter connects to *PS* by using Uniform Resource Locator (URL) for Internet channel, phone number for cellular phone or telephone channels and bar-code on voter identification card for ATM channel.
   - Voter sends authentication information to the *DS* through corresponding *PS*.
   - *DS* sends either *PAck* or *NAck* signal to the corresponding *PS* depending on successful or unsuccessful voter authentication.

- If *PS* receives *PAck* signal from *DS* then it sends electronic ballot to the requested voter depending on constituency and language chosen by the voter or else rejects the voter because of incorrect voter authentication.
- Voter sends filled electronic ballot (contain *Vid* and vote) to *DS* through corresponding *PS*.
- *DS* sends *Vid* to *EcS* for global database verification for duplicate vote.
- *EcS* checks status of *Vid* record in global database, if flag is set then *EcS* sends *NAck* signal to *DS* else *EcS* sets the flag and sends *PAck* signal to *DS*.
- *DS* stores votes in electronic ballot box and sends *PAck* signal to corresponding *PS* if it receives *PAck* signal from *EcS*, else sends *NAck* signal to corresponding *PS* and rejects vote for voter trying for duplicate vote.
- *PS* receives either *PAck* or *NAck* signal from *DS* depending on successful acceptance or rejection of vote and sends that result to voter.

8. *Counting Process*: After completing entire voting process, election authority should collect online and offline ballot boxes for each constituency, count offline votes of each participant, count online votes of each participant, add the offline and online votes and declare the result.

5.   SIMULATION

5.1   Simulation Data and Environment

Usages of online channels among various world regions, metropolitan cities of India and overall India in different years have been tabulated in *Table 2*. Internet usage data collected from International Telecommunication Union [16], telephone usage data collected from Bharat Sanchar Nigam Limited [17], cellular phone usage data collected from Videsh Sanchar Nigam Limited [18] and ATM usage data collected from Reserve Bank of India [19]. We have used these data for simulation.

The performance of MCMD voting system is simulated using Standard Template Library (STL) in C++. STL has a set of predefined classes which are used for simulation. In MCMD voting system each step such as voters arrival rate, authentication, ballot issue, database modification and vote acceptance acts as an event with separate function module. Voters arrival is denoted as random discrete event as they arrive at irregular time intervals and servers processing is denoted as deterministic discrete event as they are deterministic. The simulation is conducted with 1000 traditional voting stations and 1 million voters. The simulation is repeated by increasing number of channels (*N*) at different world regions, metropolitan cities of India and overall India. The MCMD voting system supports traditional voting model if *N=1*; if *N=2* this becomes traditional and Internet; if *N=3* this changes to traditional, Internet and cellular phone; if *N=4* it becomes traditional, Internet, cellular phone and telephone; if *N=5* system accepts traditional, Internet, cellular phone, telephone and ATM.

Table 2. Usage of online technologies

S.No	Area/Year	Internet Usage	Cellphone Usage	Telephone Usage	ATM Usage
1	Africa	1.5%	6.2%	3%	-
2	Americas	25.9%	34.1%	33.8%	-
3	Asia	6.7%	15%	13.6%	-
4	Europe	23.7%	55.4%	41%	-
5	Chennai	10%	10.4%	17.1%	44%
6	Delhi	11%	26.5%	21.8%	49%
7	Kolkata	8%	7.2%	13.9%	33%
8	Mumbai	18%	19.4%	20.1%	56%
9	2005	1.9%	7.3%	5.7%	26.4%
10	2010	3.4%	17%	8.6%	35.6%
11	2015	7%	30.4%	11.7%	42.2%

5.2   Simulation Results

The online utilization in overall India are given in *Figure 4* and voting time for world regions, metropolitan cities of India and overall India for different years are given in *Figure 5*, *Figure 6* and *Figure 7* respectively.

5.2.1   Voting Time

We define *Online utilization* (U_{online}) as the ratio of the number of voters using online channels to the number of voters using offline and online channels. The *voting time* in MCMD is defined as the time required using this system to vote for a group of people. It is inversely proportional to U_{online}. From *Figure 5* we observe that, there is a reduction of voting time in different continents like Europe, Americas, Asia and Africa with increase in number of channels in MCMD voting system. The voting time in Europe and Americas are reduced by 1/6, 1/2 and 3/4 with two, three and four channels respectively. However we find negligible reduction in Asia and Africa. From *Figure 6* we observe that, there is a reduction of voting time in different Indian metropolitan cities with increase in number of channels in MCMD voting system. The voting time in Delhi and Mumbai are reduced by 1/4, 1/2 and 3/4 with three, four and five channels respectively. For Chennai and

Kolkata it is 1/7, 1/4 and 1/2. From *Figure* 7 we observe that, there are improvements in India with usage of different channels in different years. In 2005, 2010 and 2015 the voting time is reduced by 1/9, 1/5 and 1/3 with four channels and by 1/3, 1/2 and 3/5 with five channels. There is negligible improvement with usage of two and three channels.

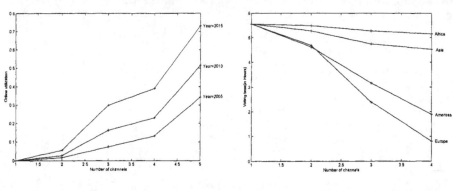

| *Figure 4.* Online utilization in India | *Figure 5.* Voting time in World regions |

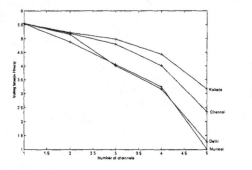
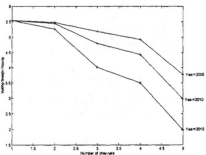

| *Figure 6.* Voting time in metropolitan cities of India | *Figure 7.* Voting time in India in different years |

5.2.2   Speed-Up Factor

The speed-up factor of MCMD system at a particular N value is defined as the ratio of voting time of MCMD system with one channel to that with N channels. Speed-up factor of MCMD voting system with multiple channels compared to traditional voting system are give in *Table 2*. We calculated the average speed for two, three, four and five channels as 1.5, 2, 2.5 and 3 respectively. The MCMD voting system with one online channel gives below average speed in places like America, Europe and poor speed in all other places. The system with two online channels gives above average speed in Europe, below average speed in America and poor speed in all other places. The system with three online channels gives good speed in Europe, above average speed in America, below average speed in Delhi and Mumbai, poor speed in all other places. The system with four online channels gives good speed in Delhi and Mumbai, average speed in Chennai and below average speed in Kolkata. The system in India with four online channels gives above average speed in year 2015, below average speed in year 2010 and poor speed in year 2005.

Table3. Speed-Up factor of MCMD voting system

S.No	Area/Year	N=2	N=3	N=4	N=5
1	Africa	1.01	1.05	1.07	-
2	America	1.2	1.75	2.93	-
3	Asia	1.05	1.17	1.22	-
4	Europe	1.18	2.32	6.9	-
5	Chennai	1.07	1.15	1.38	2.37
6	Delhi	1.07	1.38	1.75	4.36
7	Kolkata	1.06	1.11	1.25	1.75
8	Mumbai	1.13	1.36	1.71	5.4
9	2005	1.01	1.07	1.12	1.47
10	2010	1.02	1.15	1.25	1.86
11	2015	1.05	1.38	1.58	2.8

5.2.3   Cost Estimation

The cost of MCMD process (C_{mcmd}) includes cost of offline ($C_{offline}$) and cost of online voting process (C_{online}). $C_{offline}$ is product of traditional voting process cost (C_{trad}) and *Offline utilization* ($U_{offline}=1- U_{online}$). C_{online} is sum of ith ($1\leq i\leq n$) channel cost (C_i), where n is number of online channels. C_i is sum of service charge (S_i) and cost of technology (T_i) for i^{th} channel. S_i is product of number of votes casted (N_i) and cost per vote ($Cost_i$) for i^{th} channel. Number of votes casted through all online channels (N_{tot}) is sum of N_i ($1\leq i\leq n$). For simplicity we assume that the cost per vote in all online channels is same and technology enable cost for all online channels is same.

$$C_{offline} = C_{trad} * U_{offline}$$
$$= C_{trad} * (1- U_{online})$$
$$C_{online} = \sum_{i=1}^{n} C_i$$
$$= \sum_{i=1}^{n} (S_i + T_i)$$
$$= \sum_{i=1}^{n} (N_i * Cost_i + T_i)$$
$$= C * \sum_{i=1}^{n} N_i + n*T$$

(Our assumption is for all i, $Cost_i =C$ and $T_i = T$)
$$= C * U_{online} * N_{tot} + n*T$$
$$C_{mcmd} = C_{offline} + C_{online}$$
$$= C_{trad} * (1- U_{online}) + C * U_{online} * N_{tot} + n*T$$

According to Election Commission of India reports about 2004 elections, only 380 million (35% of total population) votes are casted and cost of election is 1300 Crores (Cr.) [20]. The estimated Indian population in 2005, 2010 and 2015 are 1094, 1170 and 1230 millions respectively. The assumptions made for cost calculation in MCMD are: value of T is 125 Crores, casted votes are 35% of total population and cost of elections in 2005, 2010 and 2015 are 1300, 1600 and 1900 Crores respectively. The value of U_{online} is taken from *Figure 4* and values of Cost per vote (C), C_{mcmd} are calculated by using above assumptions and formulas, and given in *Table 4*. In year 2005, cost of MCMD voting system with one or two or three or four online channels is more than traditional voting system even C is nil. In year 2010, MCMD system with one or two or three online channels is expensive than traditional voting system even if C is nil and cost of system with four online channels is less than traditional voting system if C is less then or equal to 15 INR. In year 2015, MCMD voting system with two, three and four online channels is less expensive than traditional voting system if C is less than or equal to 24 INR, 23 INR and 27 INR respectively and cost of system with one online channel is more than traditional voting system even C is nil.

Table 4. Cost estimation for MCMD voting process

S.No	Year	C_{trad} (Cr.)	n=1		n=2		n=3		n=4	
			C (INR)	C_{mcmd} (Cr.)	C (INR)	C_{mcmd} (Cr.)	C (INR)	C_{mcmd} (Cr.)	C (INR)	C_{mcmd} (Cr.)
1	2005	1300	0	1412	0	1459	0	1506	0	1358
2	2010	1600	0	1693	0	1594	0	1607	15	1597
3	2015	1900	0	1930	24	1890	23	1893	27	1882

6.   CONCLUSION AND FUTURE WORK

Offline voting system offers reasonable balance of security and reliability but it is not a scalable and feasible model for the modern world. Online voting systems promise benefits in terms of remote accessibility and ease of use. Our proposed MCMD voting system combines the advantages of both technologies, so that it enables traditional, Internet, ATM, cellular phone and telephone based voting depending on the requirement in a consistent manner. The MCMD voting system with two or three channels gives a marginal improvement in places like Europe and America and no improvement in other places due to lack of awareness of technology. The system with four channels gives a notable improvement in places like Europe and America, marginal improvement in Indian metropolitan cities and no improvement in other countries or places. The system with five channels gives a notable improvement in Indian metropolitan cities, marginal improvement in overall

India in year 2015 and no improvement in overall India in years 2010 and 2005. As long as cost per vote is within the bound given in *Table 4*, MCMD voting is cheaper compared to traditional voting. As a future work, performance of MCMD voting system on parallel servers can be studied. Fault tolerance and cost implication are to be studied when duplicate databases and redundant channels are employed. Reliability of the system can be improved with new cryptography techniques.

References

1. Mohan, J.Glidden, "The Case for Internet Voting", *Communications of ACM*, Jan 2001, Vol 44, No.1.
2. Washington, Secretary of State, News Release; http://www.secstate.wa.gov.
3. L. Mitrou, D. Gritzalis, S. Katsikas, "Revisiting Legal and Regulatory Requirements for Secure e-Voting", *Proc. of the 16th IFIP International Information Security Conference*, Kluwer Academics Publishers, May 2002.
4. Voting: What is, What Could Be, CalTech-MIT Voting Technology Project Report, 2001; http://www.vote.caltech.edu/Reports.
5. T. Kohno et.al., "Analysis of an Electronic Voting System", *In Proc. of the 2004 IEEE Symposium on Security and Privacy*, IEEE Computer Socitey Press, 2004.
6. S. Prabhakar, S. Pankanti, A. k. Jain, "Biometric Recognition: Security and Privacy Concerns", *IEEE Security and Privacy*, IEEE Computer Society Press, 2003.
7. R. Kofler, R. Krimmer, A. Prosser, "Electronic Voting: Algorithmic and Implementation Issues", *In Proc. of the 36th Hawaii International Conference on System Sciences*, IEEE Computer Society Press, 2003.
8. A. Rubin et.al, "Authentication for Remote Voting", *Workshop on Human-Computer Interaction and Security Systems*, 2003.
9. P. Bungale, S. Sridhar, "Electronic Voting-A Survey", Department of Computer Science, The Johns Hopkins University, 2001.
10. J. Benaloh, D. Tuinstra, "Receipt Free Secret-Ballot Election", *ACM Symposium on the Theory of Computing*, 1994.
11. D. Chaum, "Untraceable Electronic Mail Return Address and Digital Pseudonyms", *Communications of ACM*, Vol 24(2), 1981.
12. A. Fujioka, T. Okamoto, K. Ohta, "A Practical Secret Voting Scheme for Large Scale Elections", *Advances in Cryptology - AUSCRYPT 92*, Springer Verlag.
13. T. Okamoto, "An Electronic Voting Scheme", *Advanced IT Tools*, IFIP 96.
14. C. Lambrinoudakis et.al, "Electronic Voting Systems: Security Implications of the Administrative Workflow", *In Proc. of the 14th International Workshop on Database and Expert Systems*, IEEE Computer Society Press, 2003.
15. D. Gritzalis, "Secure Electronic Voting", *7th Computer Security Incidents Response Teams Workshop Syros*, Greece 2002.
16. *http://www.itu.int.*
17. *http://www.bsnl.co.in.*
18. *http://www.vsnl.com.*
19. *http://www.rbi.org.in.*
20. *http://www.eci.gov.in.*

PRACTITIONER BUY-IN AND RESISTANCE TO E-ENABLED INFORMATION SHARING ACROSS AGENCIES

The case of an e-government project to join up local services in England

SUSAN BAINES, PAT GANNON-LEARY AND ROB WILSON
Centre for Social and Business Informatics, University of Newcastle-upon-Tyne, Newcastle-upon-Tyne, UK

Abstract: FrAmework for Multi-agency Environments (FAME) is one of 23 national projects within the e-government strategy to reform and modernize local services in England. Six local projects each worked with an IT supplier (known as a technology partner) to produce a technical system for the exchange and management of client / patient information across agency and professional boundaries. All participants, including the technology partners, insisted that FAME was about people, organizations and change more that it was about technology. This paper draws upon the successes and setbacks of these local projects in order to report some urgent lessons for the implementation of e-government initiatives that involve new working practices for front-line practitioners.

Key words: e-social care; local government; front-line practitioners; ICT project evaluation

1.   JOINING UP LOCAL GOVERNMENT SERVICES

Numerous policies and initiatives in the UK now aim to make public services provided by different agencies more efficient, responsive and 'joined-up'. 'Joining up' has come to denote ways in which the New Labour government has reacted to the perception that complex social needs demand co-coordinated activities across organizational boundaries (Ling 2002). For example, the National Service Framework (NSF) for older people sets out standards which aim to promote older people's health and independence and ensure that services for them are joined-up and tailored to their needs. Thirty five English local authorities were awarded the status of 'Pathfinder' Children's Trusts in summer 2003. Their remit is to co-ordinate local education, social care and some health services for children and young people. The Children Act 2004 now makes it incumbent on all education, health and social service providers to work together to deliver better services focused on the child.

Fragmentation of agencies in social care and health has been blamed for poor service, inefficiency, and failures of care. A tragic instance of failure of care was the case of Victoria Climbié – an eight year old girl killed by her guardians despite being known to several agencies and services:

> Victoria Climbié came into contact with several agencies, none of which acted on the warning signs. No one built up a picture of her interactions with different services (DfES 2003).

In other words professionals who had contact with this vulnerable child failed to protect her at least partly because they did not share information they individually held.

FrAmework for Multi-agency Environments (FAME) was designed to develop a framework for sharing personal information between local authorities and other agencies. The image of the organizational and professional 'silo', in which information is inert, is ubiquitous in UK government policy documents and has come into wide usage. From within their 'silos' service workers are able to see only one aspect of an individual who may have complex needs. 'Joining up' across the silos requires personal information about users of services to be made available across organizations and agencies (including statutory bodies, voluntary groups and for-profit service providers) with different cultures, management structures, and information systems.

FAME was one of the largest and most ambitious of the national projects created to support the delivery of local e-government in England. Within FAME there were six work strands each led by an English local authority in partnership with service providers. From April 2003 to October 2004 these six local FAME projects were each required to deliver a real life example of e-enabled information sharing across agencies in a particular set of services (for example, to vulnerable older people, mental health patients, disabled children). Each strand worked with an IT supplier known as a 'technology partner'. All the strands involved Social Services. There were partners in each case from some (but not necessarily all) of the following: Health, Education, the Police, voluntary sector agencies, and other local authorities. In developing the local solutions the technology partners visited practitioners in their workplaces and held workshops with them in order to ensure that the functionality and the 'look and feel' met their needs. Each technical solution was different, reflecting local and service specific conditions and priorities. All had the remit to link participating agencies and their IT systems in order to facilitate the secure and timely exchange of information according to locally agreed protocols. We will use two examples of local FAME projects here for illustration, an electronic Single Assessment Process (SAP) for vulnerable older adults and a 'virtual integrated mental health record'.

The aim of the SAP project was to deliver a working electronic Single Assessment Tool in order to improve the way older people are jointly assessed for their health, social care and housing needs. Embedded within the electronic tool is a Department of Health accredited assessment instrument which can also be used in paper form. The SAP application allows practitioners across all participating agencies to assess the needs of elderly people by the use of the electronic version of the assessment instrument. Practitioners can then refer cases on for further, more in depth assessment electronically. Assessments are viewed via an internet browser. The information collated as a result of these assessments is fed into an 'overview assessment summary' to give a complete, holistic picture of that elderly person's needs and involvement with other agencies. Service users are asked for consent to their information being passed on to specific agencies and data accessibility is restricted to match this consent.

The FAME virtual integrated mental health record was developed across two neighboring local authority areas where community mental health teams (social care and health workers) had been integrated for more than 10 years and an integrated paper record was already in use. Electronic records, however, were still held on separate systems. The incentive to participate in FAME was described by the service manager as making technology 'catch up' with existing practice so that providers would present a seamless service to the users. This was not happening because the paper file resided with the main team dealing with the service user. Records were transported between providers across the county by courier. Liaison between teams was by telephone, email and fax and service users were likely to be asked for information they had already supplied to another professional. The FAME virtual integrated mental health record project produced an application that enables practitioners in two pilot sites to read information about service users from the existing core operational systems of the local authority and health partners. They can see names, aliases, current and previous addresses, contact numbers, and lists of when referrals have been made, by whom and to whom.

Summaries of each local strand and some of the supporting products including technical statements of requirements and integration specifications are now in the public domain. They are available from the FAME website http://www.fame-uk.org/about/strand/ as exemplars for the benefit of other local authorities and their partners. This article does not duplicate these details. It focuses upon just one key aspect of the development and implementation of local, electronic information sharing solutions for joined-up working - the responses of professional workers in the participating agencies. Unlike the technical, ethical and legal issues around information sharing this is a relatively undeveloped theme in the policy or academic literature. Yet it affects how government policy does, or does not, get translated into practice.

In addition to the six local authority led projects (known as strands) already referred to, FAME had two further strands: The Generic Framework and Learning & Evaluation – both led by a Newcastle University team of which all the authors were part. The Generic Framework identified and described nine building blocks that are essential to effective multi-agency working. (See http://www.fame-uk.org). The Learning & Evaluation team worked closely with the six local strands, exploring factors that contributed to successful delivery. This article is based upon data collected for the Learning & Evaluation strand.

Overall the evaluation of the FAME local strands was positive despite setbacks beyond the control of the local teams that led to delays in implementation (Baines et al. 2004). One of FAME's key achievements is the wealth of evidence it provides that local authorities and their partners can create multi-agency environments in which information is made accessible electronically to practitioners across traditional service boundaries. Indeed, some practitioners reported that they were able to see the 'whole' patient /client in ways that had not previously been possible. Very importantly, FAME delivers information that they value. Yet three months after new IT systems 'went live' in the two strands that implemented them on schedule, overall levels of system usage were low. The article draws upon these struggles within FAME in order to identify some urgent lessons for e-government initiatives that involve front-line professionals.

First we put the FAME experience in context by overviewing literature that has offered insight into social care and health practitioners' responses to multi-agency initiatives and IT. Then we introduce the empirical research – part of the evaluation of FAME – and describe the research methods. We give some more details about the FAME projects and report and comment upon what we learned about practitioner attitudes, experiences and behavior. Quantitative data from across FAME is reported but for reasons of space we concentrate upon qualitative material from the strands that worked with the services for vulnerable older people and mental health. Finally we reflect upon this material to point to lessons and to make recommendations for e-government projects.

2.   BUY-IN OR RESISTANCE?

The theme of 'joined-up' or 'holistic' public services is intimately associated with the modernization agenda of the New Labour government in the UK; but it is not new (6 et al. 2002; Pollitt, 2003). There is long history of joint endeavor based on shared planning, co-location of services and other physical means of attempting to promote more co-ordinated public policy and policy delivery. What is new is the *scale* of ambition of the contemporary efforts in at joining up at the level of policy implementation and service delivery. New confidence in the possibility of such joining up is substantially based on the claimed powers, and in particular the integrating capacity, of new information and communication technologies (Hudson, 2003; Geoghegan et al., 2004).

Workers who interact directly with citizens in the delivery of public services implement government policies. We refer to these people (social workers, health workers, police officers, teachers) as 'front-line practitioners'. They are the group labeled by Lipsky (1980) as the 'street level bureaucrats' through whom most citizens encounter government and whose actions constitute the services delivered by government. FAME put information systems in place at a local level in order to support the flexible and person-centered approaches now demanded of service providers in health and social care. Our participation as researchers in FAME afforded a unique opportunity to explore encounters by front-line public sector workers with IT-enabled change. As a result we have been able to open up this neglected element of the broader e-government agenda.

We look next at some evidence from earlier research on joining up in social care and health and why it is so hard to achieve at the level of front-line service delivery. Then we turn more specifically to IT and suggest selectively some approaches from a much wider literature on IT and professional working practices that can help to contextualize the experiences of social care and health workers in e-government initiatives.

Formal mechanisms put in place by agencies at a strategic level do not necessarily produce the intended cooperation on the front-line (Lupton, 2001). This may be because workers in participating agencies are not fully aware of the needs, limitations and pressures of the others (Payne et al 2002). Another practical factor is lack of time to develop relationships within project timescales (Atkinson et al. 2001). Attempts to create multi-agency information systems (whether paper or computer based) have often failed as a result of different 'mindsets', in particular different attitudes towards the recording, storage and distribution of information (Green et al. 2001). Professionalism may be perceived as under threat (Secker and Hill 2001). Such intractable barriers to multi-agency working are repeatedly labeled 'cultural'. Policy documents from central government in the UK repeatedly demand the dismantling of service 'silos' through cultural change. For example, the Green Paper *Every Child Matters* stated that local authorities are required to lead a process of 'cultural change'; new technologies for sharing information, according to this document, must be adopted but this alone will not bring about intended reforms towards more joined-up working practices (DfES 2003). The National Service Framework (NSF) for children similarly calls for a 'cultural shift' resulting in services being designed and delivered around the needs of children and families (Department of Health 2004).

The Green Paper (DfES 2003) cited above presents the sharing of personal information about citizens among the agencies that work with them as both desirable and inevitable in order to deliver benefits to individuals, families and society. Yet legal commitments to the protection of privacy are potentially in conflict with this agenda (6 et al. 2005). Exchanging personal data raises a wide range of issues about privacy and the balance between individual rights and the common good (Performance and Innovation Unit 2002). In practice tensions between information sharing and the protection of privacy are usually addressed by the use of safeguards in the form of detailed guidelines (Bellamy et al. 2005). Front-line practitioners are required to interpret such guidelines and incorporate them into their practice.

Professional expertise and IT can come into conflict on many levels. Professional workers emphasize the complex, contextual nature of front-line activities; they sometimes perceive the introduction of IT into their work as undermining their expertise and replacing it with a standardized labor process characterized by centralization of control (Haynes 2003). It has been argued that the professional care and health worker is losing authority to the citizen 'expert' as well as to the control of the state through processes of ever greater 'informatization' (Nettleton, 2003; Harrison, 2002). At the same time some reports have found that front-line practitioners believe that the caring and relational aspects of their work are threatened. One study, for example, reported that midwives saw an IT system for recording patient information as antithetical to the 'woman-centered' values of their profession (Henwood and Hart, 2003). Seemingly irrational resistance to the introduction of new technology can became understandable when examined in the light of workplace histories of technology use and earlier experiences that may have challenged workers' self image and professional relationships (Stam et al 2004).

In summary: Information systems have a vital role to play in enabling the access to timely, accurate and trusted information that is essential for joined-up working but they are likely to be only part of the solution. Other ingredients in recipes for reform are 'cultural change' (which is usually ill defined) and sets of instructions, protocols and guidelines likely to add to the ever increasing complaint of information overload. Moreover, there is evidence that from the perspectives of some front-line professional workers new information systems are not a solution at all but a threat.

3. EMPIRICAL RESEARCH: UNDERSTANDING CHANGE IN THE WORKPLACE FOR PRACTITIONERS

The overarching aim of the FAME Learning & Evaluation strand was to draw upon the experiences of the local projects in order to document, assess and report what worked, what did not work, and why. Evaluation is conventionally divided between 'summative' (to determine overall effectiveness) and 'formative' (giving feedback to people trying to improve an intervention) (Newburn 2001). There is blurring at the edge however and some commentators maintain that the distinction is often exaggerated. Our work cut across these modes with emphasis on the formative. We were guided by the principles of Theory of Change (Connel and Kubisch 1998). Central to a Theory of Change evaluation is the requirement that the evaluator works to surface the implicit theory (or theories) of action held by all participants.

The FAME Learning & Evaluation team undertook field work from July 2003 to October 2004. We consulted project managers, project board chairs and a wide range of stakeholders including service managers, service user representatives, and front-line practitioners. We undertook the following activities:

- Meetings with project managers;
- Meetings with project partners and stakeholders;
- Observation of local events, meetings, and workshops;
- Document analysis;
- Visits to pilot sites;
- A questionnaire survey and interviews with front-line practitioners;
- Report back to project teams.

All the local project teams informed us at our first meetings that 'buy-in' from practitioners was both essential and fraught with difficulty. Project managers and others typically expressed this concern in words to the effect that 'the technology will be easy – the real challenge will be changing the ways people work – changing culture'. They feared that hard pressed health care/social workers would simply 'see it as more work'. Practitioners, we were told, get blasé and weary and often suffer from 'project fatigue'. In some instances practitioners were struggling with the implementation of other new processes and systems in parallel with the FAME project. One project manager explained that she was 'dealing with reluctance and resistance.' Again and again, project managers and other team members highlighted lack of practitioner 'buy-in' as a serious risk factor. In other words their 'theories of change' were underpinned by the perception that practitioner 'resistance' must be addressed in order to ensure that the potential benefits of the projects would be realized. That is why we devoted time and resources in our evaluation to activities (observations, questionnaires and interviews) designed to elicit the experiences of practitioners across professions and agencies.

Questionnaires for practitioners prior to implementation were designed by the Learning & Evaluation team after the initial round of meetings with project managers and observation of some early work with practitioners in the strands. They were distributed to practitioners in the pilot sites by the project teams in four strands. (In two strands this was not possible because of delays in identifying which agencies and staff would participate.) The timing of this questionnaire was such that practitioners had been exposed to the aims and objectives of FAME from publicity in the workplace and from local awareness-raising events but none had yet been trained to use the system. Overall we received 108 pre-implementation questionnaires from practitioners who had been selected by project teams to be trained to use the FAME IT systems.

Response rates for the questionnaire from individual locations were variable. They ranged from an excellent 60 per cent in one strand to below 10 per cent in another. The qualitative and quantitative data we collected from practitioners prior to the implementation of FAME IT systems in four strands offer insight into attitudes, perceptions and resources that facilitate or impede multi-agency-environments and IT use. We were able to do some post-implementation evaluation work in the two strands that 'went live' in summer 2004. We also benefited from access to some local evaluation work conducted by one of the project teams. As well as a new questionnaire and interviews by telephone with selected respondents we observed post-implementation events and meetings organized by the strands.

4.   "PASSING THE PAIN BARRIER": PRACTITIONERS' EXPERIENCES AND RESPONSES

The evidence from the pre-implication questionnaire was that practitioners who had been introduced to FAME generally understood and supported its aims. Very importantly, they recognized that lack of co-ordination and exchanging information across agencies leads to less than optimal services to clients / patients.

- More than four fifths (82.5 per cent) of respondents agreed that lack of information sharing caused poor outcomes;
- More than two thirds (70 per cent) of respondents agreed that they relied on service users for information about other agencies/services;
- More than four fifths (84 per cent) of respondents agreed that increased knowledge of the work of other agencies/services would benefit their service users;
- Similarly, 86 per cent of respondents agreed that working more closely with other agencies/services would benefit their users.

Three quarters of respondents described themselves as regular IT users. Nevertheless, the prior IT experience and skills of practitioners, and their access to IT, were extremely variable. In some cases both skills and access were low. (Indeed, as later qualitative work revealed, this was a practical barrier to participation in an IT initiative.) More than two out of five respondents (42.3 per cent) reported that they lacked exclusive access to a PC in their workplace.

Only just over a third (37 per cent) indicated that they were unsure what information they were allowed to share with other agencies/services. Nearly half (47.5 per cent) indicated that they currently shared information with individual representatives of other agencies/services on an informal basis. Nevertheless, more than three quarters of all respondents (76 per cent) agreed that clearer guidelines on sharing information would be helpful to them. In respect of potential deterrents to sharing information, 45 per cent of respondents indicated that Data Protection issues deterred them, while 56 per cent were deterred by issues around client consent and confidentiality. Practitioners were asked to respond in their own words to the question 'What, in your view, are the main barriers to sharing information with other agencies/services?'

The most frequently cited responses were:

- Data Protection issues, lack of knowledge re legality, fear of litigation or of disciplinary action ;
- Lack of contact with known (knowledgeable) individuals, access to appropriate people at the right time;
- Lines of communication, different systems, delays;
- Lack of time;
- Confidentiality issues, protocols, not knowing how much to say;

- Lack of information about other agencies and services involved with clients/patients.

These findings can not of course be claimed as representative statistically of the wider population of care and health workers in the UK who are, or will become, affected by e-government initiatives. Nevertheless they are indicative of: positive attitudes to the 'joining-up' agenda; a perception that information sharing is necessary but difficult; and unevenness of IT skills and resources.

Questionnaire data were supplemented by observation of meetings, events and workshops at which practitioners were present. For example, we sat in on a selection of the workshops run by the IT partners for practitioners. In general practitioners were interested and enthusiastic about the promise of an electronic system to improve the quality and timeliness of information. Some practitioners, however, expressed anxiety that the IT system would reduce personal contact and trust. In one workshop for Health professionals, for example, it was pointed out that, where there is a history of face-to-face relationships, practitioners know a person and what s/he will do with the information. Comments made by practitioners in the workshops we observed confirmed the questionnaire evidence for shortfall in IT resources and skills. For example, school nurses reported that they had one PC between 15. Community nurses said that six of them shared a PC which crashed at least once a day. One nurse commented with heavy irony, 'my IT skills are improving every day - I now use two fingers!'

Late in the process we observed a workshop for practitioners led by the technology partner in the strand that was working towards the creation of an electronic single assessment process (SAP) for vulnerable older people. Earlier workshops had been for practitioners in specific services but this one included a mixture of health and social care workers. One of the most interesting and positive features was the interaction between the practitioners as they discussed their different practices and attitudes to service users' information. Some seemed surprised at what they heard from practitioners in other professions. For example, a district nurse explained that she always left her records with patients in their homes. A social worker commented that he would never leave any record with a client and asked her why she did so. One reason, she said, was security - it is not safe to keep confidential records in a car between visits. Another reason was to 'empower' patients - 'it is the patient's record'. This dialogue continued for some time. This was a reciprocal exchange of ideas about practice across agencies. It helps to confirm the inference from the questionnaire results that practitioners, in principle, value increased knowledge of the work of other agencies.

Our post-implementation work was limited to two FAME strands which had an IT system in use by summer 2004. There was (1) the virtual, integrated mental health record project and (2) the single assessment process (SAP) for vulnerable older people. SAP was atypical in FAME in that it included two separate (but co-operating) sites, one in the north of England and one in the south. The SAP strand involved by far the largest number of practitioners (80 in the southern site and 130 in the northern one). Unlike the virtual integrated mental health record, both the SAP systems included the facility for practitioners to write information in as well as read it.

After implementation of SAP some practitioners were extremely enthusiastic about the capacity of the new IT system to reveal the 'whole picture' of a patient/client. A psychiatric liaison officer in a hospital, for example, reported an early case where he had seen positive benefit for a patient. An elderly man had come into Accident and Emergency (A&E) with apparent memory problems but an assessment of him completed earlier gave a picture which showed that this was a result of medication and not a case of dementia. Without this assessment information A&E staff would have taken the memory loss at face value. Further positive comments from free texts answers in a questionnaire sent out after implementation in the northern SAP site included:

- '[I was] unsure about FAME to start with but as I began to use it more I could see an increased benefit for both patient and carer'
- 'When I have logged onto FAME as a duty enquiry to our department I found the information available really useful and comprehensive.'
- '[I was] able to print out an overview assessment which was completed by the Health Visitor [the] information shared led to agreed joint planning and care services...'

Overall, however, practitioners who had the opportunity were slow to adopt the system. The northern SAP site (which had trained the largest number of practitioners in any part of FAME) found that just under a third of them were using the system in any way three months later.

In order to understand and address the problem of low usage the northern SAP project team invited practitioners to a 'review day' in August 2004 in a local hotel. The Project Board Chair introduced the first session by saying, 'the steering group has gone through the pain barrier but practitioners are still in pain!' Practitioners were asked to articulate their concerns and barriers to using the system. The main points they made were:

- This is just another project – it will not last.
- Uncertainty over the IT strategy of the National Health Service discourages buy-in.
- It takes time to use the system and taking that time means giving a worse service and imposing burdens on colleagues.

- It is not easy to see direct benefits for clients/ patients from using an IT system when immediate concerns are about finite resources and expanding need. 'I worry that we will have a fantastic electronic system and no service to give people!'

Some practitioner groups are expected to put in information – at the cost of their time and effort – but will not benefit from receiving it. Some claimed that using SAP will 'punish' them. A social worker – one of the most enthusiastic SAP users – observed that the heart of the problem of low usage by colleagues is that a new 'user perspective' is needed. When you put information into SAP it benefits someone else such as an NHS worker in the hospital – 'but we must see the big picture - we are all one team'. The idea of harnessing the commitment of such individuals to animate wider interest in SAP was suggested as a way forward.

An internal evaluation questionnaire sent out to practitioners by the SAP project teams in both sites sought opinions about improvements in working practices since the introduction of SAP. In some instances double entry of data had been necessary and this, together with inexperience on the new systems, had at times slowed things down. Whilst most practitioners indicated that SAP was helping to develop 'new ways of working', there was less certainty about improving speed of access to services. These differences may be attributable to participants' particular settings (e.g. the number of persons sharing one PC as indicated in the pre-implementation survey results) as well as the project's limited scale and other factors outside of its control. On a positive note, responses to the local strand questionnaires demonstrated that trust between workers in partner organizations had improved, and 'a common language' was developing.

The FAME strand that developed a virtual integrated record for mental health also suffered from slow uptake by health and social care practitioners. This project trained 30 staff across two pilot sites and 'went live' in May 2004. When we visited one of these sites in late September 2004 the manager informed us that 13 individuals in his team had to date been trained to use the IT system but only six of them regularly did so. He attributed low usage to early technical difficulties they had experienced with access onto the system. Of the eight practitioners from that strand who responded to our post-implementation questionnaire six answered an open ended question about barriers to using FAME with reference to technical problems, for example, 'system failure, denied access' and 'time, reliability and speed of access'. Many of the practitioners nevertheless remained optimistic that in the longer term the virtual integrated mental health record will have value for them and their service users. In telephone interviews they told the Learning & Evaluation team that they liked having relevant information at their fingertips and appreciated the fact that they no longer have to wait for patients' notes to arrive on paper.

The most intractable barrier to usage of FAME IT systems is the one highlighted in the 'review day' in the northern SAP site referred to above. Putting information onto the system is perceived to represent a cost in time and resources for which there is no obvious payback. From this evidence the inequality of costs and benefits for individual practitioners and agencies appears to be a serious obstacle to the successful introduction of information systems for multi-agency working.

It was not possible to undertake post-implementation work with practitioners in the stands that did not 'go live' with their IT systems until autumn 2004. It would have been particularly valuable to contrast, in the longer term, practitioner attitudes and responses in one of these local strands, where their input into defining and designing the system was more intensive than in those discussed above. Because this could not be included in our analysis some valuable potential learning was lost.

5.   CONCLUSIONS

Our role as researchers in the Learning & Evaluation strand of FAME gave us excellent access to front-line practitioners participating in the implementation of an e-government programme. Evaluation inevitably makes demands on the evaluated (Draper 2001). We were extremely fortunate in the level of support and co-operation we received from the local project teams. Our evaluator role, however, was also a limitation in that it was tied to the time frame of an 18 month programme that suffered delays in implementation. Post-implementation evaluation was possible only in two of the six local strands. This is regrettable because local conditions, and the strategies adopted by the project teams, varied across the strands. A longer period between implementation and final reporting would have been needed in order to refine and maximize learning from the achievements of all the FAME local strands.

The main lessons from the evaluation of FAME with regard to front-line practitioners are:

- Nothing should be assumed about IT access and skills. There were serious limitations in some service providers' IT resources, as indicated in the questionnaire responses and workshops discussed above. The IT experience and skills of practitioners were extremely uneven. New projects would benefit from an early audit of IT skills and resources.

- Some practitioners complained of technical frustrations yet remained optimistic about the potential benefits of IT enabled information sharing. This evidence suggests that they can be extremely resilient to practical set-backs in technological performance when the idea of improved working practice has taken root.
- Workshops that brought together front-line practitioners from different professions and agencies stimulated interest and dialogue, inspired by a common interest in better and more timely information. There was no evidence that cultural differences per se between these groups prevented multi-agency working.
- There were however practitioners who reported that they were reluctant to become users of FAME because they saw no direct rewards for their own practice - although they recognized that other agencies may benefit. The perceived inequality of costs and benefits needs to be anticipated and managed.
- Recruiting enthusiastic and committed practitioners as 'super users' to help overcome resistance from others is one tentative solution for low practitioner uptake.
- It was often re-iterated by participants - including the technology partners – that FAME was not about IT but about people, organisations and culture. Some claimed that others (mistakenly) think it is about technology. It is our judgment (based on evidence from within and beyond the FAME strands) that the technology / practice dichotomy is misleading. Multi-agency practice and IT should be understood as two facets of the same whole.

6.   REFERENCES

6, P., Bellamy, C. and Raab C. 2005 Joined-up government and privacy in the United Kingdom: managing tensions between data protection and social policy, Part I, Public Administration, 83 (1) 111 – 133.

6, P., Leat, D., Steltzer, K. and Stoker, G. 2002 Toward Holistic Governance: the new reform agenda, Basingstoke: Palgrave.

Atkinson, M., Wilkin, A., Stott, A. and Kinder, K. 2001 Multiagency Working: an audit of activity, Slough: The National Foundation For Educational Research.

Baines, S., Gannon-Leary, P. and Walsh, S. 2004. FrAmework for Multi-Agency Environments (FAME): Final Report of the Learning & Evaluation. http://www.fame-uk.org/about/strand/

Bellamy, C., 6, P. and Raab, C. 2005. 'Joined-up government and privacy in the United Kingdom: Managing tensions between data protection and social policy. Part II.' Public Administration 83(2): 393-415.

Connell J P and Kubisch A C 1998. Applying a Theory of Change Approach to the Evaluation of Comprehensive Community Initiatives: Progress, Prospects and Problems, Aspen Institute, USA.

Department of Health 2004. NSF for Children, Young People and Maternity Services, London, Department of Health.

DfES 2003 Every Child Matters, HMSO, London.

Draper, L. 2001. 'Being evaluated: a practitioner's view', Children & Society 15(1): 46 - 52

Geoghegan, L., Lever, J. and McGimpsey, I. 2004. ICT for Social Welfare: A toolkit for managers. Bristol, The Policy Press.

Green, A., Maguire, M. and Canny, A. 2001 Keeping Track: Mapping and tracking vulnerable young people, Bristol, The Policy Press.

Harrison, S. 2002. 'New Labour, modernisation and the medical labour process.' Journal of Social Policy 31(3): 465-485.

Haynes, P. 2003. Managing Complexity in the Public Services, Maidenhead, Open University Press.

Henwood, F. and Hart, A. 2003. 'Articulating gender in the context of ICTs in health care: the case of electronic patient records in the maternity services.' Critical Social Policy 23(2): 249-267.

Hudson, J. 2003. 'E-galitarianism? The information society and New Labour's repositioning of welfare.' Critical Social Policy 23(2): 268-290.

Ling T. 2002. 'Delivering joined–up government in the UK: dimensions, issues and problems', Public Administration, 80 (4): 615-642.

Lipsky, M. 1980. Street Level Bureaucracy, New York, Russell Sage Foundation.

Lupton, C., North, N. and Khan, P. 2001. Working Together or Pulling Apart? The National Health Service and child protection networks. Bristol, The Policy Press.

Nettleton, S. and R. Burrows 2003. 'E-Scaped Medicine? Information, Reflexivity and Health.' Critical Social Policy 23(2): 165 - 185.

Newburn, T. 2001 'What do we mean by evaluation?' Children & Society 15(1): 5 - 13.

Payne, S., Kerr, C., Hawker, S., Hardey, M. and Powell, J. 2002 'The communication of information about older people between health and social care practitioners', Age and Ageing 31(2): 107-117.

Performance and Innovation Unit 2002. Privacy and data-sharing: the way forward for public services, London, Cabinet Office.

Pollitt, C. 2003. The Essential Public Manager. Maidenhead, Open University Press.

Secker, J. and Hill, K. 2001. 'Broadening the Partnerships: Experiences of Working across Community Agencies', Journal of Interprofessional Care 15 (4):341-350.

Stam, K., Stanton, J. and Guzman, R. 2004. 'Employee resistance to digital information and information technology change in a Social Service agency: A membership category approach', Journal of Digital Information, 5 (4): 10-20.

Acknowledgement

We are grateful to the Office of The Deputy Prime Minister (ODPM) for funding the research upon which this article is based. All opinions and interpretations are the responsibility of the authors.

LEGALURN: A FRAMEWORK FOR ORGANIZING AND SURFING LEGAL DOCUMENTS ON THE WEB

Caterina Lupo,[1] Luca De Santis,[1] and Carlo Batini[2]

[1] *Centro nazionale per l'informatica nella pubblica amministrazione (CNIPA)*
Via Isonzo 21/b, I-00198 Roma, Italy

{lupo,luca.desantis}@cnipa.it

[2] *Università di Milano "Bicocca"*
Via Bicocca degli Arcimboldi 9, I-20216 Milano, Italy

batini@disco.unimib.it

Abstract   Identifying resources is a critical issue in the wide web information space. Several identification systems have been defined, each tailored to a specific domain or application field, and characterized by many limitations. In this paper we describe an identification system compliant to URN specification that has been defined and implemented specifically for the legal domain, while providing several innovative features. The system allows to easily manage references to juridical documents and to automate the distributed hyperlinking building process. Moreover, the system provides a resolution service associating to the logical identifier a physical resource (e.g. URL) and other facilities to ensure semantic coherence and unambiguousness in the uniform names attribution task. Finally, we briefly outline future work concerning the opportunity to investigate other relevant properties in the legal domain by representing laws as a directed graph.

Keywords: eGovernment, uniform resource name, identification system, legal documents

1.   Introduction

The web information space consists of a huge quantity of documents, that is increasing very fast. Public administrations are among the most important sources of documents, even more nowadays as extensive e-government programmes are producing results.

In the eEurope action plan (Lisbona 2002) legislative documents have been classified as essential public information, i.e. their availability fulfills citizens' fundamental rights. Therefore several e-government initiatives are committed to provide free access to legislative documents through the Internet. Searching legislative documents in the web is a difficult task, due to the complexity of documents and the variety of data sources together with the lack of standardization. Moreover, laws contain references to other laws and often introduce modification into some part of other existing norms. This strong correlation among documents, even if issued by different authorities, requires the availability of robust hyperlinking mechanism in order to access the entire useful information. From this point of view, a legislative corpus can be seen as a net, quite similar to the web.

In this paper we describe a legislative documents identification system aimed to simplify searching and to enable automatic hyperlinking among laws references. The system has been developed within the NormeinRete (norms in the net) project, funded and coordinated by the National Center information technologies in the Public administration (CNIPA).

The rules adopted to build the laws identifiers are compliant with IETF Uniform Resource Name (URN) standard. The identifier, named *legalURN*, allows to automate the laws hypertext building process heavily reducing manual activities in detecting and marking-up references. Users can navigate through the references automatically detected by a specialized parser: a specific infrastructure is responsible to resolve URNs into physical resources, e.g. a web pages. Today, the legalURN is an Italian national standard issued as technical norm by CNIPA.

The paper is organized as follows. In Section 2 we describe the NormeinRete project. In Section 3 we report a brief description of what an identifier is expected to be, whereas in Section 4 we illustrate some of the most used digital resources identification systems. Moreover, in Section 4 we provide the motivations that have driven to the legalURN standard definition and adoption. In Section 5 and Section 6 we illustrate the legalURN syntax and semantics. In Section 7 we describe the system architecture developed to support legalURN and the related services available to use it effectively. Finally, in the Conclusions we draw some research lines and issues that are currently being investigated.

2. The NormeinRete project

Information technology is changing the way legal documents are managed and accessed. A growing number of initiatives are today in progress reaching significative results.

Public administrations and private organizations provide access to juridical documents through the web. All this cause a proliferation of sites, each with a partial set of documents. Standardization can give the opportunity to achieve interoperability among different sites.

Many standards and system enabling and simplifying juridical documents management process have been proposed (Palmirani and Brighi, 2002; Grandi et al., 2003; Boer et al., 2002a; Boer et al., 2002b). However, none, in the authors' knowledge, addresses the issues related to the identification of juridical documents as logical entities, that can have multiple editions with different value-added metadata or ensured quality standard. The NormeinRete project (Spinosa, 2001; Lupo and Batini, 2003) started in 1999 was proposed by the Italian Ministry of Justice with the aim of building a distributed cooperative system to access juridical documentation. Cooperation has been achieved through standardization. The project involves the major Italian computer science and law centers, such as ITTIG[1] and Cirsfid[2], and a number of Public administrations (e.g. Chamber of Deputies, Senate of the Republic, Italian Supreme Court of Cassation, Regions and municipalities, Authorities, several Ministries, etc.). The project has achieved the following results:

- A site providing a unique access point for searching the Italian legislative corpus. The site (`www.normeinrete.it`) offers search and retrieval services operating on all Italian laws since 1948 and utilities for automated hyperlinking. The entire project documentations and other information related to the project are also available (in Italian). The site includes also e-learning facilities, a software download section to deliver open source utilities developed by the project team,and a best-practices section to encourage experiences re-use, in order to create a virtual space for knowledge sharing within the Public administrations community. The site has more than 4000 visitors and about 7000 accesses to the search functions daily.

- a standard for norms XML representation. DTDs (Document Type Definition) for Italian legislation have been defined, able to represent metadata and all the significant information useful to automate legislative documents' life-cycle management. The availability of documents with XML mark-up according to shared DTDs definitions allows to provide advanced search and retrieval functions operating on heterogeneous data bases effectively.

- A standard for persistent identification of norms. This paper is focused on this standard.

- An infrastructure for identifier resolution and management. Currently, the mechanism to resolve identifier is centralized and provided within the site itself. For example, to resolve a generic legalURN *genericURN* it is sufficient to access to the url: `http://www.nir.it/cgi-bin/N2Ln?genericURN`. The resolution engine index manages more than 50.000 legalURNs.

3.   Background on identifiers

In this section we briefly describe some of the main features usually required for identifiers. An identifier is a sequence of symbols that can be associated to a logical or physical object unambiguously in order to distinguish it from other objects belonging to the same category: it is able to unambiguously identify a resource, when defined and used in a specific context, i.e. a namespace. Unambiguousness is a required property for an identifier. Depending on the application context for which the identifier has to be defined other properties can be required, such as uniqueness, persistence, actionability, interoperability and intelligibility. In the following paragraphs there is a brief description of these features, checked against the Uniform Resource Locator (URL), that is one of the most widely used identification system.

The uniqueness property ensures that a resource, or a class of resources, is represented by only one identifier through a one-to-one relationship. Several applications require unique identifiers: US S.S.N. or Italian fiscal code are examples of identifiers that have to be unique in their namespace. URL does not guarantee uniqueness, for it is possible to define alias; for example, the URL http://www.normeinrete.it and http://www.nir.it point to, i.e identify, the same IP address.

An identifier is persistent if it maintains the linkage to a resource even though the physical resource has been moved or some of its features have changed. For example, an URL can be used as a web page identifier, but it does not guarantee persistence, since web pages are often moved or deleted. Note that technologies can only support the persistence of identifiers and can-not ensure it.

Actionability means that the identifier can be used with a specific applicative infrastructure to obtain some result. In the simplest case, the result will be the resource bound to the identifier. URL is an actionable identifier when used with a browser; the browser exploits the domain name system (DNS) to translate it into a physical address and the HTTP protocol to obtain the resource.

Interoperability is the ability to maintain significance when the identifier is used outside the original namespace. There are different levels of interoperability: the basic one consists of the preservation of the identifier's unambiguousness in the new namespace. An URL does not guarantee interoperability.

Any dumb sequence of symbols assuring unambiguousness in a specific namespace can be used to identify a resource. When the sequence is chosen in such a way that the resulting string, or any of its substrings, has a meaning related to the resource, then it is called intelligent identifier. Analyzing the string, it is possible to extract some information about the resource. URL is an intelligent identifier composed by substrings representing the protocol used to obtain the resource, the domain of the resource and its path. A detailed description of the identifier properties reported above can be found in Paskin, 2003.

4. Related identification systems

The identification of digital resources is a problem that has been growing in interest in the last few years. Several standards, proposed for general purpose or for domain specific application, are today widely used.

The system we describe in this paper is based on the URN specification (Masinter and Sollins, 1994). URN has been initially proposed to provide a persistent alternative to the URL to identify Internet resources. The original proposal has been developed and defined more in detail afterwards. RFC 2141 (Moats, 1997) specifies the URN syntax, while guidelines for URN resolution systems, that make URN actionable, are illustrated in the RFC 2276 (Sollins, 1998). A deeper description of URN specification and its connection with URI is provided in van der Werf-Davelaar, 1999.

The Digital Object Identifier (DOI) (see DOI, 2004) is an identification system recently emerged. It allows effective identification of digital resources, providing the infrastructure needed to handle additional information related to the resources, i.e metadata, and to ensure persistence. The system is managed by the International DOI Foundation, an open membership consortium including both commercial and non-commercial partners, and has recently been accepted for standardization within ISO.

The International Standard Serial Number (ISSN ISSN, 2004) is a free of charge dumb string of 8 numerical digits used to identify periodical publications. It is managed by 77 National Centers, with a coordination center based in Paris. In order to obtain a ISSN, publisher must send a request to the appropriate agency. ISSN has been standardized by ISO (ISO 3297:1998).

The International Standard Book Number (ISBN ISBN, 2004) is an intelligent and machine-readable identification number used to unambiguously identify publications. It was approved as ISO standard in 1970 (currently ISO 2108:1992); it does not provide central repository nor searching tools. ISBN is always associated to the whole publication. To obtain a ISBN publishers must pay a minimal fee. Many other digital resource identification standard exists, such as ISRC (SICI, 2004) anf ISAN (ISAN, 2004). A detailed and complete description of the most used systems is provided in Vitielo, 2004.

5. Normative documents identification: the NormeinRete approach

Each law contains several references to other laws: one of the main problems dealing with normative documents arises from the need to retrieve all related documents. Users have to gather all the norms cited in order to correctly interpret a law and to retrieve all subsequent laws that affected the original one in order to know the complete text that is "in force".

The whole legislative corpus can be represented as a directed disconnected graph, in which laws are vertices and references among laws represent edges, defined through natural language expressions. The graph is directed because laws promulgation dates introduce a direction on the edges: a law cannot reference subsequent laws. The graph is disconnected because there are laws without references to others (for example the Constitution). Nowadays, most institutions provide systems to have access to norms by means of the Internet. Thus, nodes of the law graph are available as web resources and the hypertext of the connected part of the graph can be built using the usual web link mechanism based on resource physical address (URL). However, this approach has many drawbacks, that make it inefficient.

First of all, heavy manual activities are required, usually carried out through the following steps:

- recognizing all natural language expressions that are references to other norms;

- finding the physical address (i.e. URL) of the resource corresponding to the referred norm;

- marking-up the references inserting the physical address of the resource to be linked.

The need to modify the source document to insert the URL addresses in the appropriate locations reduces the overall document quality, because of the errors that can be introduced through manual typing. Moreover a norm could cite other norms not available on the web yet or the links inserted can become broken after a while. Thus a continuous monitoring is needed to ensure proper links behavior.

In order to build an effective and maintainable system supporting navigation through the graph a persistent, location-independent unambiguous identifier for nodes is required. This paper proposes a framework based on (i) an identifier named legalURN derived from the URN and based on (ii) a resolution system to resolve logical identifiers into physical addresses that is similar to the DNS used to resolve the self-explaining web sites names into numerical IP addresses. The mechanism used to build legalURN makes it an intelligent identifier. We illustrate legalURN syntax and semantics in Section 6 and Section 7.

The opportunity to automatically build an hypertext among laws relies on the following two considerations. The natural language expressions that refer to a norm usually contain repetitive patterns, making references automatically detectable through a specialized parser. Moreover, the URN is based on data

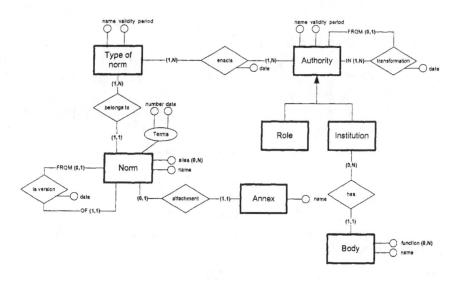

Figure 1. Entity-relationship model representing norms and related information

always included in the references and it can be built automatically. Thanks to these features, the legislative hypertext building process can be automatically performed associating the corresponding legalURN to each reference in the law. This function can be performed on the documents prior to publishing or on the fly. The parser that detects references in the text has a very high success rate (ranging from 95% to 97%).

To ensure the effectiveness of this approach some services are needed; these services provide the functionalities needed to create correct legalURNs and to resolve them. Thanks to this service, legalURN ensures actionability and persistence. We will describe the service infrastructure in Section 8.

6. LegalURN syntax

The legalURN consists of a combination of several elements. Figure 1 depicts the conceptual model on which we base our analysis, using the entity-relationship (ER) formalism. Each entity in the model has been mapped into a syntactical element. The most relevant elements are: the promulgating (enacting) authority, the type of the norm (law, decree, etc.) and the terms (i.e. date, number, etc.). The model allows to represent a set of more detailed specifications when needed, such as validity dates and alias.

The legalURN is compliant to the URN syntax. The set of rules to build a well formed legalURN has been defined by means of a formal grammar described by the Backus-Naur form. The grammar satisfies the following requirements: (i) each legalURN univocally identifies a norm and can distinguish different versions due to subsequent modifications; (ii) the rules are easy, un-ambiguous and self-explanatory; (iii) legalURNs can be built automatically.

For the sake of simplicity, we illustrate the structure of legalURN focusing our analysis to the meaning of the elements. The complete grammar, allowed characters and other rules are reported in AIPA, 2001.

The general structure of a legalURN, as defined in the current version of the standard, is the following:

```
<URN>    ::=    urn:<NID>:<NSS>
```

`<NID>` denotes the namespace identifier and assumes the arbitrary chosen value nir, that represents the acronym for Norme*in*Rete. Initially thought for the Italian context, the legalURN can handle different national legislative corpus introducing an element identifying the state where the norm has been enacted. A possible structure could be:

```
<URN>    ::=    urn:<NID>:<STT>:<NSS>
```

where element `<STT>` should contain the ISO 3166 ISO, 2004 three letter code identifying the state. For instance, DEU for Germany or ITA for Italy.

`<NSS>` is the specific part of the namespace. It is defined as follows:

```
<NSS>    ::=    <document>[@<version>]
```

The element `<document>` consists of three mandatory elements (promulgating authority, type of norm and terms) and of optional element (annexes). In most cases, these elements are sufficient to identify the norm.

```
<document>    ::=    <authority>:<type>:<terms>[:<annex>]
```

The `<authority>` element represents the public institution promulgating the norm and contains its name.

```
<authority>      ::=    <authority-name>*[+<authority-name>]
<authority-name> ::=    (<institution>*[;<body>][;<function>])|<role>
```

If several institutions enact a norm jointly, they must be all included; for example ministry.finance+ministry.justice. The element `<body>` and the element `<function>` can be used when the norm is promulgated by a department or a particular body (e.g. regional assembly, ministry department executive) of a institution; for example, ministry.finance;department.taxes or ministry.finance;department.taxes;executive.

The `<type>` element represents the typology of a norm; for example: law, constitutional law, decree, etc.

```
<type>    ::=    <typology>*[;<specification>]
```

The optional element `<specification>` contains fine granularity detail of the norm, as the common name of the norm or its classification. For instance, law;remission.official.taxes.

The `<terms>` contains the promulgation date and a unique number. Its syntax, very simple and intuitive, is the following:

```
<terms>     ::=   <dates>;<ids-norm>
<dates>     ::=   <date>*[, <date>]
<ids-norm>  ::=   <id-norm>*[,<id-norm>]
```

The number is usually that one associated with the act prior to its publication on the Official Journal. This number, in conjunction with all the other element's tokens, ensure uniqueness. However it must be taken into account that there are some kind of normative acts that have not an official number. Since there can be several acts of the same type issued by the same authority in the same date, an additional element is needed to ensure the unambiguousness of the legalURN. Therefore an internal unique number is associated to un-numbered acts when they are submitted for registration. This service is described in Section 8. These are some examples of the element `<terms>`: 2000-12-06;126, 1999-12-30,2000-01-13;p-2.

The last part of the `<document>` element is the `<annex>` element. It must be used when legalURN is built to identify a document annexed to a norm. Its syntax is the following:

```
<annex>   ::=   <id-annex>*[;<specification>]
```

Element `<version>` allows to manage different version of the same law due to subsequent changes. It contains the date of the last modifying norm that has provided modifications to be inserted in the original text. The element syntax is:

```
<version>            ::=   <norm-modifier-date>|inforce
<norm-modifier-date> ::=   <date>
```

For example, `ministry.justice:law:1961-11-15;12@1987-06-03` identifies the law number 12 enacted by the Ministry of Justice in November 15, 1961, updated with the changes introduced until June 3, 1987. Since each element is meaningful, legalURN is a so-called intelligent identifier. Information contained in the legalURNs can be exploited in order to deeply analyze the links among norms, allowing to implement applications for legislative reorder support and laws classification.

7. LegalURN semantics

In the previous section we have illustrated the legalURN limiting our attention to element definitions and providing some information about what they contain. Nevertheless syntactic rules alone does not ensure the building of meaningful legalURNs, i.e legalURNs usable in our infrastructure. For example, the following legalURNs in the Italian namespace are not "semantically" valid:

Table 1. LegalURN: rules used to normalize expressions

Normalization rules
for each expression, must be considered only nouns and adjectives, discarding all connectives, articles, etc.;
type of authority must be in first position;
nouns must come before adjectives (as usually done in italian);
spaces must be replaced by dots;
acronyms must be expanded;
abbreviations must be expanded;
generic terms must be moved at the end;
all words must be in lowercase.

```
urn:nir:aaaaa:bbbbb:1000-1-1;1;
urn:nir:ministry.defense:constitutional.law:1978-4-10;142;
urn:nir:ministry.finance:decree:2003-1-12;24;
```

These legalURNs are valid against the syntactic rules; nonetheless the first probably does not represent any law, because the elements have not any meaning. The second one has an internal inconsistency; in fact in Italy none but the Parliament can enact constitutional laws. Finally, the third one has a conflict between the authority name and the promulgation date, because Italian Finance ministry has been incorporated into the Treasure ministry in 1999.

Having regard to these aspects, two main issues can be pointed out:

- most of the legalURN elements can assume only a well defined set of value; for example, in the `<authority>` element only valid authorities names can be inserted.

- The value of each element can affect allowable values in other elements.

Internal consistency constraints, such as "norm typology must be consistent with norm date", cannot be expressed directly in the Figure 1 ER model. Moreover, since syntactical elements represent real world entities, only a limited set of valid values can be used. Each entity value needs to be *normalized* before it can be used, in order to maintain the effectiveness of the resolution system and to limit inconsistencies. In order to avoid this problem, some registries containing the up-to-date information about allowable values and a service to normalize names are provided.

Concerning normalization, the standard proposes the rules of Table 1 in order to normalize expressions: For example, the Ministry of Treasure becomes "ministry.treasure" and EU is expanded in "union.european". This approach is only one of the possible but other normalization mechanisms or rules may be used to represent names.

Some sets of values are more complicated than a simple list. In fact, it is necessary to take into account the "temporal" evolution of such values and their relationships. For example, while in the past in Italy there was a Ministry of Finance and a Ministry of Treasure, a few years ago the Ministry of Economy and Finance has taken in both. Thus, if one wants to register a legalURN for a norm of the Ministry of Finance with a year of promulgation equal to 2004, the system fires an alert message. Moreover, departments or offices often change denomination or are removed. Therefore, we need to record for each institution the name of its departments that have autonomous regulatory power, and the temporal validity of the name.

The legalURN system can discover inconsistencies and syntactical errors thanks to the presence of a centralized registry service. Registries can be used both to register legalURNs and to correctly insert persistent references to norms.

8. The NormeinRete system architecture

In this section we describe the legalURN management system implemented within the context of the NormeinRete project. Although at this stage the system adopts a simplified architecture, the successful implementation shows the benefits deriving from the proposed approach.

The system architecture aims to cover all the aspects concerning legalURN life-cycle, providing functions to easily manage and maintain the standard. The overall architecture is depicted in Figure 2. The main architectural elements are the registration services, the central registries and the legalURN resolution service. Currently, these modules are implemented in a centralized manner and are available through the NormeinRete site. Nonetheless, the modular architecture easily allows to implement an equivalent distributed system.

Administrations have two ways to share their normative data:

1 register each norm using the registration service;

2 become a NIR node, leaving to the resolution module the task to automatically indexing the norms.

In the second case, the administration legal documents must be formatted and saved with specific file system settings.

8.1 Registration services

The registration service puts at the users' disposal two functions: (i) a function to register a new legalURN or associate a new resource to an existing legalURN, and (ii) a function to register an institution as NIR node. In the former case, users actively interact with the system; whereas, in the latter case

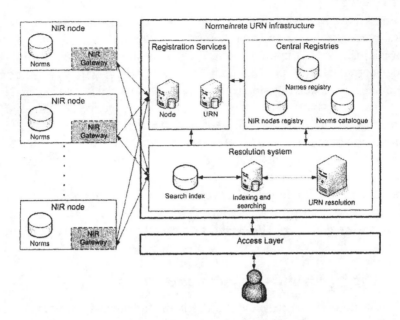

Figure 2.   The NIR legalURN system architecture

the system is responsible to load a new document on the research index and to build new legalURNs.

We think that the responsibility for legalURN registration should belong to the institution enacting the norm. In fact, it precisely knows the information needed to build the legalURN, thus avoiding mistakes or incomplete data. This rule requires a well defined inter-institutional organizational asset.

When an institution wants to make a document available by means of legalURN mechanism, it must register it on the system. At this stage additional metadata must be inserted. The system turns the inserted information into a legalURN consistent with the rules illustrated in Sections 6 and 7 and joins it to the physical resource. If the obtained URN is already present, the system associates the new physical resource to it. Beginning from this moment, the URN can be used to link a norm, using the resolution module. The institution that registers a norm must keep its physical resource aligned with the ones they have associated with the URN, in order to avoid errors in the resolution phase.

8.2   Central Registries

The central registries store information needed to allow effective standard management. The registry of official authority names is needed in order to guarantee consistency in the construction of legalURN. The registry contains the names of the institutions, name history with the periods of validity, relationships with other institutions (such as derived by, substituted with, joined in, etc.). The NIR-nodes registry contains all the information needed to allow automatic interaction between NIR agents, such as spider agent and data retrieving agent, and the application gateways located in each domain. Finally, the norms catalogue contains for each legal document a minimum set of metadata such as the title, a basic classification, associated legalURN and the list of known physical resources (such as internet addresses) where the versions of the corresponding document are published. Metadata can be used to implement more advanced services.

8.3   The legalURN Resolution service

The resolution mechanism is quite similar to the Internet domain name system (DNS). Thanks to this module, legalURN becomes an actionable identifier. Resolution service takes as input a legalURN and returns, if it exists, the related resource(s), e.g. web page or file associated to it. Currently, the system architecture is fully centralized, with one node that manages all the requests. However, the resolution system can be built both as centralized and decentralized with a hierarchical structure. We think that the architecture should be distributed, and each state or local authority should maintain its own registries and resolution services. Like DNS, the system may exploit the legalURN structure to simplify the operation and to quickly direct the search toward the right national or local level node of the search tree. Reading the <NID>, system can easily verify if the norm belongs to its domain or the request must be forwarded to another node.

Despite DNS, where the relation between the logical address and the IP address is many to one, in our case more resources can exist for the same legalURN; in other words the relation between the legalURN and the physical resource is one to many. This complicates the resolution mechanism, because the system needs a decision phase. In order to solve this problem, we are investigating a double level resolution mechanism, which allows users to specify the preferred version using a set of simply indicators, such as data source completeness or trustworthiness. This approach is similar to the one proposed in Mecella et al., 2002.

9.   Conclusions and future works

We have described the identification system for legal digital resources implemented within the Italian project NormeinRete. The proposed mechanism is based on an identifier compliant with the URN standard, named legalURN. The identifier has some important properties: it is actionable, intelligent and persistent. The system is currently working limited to the Italian legislative corpus, but can be easily extended to cover general legal documents. The implemented system has shown the effectiveness of our approach. Moreover, other European institutions have shown interest in legalURN. It is important to underline that the legalURN standard belongs to a complete legal document framework, which is able to manage the complete life-cycle of a legal document.

We are working to refine the system architecture of legalURN in order to simplify extensibility and scalability to support the standard adoption in a wide range of contexts. Many open research lines are currently being investigated; among all, a more formalized definition of the semantics rules, using logic formalism, and the introduction in the identifier of information about the document classification with respect to a semantics schema or a ontology.

Representing a legislative corpus as a graph will allow to exploit some well known graph properties and algorithms to obtain important practical results. We are working to develop systems that are able to support normative reorder, laws impact analysis and tools to simplify well done laws creation. For example, by analyzing the graph we can identify the parts of the graph characterized by an high degree of cohesion and collapse the nodes strictly connected into a unique node, thus supporting legislative reorder task. A more detailed description will be provided in a following paper.

Notes

1. http://www.ittig.cnr.it/Index.htm
2. http://www.cirfid.unibo.it/

References

AIPA (2001). Definizione delle regole per l'assegnazione dei nomi uniformi ai documenti giuridici. Circolare n. AIPA/CR/35. In Italian.

Boer, A., Hoekstra, R., Winkels, R., van Engers, T., and Willaert, F. (2002a). Proposal for a dutch legal xml standard. In Traunmüller, R. and Lenk, K., editors, *EGOV 2002 Conference*, pages 142–149, Berlin. Springer.

Boer, A., Hoekstra, R., and Winkels, R. (2002b). Metalex: Legislation in xml. In Bench-Capon, T., Daskalopulu, A., and Winkels, R., editors, *Legal Knowledge and Information Systems. Jurix 2002: The Fifteenth Annual Conference*, pages 1–10, Amsterdam. IOS Press.

DOI (2004). The digital object identifier system. http://www.doi.org/.

Grandi, F., Mandreoli, F., Tiberio, P., and Bergonzini, M. (2003). A temporal data model and management system for normative texts in xml format. In *Proceedings of the fifth ACM international workshop on Web information and data management*, pages 29–36. ACM Press.

ISAN (2004). The international standard audiovisual number. http://www.isan.org/.

ISBN (2004). The international standard book number. http://www.isbn.org/standards/home/index.asp.

ISO (2004). Standard for country names. Available on line (link checked November 2004): http://www.iso.org/iso/en/prods-services/iso3166ma/index.html.

ISSN (2004). The international standard serial number. http://www.issn.org/.

Lupo, C. and Batini, C. (2003). A federative approach to laws access by citizens: The "normein-rete" system. In Traunmuller, R., editor, *Proceedings of Second International Conference Electronic Government (EGOV)*, pages 413–416. Springer-Verlag.

Masinter, L. and Sollins, K. (1994). Functional requirements for uniform resource names, rfc 1737. Aailable on line (link checked Semptember 2004): http://www.faqs.org/rfcs/rfc1737.html.

Mecella, M., Scannapieco, M., Virgillito, A., Baldoni, R., Catarci, T., and Batini, C. (Irvine, CA, 2002). Managing Data Quality in Cooperative Information Systems. In *Proceedings of the Tenth International Conference on Cooperative Information Systems*.

Moats, R. (1997). Urn syntax, rfc 2141. Available on line (link checked Semptember 2004): http://www.faqs.org/rfcs/rfc2141.html.

Palmirani, M. and Brighi, R. (2002). Norma-system: A legal document system for managing consolidated acts. In Cicchetti, R., Hameurlain, A., and Traunmüller, R., editors, *Proceedings of the 13th International Conference DEXA*, pages 310–320. Springer-Verlag.

Paskin, N. (2003). *Digital Rights Management - Technological, Economic, Legal and Political Aspects*, chapter Components for DRM Systems: Identification and Metadata (2.3.1). Springer, Available on line (link checked September 2004):http://www.doi.org/topics/drm_paskin_20030113_b1.pdf.

SICI (2004). The international standard recording code. http://www.ifpi.org/isrc/.

Sollins, K. (1998). Architectural principles of uniform resource name resolution, rfc 2276. Available on line (link checked Semptember 2004): urlhttp://www.faqs.org/rfcs/rfc2276.html.

Spinosa, P. (2001). Identification of Legal Documents Through Urns (Uniform Resource Names). In Signore, O. and Hopgood, B., editors, *Proceedings of the Euroweb 2001 Conference "The Web in Public Administration"*.

van der Werf-Davelaar, T. (1999). Identification, location and versionoing of web-resources. URI Discussion paper, available on line (link checked Semptember 2004): http://www.kb.nl/coop/donor/rapporten/URI.html.

Vitielo, G. (2004). Identifiers and identification systems. *D-Lib Magazine*. Available on line (link checked November 2004): http://www.dlib.org/dlib/january04/vitiello/01vitiello.html.

A WEB SERVICE APPROACH TO GEOGRAPHICAL DATA DISTRIBUTION AMONG PUBLIC ADMINISTRATIONS

L. VACCARI[1], A. IVANYUCKOVICH[2] AND M. MARCHESE[2]

[1]*Provincia Autonoma di Trento, Trento, Italy*
[2]*Department of Information and Communication Technology,*
University of Trento, Trento, Italy

Abstract: In this paper a service-oriented architecture (SOA) is proposed to support the interaction with legacy Geographical Information Systems (GIS) and the implementation of value added data sharing services. In particular, we base our proposed architecture both on the standardization effort carried out by the Open Geospatial Consortium (OGC) and on current state-of-the-art Web Service middleware infrastructure. We have evaluated the proposed architecture in the context of GIS application integration in a departmental back-office scenario. The advantages of a service-oriented architecture are twofold: on one hand, it is possible to integrate several GIS application and data sources simply by wrapping their (legacy) services with appropriate interface and registering them in Web Service directories; on the other hand, this new service paradigm can be used to support the creation of completely new cartographic data sharing services.

Key words: e-Government, Geographical Information Systems, Service Oriented Architectures, Distributed Information Systems

1.   INTRODUCTION

In recent years, the domain of geographic information has experienced a rapid growth of both computational power and quantity of information. Moreover, there is an increasing necessity to share geographic information between different stakeholders (departments in public administration, professionals, citizens, etc) and diverse information systems in order to enable its coherent and contextual usage. This necessity is at the basis of a number of international and national projects, among which: (1) INSPIRE [1] that list among its main objectives: *"geographical data shall be made available for access and view free of charge by citizen and other users, with delivery, downloading and re-use on harmonized terms and conditions*; (2) the Italian "LABSITA", "Centro Interregionale" and "Intesa Stato Regioni" projects [2], focused on the issue of interoperability among existing geographical databases and related administrative procedures managed by local administrations. Furthermore, at the local level, there are specific projects that have to be coordinated with these higher level projects: for example the internal publication of the geographical data and metadata, the support to the formal exchange of the data with other public administrations within intra-departmental administrative procedures (like the Environmental Evaluation Procedure – "VIA: Valutazione di Impatto Ambientale"). It is important to reach these objectives using the most innovative technological framework and software architectures available at present and integrating them into the overall framework developed in European and national projects.

In this paper, we propose a service-oriented architecture (SOA) to support the interaction with legacy Geographical Information Systems (GIS) and the implementation of value added data sharing services. In particular, we base our proposed architecture both on the standardization effort carried out by the Open Geospatial Consortium (OGC) [3] and on current state-of-the-art Web Service middleware infrastructure. We have evaluated the proposed architecture in the context of GIS application integration in a departmental back-office scenario. The advantages of a service-oriented architecture are twofold: on one hand, it is possible to integrate several GIS applications and data sources simply by wrapping their (legacy) services with appropriate interface; on the other hand, this new service paradigm can be used to support the creation of completely new cartographic data sharing services.

The remainder of this extended abstract is organized as follows. In Section 2 we review current OGC specification addressing the GIS interoperability problem. In Section 3 we review the Service-Oriented Architectural model. In Section 4 we sketch the functionalities of the integrated GIS applications based on SOA. The discussion of results and related and future work concludes the paper.

2.   OPEN GEOSPATIAL CONSORTIUM: WMS AND WFS SPECIFICATIONS

The Open Geospatial Consortium [3] has proposed specific and detailed specifications, for the interoperability of the geographical databases that are independent from the Web application technology used in the presentation layer. The basic idea is that an increasing number of organizations will offer their geo-referenced data according to these specifications. As specifications will become a de-facto or de-jure standard, an user application will be able to request data from different geographical service providers. The advantage when using standards is that it will be easier to combine data from different suppliers. The user will be able to request specific data and customize his data to perform personalized analysis.

At present OGC is supporting a number of standard specifications. In the present work we focused on two main specifications, namely Web Map Service (WMS) [4] and Web Feature Service (WFS) [5];

- WMS can be used to produce maps of spatially referenced data dynamically from geographic information. This specification is also an International Standard and defines a "map" to be a representation of geographic information as a digital image file suitable for display on a computer screen. WMS-based maps are generally rendered in a pictorial format such as PNG, GIF or JPEG, or occasionally as vector-based graphical elements in Scalable Vector Graphics (SVG) or Web Computer Graphics Metafile (WebCGM) formats. The WMS allows a client to overlay map images for display served from multiple Web Map Services on the Internet.
- In a similar fashion, WFS allows a client to retrieve geospatial data encoded in Geography Markup Language (GML) from multiple Web Feature Services.
- WMS and WFS operations can be invoked using a standard web browser by submitting requests in the form of Uniform Resource Locators (URLs).

A server that implements the WMS specification has to support two mandatory operations (*GetCapabilities* and *GetMap*) and can support one optional operation (*GetFeatureInfo*).

- The purpose of the mandatory *GetCapabilities* operation is to obtain service metadata (an XML document), which is a machine-readable (and human-readable) description of the server's information content and acceptable request parameter values. The client can use the results of this operation to formulate the next request. Moreover, it can build a catalog useful for the user that can choose the desired geographical layer.

- The *GetMap* operation returns a map. Upon receiving a *GetMap* request, a WMS either satisfies the request or issues a service exception. The client has to send the parameters to specify, for example, the number and the name of the layers, the bounding box to be show, the projection and the coordinate system, the raster format, the display size and so on. Several layers can be picked from different servers and can be used to make a single map. The response to a valid *GetMap* request is a map of the spatially referenced information layer requested, in the desired style, and having the specified coordinate reference system, bounding box, size, format and transparency.

- *GetFeatureInfo* is an optional operation. The *GetFeatureInfo* operation is designed to provide clients of a WMS with more information about features in the pictures of maps that were returned by previous Map requests. The canonical use case for *GetFeatureInfo* is that a user sees the response of a Map request and chooses a point (I,J) on that map for which to obtain more information. The basic operation provides the ability for a client to specify which pixel is being asked about, which layer(s) should be investigated, and what format the information should be returned in. Since the WMS protocol is stateless, the *GetFeatureInfo* request indicates to the WMS what map the user is viewing by including most of the original *GetMap* request parameters (all but VERSION and REQUEST). From the spatial context information (BBOX, CRS, WIDTH, HEIGHT) in that *GetMap* request, along with the I,J position the user chose, the WMS can (possibly) return additional information about that position.

  The actual semantics of how a WMS decides what to return more information about, or what exactly to return, are left up to the WMS provider.

A server that implements the OGC WFS specification can distribute geographic features to a client application. Moreover the WFS offers the possibility to the users to load vector data only for requested layers. The state of a geographic feature is described by a set of properties where each property can be thought of as a tuple *(name, type, value)*, following [6,7]. Geographic features are those that may have at least one property that is geometry-valued. The geometries of geographic features are restricted to simple geometries, i.e. geometries for which coordinates are defined in two dimensions and the delineation of a curve is subject to linear interpolation. The traditional 0, 1 and 2-dimensional geometries defined in a 2-dimensional spatial reference system are represented by points, line strings and polygons. In addition, the OGC geometry model allows for geometries that are collections of other geometries - either homogeneous multi-point, multi-line string, and multi-polygon collections or heterogeneous geometry collections.

Finally, GML allows features that have complex or aggregate non-geometric properties.

WFS is an interfaces for describing data manipulation operations (like Create/Delete/Update/Get feature instances) on geographic features using HTTP as the distributed computing platform. In particular, a WFS request consists of a description of query or data transformation operations that are to be applied to one or more features. The request is generated on the client and is posted to a web feature server using HTTP. The web feature server then reads and (in a sense) executes the request. To support transaction and query processing, the following operations are defined in WFS:

- *GetCapabilities*. As in WMS a WFS must be able to describe its capabilities. Specifically, it must indicate which feature types it can service and what operations are supported on each feature type.
- *DescribeFeatureType*. A WFS must be able, upon request, to describe the structure of any feature type it can service.
- *GetFeature*. A WFS must be able to service a request to retrieve feature instances. In addition, the client should be able to specify which feature properties to fetch and should be able to constrain the query spatially and non-spatially.
- *Transaction*. A web feature service may be able to service transaction requests. A transaction request is composed of operations that modify features; that is create, update, and delete operations on geographic features.
- *LockFeature*. A WFS may be able to process a lock request on one or more instances of a feature type for the duration of a transaction. This ensures that serializable transactions are supported.

Based on the operation descriptions above, two classes of web feature services can be defined:

- *Basic WFS*. A basic WFS would implement the GetCapabilities, DescribeFeatureType and GetFeature operations. This would be considered a READ-ONLY web feature service.
- *Transaction WFS*. A transaction web feature service would support all the operations of a basic web feature service and in addition it would implement the Transaction operation. Optionally, a transaction WFS could implement the LockFeature operation.

3.   SERVICE ORIENTED ARCHITECTURES (SOA)

Web Services are described by a set of protocols to enable communication between independent software modules that offer their functionalities in the form of services. Current Web-Services are based on Services Oriented Architectures (SOA) [8]. In a SOA, services are self-contained, modular applications - deployed over standard middleware platforms, e.g., J2EE - that can be described, published, located, and invoked over a network. To support the realization of the service-oriented software paradigm, Web service need to be based on standardized definitions of an interoperability communication protocol, mechanisms for service description, discovery, and composition as well as a basic set of quality of service (QoS) protocols.

The most generic SOA consists of three basis actors (see Figure 1): service requester, service provider and service broker (or service registry provider). Service provider describes services and publishes them in the registry provided by service broker. Once they are published they can be found and bind by service requester, utilizing XML-based protocols (see below). Later and if needed, service requester composes discovered services to obtain the desired functionality and bind/execute them on demand.

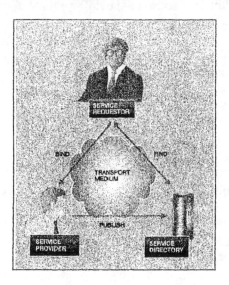

Figure 1. Basic SOA Architecture

The underlying middleware technology has already evolved to conform to the described publish-find-bind scheme: the initial trio of Web service specifications, SOAP[9], WSDL[10], and UDDI[11], provided open XML-based mechanisms for application interoperability (SOAP), service description (WSDL), and service discovery (UDDI). SOAP is now a W3C standard, and WSDL and UDDI are being considered by standard bodies. In order to implement this basic framework in real applications, mechanisms for service composition and quality of service protocols are required. Several specifications have been proposed in these areas, most notably the Business Process Execution Language for Web Service (BPEL4WS)[12] for service composition, Web service coordination (WS-Coordination) and Web service transactions (WS-Transaction) to support robust service interactions, Web service security (WS-Security), and Web service reliable messaging (WS-ReliableMessaging)[13]. The descriptive capabilities of WSDL can be enhanced by the Web Service Policy Framework (WS-Policy), which extends WSDL to allow the encoding and attachment of QoS information to services in the form of reusable service "policies." All these aspects are critical elements for meaningful services interactions.

The described Web Service protocol stack is shown in Figure 2, from [14]. On the lower level of the stack one finds transport and encoding layers, in the middle level protocols for service description, security, transaction and coordination are located, and, finally, on the top level the protocol stack has the business process composition layer. In [8] more details of the service enabling protocol stack are presented. Moreover, more comprehensive architectures have appeared recently, comprising the basic SOA and usually layered extension covering some of the vital characteristics listed above[15].

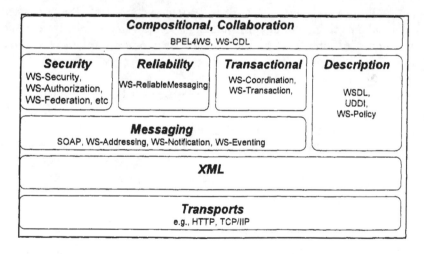

Figure 2. The Web Service protocol stack

4.   PROPOSED FRAMEWORK AND CASE STUDY

We propose to take full advantage of the SOA approach in the context of GIS by implementing the operations offered by WMS and WFS following OpenGIS Web Services initiative [16]. To this end we have used Bea Web Logic Server [17] for creating and publishing our specific Web Service interfaces. In particular Bea Web Logic Server provides support for the SOAP communication between server and the client.

We have experimented the proposed architecture in the context of integration of GIS legacy services in a back-office scenario: a user that need to navigate in a spatial database (*location search and feature layer selection*), insert a map (*download of dynamically user-specified raster image centered on searched location*), navigate the image (*pan&zoom*), insert related information in a text document (*legend insertion*) and download locally the selected feature layers in Geographic Markup Language (GML) format (*metadata extraction*). Traditionally the user would ask the assistance of a GIS technician to produce the overall data. Most of the time she will not be satisfied by the results and interactions with the GIS technician will be iterated.

In our proposed architecture the user can automatically and independently create and insert the current version of the searched geographical data in his/her document using a web service architecture based on OGC specifications. To this end we have design and implemented three main services that provide the user with the appropriate functionalities, namely:

- **TOPService**: service provider of location search by label; this service guides the user in the search of a location from all recognize labels present in the spatial database. The search is implemented in a two-step procedure: first the service searches for a particular string (user input) in the database and delivers the list of all labels that contain the string; second it locates the geographical x,y coordinates associated to a specific label (user input).
- **WMSmapService**: service provider of raster data; it wraps the functionalities defined in the WMS specification in a Web Service interface. Moreover it returns the lists of available layers. The specific supported WMS operations are: "GetCapabilities", "GetMap" and "GetLayers". In particular the last operation is implemented by analysing the XML output of "GetCapabilities" operation.
- **WFSmapService**: service provider of vector data, also in this case we have developed appropriate wrapper WS interfaces to WFS functionalities, namely "GetCapabilities", "DescribeFeature", "GetFeature".

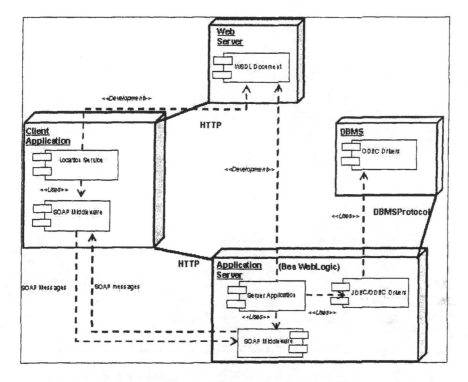

Figure 3. TOPService Component/ Deployment Diagram

In Figure 3 we provide the component and the deployment diagram for the TOPService. In the diagram we can see the various components of our SOA, namely:

- the WSDL file to define the interface of the service
- the use of the SOAP standard for messaging exchanges
- the connection of the SOAP middleware to the appropriate database driver (JDBC/ODBC)
- the DBMS system that implements the SQL query and format the result

Figure 4 provides the component and the deployment diagram for both WMSmapService and WFSmapService. In fact the two services share the same component and message structure and differ only in the specific procedures implementation. Moreover the only difference with the previous diagram for the TOPService is in the connection of the SOAP middleware to the MapServer component driver. This connection is implemented by means of appropriate calls following WMS/WFS specifications. The MapServer then implements the database queries and format the results.

A central role in the proposed architecture is played by the WSDL file created for each implemented service.

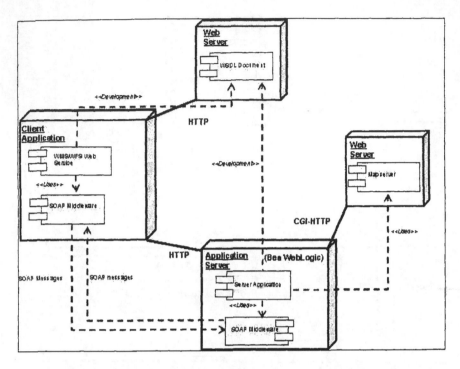

Figure 4. WMSmapService and WFSmapService Component/ Deployment Diagram

The WSDL files are XML documents that describe the mechanics of interacting with the specific web service. Although a web service description in WSDL is written solely from the point of view of the web service (or the service provider that realizes that service), it is inherently intended to constrain both the service provider and the service requester that makes use of that service. This implies that WSDL represents a "contract" between the service requester and the service provider, in much the same way that an interface in an object-oriented programming language, e.g., Java, represents a contract between client code and the actual object itself.

In order to implement a single GIS Web Service, the following steps have to be completed:

- locate an appropriate spatial data base (in our case the GIS of Provincia Autonoma di Trento, PAT)
- define some interesting WMS and WFS services (to this end we have used MapServer for the implementation)
- define the related WSDL files, that expose to the user the offered functionalities
- create server side applications (Web Services providers)
- create client side applications (Web Service requesters)

To support aggregate services, we have first to model the appropriate sequence of processes and then implement them in the service architecture framework. This is possible in two ways: statically, by using proper tools to link the various services needed in the process workflow, or dynamically by describing the workflow in appropriate and adequately expressive languages (such as BPEL4WS [7]).

In our first evaluation of the proposed framework, we have developed a number of aggregate services statically, using the Microsoft Office 2003 Web Services Toolkit to develop the client application. It is worthwhile to note that this choice has been driven by compatibility issues related to the specific back-office development environment used in the local public administration. A similar toolkit is also available in Open Source environment such as Open Office. Figure 5 provides an example of workflow for a typical back-office aggregate service, where the involved services and process flow have been specified. The final result is presented in figure 6, where we show the final outcome of the user request: the inclusion of the requested map in the current document as well as the navigation bar that permits the user a personalization of the graphical appearance.

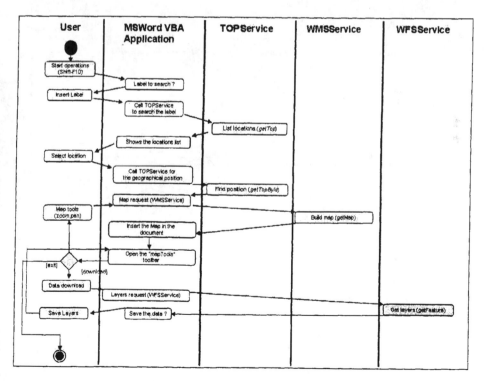

Figure 5. Example of workflow of back-office aggregate service

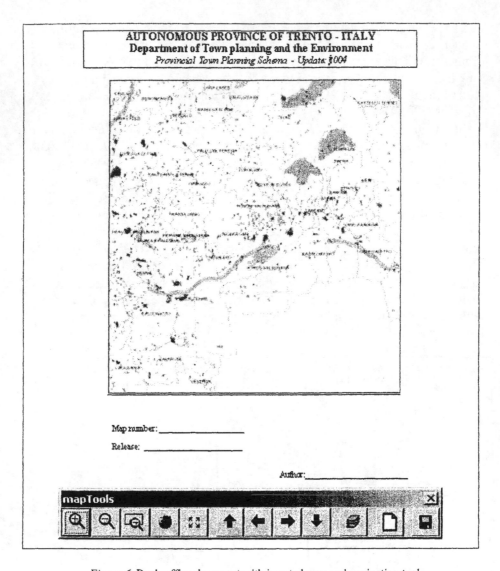

Figure 6. Back-office document with inserted map and navigation tool

5.   RELATED WORK

Currently geographical data are shared through stand-alone or web client/server applications based on OGC specifications. A number of geographical servers are present in the market, among which "*MapServer*" (used in our implementation), "*Autodesk MapGuide*", "*ESRI ARCIMS*",

"CubeWerx CubeSERV WMS", *"JUMP"*, *"OPENMAP"*, *"MYSQL Spatial"*. Among client implementations we mention: *"Chameleon"*, *"Intergraph WMS Viewer"*, *"J2ME OGC WMS Client"*, *"NASA Web Map Viewer"*. For details of the various implementations see [18,20].

On the other hand Web Service implementation of OGC specifications are still under evaluation and standardization from the OGC consortium. One of the few commercial implementation is the ESRI Business Analyst Web Services [20] http://www.esribis.com/solutions/index.html: they comprise a set of centralized services delivered online and delivered to custom Web applications. In particular the user must rely on ESRI geographical database and not on his own data.

OGC is currently investigating SOA in the OpenGis Web Services (OWS) Initiative: an interoperability program designed for rapid development and delivery of proven candidate Web Service specifications into OGC's Specification program which can then be formalized for public release. In particular we recall here a list of relevant initiatives related to our current work:

- OWS 1.2 SOAP Experiment Report [21]: this document describes how OWS services can be ported to Web Services and highlight various issues/problems that have been discovered and need further discussion.
- OWS 1.2 UDDI Experiment [22]: this document lists the design principles, requirements, and experimental results for future versions of a potential OGC – UDDI (Universal Discovery, Description, and Integration) implementation specification.
- OpenGIS® Web Service Architecture [23]: this document is an Interoperability Program Report from the OGC Open Web Services (OWS1.2) Testbed. It specifies and discusses a common architectural framework for OGC Web Services.

6.   CONCLUSIONS AND FUTURE WORK

With the evolution of applications dedicated to geographic information and current networking infrastructures, spatial data are required to be accessible to an increasing number of users. Standards bodies are working together to define appropriate interface specifications to support sharing and interoperability between various spatial data platforms. At the same time, the advance of Service Oriented Architectures is contributing to solve a number of limitations of traditional distributed systems. In this work, we have focused on the use of state-of-the-art Web Services technologies to support and extend current GIS applications.

From a preliminary analysis of the results of our case study we believe that several advantages can be obtained by introducing service oriented architectures into the GIS environment:

- the interoperability between different system can be enhanced
- the availability and usability of geographical information can be improved
- the creation of new valued-added services out of a number of legacy GIS application can be supported

In future work, we will also consider:

- performance issues: since multimedia objects, like maps, can be of relevant size, specific compression algorithms must be considered for data transmission
- security issues: adequate security policies must be established for the deployment of a secure distributed service environment. User can be allowed to query and browse the geographical database, but only authenticated users must be able to actually change the data. This can be achieved with the implementation of the suitable WS-security and WS-Policy framework.

7.   REFERENCES

[1]   N. Land, Building Europe's Spatial Data Infrastructure (ESDI), Cambridge Conference, 2003. See also http://inspire.jrc.it

[2]   for more information on some current Italian projects see. http://labsita.arc.uniroma1.it; http://www.centrointerregionale.it; http://www.intesagis.it

[3]   OGC (Open Geospatial Consortium) web site http://www.opengeospatial.org

[4]   ISO/TC 211 19128 Geographic information — Web Map Server Interface

[5]   P. A. Vretanos, A. Doyle, May 2002, Web Feature Service Implementation Specification, ref. document OGC 02-58, OGC.

[6]   S. Cox, A. CuthBert, R. Lake, R. Martell, 2003, Geography Markup Language Implementation Specification OGC 02-023r4, Open GIS Consortium Inc. http://www.opengis.org/techno/documents/02-023r4.pdf

[7]   http://www.opengis.org/techno/spec.htm

[8]   M.P. Papazoglou, D. Georgakopoulos, Ottobre 2003,Service Oriented Computing, Communication of the ACM, Vol. 46, No. 10.

[9]   http://www.w3.org/TR/soap

[10] http://www.w3.org/TR/wsdl

[11] http://www.uddi.org

[12] http://www-106.ibm.com/developerworks/library/ws-bpel

[13] http://www-106.ibm.com/developerworks/library/ws-coord; http://www-106.ibm.com/developerworks/webservices/library/ws-transpec; http://www-106.ibm.com/developerworks/webservices/library/ws-security.

[14]   Curbera, F., Khalaf, R., Mukhi, N., Tai, S., and Weerawarana, S., 2003. The next step in web services. In Papazoglou and Georgakopoulos (2003), pages 29–34

[15]   M. Papazoglou, J. Dubray, Giugno 2004, A Survey Of Web Service Technology, Technical report of Università di Trento,

[16]   http://www.opengeospatial.org/initiatives

[17]   http://dev2dev.bea.com

[18]   geographical servers implementations:
http://demo.cubewerx.com/demo/cubeserv/cubeserv.cgi;
http://www.vividsolutions.com/jump;
http://www.vividsolutions.com/jump;
http://dev.mysql.com/doc/mysql/en/Spatial_extensions_in_MySQL;

[19]   geographical clients implementations: http://www.maptools.org/chameleon;
http://ogc.intergraph.com/webmapviewer/main.asp;
http://www.boege.net/wmsclient_en.html;
http://viewer.digitalearth.gov/

[20]   ESRI Business Analyst Web Services: http://www.esribis.com/solutions/index.html

[21]   J. Sonnet, C. Savage, 15th January 2003, OWS 1.2 SOAP Experiment Report, Reference document OGC 03-14, Open GIS Consortium Inc. .

[22]   J. Lieberman, L. Reich, P. Vretanos, 17th January 2003, OWS1.2 UDDI Experiment, Reference document OGC 02-054r1, Open GIS Consortium Inc. .

[23]   J. Lieberman, 18th January 2003, OpenGIS® Web Services Architecture, Reference document OGC 03-025, Open GIS Consortium Inc. .

Second generation micropayment systems: lessons learned

Róbert Párhonyi, Lambert J.M. Nieuwenhuis, Aiko Pras
University of Twente, Faculty of Electrical Engineering, Mathematics and Computer Science
P.O. Box 217, 7500AE Enschede, The Netherlands
{parhonyi, l.j.m.nieuwenhuis, pras}@ewi.utwente.nl

Abstract: In the next years the market for low value products such as online music and videos and the role of micropayment systems for selling such products are expected to grow substantially. The first generation micropayment systems appeared around 1994, with systems such as eCash, MilliCent and CyberCoin. These systems were unable to gain market share, however, and disappeared slowly in the late 1990s. The second generation micropayment systems appeared around 1999-2000, and are still operational. In this paper we present an overview of first and second generation micropayment systems, and compare their key characteristics to determine their success or failure. This paper explains why the first generation systems failed and concludes that second generation systems have a better chance for success than their predecessors.

Keywords: micropayments; micropayment system; state of the art of micropayment systems; online payments; electronic payment system; e-commerce

1   INTRODUCTION

Market research companies expect that sales of low value products such as online music and videos will grow in the years to come (Leong 2003). The revenues will mostly add up from individual product payments rather than subscriptions (Ulph Jennings 2003). Reports of Online Publishers Association show that the share of content subscriptions dropped from 89% in 2003 to 84,6% in 2004. Among the individual content payments, the share of micropayments increased from 7,4% in 2003 to 17,9% in 2004. Almost US$50 million was paid with micropayment systems in 2004 (OPA 2004 and 2005). Hence, micropayment systems usage increases.

In the short history of micropayment systems two generations are distinguished (Böhle 2002). The first generation of micropayment systems began around 1994[1] and lasted until the end of the 1990's. The developers of these systems primarily aimed at the introduction of the electronic form of cash

---

[1] Actually, work on topics closely related to micropayments had already started in the 1980's. David Chaum published later his work on untraceable electronic cash (Chaum 1990).

(called e-cash, e-coins, digital cash or tokens) on the Internet. They focussed on the generation of e-coins or tokens, secure, anonymous and untraceable exchange of them, validation and fraud avoidance. Others developed account-based systems transferring money from customer accounts into merchant accounts similarly to banking systems. Nevertheless, all first generation systems failed one after the other, stopped after a public trial or remained at a theoretical description level.

The second generation (or current) micropayment systems emerged in 1999-2000. These systems are almost without exceptions account-based.

In this paper, we discuss the chance that the second generation system will become more successful than their predecessors and to what extent do these systems solve or avoid problems causing the failure of the first generation systems. We show that most failure causes are avoided in the second generation, and conclude that these systems have a much better chance to be successful than their predecessors.

We define first the characteristics of micropayment systems and present an overview of both generation systems to indicate the differences between them. Afterwards, based on the key characteristics that determine the success of micropayment systems, we discuss why the first generation failed and analyze the chance for success of the second generation systems.

The structure of this paper is as follows. Section 2 defines the characteristics of micropayment systems. Section 3 and Section 4 presents the overviews of the first and second generation systems, respectively. Section 5 discusses differences and analyses the chances for the second generation micropayment systems. Section 6 presents the conclusions.

2   CHARACTERISTICS OF MICROPAYMENT SYSTEMS

Models presented in literature define a number of characteristics, mostly classified in different groups: user and technology related characteristics (Abrazhevich 2001), economical and technical characteristics (Weber 1998). A list of characteristics is presented in (Kniberg 2002). In this paper, we distinguish technical and non-technical characteristics.

2.1   Technical characteristics

The technical characteristics describe the internal structure and functionality of micropayment systems. The following characteristics are considered:

- *Token-based* or *account-based* specifies the medium of value exchange. Token-based systems use tokens or e-coins, which provide buying power. In general, customers "buy" tokens from a broker to pay the merchants. Afterwards, merchants send the received tokens to the broker that "pays" the merchants. In account-based systems customers and merchants have accounts at a broker or bank, and customers authorize the broker to transfer money to merchant accounts.

■ *Ease of use* or *convenience* relates to both subscription to and usage of a system for both new and experienced users, and typically relates to the user interfaces and underlying hardware and software systems.

■ *Anonymity* is relevant only to customers. We distinguish between anonymity with respect to the merchants and the micropayment system operators (MPSOs). Merchants are never anonymous.

■ *Scalability* specifies whether a micropayment system is able to cope with increasing payment volume and user base without significant performance degradation.

■ *Validation* determines whether a payment system is able to process payments with or without online contact with a third party (e.g., broker or MPSO). Online validation means that such a party is involved for each payment. Semi-online means that a party is involved, but not for each payment. Offline validation means that payments can be made without a third party (e.g., cash payments).

■ *Security* prevents and detects attacks on a payment systems and fraud attempts, and protects sensible payment information. It is needed because attacks and attempts for misusing a payment system to commit fraud on the Internet are common (Abrazhevich 2004). Security is to a certain extent a subjective concept, and felt differently by each user. Users often interpret security as an equivalent for guarantee: customers feel secure if they receive the paid products, while merchants feel secure if they get the money for the delivered products. The main security concerns are the non-repudiation, authentication and authorization, data integrity, and confidentiality (MPF 2002).

■ *Interoperability* allows users of one payment system to pay or get paid by users of another system. Standardization defines a set of criteria or rules that assure the interoperability and compatibility of micropayment systems. Interoperability also means the convertibility of currencies. A currency is convertible if it is also accepted by other systems.

2.2   Non-technical characteristics

The non-technical characteristics are related to aspects such as the economics and usability of micropayment systems, so they are visible and perceptible for the customers and merchants (users). The following characteristics are considered:

- *Trust* defines users' confidence with respect to the trustworthiness of the micropayment system and its operator. Trust can be developed if users know that the MPSO is bearing most of the risks. Security techniques increase the trust users feel. Trust is considered a pre-condition for a blooming e-commerce (Böhle 2000).

- *Coverage* expresses the percentage (or number) of merchants and customers that can use the payment system. In literature the terms acceptability and penetration are synonyms of coverage (Weber 1998, Abrazhevich 2001, Kniberg 2002).

- *Privacy* relates to the protection of personal and payment information. A payment system provides privacy protection depending on the type of information.

- *Pre-paid* or *post-paid* determines how customers use a payment system. Pre-paid systems require customers to transfer money to the system before they can initiate micropayments. Post-paid systems authorizes customers to initiate micropayments up front and pay later.

- *Range of payments* and *multicurrency support* specify the minimum and maximum payment values supported by a system, and whether a system supports multiple currencies or not.

3   1ST GENERATION MICROPAYMENT SYSTEMS

This section presents an overview of the first generation micropayment systems based on the characteristics defined in Section 2. Detailed information about these systems can be found in (O'Mahony 1997, Weber 1998).

Token-based and account-based

Motivated by the overwhelming popularity of cash in the retail commerce, most first generation systems were token-based. These systems would have liked to introduce e-cash with the main attributes of cash: widespread acceptability, guaranteed payment, no transaction fees and anonymity (O'Mahony 1997). Examples of such systems are Millicent (developed by Digital Equipment Corporation in 1995), ECash (developed by DigiCash in 1996), MicroMint and PayWord (developed by R. Rivest and A. Shamir in 1995-96), SubScrip (developed by Newcastle University, Australia in 1996), NetCash (developed at the University of Southern California in 1996), and *i*KP (developed by IBM in 1997). We also found a few account-based systems: Mondex (developed by MasterCard in 1995), CyberCoin (developed by CyberCash Inc. in 1996), Mini-Pay (developed by A. Herzberg and IBM in 1997).

Ease of use

First generation systems were very inconvenient for users, who were forced to use cumbersome interfaces and difficult wallet and e-coin management operations. It was almost impossible to use these systems without thorough technical knowledge of technologies such as RSA encryption, digital signatures, transport protocols, host names, mint and withdraw e-coins, etc. In some cases also special hardware was needed, e.g., Mondex required contact chip cards and special card readers or a specially

*Figure 1.*Millicent wallet screen shot

adapted mobile phone. Figure 1. illustrates the interface of the Millicent wallet revealing all details: two panels for wallet information, two for the vendor (i.e., merchant) and broker (i.e., currency issuer) policies, and finally two panels for the customer's activity information.

Figure 2. shows that dedicated software was required and moreover, knowledge about transport protocols is needed to use ECash.

Figure 3. illustrates the list of coins in ECash (in German). The first column specifies the quantity, the second the value, the third the total value, and the fourth the expiration date of e-coins. Unspent e-

*Figure 2.*ECash wallet screen shot

coins needed to be returned back to the minting server before their expiration date and had to be replaced with new e-coins. Additionally, payments took a long time to complete. Especially, for micropayments, the time and effort required from many ECash users was too much (Drehmann 2002). Also CyberCash had a very high latency: 15-20 seconds/transaction (Weber 1998).

Lack of portability was another inconvenient usage issue. Because most systems required wallet software to be installed by customers, the customers could only use the payment systems from the computer on which the wallet was installed and where the tokens were stored.

Anzahl	Wert	Betrag	Verfallsdatum
8 x	0,01 =	0,08	22.10.01
8 x	0,02 =	0,16	22.10.01
5 x	0,04 =	0,20	22.10.01
9 x	0,08 =	0,72	22.10.01
5 x	0,16 =	0,80	22.10.01
8 x	0,32 =	2,56	22.10.01
7 x	0,64 =	4,48	22.10.01

*Figure 3.*List of ECash coins

Anonymity

Many systems were not anonymous in any way and a few provided anonymity only with respect to merchants. Systems like Millicent, Mondex, *i*KP, PayWord did not provide any kind of anonymity, NetCash and MicroMint allowed customers to remain anonymous only to merchants. Only ECash provided full anonymity together with the untraceability of payments.

Scalability

Especially token-based first generation systems had scalability problems, originating from the fact that they had a central administration for the issued or received e-coins or tokens. In general, brokers registered the issued tokens in a central database. ECash is an example of such a payment system.

Other systems distributed the central administration of tokens. MilliCent and SubScrip, for instance, used specific tokens issued by broker and merchants, and the issuing party needed to keep the administration of the tokens.

Account-based coped better with scalability, because the number of accounts to be administrated was much lower than of the issued tokens.

Validation

Most first generation systems used online validation. Examples are ECash, NetCash, MagicMoney, PayMe, *i*KP, CyberCoin. Several systems used offline validation. In the case of PayWord, SubScrip, MicroMint, for instance, merchants validated the tokens, Mondex merchants had special hardware that validated alone the payments. Only a few systems used semi-online validation, e.g., a MilliCent broker was involved to process an initial macropayment and subsequent micropayments involved only customers and merchants, a Mini-Pay broker was involved when a certain spending limit of the customer had been reached, Polling used probabilistic intervals to validate payments.

Security

First generation micropayment systems used variable security techniques. Some systems, e.g., ECash, CyberCoin and NetCash, used heavy security techniques such as RSA and/or DEC cryptographic algorithms, digital signatures and passphrases. These techniques were expensive and needed to be understood to a certain extent by both customers and merchants. Other systems, e.g., Millicent and Payword, relied on lightweight security techniques such as hash functions and passphrases and were vulnerable for attacks. Finally, there were systems, e.g., MicroMint, that did not provide any protection of payments, so fraud (e.g., double-spending) was possible. Such systems were not accepted by users, even if the developers of these systems stated or proved mathematically that attacks are difficult to commit.

Interoperability

Interoperability between first generation micropayment systems was never provided nor addressed. Token-based systems created their own currencies (e.g., e-coins, scrip, subscrip, payword, coupons, merchant-specific tokens) and did not define exchange rules or rates. Some systems, e.g., SubScrip, needed extensions enabling customers to withdraw their money and exchange them back to US$. Another example is Millicent, requiring customers to buy specific scrips for each merchant they wanted to pay. Yet another example is ECash, positioned as a system offering the possibility to pay anywhere on the Internet. ECash licenses, however, covered only the customers and merchants of a particular bank, so customers could pay only merchants that were affiliated to the same bank (Drehmann 2002).

The World Wide Web Consortium (W3C) set up a Micropayment Markup Working Group, which developed a Micropayment Transfer Protocol (MPTP 1995) and the Common Mark-up for Micropayment per-fee-links language (Michel 1999). Neither the protocol nor the language became full standards, and the activity of this working group was terminated around 1999.

Trust

MPSOs of deployed systems did not manage to persuade the users that their systems are trustworthy. One reason for this is that users tend not to trust new systems without established positive reputation (Abrazhevich 2004). Additionally, these systems emerged in a period when proper legislation for customer protection, privacy and supervision from financial authorities was lacking. The NetCash software, for instance, was online available for download and deployment. Such factors further diminished the trust of users in these systems.

Coverage

First generation systems had a low coverage. One of the reasons was of course that in general the acceptance and penetration of payment systems develops slowly, as was the case of credit cards (Odlyzko 2003). MPSOs underestimated the marketing efforts needed to acquire merchants and customers. MilliCent did not actively approach customers and merchants, and started in 1997 its trial with only 7000 customers and 24 merchants (wired.com). Another reason was that customers expected that they could use the system for free, as is the case for paying with cash (Hille 2000). Ecash, however, charged US$11 as setup fee, US$1 monthly fees, and transaction costs (Weber 1998).

An example of low coverage is the trial of CyberBucks (of DigiCash) in 1995, in which 30.000 customers and 50-60 merchants were registered, and four banks were issuing the CyberBucks (Weber 1998). One year later DigiCash started to license ECash to banks such as Mark Twain Bank (USA), Merita Bank (Finland), Deutsche Bank (Germany), Advance Bank (Australia) and the Swedish Post. Mark Twain Bank had just over 3000 ECash customers. DigiCash went bankrupt in 1998. Another example is CyberCoins, which was one of the systems operated by CyberCash. CyberCash had relationship with 3.000 merchants who used or planned to use its payment systems.

Privacy

Little is known about privacy, because mostly technical descriptions are available about systems of this generation. In general, MPSOs promise privacy to customers to earn their trust. ECash, for instance, provided high privacy to customers, who could make payments without merchants and ECash banks being able to find out the identity of the customers.

Pre-paid and post-paid

Token-based systems were pre-paid, because tokens could only be withdrawn or received if a macropayment occurred before to cover the value of the tokens. This means that the majority of the systems were pre-paid, e.g., MilliCent, ECash, SubScrip, PayWord, NetCash, and MicroMint. There were also pre-paid account-based systems like Mondex and CyberCoin.

We have not found post-paid system among the first generation systems.

Range of payments and multicurrency support

The range of payments varies a lot. MilliCent supported payments from US$0,001, which is very unusual because in practice products are always much more expensive. CyberCoin and CyberCash supported payments between US$0,25 up to US$10. CyberCent supported payments from US$0,01. Each PayWord token was US$0,01 worth, unless a special deal was made between customers and merchants to raise this value.

The majority of systems supported US Dollars and processed payments with this currency as they were mainly available in the USA. Several token-based systems (e.g., SubScrip, PayWord, each MilliCent merchant had its own currency) created their own currencies besides national currencies. None of these systems had multicurrency support although CyberCash and CyberCoin were also available outside of the USA and ECash was deployed in several countries.

4   2ND GENERATION MICROPAYMENT SYSTEMS

This overview is based on our own extensive study on these systems. The studied systems were found in a research report of the Dutch Ministry of Economical Affairs (DMEA 2003), the payment systems repository of the Electronic Payment Systems Observatory (http://epso.jrc.es), on the EPayNews.com web site, which is a payment news and resource centre, and in the Google directories on payment and micropayment systems.

We observed that, in contrast with the first generation systems, very little information is provided regarding the technical characteristics of the systems. Instead, the information revealed mainly the non-technical characteristics.

Token-based and account-based

We found only two token-based systems in the second generation systems: Beenz and Flooz. The large majority of the current systems is account-based. Reasons for this development are the easier administration of accounts than of tokens, and no monetary value has to be transmitted over the Internet.

Ease of use

A few current systems require a rather long subscription from their customers (e.g., click&buy). This is due to the laws and regulations that require MPSOs to collect detailed customers information to combat fraud better.

Current systems improved significantly with respect to usage convenience. In general, they require two or three simple interactions with customers to process payments. Additionally, these systems use web interfaces rather than special software. Most merchants need common web servers to receive payment confirmations. Peppercoin is an exception, requiring customers and merchants to use dedicated application software.

Figure 4. depicts screen shots of three interactions, in which a Wallie customer pays a merchant (*Film, Music & Games b.v.*) using a web interface. In the first interaction the customer (who previously selected content for €4,50) fills in her account number for authentication. In the second interaction she sees that her account balance is €20 (and will become €15,50 after this payment), and confirms the payment. Finally, she receives a receipt and the payment was processed. Right away also the merchant receives a confirmation.

*Figure 4.*Screen shots of the Wallie payment process

Another advantage of the web interface is that the system is accessible from any computer connected to the Internet and the portability issue is solved. Most systems have similar interactions in proprietary interfaces.

Anonymity

Without exceptions, current micropayment systems allow customers to remain anonymous to merchants. However, only a few systems allow anonymity with respect to the payment systems and MPSOs as well. These payment systems use physical cards bought with cash (e.g., PaySafeCard, Wallie).

Scalability

The large majority of current systems is account-based. Hence, their scalability potential increased compared to the token-based systems (Abrazhevich 2001). Firstgate, the operator of click&buy, declared in November 2004 that click&buy has more than 3 million customers and 2500 merchants in Europe, new customers and merchants can subscribe at any moment and the system copes with scalability (Siegel 2004). Wallie's operator declared that the payment volume reached 15.000 transactions in February 2005 and is monthly increasing with 15%, which is apparently supported by Wallie (emerce.nl).

Validation

All second generation systems use online validation. A reason for this is that merchants often consider these system more trusted and secure, because they are guaranteed the receipt of the processed payments. The attempt to create fraud by double-spending is therefore prevented.

Security

The second generation systems do not use the heavy security measures required for token-based systems. Today transparent security techniques are used. Take, for instance, the authentication techniques, which in general use an e-mail address and password combination (e.g., Way2Pay), user name and password (e.g., WebCent), an account identifier number (e.g., Micromoney, PaySafeCard), an account identifier and pin code (e.g., Teletik SafePay). Merchants are transparently identified for each payment by these systems based on their account or registration number (issued by the systems as well).

The majority of systems uses the de facto HTTPS web protocol, which provides safe data transmission. This protocol requires authentication of the communicating parties, encrypts and decrypts data. Customers have no trouble using this protocol, because all browsers support HTTPS.

Current systems and their MPSOs are obliged by law to generate audit information. Such information can be used to prevent non-repudiation, and trace back and verify payments in case of complaints or fraud attempts.

Generally customers need to complain at the merchants if the delivered products differ from the offered. MPSOs do not get involved and refunds hardly ever occur. A reason for this is that the costs of chargebacks are huge compared to the payment values. Firstgate is an exception, however.

Interoperability

The interoperability between current micropayment systems is not solved yet and there are still no micropayment standards. However, almost none of the current systems introduced new currencies, and the amounts of money stored by these systems can be withdrawn and exchanged into other forms of money, except in the case of physical card-based systems (e.g., Wallie, Microeuro, PaySafeCard). Exceptions exists, however, Beenz and Flooz created new currencies called beenz and flooz, respectively.

Trust

The trust of customers and merchants increased significantly. This can be partially attributed to the definition of proper legislation by authorities such as the European Central Bank (ECB), European Commission (EC), Federal Reserve. Although the legislation varies from country to country, laws require licenses for MPSOs and auditable systems, define obligations, liabilities, the security level of the systems, the right for privacy, etc. Such laws are, for instance, the Federal Internet Privacy Protection Act in 1997, Recommendation 489/EC in 1997, Directive 46/EC on e-money in 2000, Uniform Money Service Act in 2000, Electronic Fund Transfer Act in 2001.

Another factor that increased trust is the partnerships or affiliations of MPSOs with banks, financial institutions, or well-established organizations with a very large customer-base. For instance, the Deutsche Telekom operates Micromoney, the Rabo Bank Minitix, Visa and Mastercard are partners of PayNova, the Commerzbank A.G. and BAWAG are partners of PaySafeCard, Swisscom and British Telecom are involved in the operation of click&buy.

Coverage

Second generation micropayment systems have a high coverage because the behaviour of customers changed. They are more used to work on the Internet and have embraced the idea to pay for content. Their willingness to pay for low value content such as database search, software downloads, archived information, economics and financial content, online banking and brokerage, consumer reports increases (VDZ 2002). The number of merchants using second generation systems has increased significantly. Click&buy has more than 3 million customers and 2500 merchants (Siegel 2004). PaySafeCard had over 2000 merchants in 2004. Bitpass registered over 1900 content merchants in January 2005. Currently, customers can use the majority of these systems for free. Exceptions are PayNova and Centipix charging for specific transactions. The merchants are those who pay for the usage.

Privacy

Nowadays, MPSOs need to protect the privacy of their customers. This protection is enforced by the legislation. The EC, for instance, issued the Directive 95/46 "on the protection of individuals (end-users) with regard to the processing of personal data and on the free movement of such data".

MPSOs always publish privacy statements that describe what kind of user and payment information MPSOs collect and for what purpose, and that state the conditions for doing business with customers and merchants.

Pre-paid and post-paid

The majority of current systems is pre-paid. Examples are Minitix, Bitpass, Wallie, PaySafeCard, WebCent, MicroMoney, Softpay. Among the reasons for the increasing number of pre-paid systems is to limit the fraud possibilities by guaranteeing the payments to providers. It is also important to notice that post-paid systems require a (long-term) contract with consumers in which a steady money source should be provided. This fact makes it more difficult for minors, who have no such money sources, to become users of a post-paid system. Examples of post-paid systems are click&buy and Peppercoin.

Range of payments and multicurrency support

The range of payments varies a lot. Examples of minimum payment values are €0,01 for PaySafeCard, €0,10 for Minitix, US$0,01 for Bitpass, US$0,25 for PayNova. Examples of maximum payment values are €10 for Minitix, €150 for Wallie, and €1.000 for PaySafeCard.

The majority of the systems support a single currency, most often the US$ and the Euro. System supporting the US$ also have an international reach (e.g., Bitpass, Peppercoin and PayStone). Systems supporting the Euro are mainly available within national borders (e.g., Micromoney, Microeuro and WebCent in Germany, Teletik Safepay, Wallie, Minitix, Way2Pay in the Netherlands).

Only a few systems support multiple currencies (e.g., PayNova also supports Great Britain Pounds, Swedish Crowns, Danish Crowns, Norwegian Crowns, Australian Dollars, and Swiss Franks, click&buy supports both the US$ and Euro). Such systems are also internationally available.

5   DISCUSSION

In literature, two extensive studies present the key characteristics and factors responsible for the success of micropayment systems. In one study, interviews were conducted with merchants and MPSOs in Sweden, Japan and the US (Kniberg 2002). In the other study, interviews were conducted and workshops organized for banks, payment system operators, IT and telecom companies, and desk research focused on Dutch and international payment initiatives (DMEA 2003).

Table 1. presents these key characteristics and factors, which are then compared for the two generations in the following sub-sections. Several related characteristics and factors are discussed together.

Table 1.   Key characteristics and factors

(Kniberg 2002)	*(DMEA 2003)*
trust	*who are the system developers and MPSOs?*
ease of use (convenience)	*laws and legislation*
coverage	*influence of standardization bodies*
fixed transaction costs	*demand for micropayments*
processing speed	*ease of use*
	guaranteed delivery of paid products and receive of paid money
	trust
	security
	coverage
	processing speed
	anonymity
	transparent transaction costs, no extra or hidden costs

High level of trust
The trust of customers and merchants in second generation systems increased significantly. MPSOs and their systems enjoy a high level of trust, which is owed to the definition of proper legislation by authorities and to the partnerships or affiliations of MPSOs with banks, financial institutions, etc.

Increasing coverage
The value of a payment system depends on the number of users (customers and merchants), as in case of communication networks. The value of the network increases more than proportional with the number of the users (as expressed for instance by Metcalfe's law). MPSOs needed a certain minimal number of participants that generate sufficient transaction volume (called critical mass) and through that revenues. None of the first generation systems reached that number, so MPSOs went bankrupt without profits.

Second generation systems have a significantly higher coverage than the first generation systems, and the coverage shows an increasing tendency. The number of merchants is rather high, which means that lots of low value products are offered and the demand for micropayment systems increases.

The increasing coverage requires cross-border potential from current micropayment systems. Because of the increasing international reach and multicurrency support, this potential is much higher than before.

Convenient and user-friendly systems
The significantly increased convenience and user-friendliness of current systems is primarily owed to the simple and easily understandable web interfaces of these systems. Note that, in the 1990s, the technology often failed to convince the social groups that it could be used without difficulties. SET (Secure Electronic Transactions), a well engineered protocol for online credit card payments developed by Visa, MasterCard and technology vendors, failed due to extremely complicated and inconvenient usage (Øygarden 2001).

Adequate level of security
Micropayment systems only need lightweight security techniques because the risks are manageable due to the limited value per transaction. First generation systems used security techniques that oscillated between no security at all and heavy security techniques, so they were either exposed to attacks or too expensive and too difficult to understand for their users. Current systems use adequate authentication, identification, non-repudiation techniques, and secure communication channels, which increase the security felt by users. Because of the audit support, customers and merchants are guaranteed that they will receive the paid products (according to their expectation) and the transferred money, respectively.

Fraud attempts are not mentioned in the literature. Reasons for this could be the low payment values and that these systems did not reach yet a large coverage as credit card systems did.

High degree of anonymity

Current payment systems provide customers a high degree of anonymity because they always remain anonymous to merchants and in some cases also to the MPSOs. Laws and regulation limit in some cases the anonymity.

Processing speed

Compared to their predecessors, current payment systems take advantage of faster and more developed Internet and IT technologies. According to Moore's law, the processing power of computers doubles every 18 months, and the bandwidth of communication networks increases even faster (Coffman 2002).

Influence of standardization bodies

The influence of standardization is limited. A reason for this is that many operators deployed proprietary systems and do not want to make large changes if a standard emerges (Böhle 2000).

Note that, the interoperability between current micropayment systems is still not solved. Customers using one system are not able to pay merchants using another system. Current practice shows that, merchants use several payment systems to attract as many customers as possible (VDZ 2002), and customers need to be prepared to pay with any system the merchants use. As a consequence, customers and merchants are in a very unpleasant situation because they need to learn the usage of several systems, manage multiple accounts, remember multiple passwords, trust different MPSOs and so on.

6 CONCLUSIONS

In this paper we identified the key characteristics of micropayment systems, and used these characteristics to compare the first and second generation systems and determine the possible success of the second generation systems.

Our analysis shows that the second generation micropayment systems have a better chance for success than the first generation. In many cases the developers and operators of the new systems learned from the failures of the previous systems. In some cases, however, the same mistakes were made again, so even some second generation systems failed. Beenz, for example, operated between 1999 and 2001 and raised US$89 million from investors, but could not win sufficient user trust and credibility, and thus failed. Its main mistake was the introduction of an unconvertible currency, which users could lose without being notified (Kniberg 2002). The failure story of Flooz is similar.

Just like what happened with credit card systems, the end effect of competition will be that only a few, globally accepted micropayment systems will survive. Until then, and due to the lack of standardization results, regional payment systems will have to interoperate to facilitate world-wide micropayments.

References

Abrazhevich, D., Classification and characteristics of electronic payment systems, Proceedings of the Second Int. Conf. on E-Commerce and Web Technologies, Bauknecht, K. et al. eds., LNCS 2115, ISBN 3-540-42517-9, Springer, 2001

Abrazhevich, D., Electronic payment systems: A user-centered perspective and interaction design, PhD Thesis, Technical University of Eindhoven, ISBN 90-386-1948-0, 2004

Böhle, K. et al., Electronic payment systems - Strategic and technical issues, Background paper Nr. 1 of the EPSO, Institute for Prospective Technological Studies, December 2000

Böhle, K., The innovation dynamics of internet payment systems development, Report Nr. 63, Institute for Prospective Technological Studies, April 2002

Chaum, D. et al., Untraceable electronic cash, Proceeding of the 8th Int. Cryptology Conf., Shafi Goldwasser ed., LNCS 403, ISBN 3-540-97196-3, Springer, 1990

Coffman, K.G. and Odlyzko, A., Growth of the Internet, In Optical Fiber Telecommunications IV B: Systems and Impairments, I. P. Kaminow and T. Li, eds. Academic Press, 2002

Drehmann, M., et al., The challenges facing currency usage, Economic Policy, Volume 17, Issue 34, ISSN 0266-4658, Blackwell Publishers, April 2002

Dutch Ministry of Economic Affairs (DMEA), Betalen via Nieuwe Media (Pay via new media), Research report, The Hague, October 2003

Hille, S., Legal and regulatory requirements on accounting, billing and payment, Deliverable 1.4 of the GigaABP project of the Telematics Institute, Enschede, November 2000

Kniberg H., What makes a micropayment solution succeed, Master thesis, Kungliga Tekniska Högskolan, Stockholm, November 2002

Leong, L., Global Internet offers big opportunities for growth, Report of Gartner, June 2003

Michel, T., Common Markup for micropayment per-fee-links, W3C, August 1999

Micro Payment Transfer Protocol (MPTP) Version 0.1, W3C, November 1995

Mobile Payment Forum (MPF), Enabling secure, interoperable, and user friendly mobile systems, White paper, December 2002

Odlyzko, A., The case against micropayment systems, Proceedings of the 7th Int. Conf. on Financial Cryptography, Wright, R.N. ed., LNCS 2742, Springer, 2003

O'Mahony, D., et al., Electronic payment systems, Artech House, ISBN 0-89006-925-5, 1997

Online Publishers Association (OPA), Paid content market - US market spending report, Research reports for 2003, May 2004

Online Publishers Association (OPA), Paid content market - US market spending report, Research reports for 2004, March 2005

Øygarden, K., Constructing security - The implementation of the SET technology in Norway, Master thesis, University of Oslo, 2001

Siegel, F., E-payments in Europe - a payment scheme's perspective, Presentation at the "E-payments without frontiers" conference of the ECB, Frankfurt, November 2004

Ulph Jennings, R. et al., Downloads: 13% of Europe's music market in 2007, Report of Forrester Research, May 2003

Verband Deutscher Zeitschriftenverleger (VDZ) and Sapient, Paid content market in Germany, Berlin, December 2002 (http://www.paidcontent.org/germarket1.ppt)

Weber, R., Chablis - Market analysis of Digital payment systems, Technical report, TUM-I9819, Technical University of München, August 1998

VALUE ANALYSIS OF RETAIL ELECTRONIC PAYMENTS MARKET
A generic value framework for electronic payment services providers

Rigopoulos George, Psarras John and Askounis Dimitrios
National Technical University of Athens, School of Electrical & Computer Engineering, Management & Decision Support Systems Lab, {grigop, john, askous}@epu.ntua.gr

Abstract: Rapid developments in retail electronic payments industry increase complexity and result in fragmented view of the market. Key players in the domain need compact tools for analysis and decision support. This paper proposes a generic value framework for retail electronic payments industry, which is based on the concept of value network and consists part of an ongoing work towards an integrated decision support environment for actors in the payments industry. We use value network approach for the analysis of retail electronic payments aiming to provide a useful tool for better understanding of payments domain.

Key words: value creation; value chain; value store; value network; electronic payments.

1.   INTRODUCTION

Payments data (Markose and Loke, 2000) demonstrate a clear trend towards replacement of cash instruments by non-cash ones and digitization of payment processes. Traditional forms of money are being transformed into their digital analogues. New payment methods and instruments are competing with traditional cash. Initially, electronic retail payments were born from electronic commerce evolution, as a demand for retail payments over Internet. Nowadays, evolution of mobile devices is expanding needs to mobile retail payments, and future technologies may also impose new needs in payments (Schapp and Cornelius, 2000). Researchers are studying issues deriving from emerging payment methods and instruments. So far, analysis of payment systems is based on financial (econometric models, cost), legislative (policy), or technical perspective (security, internet and mobile technologies, software design), mostly affected by the orientation of researchers. Several complementary views of the payment scene exist, increasing complexity that is already present.

Our research focuses on the subsection of electronic retail payments, which according to Rice and Stanton (2003) contribute at a large percentage at banks' revenues although it is not always obvious. In this paper we present a framework for value analysis of the payments industry, based on the concepts of value chain (Porter, 1985), value shop and value network (Stabell and Fjeldstad, 1998). We identify the basic value entities and argue that value network model is appropriate for a value analysis of the domain. We provide a preliminary approach towards a value framework for payment industry, which is part of an ongoing work towards an integrated decision support tool for the actors in the domain. Though an extensive value analysis of the payments domain is necessary, we limit the scope of this paper and present only an overview of our approach.

In the remainder of this paper we provide some background theory and relevant literature (Section 2), present the value network configuration (Section 3), and conclude with future directions of this project (Section 4).

2.   BACKGROUND AND RELEVANT WORK

In this section we provide some background on payments terminology (Section 2.1), on firm's value theory (Section 2.2) and selective relevant literature references on payments with emphasis on network economics (Section 2.3).

2.1   Payments

Money is the central concept behind all payments, traditional or digital. Though money is a term that is trivial in our everyday life, it is not easy to define it. Stenkula (2003) proposes that we may define it by what it is and by what it does. A commonly accepted definition is that "money is anything that is generally accepted as payment for goods and services and in settlement of debts". Money also fulfills three functions: a medium of exchange, a unit of account and a store of value. Shamos (2002) combines both views and defines money as "something generally accepted as a medium of exchange, a measure of value, or a means of payment".

The above definitions reflect traditional view of money as an economic phenomenon related to the market alone. According to this, money is a commodity universal and homogenous, which is distinguished by quantity. However, during last decade, sociology of money (Zelizer, 1994) has shown that money is not an economic phenomenon but a social one that belongs to both market and non-market aspects of social life (Singh, 2004). Dodd (1994) contributes to social approach of money, defining that what distinguishes money from non-money is a person's use and perception of money, arguing that money has to be part of a social network of trust.

The term *payment* is defined as "the payer's transfer of a monetary claim on a party acceptable to the payee. Typically, claims take the form of banknotes or deposit balances held at a financial institution or at a central bank" (ECB, 2001). *Payment system* is defined as "a set of instruments, banking procedures and, typically, interbank funds transfer systems which facilitate the circulation of money" (ECB, 2001; Soramäki and Hanssens, 2003). A *payment instrument* is defined as "any instrument enabling the holder/user to transfer funds" (ECB, 2001). *Electronic payments* are defined as "payments that are initiated, processed and received electronically. For electronic payments, the monetary claims (electronic means of payment) are held, processed and received in the form of digital information, and their transfer is initiated via electronic payment instruments" (ECB, 2004). *Mobile payments* are defined as "payments initiated through mobile phones. They are a sub-group of electronic payments" (ECB, 2004). *Clearing* is the process of transmitting, reconciling and, in some cases, confirming payment orders prior to settlement. *Settlement* is an act of discharging obligations related to payment transactions between two or more parties.

Payments have evolved during the previous hundreds of years, from barter to electronic money, through hard money, paper money and checks, in parallel with the available technology. We may analyze this process in two vertical axes, depicting degree of technology abstraction and degree of adoption respectively (Fig. 1).

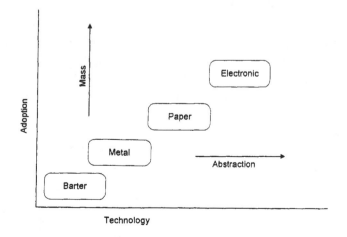

Figure 1. Evolution of payments

This process is continuing today and is due to both social and technological drivers. Social drivers include the various needs of involved parties in the payment process. Some major drivers of change include universal acceptance, reliable value, portability, ease of use, safe storage and transport. Technological drivers include all the innovations that transform the money format and the payment process towards abstraction.

2.2   Value creation theory

In this section we provide some background on value theory as a tool for understanding value creation at firm level. The value concept is important in the analysis of how a firm creates and transfers value to its customers.

Porter (1985) introduced the value chain framework as a framework for value creation analysis at firm level. Stabell and Fjeldstad (1998) proposed value shop and value network models in addition to Porter's value chain. All value models are based on Thompson's (1967) typology of long-linked, intensive, and mediating technologies. An overview of the three models is following.

The value chain model is based on the logic of value creation through transformation of inputs to products mainly through sequential process. It is consisted of primary and support activities. Primary activities are directly involved in creating and bringing value to customers. Porter's (1985) five generic primary activities of a value chain are, *inbound logistics, operations, outbound logistics, marketing and sales,* and *service.* Support activities that enable and improve the performance of the primary activities are, procurement, technology development, human resource management and firm infrastructure (Porter, 1985).

Value shop model is based on the logic of value creation through problem solving. Value is created by mobilizing resources and activities to resolve a particular customer problem (Stabell and Fjeldstad, 1998). Customer value is not related to the solution itself, but to the value of solving the problem. The primary activities of a value shop are, *problem-finding and acquisition, problem-solving, choice, execution* and *control and evaluation* (Stabell and Fjeldstad, 1998).

Value network model is based in the logic of value creation through linking customers. Value networks rely on a mediating technology to link independent customers. The primary activities of a value network are *network promotion and contract management, service provisioning,* and *network infrastructure operations* (Stabell and Fjeldstad, 1998). The primary activity network promotion and contract management consists of activities related to attracting and selecting customers and to managing the customer relationship, in particular contracts related to governing service provisioning and pricing. Service provisioning is linking customers to one another and charging for the services provided. Network infrastructure operation consists of activities related to maintaining a physical and informational infrastructure (Stabell and Fjeldstad, 1998). Value creation, can be direct between two customers, or indirect where one customer is not linked directly to another customer but linked through a pool.

2.3 Relevant literature

During previous years we may notice increasing research interest in retail electronic payments from players in the domain. We may find a lot of discussion in electronic payment systems concerning analysis and taxonomies (Yu et al 2002), classification schemes (Zmijewska et al, 2004), critical success factors (Hort et al, 2002) and adoption studies (Plouffe et al 2000, 2001a, 2001b), to name a few.

However, there is no clear value framework proposed for the analysis of payments domain. The main reason for this is that researchers, policy makers, business owners, and other actors in the domain, approach the subject according to their own perspective. Additionally, domination of banks in retail payments services provision until recently was also a limiting factor for interest from other firms. Nowadays, that payment services are being deregulated and competition from new firms is increasing (Bossone, 2001), such an approach is necessary (Chakravorti and Kobor 2003). Literature contributing to our work may be classified in two major categories.

The first category is consisted from network economics studies related to payments. Network economics (Economides, 1996) is a research field that contributes towards our value network approach. Researchers in the field approach payments domain from a network economics perspective (Chakravorti, 2003; Chakravorti and Roson, 2004) emphasizing in network effects that are present in such industries (Guibourg, 2001), or studying adoption (Saloner and Shephard, 1995) under the presence of network effects. These studies though focus on economic issues, provide evidence for the network characteristics of payment firms and instruments.

The second category is consisted from studies with similar approaches. A framework towards payment services provision is presented by Kannen et al (2003), which analyses the payment process in phases based on Lelieveldt's (2001) generic B2C purchase process analysis. A value network approach is presented in Sannes (2001), who proposes such a model for self-service banking based on firm's value theory (Stabell and Fjeldstad, 1998). Camponovo and Pigneur (2003) also utilize value network theory in their analysis of mobile business.

From a selective review of literature on the field, we notice relative lack in theoretical work towards an integrated value analysis framework for electronic retail payments. Extensive studies related to technology and security issues, user requirements (Abrazhevich, 2001a, 2001b, 2001c, 2002), adoption and diffusion, provide extensive knowledge to researchers, but they are not practical for the decision makers in the domain, that need integrated analysis tools. Our work aims to contribute in the above, providing a value analysis framework for retail electronic payments domain.

3.   THE PROPOSED VALUE FRAMEWORK

Electronic payments transform the entire internet business sector. Not only traditional financial institutions, like banks, face new challenges from new competitors (Bradford et al 2002), but also consumers face increasing complexity in their interaction at the point of sale. Absence of an integrated value analysis framework is a serious drawback for payment industry, since multiple views increase complexity and result in limited understanding and failure of payment innovations.

The proposed framework is part of our ongoing work towards an integrated decision support tool for decision makers in the domain and is focusing on retail electronic payments, which are designed with the main purpose to facilitate payments for consumer e-commerce.

Within the limited scope of this paper we present an overview of the analysis of retail payment services provision (Section 3.1), a brief analysis of actors in the domain (Section 3.2) and the proposed value framework (Section 3.3).

3.1   Payment layers

Retail electronic payment is a part of customers' online buying activities as described by the Consumer Mercantile Activities Model, (Kalakota and Whinston, 1997). The model comprises pre-purchase interaction, purchase consummation and post-purchase interaction phases. The payment activity takes place within the purchase consummation phase. Such an activity is based on a number of payment services offered by various actors in the domain. Bradford et al (2002) group payment services provided by banks and non-banks in three major activities: payment instrument provision, payment processing and authorization. Camponovo and Pigneur (2003) propose tree axes: device, network and services and content, for an m-business analysis framework. Ondrus (2003) utilizes this framework for mobile payments domain analysis.

Based on concepts from previous similar approaches and value network theory (Section 2.2), we approach retail electronic payments as a network product, which is offered to consumers as a bundle of services from a number of involved actors. Despite the complexity of different technologies and services, we model payments as a three-layer structure: core services, network infrastructure and payment services (Fig. 2).

Each layer comprises services provided from corresponding actors that are either essential for the payment activity or facilitate the payment process. Each service incorporates a value offer to consumers or users of payment service. Below we present some key services indicative for each layer.

Core services layer comprises all the necessary prerequisite services for payment transactions. Such services include: social contract about what is accepted as money (e.g. metal, paper), customer trust building (e.g. by payment risk reduction), payment instruments issuing (e.g. debit cards, credit cards) and account provision. .

Network infrastructure layer is based on top of the previous layer and comprises services that connect users of *core services* in a network. Such services include: internet services, and mobile network services.

Payment services layer comprises all services that are built upon the network infrastructure layer such as withdrawals, deposits, account transfers and bill payments.

Payment Layers	Provided Services
Payment Services	Payment services built on the network infrastructure (e.g. withdrawal, deposit, payment)
Network Infrastructure	Existing or new network services that connect users of core services (e.g. telephone, internet)
Core Services	Social contract about "what is accepted as money" (e.g. metal, paper, check, plastic), instrument issuing, trust building, account provision

Figure 2. Layers of payments

Actors in the domain should identify and improve the value offer for each service in order to obtaining competitive advantage (Porter, 1985).

3.2   Actors

Deregulation of payments, though not complete, is challenging new players to enter the promising market of retail payments. Payments industry has evolved through the years as a collection of specialized products built around single purpose networks. Various players operate in retail electronic payments industry today, ranging from traditional banks to non-bank payment service providers (Bradford et al, 2002). Below we present an overview of key actors in the domain focusing on payment services provision and not in the related industry of software and hardware solutions vendors, despite their contribution in payments evolution. In our analysis we focus on the supply side of payment services referring to corresponding actors, and not on demand side where consumers and merchants are the major users of payment services as payers and payees. Major actors that provide payment services based on the previous payment layers approach (Section 3.1) are banks, telecommunication companies, payment service providers, network providers and regulators. Each actor operates within one or more payment layers providing corresponding services as depicted below (Fig. 3).

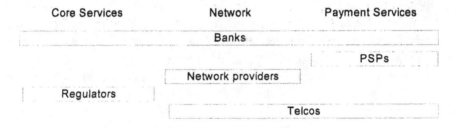

Figure 3. Major actors in the payments domain

Banks provide a full range of payment services covering all three layers, and keep an outstanding role in the domain. Though new entrants threaten their revenues, their exclusive access to core services layer provides them unique competitive advantages. Banks also operate in the network and payment services layers providing total payment solutions to their customers.

Telecommunication companies started to offer payment services in the domain based on their own networks infrastructure. Till now they are the major competitors of banks, but not able to provide total solutions due to restricted access to core services.

Payment service providers (PSPs) have evolved as intermediaries or aggregators providing only payment services in collaboration with actors that operate in network and core services layer. For example, a PSP may provide payers a single gateway to multiple payment networks (e.g. electronic, mobile) and payment instruments (e.g. credit card, debit card).

Network providers act as intermediaries connecting actors operating in the other two layers. They provide network infrastructure for wired and wireless communication and electronic payments.

Regulators operate mostly in the core services layer in close relationship mostly with banks. They set rules for the entire payments domain operation, and supervise their application. Governments and international institutions comprise the most important ones.

3.3 Value network configuration

Based on value theory (Section 2.2) we consider a payment services provider as a firm that relies on a mediating technology and links its customers in a network pool, and thus is best modeled by the model of value network. Payment service provision is offered to a pool of users connected through a facilitating network structure. Traditionally, payment services provision from a bank was rather an indirect offer to its customers and not a separate service. Today, as we may notice from previous analysis (Sections 3.1, 3.2) payment services have been transformed to a value offer from different competing actors to consumers. Our focus is on retail electronic payments only, since B2B payments require extensive analysis for the limited scope of this paper.

In order to identify competitive advantages leading to market leadership we propose a value framework that integrates value network concepts (Section 2.2) and payment layers (Section 3.1) into a value matrix (Fig. 4), where we identify major value creation entities for every part of the transaction process.

First, we map each payment layer (Section 3.1) to a primary activity as is defined in value network configuration (Section 2.2). *Payment services*, *network* and *core services* layers are mapped to *service provisioning*, *infrastructure operation* and *network promotion and contract management* activities respectively.

Next, following a similar approach to Kannen et al (2003) who propose a phase model for electronic payments, we divide a retail electronic payment in three phases: pre-payment, payment and post-payment phase.

Pre-payment phase includes all the initial actions prerequisite for the execution of a payment. For example involved parties must keep accounts to banks or third parties should guarantee for the involved parties.

Payment phase includes the initiation of transaction and actions necessary for the payment process such as payment instrument, payment mode, and payment channel selection. It also includes actions of the payment process such as authorization and payment.

Post-payment phase includes the end of transaction and actions after the completion of payment process such as clearing and settlement.

Finally, following the value network theory (Stabell and Fjeldstad, 1998) and deriving concepts from similar approaches (Sannes, 2001), we identify a value entity for each primary activity and payment phase box of the matrix, resulting in a generic value matrix.

Pre-payment services, transaction services and *post payment services* are the value creation entities for the service provisioning primary activity. These entities cover all the high-level payment services such as withdrawals, deposits, account transfers and bill payments. *Availability, accessibility* and *customer training* are the value creation entities for the infrastructure operation primary activity. *Services bundling, channel integration* and *customer service* are the value creation entities for the network promotion and contract management primary activity.

Actors in the domain (Section 3.2) that offer their services within a payment layer should enhance them by increasing the corresponding value entity.

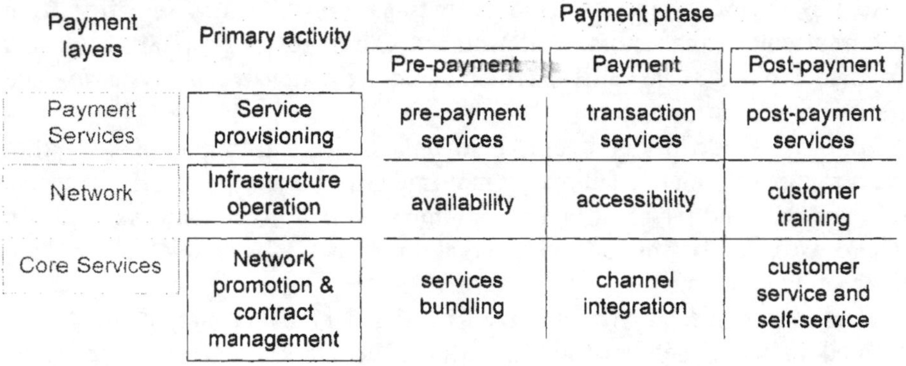

Payment layers	Primary activity	Payment phase		
		Pre-payment	Payment	Post-payment
Payment Services	Service provisioning	pre-payment services	transaction services	post-payment services
Network	Infrastructure operation	availability	accessibility	customer training
Core Services	Network promotion & contract management	services bundling	channel integration	customer service and self-service

Figure 4. Value network configuration for payments

From the above analysis appears that a payment system or innovation is not a competitive advantage by itself. Competitive advantage comes from built around services and customer service. Present complexity in the domain requires an integrated view, helpful for the decision makers.

4. CONCLUSION

In this paper we presented our approach towards a value analysis framework for the retail electronic payments domain. It is part of an ongoing work towards building integrated decision support tool for actors in the domain. The aim of the paper was to demonstrate our approach, so it was not provided extensive value analysis of the domain. We also focused on theoretical presentation and did not examine current practices in the domain.

However, from our analysis, value network approach provides a valuable analysis tool for the domain.

Future directions of our work include extensive value analysis of the electronic payments industry and enhancement of our framework with contributions from real cases. Due to increasing impact of technology to retail payments and their contribution to banks' revenues we aim to provide a helpful tool for decision makers in the retail electronic payments domain.

5. REFERENCES

Abrazhevich, D., 2001a, A survey of user attitudes towards electronic payment systems, *The 15th Annual Conference of the Human Computer Interaction Group of the British Computer Society, IHM-HCI-2001*, **2**:69-71.

Abrazhevich, D., 2001b, Classification and characteristics of electronic payment systems, in *Lecture Notes in Computer Science 2115*, K. Bauknecht, S. K. Madria, and G. Pernul, eds., Springer-Verlag, Berlin, pp. 81-90.

Abrazhevich, D., 2001c, Electronic payment systems: issues of user acceptance, in *E-work and E-commerce*, B. Stanford-Smith and E. Chiozza, eds., IOS Press , pp. 354-360.

Abrazhevich, D., 2002, Importance of user-related factors in electronic payment systems, in *Trust in Electronic Commerce - The Role of Trust From a Legal, an Organisational and a Technical Point of View*, J.E.J. Prins, P.M.A. Ribbers, H.C.A. van Tilborg, A.F.L. Veth, and J.G.L. van der Wees, eds., Kluwer Law International, The Hague.

Bossone, B., 2001, Do banks have a future?: A study on banking and finance as we move into the third millennium, *Journal of Banking & Finance*, **25**(12):2239-2276.

Bradford, T., Davies, M., and Weiner, S.E., 2002, Nonbanks in the payments system, *Payments System Research Working Paper WP 02-02*, Federal Reserve Bank of Kansas City.

Camponovo G., and Pigneur, Y., 2003, Analyzing the m-Business Landscape, *Annals of Telecommunications*, vol. **58**, no. 1-2.

Chakravorti, S., and Kobor, E., 2003, Why invest in payment innovations?, *Emerging Issues*, Federal Reserve Bank of Chicago.

Chakravorti, S., 2003, Theory of Credit Card Networks: A Survey of the Literature, *Review of Network Economics*, **2**:50-68.

Chakravorti, S., and Roson, R., 2004, Platform competition in two-sided markets: the case of payment networks, *Working Paper Series WP-04-09*, Federal Reserve Bank of Chicago.

Dodd, N., 1994, *The Sociology of Money: Economics, Reason and Contemporary Society*, Polity Press, Cambridge.

ECB, 2001, Blue Book - Payment and securities settlement systems in the European Union, European Central Bank, (July 04 2005); http://www.ecb.int/paym/pdf/market/blue/bluebook2001.pdf.

ECB, 2004, E-payments in Europe - the Eurosystem's perspective, European Central Bank, (July 04 2005); http://www.ecb.int/events/pdf/conferences/epayments.pdf.

Economides, N., 1996, The economics of networks, *International Journal of Industrial Organization*, **14**(6):673-699.

Guibourg, G., 2001, Interoperability and Network Externalities in Electronic Payments, *Working Paper Series 126*, Sveriges Riksbank (Central Bank of Sweden).

Hort, C., Gross, S., Fleisch, E., 2002, Critical Success Factors of Mobile Payment, *M-Lab working paper,* University of St. Gallen, Institute of Technology Management.

Kalakota, R., Whinston, A., 1997, *Electronic commerce: a manager's guide,* Addison-Wesley, Reading, MA.

Kannen M., Leischner M., Stein T., 2003, A Framework for Providing Electronic Payment Services, in: *HP OpenView University Association, Proceedings of the 10th Workshop,* University of Geneva.

Lelieveldt, S., 2001, Research study on the integration of e-payments into the online transaction process, *IPTS/ePSO workshop,* Amsterdam (July 04 2005); http://epso.jrc.es/project/IntegrationwholeTPfinalreportres.pdf.

Markose S., and Loke, Y., 2000, Changing trends in payment systems for selected G10 and EU countries 1990-1998, *Economics Discussion Papers,* 508, University of Essex, Department of Economics.

Ondrus, J., 2003, Mobile Payments: A Tool Kit For A Better Understanding Of The Market, *License Thesis,* University of Lausanne, Ecole des HEC.

Plouffe, C. R., Vandenbosch, M. and Hulland, J., 2000, Why Smart Cards Have Failed: Looking to Consumer and Merchant Reactions to a New Payment Technology, *International Journal of Bank Marketing,* **18**:112-123.

Plouffe, C.R., Hulland, J.S. and Vandenbosch, M., 2001a, Research Report: Richness Versus Parsimony in Modeling Technology Adoption Decisions - Understanding Merchant Adoption of a Smart Card-Based Payment System, *Information Systems Research,* **12**(2):208-222.

Plouffe, C. R., Vandenbosch, M., and Hulland, J., 2001b, Intermediating Technologies and Multi-Group Adoption: A Comparison of Consumer and Merchant Adoption Intentions Toward a New Electronic Payment System, *Journal of Product Innovation Management,* **18**:65-81.

Porter, M. E., 1985, *Competitive Advantage: Creating and Sustaining Superior Performance,* The Free Press, New York.

Rice, T., Stanton, K., 2003, Estimating the Volume of Payments-Driven Revenues, *Emerging Issues,* Federal Reserve Bank of Chicago.

Saloner, G., and Shephard, A., 1995, Adoption of Technologies with Network Effects: An Empirical Examination of the Adoption of Automated Teller Machines, *RAND Journal of Economics,* **26**:479-501.

Sannes, R., 2001, Self-Service Banking; Value Creation Models and Information Exchange, *Informing Science,* **4**(4):139-148.

Schapp, S. and Cornelius, D. R., 2000, Leading the New World of Payments: U-Commerce, *VISA International, White paper,* (July 04 2005); http://www.corporate.visa.com/md/dl/documents/downloads/u_whitepaper.pdf.

Shamos, M. I., 2002, Electronic Payment Systems (20-763), Carnegie Mellon University, (July 04 2005); http://euro.ecom.cmu.edu/program/courses/tcr763/index.shtml.

Singh, S., 2004, Impersonalisation of electronic money: implications for bank marketing, *The International Journal of Bank Marketing,* **22**(7):504-521.

Soramäki K., Hanssens, B., 2003, E-payments: what are they and what makes them different?, *ePSO Discussion Starter1 No. 1,* (July 04 2005); http://epso.intrasoft.lu/papers/ePSO-DS-no1.pdf.

Stabell, C. B., Fjeldstad, Ø. D., 1998, Configuring value for competitive advantage: On chains, shops, and networks, *Strategic Management Journal,* **19**(5):413-437.

Stenkula, M., 2003, Essays on Network Effects and Money, Doctoral Dissertation, Lund University, Faculty of Economics and Management, Sweden.

Thompson, J. D., 1967, *Organizations in Action,* McGraw-Hill, New York.

Yu, H.C., Hsia, K.H., Kuo, P.J., 2002, An Analysis and Comparison of Different Types of Electronic Payment Systems, *Technology in Society*, **24**(3):331-347.

Zmijewska, A., Lawrence, E., and Steele, R., 2004, Classifying m-payments - a user-centric model, *Proceedings of the Third International Conference on Mobile Business, M-Business 2004*.

Zelizer, V., 1994, *The Social Meaning of Money*, Basic Books, New York.

PERSONALIZED DISCOUNT - A FUZZY LOGIC APPROACH

Nicolas Werro, Henrik Stormer and Andreas Meier
University of Fribourg, Department of Informatics, Rue Faucigny 2, 1700 Fribourg, Switzerland

Abstract: A growing challenge for the companies in the e-business era is customer retention. In today's global economy this task is getting, at the same time, more difficult and more important. In order to retain the potentially good customers and to improve their buying attitude this paper proposes to calculate personalized discounts. This calculus is based on a fuzzy classification which can derive the customers' value for an enterprise. This approach allows the company to drive the customer equity which treats the customers according to their real value in order to maximize its profit.

Key words: CRM, Discount Management, Customer Equity, Fuzzy Classification, Query Language, Relational Databases

1. INTRODUCTION

The growing importance of the e-business in today's economy forces the enterprises to adapt their behavior towards the different actors of the market. This is particularly true for the customer relationship management (CRM) as the traditional means based on the human relationship are no more available. In this area, the customer retention is a special issue because the global economy enabled by the Internet allows, on the one hand, the companies to offer their products or services worldwide and, on the other hand, also allows the customers to easily compare the different products/services and their prices.

When buying on the Internet the price is certainly one of the most important decision factors. For this reason companies are using different discount strategies in order to attract and retain their customers. Standard discount methods are based either on the *customer* (fixed discount per customer sometimes calculated for customer segments), on the *quantity* (scale price in regard to the quantity of the purchased items), on the *time* (promotional price for a given timeframe), on the *region* (discount depending on the region) or on *other products* (special price for a bundle of items).

A company can combine those different methods in order to fit its price strategy (see Inoue et al., 2001). By doing so, the company may encounter the following difficulties:

- Each method has to be defined manually and independently of the other chosen methods.
- The maintenance and adaptation of the discount methods can be difficult since new customers and products are regularly added.
- The combination of several methods may lead to discount collisions which have to be solved.
- With several independent discount methods it is almost impossible to maintain a consistent price strategy on the long run.

To avoid the mentioned problems and to improve the customer retention, a global discount method considering all the aspects of the customers, including the customer's buying attitude and potential, is needed.

This article presents a simple way of calculating personalized discounts in order to improve the retention rate of the potentially good customers. Based on a fuzzy classification, our approach can derive the customers' value according to an enterprise and, this way, can give each customer the discount he deserves. This approach, often called customer equity (see Blattberg et al., 2001; Rust et al., 2000), allows the company to reinforce the customers' loyalty and also encourages the customers to improve their buying attitude.

The reminder of the present paper has the following structure: Section 2 introduces the fuzziness with relational databases as well as the fuzzy classification concept, query language and implementation. Based on a fuzzy classification, the concept of customer equity and the calculation of personalized discounts are explained in section 3, which also presents the aggregated concept of customer loyalty and discusses the combination of the personalized discount approach with other discount methods in order to include the customer acquisition problematic. Finally, section 4 gives a conclusion and an outlook.

2. FUZZY CLASSIFICATION

2.1 Databases & Fuzziness

In practice, information systems are often based on very large data collections, mostly stored in relational databases. Due to an information overload, it is becoming increasingly difficult to analyze these collections and to generate marketing decisions.

In this context, a toolkit for the analysis of customer relationships which combines relational databases and fuzzy logic is proposed. Fuzzy logic, unlike statistical data mining techniques such as cluster or regression analysis, enables the use of non-numerical values and introduces the notion of linguistic variables. Using linguistic terms and variables will result in a more human oriented querying process.

The proposed toolkit reduces the complexity of customer data and extracts valuable hidden information through a fuzzy classification. The main advantage of a fuzzy classification compared to a classical one is that an element is not limited to a single class but can be assigned to several classes. Furthermore, each element has one or more membership degrees which illustrate to what extend this element belongs to the classes it has been assigned to. The notion of membership gives a much better description of the classified elements and also helps to find out the potential or the possible weaknesses of the considered elements.

In everyday business life, many examples can be found where fuzzy classification would be useful. In the customer relationship management for instance, a standard classification would sharply classify customers of a company into a certain segment depending on their buying power, age and other attributes. If the client's potential of development is taken into account, the clients often cannot be classified into only one segment anymore, i.e. customer equity. Other examples are risk management in an insurance company or client's credit worthiness in a bank. In the last case, studies have shown that with a sharp classification, clients with almost similar risks were classified very differently. The opposite happened too, that is with clearly different properties the clients' overall judgment was very similar.

The fuzzy classification is achieved by extending the relational database schema with a context model. A fuzzy Classification Query Language (fCQL) can directly operate on the underlying database so that no migration of the raw data is needed. In addition, fCQL allows marketers to formulate unsharp queries on a linguistic level. To implement this, an fCQL interpreter which transforms fCQL queries into SQL (Structured Query Language) statements for the sharp databases has been developed.

2.2 Fuzzy Classification with Linguistic Variables

In order to define classes in the relational database schema, we extend the relational model by a context model proposed by Chen (1998). This means that to every attribute A_j defined by a domain $D(A_j)$, we add a context $K(A_j)$. A context $K(A_j)$ is a partition of $D(A_j)$ into equivalence classes. A relational database schema with contexts $R(A,K)$ is then the set $A=(A_1,...,A_n)$ of attributes with associated contexts $K=(K_1(A_1),...,K_n(A_n))$ (see Shenoi, 1995).

Throughout this paper, a simple example of relationship management is used. In this example, customers will be evaluated by only two attributes, turnover and payment time. In addition, these two qualifying attributes for customer equity will be partitioned into only two equivalence classes. The pertinent attributes and contexts for relationship management are:

- *Turnover* in dollars per month: The attribute domain is defined by [0,1000] and divided into the equivalence classes [0..499] for low turnover and [500..1000] for high turnover.
- *Payment time* in days: The domain of the attribute is defined by [-9,10] with its equivalence classes [-9..0] for a positive payment time and [1..10] for a negative one. A payment time of -3 means that the customer pays bills three days before the payment deadline.

To derive fuzzy classes from sharp contexts, the qualifying attributes are considered as linguistic variables, and verbal terms are assigned to each equivalence class (see Zimmermann, 1992). With the help of linguistic variables, the equivalence classes of the attributes can be described more intuitively (see Fig. 1). In addition, every term of a linguistic variable represents a fuzzy set. Each fuzzy set is determined by a membership function μ over the domain of the corresponding attribute (see Fig. 2).

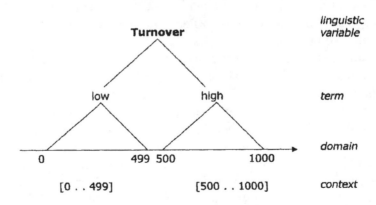

Figure 1. Concept of linguistic variable

The definition of the equivalence classes of the attributes turnover and payment time determines a two-dimensional classification space shown in Fig. 2. The four resulting classes C1 to C4 could be characterized by marketing strategies such as 'Commit Customer' (C1), 'Improve Loyalty' (C2), 'Augment Turnover' (C3), and 'Don't Invest' (C4).

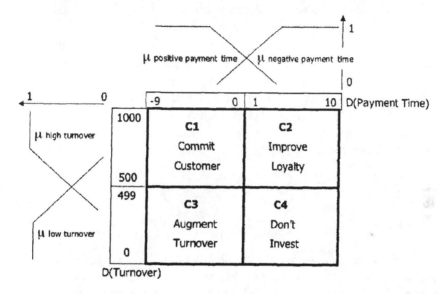

Figure 2. Fuzzy classification space defined by turnover and payment delay

With the context model, the usage of linguistic variables and membership functions, the classification space becomes fuzzy. This fuzzy partition has an important outcome, it implies the disappearance of the classes' sharp orders, i.e. there are continuous transitions between the different classes. This means that a customer can belong to more than one class at the same time and that his membership degrees in the different classes can be calculated. This precise information on the customers allows a company to correctly judge its customers and to apply the customer equity by treating the customers according to their real value (see section 3.1).

The selection of qualifying attributes, the introduction of equivalence classes and the choice of appropriate membership functions are important design issues. Database architects and marketing specialists have to work together in order to define an adequate fuzzy classification which will correctly express the company's viewpoint.

2.3   Fuzzy Classification Query Language fCQL

The Structured Query Language SQL is the standard for defining and querying relational databases. By adding to the relational database schema a context model with linguistic variables and fuzzy sets, the query language has to be extended. The proposed extension is the fuzzy Classification Query Language fCQL, originally described by Schindler (1998).

The classification language fCQL is designed in the spirit of SQL. Instead of specifying the attribute list in the select-clause, the name of the object column to be classified is given in the classify-clause. The from-clause specifies the considered relation, just as in SQL. Finally, the where-clause is changed into a with-clause which does not specify a predicate for a selection but a predicate for a classification. An example in customer relationship management could be given as follows:

```
classify     Customer
from         CustomerRelation
with         Turnover is high
             and PaymentTime is positive
```

This classification query would return the class C1, i.e. the class with the semantic 'Commit Customer'. This class was defined as the aggregation of the terms 'high' and 'positive'. The chosen aggregation operator is the γ-operator which was suggested as compensatory and was empirically tested by Zimmermann and Zysno (1980).

In this simple example, specifying linguistic variables in the with-clause is straightforward. In addition, if customers have to be classified on three or more attributes, the capability of fCQL for a multi-dimensional classification space is increased. This can be seen as an extension of the classical slicing and dicing operators on a multidimensional data cube.

2.4   Architecture of the fCQL Toolkit

As noted above, the fuzzy classification is achieved by extending the relational database schema. This extension consists of meta-tables added to the system catalogue. These meta-tables contain the name and the definition of the equivalence classes, the description of the classes and all the meta-information regarding the membership functions.

The architecture of the fCQL toolkit shown in Fig. 3 illustrates the interactions between the user and the different fCQL components. The fCQL toolkit is an additional layer above the relational database system. This particularity makes fCQL independent of underlying database systems and thus enables fCQL to operate with every RDBMS. It also implies that the user can always query the database with standard SQL (see case 1 in Fig. 3).

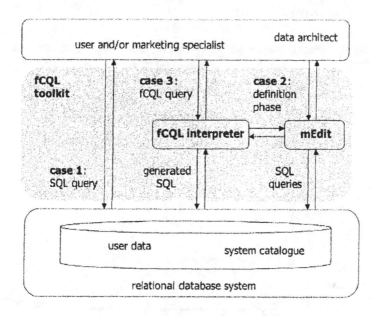

Figure 3. Overview of the fCQL toolkit

The architecture of the fCQL toolkit consists of two main components, the fCQL interpreter and the mEdit editor. mEdit, for membership function editor (see case 2), helps the data architect to select the appropriate attributes and to define the equivalence classes, the linguistic variables and the linguistic terms. Its main functionality is to allow the user to graphically define the membership functions by using linear and S-shaped functions (see Dombi, 1991). The mEdit editor finally communicates with the underlying database via classical SQL statements.

The fCQL interpreter allows the user to formulate unsharp queries (case 3). Those queries are analyzed and translated into corresponding SQL statements for the RDBMS. The interpreter also communicates with mEdit in order to retrieve the membership degrees of the classified elements regarding the previously defined membership functions. With the information returned by the database system and the mEdit data, the fCQL interpreter computes the membership degrees of the elements in the final classes and provides the fuzzy classification to the user.

For more details on the concept and the implementation of the fCQL toolkit, see Werro et al. (2005).

3.   FUZZY CUSTOMER CLASSES

3.1   Customer Equity

Managing customers as an asset requires measuring them and treating them according to their real value (see Blattberg et al., 2001). With sharp classes, i.e. traditional customer segments, this is not possible. In Fig. 4 for instance, customers Brown and Ford have similar turnover as well as similar willingness to pay. However, Brown and Ford are treated differently: Brown belongs to the winner class C1 (Commit Customer) and Ford to the loser class C4 (Don't Invest). In addition, a traditional customer segment strategy treats the top rating customer Smith the same way as Brown, who is close to the loser Ford.

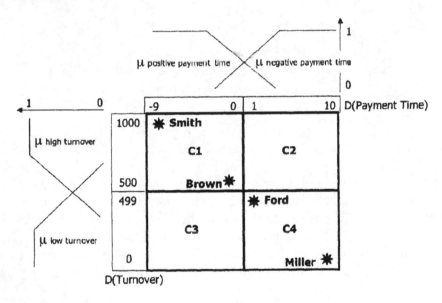

Figure 4. Customer equity example based on turnover and willingness to pay

With a sharp classification, the following effects may happen:

- Customer Brown has no advantage of improving his turnover or his payment time as he already gets the privileges of the class C1.
- Brown may also be surprised and disappointed to be suddenly treated very differently if his turnover and payment time would slightly decrease.
- Customer Ford, who is a potentially good customer classified in the loser class, may find better opportunities elsewhere.
- More critical for the company is the fact that Smith, the most profitable customer, not being treated accordingly to his value could leave the company.

Those dilemmas can be adequately solved by the use of a fuzzy classification where the customers can belong to several classes. The notion of membership functions brings the disappearance of the sharp borders between the customer segments. Fuzzy customer classes better reflect the reality and allow companies to treat customers according to their real value. By driving the customer equity, a company can significantly improve the retention rate of potentially good to top customers and, by this mean, maximize its profit.

3.2   Personalized Discount

According to the customer equity principle, customers personalized discounts can be easily derived from the fuzzy classification shown in Fig. 4. Indeed the membership degrees of the customers in the different classes can precisely determine the privileges they deserve, i.e. a personalized discount reflecting their real value for the enterprise. For that purpose, a discount rate can be associated with each fuzzy class: for instance C1 gets a discount rate of 10% (Commit Customer), C2 one of 5% (Improve Loyalty), C3 3% (Augment Turnover), and C4 0% (Don't Invest). The individual discount of a customer can then be calculated by the aggregation of the discount of the classes he belongs to in proportion to his membership degrees.

The top rating customer Smith belongs 100% to class C1 because he has the highest possible turnover as well as the best paying behavior; the membership of Smith in class C1 would be written as Smith (C1:1.0). Customer Brown belongs to all four classes and would be rated as (C1:0.28, C2:0.25, C3:0.25, C4:0.22). With fuzzy classification, the customers of Fig. 4 get the following discounts:

- Smith (C1:1.0, C2:0, C3:0, C4:0):
  $(1.0 * 10\%) + (0 * 5\%) + (0 * 3\%) + (0 * 0\%) = 10\%$
- Brown (C1:0.28, C2:0.25, C3:0.25, C4:0.22):
  $(0.28 * 10\%) + (0.25 * 5\%) + (0.25 * 3\%) + (0.22 * 0\%) = 4.8\%$
- Ford (C1:0.22, C2:0.25, C3:0.25, C4:0.28):
  $(0.22 * 10\%) + (0.25 * 5\%) + (0.25 * 3\%) + (0.28 * 0\%) = 4.2\%$
- Miller (C1:0, C2:0, C3:0, C4:1.0):
  $(0 * 10\%) + (0 * 5\%) + (0 * 3\%) + (1.0 * 0\%) = 0\%$

Using a fuzzy classification leads to a transparent and fair judgment: Smith gets the maximum discount and a better discount than Brown who belongs to the same customer class. Brown and Ford get nearly the same discount rate. They have comparable customer values although they belong to opposite classes. Miller, who sits in the same class as Ford, does not benefit from a discount.

Applying the customer equity with personalized discounts has two positive side effects apart being fair with the customers. The first one is to motivate all the customers to improve their buying attitude. For instance, with a sharp classification the customer Brown, being in the best class, has no interest of getting better. With a fuzzy classification he can on the one hand get better privileges by improving his buying behaviour and, on the other hand, he can concretely see his progression. The second side effect comes from the fact that only a small group of the customers in the winner class C1 (Commit Customer) gets the best discount. So if an enterprise gave 10% discount to all the customers in the sharp class C1, with a fuzzy classification it can give to its very best customers a greater discount (20% for example) within the same discount budget. By treating accordingly the top customers, this approach reinforces their loyalty toward the company.

3.3   Customer Loyalty

Customers can be classified based on several information or attributes. In the classification example shown in Fig. 4, customers were only evaluated regarding the turnover and the willingness to pay on time. This simple example cannot be effective in the real world. Some other perspectives like the number of items bought, the purchase intervals, the customer's age and region and so on can be included into the classification in order to reflect the customers' value. It is important to note that each company will consider different attributes to judge its customers depending on the data available and the company's definition of the value of a customer.

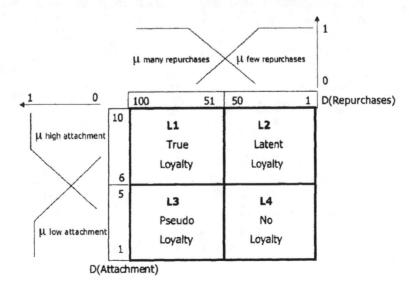

Figure 5. Fuzzy concept for loyalty

A specifically central perspective for a company is the customer loyalty. Many loyalty concepts have been proposed in the marketing literature. Harrison (2000), for instance, proposes two important dimensions, attachment and behavior of customers. For simplicity again, only two attributes (attachment, repurchases) and four classes will be considered: Class L1 (True Loyalty) with high attachment and numerous repurchases, class L2 (Latent Loyalty) with high attachment but few repurchases, class L3 (Pseudo Loyalty) with low attachment but many repurchases, and finally, L4 (No Loyalty) with low attachment and few repurchases. The four fuzzy classes for customer loyalty with appropriate membership functions are illustrated in Fig. 5.

This classification scheme can be used to improve the original customer classes of Fig. 2. For instance, the attribute payment time can be replaced by a loyalty rate calculated the same way as the personalized discount. This mechanism allows the companies to merge several attributes in order to build more consistent and valuable concepts. Those new dimensions can be then integrated in the final classification space (see Fig. 6).

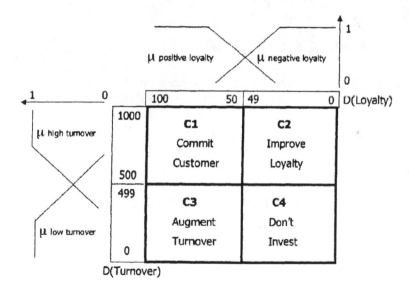

Figure 6. Fuzzy classification space integrating the concept of loyalty

The loyalty concept beneficially replaces the attribute payment time which was too weak to express the fidelity of the customers. Therefore, by combining attributes and calculated concepts, a company can effectively define a fuzzy classification scheme which will be able to calculate the real value of its customers.

3.4   Customer Acquisition

The personalized discount approach is primarily focused on the customer retention by trying to keep the best customer and by motivating them to improve their buying attitude. For this reason it is necessary to combine this approach with other strategies in order to integrate the customer acquisition process.

For this sake, the discount methods mentioned in the introduction based on the time or on bundle of products can be well combined with the personalized discounts in order to attract new customers and, at the same time, better retain the already loyal customers. The combination of other discount methods with the personalized discounts should not lead to discount collisions because all the resulting discounts should be simply summed.

By combining the time and bundle discounts with the personalized discount, a company can build and easily maintain a consistent and effective price strategy which will allow it to fully benefit from the opportunities offered by the e-business era.

4.   CONCLUSION AND OUTLOOK

The personalized discount approach allows the companies to effectively retain the good customers by driving the customer equity. The main advantage of this approach is to have a fully automatic and fair discount method once the fuzzy classification has been set. This precise and transparent evaluation of the customers is made regarding the companies' criteria. By combining this approach with other discount methods which enable the customer acquisition, an enterprise can manage a consistent and effective price strategy in order to maximize its profit, especially through the digital channels.

The strength of a fuzzy classification is not limited to the calculation of a personalized discount. Some other CRM techniques taking advantage of a fuzzy classification like the selection of the most appropriate customers for a marketing campaign or the ability of precisely observe the customers' evolution, are foreseen. The objective is to achieve a CRM framework entirely based on a fuzzy classification.

The personalized discount will be implemented in the eSarine Webshop (see Werro et al., 2004) as alternative discount method. More generally, the fuzzy classification of customers is actually tested in a major Swiss company and will be compared to clustering methods. The results of this experimentation will show the advantages (resp. disadvantages) of a fuzzy classification versus the standard data mining methods.

5.   REFERENCES

Blattberg, R. C., Getz, G., and Thomas, J. S., 2001, *Customer Equity - Building and Managing Relationships as Valuable Assets*, Harvard Business School Press, Boston.

Bosc, P., Pivert, O., 2000, SQLf query functionality on top of a regular relational database management system, in: *Knowledge Management in Fuzzy Databases*, O. Pons, M. A. Vila, J. Kacprzyk, Physica Publisher, Heidelberg, pp. 171-190.

Chen, G., 1998, *Fuzzy Logic in Data Modeling – Semantics, Constraints and Database Design*, Kluwer Academic Publishers, London.

Dombi, J., 1991, Membership function as an evaluation, *FSS* **35**:1-21.

Harrison, T., 2000, *Financial Services Marketing*, Pearson Education, Essex.

Inoue, K., Nakajima, H., and Yoshikawa, N., 2001, Pricing strategies in the e-business age, *NRI Papers 23*.

Kacprzyk, J., Zadrozny, 2000, S., Data mining via fuzzy querying over the internet, in: *Knowledge Management in Fuzzy Databases*, O. Pons, M. A. Vila, J. Kacprzyk, Physica Publisher, Heidelberg, pp. 211-233.

Rust, R. T., Zeithaml, V. A., and Lemon, K. N., 2000, *Driving Customer Equity*, Free Press, New York.

Schindler, G., 1998, *Fuzzy Datenanalyse durch Kontexbasierte Datenbankanfragen* (Fuzzy Data Analysis Through Context-Based Database Queries), Deutscher Universitäts-Verlag, Wiesbaden.

Shenoi, S., 1995, Fuzzy sets, information clouding and database security, in: *Fuzziness in Database Management Systems*, P. Bosc, and J. Kacprzyk, Physica Publisher, Heidelberg, pp. 207-228.

Werro, N., Stormer, H., Frauchiger, D., and Meier, A., 2004, eSarine - A struts-based webshop for small and medium-sized enterprises, in: *Proc. of the EMISA Conference - Information Systems in E-Business and E Government*, Luxembourg.

Werro, N., Meier, A., Mezger, C., and Schindler, G., 2005, Concept and implementation of a fuzzy classification query language, in: *Proc. of the International Conference on Data Mining*, World Congress in Applied Computing, Las Vegas.

Takahashi, Y., 1995, A fuzzy query language for relational databases, in: *Fuzziness in Database Management Systems*, P. Bosc, and J. Kacprzyk, Physica Publisher, Heidelberg, pp. 365-384.

Zimmerman, H.-J., Zysno, P., 1980, Latent connectives in human decision making, *FSS* **4**:37-51.

Zimmermann, H.-J., 1992, *Fuzzy Set Theory – and Its Applications*, 2nd ed., Kluwer Academic Publishers, London.

DYNAMIC MODEL HARMONIZATION BETWEEN UNKNOWN eBUSINESS SYSTEMS

Makoto Oya and Masumi Ito
Graduate School of Information Science and Technology, Hokkaido University, N14, W9, Kita-ku, Sapporo, 060-0814, Japan

Abstract: It is usually assumed that systems share an agreed model of business protocol to implement consistent exchange of series of business messages between eBusiness processes. R&Ds based on this approach are making progress such as model repository technology, business process modeling and business process description languages. This assumption, however, is not always satisfied when considering flexible and free dealings among independent and autonomous eBusiness systems demanded in future eBusiness environment, where systems having their own way of feasible interactions without an agreed business protocol model unexpectedly encounter each other, and want to execute business conversation using their best efforts.

We propose a solution to the above challenge in this paper, taking an approach: Each system exposes a model specifying possible interfaces and behavior; Systems exchange exposed models; Each system reduces its exposed model adjusting to the opponent system; Then, systems begin business conversation if both models were successfully reduced. The paper provides a formal definition of exposed models and an algorithm to reduce exposed models, and presents results using experimental implementation showing appropriateness of the proposed definition and algorithm. It also discusses matching methods of business resource definitions used in the algorithm. The results firstly target eBusiness application but are also applicable to dynamic protocol generations in other areas including robots, mobile devices and ubiquitous environments.

Key words: model harmonization; business protocol; exposed model; interface; behavior; business resource definition; model reduction algorithm.

1.   INTRODUCTION

As Web Services expand from simple request-response technology to flexible message-based bidirectional conversation technology, alignment of business protocol among eBusiness systems becomes an urgent key issue.

Web Services basic protocol stacks, consisting of SOAP[1,] WSDL[2] and relevant specifications, are standardized, implemented by many products, and already used widely. Messaging protocols such as ebXML messaging[4] and WS-Reliability[5] are standardized and expected to be supported soon by many infrastructure products with relevant technologies including WS-Transaction and BTP[6]. Based on these technologies, researches and standardizations about business process modeling are underway including description languages such as WS-BPEL[7,8] and WS-CDL[9], and business process modeling notations such as BPNM[14] and BPML[15].

It is usually assumed that systems share an agreed model of business protocol to execute consistent exchange of series of business messages. Sharing or standardization of business protocol specification is generally possible in an enterprise, an enterprise group, a particular domain group, or a community with a well-defined scope such as RossetaNet. Most of current studies including the above business process modeling studies are based on this assumption. Repository technology to share models or meta-models is researched and standardized (ebXML[10], MOF[12]). Sharing technology of reusable assets including models at development stage is also advancing (e.g., RAS[13]) and being implemented by IDEs such as Eclipse.

The assumption that systems can share pre-agreed model of business protocol, however, is not always satisfied. eBusiness systems scattered over the world in the Internet environment do not always share a complete agreed business process model even if they may share portions of model, meta-model and meta-data. It is desired that such independent and autonomous systems are able to communicate using their best efforts when they encounter. In addition to the current R&D based on the shared model assumption, dynamic harmonization of different business process models must be researched at the same time, to realize flexible and free dealing required in the future eBusiness systems. This requirement is come out not only from eBusiness application field but also from other application fields such as robot communication[16] and ubiquitous application.

In this paper, we propose a solution to this challenge, called *model harmonization*, extending dynamic business protocol generation[17,18] from a model harmonization view point. The approach is as follows:

• Each eBusiness system exposes a model specifying feasible interfaces and behaviors.
• Systems exchange exposed models when encountered.

- Each system reduces its exposed model adjusting to the opponent system.
- Systems begin business conversation if both reduced models are not null.

The main proposal of this paper is to formalize exposed models under this approach and propose the *model reduction algorithm* used in the third step. The model reduction algorithm uses matching of business resource definitions appeared in exposed models. We also propose an early stage solution for their matching method using Web ontology. Note that, however, the model reduction algorithm does not assume full solution for business resource definitions matching, and enough effective with rather primitive matching methods.

The structure of this paper is: Section 2 explains the concepts and defines terminology. Section 3 is the main section and provides a formal definition of models exposed by systems and an algorithm to reduce exposed models. Section 4 provides some solution for business resource definitions matching required during model harmonization. Section 5 shows results of experimentation using experimental implementation. Section 6 discusses the whole results and future issues. Section 7 gives short conclusions.

2. MODEL HARMONIZATION

Model harmonization is based on the following concepts regarding eBusiness systems in open network such as the Internet/Web:

1. A system is modeled as an *internal model* and an *exposed model*. An internal model is a design model of the system, describing functionality used inside of the system or in its internal operational environment, and having a key role in its implementation process. An exposed model is to externally declare the system's functionality to other systems that may be encountered some time. Other systems interact with the system through its exposed model. Model harmonization concerns about exposed models. An exposed model may be simply called a model in this paper.

2. An exposed model consists of an *interface model* and a *behavior model*. An interface model includes a set of operation signature specifications and relating attributes like as IDL or WSDL portType. A behavior model describes behavioral specification of operations.

3. *Business resource definitions* (or *BRDs*) are used in an exposed model to specify types of business elements in messages such as product id, price, invoice, and shipment notification. A business resource definition is an object defining business resource, and has a unique identifier called a *business resource definition identifier* (or *BRD identifier*). By specifying business resource definition identifiers in an exposed model, the

definition bodies of business resource and its reference are separated. A business resource definition identifier typically has a form of URI.
4. *Model harmonization* is defined as a process to automatically adjust exposed models between encountering systems.

3.   MODEL DESCRIPTION AND HARMONIZATION ALGORITHM

This section is the main part of this paper, proposing a way to describe exposed models and an algorithm to dynamically harmonize exposed models.

3.1   Model Description

Figure 1 shows a formal definition of exposed models. It is a kind of meta-model and also definable using other meta-model languages such as MOF, UML profile and XML schema. We here use a traditional style of formal definition to concentrate on essential arguments.

$M = (IM, BM)$
    IM : An interface model defined below.
    BM : A behavior model defined below.

$IM = (U, T, D)$
    U : A finite set. (Operations)
    $T : U \rightarrow \{ I, O, (I, O), (O, I) \}$
    $D : U \times \{ I, O \} \rightarrow \{ (BRD, ..., BRD) \}$

$BM = (B)$
    B : A regular expression on U.

Figure 1. Definition of Exposed Models

An exposed model M consists of an interface model IM and a behavior model BM. U is a set of operations. T is a mapping from each operation to its *message exchange pattern*, specifying I (input-only), O (output-only), (I, O) (input-output) or (O, I) (output-input), abstracted form WSDL2.0 Part 2[3]. D specifies a sequence of business resource definitions defining elements of each message. Each BRD is given by a business resource definition identifier. BM consists of a *behavior pattern B*, expressed by a regular expression of operations.

Figure 2 shows an example, optionally querying price, then, requesting an order and receiving a confirmation of order acceptance, if the order is accepted, receiving a bill and notifying payment, then receiving a delivery notice and sending an acceptance notification. Business resource definitions are specified by URIs in a name space ns = 'http://www.examp.org/brd008/'.

```
U = { PriceQuery, GetPrice, Order, Response, Bill, PaymentNotice, Delivery, Acceptance }
T(PriceQuery)=O, T(GetPrice)=I, T(Order)=O, T(Response)=I,
T(Bill)=I, T(PaymentNotice)=O, T(Delivery)=I, T(Acceptance)=O
D(PriceQuery,O)= 'ns:price.ask', D(GetPrice,I)='ns:price.ans',
D(Order,O)='ns:form.order', T(Response,I)='ns:form.order_response',
D(Bill,I)='ns:form.bill', D(PaymentNotice,O)='ns:notice.conf',
D(Delivery,I)='ns:notice.shipment', D(Acceptance,O)='ns:notice.conf'
B = ( SEQ,
        ( OPT, (SEQ, PriceQuery, GetPrice) ),
        Order, Response,
        ( OPT, ( SEQ, Bill, PaymentNotice, Delivery, Acceptance ) )    )
```

Figure 2. Example of Exposed Model

Note that this formal definition is designed considering application to Web Services. *Fig. 3* is an example of a mapping result from the model described in *Fig. 2* to WSDL style.

```
<definitions name= "Model_PS" xmlns:ns="http://www.examp.org/brd008/">
    <message name="Message1">
        <part name="pt_1" element="ns:price.ask"/>
    </message>
    <message name="Message2">
        <part name="pt_1" element="ns:price.ans"/>
    </message>
    .....
    <portType name="Model_PS_interface">
        <operation name="PriceQuery">
            <output message="Message1">
        </operation>
        <operation name="GetPrice">
            <input message="Message2">
        </operation>
    .....
    </portType>
    <behavior>
        <SEQ>
            <OPT>
                <SEQ> "PriceQuery" "GetPrice" </SEQ>
            </OPT>
            "Order" "Response"
            <OPT>
                <SEQ> "Bill" "PaymentNotice" "Delivery" "Acceptance"
</SEQ>
            </OPT>
        </SEQ>
    </behavior>
</definitions>
```

Figure 3. Example Mapping to WSDL Style

3.2   Model Harmonization Algorithm

Suppose two systems S and T have encountered. Assume S exposes a
model P with an interface model IM_P and a behavior model BM_P, and T does
Q with IM_Q and BM_Q (see *Fig. 4*). Model harmonization algorithm, the main
result of this paper, is explained below. To simplify the explanation without
losing generality, we limit a message exchange pattern is always I or O,
because (I, O) and (O, I) are equivalent to successive two operations whose
message patterns are I and O. We also limit only one business resource
definition is specified for each operation in D.

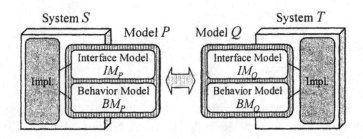

Figure 4. Model Harmonization

3.2.1   Top-level Algorithm

Step a :
  exchange P and Q between S and T
Step b :
  At S,
    reduce P adjusting to Q, using the model reduction algorithm
    suspend execution if the resulted model *newP* is ϕ
Step c :
  At T,
    reduce Q adjusting to P, using the model reduction algorithm
    suspend execution if the resulted model *newQ* is ϕ
Step d :
  start conversation between S and T using the reduced models

---

Figure 5. Top-level Algorithm

The top-level algorithm is shown in *Fig. 5*. The model reduction
algorithm used in step b and c is explained in the next subsection. Note that
steps b and c may be executed in parallel at each system.

3.2.2   Model Reduction Algorithm

The proposed algorithm, called *model reduction algorithm*, is shown in *Fig. 6*. Note that *Fig. 6* describes the process executed at S, i.e., in Step b in *Fig. 5*. The process executed at T, i.e., in Step c, is similar except that P and Q are swapped. The following notations are used:

$P = (IM_P, BM_P)$, $IM_P = (U, T_P, D_P)$, $BM_P = (B_P)$, $Q = (IM_Q, BM_Q)$, $IM_Q = (U, T_Q, D_Q)$, $BM_Q = (B_Q)$. ϕ is an empty set, $\cap$ denotes intersection, and $(A)^*$ means a power set of A. ε is a null string, $+$ is concatenation of strings, and "|" denotes a 'choice' operator in regular expressions. $L(R)$ denotes a set of all strings matching to a regular expression R.

A function *match*(), called a *business resource definition matching function*, is used in the algorithm. *match(from, to)* examines, in its execution context, a business resource definitions BRD_f specified by *from* and BRD_t specified by *to*, and detects inclusion relationship between $I(BRD_f)$ and $I(BRD_t)$ as follows, where $I(brd)$ is a set of all instances of a business resource definition *brd*:

$$match\ (from,\ to) \quad = \quad T(rue) \quad\quad (\text{if } I(BRD_f) \subset I(BRD_t) \text{ is detected}),$$
$$F(alse) \quad\quad (\text{if } I(BRD_f) \not\subset I(BRD_t) \text{ is detected}),$$
$$U(nknown) \quad (\text{otherwise, i.e., neither is detected})$$

The algorithm has two versions, *strict* and *optimistic*. The algorithm in *Fig. 6* is the strict version. In the optimistic version, four invocations of *match*() in Step 1 are replaced by

$$match\ (D_P\,(u,O),\ D_Q\,(v,I)) = True \text{ or } Unknown,$$
$$match\ (D_Q\,(v,O),\ D_P\,(u,I)) = True \text{ or } Unknown,$$
$$match\ (D_Q\,(v,O),\ D_P\,(u,I)) = True \text{ or } Unknown, \text{ and}$$
$$match\ (D_P\,(u,O),\ D_Q\,(v,I)) = True \text{ or } Unknown.$$

Step 1 compares U and V, and decides possible pairs of operations whose business resource definitions are matched (or not not matched in the optimistic version). $\Phi_P(u)$ is a set of operations in V that match to u in U, and $\Phi_Q(v)$ is a set of operations in U that match to v in V. Step 2 removes unmatched operations from original behavior patterns B_P and B_Q, and computes revised behavior patterns B'_P and B'_Q. Step 3 is the main part of this algorithm. Operations in the behavior pattern exposed by the opponent system T is replaced by corresponding possible operations in S, and an intersection with the own behavior pattern is taken. $G(v)$ is a regular expression created by connecting all operations in $\Phi_Q(v)$ using choice ("|"). After replacing all V operations in B'_Q by $G(v)$, a regular expression $newB_P$ giving an intersection of $L(B'_P) \cap L(B'_Q)$ is calculated. Step 4 finally generates a reduced model *newP*.

<u>Step 1</u> :
  for each u **in** U :
    $\Phi_P(u) = \{\ v\ |\ T_P(u){=}O$ **and** $T_Q(v){=}I$ **and** *match* $(\ D_P(u,O), D_Q(v,I)\ )$
            or $T_P(u){=}I$ **and** $T_Q(v){=}O$ **and** *match* $(\ D_Q(v,O), D_P(u,I)\ )\ \}$
  for each v **in** V :
    $\Phi_Q(v) = \{\ u\ |\ T_Q(v){=}O$ **and** $T_P(u){=}I$ **and** *match* $(\ D_Q(v,O), D_P(u,I)\ )$
            or $T_Q(v){=}I$ **and** $T_P(u){=}O$ **and** *match* $(\ D_P(u,O), D_Q(v,I)\ )\ \}$
  $U' = \{\ u\ |\ u \in U$ **and** $\Phi_P(u) \neq \phi\ \};\ V' = \{\ v\ |\ v \in V$ **and** $\Phi_Q(v) \neq \phi\ \}$
  if $U' = \phi$ **or** $V' = \phi$ **then exit** (suspend)

<u>Step 2</u> :
  obtain B'_P **satisfying** $L(B'_P) = L(B_P) \cap (U')^*$
  obtain B'_Q **satisfying** $L(B'_Q) = L(B_Q) \cap (V')^*$
  if $L(B'_P) = \phi$ **or** $L(B'_Q) = \phi$ **then exit** (suspend)

<u>Step 3</u> :
  for each v **in** V' :
    $G(v) = \varepsilon$
    for each u **in** $\Phi_Q(v) : G(v) = G(v) + "|" + u$
  replace all v **in** B'_Q **by** $G(v)$
  obtain $newB_P$ **satisfying** $L(newB_P) = L(B'_P) \cap L(B'_Q)$
  if $L(newB_P) = \phi$ **then exit** (suspend)

<u>Step 4</u> :
  $newU = \{\ u\ |\ u \in U'$ **and** $(u$ in $newB_P)\ \}$
  if $newU = \phi$ **then exit** (suspend)
  $newT_P = T_P$ **restricted in** $newU;\ newD_P = D_P$ **restricted in** $newU$
  $newIM_P = (\ newU, newT_P, newD_P\ );\ newBM_P = (\ newB_P\ )$
  $newP = (\ newIM_P, newBM_P\ )$
  return $newP$

Figure 6. Model Reduction Algorithm

4. BUSINESS RESOURCE DEFINITION MATCHING

match(from, to) is implemented in various ways. A trivial implementation is to return T if *from=to*, F if *from≠to* and both are in the same name space, and U otherwise. The model harmonization algorithm effectively works even using such a trivial matching method as shown in

Section 5. This section discusses a more improved method based on the following approach.

Definitions of business resource cannot always be processed by machines because they are defined in various forms, sometimes in natural language. We associate information describing a BRD (business resource definition) as its proxy, called a BRD description, having an identifier of the BRD. A BRD description is expressed using Web ontology, which may exist at some place in the Internet, and maintains binary relations between the BRD and other BRDs. In the proposed method, *match(from, to)* is calculated by inspecting paths of BRDs from *from* to *to*.

4.1 BRD Description

A BRD description includes descriptions of binary relation and structure. *Fig. 7* shows an example. A binary relation description specifies relationship between the concerning BRD and another BRD such as equivalence, subsumption (inclusion) and disjointness (exclusion). A structure description expresses structural characteristics of the BRD. Both are described using OWL[21] in RDF/XML[22] Syntax. Binary relations are expressed using owl:equivalentClass, owl:subClassOf and owl:disjointWith. The algorithm mentioned below focuses on these three binary relations.

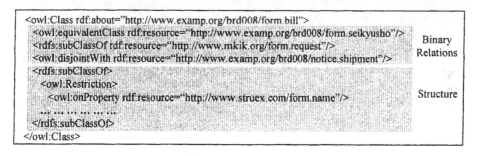

```
<owl:Class rdf:about="http://www.examp.org/brd008/form.bill">
    <owl:equivalentClass rdf:resource="http://www.examp.org/brd008/form.seikyusho"/>
    <rdfs:subClassOf rdf:resource="http://www.mkik.org/form.request"/>
    <owl:disjointWith rdf:resource="http://www.examp.org/brd008/notice.shipment"/>
    <rdfs:subClassOf>
      <owl:Restriction>
        <owl:onProperty rdf:resource="http://www.struex.com/form.name"/>
        ... ... ... ... ... ...
    </rdfs:subClassOf>
</owl:Class>
```

Binary Relations

Structure

Figure 7. Example of BRD Description

4.2 BRD Matching Algorithm

Figure 8 shows the algorithm. BRD_f and BRD_t are BRDs specified respectively by *from* and *to*. B_{fe}, B_{fs}, B_{fd}, B_{te}, B_{ts} and B_{td} are sets of BRDs. BRDs determined as equivalent with BRD_f, as subsumed by BRD_f and as disjoint with BRD_f are respectively stored in B_{fe}, B_{fs}, and B_{fd} in Step 1. BRDs determined as equivalent with BRD_t, as subsumed by BRD_t and as disjoint with BRD_t are respectively stored in B_{te}, B_{ts}, and B_{td} in Step 2. *visible(brd)* is a function that determines whether a BRD description *brd* is referable in this execution context. *equivalentClass(brd)*, *subClassOf(brd)* and *disjointWith(brd)* are functions returning sets of BRDs specified in owl:equivalentClass, owl:subClassOf and owl:disjointWith in *brd*.

Step 1 :
  $B_{fe} = \{from\}$; $B_{fs} = \phi$; $B_{fd} = \phi$
  $sort(from, B_{fe}, B_{fs}, B_{fd})$
Step 2 :
  $Bte = \{to\}$; $B_{ts} = \phi$; $B_{td} = \phi$
  $sort(to, B_{te}, B_{ts}, B_{td})$
Step 3 :
  if $B_{fe} \cap B_{te} \neq \phi$ then return T
  if $B_{fs} \cap B_{te} \neq \phi$ then return T
  if $B_{fe} \cap B_{td} \neq \phi$ then return F
  if $B_{fs} \cap B_{td} \neq \phi$ then return F
  if $B_{fd} \cap B_{te} \neq \phi$ then return F
  if $B_{fd} \cap B_{ts} \neq \phi$ then return F
  if $B_{fe} \cap B_{ts} \neq \phi$ then return U
  if $B_{fs} \cap B_{ts} \neq \phi$ then return U
  if $B_{fd} \cap B_{td} \neq \phi$ then return U
  return U

$sort(b, E, S, D)$
  if not *visible*(b) then return
  for each $c \in equivalentClass(b)$ and $c \notin E \cup S \cup D$:
    if $b \in E$ then add c to E; $sort(c, E, S, D)$
    if $b \in S$ then add c to S; $sort(c, E, S, D)$
    if $b \in D$ then add c to D; $sort(c, E, S, D)$
  for each $c \in subClassOf(b)$ and $c \notin E \cup S \cup D$:
    if $b \in E$ then add c to S; $sort(c, E, S, D)$
    if $b \in S$ then add c to S; $sort(c, E, S, D)$
  for each $c \in disjointWith(b)$ and $c \notin E \cup S \cup D$:
    if $b \in E$ then add c to D; $sort(c, E, S, D)$
    if $b \in S$ then add c to D; $sort(c, E, S, D)$
  return

Note: Parameters E, S and D are used as "call by reference".

Figure 8. BRD Matching Algorithm

In Step 1 and 2, *sort*() recursively searches BRDs started from BRD_f or BRD_t and stores them into appropriate sets B_{fe}, B_{fs}, B_{fd}, B_{te}, B_{ts} or B_{td}. Step 3 makes a final decision inspecting these six sets.

Note that the above is to show the essential algorithm. Practically, it is not necessary to fully complete Step 1 and 2 before execution of Step 3. Step 1 and 2 may incrementally run in parallel, and Step 3 may be executed each time when a new BRD is added.

5.   EXPERIMENT

This section shows result of experiment using MD_REDUCE, an experimental implementation of the model reduction algorithm. MD_REDUCE is developed using Python and the whole algorithm mentioned in Section 3.2 is implemented with necessary background processes including set operations and automata transformations. Models are expressed by Python objects, making independent of middleware platforms and transformable to specific platforms such as XML/WSDL.

Figure 9 and *10* shows an example case. A buyer's system and a provider's system having unadjusted exposed models P and Q try to start conversation. P has nine operations, PriceQuery to ask price, GetPrice to receive price, Order to order, Response to know result of order, AnsQuestion to answer a question from provider during order process, Delivery to get a delivery notification, Acceptance to answer completion of acceptance, Bill to receive a bill, and PaymentNotice to notify payment. Business resource definition identifiers are given to each message as in *Fig. 10*.

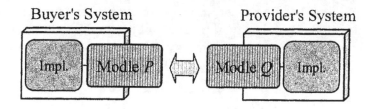

Figure 9. Example Case

Model P

NameSpaces:
ns1=http://www.examp.org/brd008/, ns2=http://www.mkik.org/brdef/
U, T, D:
PriceQuery[O]=ns2:price.ask, GetPrice[I]=ns2:price.ans,
Order[O]=ns2:form.order, Response[I]=ns2:form.order_response, AnsQuestion[O]=ns2:form.order,
Bill[I]=ns1:form.bill, PaymentNotice[O]=ns1:notice.conf,
Delivery[I]=ns1:notice.shipment, Acceptance[O]=ns1:notice.conf
B:
(SEQ,
    (OPT, (SEQ, PriceQuery, GetPrice)), Order,
    (CHO,
        Response,
        (SEQ, Response, AnsQuestion, Response),
        (SEQ,
           (CHO,
             Response,
             (SEQ, Response, AnsQuestion, Response)),
          Delivery, Acceptance, Bill, PaymentNotice   )
)))

Model Q

NameSpaces:
NS=http://www.examp.org/brd008/, mk=http://www.mkik.org/brdef/
U, T, D:
EstPrice[I]=mk:price.ask, AnsPrice[O]=mk:price.ans, Preordered[I]=NS:notice.preorderID,
Order[I]=mk:form.order, Question[O]=mk:form.order_response,
AcceptOrder[O]=mk:form.order_response,
DenyOrder[O]=mk:form.order_response,
Bill[O]=NS:form.bill, ConfPayment[I]=NS:notice.conf
Ship[O]=NS:notice.shipment, ConfDelivery[I]=NS:notice.conf,
B:
(SEQ,
    (CHO, (SEQ, EstPrice, AnsPrice), Preordered),
    Order,
    (REP, (SEQ, Question, Order)),
    (CHO,
        DenyOrder,
        (SEQ, AcceptOrder,
           (CHO, (SEQ, Bill, ConfPayment, Ship, ConfDelivery),
               (SEQ, Ship, ConfDelivery, Bill, ConfPayment))   )
))

Figure 10. Model P and Q (before reduction)

Note that *U, T* and *D* in the formal definition are expressed in a short form in *Fig. 10* as "uuuu[t]=dddd" where uuuu is an operation name, t is a message exchange pattern, I or O, and dddd is a business resource definition identifier. Q has ten operations whose names are not compatible with P. Behavior of P and Q is not aligned. Q always requires price estimation or pre-order ID before starting order, may ask back questions more than zero times to close order, and may ship after billing or bill after shipment. Whereas, P may skip price query process before ordering, accept question only once, and requires shipment before billing.

```
Model    NameSpaces:
  P        ns1=http://www.examp.org/brd008/, ns2=http://www.mkik.org/brdef/
         U, T, D:
           PriceQuery[O]=ns2:price.ask, GetPrice[I]=ns2:price.ans,
           Order[O]=ns2:form.order, Response[I]=ns2:form.order_response, AnsQuestion[O]=ns2:form.order,
           Bill[I]=ns1:form.bill, PaymentNotice[O]=ns1:notice.conf,
           Delivery[I]=ns1:notice.shipment, Acceptance[O]=ns1:notice.conf
         B:
           ( SEQ,
             PriceQuery, GetPrice, Order,
             ( CHO,
                 Response,
                 ( SEQ, Response, AnsQuestion, Response ),
                 ( SEQ,
                     ( CHO,
                         Response,
                         ( SEQ, Response, AnsQuestion, Response )  ),
                     Delivery, Acceptance, Bill, PaymentNotice          )
           )   )   )
```

```
Model    NameSpaces:
  Q        NS=http://www.examp.org/brd008/, mk=http://www.mkik.org/brdef/
         U, T, D:
           EstPrice[I]=mk:price.ask, AnsPrice[O]=mk:price.ans,
           Order[I]=mk:form.order, Question[O]=mk:form.order_response,
           AcceptOrder[O]=mk:form.order_response,
           DenyOrder[O]=mk:form.order_response,
           Bill[O]=NS:form.bill, ConfPayment[I]=NS:notice.conf
           Ship[O]=NS:notice.shipment, ConfDelivery[I]=NS:notice.conf,
         B:
           ( SEQ,
             EstPrice, AnsPrice,
             Order,
             ( CHO,
                 DenyOrder,
                 ( SEQ, Question, Order, DenyOrder),
                 ( SEQ,
                     ( CHO,
                         AcceptOrder,
                         ( SEQ, Question, Order, AcceptOrder) ),
                     Ship, ConfDelivery, Bill, ConfPayment         )
           )   )
```

Figure 11. Model P and Q (after reduction)

Figure 11 is the execution result of MD_REDUCE. Hatchings show modified parts by the model harmonization algorithm. Price query process in *P* has been mandated. Preorder option in *Q* has been removed. Repetition of questions in Q has been limited. These results show the algorithm effectively reduce both models.

In this experiment, a trivial *match*() mentioned in Section 4 is used, which indicates that the model harmonization algorithm is effective even without refined business resource definition matching algorithms.

6.　　DISCUSSION

The appropriateness of the model description definition and the model harmonization algorithm mentioned in Section 3 is verified through experiment using MD_REDUCE.

Table 1 is a simulation result showing the model harmonization algorithm effectively removes invalid protocol sequences in several sample cases. "Total" is a total number of possible message sequences produced by System 1 or 2. "Errors" is a number of message sequences within the "Total" causing intermediate suspension because one side receives a message in a format it cannot process. Internal errors in implementation are not counted. The trivial business resource matching is applied and the strict version is used. As shown, the model reduction algorithm effectively removes unnecessary protocol errors.

Table 1. Simulation Result

| | without model reduction | | | | after model reduction | | | |
| | System 1 | | System 2 | | System 1 | | System 2 | |
	Total	Errors	Total	Errors	Total	Errors	Total	Errors
Case 1	72	48	24	0	24	0	24	0
Case 2	12	8	4	0	4	0	4	0
Case 3	18	14	24	20	4	0	4	0
Case 4	16	14	18	16	2	0	2	0
Case 5	4	4	4	4	0	0	0	0

Future issues on model harmonization algorithm include the followings: 1) Expansion of expression of behavior patterns. The model description in this paper limits expression of behavior patterns as regular expression, i.e. automata, in order to ensure decidability of the algorithm. Even in such limitation, model harmonization takes effect as discussed. To make it further effective, state machine expressions with appropriate restriction is to be introduced. 2) Internal error handling: In this algorithm internal errors that occur during actual process in implementation are ignored. Exception mechanism needs to be studied.

Business resource definition matching in Section 4 is still at an early stage. Though refined business resource matching is not a prerequisite of the model harmonization algorithm, improvement of business resource definition matching needs further study. A major issue is to find an effective and practical matching algorithm traversing through BRD descriptions scattered in the Internet space. Reliability of each BRD description may need to be evaluated during execution of the algorithm. Another issue is to expand BRD descriptions beyond three types of binary relations as mentioned in Section 4.1. A certain subset of OWL DL[19] may need to be introduced considering appropriate balance between expressiveness and complexity of reasoning.

The model harmonization proposed in this paper may be positioned as an extension of OMG/MDA[11]. An exposed model is a PIM (Platform Independent Model) able to map to PSMs (Platform Specific Models), and, at the same time, is a PSM over a specific business process platform. The model harmonization is an approach to dynamically generate a PIM common to concerning business process platforms. The further study should be done from this point.

7.   CONCLUSIONS

We have shown a method to dynamically align business protocol with best effort between eBusiness systems not sharing a pre-agreed business process model, by exchanging and harmonizing models exposed by unexpectedly encountering systems. Definition and algorithm have been given, and verified through experimental implementation. Business resource definition matching has discussed and an early stage solution has been proposed. Future eBusiness communication must allow both cases when pre-agreed business protocol models exist and when do not or are partially given. The results of this paper give an initial step for its realization.

REFERENCES

1. M. Gudgin, M. Hadley, N. Mendelsohn, J. Moreau and H. Nielsen, SOAP Version 1.2 Part1: Messaging Framework, W3C Recommendation, 2003.
2. R. Chinnici, J. Moreau, A. Ryman and S. Weerawarana, Web Services Description Language (WSDL) Version 2.0 Part 1: Core Language, W3C Working Draft, 2005.
3. M. Gudgin, A.Lewis and J. Shlimmer, Web Services Description Language (WSDL) Version 2.0 Part 2: Adjuncts, W3C Working Draft, 2005.
4. ebXML, Message Service Specification Version 2.0, OASIS, 2002.
5. K. Iwasa (ed.), et al, WS-Reliability 1.1, OASIS, 2004.
6. S. Dalal, T. Fletcher, A. Green, B. Haugen, A. Ceponkus and B. Pope, Business Transaction Protocol Version 1.1.0, OASIS, 2004.

7. A. Arkin, S. Askary, B. Bloch, F. Curbera, Y. Goland, N. Kartha, C. Kevin, S. Thatte, P. Yendluri and A. Yiu, Web Services Business Process Execution Language Version 2.0, OASIS Working Draft, 2005.
8. T. Andrews, Francisco Curbera, et al, Business Process Execution Language for Web Services Version 1.1, 2003, ftp://www6.software.ibm.com/software/developer/library/ws-bpel.pdf
9. N. Kavantzas, D. Burdett, G. Ritzinger, T. Fletcher and Y. Lafon, Web Services Choreography Description Language Version 1.0, W3C Working Draft, 2004.
10. ebXML, Collaboration-Protocol Profile and Agreement Specification Version 2.0, OASIS, 2002.
11. J. Miller, J. Mukerji, et al, "MDA guide version 1.0", OMG omg/2003-05-01, May 2003.
12. OMG, Meta Object Facility (MOF) 2.0 Core Specification, OMG, ptc/03-10-04, 2003
13. OMG, Reusable Asset Specification, OMG, ptc/04-06-06, 2004.
14. S. White (ed.), et al, Business Process Modeling Notation (BPMN), BPMI.org, 2004.
15. A. Arkin, Business Process Modeling Language, BPMI.org, 2002.
16. M. Oya, K. Naruse, M. Narita, T. Okuno, M. Kinoshita and Y. Kakazu., Loose Robot Communication over the Internet, Journal of Robotics and Mechatronics, Vol.16, No.6, pp. 626-634, 2004.
17. M. Oya, and Y. Kakazu., Automatic Business Process Generation in the Autonomous Web Services Environment, IAS-8, pp.112-119, 2004.
18. M. Oya, M. Kinoshita, Y. Kakazu, "On Dynamic Generation of Business Protocols in Autonomous Web Services", The IEICE Transaction on Information and Systems, Vol. J87-D-I, No.8, pp.824-832, 2004. (in Japanese)
19. T. Berners-Lee, J. Hendler and O. Lassila, The semantic web, Scientific American, 2001.
20. F. Baader, D. Calvanese, D. McGuinness, D. Nardi and P. Patel-Schneider, The Description Logic Handbook, Cambridge University Press, 2003.
21. P. Patel-Schneider, P. Hayes and I. Horrocks, OWL Web Ontology Language Semantics and Abstract Syntax, W3C Recommendation, 2004.
22. G. Klyne and J. Carroll, Resource Description Framework (RDF): Concepts and Abstract Syntax, W3C Recommendation, 2004.

ACTIVE ADVERTISEMENT IN SUPERMARKETS USING PERSONAL AGENTS

Jarogniew Rykowski
Department of Information Technology, Poznan University of Economics
Mansfelda 4, 60-854 Poznan, Poland
e-mail:rykowski@kti.ae.poznan.pl

Abstract: In this paper we present our approach to active marketing in supermarkets, with an extensive use of radio-frequency identifiers (RFIDs) of goods and locations, and personal, mobile communication devices of clients. Our solution is based on personalized filtering of RFID-related marketing info by the use of software agents. As an implementation base we use the Agent Computing Environment (ACE) framework. ACE agents are partially executed in clients' mobile devices, and partially in the local area network of a supermarket. These agents are able to filter broadcasted marketing information according to detailed user needs, technical restrictions for end-user device, date and time, previous contacts, etc. Several strategies are proposed to use ACE agents to support everyday shopping in a supermarket, including maintaining shopping lists, personal marketing firewalls, and monitoring for changes.

Key words: Software agents, personalization, targeted marketing, RFID

1. INTRODUCTION

Recently we observe two basic trends in modern economy: the globalization, and mass applying of new information and telecommunication technologies. The globalization stands for world-wide market competition regardless time and geographical limitations. Fighting off this competition forced remarkable business changes. Rather than cutting a price, that is already lowered to the maximum extent, one has to compete by other means, for example by broadening and personalizing an offer. However, mass production and selling of personalized goods and services is putting out a great technical and organizational challenge. To this goal, modern technologies must be applied, at each stage of the production and distribution process, including design, logistics, marketing, etc. All these technologies require an efficient information flow and flexible system architecture. Recently, mass tele- and radio-communication systems seem to be the most promising in that domain, mainly mobile telecommunication systems from a client point of view, and bar codes and radio-based automatic identification of goods (RFID identification [16]) for supplying mass production and logistics. Many world-wide companies targeted on mass clients, as owners of supermarket networks for example, widely applied such technologies to cut overall costs, to improve contacts with clients, etc.

So far, a process of applying the above-mentioned modern technologies was transparent for ordinary users – market clients. These technologies were reserved for internal production, logistics, and distribution stages, with limited interaction with end-users [12]. However, there is huge clients' expectancy to change this situation as a result of mass introduction of personal communication devices and portable computers. Returning to supermarkets, the clients are interested in using mobile information technologies to support their everyday shopping. However, so far mass usage of personal clients' devices is not supported by supermarkets, except for very few examples and testbeds, e.g., automatic payment systems in WalMart network [7], and "intelligent" shopping carts [15].

In this paper, we propose to use two modern technologies: personal software agents, and radio-frequency identifiers (RFIDs), to improve the way of shopping in supermarkets. We propose to support the whole process of choosing goods (marketing and comparison of different offers), finding them in the supermarket, and finally buying them. At the same time, our technology may be used for distributing marketing information among clients, as well as for improving internal management of a supermarket. The main goal of this paper is to propose a framework for targeted marketing inside a supermarket, based on RFIDs of goods and locations, and intelligent filtering of incoming marketing information by client's personal (mobile) devices. We propose to use agent-based ACE framework, developed by us and already used with success in many application areas, to create an efficient and safe environment for preparing, storing and executing agents.

The remainder of the paper is organized as follows. In Section 2, some basic information about radio communication and RFID technology is given. In Section 3, agent technology is described, and the ACE (Agent Computing Environment) is presented. In Section 4, an overall architecture of the system is presented. In Section 5, some basic strategies are given of using ACE agents for targeted marketing and personal filtering of marketing information. In addition, some tips are given of using ACE agents for improving supermarket management. In Section 6, a short comparison with some related work is presented. Section 7 concludes the paper.

2. RADIO COMMUNICATION AND RFID IDENTIFIERS

Radio communication systems were traditionally divided into two basic groups: systems devoted to human-to-human voice communication, and computer networks. The human-related communication networks evolved during last twenty years from small analog networks with proprietary solutions to world-wide GSM standard. At the same time computer networks evolve, by introducing new protocols and hardware for radio-based data transfer, mainly for personal (BlueTooth) and local networks (WiFi). Recently, we observe a trend of mixing the above mentioned communication systems into a single, universal, multimedia network (the UMTS idea). The same end-user device and networking equipment is used for voice (recently multimedia) communication, and data transfer. Thus, a user is able to communicate via different standards, according to current situation, environment, technical and economical limitations, etc.

Apart radio-communication systems for humans, there is a large application area of using such systems for automatic wireless connections among different devices. Among others, radio frequency identification (RFID) is one of the hottest research topics. RFID is a generic term that is used to describe a system that transmits the identity of an object or person wirelessly, using tags accessible by radio transmission [16]. A typical RFID tag consists of a microchip attached to a radio antenna mounted on a substrate.

So far, RFID tags are not compatible with Bluetooth/WiFi communication standards. Thus, some additional equipment (a specialized reader) is needed. Such a reader must be mobile, thus it is usually equipped with a radio communication link to a personal/local computer network (WiFi/DECT). The RFID readers are not cheap, however, despite RFID tags, such readers may be reused. For example, a Bluetooth-compliant two-system reader may be applied to a shopping cart in a supermarket. Then, an owner of a mobile phone with Bluetooth connection may take full profits of RFID identification as long as he/she is close to the cart. Note that the connection and communication may be fully automated, and the data transfer is free of charge. Note also that the network is not overloaded due to small size of Bluetooth cells and thus limited number of local signal (frequency) conflicts.

Shopping carts with Bluetooth(WiFi)/RFID readers may be also used by supermarket staff, to transparently track clients and their shopping customs, timings, to compute some anonymous statistics, to improve internal management, etc. Moreover, such carts may automatically inform clients about current price of all the collected goods, send some advertisement info while passing by some goods/locations, support final checkout, etc.

3. AGENT TECHNOLOGY

In our approach, we used a classical definition of a software agent, as presented in [4, 6, 17]. A software agent is a program, executed at a given place, characterized by: (1) autonomy – agents process their work independently without the need for human management, (2) communication – agents are able to communicate with one another, as well as with humans, and (3) learning – agents are able to learn as they react with their environment and other agents or humans. As follows from the above definition, an agent may be programmed by its owner, thus allowing unrestricted personalization of behavior of this agent [1]. Agents may be executed in different places, according to owners' needs and possibilities of the end-user hardware [5].

The ACE framework is based on a set of distributed Agent Servers [8-11], each of them capable of storing and executing software agents. The agents may be moved among Agent Servers. There are "light" Agent Servers with limited functionality to be executed in a "thin" hardware/software environment (e.g., mobile phones), and "thick", massively used Agent Servers located in stationary network hosts. The "light" servers are mainly used for executing individual agents of an owner of a mobile device, while the "thick" ones are used by many users in parallel, usually to access certain services, external software systems, and public communication channels.

There are two basic classes of ACE agents: public System Agents, and Private Agents. Public *System Agents* SAs are created by trusted users (usually system designers), to be used in a mass manner by many users, providing information in a standardized form and with optimum effort. As overall efficiency is of primary concern, SAs are programmed in Java. A way of usage of a given SA cannot be changed by an ordinary user, however, it may be parameterized during the invocation [8, 10].

The *Private Agents* PAs are created and controlled by their human owners. Unless directly ordered by its owner, the agent cannot be accessed by any other agent. For private agents, the main problem is to achieve a reasonable trade-off between overall system security and a need for remote (i.e., server-side) execution of user-defined, thus „untrusted" (from the local administrator point of view) code. Several restrictions and limitations must be applied to user-defined code, protecting the system from (intentional or accidental) damages. Thus, a specialized language is proposed to program agent behavior, based on XML and equipped with several non-standard mechanisms like run-time monitoring of CPU time and memory allocation [8]. The language is of imperative type, thus allowing much wider personalization of the agent code in comparison with the classical declarative approach. XML-programmed private agents may invoke huge library of on-site, residential, Java-based system agents: communicators, services, brokers to external software systems, tools and utilities, etc. Usually, a small private agent, being a "light" mobile entity, is able to use (i.e., execute) several system agents, to achieve different goals. From the user point of view, the system is effective and powerful, and even small private agents are "intelligent" enough to fulfill complex requirements. From the system point of view, private agents executed at server-side do not pose a threat to local environment and other agents.

A typical Agent Server is equipped with several specialized system agents, so called input/output gateways, able to communicate with an external world (including other Agent Servers, local and remote software, and humans) via communication channels of different type and purpose. In general, two basic types of human-agent communication gateways are available: textual and Web-based. A *textual gateway* is able to exchange flat (unformatted) text messages, usually among humans and agents. Physically, textual gateways may use such means as an e-mail connection, SMS/MMS connection with a telecommunication network, a voice gateway, etc. Once sent by a textual message, an ACE agent may act as a chatterbot, analyzing the message via keyword extraction and analysis [9]. The chatterbot interface is useful for non-advanced users, and for users temporary handicapped due to limited hardware possibilities and communication costs.

Web-based gateways are used to access an agent via a WWW/WAP page, and from specialized ACE applications. For semi-automatic formatting of both contents and presentation of the data to be sent, XSL-T technology was adopted with XSL transformations defined in a personal manner and stored in private agent variables [11]. To improve data formatting and presentation, automatic detection of end-user device may be applied, allowing auto-adjustment to the availabilities and technical possibilities of both communication means and end-user devices.

Gateways to external data sources are mainly used for automatic monitoring of information changes. As a change is reported by an external data source, a gateway invokes a selected agent. The agent may next pass the notification about "interesting" changes to user(s), via certain tele-communication gateways. What is "interesting" for the user is programmed by him/her in the code of the private agents [8]. Thus, a set of user's agents is an "intelligent", personalized filter of changes of monitored data.

4. SYSTEM ARCHITECTURE

Overall system architecture is presented in Fig. 1. The architecture consists in using a set of Agent Servers: mobile, light-weight Agent Servers in clients' mobile devices, and a public Agent Server of the supermarket.

The personal Agent Servers are used to execute private agents only. The public Agent Server is able to execute both private and public (system) agents, by the use of two distinguished agent pools: a user pool, linked with clients' personal devices and shopping carts, and a system pool, linked with external software systems of a supermarket (and possibly the Internet).

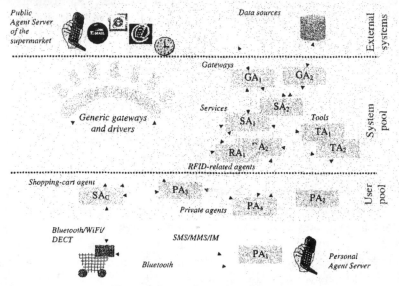

Figure 1. Layered system architecture

The *system pool* of the public Agent Server is devoted to four basic classes of agents: system gateways, services, tools and utilities, and agents related with RFID tags. *Gateways* are specialized agents able to connect with an external software system (cf. Section 3). *Public services, tools and utilities* are system agents prepared by the supermarket staff to be massively used by the clients' agents. These agents are characterized by a stable, well-defined functionality. One of the system agents may act as a directory-agent, providing implementation and access details about other agents. Some agents may be also related with supermarket services, information sources, databases, Internet access, etc.

The public Agent Server is linked with a centralized database of RFIDs related with descriptions of products/goods/locations. The database is usually located inside the local area network of the supermarket, however, it may be accessed via a public communication network as well. The basic functionality of the database is to provide a description/characteristics/ marketing info about a product/piece related with given RFID tag. This basic functionality may be extended, for example by searching for "similar" products/goods, finding an RFID identifier according to some keywords (textual characteristics) provided by end-users, etc. A WAP/WWW server may be provided to access the database from the Internet (e.g., using GPRS radio-connection and WAP/WWW interfaces of a mobile PDA/phone).

There is a possibility to access other Internet/extranet/intranet data sources, using agent-gateways of the public Agent Server as brokers and wrappers. Note, that the outcoming network traffic is controlled by a system agent, thus an access to public resources may be (automatically) moderated.

RFID agents are directly related with RFID tags, and indirectly, with goods and locations. A typical RFID agent is uniquely identified by its corresponding RFID "serial number". The agent is responsible for giving some information about the product/piece/location related with the RFID tag. To this goal, the agent is able to contact an internal database of RFID tags of the supermarket, and, if needed, the Internet.

The *user pool* is devoted to store and execute two basic classes of agents: agents related with shopping carts, and private agents of supermarket clients. Each *shopping-cart agent* is related with a single radio device located inside a given cart. The device is able to communicate with RFID tags (usually a proprietary supermarket standard), as well with mobile devices of supermarket clients (using Bluetooth and/or WiFi). The agent starts to work once the cart enters the supermarket, and is stopped after client's checkout. The main role of this agent is twofold. First, the agent is used as a broker between the RFID tags and the rest of the system. The notifications about detecting RFID tags passing-by are sent to shopping-cart agent, and in turn, to private agents of the client. It is up to the user agents to use such notifications or to ignore it. Second, the agent is a wrapper to the communication between the client's mobile device and the agents from the user or system pool of the public Agent Server. The client may register its mobile equipment in the shopping-cart communication device, e.g., by establishing a Bluetooth link. After registration, the client is able to register and execute his/her personal agents. Personal agents are identified by the use of a physical identifier of an end-user device – a network (usually MAC or Bluetooth-ID) address of a portable/pocket computer, and a phone number for mobile phones. Such way of identification ensures that (1) the identifiers of private agents are unique, (2) the identifiers are stable, and they survive a time of single shopping. Thus, the same identifier may be used next time the client is entering the supermarket. This creates a possibility of using resident, autonomous agents, monitoring selected goods/prices all the time and informing clients if anything "interesting" happens, even if the client is not visiting the supermarket at the moment (cf. Section 5).

Mobile *private agents* are able to move themselves, and they change their position as their owners move (both globally, from a supermarket to another one, and locally, inside a supermarket, from one Agent Server to another). However, a mobile equipment is not powerful enough to execute such complicated software, thus most of the private agents must operate in the stationary network, as close to their owners as possible, to limit the network traffic and system response time. For example, a private agent registers in the supermarket network once its owner enters the supermarket. During check-out, the agent either moves back to the private equipment, or freezes itself waiting for the next visit of the client. Once the client is back, the agent is automatically awaken and ready to serve client's requests.

In contrast to public agents related with system services and RFID tags, personal agents are not characterized by well-defined, stable functionality. Instead, a detailed functionality of a given private agent is under exclusive control of the agent's owner. Thus, we cannot provide here a detailed description of agent's architecture. Instead, we propose a strategy of using private agents for active marketing and on-line comparison of goods (cf. Section 5). However, this is up to particular clients to decide whether to use this strategy or not. The ACE framework is open for introducing any number of other strategies, individualized for both clients and products/producers.

For some less-advanced users with limited ability to program individual agent's behaviour, a standard agent may be created, e.g., implementing the above-mentioned strategy. More advanced clients, however, have a possibility of adjusting the strategy to their own expectations and current requirements. The experts are able to implement their own strategies, fully controlling agent's behaviour and state (cf. Section 3). Note that standard agents may be created automatically once the client is entering the supermarket, and disposed while he/she finishes shopping. Note also that such agents may use some supermarket's hardware only, as for example "intelligent", interactive shopping carts with LCD displays.

4.1   Using RFID tags

Unlike typical applications for logistics and management, we propose to use RFID tags to identify not only goods, but also selected locations inside a supermarket. The standard solution with simple RFID tags applied to goods only is quite expensive, and may generate huge network traffic. First, simple RFID tags cannot be reused, for obvious reasons. Second, for lots of pieces of the same product laying on a shelf, detailed serial numbers of these pieces are of no use, the client is rather interested in getting some general info about the product. However, when lots of tags of the same type are trying to register to a single reader providing similar information, continuous, huge network traffic is generated. Thus, an additional filtering mechanism is needed, and some generalization (i.e., a mapping from identifiers of pieces to identifiers of products) must be provided. Taking into account the above limitations, we propose to use simple RFID tags only for single-piece, usually expensive products, as for example TV sets, audio-video equipment, etc. To identify "ordinary" goods we propose to use RFID tags related with locations, i.e., places inside a supermarket where these goods are displayed on the shelves. In such case, a single tag is used to identify any piece of a product, and any piece of the same product is treated in the same manner.

There are several advantages of linking RFID tags with locations rather than pieces of goods. First, the tags are reused, thus the whole system is quite cheap. Second, the reused tags may be technically more complicated than simple RFID tags. In particular, a proprietary radio communication may be replaced by standardized networking connection (Bluetooth, WiFi, etc.). Thus, such a tag may be accessed by standard mobile equipment, including most of PDAs and mobile phones, without a need for dedicated RFID reader. In the case of simple RFID tags related with goods, an additional hardware broker is needed, usually located in a shopping cart. Such broker is responsible for contacting RFID tags, eliminating repetitive requests, and providing a standardized interface. Note, however, that the broker, in contrast to simple RFID tags, is reused, so its cost (even high) is not critical.

In the case of location-aware RFID tags, general system functionality is reduced in comparison with simple tags related with pieces. This is due to a fact that unique "serial numbers" of pieces are not tracked. This limitation is important, however, only from the supermarket point of view. For example, an automatic payment system based on collecting RFIDs of goods from the shopping cart cannot be applied. Similarly, any tool for tracking pieces (statistics, internal supermarket management) cannot be used. However, from a client point of view, these features are not of a great importance. Moreover, a mixed solution may be implemented. One start with location-aware tags, and apply simple tags only to the most expensive goods. Once the simple RFID tags are going cheaper, more and more products are equipped with unique tags, and the system functionality grows.

4.2   Network connections

A technical question arises for choosing the most adequate networking standard to contact end-user devices and the local area network of a supermarket. Two radio-communication standards dominated today's market: Bluetooth, and WiFi. Bluetooth piconets are better for reducing local network traffic and automatic detection of devices in range. Automatic interaction of WiFi devices in range is hard to maintain, and overall traffic inside a WiFi cell may be huge, as the cell size grows (WiFi cells provide useful radio signal at a distance of 50-100 meters, in comparison with 10-meter-sized piconets). However, WiFi is more universal, as at the same time it may be used to connect to a local area network – for Bluetooth one needs a specialized router (however, such router may be linked to a shopping cart). The mixed solution, with Bluetooth piconets and WiFi access to a local area network seems to be the best idea. More and more mobile devices are equipped with both interfaces. Thus, we assume that the system (mainly communicating devices in the shopping carts) accepts a network traffic in both standards, and that the clients' devices are equipped with either Bluetooth, or WiFi radio communication (preferably both).

5.   BASIC STRATEGY OF USING ACE AGENTS FOR ACTIVE MARKETING

A connection of ACE agents and RFID identifiers makes it possible to change a traditional way of shopping. Usually, the goods are lying on a shop shelf, passively waiting for clients. A client is informed about given goods mainly via previously watched/read advertisements, in TV, newspapers, etc. A real comparison with other similar products is limited, not to say impossible (especially inside a supermarket, at shopping time). We propose to change this situation by introducing an active marketing – "hunting" for clients. Active goods/products are trying to access client's personal communication device in order to present themselves and to persuade the client to buy them. To this goal, RFID tags are used to identify goods and places(locations), and an internal supermarket database of goods is used to collect an on-line information about goods. From the client point of view, the main technical problem lies in intelligent filtering of all incoming offers to restrict such offers only to those interested for the client at the moment. This is a task for client's personal agent, residing in client's personal device and migrating to the supermarket network for requested information. The agent informs its owner about new "interesting" offers. What is "interesting" for a given client is programmed for/by him in the code and variables of his/her personal agents. The agents may also take into consideration such features, as actual client's position, battery time, costs of a connection, etc.

Note that the active marketing is not treated as yet-another version of irritating spam, because all the information coming to the client is filtered by his/her personal agent, and probably the client is waiting for such information. As the client is targeted on "interesting" marketing information, such way of contacts will probably substantially reduce client's individual level of irritation. Moreover, a personal agent will be treated as an advisor rather than yet-again source of useless marketing information. Note also, that the time period between sending a marketing info and buying some goods is very little (seconds or minutes), comparing with traditional marketing in newspapers and TV (a delay counted in days or even weeks).

Personalized interaction of the client's device and different goods makes it also possible to implement individual targeted marketing. A "special" offer sent to a client may be personalized according to (1) the current situation, and (2) a history of contacts with this client. Note that today's "special offers" are not targeted on particular clients except for high-cost, rarely selling goods – a typical "special offer" of a supermarket is addressed to all the supermarket clients, regardless time and money already spent by the client. Our "special offers" may be addressed to individual, however, anonymous (unknown by name/real address, not by phone number) persons.

The above described strategy of active marketing makes it is possible to reverse a traditional way of marketing and shopping. Instead of huge amount of useless marketing information, flooding clients all the day regardless time and place, we propose to search automatically marketing info looking for something "interesting" (from a particular user point of view) at given place and time. We expect at least four scenarios of using the active marketing strategy.

- *Dynamic scenario*: a client stores a list of products he/she wants to buy at the moment. Passing given product from the list, the client is informed by a pop-up message. Then, the client may collect an item of the product to automatically "free" its corresponding position from the list. During searching for products, the client may be guided to certain locations. It is also possible to search for similar products, to compare products according to users' opinions, current price, functionality, etc. Note that no direct interaction is needed except for storing the list – the rest is performed automatically with the help of ACE agents, and RFIDs passing by.

- *Personal Marketing Firewall*: a client stores a list of "needed" and "unwanted" products, to pass/immediately block any marketing information related with these products. Thus, an amount of advertisement may be substantially reduced. The list of "needed"/"unwanted" products may be set up dynamically, similar to the list of IP/DNS sites for Personal Network Firewalls, by answering simple questions once a new advertisement is displayed, e.g. "Accept? Yes/No/Always yes/Always no".

- *Static scenario*: a client chose already a product, however its price (or other conditions) is not satisfactory yet. Then, the client instructs his/her agent to continuously monitor the product/price. Once the price drops below certain limit, the client is immediately informed, for example by an e-mail or SMS message. Note that the monitoring agent resides in the supermarket network for a long time, not only at client's shopping time, waiting for a selected change in supermarket database of products. Note also that such agent is executed autonomously, with no on-line connection with its owner.

- *Hunting for promotions*: a scenario similar to the above static scenario, except the agent is monitoring a group of products rather that a single product. As soon as a promotion arrives concerning any product from the group, the agent owner is immediately informed.

Note that at least two last scenarios may be implemented with agents working in the Internet rather than in internal network of a supermarket. Thus, an offer of several supermarkets may be compared, and client's choice is significantly extended.

A supermarket may also take some profits, tracking an "interaction" among client's personal agent and different goods. A statistical (anonymous) information obtained in such a way may be used to improve an internal organization of a supermarket (positions of goods, mutual relations among different goods, clients' choices, etc.). Note that this a real, on-line information rather that estimated results obtained by specialized research on chosen clients/situations/goods. Such real immediate information is very important not only for supermarket owners, but also for producers, marketing managers, etc. Among others, a few useful scenarios of using ACE agents to improve an internal organization of a supermarket are given below, both apparent (i.e., with some results visible for clients) and transparent (visible only for the staff):

- tracking client choices,
- tracking client positions and timings,
- computing global statistics concerning the above (and similar) scenarios,
- taking care about some special products, e.g., RFID tags with thermometer/pressure meter, to inform about "bad" conditions while storing and transporting given goods,
- tracking persons with temporary/stable RFIDs, for example children and other family members, tracking positions of shopping carts, etc.,
- tracking and monitoring supermarket staff,
- anti-thief systems,
- automatic counters of shopping carts, clients, goods bought by clients, etc.

6. RELATED WORK

To our best knowledge, a system for supporting everyday shopping in supermarkets has not been proposed so far. Except for some proprietary prototypes, as for example "intelligent shopping cart", "intelligent refrigerator", and some automatic payment systems [7], not a single global solution exists. Moreover, the above mentioned prototypes are not personalized, except for very limited parameterization (the same functionality for everybody). Thus, we think that our idea of active marketing and personalized filtering of advertisement info is pretty new.

Similar, the software agents technology has not been used for shopping support. Typical solutions [2, 14], based on descriptive approach to agent programming [13], are not universal enough. The environments with imperatively programmed agents are "heavy" and less secured [10]. A popular idea of an "intelligent" personal agent [3], introduced a few years ago, is quite different of our approach. First, typical "intelligent" agents are pre-programmed by system designers, and their architecture and functionality is fixed (from an end-user point of view). Second, these agents are not highly mobile, and their code is "thick" – they need a powerful environment to be executed efficiently. As a consequence, a typical personal agent is executed in a stationary, fixed host (usually a private host of an agent owner). Mobile devices, characterized by small memory, display, and keyboard, are not powerful enough to fulfill the agent's expectations. A local area network of a supermarket is also not a good place for such an agent, mainly due to security and compatibility restrictions. In contrast, imperative ACE agents are mobile and distributed, with "light" mobile and "thick" stationary parts. At the same time, private agents may be personalized by their owners, still having a possibility of using other agents, mainly system agents predefined by "trusted" system designers.

A personalized functionality of private ACE agents cannot be implemented using classical programming techniques, mainly WWW servers and centralized, multi-user and multi-access databases. All such techniques assume that there is one single software common for all the users, executed in a certain place and with certain access limits. Even parameterized, such software is not able to satisfy any user. Moreover, a level of parameterization is usually low, due to technical and economical reasons. To effectively filter the marketing information flooding the clients, one needs a specialized, personalized software, adjusted to his/her personal communication device. On the other end, every product is different, and its marketing should be different and addressed to different clients, thus an individualization is needed as well.

Using RFID tags for marketing support was not considered so far. Note that the popular bar codes are not used to this goal as well. Our idea of using RFID tags for broadcasting an automatic info about passing by an "interesting" product/place looks quite new. The technology used is "light" and may be easily applied for today's radio communication systems and existing personal communication devices.

7.   CONCLUSIONS

In this paper we present our approach to active marketing in supermarkets, with an extensive use of radio-frequency identifiers (RFIDs) of goods and locations, and personal, mobile communication devices of supermarket clients. Our solution is based on personalized filtering of RDIF-related marketing info by the use of software agents. To this goal, we adopt our Agent Computing Environment ACE framework, previously used for personalizing an access to Web Services and Internet data sources. ACE agents are partially executed in clients' mobile devices, and partially in the local area network of a supermarket. These agents are able to filter broadcasted marketing information according to detailed user needs, and current situation – technical restrictions for end-user device, date and time, previous contacts, etc. Several strategies are proposed to use ACE agents to support everyday shopping in a supermarket, including maintaining shopping lists, personal marketing firewalls, and continuous monitoring and asynchronous notification about changes (promotions, discounts, etc.). Basic functionality of the system may be extended at any time and for any user, for example by enabling contacts with other users, by tracking current locations of persons (e.g., children) and shopping carts, etc. The agents and RFID tags may be also used by supermarket staff in a transparent (from a client point of view) manner, to support internal management of the supermarket.

ACE agents may be executed in an autonomic manner, and it is possible to implement an asynchronous way of information access – this is the agent informing its owner that something interesting just happened. What is "interesting" for a given user is programmed by this user in the agent's code. ACE agents may be executed in arbitrary chosen (by users) places, including stationary network servers and users' private mobile devices. Moreover, a place of an execution of an ACE agent may be dynamically adjusted to current situation/user localization/date and time, etc. As agents may be executed at different places, there is no huge demand for high computational power, neither at server-, nor at the client-side. Due to distribution of network resources and devices, and small sizes of Bluetooth piconets and coverage areas of WiFi access points, an overall network saturation is reasonably small.

The system is flexible and open, not only for new clients and products, but also for new services, communication standards, etc. Due to brokerage of public agents, the new products, services and communication protocols may be added in an invisible (for an ordinary user) way.

Although the ACE framework is fully implemented and industry-tested [10, 11], we could not test the proposed application in a real supermarket. Thus, we developed a simulator, being a set of ACE agents, to model a behavior of a set of RFID tags and different supermarket clients. Even this simplified simulator showed that the system would be very useful, both for supermarket clients, and for supermarket staff. The implementation costs are quite low (a single PC as a server, and a set of Bluetooth/WiFi devices), in comparison with other parts of a local area network of a typical supermarket. We are looking now for a supermarket ready to implement and test our approach with real clients, products, and services.

REFERENCES

[1] Bonett, M., Personalization of Web Services: Opportunities and Challenges, 2001, Ariadne Issue 28, http://www.ariadne.ac.uk /issue28/personalization/intro.html

[2] DARPA Agent Markup Language Homepage, http://www.daml.org/

[3] FIPA Personal Assistant Specification, http://www.fipa.org/specs/fipa00083/XC00083B.html

[4] Franklin S., Graesser A. Is it an Agent, or just a Program? A Taxonomy for Autonomous Agents, 3rd Int. Workshop on Agent Theories, and Architectures, Springer-Verlag, 1996

[5] Milojicic D., Trend Wars - mobile agent applications, IEEE Concurr., 1999, pp. 80-90.

[6] Nwana, H., "Software Agents: an overview", Knowledge Engineering Review 11 (1996) 3, pp. 205-244

[7] RFID Payment Processing Drives Customer Throughput at POS, RFID Technology info, http://www.rfida.com/weblog/2005/01/rfid-payment-processing-drives.ht

[8] Rykowski J., "Agent Technology for Secure Personalized Web Services", 24th International Scientific School ISAT 2003, Szklarska Poręba (Poland); September 2003; pp. 185-193

[9] Rykowski, J., Using software agents to personalize natural-language access to Internet services in a chatterbot manner, 2nd International Conference Language And Technology L&T'05, Poznan, Poland, April 2005, pp. 269-273

[10] Rykowski J., Cellary W., Virtual Web Services - Application of Software Agents to Personalization of Web Services, 6th International Conference on Electronic Commerce ICEC 2004, Delft (The Nether-lands), 2004 ; ACM Publishers; pp. 409-418

[11] Rykowski, J., Juszkiewicz, A., Personalization of Information Delivery by the Use of Agents, IADIS Int. Conference WWW/Internet 2003, Algarve, Portugal, 2003, pp. 1056-1059

[12] Secure Logistics, RFID centre, http://rfid.bemrosebooth.com/secure_logistics.php courier mail

[13] Shoham, Y. Agent-oriented programming. Artificial Intelligence, 60(1):51-92

[14] Specification of the KQML Agent-Communication Language, the DARPA Knowledge Sharing Initiative, External Interfaces Working Group, http://www.cs.umbc.edu/kqml/kqmlspec/spec.html

[15] Thomas D., IT move in store for new Tesco shops, VVU network technical info, http://www.vnunet.com/news/1152559

[16] What is RFID, RFID Journal, http://www.rfidjournal.com/article/articleview/1339/1/129/

[17] Wooldridge, M., Jennings, N.R., "Intelligent agents: theory and practice", Knowledge Engineering Review 10 (1995) 2, pp. 115-152

A SMART HTTP COMMUNICATOR: SMACH

Yosuke Murakami, Yusuke Takada and Makoto Oya
Graduate School of Information Science and Technology, Hokkaido University, N14, W9, Kita-ku, Sapporo, 060-0814, Japan

Abstract: Most developments and applications of current eBusiness systems focus on large enterprise systems. HTTP based full implementation of the Internet/Web protocol stack is used in such environment. On the other hand, small businesses or community works require simpler and smaller implementation not assuming big computer resource. This requirement exists also in other business-like environments such as robot communication, mobile devices and ubiquitous environment. Essential requirements for HTTP infrastructure are (1) to support HTTP protocol, and (2) to enable peer-to-peer communication. Currently existing infrastructures such as Apache and Mozilla, however, support more and do not fit to smaller and simpler applications. They were originally developed considering Web document access applications and have large functionality unnecessary for eBusiness communication. To solve this problem, we developed a new open source middleware essentially supporting HTTP and having both server and client feature called SMACH (Smart Communicator for HTTP). SMACH is designed based on three policies: small, bidirectional, and HTTP protocol focused. It supports minimum but enough HTTP communication function and symmetric APIs for server and client applications, having multi-threading based architecture with persistent TCP/IP connection pursuing maximum performance in small memory environments. SMACH can communicate with major existing products including Apache, IIS, Mozilla and IE, achieving high performance and small executable size. This paper provides its development policy, function, architecture, and results of interoperability tests and performance evaluation.

Key words: HTTP, Web service, equal distributed system, bidirectional communication, Inter-organizational communication

1.   INTRODUCTION

Most developments and applications of current eBusiness systems focus on large enterprise systems including complex trade systems, supply chain management systems, sales force systems. HTTP[1] based full implementation of the Internet/Web protocol stack is used in such environment. On the other hand, small businesses or community works require simpler and smaller implementation not assuming big computer capability. This requirement exists also in other business-like environments such as robot communication, mobile devices and ubiquitous environment.

eBusiness basic protocol is HTTP[1]. Essential requirements for the infrastructure are (1) to support HTTP protocol, and (2) to enable peer-to-peer communication. Currently existing infrastructures such as Apache and Mozilla, however, do not fit to smaller and simpler applications. They were originally developed mainly for Web document access applications and having large functionality for document processing such as HTML handling and rendering, which makes whole system too large for smaller applications. In addition, each infrastructure supports either server function or client function, resulting application development difficult, because eBusiness applications have both server and client functions as their nature.

To solve the above problem, we developed a new open source middleware essentially supporting HTTP and having server and client feature called SMACH (Smart Communicator for HTTP). This paper provides its development policy, function, architecture, and results of interoperability tests and performance evaluation.

SMACH is designed based on three policies: compact build, bidirectional, and HTTP protocol focused. It supports minimum but enough HTTP communication function and symmetric APIs for server and client applications, having multi-threading based architecture with persistent TCP/IP connection pursuing maximum performance in small memory environment. SMACH can communicate with major existing products including Apache[4], IIS, Mozilla, IE, and language clients such as Java. Client is 36-65% faster than Java client library, server is 16-60% faster than Apache/CGI. Size of executable is half of thttpd [5] and 1/26 of Apache.

2. DEVELOPMENT POLICY

SMACH was designed and developed based on the following policies:

- To minimize its functionality enough to support HTTP protocol execution.
- To prepare enough APIs for application programs to implement higher-layer protocol and functions, e.g., document processing, file handing, SOAP processing, messaging.
- To Support both client and server function.
- To prepare symmetrically designed APIs for client and server, which make implementation of bidirectional communication easier.
- To comply with latest specification, HTTP/1.1.

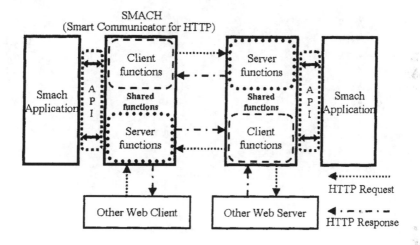

Figure 1. SMACH Overview

Figure 1 shows overview of SMACH. SMACH has client and server function and communicates using HTTP/1.1. Applications use SMACH functions through using originally designed APIs. In addition, SMACH client and server can communicate with existing HTTP client and server software. Client function will be used by library in three patterns:

- Execution as library function
- Execution as SMACH child process
- Execution as another process

3.   FUNCTION AND API

3.1   Functions

Table 1 shows functions supported by SMACH. Following functions are excluded based on the development policy.
- Responding a file specified by URL when client requests it.
- Rendering and displaying HTML documents.

Table 1. Client and Server Function

Function	support
Server	
parsing request line and header field	*supported*
setting status line and header field	*supported*
getting file specified by URL	*API*
CGI	*API*
BASIC Authentication	*supported*
Logging	*supported*
Client	
setting request line and header field	*supported*
parsing status line and header field	*supported*
rendering the HTML file	*API*
Common	
Content negotiation	*supported*
Persistent Connection	*supported*
Chunked Encoding	*supported*
Cache	*API*
Cookie	*API*

3.2   Application Program Interface

This section mentions about two major design results, symmetry between client APIs and server APIs, and protocol hiding.

3.2.1   Symmetry between client APIs and server APIs

SMACH realizes both HTTP client and HTTP server functions in single software. Sending and receiving messages in HTTP communication using symmetric APIs. *Table 2* shows major APIs.

Table 2. SMACH APIs

Client API
API for creating request message (excerpt)
sma_set_request_line(void *h, int method, char *url)
sma_set_req_content_language(void *h, char *language)
API for sending request message
sma_send_request(void *h, char *body, int size)
API for receiving response message
sma_receive_response(void *h, char *body, int size)
API for parsing response message
sma_get_status_code(void *h)
sma_get_res_content_type(void *h, char *language);

Server API
API for receiving request message
sma_receive_request(void *h, char *body, int size)
API for parsing request message
sma_get_abs_path(void *h, char *abs_path)
sma_get_req_content_type(void *h, char *language);
API for creating response message (excerpt)
sma_set_status_line(void *h, int method, int status_code)
sma_set_res_content_language(void *h, char *language)
API for sending response message
sma_send_response(void *h, char *body, int size)

3.2.2   Hiding Protocol and Memory Management

1. Hiding message form

HTTP message is consisted of startline, header field, and body field. They have to follow the message form defined in HTTP/1.1. This form is hidden from the application using SMACH API. The Application can create HTTP message if it passes only data to SMACH. In parsing message, applications need not to parse HTTP messages, but only to get values.

2. Hiding message flow

Application is hidden from actual data flow. This enables the application to send and receive messages at any time in any size.

3. Hiding memory management

The data used in sending and receiving message don't have to be managed by the application. Memory allocation and free memory is managed by SMACH. So memory management is hidden from application.

Followings are examples of client and server application using API (attaching prefix, "sma_").

- Example Of Client Application

```
int client_application(void) {
    void *handle;
    int size = 1024;
  char res_body[1024];
  char req_body1[] = "<?xml version = ...>";
  char req_body2[] = "<soapenv:Envelope...>";
  char req_body3[] = "</soapenv:Envelope>";
  char uri[] = "www.smach.com";
  char language[10] ;
    /*establishing connection*/
  sma_bind(&handle, uri, 80);
    /*initializing*/
    sma_initialize(handle);
    /*process for request message*/
    /*setting request line*/
    sma_set_request_line(handle,POST,"/service");
    /*setting request header*/
    sma_set_req_content_language(handle, "ja");
    /*setting request body*/
    sma_send_request(handle, body1, strlen(body1));
    sma_send_request(handle, body2, strlen(body2));
    sma_send_request(handle, body3, strlen(body3));
    sma_send_request(handle, NULL, 0);
    /*process for response message*/
    /*getting response header*/
    sma_get_res_content_type(handle, language);
/*getting response body*/
    while(1) {
rval = sma_receive_response(handle, body, size);
        if (rval == 0) break;
    }
  /*closing connection*/
  sma_close(handle);
  return (0);
    }
```

- Example of Server Application

```
int server_application(const void *handle) {
    int rval = 0;
    char language[10];
  int size = 1024;
  char req_body[1024];
  char res_body1[] = "<?xml version = ...>";
  char res_body2[] = "<soapenv:Envelope...>";
  char res_body3[] = "</soapenv:Envelope>";
    /*process for request message*/
    /*getting request header value*/
  sma_get_accept_language(handle, &language);
    /*getting request body message*/
    while(1) {
rval = sma_receive_request(handle, body, size);
        if (rval == 0) break;
    }
    /*process for response message */
    /*setting status line*/
    sma_set_status_line(handle, 200);
    /*setting response header */
    sma_set_res_content_language(handle, "ja");
    /*setting response body message*/
    sma_send_response(handle, res_body1,strlen(res_body1));
    sma_send_response(handle, res_body2,strlen(res_body2));
```

```
    sma_send_response(handle, res_body3,strlen(res_body3));
    sma_send_response(handle, NULL, 0);
    return(0);
}
```

4.   SMACH ARCHITECTURE

4.1   Architecture Design

Architecture is designed on the following policies.
- Compact Size

By galvanizing functions from HTTP/1.1 (RFC2616), and separating them for client and server, we picked out common processes. They enable SMACH to cut off redundant processes between modules, and realize compact size.
- Loose Coupling Between Modules

Modules are designed not to influence intricately, but to have simple relation each other. They are also designed to be loosely coupled.

On the basis of these, we designed as *Figure 2*. The above is client architecture, and the below is server architecture. *Table 3* shows roles of each module.

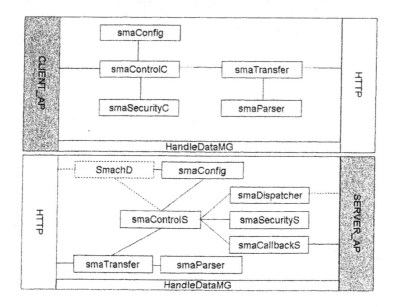

Figure 2. Architecture

Processes of both client and server system is controlled by smaControlC/S. This control part becomes the hub, and makes it easy to enhance when new processing is added. HTTP has symmetrical characters in sending and receiving, and structure of HTTP message. Therefore common processing becomes possible, and SMACH client and server are implemented by them. Other parts that can't be shared are used in original modules.

Table 3. Module

Client Module	
SmaControlC	Client Protocol Control
SmaSecurityC	Process Of security
Server Module	
SmachD	Establishment of TCP Connection, Forking Thread
SmaControlS	Server Protocol Control
SmaDispatcher	Application Dispatch
SmaCallbackS	Control of Callback
SmaSecurityS	Process Of security
Common Module	
smaTransfer	Control Of sending and Receiving
smaParser	Parser
smaConfig	Setting Up Configuration
HandleDataMG	Getter And Setter of data

4.2   Module Implementation

- Server Multiplexing

To respond to two or more requests, the server is multiplexed. There are three ways to realize multiplexing.
  - Using process
  - Using thread
  - Using both process and thread

If something goes wrong with the parent process or thread, all threads come under the influence of the problem. So threads could compromise stability. But using thread has following merits.
  - small consumption of memory
  - short time in starting and stopping

SMACH uses thread from small and lightweight point of view. *Figure 5* shows the mode of multiplex processing. SmachD forks smaControlS as thread. Therefore smaDispatcher, smaSecurityS, smaCallbackS, smaTransfer, smaParser, HandleDataMG are multiplexed.

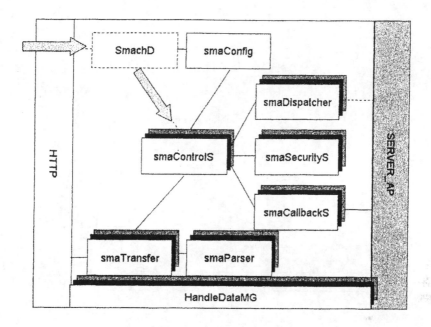

Figure 3. Server Multiplexing

- Callback from application

Server application which is implemented on SMACH Server is called from SMACH as library. But Server application needs to use SMACH inner functions to respond. SMACH uses Callback functions to resolve this problem. SMACH server passes the Function Vector including pointer to SMACH Server API when smaDispatcher calls for Server application. It realizes callback. smaCallbackS makes Function Vector, and treats callback processes. *Figure 4* shows callback process.

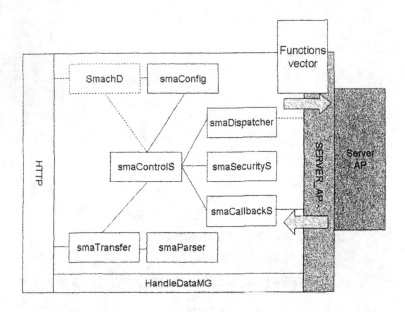

Figure 4. Callback Process

• Persistent connection

SMACH supports persistent connection[6]. SMACH can realize closing TCP connection when "Connection: Close" Header is attached. This enables SMACH Server to kill the thread in appropriate time, so this achieves small size structure.

5.   EVALUATION

This section shows evaluation results of developed SMACH. The following configuration was used:

Server:
• OS: Fedora Core 3(2.6.10-1.760-FC3)
• Memory : 384MB
• CPU: Athlon(tm) XP1700 + 1466.601MHz
Client:
• OS : Redhat 9(2.4.20-8)
• Memory : 192MB
• CPU: Pentium III Coppermine (597.416MHz)

Fedora Core 3 and Redhat 9 were elected as OS based on the fact that SMACH chiefly targeted Linux, which is widely used well.

5.1 Interoperability Test

The following three tests were done.

TEST1: Connected experiment of client AP and server AP that uses SMACH API.

TEST2: Connected experiment of client AP that uses SMACH API and existing server (Apache, IIS).

TEST3: Connected experiment of existing client (Mozilla, Internet Explorer, and JAVA HTTP class) and server AP that uses SMACH API.

Table 4. Interoperability

	Client	Server	Result
TETS 1	SMACH –C+ AP	SMACH-S + AP	Connected
TEST 2	SMACH-C + AP	Apache	Connected
	SMACH-C + AP	IIS	Connected
TEST 3	Internet Explorer	SMACH-S + AP	Connected
	Mozilla	SMACH-S + AP	Connected
	Java HTTP Class	SMACH-S + AP	Connected

The connectivity of SMACH could be proven from the result of TEST1.Moreover; the connectivity with existing Server/Client can be proven from the result of TEST2 and TEST3.

5.2   Performance

5.2.1   Client performance

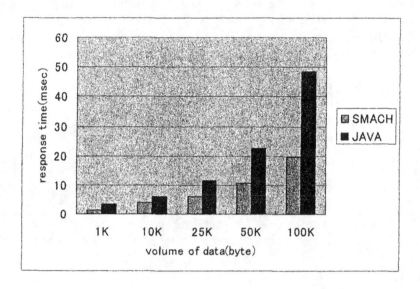

Figure 5. Client Performance

Figure 5 shows the result of measuring the performance with Java. The server is Apache. The performance of SMACH is 36-65% faster than that of Java. Java encodes data to Unicode once. I speculate that it becomes an overhead. Moreover, Java should have Java-VM, so there is a not suitable part for small equipment.

5.2.2 Server performance

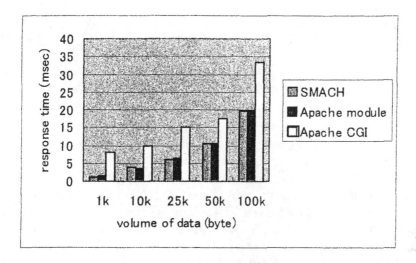

Figure 6. Server Performance

Figure 6 shows the result of measuring the performance of the server. The client is SMACH. The performance of SMACH is 16-60% faster than Apache CGI, and at the same level as the Apache modules. The overhead of CGI start cannot be disregarded when comparing it with Apache CGI because SMACH AP is called from SMACH statically. But it is a comparison result profitable because generally CGI is used when server AP is made with Apache. A general engineer has a difficult part by the AP development as the Apache module. Therefore, it can be said that there is an advantage in which SMACH is used from the comparison result with the Apache module.

5.3 Program Size

The comparison among the number of source files, the number of source lines, and the size of the execution file were done for Apache and thttpd. *Table 5* shows the result. Because the function of SMACH, Apache, and thttpd is different, SMACH is not necessarily simply smallest. However, it can be said that SMACH was able to achieve the target policy, considering containing both the client and the server.

Table 5. Performance Comparison Concernig Small Size

Software	Version	Source files	Source lines	exe (byte)
SMACH	1.0b	20	6697	46,385
thttpd	2.25b	21	11129	85,596
Apache	2.0.53	608	264505	1,222,809

6.   CONCLUSIONS

SMACH has been designed based on three policies: small build, bidirectional, and HTTP protocol focused. It supports number of, yet enough HTTP communication function and symmetric APIs for server and client applications. It has multi-threading based architecture with persistent TCP/IP connection pursuing maximum performance in small memory environments. Interoperability test shows SMACH can communicate with major existing products including Apache, IIS, Mozilla, IE, and language clients such as Java. As for it performance, client is 36-65% faster than Java client library, the server is 16-60% faster than Apache/CGI. The developed implementation has achieved enough compactness HTTP infrastructure used in small eBusiness systems.

REFERENCES

1. Fielding, R., Gettys, J., Mogul, J., Frystyk, H., Masinter, L., Leach, P. and T. Berners-Lee, "Hypertext Transfer Protocol -- HTTP/1.1", RFC 2616, June 1999.
2. Fielding, R., Gettys, J., Mogul, J., Frystyk, H. and T. Berners-Lee, "Hypertext Transfer Protocol -- HTTP/1.1", RFC 2068, January 1997.
3. Berners-Lee, T., Fielding, R. and H. Frystyk, "Hypertext Transfer Protocol -- HTTP/1.0", RFC 1945, May 1996.
4. The Apache Team, "The Apache Software Foundation" http://www.apache.org/
5. Jef Poskanzer. "thttpd - tiny/turbo/throttling HTTP server. Acme Laboratories", May 2005. http://www.acme.com/software/thttpd/
6. Joe Touch John Heidemann and Katia Obraczka, "Analysis of HTTP Performance", 1998
7. Andrew S. Tanenbaum., Maarten van Steen, "Distributed Systems"
8. Takada, Y., Murakami, Y. and Oya, M., "Design and Development of SMACH (Smart Communicator for HTTP)", IEICE/IPSJ Information Technology Letters, vol.4, 2005 (to appear). (in Japanese)
9. Murakami, Y., Takada, Y. and Oya, M., "Architecture of SMACH (Smart Communicator for HTTP)", IEICE/IPSJ Information Technology Letters, vol.4, 2005 (to appear). (in Japanese)

MOBILE PORTAL IMPLEMENTATION STRATEGY: A THEORETICAL EXPLORATION

Ping Gao and Jan Damsgaard
Deformant of Informatics, Copenhagen Business School

Abstract: Mobile portal plays an important role in mobile commerce market. Current literature focuses on static analysis on the value chain of mobile portals. This article provides a dynamic perspective on mobile portal strategy. Drawing upon network economics, we describe mobile portal implementation as a four-phase process. In different phase, a portal provider has various challenges to overcome and adopt diverse strategies, and correspondingly the regulator has different foci. The conceptual framework proposed in this article offers a basis for further analyses on the market dynamics of mobile commerce, and can be generalized to studying other networked technologies.

Key words: mobile commerce, mobile portal, network economics, strategy

1. INTRODUCTION

Technology advance begets a new business model called mobile commerce, which is an application potentially to bring wireless telecommunications and the Internet to the customers (Louis, 2001). It is expected that mobile commerce will be boomed by the deployment of 3G networks that enable a wideband, high-speed wireless access to Internet. Led by Japan, Korea and some European countries, the future of 3G market is about to unfold globally (Maitland et al., 2002). An academic analysis on mobile commerce implementation is of practical importance. As a new research field, deep theoretical studies on this topic are seldom found.

This paper reports the result of such a research. Particularly, as in the whole value chain of mobile commerce the mobile portal plays a key role (Li and Whalley, 2002), it will be our study focus. Current literature focuses on static analysis on the value chain of mobile portals (Kim and Kim, 2003; Sterling, 2002). Whilst such research efforts help us understand the positions of different mobile market actors in providing portal services, we lack a dynamic perspective on the strategy by a mobile portal provider. Drawing upon network economics, this article describes mobile portal development as a four-phase process. In different phase, the portal provider has various challenges to overcome and adopt diverse strategies, and correspondingly the regulator takes different measures to support the development of the mobile portal.

This paper proposes a conceptual framework for analyzing the strategies of mobile portal. It has five sections. The second section describes the characteristics of the mobile portals. The third section introduces the theoretical foundation. The fourth section is main body of analysis. Here we will answer two questions: in a specific stage of market and technological situation, what kind of an implementation strategy should the portal providers choose? What sort of a role should the regulator play? Finally, in the fifth section we conduct discussion and draw conclusions.

2.   MOBILE PORTAL

A portal is commonly defined as a website that offers a set of services that helps users navigate the Internet. For Internet users it is a gateway to a variety of resources or data (Ward and Gardner, 2000). Mobile portal enables an extension of services from Internet to mobile devices. It presents contents that mobile phone users are able to access. Formed by aggregating applications (e-mail, instant messaging etc) and contents from various sources, a portal sets the business model of mobile commerce services (Kim and Kim, 2002). Mobile portal is not a replication of web on the mobile networks. Compared with a normal Internet portal, the mobile portal is characterized by supporting personalization and localization. Because mobile phones have small screens, mobile portals are particularly important for mobile commerce (Barnett et al., 2000).

In the value chain of mobile commerce, which is composed by venders, application developers, content providers, content aggregators, portal providers, network operators and service providers (Muller-Veerse, 2000), mobile portal providers play a specifically important role. In nature, mobile commerce is transactions with a monetary value that are conducted via mobile networks. As Muller-Veerse (2000) puts it, mobile commerce is all about applications and services on the mobile phones; it is about contents, rather than technological capability. Having direct contacts with customers and providing them a gateway to access the contents, a mobile portal gains a strategic importance in mobile commerce implementation. To fuel subscriber growth and hold customer loyalty, which is critical for generating more traffic revenue, network operators (e.g. DoCoMo and Sonera) have been keen to develop their mobile portals. Meanwhile, regarding mobile portals as an opportunity to reach customers at anytime and anywhere with personalized services which means high income, traditional web portals (Yahoo!, AOL etc) and many new independent content providers are active to have a share in mobile portal market (Sterling, 2002). The integration of Internet portal and mobile portal means the convergence of fixed and mobile market. Portal market is currently undergoing significant expansion, and the ownership and operation of portals is becoming an area of fierce competition. For users, mobile portals are the prime suppliers for web-based information that is delivered to their mobile terminals. There is an increased reliance on mobile portal by customers hence it is gaining importance (Barnett et al., 2000).

In theory, institution intermediary is assumed to play a key role in promoting technology implementation (King et al., 1994). In practice, a fair, efficient regulation has been necessary for telecommunications industry (Melody, 1999). Because the mobile network operator is capable to control access to portals hence it may hinder portal competition, in mobile commerce market the role of the regulators is specifically important in terms of securing a competition to protect the interests of customers and other portal providers (Maitland et al., 2002). Hence, while the strategy of portal providers is the major concern of this paper, the role of regulator in promoting mobile portal development will also be examined.

3. THEORETICAL FOUNDATION

According to Lyytinen and Damsgaard (2001), it is critical to consider the underlying specifies of the technology in order to decide the theoretical tool for analyzing its implementation. Mobile commerce is based on mobile access and Internet networks as standard technologies. Mobile portals must offer their customers the social interaction possibility hence will establish user community around services like dating services, gaming services etc (Sterling, 2002). Consequently network economics serves as an appropriate tool for our analytical purpose. Followings are major concepts to be drawn upon in our analysis.

3.1   Lock-in effect

In network economics, lock-in effects capture the fact that the use of certain technology or service becomes a habit that is hard to break (Shapiro and Varian, 1999). To operate a technology efficiently, a user needs to invest time and other resources so as to get acquainted with it. When a technology becomes well known to the user, she no longer pays attention to it or the dependency she has developed. Technology has become an extension of herself that is ready-at-hand. A clear example is the layout of the keyboard. We know where the different keys are located and we can operate the keyboard seamlessly in our endeavor to write. We do not need to know with what purposes the keys are ordered in the particular QWERTY way (David, 1985).

It is nuisance to change from something known well to something new and different. Network economics seeks to price this nuisance. In line with Shapiro and Varian (1999), a user that is locked into a standard technology or service must incur certain cost, if she wishes to switch to a new one. The magnitude of switch cost of a service decides the lock-in effects. The service providers must flexibly use lock-in strategies in their operations. On the one hand, they would create barriers that prevent the users from switching. On the other hand, in moving to new services, they must facilitate their incumbent customers to break the barriers set by traditional services.

3.2   Network externality

Shapiro and Varian (1999) identify the major sources of lock-in as the habit of using a technology and dependency to it. These lock-in effects are in an individual level, thus they omit switching costs related to a community of interacting agents that communicate with one another using the standard technology or service like online chat. In this case, a switch to a different service provider must incur cost for breaking relation with the community. Once a community has been locked in, the provider can "tax" its members. If the community is concentrated around one provider, this is specifically painful for a user. It should be the target of regulation to avoid the existence of market monopoly that may exert an over-taxation on the users.

The network externality emphasizes the value of a community to the service provider by its scale, and the costs of switch from the community for a user. The installed base of users is the most valuable asset of a provider (Markus, 1987). Community is an efficient way to create a critical mass of the installed base. How to make itself a community hub that may lock in customers to establish an installed base beyond a critical mass and take advantage of network externality, this is the strategic issue for a provider to survive. In providing telecommunications services, operators may promote network externalities by allowing interconnections between networks (Liebowitz and Margolis, 1999).

3.3   Implementation of networked-technology

According to Besen and Farrell (1994), when firms compete for user communities around some standard technologies, they use three combinations of strategies. In the first combination each company wants to set its own standard for a given technology and both are willing to fight for it. Besen and Farrell call this strategy as *Tweedledum and Tweedledee*. In the second combination, each company prefers its own standard technology but is willing to compromise rather than to go solo. This strategy is referred as the *Battle of the sexes*. Finally, there is the situation where one company prefers its own standard technology while the contestant, called as *Pesky little brother*, wishes to join the established network of technology users.

In studying the implementation of networked-technology, Damsgaard (2002) observes a fourth strategy. He defines it as *Big brother* as opposite to *Pesky little brother*. In the case of portal market, it denotes one portal has won the dominant position and does not want to share its community with the young contestants. These four types of strategies defined by Besen and Farrell (1994) and Damsgaard (2002) form the conceptual basis for us to examine the strategies of portal service providers, and the role of the regulator in the process of implementing mobile portals.

4.   A FRAMEWORK OF MOBILE PORTAL STRATEGY

We argue to classify the whole process of implementing a mobile portal to attraction, contagion, entrenchment and defense phases. This four-stage model idealizes a successful implementation process from genesis to domination. Each stage poses a key challenge that must be overcome in order to proceed to the next one. If a challenge is not resolved properly, the mobile portal cannot evolve but will stagnate. The first three stages are transitional ones. In this time the "burn rate" of investment needs to be controlled (Lamont, 2001), and a safe transfer to the last stage should be realized within a reasonable period. In different phases, a mobile portal provider adopts various strategies as defined by Besen and Farrell (1994) and Damsgaard (2002), and the regulator has different concerns to promote mobile portal development. For simplification in this article we examine the market with only two portals. The analytical results are condensed in Table 1.

Table 1. Mobile portal implementation strategy

	Attraction phase	Contagion phase	Entrenchment phase	Defense phase
Portal provider	*Pesky little brother* Attract users and get them to return. Facilitating users to switch from normal Internet portals and 2G services. Follow the incumbent in service and network standard	*Battle of the sexes* Try to build up user base around different services over network. Extend the user base toward a critical mass	*Tweedledum and Tweedledee* Build and diffuse proprietary service that may lead to a dominance	*Big brother* Evolve with backward compatibility. Keep innovation in services and technology so as to hold customers
Regulator	Encourage a common standard in network. Support an operator to develop its own portal	Enforce interconnection, interoperation to adapt to service cooperation	Monitor fair competition and equal access to networks from all portals. Adopt an "arm's length" policy	Supervise fair competition. Beware over-taxation

4.1   Mobile portal provider

Attraction phase. A mobile portal develops from the attraction phase. In this initial stage, the primary objective of a mobile portal provider is to attract users and let them try out its services. In the situation where there already exists an overlapping portal with a certain size of user base, the simplest strategy for the young provider is to imitate the established one in services in the hope to share the market that has been proven lucrative. The new portal can also provide services that the established one cannot offer, or add values to the incumbent's services to form its own products. Yet, to reduce users' cost of switching from the incumbent, in the method of using services an imitation to the established provider is necessary. The new provider can also take facility measures for example providing a help function for browsing its website. In the words of Besen and Farrell (1994), it will adopt a *Pesky little brother* strategy.

In this phase the lock-in degree of users to portals is generally low. The young portal will initiate the lock-in strategy by exploring a service that may set up its own user community, or share a community with the incumbent. At this stage the challenge for the new portal revolves around getting users interested in what it offers and making them want to return for more. Successful progression to the next stage depends on that there are enough users to continue using its services. For the established provider, the challenge from new services based on new technology should be its attention. For which it may also consider to initiate the *Pesky little brother* strategy in due time. But a backward compatibility must be guaranteed to let its customers to co-evolve alongside with it as innovation of service and technology proceeds.

As observed by Sterling (2002) a network operator and normal Internet portal are the most active providers of mobile portals. For an operator, if it has an installed base of 2G users it must make efforts to design its services to be backward compatible. In case this is infeasible in technology, a facilitating function should be provided to enable a smooth switch for the customer community. For a mobile portal developing from a normal Internet portal, the innovation should be based on current services so that the user base may go along with it to the mobile market. This is possible as users may like the services by Internet portal also be available via mobile devices (Kim and Kim, 2003).

Meanwhile, a network provider is also the owner of networks. The very first decision for it to make is the selection of network standard. The new operator may adopt a *Pesky little brother* strategy to follow the incumbent. This strategy favors network interconnection and service interoperation, which gives the new operator an opportunity of sharing a portal community with the incumbent. But in some cases this will invalid the smooth transfer in technologies from old standard to the new one, as what has happened in Japan. In this case, to bring their customer bases along, different operators may separately go for two standards (Pikula, 2001).

Content and portal market allows the existence of a lot of providers. In contrast, because of limitation of frequency resource and the need of a huge investment, the network market is restricted to competition within limited companies by the state based on a license system. At the beginning period there may be only one 3G operator in the market. Whilst cooperation with social portals will happen, in this time the operator may major rely on self to explore content and create its affiliated portal (Funk, 2001). This is efficient in time and necessary to avoid the risk of without profitable contents for the customers. Later on more providers will swarm in and form a competition with network operator in providing portals, and other competitive networks will also appear and join in mobile portal market.

Contagion phase. The contagion phase is a period of expending the user size. In this second phase of implementation, the focus of a mobile portal is to "infect" the recruited users so that they become carriers to help attract more users to join in. At this time the degree of lock-in of the user community to a provider is only moderate. Relatively the users can easily leave and participate in a rival. For a portal provider the successful progression to the next stage is dependent on achieving the critical mass (Markus, 1987). An existential crisis occurs if one portal cannot attract a sufficiently large number of users. In this stage while the users are not locked in yet and no provider has achieved a critical mass of users, there is no reason for them to engage in a battle, which is risky for both. Each provider is planning a good future and is paying attention to extend its user community, for which each one is willing to cooperate. The mobile portal providers will prefer an open-access between portals to a "walled-garden strategy (Barnett et al., 2000; Sterling, 2002). The open-access strategy creates value for end users, which may allow both portals to have more customers which may finally reach a critical mass. Hence *Battle of the sexes* is a proper strategy in the contagion phase.

In running the networks and providing portal services, the operators will abide by a *Battle of the sexes* strategy by promoting interconnection and interoperation, which is right out there in technology if a common standard is adopted in the attraction phase. For a user the major switching costs from a portal is being a member of a community around some services that allow active interactions among members, and the habits of using them (Shapiro and Varian, 1999). Because of interconnection, compared with services, the network creates a less significant switching cost. The switching cost from network is major due to the financial elements, i.e. the users need to pay an interconnection fee extra to the normal expense to get access to the community around previous operator, and bear a cost of opening a new account. Interconnection and interoperation allows social portals and customers a higher freedom of selecting network operators based on services. It is also good for an operator to diffuse services and extend network in terms that the customers will be not scared away for being locked-in to its network. Interconnection and interoperation encourages mobile commerce market to develop based on competition in portal services, and avoid the network market to move to a monopoly (Liebowitz and Margolis, 1999).

Entrenchment phase. The first two phases are periods of accumulating knowledge about market, and trying services so as to build up user community around some of them. Ideally in this entrenchment phase this work moves further to the step that a specific mobile portal has formed proprietary services of itself. By making the users adopt the proprietary services the community is locked in to a higher degree. If the portal fails in installing its proprietary services, its users will remain to have a high freedom to leave attracted by the competitive provider. This is the time to fight for the control of the community. When all firms choose to compete they decide to have a battle. Following Besen and Farrell (1994) they adopt a strategy of *Tweedledum and Tweedledee*. Every competitor attempts to win the dominant position by building a community around specific proprietary services that are able to lure over users from the rival's community and win over the "free" users. Moreover, the portal can use pricing strategy to dominate a niche of market. For example in Finland, because of low cost in investment, generally the service price of local mobile network operators is lower than that with cross-country networks; thus the market is differentiated between normal residents and these who need to travel frequently (Manninen, 2002).

Defense phase. The proprietary services will help a portal to dominate a niche market. Consequently the implementation of a mobile portal moves to the fourth phase of defending the market dominance. In the defense phase one has won the dominant position and does not want to share its community with the young contestants. In terms of Damsgaard (2002), the mobile portal adopts the strategy of *Big Brother*. Yet, facing technology innovation and the appearance of disruptive technologies, the dominance built around proprietary services is at the risk. Once a community is well established around a proprietary service there is an ongoing need to nurture it. What keep the community together are services, community features and switching costs. The community is not a static entity so at all times there are some users come and go as their natural contexts change. This is natural and will not affect the market structure in general. But if users are willing to leave for the competitor's services as perceived as more attractive the provider should be alert. The danger from disruptive technologies and services is real and it can bring giants down (Christensen, 1997). In this phase the challenge is to keep evolution going and incorporate new services and technologies, and avoid revolutions caused by disruptive ones. The idea is to move ahead while stay backward compatible (Shapiro and Varian, 1999).

4.2   Regulator

In general the governmental regulation should facilitate service competition by portals. Owing the networks, a network operator meanwhile as a portal provider has the advantage of establishing the dominance and jeopardizing a fair competition in portal service market. Hence the network owner should be the focal point of regulation (Melody, 1999). In principle, the regulator should foster the content as the "king" rather than allow the network owner to steer the market (Muller-Veerse, 2000). As a portal provider adopts different strategies by phases, the regulator should support its development by accordingly adjust its concentration as the implementation proceeds.

A common standard in networks facilitates interconnection and interoperation, which is to the benefit of customers as well as portals. A common standard may relieve the concern of the first mover that a future comer may surpass it through adopting a more advanced technology; hence it promotes the early investment on mobile commerce networks. This implies that in general the regulator should promote adopting a common standard in issuing network operating licenses. Yet, it must account the specific market situation that operators have already used different networks of last generation. For example in China, as two mobile operators respectively use GSM and CDMA systems, the regulator is considering to accordingly issue WCDMA and CDMA2000 licenses to them so that their networks can economically upgrade from the second to the third generation (Lamont, 2001; Zhang and Prybutok, 2005).

Moreover, the regulator should support the operator to build its affiliated portal. This is necessary to encourage the operator to invest on mobile commerce without the concern of content unavailability, hence is an efficient measure to nurture the mobile commerce market to develop.

In the contagion phase, the market is characterized by cooperation between competitors. While interconnection and interoperation might have been primarily promised in technology by adopting a common standard in last phase, at this phase the regulator must guarantee its practical enforcement. Though market force should play main role in normalizing the market structure, fair and efficient regulation is necessary in cases for example when two portals cannot reach an agreement over interconnection fees.

In the third phase the competitors fight for the user community. The focus of regulation is to guarantee a fair competition between the portals affiliated to an operator and these without networks. Ideally the portal services and network operation of a network operator are kept an "arm's length". It is advised to prohibit cross subsidies for example from voice communications to mobile commerce services. Network operators must allow their networks to be accessible to all portals at reasonable prices, including that of competitive operators. In fact, this will generate more traffic sources for network operators hence is also to their benefit, as is demonstrated by DoCoMo and Telia (Muller-Veerse, 2000). The operators have a privilege of controlling the portals that are pre-set on a SIM card when it is distributed. For a customer to access contents of network operator's own portal and that of other providers', the operator should be not allowed to set difference in convenience and efficiency, and discrimination in price. In short, the regulator should guarantee that the networks are neutral platforms for competition in providing mobile commerce.

The defense phase sees a differentiated market that has locked in customers around different services to a high degree. While still keeping an eye on fair competition, the regulator needs to warrant that over-taxation on locked-in customers would not happen.

5.   DISCUSSION AND CONCLUSION

Drawing upon network economics, we have theorized the strategy of portal providers, and the role of a regulator in implementing mobile portals. We argue a portal provider must overcome four existential crises. First, if visitors do not return to its services it cannot evolve. Second, if a critical mass of users cannot be reached, implementation will stagnate. Third, if proprietary services cannot be established to lock in the customers, the user community remains open for competitors to poach. Finally, whenever new innovations occur, they must incorporate them into their services to avoid a situation where users will have to leave so as to use new services.

The role of regulation should be to prevent a network operator to take advantage of its network to dominate the service market. In the whole process of implementing mobile services, the focus of a regulator evolves by phases to adapt to the different strategy of portal providers. At the beginning, the regulator should encourage a single network standard in issuing licenses, and promote investment on networks by allowing the operators to build their own portals. In the second phase, the focus is to guarantee interconnection and interoperation, and promote the *Battle of the sexes* strategy of portal providers. In the third phase, to adapt to the *Tweedledum and Tweedledee* strategy of the portals, the regulator should facilitate service competition by warranting that a network allows an equal access by its affiliated portal and the independent ones, and encouraging the subscribers of a network to access other portals. In the final phase, its major task is to prevent an over-taxation to happen.

An "all or nothing" characteristic of interactive technology implementation has been noticed in literature (Markus, 1987). Similarly, the competition will make the portal market to become tippy. Some providers may leave the market without reaching the fourth phase of life cycle, while few dominant others stay to share the market. Moreover, because a portal can provide many different services, the failure in some mobile commerce services does not mean its collapse. The market can be differentiated by services.

At present the critical problem of mobile commerce development is to start 3G networks. Then the *Pesky little brother* strategy may lead to a "penguin phenomenon", which describes a swarm of penguins walk around the beach and hesitate to jump into the sea; but as a leader appears the rest will follow. At the start the power is on the side of network operators, as without a network the services cannot be realized hence no one will establish the mobile portal. Operators are in a critical position to form an "ecosystem" which is the cooperation within the provider community to create profitable mobile commerce models (Costello, 2002). The first mover is potentially to have advantage, but is also adventurous in that a huge investment in network can be repaid only by good services. Hence an operator should be encouraged to explore contents and portal services. The good start of network operators will lead content market to develop, which in turn may bring mobile commerce market to soar (Sterling, 2002).

This study is theoretically exploratory by nature. We move one step towards forming a conceptual framework that dynamically describes mobile portal implementation. The conceptual framework proposed offers a basis for further analyses on the market dynamics of mobile commerce. It can be generalized to studying other networked technologies that allow the establishment of a user community.

We have only considered a simplified market with only two competitors. As mobile market is becoming complex in terms of services, technologies, and participants of market and the relationship among them, in future study the influence of broad market elements on portal strategy should be put into consideration (Li and Whalley, 2002). It is a research opportunity of incorporating present literature of mobile portal value chain with our framework. Moreover empirical work is needed to validate our arguments.

6.   REFERENCES

Barnett N., Hodges, S., Wilshire, M.J. "M-Commerce: An Operator's Manual", *The McKinsey Quarterly*, (37:3), 2000, pp.163-173.

Besen, S.M., Farrell, F. "Choosing How to Compete: Strategies and Tactics in Standardization", *Journal of Economic Perspectives*, (8:2), 1994, pp. 117-131.

Christensen, C.M. *The Innovator's Dilemma: When New Technologies Cause Great Firms to Fail*, Harvard Business School Press, 1997.

Costello, J. *Partnering: The Essential 3G Challenge*. Ernest & Young Report. Available at http://www.cgey.com/tmn/nmi/3g/downloads/3g_partners.pdf, 2002.

Damsgaard, J. "Managing An Internet Portal", *Communications of AIS*, (9), 2002, pp.408-420

David, P.A. "Clio and the Economics of QWERTY", *The American Economic Review*, (75:2), 1985, pp.332-337

Funk, J.L. *The Mobile Internet: How Japan Dialed Up and the West Disconnected*, ISI Publications, 2001.

Kim, G., Kim, K. "Two-way Convergence of the Korean Portal Market: Competitive Responses to the New Mobile Internet Technology", *Proceedings of Second International Conference on Mobile Business*, 2003, pp. 261-270.

King, J.L., Gurbaxani, V., Kraemer, K.L., McFarlan, F.W., Raman, K.S. Yap, C.S. "Institutional Factors in Information Technology Innovation", *Information Systems Research*, (5:2), 1994, pp. 139-169.

Lamont, D. *Conquering the Wireless World: The Age of M-Commerce*, Capstone, 2001

Li, F., Whalley, J. "Deconstruction of the Telecommunications Industry: from Value Chains to Value Networks", *Telecommunications Policy*, (26), 2002, pp. 451–472.

Liebowitz, S.J., Margolis, S.E. *Winners, Losers & Microsoft: Competition and Antitrust in High Technology*, The Independent Institute, Oakland, CA, 1999.

Louis, P. J. *M-Commerce Crash Course: The Technology and Business of Next Generation Internet Services*, McGraw-Hill, 2001.

Lyytinen, K., Damsgaard,J. "What's Wrong with the Diffusion of Innovation Theory". In *Diffusing Software Product and Process Innovations*, M.A. Ardis and B.L. Marcolin Ed., 2001, pp. 173-190. Kluwer Academic Publishers.

Maitland, C.F., Bauer, J.M., Westerveld, R. "The European Market for Mobile Data", *Telecommunications Policy*, (26), 2002, pp. 485–504.

Manninen A. *Standardization of 2G Mobile Communications*. Unpublished Dissertation. Faculty of Information Technology, University of Jyväskylä, Finland, 2002.

Markus, M.L. "Towards a Critical Mass Theory of Interactive Media: Universal Access, Interdependence and Diffusion", *Communications Research*, (14:5), 1987, pp. 491-511.

Melody, W.H. "Telecom Reform: Progress and Prospects", *Telecommunications Policy*, (23:1), 1999, pp. 7-34.

Muller-Veerse, F. *Mobile Commerce Report*, Durlacher Research Ltd, London, 2000.

Pikula, V. *Mobile Internet Services in Japan: Identifying Industrial Organization as a Key Factor for Success*, Master degree thesis, Erasmus University Rotterdam, 2001.

Shapiro, C., Varian, H.R. *Information Rules: A Strategic Guide to the Network Economy*, Harvard Business School Press

Sterling, D. *Mobile Portal Strategy: When Did Business Partnerships Become So Critical to Customer Value?* IBM Institute for Business Value Report, Available at http://www-1.ibm.com/services/files/ibv_mobileportal.pdf, 2002

Ward, H.J., Gardner, M. "Portals: Their Role in the Emerging Networked Economy", *Journal of the Institution of British Telecommunications Engineers*, (1:4), 2000, pp.14-21.

Zhang, X., Prybutok, V.R. "How the Mobile Communication Markets Differ in China, the U.S., and Europe", *Communications of the ACM*, (48:3), 2005, pp.111-114.

CROSS-ORGANIZATIONAL WORKFLOWS: A CLASSIFICATION OF DESIGN DECISIONS *

Pascal van Eck,[1] Rieko Yamamoto,[2] Jaap Gordijn,[3] Roel Wieringa[1]

[1] *Department of Computer Science, University of Twente*
P.O. Box 217, 7500 AE Enschede, The Netherlands.
vaneck,roelw@cs.utwente.nl

[2] *Fujitsu Laboratories Ltd., IT Core Laboratory*
4-1-1 Kamikodanaka, Nakahara-ku, Kawasaki
Kanagawa, 211-8588, Japan.
r.yamamoto@jp.fujitsu.com

[3] *Department of Computer Science, Vrije Universiteit Amsterdam*
De Boelelaan 1081, 1081 HV Amsterdam, The Netherlands.
gordijn@cs.vu.nl

Abstract   Web service technology enables organizations to open up their business processes and engage in tightly coupled business networks to jointly offer goods and services. This paper systematically investigates all decisions that have to be made in the design of such networks and the processes carried out by its participants. Three areas of different kinds of design decisions are identified: the value modeling area, which addresses economic viability of the network, the collaboration modeling area, which addresses how business partners interact to produce the goods or services identified in the value modeling area, and the workflow modeling area, which addresses the design of internal processes needed for the interactions identified in the collaboration modeling area. We show, by reporting on a real-world case study, that there are significant differences between these areas: design decisions are unique for each area, IT support for collaboration processes is orthogonal to IT support for workflows, and the role of web choreography standards such as BPEL4WS differs for both of them.

Keywords: cross-organizational workflows, process design, web services

*This work is part of the Freeband A-MUSE and FRUX projects. Freeband (http://www.freeband.nl) is sponsored by the Dutch government under contract BSIK 03025.

1.   Introduction

Recently, a number of standards have been proposed for machine-readable specification of inter-organizational coordination processes, such as ebXML BPSS, BPEL, and WSCI (Alonso et al., 2004). Although these formalisms differ in many respects, they are all based on the same idea: they provide (and only provide) XML-based syntactic constructs to specify valid sequences of web service invocations of some business partners. Currently, not much is known about guidelines for actually designing cross-organizational processes. In this paper, we report on our research on these design guidelines. Our guidelines are compatible with any of the known web service choreography standards, because they should be used before the designer considers using one of these standards. Briefly, these decisions concern the commercial viability of the business activities being coordinated, the coordination mechanisms required to realize these commercial activities, and the workflows for each participating organization to support this coordination.

In the next section, we introduce the running example used throughout the paper. Is is based on a real-life industry project (Yamamoto et al., 2004). In section 3 we describe our design approach and in the following sections, we describe the decisions made in each of the three views: commercial viability, coordination process, workflow processes.

2.   Case study: A portal for music fans

Fans of a particular artist are interested in information about the artist, merchandise, and song scores, but also want to chat about their favorite artist. Our task is to build a *portal* that organizes information and services related to the artist. In March 2003, a Japanese project developed two such portals by integrating various e-services delivering content, merchandise and more, from different providers. The services provided included information about the singers' schedules, the sale of song scores, the sale of goods (T-shirts, pens, CDs, photographic prints, etc.), the management of fan clubs, the mailing of fan club news and birthday congratulations, and accounting for members' fees. As we will see, the portal is actually a constellation of enterprises, which collaborate to create a portal for a specific artist, with interesting services and content for fans.

3.   Design decisions

Before committing considerable resources to creating a collaboration with another organization, an organization usually seeks answers to the following two questions: is the collaboration commercially viable (e.g., generating a positive cash flow), and is the collaboration feasible (e.g., does it not overextend organizational and IT support change capabilities). We approach these questions by dividing them in three areas of concern: value modeling (economic viability), coordination modeling (feasibility/impact with respect to relations of organizations with each other), and workflow modeling (feasibility/impact with respect to internal structure and processes).

In the *value modeling* area, we address the enterprises and final customers that participate in the collaboration. As such, the value model presents who is offering *what* of *economic value* to whom and expects *what* in return. The latter refers to the notion of economic reciprocity; an important notion in commercial trade. In addition, the value model shows whether valuable objects are offered as a bundle (potentially by different suppliers) or not. *Bundling* (Choi et al., 1997) is an important notion in business to increase total sales and is in e-business settings of specific interest because information integration enable multi-supplier bundles. Finally, a value model shows the assignment of value activities (activities that yield profit) to performing actors. In the recent past, we have seen in the context of e-business many shifts of such activities from the one enterprise to another enterprise. All these design decisions are quantified in terms on revenues and expenses and are summarized in *profitability sheets*, representing the net cash flow for each actor involved. A discounted net cash flow analysis known from investment theory (see e.g. Horngren and Foster, 1987) can then be used to decide whether to invest in the collaboration or not.

We distinguish between on the one hand, coordination process by which business coordinate their behavior in a collaboration (*coordination modeling* area), and on the other hand, internal processes of each of the businesses participating in a collaboration (*workflow modeling* area). A *coordination process* consists only of interactions between two or more parties in the collaboration. These interactions involve externally visible behavior of each of the coordinating businesses. The set of all interactions of one business is called its *abstract business process*. In general, there will be one or more *internal business processes* that jointly realize the abstract process of a business. Most of these internal processes will be confidential, as it contains confidential business rules and uses confidential data. The distinction between coordination processes, abstract business processes and internal business processes is also made in the BPMN standard (White, 2004). A similar distinction is also made by van der Aalst and Weske, 2001.

Traditionally, when a business manager negotiates a collaboration agreement with other businesses, no technical knowledge is needed. However, when digital services are traded, the value network will be implemented as a computer network and almost all activities will be performed by software. In this case, the value model is a requirements specification for a network of communicating software systems, and the business manager needs the assistance of the software requirements engineer to point out opportunities for allocating tasks to business actors, and for guarding the implementability of the value model. If a software requirements engineer would not participate in the negotiation about the value model, then the manager would unwittingly make software engineering decisions. Moreover, unrealizable parts of the value model would get changed later on in the implementation process, and those decisions would be made by software engineers, not by managers. Consequences of these changes for the value model would go unnoticed, and in effect a software engineer would then change the value model without giving a commercial motivation for this. By having a software requirements engineer participate in value modeling, we ensure that commercial decisions are made in the value modeling task only, and technical decisions are made in the software engineering task only.

4.   Value modeling

Value modeling design decisions

We represent the outcome of value modeling decisions using the e^3-*value* notation described in Gordijn and Akkermans, 2003; Gordijn and Akkermans, 2001. The purpose of the e^3-*value* method is to represent enterprises (actors) who exchange things of *economic value* with each other, in an economically reciprocal way. Reciprocity expresses economic rationality: An enterprise offers something of value but requires something of value in return. e^3-*value* contains tools to assess profitability for each actor. In previous work (van Eck et al., 2004), we identified a series of design decisions to be taken on the business value level:

- Which *consumer needs* do exist? A customer need is a state of felt deprivation of some basic satisfaction (Kotler, 1988).

- How are these consumer needs *satisfied* by *value objects*? Value objects are things that can be produced or consumed by enterprises and end-customers, and are by definition of *economic value*.

- Who is *offering/requesting* value objects to/from the environment? Each enterprise or end-customer produces/consumes value objects to create profit or to increase economic utility.

- What are the *reciprocal* value object exchanged between enterprise/end-customers? If an enterprise/end-customers requests a value object from its environment, what is offered in return for that.

- What *bundles* of value objects exist? Many e-business practices (Choi et al., 1997) are characterized by good or service (un)bundling. Bundling refers to offering a set of value object as one, because of higher profits, or because of a better need satisfaction.

- What *partnerships* do exist? This closely refers to bundling as objects in a bundle are often offered by more than one enterprise.

Similar to a so-called Computation-Independent Model (CIM) in OMG's Model Driven Architecture (MDA), a value model completely abstracts from the internal structure of any software artifact in the domain. However, a value model seems to be broader than a CIM: in our opinion, a CIM focuses on a specific software artifact while a value model focuses on a constellation of net-worked businesses that may employ tens if not hundreds of software artifacts.

Case study value model

These design decisions can be represented by an e^3-*value* value model (see Fig. 1). e^3-*value* represents *actors* (enterprises and final customers) that exchange *value objects* (goods and services) with each other through *value interfaces*. These interfaces consist of *ports* offering or requesting value objects. Final customers have a customer *need*. To satisfy such a need, a set of value exchanges need to be executed by all enterprises collaborating in satisfying that need. We represent these exchanges by a *dependency path*. A dependency path consists of the need, the interfaces exchanging objects contributing to need satisfaction, and internal actor dependencies between interfaces. If an actor has a *need*, he will exchange objects of value through one of his interfaces to satisfy the need. Additionally, exchanges via an interface may cause exchanges via another interface of such an actor (e.g. to buy raw materials to produce to object requested). So, the focus is on *what* actors exchange of *economic value*, and not *how* they do so from a business process perspective.

The value model shows two portals for two artists, each of which offers services to fans of that artist. Each artist portal integrates a number of services offered by so-called function providers. Since each artist portal promotes music of a particular artist, it is paid for by the record companies of the artist. In order to use the Akinori Nakagawa portal, one has to be a member. In contrast, the Kitaro portal offers also some goods to non-members in addition to providing member services.

A member of the Akinori Nakagawa portal can do two things: (1) use member services (e.g. viewing content of a specific artist), and (2) buy merchandise related to the artist. There are two kinds of membership services: (1) member management services, which are about joining the portal, canceling membership, changing personal information and more, and (2) content services, which consist of a database of freely available content such as photographs taken by and from the artist, pieces of music, etc. These services are themselves outsourced. The portal only integrates them and adds the branding of the spe-

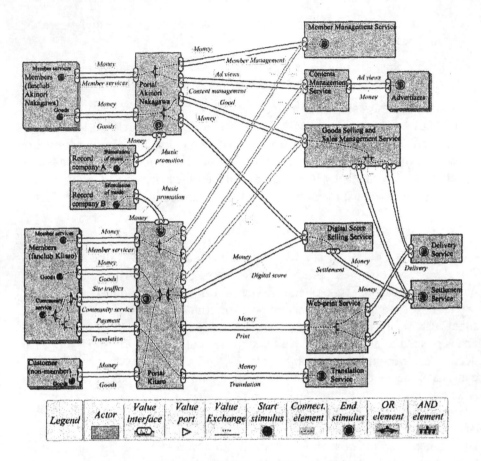

Figure 1.   Value Model of the case study.

cific artist. The portal pays for member management services and obtains this money from members. The content provider obtains money from the portal and is financed by selling ads surrounding the content. For the fan, content is free.

A member can also buy goods (merchandise of an artist). For doing so, a service is needed that handles the sales of goods. We distinguish two types; merchandise goods and digital scores. The sale of both types of goods is outsourced to external parties by the portal. Selling goods requires payment (settlement) services (e.g. a credit card service). Consequently the goods selling and scores selling services require a payment service. Additionally, 'goods selling' requires delivery of the physical goods. As can be seen, the goods selling service uses a delivery service for doing so.

The Kitaro portal looks like the Akinori Nakagawa portal but has some additional services. First there is a web-print service. Members can use this service to print various materials such as photographs. Also, the Kitaro portal has a community service (basically a discussion list). This service comes in two flavors. First, there is a discussion service for Japanese users in the Japanese language. The second service adds a paid translation service. For translation, an additional function provider is used.

The e^3-*value* model illustrates that even seemingly simple services can involve a network of businesses that operate according to complex business models. The profitability of these business models for all cooperating businesses can be estimated if we we assign *valuation functions* (basically a pricing formula) to all the ports exchanging money, and if we estimate the number of customer needs per timeframe, we can generate out of the model profitability sheets on a per actor basis. These sheets can be used to assess the potential for profit generation for each actor involved. It is a requirement that all actors can make a profit; otherwise the *model* is considered not sustainable. Due to lack of space, we do not present the sheets for the case at hand; the interested reader is referred to Gordijn and Akkermans, 2003 for the construction of such sheets.

5.   Coordination modeling

Coordination modeling design decisions

A dependency path in an e^3-*value* model shows which value exchanges are triggered by the occurrence of a consumer need, but it does not show how these exchanges are coordinated. Coordination is the interaction between a number of actors needed to produce a result. In the design of a coordination processes, the following choices have to be made. These choices are all relative to the design decisions made in the value model.

- Which information is exchanged between business partners, and in which order?

- What are the trust relations between the actors?

- Are additional actors needed to resolve trust issues (e.g., trusted third parties?)

- Who is responsible for the coordination activities at each business partner?

In this paper, we ignore trust relations (Wieringa and Gordijn, 2005) and focus on the coordination required to implement the value model under the assumption that all partners trust each other.

Exchange	Description
Members - Portal Kitaro	Low trust. The coordination process must ensure that for each transaction, payment is guaranteed: ■ Goods transfer from portal provider to members: goods are delivered via the delivery service on behalf of the portal provider after payment is confirmed by the settlement service. ■ Money transfer from members to portal provider: members have to use the settlement service for each order.
Portal Kitaro - Web-print service	High trust. There is a long-term custom contract between the portal provider and the web-print service provider. ■ Print ordering by portal provider: portal provider is expected to order prints one by one, for each client order. ■ Money transfer from portal provider to web-print service provider: The web-print service provider sends invoices at his discretion, which is payed by the portal provider's financial department.
Web-print service - settlement service	High trust. Business is conducted according to the standard business procedure defined by the settlement service provider. ■ Delivery of settlement service: the settlement service is provided to the members on behalf of the web-print service. ■ Money transfer from web-print service provider to settlement service provider: The settlement service sends a monthly subscription invoice.

Table 1. Value exchanges in the dependency path from Members via the Kitaro Portal and Web-print service to the settlement service. Exchanges refer to actors in Fig. 1.

Case study coordination processes

We take as an example the dependency path for goods that starts at the members of the Kitaro fanclub, goes through the Kitaro portal and the Web-print service and ends in the delivery and settlement service. The value exchanges that make up this dependency path are listed in Table 1.

A coordination process shows us how to deliver goods or services to one specific customer. However, some of the value exchanges to be implemented by the coordination process do not have to be carried out for each specific customer-driven instance of the process. This is the case for the entire exchange between the web-print service provider and the settlement service provider (both directions) and for the money transfer from the portal provider to

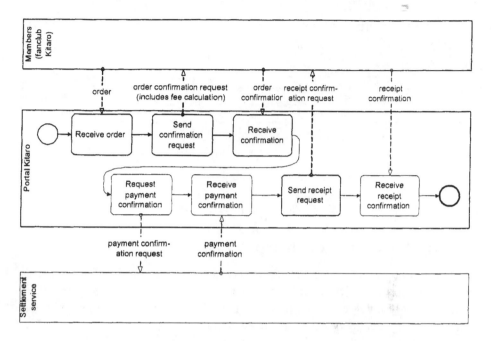

Figure 2.   Coordination process of fanclub member and portal. See Fig. 3 for legend.

the web-print provider: they are aggregated in time-triggered processes as indicated in Table 1.

We assume that (secondary) business processes are already in place for sending invoices (settlement service provider and web-print service) and receiving and paying them (web-print service provider and portal provider) mentioned in Table 1. Therefore, they do not have to be taken into account in the design of the coordination processes for realizing the dependency path that we focus on.

Fig. 2 shows the coordination process (in BPMN notation, see White, 2004) that is being used in the case study between a member of the Kitaro fanclub and the Kitaro portal. The fanclub member starts by submitting an order. The portal receives this order and answers with a request for an order confirmation. The fanclub member confirms his order and receives a request to confirm receipt of the goods. The actual receipt of the goods is not in the figure, as this figure only contains information exchange, not the exchange of physical goods. After receipt of the goods, the fanclub member sends a confirmation. Because of space restrictions, we have chosen to only depict information exchange for a successful execution of the process.

The portal in turn coordinates its activities with the web-print service. This coordination process is depicted in Fig. 3.

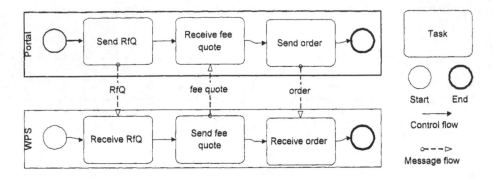

Figure 3.   Coordination process of portal and web-print service (WPS).

IT support for coordination processes

The collaboration processes described above consist only of information exchange activities of business partners. IT support for coordination processes therefore only involves IT support for these information exchange activities. The following design choices have to be made:

- What technology to use (e.g., HTML forms, web services)?

- Synchronous or asynchronous information exchange?

- What is the format of the message data exchanged?

In our case study, information exchange with the fanclub members is based on HTML forms, as fanclub members (who are human end consumers) want to interact with the portal directly. The portal software designers have complete freedom in designing these forms.

Information exchange with the settlement service is most probably governed by the standard procedures published by the settlement service provider. In this case study, all relevant member data for payment is already collected in the first information exchange in the coordination process. This data is forwarded to the settlement service. Another possibility is that members are redirected to a website of the settlement service where they have to enter payment data.

We assume that information exchange between the portal provider and the web-print service provider is within the design charter of our case study and that there is an interest in using web service technology for this. In its basic form, web service technology is based on an asymmetric paradigm: a web service client calls a passive web service. The process depicted in Fig. 3, however, is symmetric. Therefore, choices have to be made as to who is the client and who is the server. There are two options: (1) The web-print service provider is always the server and provides a web service with two operations: one to receive a quote and one to submit an order. (2) A web service with one operation is defined for each message flow arrow in Fig. 3; the web service is offered by the partner at the receiving end of the message flow arrow and called by the partner at the sending end of the message flow arrow. The number of operations in each option is influenced by choices with respect to whether operations are called synchronously or asynchronously: each asynchronously defined operation results in one additional operation, namely the callback operation. For this case study, we proceed with the first option, which results in the following web services (defined using WSDL; details left out):

```
<wsdl:definitions>                      <operation name="submitRfQ">
   <message name="orderDataMsg">          <input message="orderDataMsg"/>
      <part name="..." type="..."/>       <output message="feeQuoteMsg"/>
      ...                                </operation>
   </message>                           <operation name="submitOrder">
   <message name="feeQuoteMsg">           <input message="orderDataMsg"/>
      ...                                </operation>
   </message>                          </portType>
   <portType name="portalPT">        </wsdl:definitions>
```

We use a BPEL4WS abstract business process to specify the choreography associated with these operations as follows:

```
<process name="portal2WPScoordination" abstractprocess="yes">
   <partnerlinks>
      <partnerlink name="portal2WPS" partnerLinkType="..."
                   myRole="WPS" partnerRole="portal"/>
   </partnerlinks>
   <sequence>
      <receive partnerLink="portal2WPS" portType="portalPT" operation="submitRfQ"/>
      <reply partnerLink="portal2WPS" portType="portalPT" operation="submitRfQ"/>
      <receive partnerLink="portal2WPS" portType="portalPT" operation="submitOrder"/>
   </sequence>
</process>
```

As this is an abstract business process, the internal workflow executed to determine what to reply (second item in the sequence) to the received message (first item in the sequence) is left unspecified.

The above WSDL and BPEL fragments are sufficient to represent IT support for the coordination process depicted in Fig. 3. These fragments can be published by the web-print service provider and downloaded by the portal provider to find out how to conduct business. It is also possible to specify the process that the portal provider executes:

```
<process name="portal2WPScoordination" abstractprocess="yes">
   <partnerlinks>
      <partnerlink name="portal2WPS" partnerLinkType="..."
                   myRole="portal" partnerRole="WPS"/>
   </partnerlinks>
   <sequence>
      <invoke partnerLink="portal2WPS" portType="WPSport" operation="submitRfQ"/>
      <invoke partnerLink="portal2WPS" portType="WPSport" operation="submitOrder"/>
   </sequence>
</process>
```

This fragment would be put in a separate BPEL4WS document; the relation with the BPEL4WS process description of the web-print service providers is only implied by the shared WSDL definition. This is a consequence of a fundamental design decision in BPEL4WS: BPEL4WS can only represent executable business processes (i.e., internal workflows, which will be treated in the next section) and abstract business processes, but not coordination processes (see Section 3 for the distinction between these three kinds of processes). The business process specification part of ebXML, as well as WSCI, do allow specification of coordination processes.

As we can learn from this example, a complex business collaboration as described by the dependency path that we have focused on in our case results in a number of relatively small web service choreography specifications such as the BPEL4WS fragments presented above. At least BPEL4WS does not allow a full specification of the entire coordination process associated with the dependency path (but other choreography standards may allow this). No notation that we are aware of would allow coordination actions that do not result in message exchange, such as physical delivery of goods.

6.   Workflow modeling

Workflow design decisions

The coordination processes presented in the previous section only present message exchange between business partners. Workflow modeling focuses on the internal processes of each partner and determines how each partner brings about the exchanges specified in the coordination processes. Guidelines for design choices in workflow design can be found in organization theory (Daft, 1998), process design (Ould, 1995), and operations management (Slack et al., 1998). We do not summarize all of this but point out one of them:

- Are orders satisfied by taking the items ordered from stock or by manufacturing them at the moment the order arrives?

This question concerns the so-called customer order decoupling point (CODP), which is the place in the workflow beyond which the workflow is no longer for a specific client order.

Case study workflow processes

In our case study, decided where the CODP lies comes down to deciding who keeps printed material on stock. There are three possibilities: (1) The portal orders printed material in batches of say 1000 copies and keeps them on stock (CODP is at the portal). (2) The web-print service prints the material in batches and keeps them on stock. The portal orders printed material per copy (one for each client request) and does not keep them on stock (CODP is at

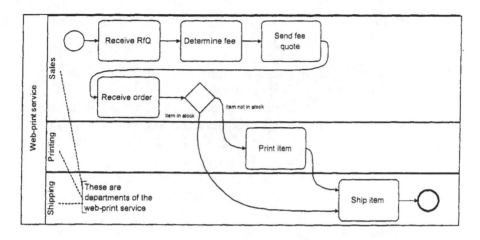

Figure 4. Web-print service internal process.

the web-print service). (3) Neither the portal nor the web-print service keeps printed material on stock. Instead, copies are printed in batches of size 1, with one batch per client order (no CODP).

The best alternative in this domain is usually determined by the printing technology used. E.g., it is prohibitively costly to run very small full-color offset printing jobs. For larger jobs, printing price per copy is low. With color laser printing, however, price per copy is constant, even for batches of size 1. The price per copy is, however, higher than for offset printing.

For commercial reasons, we cannot disclose the choice made in this case study, but we assume that the printer has chosen option (2). This gives us the workflow shown in Fig. 4. The workflow for the portal is trivial: it just relays messages between the fanclub member and the web-print service. This relaying is already fully captured in the middle part of Fig. 2, and is also presented in Yamamoto et al., 2004.

IT support for workflow processes

A workflow describes a process that is carried out by actors who work in one or more departments of one business. Although nowadays most workflow steps will be at least supported by information systems if not completely executed by it, one still has to consider exactly what steps need support from information technology and what this support entails. So, a workflow should not be confused with a specification of the behavior of one or more information systems. The main IT support design decisions are:

- Which workflow steps need support from information systems?

- What functions do these information systems need to offer?

- Distribution decisions, e.g. central IT facilities or facilities per location

These questions are fairly standard information systems design questions for which many design methods are available.

There are two different roles for a web service choreography standard such as BPEL4WS. First, there is an implementation relation between collaboration processes (which may be described in BPEL4WS) and internal workflows. So, a BPEL4WS description can be considered a partial specification of the workflows that have to be designed. Second, in a number of cases, internal workflows have to be formally specified and supported by workflow management systems. In these cases, the workflows can be described as BPEL4WS executable processes and executed by the BPEL4WS execution engines that are currently emerging in the market.

7.   Conclusion

In this paper, we have systematically identified all design decisions that need to be made when designing multi-party collaborations. This revealed a clear distinction between value modeling, coordination modeling and modeling internal workflows. IT support is different for each of the latter two, as is the role of web service technology and choreography standards. For each type of modeling, we have shown examples (using our case study) of modeling techniques such as e^3-*value* and BPMN. These modeling techniques are relatively lightweight while still providing enough insight to support design decisions. Moreover, these techniques are simple enough to be understood by non-technical stakeholders, which is important as design decisions made by software engineers influence design decisions that have to be made by business stakeholders and the other way around.

Many papers on web service technology that are currently being published focus on automatic service discovery and composition. We have not used any of this. One could argue that our case study is too conservative and should have used e.g. web service discovery to dynamically find a suitable settlement service and web service composition to dynamically create the collaborations instead of statically at design time. However, it is currently much too early to employ these technologies in real-world case studies. More importantly, we think that it is essential to first fully understand the static case before moving on to dynamic composition of business collaborations. As an aside, in a case like this which involves marketing mass-produced goods, a need remains for static, long-running relations for reasons of logistic and manufacturing efficiency.

Further work includes a validation of our approach on more case studies, and an analysis of the correctness relationship between a coordination process and a value model (when does a coordination model correctly implements a value model?) and between an internal and an abstract business process (when does an internal business process correctly implement an abstract process?)

References

Alonso, G., Casati, F., Kuno, H., and Machiraju, V. (2004). *Web Services: Concepts, Architectures and Applications.* Springer-Verlag.

Choi, S.-Y., Stahl, D. O., and Whinston, A. B. (1997). *The Economics of Doing Business in the Electronic Marketplace.* MACMillan Technical Publishing, Indianapolis, IN.

Daft, R. L. (1998). *Organization Theory and Design.* Thomson Publishing, sixth edition.

Gordijn, J. and Akkermans, J. (2003). Value-based requirements engineering: Exploring innovative e-commerce ideas. *Requirements Engineering Journal,* 8(2):114–134.

Gordijn, J. and Akkermans, J. M. (2001). Designing and evaluating e-Business models. *IEEE Intelligent Systems - Intelligent e-Business,* 16(4):11–17.

Horngren, C. T. and Foster, G. (1987). *Cost Accounting: A Managerial Emphasis, sixth edition.* Prentice-Hall, Englewood Cliffs, NJ.

Kotler, P. (1988). *Marketing Management: Analysis, Planning, Implementation and Control, 6th edition.* Prentice Hall, Englewood Cliffs, NJ.

Ould, M. A. (1995). *Business Processes–Modelling and Analysis for Re-engineering and Improvement.* Wiley.

Slack, N., Chambers, S., Harland, C., Harrison, A., and Johnston, R. (1998). *Operations Management.* Pitman Publishing, second edition. ISBN: 0-273-62688-4.

van der Aalst, W. M. P. and Weske, M. (2001). The P2P approach to interorganizational workflows. In Dittrich, K. R., Geppert, A., and Norrie, M. C., editors, *Advanced Information Systems Engineering: 13th International Conference, CAiSE 2001,* volume 2068 of *Lecture Notes in Computer Science,* pages 140–156.

van Eck, P., Gordijn, J., and Wieringa, R. (2004). Value-based design of collaboration processes for e-commerce. In Yuan, S.-T. and Liu, J., editors, *Proceedings 2004 IEEE International Conference on e-Technology, e-Commerce and e-Service, EEE'04,* pages 349–358. IEEE Press.

White, S. (2004). Business process modeling notation (BPMN). http://www.bpmn.org/Documents/ BPMN%20V1-0%20May%203%202004.pdf, visited 20041123.

Wieringa, R. J. and Gordijn, J. (2005). Value-oriented design of service coordination processes: Correctness and trust. In *Accepted for Proceedings of the ACM Symposium on Applied Computing, Organizational Engineering Track.* http://www.cs.vu.nl/~gordijn/sac05-submitted. pdf.

Yamamoto, R., Ohashi, K., Yamamoto, K., Inomata, J., and Matsuda, T. (2004). Lessons learned from requirements analysis for implementing integrated services. In *Proceedings of the International Workshop on Service-Oriented Requirements Engineering – SORE 2004.*

BIOVAULT: SOLVING THE PROBLEM OF REPLAY IN BIOMETRICS
An electronic commerce example

Prof Basie von Solms & Bobby Tait
Johannesburg University

Basie@adam.rau.ac.za, bobby@csrau.rau.ac.za

Abstract: One of the major risks involved in using biometrics for identification and authentication over open public networks, is the danger that the electronic biometric token (for e.g. a fingerprint or iris) can be intercepted and replayed by an unauthorized party. Furthermore, it is possible to make an unauthorized copy of a biometric token, without the permission and knowledge of the real owner, and use that for unauthorized transactions. This can for e.g. happen when a fingerprint is 'lifted' from an object the owner has used, and a latex copy is made from this token [5].This paper reports on a system in development, called Biovault, which addresses precisely the problems mentioned above, and which may help to make biometric tokens much safer to use over open public networks, for specific application in electronic commerce.

Key words: Electronic Commerce, Biometrics, Biometric Tokens, Identification, Authentication, Replay, Identity theft

1.   INTRODUCTION

Identification and authentication over insecure networks had always been a problem that caused serious information security risks. Several reasons for this can be identified, but the two discussed below are amongst the most serious ones.

Firstly, a password, even in encrypted form, can be intercepted by a third party, and reused or replayed at a later stage without the knowledge of the owner of the password.

The system which performs the authentication will never know whether the password is the original version originating from the real owner, or whether it is a replayed version of the password [4].

Supporting technologies like time stamps may help, but do not solve the problem completely.

Digital Identities, allowing the use of digital signatures, do offer some help, but do also not solve the problem, as there is no real relationship between the user and his digital identity.

Secondly, with both passwords and digital signatures, the real owner is not authenticated – rather the person who is in possession of the password or private key needed to create the digital signature, is authenticated [1]. If the password or private key had been compromised in any way, unauthorized people may masquerade as the real owner, and the computer system will not be able to identify this masquerading. The bottom line is that the system doing the authentication cannot determine whether the real owner, or a masquerader, is offering the password, token or digital signature.

Biometrics, of course, goes a long way in solving the second problem discussed above [2]. In most cases, the real owner of the biometric token must be present when the token is 'taken', for e.g. when a fingerprint is scanned on a digital fingerprint reader. Therefore the token is directly linked to the owner, and cannot be used by someone else [4].

Again, this is however not always true. A biometric token can be 'lifted' from an object handled by some person, and techniques do exist to make a copy of that lifted token and use it in a replay situation [5].

Furthermore, even when using biometric tokens, the same risks as for passwords exist. A biometric token send over an insecure network can be intercepted, and replayed at a later stage, without the knowledge and authorization of the real owner.

As in the case of the password, the computer system will not know whether the token is supplied by the real owner, or by a masquerading person.

The problems discussed above are some of the major reasons why biometrics had not yet moved into the mainstream for identification and authentication over insecure networks.

The system described in this paper, Biovault, goes a long way in addressing the problems identified above.

In the following paragraphs, we will describe how Biovault does address these problems, and what future research and development are envisaged to use Biovault as a secure biometrically based identification and authentication mechanism for e-commerce over insecure networks.

2. THE BASIS OF BIOVAULT

The basic design pillar, on which Biovault is based, has to do with what we call the symmetry and asymmetry differences between password and biometric tokens.

2.1 Symmetry

When an offered password is matched by a computer system to a stored version of the specific password, a 100% match is required, i.e. the offered version must exactly match the stored version – we call this symmetric matching because the error acceptance ratio between the 2 versions must be zero to accept the offered version as valid.

2.2 Asymmetry

When an offered biometric token is matched by a computer system to a stored version of the specific biometric token, a 100% match is not required – actually the chances of a 100% match is anyway very slim. This is inherent in the mathematical algorithms used to create and match biometric tokens. The algorithms must make provision for the fact that, for e.g. a fingerprint, can be positioned a little differently on the reader as when the stored master copy was read. The error acceptance ratio between the offered and stored versions is therefore greater than zero – the precise ratio can be set, and any offered token differing form the stored version within the error acceptance ratio, will be accepted as a match, and therefore lead to valid authentication. For this reason we call this asymmetric matching

2.3   The Token Archive (TA)

Biovault makes use of the fact that if an offered biometric token and any stored biometric token matches 100%, the chances that the offered biometric token is a replay of a previously used biometric token, is very high, and the offered biometric token is not accepted.

For this model to function a Token Archive (TA) is introduced on the Authentication Server. This TA will store all biometric tokens that the user ever used in his life time. It is quite clear that this TA might become very big, hence take long to search and match the offered token with the whole TA.

In order to speed up the searching of possible 100% matches in the TA, all biometric tokens will be sorted ascending in the TA, making it possible to do binary searching inside the TA. Using Binary Searching will allow the server to detect a possible 100% match at incredible speeds. The matching speed is described by the function O(LogN) [6]. This function demonstrates that as data becomes larger, there is no significant rise in search time

The following paragraph describes the first (initial) version of Biovault.

3.   BIOVAULT VERSION 1

This initial version made provision for a Biovault master copy of the owner's biometric token stored during the registration phase, as well as a Biovault Token Archive (TA) stored on the computer system.

Whenever a token is offered to the computer system, the offered token is first compared with the Biovault master copy of the token stored during registration of the user. If a non-identical match within the acceptance ratio is determined, the offered token is then compared with all versions stored in the TA. If an identical match is found with any version stored in the TA, the offered version is rejected, and the user is requested to offer another copy. The process is then repeated with the new offered copy received.

If no identical match is found between the offered copy and any version stored in the TA, the offered version is stored in the TA, and the offered version is accepted as a valid token, and the user is authenticated.

Figures 1 illustrates this operation

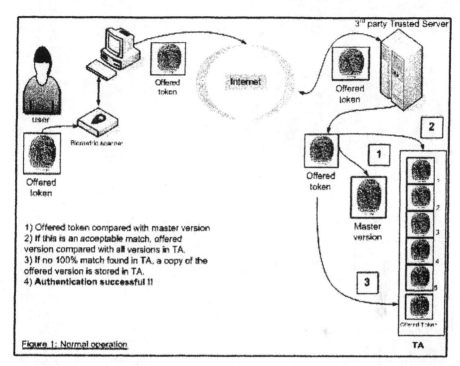

Figure 1. Normal Operation

If the offered token was intercepted while being sent to the computer system, this intercepted version could be replayed at a later stage to try to masquerade as the real owner.

Biovault Version 1 however, recognizes this replay attempt. When the replayed version was received by the computer system, it was first compared to the stored master version. If an acceptable match was found, it was compared to all versions stored in the TA. In this case a 100% would be found, because the original offered version, of which a copy was intercepted, had been stored in the TA. The replayed version would then be rejected.

This is illustrated in Figure 2.

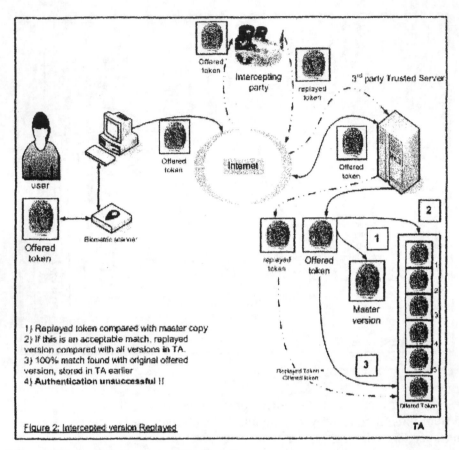

Figure 2. Intercepted version Replayed

The developed system works perfectly. It was proved easily that if an offered token is intercepted during a transaction, and the interception does not cause the aborting or termination of the transaction – ie the offered token does reach the computer system, replay of the intercepted token at a later stage, results in the replayed token being recognized as such and rejected.

The concept of the TA therefore seemed to solve some of the major problems.

However, some other problems still could not be solved.

Firstly, if a unauthorized token, 'lifted' from some object is replayed into the system, Biovault Version 1 accepted the lifted version, because it did not have an identical copy of the lifted version in its TA, and therefore assumed this version to be 'unblemished'. Biovault Version 1 could not determine whether this version really came from the real owner – all it could determine is that it had not received this version of the token before. This is illustrated in Figure 3.

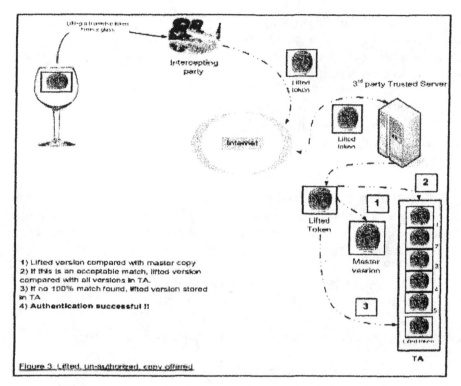

*Figure 3.*Lifted, un-authorized, copy offered

Secondly, it was determined that if a (clear text) token is intercepted, it is possible to 'tweak' the electronic version of the intercepted token in such a way that it differs from the original version just enough to be accepted by the computer system. The tweaking resulted in another version of the original token, differing just enough to still fall within the error acceptance ratio.

Biovault Version 2 addressed both problems by using encryption.

4.   BIOVAULT VERSION 2

This version ensured that the offered version, ie the one acquired directly from the owner, was first 'digitally signed' by the owner, by encrypting it with the private key of the owner. The computer system then first decrypted the offered version with the public key of the owner. (The reader is assumed to be up to date on the theory of Public Key encryption).

This approach solved both problems identified in Version 1.

Firstly, any 'lifted' version was not digitally signed by the owner, and when decrypted by the computer system using the public key of the owner, always resulted in an electronic string which fell outside the error acceptance ratio, and was therefore always rejected.

Secondly, trying to 'tweak' the digitally signed version of the offered token always resulted in a string which was rejected. Tweaking an encrypted version of the offered token was exceedingly more difficult than tweaking the clear text version.

Note that if a digitally signed version of the offered token was intercepted and replayed, it would immediately be recognized as a reply, because the offered version itself would by that time, be stored in the TA. This is just a more advanced case of the situation described in paragraph 3 above.

Biovault Version 2 worked perfectly, and solved many of the problems inherent in Biovault Version 1.

However, some more problems and difficulties were identified.

Firstly, requiring all participants to have a Public/Private key pair in order to digitally sign biometric tokens, placed a significant burden on potential rollout of Biovault. Furthermore this did not really improve on systems that uses biometrics to gain access to one's private key [7]. All that Biovault 2 accomplished was merely to use ones private key to gain access to your biometric token.

Secondly, we were still worried that a token, digitally signed by the owner, could be intercepted, and the transaction in some way aborted or terminated before the offered token reached the computer system. If this happened, the offered token would not become part of the TA (because the computer system never received it), and the intercepted version could then successfully be replayed at a later stage. This is illustrated in Figure 4.

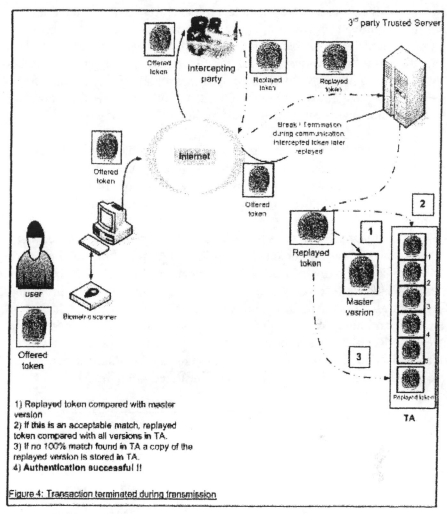

Figure 4. Transaction terminated during transmission

This resulted in Biovault Version 3

5.   BIOVAULT VERSION 3

The inherent problem with Biovault Version 2 was that if a biometric token is created with the involvement of the real owner, ie a token that the owner really wants to offer to the computer system for identification and authentication purposes, the moment this token leaves the workstation of the owner, the owner has no copy or record of that token. If the token successfully reached the computer system, a copy will be stored in the TA.

However, if the offered token is intercepted during transit, and does not reach the computer system, as mentioned at the end of the previous paragraph, neither the owner nor the computer system has a copy. This means there is a 'hot' copy of the offered token, the intercepted version, out in the open. This hot copy can then be used in a replay effort at a later stage. Such an effort will most probably be successful, because the computer system does not have a copy in Biovault master TA.

As an initial option (version 3A) in solving this problem of a hot copy , a personal TA will be created on the workstation of the user, in which a copy of every token sent to the computer system was first stored locally before it was sent to the computer system and offered for identification and authentication.

This meant that no unrecorded 'hot' copies of offered tokens could exist.

By synchronizing the personal and master TA from time to time, it is possible to identify any offered tokens which was sent to the computer system, and never received by the computer system. This synchronizing effort updates the system TA, and caused any offered copy which was intercepted and never reached the computer system, to be included in the master TA. Replaying such an intercepted copy at a later stage, would the result in rejection. The reader should be able to see that this solution solves the problem illustrated in Figure 4. This is illustrated in Figure 5

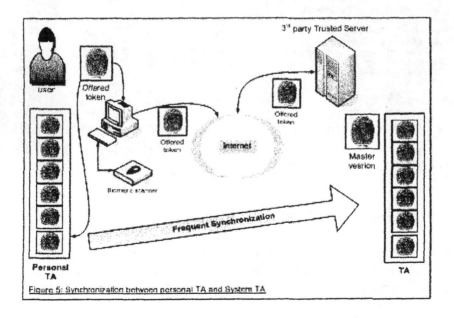

Figure 5: Synchronization between personal TA and System TA

Figure 5. Synchronization between personal TA and System TA

6. A PRACTICAL E-COMMERCE APPLICATION OF BIOVAULT.

One of the primary objectives during the development and research of Biovault was that the developed system must be usable for electronic commerce. Electronic commerce can benefit from an environment where the client can be sure that his money will only be paid from his account on his request. The money vendor like Visa card [8], wants to be sure that the request to pay money, came from a authentic account holder, and a seller like Amazon [9] want to be ensured that they will get their money, and preferably not be informed that the transaction was fraudulent, after goods have been dispatched.

With the development of Biovault, the possibility of biometric replay is not of much concern. In order to demonstrate the usage of Biovault during an online purchase, the process will be discussed in two phases. Figure 6 illustrates the first phase of purchasing a book from Amazon [9]

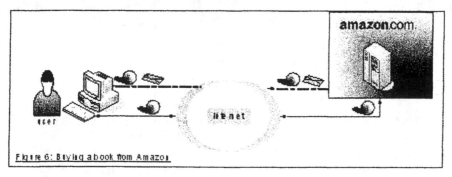

Figure 6. Buying a book from Amazon

During this phase the user will visit the website of Amazon as shown in step 1. The user will then find the book that he wishes to buy, place it in his shopping cart, and proceed to the checkout section on Amazon's website.

Amazon will then inform the user the total amount payable, including shipping and handling, this is illustrated by the little envelope in step 2. This is a familiar process to everybody that buys a book from Amazon. The next phase will demonstrate how the user will use the Biovault model to pay for the book. Currently, when a user uses a token like a credit card to pay for a transaction, the Visa Card server is contacted by the seller to ensure that the credit card is authentic and that the card is not reported as stolen. Once the authenticity is verified, Visa will inform the seller that the money will be paid, and an authorization code is supplied [8] to the seller. With the Biovault environment the same basic model will be used, and is illustrated in figure 7

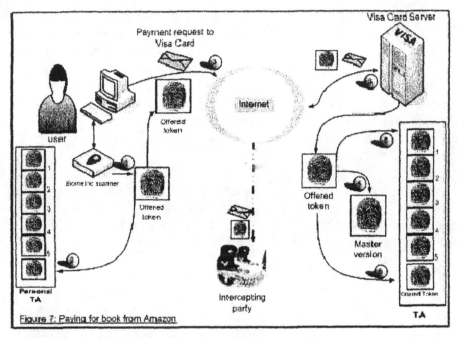

Figure 7. Paying for a book from Amazon

During the first step the user provides a fresh biometric token, this fresh biometric token will be placed in the personal TA during step 2. This will ensure that one keeps track of all biometric tokens destined for payment. The user will then submit the payment request and fresh biometric token to his money vendor, in this example Visa, during step 3.

Take note that the offered biometric token and payment request to Visa is sniffed by an intercepting party during transmission. Step 4 illustrates how the Biovault mechanism authenticates the user against the master version of the biometric token. If the matching algorithm is satisfied with the offered biometric token, the system will proceed to step 5 to confirm weather this offered token is unique and not a replayed old token already in the TA.

If the system did not discover an identical copy in the TA, the new offered token will be added in to the TA in the last step.

At this stage the Visa server is satisfied that it is the authentic user that is requesting money to be paid to Amazon. The Visa server will typically now confirm that the user has the necessary funds available to pay for the Amazon transaction.

If the funds are available, the Visa server will provide Amazon with an authentication code (step 2), for the amount payable. The user will receive a transaction result directly from the Visa Server in step 3. This is illustrated in Figure 8.

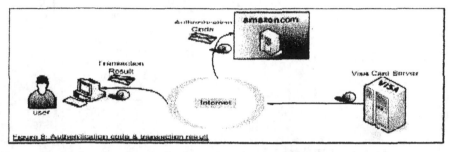

Figure 8. Authentication code & transaction result

7. REPLAY OF INTERCEPTED BIOMETRIC TOKEN.

In order to complete the electronic commerce example, figure 9 illustrates the scenario of a hacker replaying the sniffed biometric token procured earlier in figure 7.

The intercepting party would typically alter the payment request for Visa in such a way that the money must be paid to a Swiss bank account, this results in an updated payment request. The intercepting party will then submit the replayed biometric token and updated payment request to the Visa server indicated by step 1, figure 9.

The Visa server will receive the payment request and biometric token (step 2 in figure 9) and match the replayed token to the master version (step 3 in figure 9). If the matching algorithm is satisfied with the matching ratio, the replayed version will be compared to all the old biometric tokens in the TA (step 4 in figure 9). Step 5 in figure 9 indicates that the token supplied is a token that has been used at an earlier stage, because a 100% is found with a biometric token in the TA.

For this reason the Authenticity of the user is rejected and the transaction is unsuccessful.

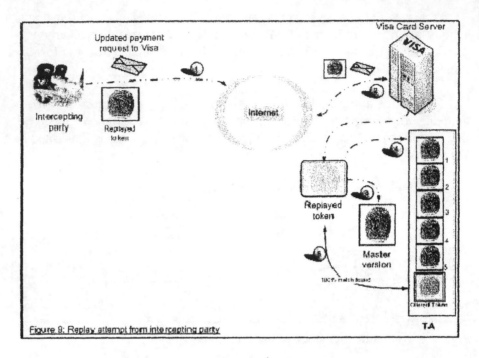

Figure 9. Replay attempt from intercepting party

The reader may reason that in figure 7, if the interception takes place successfully, but the offered token does not reach the Visa card server, a replay of the intercepted token (hot copy), may be successful, because the offered token did not reach the server's TA.

This issue is addressed by the synchronization step illustrated in figure 5, and also extensively addressed in Biovault version 4.

We will not expand on this issue at this point.

8.   BIOVAULT VERSION 4

Biovault Version 3 is fully operational. Biovault Version 4 is being designed at present. This version will use Biovault to implement the concept of 'biometric digital signatures'.

Furthermore in version 4 the user will not need to frequently synchronize the personal TA with the server. This version of Biovault will be much easier to roll out, and will not need much additional hardware to function. Version 4 we also address a number of problems still inherent in version 3.

Using this version 4, it is investigated that unique digital signatures can be created using biometric tokens.

9. SUMMARY

We are convinced that Biovault is addressing many, if not all, of the problems which had prevented the very powerful technology of Biometrics to be used properly for identification and authentication over insecure public networks. Biovault allows for applications in many domains, including electronic commerce (as demonstrated), Point of sales transactions, and even Automated teller machine transactions. During the presentation of Biovault, a demonstration of Biovault version 3 will be given as proof of concept.

10. REFERENCES

[1] Secrets and Lies – Digital security in a Networked World. Bruce Schneier.

[2] Namitech – http://www.namitech.co.za

[3] Biometrics – A look inside. John D. Woodward Jr. ISBN 0-07-222227-1

[4] Biometrics: Advanced Identify Verification: The Complete Guide - Julian D. M. Ashbourn

[5] T. Matsumoto, H. Matsumoto, K Yamada, S. Hoshino, 2002, "Impact of artificial gummy fingers of fingerprint systems" Proceedings of SPIE Vol #4677, Optical security and counterfeit deterrence techniques IV.

[6] http://www.ics.uci.edu/~eppstein/261/f03-outline/11.fraccasc

[7] http://www.activcard.com

[8] http://www.Visacard.com

[9] http://www.amazon.com

INTEGRATION OF XML DATA IN PEER-TO-PEER E-COMMERCE APPLICATIONS

Tadeusz Pankowski [1,2]

[1] *Institute of Control and Information Engineering*
Poznan University of Technology
Pl. M.S.-Curie 5, 60-965 Poznan
Tadeusz.Pankowski@put.poznan.pl

[2] *Faculty of Mathematics and Computer Science*
Adam Mickiewicz University
ul. Umultowska 87, 61-614 Poznan
tpankow@amu.edu.pl

Abstract   E-commerce applications need new solutions in the field of integration, interchange and transformation of data across the global marketplace. Such advanced data management features, which are expected to function automatically
or semi-automatically, are necessary when a party looks for potential business
partners, a buyer wants to find relevant supplier of the products, a seller wants
to find potential customers or business partners negotiate a deal, and so on.
In these e-commerce applications distributed systems based on the traditional
client-server paradigm are nowadays replaced by peer-to-peer (P2P) systems.
The goal of data management in P2P systems is to make use of a decentralized, easily extensible architecture in which any user can contribute new data or
new schemas and mappings between other peer's schemas. P2P data management systems replace traditional data integration systems based on single global
schema with an interlinked collection of semantic mappings between peers' individual schemas. The paper discusses this kind of P2P data management in
e-commerce settings. A new proposal concerning schema mapping specification and query reformulation is presented.

Keywords: Data integration, XML databases, query reformulation, schema mapping, Peer
Database Management Systems, P2P e-commerce

1.   Introduction

E-commerce (*electronic commerce*) covers trading activities that are supported by variety of information and communication technologies. A new generation of e-commerce applications such as B2B (*Business-To-Business*) and
EAI (*Enterprise Application Integration*) requires new standards and new tech-

nologies. Such new technologies are developed and provided among others by P2P (*Peer-to-Peer*) computing and PDMS (*Peer Data Management Systems*) [Bernstein et al., 2002; Tatarinov and Halevy, 2004]. B2B P2P e-commerce opens up new possibilities of trade, where new business partners from around the globe can be found, their offers can be compared, even complex negotiations can be conducted electronically, and a contract can be drown up and fulfilled via an electronic marketplace. Thus, market places for B2B e-commerce require integration and interoperation of several systems (e.g. product databases, order processing systems) across multiple organizations. E-commerce is carried out in a highly dynamic environment where companies enter the marketplace some others drop out. The data flow is bi-directional, i.e. data has to be transferred back to participants as well (orders, product lists). The system must be adaptable for different environments, as the electronic marketplace covers many countries with different languages and different legal regulations.

A basic functionality of a system supporting e-commerce applications is the integration of external data sources or data services. To solve the problem of data integration one can use the idea of federated database system [Sheth and Larson, 1990]. In this scenario a global business data repository is a key component of a federated system where it plays the role of a global schema (mediator): all requests by the client application are sent to the repository. The mediator then looks up its resources (metadata repository) and sends the query to the appropriate source. The result is received by the mediator and then sent back to the client application in the desired format. Such a solution was proposed in [Quix et al., 2002]. This approach is based on a centralized client-server architecture in which servers represent vendors or marketplaces and customers are represented by clients.

Nowadays and after the great success of file sharing systems, such as Napster, Gnutella and BitTorrent, another more decentralized approach referred to as Peer-to-Peer comes into use [Bernstein et al., 2002; Calvanese et al., 2004]. P2P systems are characterized by an architecture constituted by various autonomous nodes (called *peers*) which hold information, and which are linked to other nodes by means of mappings. In P2P data sharing and data integration each peer exports data in terms of its own schema, and data interoperation is achieved by means of mappings among the peer schemas. One of the challenges in these systems is answering queries posed to one peer while taking into account the mappings. This can be achieved by so called *query reformulation* [Halevy, 2001],[Lenzerini, 2002],[Madhavan and Halevy, 2003], [Pankowski, 2005],[Tatarinov and Halevy, 2004],[Yu and Popa, 2004].

A system supporting query reformulation does not need to materialize a target view over sources. Instead, a *target query* is reformulated into a set of *source queries* that can be processed in underlying sources, and partial answers are merged to obtain the final result. In both cases, the central problem is how to describe the correspondence or *mappings* between the source data and the target data. Mappings are usually specified as high-level assertions that state how source elements correspond to target elements at schema and/or instance level. So, a distinction can be drawn between schema-level, instance-level or hybrid approaches to source-target mappings [Rahm and Bernstein, 2001]. In the case of schema mapping only schema information, not instance data, is taken into account. Schema mappings can be given manually, perhaps supported by a graphical user interface, or they can be derived semi-automatically [Miller et al., 2000; Popa et al., 2002] based on schema matching algorithms [Rahm and Bernstein, 2001]. For query reformulation in relational data integration systems, schema mappings have been defined using GAV (*global-as-view*), LAV (*local-as-view*) or GLAV (*global-and-local-as-view*) approaches [Calvanese et al., 2004; Halevy, 2001; Lenzerini, 2002; Ullman, 1997].

The main contributions of this paper are the following. We propose a method for specifying mappings between schemas of peer XML data repositories. The source-to-target mapping specification is based on Skolem functions. Any invocation $SF(x_1, ..., x_n)$ of a Skolem function SF returns the same node identifier for the same values of arguments $x_1, ..., x_n$. For different Skolem functions and for different values of arguments returned identifiers (nodes) are distinct. Arguments of a Skolem function are defined by means of path expressions returning text values. The mapping is specified as an expression of a mapping language that asserts source-to-target dependencies [Fagin et al., 2004]. Two kinds of dependencies are taken into account: *(a) source-to-target node generating dependencies*, where a Skolem function is assign to each absolute target path (i.e. a path starting from the root of a target schema) and establishes a one-to-one relationship (modulo the function name) between tuples of text values of source nodes and target nodes; and *(b) source-to-target value dependencies* that constrain relationships between leaf node text values in source and target data trees. Next, we propose *rewriting rules for query reformulation*. A query reformulation is defined as a rewriting process leading from a target query to a required source query. Both mapping specification and query reformulation are illustrated by examples relevant to e-commerce applications.

The paper is structured as follows. In Section 2 we introduce some concepts concerning XML data and XML path expressions. Then we define a method to specify schema mappings based on Skolem functions. Classes of source-to-target and value dependences are discussed and illustrated by an example. In Section 3 we propose rewriting rules for query reformulation. Application of these rules is illustrated in Section 4. Section 5 concludes the paper.

2.   Specification of schema mapping

In data integration systems, there are one target (or mediated) schema and a number of source schemas. In a P2P computation, a role of the target schema can be played any peer that can be arbitrary chosen by the user. The target schema is commonly treated as a virtual view over sources, and source schemas describe real data stored in source repositories. We assume that both source and target data conform to XML format.

2.1   XML data and path expressions

An XML document is a textual representation of data and consists of hier-archically nested element structure starting with a root element. In the DOM Data Model proposed by the W3C [XQuery 1.0 and XPath 2.0 Data Model. W3C Working Draft, 2002], an XML document is represented by an ordered node-labeled tree (or *instance*) that includes a concept of node identity. Similarly, the schema of an XML document can be described by a node-labeled tree, where multiplicity qualifiers (?, +, or ∗) are assigned with nodes.

We adopt an unordered tree model for XML schemas and instances, where the leaves can be element nodes with text values. We will use a simple path language for data tree navigation and we assume traversing only along the child (/) axis. Variables will be bound to individual nodes (node identifiers). The following categories of expressions are in our path language:

$root$	::=	@doc | $\$x$	*an absolute (@doc) or a relative ($x) root*
P	::=	l | $root/l$ | P/l	*a path ,*
G	::=	$\$x$ in P	*a range,*

where @doc identifies document schema tree and points to the (absolute) root of a document data tree being an instance of the schema; $\$x$ is a node variable and its value is referred to as a relative root; l is an XML node label (element tag); a path P is referred to as an absolute or a relative path depending on its starting node; G can be an absolute range (if P is an absolute path) or a relative range (if P is a relative path).

The type, $type(p)$, of a path expression p is defined as follows:

$type(p)$	=	$p,$	for a variable-free expression,
$type(\$x)$	=	$type(P),$	for $\$x$ defined in a range $\$x$ in P,
$type(\$x/P)$	=	$type(\$x)/P.$	

In Figure 1 there are five XML document schemas (written as schema trees) that will be used as a running example to illustrate schema mapping and query reformulation in a data integration scenario. Along with schemas, text values of leaf nodes are also given. It is quite obvious, how from this simplified presentation, proper XML document instances should be derived. E.g. @P3 has the instance given in Figure 2.

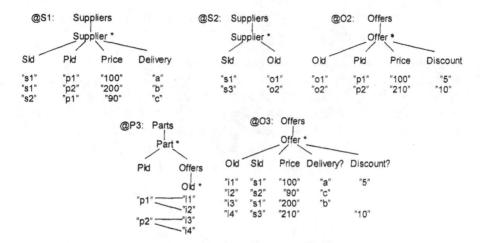

Figure 1. Schemas and leaf values of sample XML documents

```
@P3:
    <Parts>                              <Part>
        <Part>                               <PId>p2</PId>
            <PId>p1</PId>                     <Offers>
            <Offers>                             <OId>i3</OId>
                <OId>i1</OId>                     <OId>i4</OId>
                <OId>i2</OId>                 </Offers>
            </Offers>                        </Part>
        </Part>                          </Parts>
```

Figure 2. Instance of the document schema @P3 from Figure 1

All the documents represent information about suppliers and parts. Elements SId, PId, Price, Delivery, and Discount represent, respectively, supplier identifier, part identifier, price of a part being supplied, information about delivery time, and about discount. The attribute OId is used to link suppliers with their offers (in documents @S2 and @O2) or to link parts with offers concerning these parts (in documents @P3 and @O3).

Note that information in two sources, i.e. in (@S1), and in (@S2,@O2), may overlap. If an offer appears only in one source, then we can have incomplete information in the target (the lack of values for Delivery or Discount). In the rest of the paper instances of @P3 and @O3 will be treated as canonical virtual instances derived from real instances of @S1, @S2 and @O2. It means that these instances are not materialized. Further on it will be assumed that there are three peers, P_1, P_2, and P_3, in a P2P system. Peers P_1 and P_2 are *source peers* that store data with schemas, respectively, {@S1} and {@S2,@O2}. P_3 does not store any data but provides the schema {@P3,@O3}.

2.2   Schema mapping specification based on Skolem functions

The basic idea of our approach to schema mapping is shown in Figure 3. A source schema consists of two document schemas @S2 and @O2, and a target schema has also two document schemas @P3 and @O3 (see Figure 1). There are four mapping functions shown in Figure 3, the total number of functions is equal to the number of mapped nodes in the target schema trees, i.e. 13, 2 for root nodes (root nodes are not visible) and 11 for ordinary labeled nodes (the node Delivery will be not mapped for this source schema).

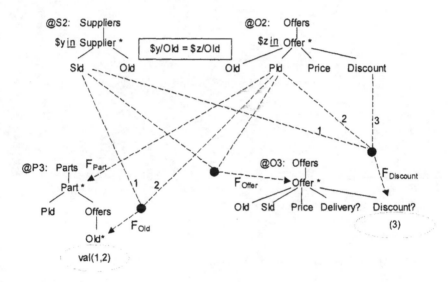

Figure 3.   Graphical illustration of schema mapping based on Skolem functions

Variables \$y and \$z are defined over the source schema, and their ranges are sets of nodes determined by @S2/Suppliers and @O2/Offers/Offer, respectively. A constraint can be imposed on variable values (in the box). We assume that there is a Skolem function for any node type from a target schema tree. The function generates instances of this node type, i.e. nodes of this type in a target data tree. In our approach, we are interested in arguments of the function and not in how the function works. It is only important that a Skolem function returns different nodes (node identifiers) for different arguments, and the same values for equal arguments. It means that the value is uniquely determined by the function name and the value of argument list. Moreover, if two functions have different names they will never return the same value [Abiteboul et al., 2000]. In our approach, if a list of arguments is not empty then every argument is the text value of a leaf node from a source data tree. This value is determined by a path expression specified over source schema tree. In Figure 3, we have:

- F_{Part}($z/PID) generates instances of @P3/Parts/Part,

- F_{OId}($y/SId,$z/PID) generates instances of @P3/Parts/Part/Offers/OId, and so on.

Additionally, if a target node is a leaf node we also specify the text value for it. The value is a text-valued function over arguments of the Skolem function generating this node. Arguments of a text-valued function will be denoted by indices of arguments in the argument list of the corresponding Skolem function. If the text-valued function is the identity function its name will be omitted. In Figure 3 specifications of text values for leaf nodes are depicted in ovals. If a Skolem function has more arguments then one, we index them by integers labeling appropriate edges in Figure 3.

The following definition lays out the notational convention used for specifying schema mappings.

DEFINITION 1 *A mapping between a source schema* **S** *and a target schema* **T** *is an expression conforming to the following syntax*

$\mathcal{M}_{\mathbf{S,T}}$ ::=
  foreach $f_1, ..., f_n$
  where Φ
  exists sk_1 **in** P_1 [**with** $val_1(idx\text{-}seq_1)$],
     ...,
     sk_m **in** P_m [**with** $val_m(idx\text{-}seq_m)$]

where f_i *is a range over* **S**, Φ *is a conjunction of atomic formulas,* sk_i *is a Skolem function expression over* **S**, P_i *is an absolute path in* **T**, val_i *is a text-valued function,* $idx\text{-}seq_i$ *is a sequence of indices of arguments of the Skolem function occurring in* sk_i *(applicable only if* P_i *leads to a leaf node).*

To explain our approach to schema mapping, we will use schemas from Figure 1. Let us assume the following notations:

S_1={@S1}, and S_2={@S2,@O2} – source schemas,
S_3={@P3,@O3} – target schema,
$I_1 = \{I^{@S1}\}$, and $I_2 = \{I^{@S2}, I^{@O2}\}$ – source instances,
$\mathcal{M}_{1,3}, \mathcal{M}_{2,3}$ – mappings from S_1 and S_2, respectively, to S_3.

Mappings $\mathcal{M}_{1,3}$ and $\mathcal{M}_{2,3}$ are specified in Figure 4 and Figure 5, respectively. The mappings specify how elements from source XML data relate to elements in the target.

According to these specifications, the root node @$P3$/ is obtained by invocation of the Skolem function $F_{P3}()$ (with the empty list of arguments). The unique node of type @P3/Parts is obtained by invocation of $F_{Parts}()$.

$\mathcal{M}_{1,3}$:

foreach \$x <u>in</u> @S1/Suppliers/Supplier
exists

$F_{P3}()$ **in** @P3/
$F_{Parts}()$ **in** @P3/Parts
$F_{Part}(\$x/PId)$ **in** @P3/Parts/Part
$F_{PId}(\$x/PId)$ **in** @P3/Parts/Part/PId **with** (1)
$F_{Offers}(\$x/PId)$ **in** @P3/Parts/Part/Offers
$F_{OId}(\$x/SId,\$x/PId)$ **in** @P3/Parts/Part/Offers/OId **with** val(1,2)
$F_{O3}()$ **in** @O3/
$F'_{Offers}()$ **in** @O3/Offers
$F_{Offer}(\$x/SId,\$x/PId)$ **in** @O3/Offers/Offer
$F'_{OId}(\$x/SId,\$x/PId)$ **in** @O3/Offers/Offer/OId **with** val(1,2)
$F_{SId}(\$x/SId,\$x/PId)$ **in** @O3/Offers/Offer/SId **with** (1)
$F_{Price}(\$x/SId,\$x/PId,\$x/Price)$ **in** @O3/Offers/Offer/Price **with** (3)
$F_{Delivery}(\$x/SId,\$x/PId,\$x/Delivery)$ **in** @O3/Offers/Offer/Delivery
        with (3)

Figure 4.   Mapping from source schema @S1 to target schema (@P3,@O3)

Note that in @S1/Suppliers/Supplier/PId there can be many nodes of type PId corresponding to the same real world *part*. In @P3, however, we want to have exactly one node of type PId for one *part*. Thus, we assign the Skolem function $F_{PId}(\$x/PId)$ with the path @P3/Parts/Part/PId. The function will return as many new nodes as many different values the expression $\$x/PId$ has. In this way we *merge* source nodes with the same *PId*. In general, in our approach criteria for merging are specified by appropriate construction of path expressions determining arguments of Skolem functions.

The mapping specification allows for partial specification, i.e. some target absolute path might not be constraint in a mapping from a source schema that does not have any corresponding information. For example, there is no node generating dependency for the path @O3/Offers/Offer/Discount in the mapping $\mathcal{M}_{1,3}$, because there is no Discount element in @S1. Similarly for @O3/Offers/Offer/Delivery in mapping $\mathcal{M}_{2,3}$. The advantage of these approach is that we can add, or remove the mapping constraints, when the source schema is changed [Yu and Popa, 2004].

A **with** clause specifies text value for an absolute path leading to a leaf node. The value is obtained from arguments of the Skolem function indicated by a sequence of integers written on the right hand side of the keyword **with**. If the sequence is $(k_1, ..., k_h)$ it means that the value is obtained by $value(E_{k_1}, ..., E_{k_h})$, where E_i is the *i-th* argument of a corresponding Skolem function, and $value()$ is a text-valued function. For $h = 1$ we assume that $value()$ is the identity function and its name will be omitted. For example: $F_{OId}(\$x/SId,\$x/PId)$ **in** @P3/Parts/Part/Offers/OId **with** $val(1,2)$

specifies that the text value of the path @O3/Offers/Offer/OId is equal to $val(\$x/SId, \$x/PId)$, so, it is determined by the first and the second arguments of the Skolem function F_{OId}.

Value constraints can impose equalities between some target values. For example (see Figure 5), values of nodes in

@P3/Parts/Part/Offers/OId, and in

@O3/Offers/Offer/OId

are determined by the expression $val(\$y/SId, \$z/PId)$. Thus, the value equality between leaf nodes from these two different paths is imposed. That allows for joining corresponding target elements.

$\mathcal{M}_{2,3}$:

foreach $y:@S2/Suppliers/Supplier
        $z:@O2/Offers/Offer
where
        $y/OId=$z/Oid
exists

   $F_{P3}()$ **in** @P3/
   $F_{Parts}()$ **in** @P3/Parts
   $F_{Part}(\$z/PId)$ **in** @P3/Parts/Part
   $F_{PId}(\$z/PId)$ **in** @P3/Parts/Part/PId **with** (1)
   $F_{Offers}(\$z/PId)$ **in** @P3/Parts/Part/Offers
   $F_{OId}(\$y/SId,\$z/PId)$ **in** @P3/Parts/Part/Offers/OId **with** val(1,2)
   $F_{O3}()$ **in** @O3/
   $F'_{Offers}()$ **in** @O3/Offers
   $F_{Offer}(\$y/SId,\$z/PId)$ **in** @O3/Offers/Offer
   $F'_{OId}(\$y/SId,\$z/PId)$ **in** @O3/Offers/Offer/OId **with** val(1,2)
   $F_{SId}(\$y/SId,\$z/PId)$ **in** @O3/Offers/Offer/SId **with** (1)
   $F_{Price}(\$y/SId,\$z/PId,\$z/Price)$ **in** @O3/Offers/Offer/Price **with** (3)
   $F_{Discount}(\$y/SId,\$z/PId,\$z/Discount)$ **in** @O3/Offers/Offer/Discount
        with (3)

Figure 5.   Mapping from source schema (@S2,@O2) to target schema (@P3,@O3)

3.   Rewriting rules

Rewriting rules determine how a target query (on a target schema **T**) should be translated into a source query (on a target schema **S**) taking into account a mapping between these source and target schemas. For our running example we have the following interpretation.

Let Q be a target query over $\mathbf{S}_3$. We want to find rewritings $\tau_{\mathcal{M}_{1,3}}$, and $\tau_{\mathcal{M}_{2,3}}$ such that: $\tau_{\mathcal{M}_{1,3}}(Q)$ is a source query over $\mathbf{S}_1$, $\tau_{\mathcal{M}_{2,3}}(Q)$ is a source query over $\mathbf{S}_2$, and for any instances I_1 and I_2 of schemas $\mathbf{S}_1$ and $\mathbf{S}_2$, respectively, the following equality holds:

$$Q(\mathcal{M}_{1,3}(I_1) \cup \mathcal{M}_{2,3}(I_2)) = \tau_{\mathcal{M}_{1,3}}(Q)(I_1) \cup \tau_{\mathcal{M}_{2,3}}(Q)(I_2),$$

where $\mathcal{M}(\mathrm{I})$ denotes the canonical target instance corresponding to I with respect to $\mathcal{M}$, and $\cup$ denotes an operation of merging two XML documents.

We will consider queries that have the following XQuery-like form [XQuery 1.0: An XML Query Language. W3C Working Draft, 2002]:

DEFINITION 2 *A query is an expression of the form*

$$q \quad ::= \quad <tag> \text{ for } f_1, ..., f_2$$
$$\text{where } w_1 \wedge ... \wedge w_m$$
$$\text{return } r</tag>$$

where each f_i is a range, the **where** *clause is a conjunction of atomic formulas, and* **return** *clause is an expression defined by the grammar* $r ::= <tag>r</tag> | e | e \ r | q$, *where* $e ::= <tag>\$x/P</tag>$, *and the path* $\$x/P$ *ends at a leaf node. Each variable occurring in q is defined either in a range f_i or in a superquery in which q is nested.*

In Figure 6 we define rewriting rules for reformulating a target query into a source query based on a mapping specification. A rewriting rule is a collection of *premises* and *conclusions*, written respectively above and below a dividing line. The premise part of a rule is a set of conditions which implies rewriting actions connected with the conclusion part.

There are three type of conditions: *target query conditions, mapping conditions*, and *variable mapping conditions* (by A we denote an absolute path).

1. *A target query condition* is an expression of one of the following forms $F_t : e$, $W_t : e$, or $R_t : e$, and asserts that e is an expression within, respectively, the **for, where**, or **return** part of the target query. The e expression is to be rewritten by a (sequence of) source query expression(s) defined in the conclusion of the rule.

2. *A mapping condition* is an expression of one of the following forms $\mathcal{M}^f : d, \mathcal{M}^w : d, \mathcal{M}^e : d$ or $\mathcal{M}^v : d$, and asserts that d is an expression occurring in the mapping specification under consideration. The expression d may be: a source range occurring in the **foreach** part of $\mathcal{M}$, a conjunction of atomic formulas occurring in the **where** part of $\mathcal{M}$, a node generating dependency $SF(...)$ in P, occurring in the **exists-in** part of $\mathcal{M}$ or a value dependency P with $val(...)$ occurring in the **exists-with** part of $\mathcal{M}$. The superscript of $\mathcal{M}$ denotes the kind of d.

3. *A variable mapping condition* is an expression of the form ω [$\$t \mapsto (\$s_1, ..., \$s_n)$], where $\$t$ is a target variable defined in the target query Q_t, and $\$s_1, ..., \$s_n$ are source variables invented for the source query Q_s. The premise is valid if the mapping [$\$t \mapsto (\$s_1, ..., \$s_n)$] has been defined in a conclusion part of a preceding rewriting rule.

$(R1)$
$$\frac{\begin{array}{l} F_t : \$t \underline{in} \ A \\ \mathcal{M}^e : SF(\$x_1/P_1, ..., \$x_n/P_n) \text{ in } A \\ \mathcal{M}^f : \$x_1 \underline{in} \ A_1, ..., \$x_n \underline{in} \ A_n \\ \mathcal{M}^w : \Phi_{\$x_1,...,\$x_n} \end{array}}{\begin{array}{l} \omega : [\$t \mapsto (\$s_1, ..., \$s_n)] \\ F_s : \mathcal{M}^f[\$x_1 \to \$s_1, ..., \$x_n \to \$s_n] \\ W_s : \mathcal{M}^w[\$x_1 \to \$s_1, ..., \$x_n \to \$s_n] \end{array}}$$

$(R2)$
$$\frac{\begin{array}{l} F_t : \$t \underline{in} \ \$t'/P \\ \mathcal{M}^e : SF_1(\$x_1/P_1, ..., \$x_n/P_n) \text{ in } type(\$t) \\ \mathcal{M}^e : SF_2(\$x_1/P_1, ..., \$x_{n-k}/P_{n-k}) \text{ in } type(\$t') \\ \mathcal{M}^f : \$x_1 \underline{in} \ A_1, ..., \$x_n \underline{in} \ A_n \\ \mathcal{M}^w : \Phi_{\$x_1,...,\$x_n} \\ \omega : [\$t' \mapsto (\$s'_1, ..., \$s'_{n-k})] \end{array}}{\begin{array}{l} \omega : [\$t \mapsto (\$s_1, ..., \$s_n)] \\ F_s : \mathcal{M}^f[\$x_1 \to \$s_1, ..., \$x_n \to \$s_n] \\ W_s : \mathcal{M}^w[\$x_1 \to \$s_1, ..., \$x_n \to \$s_n] \wedge \\ \quad \wedge \ \$s_1/P_1 = \$s'_1/P_1 \wedge \ ... \ \wedge \ \$s_{n-k}/P_{n-k} = \$s'_{n-k}/P_{n-k} \end{array}}$$

$(R3)$
$$\frac{W_t : \$t_1/P_1 = \$t_2/P_2}{\begin{array}{l} F_s : R5(\$t_1/P_1).F; \ F_s : R5(\$t_2/P_2).F \\ W_s : R5(\$t_1/P_1).W \wedge R5(\$t_2/P_2).W \\ W_s : R5(\$t_1/P_1).R = R5(\$t_2/P_2).R \end{array}}$$

$(R4)$
$$\frac{\begin{array}{l} R_t : \$t/P \\ \mathcal{M}^e : SF(\$x_1/P_1, ..., \$x_n/P_n) \text{ in } type(\$t/P) \\ \mathcal{M}^v : type(\$t/P) \text{ with } value(k_1, ..., k_h) \end{array}}{\begin{array}{l} F_s : R5(\$t/P).F \\ W_s : R5(\$t/P).W \\ R_s : value((R5(\$t/P).R)[k_1, ..., k_h]) \end{array}}$$

$(R5)$
$$\frac{\begin{array}{l} Val : \$t/P \\ \mathcal{M}^e : SF_1(\$x_1/P_1, ..., \$x_n/P_n) \text{ in } type(\$t/P) \\ \mathcal{M}^e : SF_2(\$x_1/P_1, ..., \$x_{n-k}/P_{n-k}) \text{ in } type(\$t) \\ \mathcal{M}^f : \$x_1 \underline{in} \ A_1, ..., \$x_n \underline{in} \ A_n \\ \mathcal{M}^w : \Phi_{\$x_1,...,\$x_n} \\ \omega : [\$t \mapsto (\$s_1, ..., \$s_{n-k})] \end{array}}{\begin{array}{l} F : \$s'_{n-k+1} \underline{in} \ A_{n-k+1}, ..., \$s'_n \underline{in} \ A_n \\ W : \mathcal{M}^w[\$x_1 \to \$s_1, ..., \$x_{n-k} \to \$s_{n-k}, \\ \quad \$x_{n-k+1} \to \$s'_{n-k+1}, ..., \$x_n \to \$s'_n] \\ R : (\$s_1/P_1, ..., \$s_{n-k}/P_{n-k}, \$s'_{n-k+1}/P_{n-k+1}, ..., \$s'_n/P_n) \end{array}}$$

Figure 6. Rewriting rules for query reformulation

The conclusion part of a rule consists of a variable mapping and a set of source query elements that are of the form $F_s : e_f$, $W_s : e_w$, or $R_s : e_r$, and represent the **for**, **where**, or **return** parts of a source query, respectively.

4.   Example of rewriting

Now, we will show how rewriting rules from Figure 6 can be used to reformulate a target query. The query Q from Figure 7 is a target query over target schema (@P3,@O3). Some steps of reformulating Q according to schema mapping $\mathcal{M}_{1,3}$ using rewriting rules (R1)-(R4) and the auxiliary rule (R5), are given in Figure 10. The result of rewriting is the query in Figure 9.

Q :
```
<Result>
    for $p in @P3/Parts/Part
        $s in $p/Offers
        $o in @O3/Offers/Offer
    where  $s/OId = $o/OId
    return
    <Part>
        <PartId>$p/PId</PartId>
        <Supplier>$o/SId</Supplier>
        <Price>$o/Price</Price>
        <Discount>$o/Discount</Discount>
    </Part>
</Result>
```

Figure 7.   Example of a target query

In Figure 8 we show three kinds of data integration scenarios that can be realized within our approach to P2P data sharing systems.

We assume that P_3 provides a schema S_3. There are two other peers, P_1 and P_2, that store local data with schemas S_1 and S_2, respectively. We also assume that there are schema mappings $\mathcal{M}_{1,3}$, $\mathcal{M}_{2,3}$ and $\mathcal{M}_{1,2}$ globally available to all peers.

When P_3 receives a query Q formulated over its schema (a target query) then the following situations may occur [Tatarinov and Halevy, 2004]:

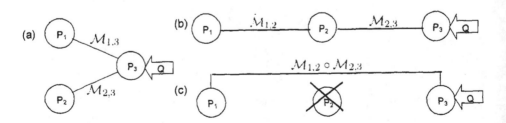

Figure 8.   Three scenarios of data integration in P2P -system

(a) P_3 starts from the querying its own data (if it stores any) and reformulates Q over its immediate neighbors, Figure 8(a). This reformulation can be performed using available schema mappings. In our case $\mathcal{M}_{1,3}$ and $\mathcal{M}_{2,3}$ are used to obtain Q' (a source query over P_1) and Q'' (a source query over P_2). The reformulation processes for Q with respect to mapping $\mathcal{M}_{1,3}$ is illustrated in Figure 10.

(b) P_3 reformulates Q over some neighbor peers (P_2 in our case). Each such a peer can also play the role of mediator and reformulates obtained query Q' over its neighbor peers (P_1 in our case), and so on, until all the relevant data sources are reached, Figure 8(b). In this way the initial query Q is reformulated across all peers participating in the data sharing system, and answers are in turn merged and sent back to the starting peer.

(c) It may happen that instead of successive reformulation we have to perform reformulation based on a composition of mappings, as was illustrated in Figure 8(c), where peer P_2 is not available. Composing schema mappings is a new challenging problem formulated recently in [Fagin et al., 2004; Madhavan and Halevy, 2003]: given a schema mapping $\mathcal{M}_{1,2}$ from schema $\mathbf{S}_1$ to schema $\mathbf{S}_2$, and a schema mapping $\mathcal{M}_{2,3}$ from schema $\mathbf{S}_2$ to schema $\mathbf{S}_3$, derive a schema mapping $\mathcal{M}_{1,3}$ from schema $\mathbf{S}_1$ to schema $\mathbf{S}_3$ that is "equivalent" to the successive application of $\mathcal{M}_{2,3}$ and $\mathcal{M}_{1,2}$, i.e. $\mathcal{M}_{1,3} = \mathcal{M}_{1,2} \circ \mathcal{M}_{2,3}$. (Schema composition is not addressed in this paper.)

Q' :
```
<Result>
    for $p' in @S1/Suppliers/Supplier
        $s' in @S1/Suppliers/Supplier,
        $o' in @S1/Suppliers/Supplier
    where  $p'/PId = $s'/PId and $s'/OId = $o'/OId and $s'/SId = $o'/SId
    return
    <Part>
        <PartId>$p'/PId</PartId>
        <Supplier>$o'/SId</Supplier>
        <Price>$o'/Price</Price>
    </Part>
</Result>
```

Figure 9.   Reformulated query Q with respect to mapping $\mathcal{M}_{1,3}$

$$
(R1\text{--}1) \quad \frac{\begin{array}{l} F_t : \$p \ \underline{in} \ @P3/Parts/Part \\ \mathcal{M}^e : F_{Part}(\$x/\texttt{PId}) \ \text{in} \ @P3/Parts/Part \\ \mathcal{M}^f : \$x \ \underline{in} \ @S1/Suppliers/Supplier \end{array}}{\omega : [\$p \mapsto \$p']; \ F_s : \$p' \ \underline{in} \ @S1/Suppliers/Supplier}
$$

$$
(R2\text{--}2) \quad \frac{\begin{array}{l} F_t : \$s \ \underline{in} \ \$p/Offers \\ \mathcal{M}^e : F_{Offers}(\$x/\texttt{PId}) \ \text{in} \ @P3/Parts/Part/Offers \\ \mathcal{M}^e : F_{Part}(\$x/\texttt{PId}) \ \text{in} \ @P3/Parts/Part \\ \mathcal{M}^f : \$x \ \underline{in} \ @S1/Suppliers/Supplier; \ \omega : [\$p \mapsto \$p'] \end{array}}{\begin{array}{l} \omega : [\$s \mapsto \$s']; \ F_s : \$s' \ \underline{in} \ @S1/Suppliers/Supplier \\ W_s : \$p'/PId = \$s'/PId \end{array}}
$$

$$
(R1\text{--}3) \quad \frac{\begin{array}{l} F_t : \$o \ \underline{in} \ @O3/Offers/Offer \\ \mathcal{M}^e : F_{Offer}(\$x/\texttt{SId}, \$x/\texttt{PId}) \ \text{in} \ @O3/Offers/Offer \\ \mathcal{M}^f : \$x \ \underline{in} \ @S1/Suppliers/Supplier \end{array}}{\omega : [\$o \mapsto \$o']; \ F_s : \$o' \ \underline{in} \ @S1/Suppliers/Supplier}
$$

$$
(R3\text{--}4) \quad \frac{W_t : \$s/OId = \$o/OId}{W_s : \$s'/PId = \$o'/PId \wedge \$s'/SId = \$o'/SId}
$$

$$
(R5\text{--}4) \quad \frac{\begin{array}{l} Val : \$s/OId \\ \mathcal{M}^e : F_{OId}(\$x/\texttt{SId}, \$x/\texttt{PId}) \ \text{in} \ @P3/Parts/Part/Offers/OId \\ \mathcal{M}^e : F_{Offers}(\$x/\texttt{PId}) \ \text{in} \ @P3/Parts/Part/Offers \\ \mathcal{M}^f : \$x \ \underline{in} \ @S1/Suppliers/Supplier; \ \omega : [\$s \mapsto \$s'] \end{array}}{R : (\$s'/SId, \$s'/PId)}
$$

$$
(R4\text{--}5) \quad \frac{\begin{array}{l} R_t : \$p/PId \\ \mathcal{M}^e : F_{PId}(\$x/\texttt{PId}) \ \text{in} \ @P3/Parts/Part/PId \\ \mathcal{M}^v : @P3/Parts/Part/PId = (1) \end{array}}{R_s : \$p'/PId}
$$

Figure 10. Reformulation of query Q using mapping $\mathcal{M}_{1,3}$ and rewriting rules from Figure 6

5. Conclusion

This paper presents a novel approach to XML query reformulation based on Skolem functions and its application to data integration and data sharing in the context of P2P e-commerce systems. We propose a new method for schema mapping specification between heterogeneous data sources and rewriting rules for query reformulation in an environment of cooperating peers. Such advanced data management features provide a new facility in the field of integration, interchange and transformation of data across global marketplace. The described method is a part of our work on data integration [Pankowski and Hunt, 2005] and transformation of heterogeneous data sources [Pankowski, 2004]. Current work is devoted to evaluate algorithms in real word scenarios.

References

Abiteboul, S., Buneman, P., and Suciu, D. (2000). *Data on the Web. From Relational to Semistructured Data and XML*. Morgan Kaufmann, San Francisco.

Bernstein, P. A., Giunchiglia, F., Kementsietsidis, A., Mylopoulos, J., Serafini, L., and Zaihrayeu, I. (2002). Data management for peer-to-peer computing: A vision. In *Proc. of the 5th International Workshop on the Web and Databases (WebDB 2002)*, pages 1–6.

Calvanese, D., Giacomo, G. D., Lenzerini, M., and Rosati, R. (2004). Logical Foundations of Peer-To-Peer Data Integration. In *Proc. of the 23rd ACM SIGMOD Symposium on Principles of Database Systems (PODS 2004)*, pages 241–251.

Fagin, R., Popa, L., Kolaitis, P., and Tan, W.-C. (2004). Composing schema mappings: Second-order dependencies to the rescue. In *Proc. of the 23th ACM SIGMOD Symposium on Principles of Database Systems (PODS 2004)*, pages 83–94.

Halevy, A. Y. (2001). Answering queries using views: A survey. *VLDB Journal*, 10(4):270–294.

Lenzerini, M. (2002). Data integration: a theoretical perspective. In *Proc. of the 21th ACM SIGMOD Symposium on Principles of Database Systems (PODS 2002)*, pages 233–246.

Madhavan, J. and Halevy, A. Y. (2003). Composing mappings among data sources. In *Proc. of the 29th International Conference on Very Large Data Bases, VLDB 2003, Berlin, Germany*, pages 572–583.

Miller, R. J., Haas, L. M., and Hernandez:, M. A. (2000). Schema mapping as query discovery. In *Proc. of the 26th International Conference on Very Large Data Bases, VLDB 2000, Cairo, Egypt*, pages 77–88.

Pankowski, T. (2004). A High-Level Language for Specifying XML Data Transformations, In: Advances in Databases and Information Systems, ADBIS 2004. *Lecture Notes in Computer Science*, 3255:159–172.

Pankowski, T. (2005). Specifying Schema Mappings for Query Reformulation in Data Integration Systems. In *Proc. of the 3-rd Atlantic Web Intelligence Conference - AWIC'2005*, Lecture Notes in Artificial Intelligence 3528, Springer-Verlag, pages 361–365.

Pankowski, T. and Hunt, E. (2005). Data merging in life science data integration systems. In *Intelligent Information Systems, New Trends in Intelligent Information Processing and Web Mining*. Advances in Soft Computing, Springer Verlag, pages 279–288.

Popa, L., Velegrakis, Y., Miller, R. J., Hernandez, M. A., and Fagin, R. (2002). Translating web data. In *Proc. of the 28th International Conference on Very Large Data Bases, VLDB 2002, Hong Kong, China*, pages 598–609.

Quix, C., Schoop, M., and Jeusfeld, M. A. (2002). Business Data Management for B2B Electronic Commerce. *SIGMOD Record*, 31(1):49–54.

Rahm, E. and Bernstein, P. A. (2001). A survey of approaches to automatic schema matching. *The VLDB Journal*, 10(4):334–350.

Sheth, A. P. and Larson, J. A. (1990). Federated database systems for managing distributed, heterogeneous, and autonomous databases. *ACM Computing Surveys*, 22(3):183–236.

Tatarinov, I. and Halevy, A. (2004). Efficient query reformulation in peer data management systems. In *Proc. of the 2004 ACM SIGMOD International Conference on Management of Data*, pages 539–550.

Ullman, J. D. (1997). Information integration using logical views. in: Database Theory - ICDT 1997. *Lecture Notes in Computer Science*, 1186:19–40.

XQuery 1.0: An XML Query Language. W3C Working Draft (2002). www.w3.org/TR/ xquery.

XQuery 1.0 and XPath 2.0 Data Model. W3C Working Draft (2002). www.w3.org/TR/ query-datamodel.

Yu, C. and Popa, L. (2004). Constraint-based XML query rewriting for data integration. In *Proc. of the 2004 ACM SIGMOD Conference*, pages 371–382.

USING ebXML FOR SUPPLY CHAIN TRACEABILITY
Pitfalls, solutions and experiences

A. Bechini, M.G.C.A. Cimino, A. Tomasi
Dipartimento di Ingegneria dell'Informazione: Elettronica, Informatica, Telecomunicazioni. University of Pisa, Via Diotisalvi 2, 56122 Pisa (Italy). Fax: +39 050 2217600; tel: +39 050 2217599; e-mail: {a.bechini, m.cimino, a.tomasi}@iet.unipi.it

Abstract: In this paper, we analyze the main issues of traceability along the supply chain: architectural solutions, business process interaction, lot identification, traceability information management, and communication standards. In particular, the employment in this setting of two different standards for inter-enterprise business collaboration (as ebXML and Web Services) is discussed. Moreover, different standards for lot identification and data capture, as EPC for RFID and EAN/UCC for bar code are taken into account, uncovering their potential contributions in reducing the cost of procedures for tracking goods. The Cerere project experience is finally reported: it is shown that the architecture of a Web Information System framework (developed to assess food supply requirements) witnesses the actual possibility to support process integration and semantic interoperability via XML-based technologies.

Key words: Traceability, Information Systems, Web Services, ebXML.

1.   INTRODUCTION

Traceability may be defined in general as the "ability to trace and follow any product through all stages of production, processing and distribution"[1]. Traceability systems are constituted by three basic elements[2]: i) univocal identification of units/batches (denoted as *lots* in the following) of every product components, ii) information collection about time and location for every lot transfer/transformation, and iii) a method to relate this kind of data. In practice, traceability systems are record-keeping procedures that store information about and show the path of a particular product/component from the supplier(s) into the business, throughout all the intermediate steps (which process and combine components into new products) and all through the supply chain to the end consumers.

Therefore, both products and processes form key components in a traceability system, which is in charge of storing information about them. Information representation and data flows may be dissimilar in distinct actual traceability systems, depending on the particular functional specifications coming from legal requirements, certification needs for the target system, incidents prevention policies or practices for quality improvement. The availability of existing information systems along the supply chain stages have to be taken into account, both in the definition of the data model and in the implementation of the message interactions, as well as in the choice of the communication structure and protocols.

The traceability information flow can follow the product flow along the supply chain, embedded in it, or can be passed through data repositories of any kind, external to the supply chain. The traceability information flow can be directly linked to the product flow by leveraging a proper lot identification mechanism. The more straightforward form of identification is based on the assignment of a numeric or alphanumeric string to every lot. Such a string actually gives no information about the lot, but it is intended to provide a univocal key to retrieve traceability data stored elsewhere. To guarantee the uniqueness of this string, standard systems have been introduced, as will be discussed in sect. 3.

Once the lot identification has been performed in some way, the retrieval of information crucial to traceability asks for established standards for the elicitation, representation, and storage of the required data. Considering that a large number of companies along a target supply chain might hold their own information systems, possibly containing data relevant to traceability as well, the crucial role played by communication and information exchange facilities becomes particularly evident: in this setting, the communication infrastructure is thus required to overcome the heterogeneity of the involved information systems. Technologies for XML-based business interchanges[2,4] can serve as the framework for defining new process cooperation paradigms. Among such paradigms, ebXML[5,6,7] enables enterprises to conduct business over the Internet in more straightforward and efficient ways. The ebXML modular suite of specifications provides organizations with a common, automated method of exchanging business messages, conducting trading relationships, communicating data using common terms, and defining and registering business processes — such as ordering, shipping, and invoicing[8]. The ebXML Message Service (ebMS) defines the message enveloping and header document schema used to transfer ebXML messages over a communication protocol such as HTTP or SMTP, and the behavior of software sending and receiving ebXML messages. The use of ebXML-related solutions can be evaluated by comparison with other technological approaches, i.e. based on the Web Services stack, facing with integration and interoperability requirements. A discussion on these topics is presented in sect. 3 and sect. 4.

Article 3 of the EU General Food Regulation (178/2002), which is in appliance since 1 January 2005, forces traceability concerns to the food supply[1]. A generic supply chain technical disciplinary have to accurately set the rules for each certified food supply chain, with regard to material flow, production process management and execution, document flow and business process collaboration through partners agreement, and responsibility assumptions. Traceability requirements are stated as well as quality and safety goals.

Nevertheless, a preliminary analysis of existing traceability systems reveals some open problems[9,10]. For instance, typically only a few stages of a supply chain are supported by a traceability information system, and in many cases no kind of information system is used at all. Whenever present, often the information system is a legacy one, hampering both integration and interoperability. Answering to many of the above-mentioned issues, the main goal of the project named *Cerere* at the University of Pisa is the development of a robust and efficient traceability framework, implementing a Web Information System applied to the food supply. The overall architecture of the underlying data repositories is discussed in the next section, and the Cerere Traceability WIS is briefly depicted in sect. 5.

2. TRACEABILITY INFORMATION MANAGEMENT ON THE SUPPLY CHAIN

An abstraction of traceability information systems can envision a massive, centralized database capturing in a single location all the information about each lot at each stage of the supply chain. The logical view of a lot contains attributes for each feature of every product and its components, as well as details of the processing phases. Any actual traceability system adopting a centralized solution can be regarded as an implementation of the so-called *push* model[11]. According to this paradigm, as soon as each actor in the supply chain collects traceability data, it pushes these data into the centralized traceability database; each single data recording that is relevant to traceability is completely transferred from the actor to the central database. However, the implementation of a centralized traceability database is neither realistic nor efficient in most actual settings.

In fact, we should keep logically separated the traceability information (related to product transformations and flows on the chain) and other kinds of product characteristics (either constant or variable over time): while the former can be managed through a centralized system, the latter are suitable to be stored just once at the source site. Moreover, the involved data repositories can be proficiently associated with different stages or with external data trustees, thus obtaining a physically distributed architecture encompassing different nodes, each of them possibly addressing local specific implementation problems.

Indeed, food supply chain is characterized by a number of peculiarities that can be summarized as follows[12]:

i) Heterogeneous Structure and Naming of Data. For several years, important agricultural communities have wrestled with the task of identifying the relevant information to be captured and stored in an agricultural database for a given product, and developing a standard naming convention for each data element in that database. Producers have failed in building consensus for any single standard for any single commodity, and there is no reason to believe that consensus will ever be reached.

ii) Confidentiality and Control of Data. Food chain participants, at all segments of production, are often highly protective of their own data, thus they would not agree on sharing their company's data. The industry is concerned that a centralized database would create issues of data confidentiality and trade disruption. Ownership, movement, and location data, might be used for purpose other than the goal of traceability. Further, there are potential data integrity issues.

Given the obvious benefits from value traceability for increasing corporate profitability, the implementation of a logically centralized database should consider possible alternatives. The architectural solution that is achieving widespread consensus accounts for the distribution of traceability information among different robust databases along the supply chain, and allow for a connectivity backbone between such databases. Actually, the system is not required to operate with constant connectivity. Data may be held locally either within the management system of each actor of the supply chain or associated with the lot itself. When connectivity is achieved at a key point of the chain, the cache of information on the lot is updated. Thus, different actors can use different structure and naming of data and agree on a common vocabulary only when interaction is required. Further, each actor is responsible for confidentiality of its data and will provide the other actors with only the information concerning the traceability. Typically, the distributed architecture uses intermediate data trustee. A data trustee is a private, third party intermediary between the responsibility actors each to other and with other entities: companies, government, individuals, or associated consumers. Each actor transfers its location and ownership data to a data trustee. The data trustee acts like an escrow agent, holding the actor's data until a legitimate product health investigation need would be established.

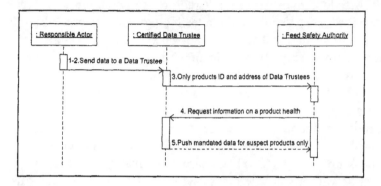

Figure 1. "Pull" model: in this paradigm, the actor is expected to send all the required data towards a certified data trustee.

Figure 1 introduces the "pull" model by means of an UML sequence diagram, where the data flow is handled in a five-step process. First, the actor inputs data into its private software system normally used to manage the operation. Second, this software system is linked to a data trustee chosen by the actor. Obviously the two initial phases can be accomplished manually if there is not an information system. Third, mandated data (no commercial or production data) are pushed to the data trustee, who exposes only the product's identification number to external databases. No other ownership, location or movement information is sent at this point. Fourth, authorized users or government officials request information on the food, as in the case of detecting a consumer's health incident. Fifth, the data trustee publishes to the requester the mandated data for suspect food only.

We anticipate that there would be multiple data trustees, and these trustees would be certified and audited by the government or the government's appointed agency, such as a trade association of a certain class of food product. Actors are free to choose which data trustees they wish to collect and store their data. Larger actors might even choose to apply for certification as a data trustee similar to the self-insurance approach many large corporations use for risk management.

In the "pull" architecture, there can be still a single, central database. However, this database would store only the identifiers of the product and of the data trustees where the location, ownership, and movement of the product were stored. Information on a product might be stored at more than one data trustee. The identifier can allow to know where the data on each product were stored, thus safeguarding business information. Of course, the system could be checked to determine that each data trustee is performing its obligations.

This "pull" architecture has proved to be effective in other fields such as the global credit card organization. Credit card transactions can occur within a matter of seconds even though the technology must seamlessly link a large number of separate databases. This is also the architecture used in the Brazilian national animal identification program, which covers a national herd roughly twice the size of that in the United States[13].

A "pull" database strategy can also equally meet or exceed the trace-back standard and address the privacy and data mining concerns raised above. Some producers and processors may still opt to "push" their data in a global public database, e.g. for enhancing the value of their products by information about the source origin, or about particular quality features, or about the identification with a valuable brand. However, the use of a data trustee will provide an alternative, helping actors protect the confidentiality of their data, protect the integrity of their existing trading relationships, and increase data integrity within the system.

3. BUSINESS PROCESS INTEGRATION INFRASTRUCTURE

Retailers are not going to be willing to have interconnections with a huge number of disparate traceability systems. A fast food outlet, for example, would not like to use a separate system for their meat, their baked goods, their dairy products, their lettuce, their tomatoes, their catsup, and so forth. They would prefer to access a single system able to provide all the necessary information.

The best solution is to build independent, private data sharing networks that are very loosely interconnected. A private data sharing network[12] begins with one sponsoring company at any segment of production, and proceeds linking to individual supplier and customer companies, inter-connecting with each to expand the initial network.

Typically, private data sharing networks focus on a certain class of food product. In an ideal future, there would be many such private data sharing networks for each commodity. Once built, each independent, private data sharing network could operate autonomously and also be loosely linked with other such independent networks via technology that makes the system appear a single to a downstream customer without exposing the data from one independent system to another.

To raise the optimal way for designing a given independent private data-sharing network, first of all one must avoid point-to-point connections. A strong temptation is to begin from connecting one application to another using standard application program interfaces (API's), XML data structures and SOAP (Simple Object Access Protocol). However, this road leads to significant problems. When there are only two applications to be connected, there is only one interface that needs to be built, but as number of participants increases to n, all the n would need to write software interfaces with each other so that leading to a total of n x n interfaces. The problem gets even worse if at each segment of production there is more than one pre-existing application program that will need to be interconnected (e.g., procurement system and separate manufacturing system). The bottom line is that the point-to-point method of connection just is not sustainable.

This instability becomes even more apparent when one of the participating applications changes. A single change in the application requires that all point-to-point interfaces from that application be changed. The cost of maintaining such a system is staggering.

A much better approach is to connect each connection of third-party applications in a private data-sharing network to an Enterprise Service Bus (ESB), an integration middleware, standards-based, service-oriented backbone capable of connecting hundreds of application endpoints. ESBs combine messaging, Web services, XML, data transformation and management to reliably connect and coordinate application interaction. In our scenario, ESB would translate data from one third-party system (say a producer system) to an internal "data bus" format, and then retranslate this information to another third-party system, such as the first stage processor's system. The "data bus" approach requires developing only an interface between each third-party application and the "data bus", thus reducing the complexity of the integration. Further, the infrastructure is more resilient to application and business changes.

Theoretically, each company publishing its data in a common language (e.g., XML) using the same data tag names would accomplish the task of building a private data sharing network. However, such an approach would still result in some serious problems. The first problem is that each participant in the chain has to agree on the naming convention for each data element in the XML structure. And when the supply chain crosses national boundaries, the introduction of a different language adds even more complexity. These observations suggest that the ESB has to take naming translation into charge, mapping one data element from one application system to another. Thus, each application program can use its own terminology for each data element. Figure 2 shows the generic functional components of an Enterprise Service Bus using a UML notation. Here, a

Responsible Actor, a Feed Safety Authority, or a Data Trustee interacts each other with own private interface (the lollypop symbols in the Figure) through the ESB. The Messaging Oriented Middleware (MOM) facilities provide a software infrastructure to support an asynchronous interchange of information. The ESB also offers integration with the broad spectrum of components likely to be encountered through the use of various 'standard' binding approaches such as Web Services, J2EE Connector Architecture, JMS, COM, and other common mechanisms. This integration is dealt with by the ESB in a standard, service-oriented way, independent of the particular binding technologies. The ESB also offers a level of transformation capabilities and XML services to address the problem of differing data format requirements in the heterogeneous components, and intelligent routing facilities to govern the flow between components.

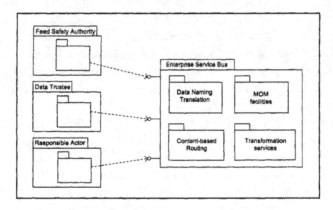

Figure 2. Generic functional components of an Enterprise Service Bus for traceability purposes.

To make traceability effective often means managing a lot of information on each product reference, each production batch, each stock movement, each shipment, etc. We underline that traceability is a tool intended for follow the path of a specified physical unit of goods. Thus labeling and automatic identification are often a bottleneck within a company, as well as between partners in supply chains. The strong separation between product information (e.g. related to quality features) and traceability information (identifiers and links between them) brings along many advantages. Actually it enables a better management of a traceability system as a more separated subsystem with respect to the individual Information Systems of each responsible actor.

Linking together the two information flows implies the use of a unique identifier for the lot. The simplest form of identification consists in a numeric or alphanumeric string. The string gives no information about the lot, but provides a univocal key to retrieve traceability data stored elsewhere. To guarantee the uniqueness of this string, standard systems have been introduced. The most promising is certainly the EAN/UCC system[14,15]. By administering the assignment of company prefixes and coordinating the accompanying standards, EAN/UCC maintains the most robust lot identification system in the world. As regards traceability, the numbering structures of immediate interest are the Global Trade Item Number, which identifies uniquely each commercial unit, the Serial Shipping Container Code which identifies uniquely a logistic unit (dispatch unit), the Global Location Number which identifies any legal, functional or physical location within a business or organizational entity[16]. More complex form of identification can however be realized, by introducing descriptions of the key features of the item[17]. Another emerging numbering standard is the Electronic Product Code (EPC), under development by the UCC too[18]. It is a scheme for universally identifying physical objects via RFID tags and other means. The EPC Identifier is a meta-coding scheme designed to support the needs of various industries by accommodating both existing coding schemes where possible and defining new schemes where necessary.

The most used technologies for automatic identification are certainly the one-dimensional and two-dimensional (or matrix) barcodes, and the radio frequency identification (RFID). Unlike the one-dimensional barcodes, which have a very limited storing capacity, the matrix barcode can encode more than a kilobyte of data. The achievement of this performance, however, requires a very high print quality and consequently expensive printers. RFID identifiers (tags) consist of a chip, which can be attached onto or implanted into any surface of an item[19,20,21]. Apposite devices can read data from and possibly write data into the tags. RFID tags can be passive, i.e., are powered by a remote energy source, or active, i.e., contain their own energy source. Active tags have greater storage capacity and greater read range than passive tags[22]. On the other hand, they are physically larger and more expensive than passive tags. Further, their life depends on the duration of the energy source (approximately 6-10 years). As regards food traceability, RFID technology appears to be very promising, because it allows to store incremental information during the processing steps, but it is currently unsatisfactory, especially for cost and read range[23,24,25]. Unlike barcodes technology, for instance, RFID allows acquiring information from several (up to 1000) tags concurrently.

4.   BUSINESS PROCESS INTEROPERABILILITY

An important standard for business-to-business communication has been used for almost a quarter of a century, Electronic Data Interchange (EDI). EDI has been applied as a fast and reliable means of achieving electronic, computer-to-computer exchange of information between trading partners[26]. Though EDI techniques work well, they are difficult and expensive to implement. Therefore, use of these techniques has been normally limited to large enterprises possessing mature information technology capabilities. The proliferation of XML-based business interchanges[2,4] has served as the catalyst for defining a new global paradigm that ensured all business activities, regardless of size, could engage in electronic business activities. Such paradigm, denoted electronic business eXtensible Markup Language (ebXML) is an international initiative established by the United Nations Centre for Trade Facilitation and Electronic Business (UN/CEFACT)[8] and the Organization for the Advancement of Structured Information Standards (OASIS)[27].

Technically speaking, two enterprises willing to do business with each other need to agree on ways how to invoke business services or business processes on a business partner's system and how to exchange data. Obviously, both business partners need to have a common understanding of protocols and formats, as well as message content.

Of course, inter-enterprise business collaboration must take potential failure into account. For example, company A sends a message to company B, which is received. Then, however, due to a communication problem, company B cannot send a response back to company A, which leaves company A in the dark about whether the message got through or not. If company A sends the message again, it may receive two shipments. Potential failure conditions are numerous. Now, the question is if and to what extent Web services and ebXML meet the requirements that result from business collaboration characteristics and business service types. Roughly speaking, Web services are request/response with no business process semantics. This is in keeping with the three specifications that enjoy broad acceptance in the vendor community: SOAP, WSDL, and UDDI. Figure 3 shows the stack of technologies. In addition, there is BPEL, a language specification introduced in May 2003. It aims to describe how to coordinate Web Services within a process flow.

In inter-enterprise scenarios, a requester would invoke a remote service. Technically speaking, this is no issue and has already been proven to work in many cases. However, the question is how to cope with potential failure conditions: there is no way to discover a Web service implementation unavailability or modification before service invocation. Also, WSDL and

SOAP provide for technical interoperability but not for semantic interoperability[28]. Web services technology is about loose coupling in the technical sense. However, it is tight coupling in a conceptual sense. The use of a Web service does not require an agreement between requester and provider.

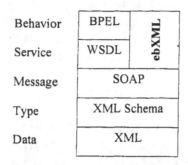

Behavior	BPEL	ebXML
Service	WSDL	
Message	SOAP	
Type	XML Schema	
Data	XML	

Figure 3. Web Services and ebXML standards.

ebXML represents a set of modular business collaboration-oriented specifications. Business collaboration requires a solid and consistent conceptual foundation, encompassing the concept of inter-enterprise business collaboration based on mutually accepted trading partner agreements, as well as the concept of a technical infrastructure which enables businesses to find each other and provides for the reliable and secure exchange of business messages between collaborating business partners. Of course, business partners can also be represented by functional units within the enterprise. Like Web services technology, ebXML provides technical interoperability through a vendor-neutral protocol. ebXML uses Collaboration Protocol Agreements (CPAs) to declare bindings to business collaboration specifications. ebXML requires collaborating partners to mutually agree upon the formats and semantics of business documents, which are XML-encoded. However, it is not an actual constraint to only allow XML-encoded messages within ebXML, which would even leave room for transmitting EDI messages. In an inter-enterprise business collaboration scenario, both business partners would use the ebXML Message Service (ebMS) to securely and reliably transport business documents. The ebMS is defined as a set of layered extensions to the base Simple Object Access Protocol (SOAP) and SOAP Messages with Attachments (SOAPAttach) specifications[29], defined by the W3C organization[30].

However, the ebMS just represents the message envelope. It requires an additional content standard to define the semantics of a business document (which represents the content of the envelope, i.e. the message payload). As there are several horizontal and vertical content standards in existence, a novel initiative, called Universal Business Language, it is in achieving a universal XML business language over ebXML. ebXML-based business collaboration assures a reliable and recoverable message exchange as well. Business level failures are completely taken into account with the Business Process Specification Schema (BPSS). For example, if a party fails to respond within a pre-defined time period, then the BPSS reverts to the previously known secure state. The message-exchange agreement between two business partners is described by means of a Collaboration-Protocol Agreement (CPA). However, if one business partner afterwards changes the interface of a business service identified in the CPA, it renders the CPA invalid and requires a new CPA to be built. However, it doesn't affect the technical message exchange. Hence, the sender can be sure that the message gets delivered and the recipient has to deal with a potential problem. ebXML has its major strengths when it comes to inter-enterprise business process integration. However, ebXML is also suitable for intra-enterprise business process integration in that functional units (e.g. divisions) are treated as separate mini-enterprises. In B2B scenarios, the specific strengths of ebXML and Web services can be combined in that ebXML is used for managing enterprise-spanning business transaction services in the context of collaborative business, while Web services find their place in intra-enterprise integration of back-end systems.

In this perspective, the Cerere project has designed an interoperability architecture for traceability systems based on the ebXML technology as the reference specification in defining and exchanging business documents. Figure 4 shows the Cerere architecture, which is general enough to be applied to systems in different contexts; in particular, it has been used in a case study involving the food chain. It is worth pinpointing that the main component of the message switching system is the Message Service Handler (MSH): it takes care to validate Cerere documents and to send and receive them over the Internet using HTTP as its transport protocol. Furthermore, it provides error-handling facilities for a number of situations that may arise in real life.

Finally, a final consumer is able to access traceability information through a Web Interface connected to the database by means of a Web Services based infrastructure. Whenever Process Collaboration is the main goal, MSH System provides the proper interaction protocol among peers, as a document-centric approach is followed[28]. On the other hand, the access to Business Information Services can be proficiently achieved via Web Services, able to provide an efficient and lightweight RPC-based interaction. Registration and authentication services are provided for different classes of users, and are implemented within a Web Application module. The support for publication is implemented by a Content Management System (namely OpenCms v. 5.0.1).

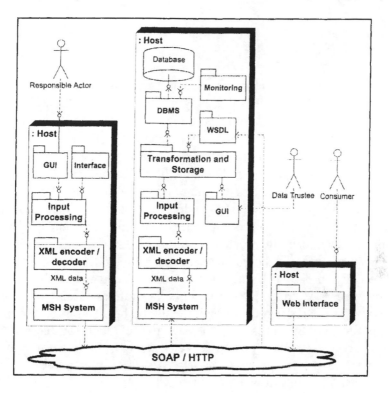

Figure 4. In the Cerere architecture shown above, the communication infrastructure leverages a Message Service Handler for exchanging and validating documents among the involved nodes.

The overall architecture has been designed to provide a clear, well-structured organization for the modules involved in a traceability system, addressing the typical issues for this broad category of information systems. Anyway, we must also underline that each specific domain covered by actual traceability systems presents particular challenges in obtaining the required performance level. Although performance is not the main focus in the presented architectural design, it must be always taken into account: from this standpoint, we can easily note that the messaging modules represent the main bottleneck. Thus, any attempt to improve performance (and subsequently scalability) must solely concentrate on the design, implementation, and configuration of the messaging subsystem. Although at first sight the treatment of XML documents might seem a computing-intensive activity, today the employment of highly optimized libraries for this kind of tasks can easily overcome any performance problem from the XML-processing modules.

5.   CONCLUSION

The food production environment is largely composed of a wide set of small and medium enterprises that play different roles in the supply chain, with different levels in technological competence, economic resources, and human skills. In order to achieve data interoperability along the supply chain for traceability purposes, a common, widely accepted set of specifications for collaboration is required. In this context, XML and SOAP can be surely regarded as emerging enabling technologies. Anyway, the plain help from XML and SOAP is not sufficient to address all the semantic aspects of each document exchange (which process generates the data exchange, what is the meaning of each data item, etc): document communication and sharing among business partners should be unambiguously modeled.

A recently proposed standard to provide semantics, elements, and properties necessary to define business collaborations is ebXML: thus, its employment in the context of traceability should be taken into account. The goal of the ebXML Specification Schema is to provide the bridge between e-business process modeling and specification of e-business software components. Business process models describe interoperable business processes that allow business partners to collaborate.

The Cerere project has developed a Traceability Web Information System for the food chain, and the ebXML technology has been successfully adopted to support collaboration among all the involved actors at different stages of the supply chain. The dictionary of XML business components and the set of document types built upon them are the first step of the Cerere data model definition[2]. The supply chain processes are defined by means of CPA documents and messages are delivered to a data trustee repository using ebXML mechanisms. The front-end interface of the Traceability Information System is implemented by a Web Application, and it has been tested on a specific food supply of typical Tuscany products.

6.   ACKNOWLEDGMENTS

The Cerere project is partially supported by The Foundation Cassa di Risparmio di Pisa under contract 2003.0132

7.   REFERENCES

1. Regulation (EC) n. 178/2002, European Parliament and Council of 28 Jan 2002, ch. I,V.
2. A. Bechini, M.G.C.A. Cimino, B. Lazzerini, F. Marcelloni, A. Tomasi, "A general framework for food traceability", IEEE SAINT 2005 Workshops, Proceedings pagg. 366-369, January-February 2005, Trento, Italy.
3. C. Binstock, D. Peterson, M. Smith, M. Wooding, C. Dix, C. Galtenberg, "The XML Schema Complete Reference", Addison Wesley Professional, 2003.
4. eXtensible Markup Language (XML), XMLhttp://www.w3.org/XML/.
5. ebXML official website – http://www.ebxml.org.
6. B. Gibbs, S. Damodaran, "ebXML Concepts and Application", John Wiley & Sons, 2002.
7. A. Kotok, D.R.R. Webber, "ebXML: The New Global Standard for Doing Business on the Internet", New Riders Publishing, 2001.
8. UN/CEFACT – United Nations Centre for Trade Facilitation and Electronic Business, http://www.unece.org/ cefact/.
9. M. de Castro Neto, M.B. Lima Rodrigues, P. Aguiar Pinto, I. Berger, "Traceability on the web – a prototype for the Portuguese beef sector", EFITA 2003 Conference, 5-9 July 2003, Debrecen, Hungary, pp. 607-611.
10. C.A. van Dorp, "Tracking and Tracing Business Cases: Incidents, Accidents and Opportunities", EFITA 03 Conference, 5-9 July 2003, Debrecen, Hungary, pp. 601-606.
11. W.R. Pape, B. Jorgenson, R.D. Boyle, J. Pauwels, "Let's get animal traceback right the first time", Food Traceability Report, Feb 2004, pagg.14-15.
12. W.R. Pape, B. Jorgenson, R.D. Boyle, J. Pauwels, "Selecting the most appropriate database architecture", Food Traceability Report, Feb 2003, pagg.21-23.
13. M. de Mello, P. de Azevedo, "Effects of Traceability on the Brazilian Beef Agribusiness System", Virtual Library Osvaldo "Bebe" Silva, Quilmes, Argentina 2000.
14. EAN/UCC official website – http://www.ean-ucc.org/.
15. EAN International, "EAN•UCC Traceability Implementation", february 2003.
16. EAN Belgium-Luxembourg, "EAN/UCC standards for shared supply chain traceability", http://www.eanbelgilux.be/ PAGE/brochure_tracability.pdf.
17. The Ministry of Agriculture, Forestry and Fisheries of Japan, "Guidelines for Introduction of Food Traceability Systems", March 2003, http://www.maff.go.jp/trace/ guide_en.pdf.
18. EPCglobal official website – http://www.epcglobalinc. org/.
19. K. Finkenzeller, "RFID Handbook", Carl Hanser Verlag Munich, 1998.
20. R. M. Hornby, "RFID solutions for the express parcel and airline baggage industry", Proc. IEE Colloq. RFID Technology, London, U.K. Oct 1999
21. U. Karthaus and M. Fischer, "Fully Integrated Passive UHF RFID Transponder IC With 16.7-µW Minimum RF Input Power", IEEE Journal of solid state Circuits, Vol. 38, No 10, 2003, pp. 1602-1608.
22. A.L. Annala, I. Oy, U. Friedrich, "PALOMAR Passive, Long range Multiple Access high frequency RFID system", IST-1999-10339.
23. Matrics Inc., "Matrics UHF RFID Tag Family", 2004, pp. 5.
24. Philips Semiconductors, "I CODE1 label ICs Protocol Air Interface", May 2002, pp. 42.
25. Philips Semiconductors, "UCODE HSL", Oct. 2003, pp. 9.
26. UN/EDIFACT - United Nations Directories for Electronic Data Interchange for Administration, Commerce, Transport, http://www.unece.org/trade/untdid/welcome. htm.
27. OASIS - Organization for the Advancement of Structured Information Standards, http://www.oasis-open.org.
28. Dieter E. Jenz, "ebXML and Web Services - Friends or Foes?", 27.06.2002, http://www.mywebservices.org/index. php/article/articleview/451/1/1/.
29. SOAP, http://www.w3.org/TR/soap/.
30. W3C – World Wide Web Consortium, http://www.w3. org/.

AN XML-BASED DATA MODEL FOR VULNERABILITY ASSESSMENT REPORTS

George Valvis[1]and Despina Polemi[2]

[1] *University of Pireaus, Informatics Department, Karaoli & Dimitriou 80 Pireaus 18534, Greece gvalvis@bankofgreece.gr;* [2] *University of Pireaus, Informatics Department, Karaoli & Dimitriou 80 Pireaus 18534, Greece dpolemi@unipi.gr*

Abstract: Periodic vulnerability assessment (VA), used to uncover and correct vulnerabilities, is a common intrusion prevention technique. Although the VA tools that perform those assessments, report similar information, there are tool specific differences. Unfortunately, trying to combine the output of these tools would require separate parsing tools to address the significant low-level differences. A new data model (Vulnerability Assessment Report Format - VARF) is presented in this paper in order to define data formats for sharing information of interest to VA and to facilitate the interaction with the risk management process. As a proof of concept a set of XSLT transformations was built in order to transform the results of an open source VA tool to a VARF compliant report enabling further processing of the results.

Key words: Vulnerability assessment, XML modeling

1.   INTRODUCTION

Although organizations understand the consequences of being insecure, their response time to the security challenges, by finding and applying appropriate security fixes or configurations, is not prompt. With the increasing sophistication and scalability of attacks [1], such an approach will provide diminishing returns.

A major challenge when performing a vulnerability analysis of a business-critical system today is the fact that the surrounding IT infrastructure undergoes continuous changes, the risk analysis and remediation planning are based primarily on human resources and the correlation of the technical vulnerabilities and exposures to business impact is complex.

Vulnerability assessment tools are a valuable aid in this area, as they automate the process of identifying vulnerabilities. However, vulnerability assessment tools reveal a large volume of known weaknesses, the majority of which are not critical. This leaves the task to prioritize the mitigation of the vulnerabilities to the security personnel; a task that takes time to deliver, producing a long window of exposure.

Also, various vendors of vulnerability assessment tools use different terminology to explain the same issue and there is a lack of machine-readable information. Thus, although the data provided by vulnerability assessment reports are detailed, are presented in an ambiguous textual form or in a proprietary data format. The effect is that a vulnerability report has become tightly coupled to specific tool and cannot easily be shared across different tools. This lack of common ground has hampered the ability to integrate diverse sources of available security data more effectively. The result is twofold: the security personnel are overloaded with redundant data and it is not feasible to fully utilize all possibly available data in making the most accurate diagnosis. On the other hand the development of commonly agreed or standardised and extensible exchange formats will enable interoperability between commercial, open source, and research systems, allowing users to deploy their preferred systems according to their advantages in order to obtain an optimal implementation with improved response time. In general, a standardised format in vulnerability assessment will provide increased efficiency of vulnerability assessment results:

- *Extensibility* and *flexibility*: providing data in extensible and flexible format could facilitate the collaboration and simplify the integration of information generated by heterogeneous sources.
- *Broader analysis*: the co-use and combination of more than one complementary vulnerability assessment tools increases the likelihood that more reported vulnerabilities are taken into consideration.

Our goal in this paper is to propose a "common ground" in the vulnerability assessment area providing the Vulnerability Assessment Report Format (VARF) data model. VARF based on emerging standardization efforts in the security field, outputs assessment information in XML. It is designed to facilitate the extraction of meaningful, tool-independent information to address the vulnerability assessment needs. This paper has been organised as follows: In section 2 we present a condensed overview of standardization efforts on vulnerability schemes and description languages. Section 3 describes the VARF model and subsequently section 4 demonstrates some applications of the model. The last section concludes with some experience statements and a rough outlook on future directions.

2. STANDARDIZATION ACTIVITIES

This section introduces the main standardization and research efforts on XML-based vulnerability schemes and description languages.

2.1 Common Vulnerabilities and Exposures (CVE)

CVE [2] is a dictionary of information security vulnerabilities and exposures that aims to provide common names for publicly known weaknesses. The goal of CVE is to standardize the names of vulnerabilities and make it easier to share data across separate vulnerability databases and security tools.

2.2 Open Vulnerability Assessment Language (OVAL)

OVAL [3] standardizes how to test for the existence of those vulnerabilities, based on system configuration information. The vulnerabilities are identified with a CVE number by OVAL queries, which perform the checks. A synopsis section accompanies the OVAL query that should include information related to two main items: the vulnerable software and the vulnerable configuration(s). Currently individual platform-specific XML schemas have been developed. In order to use OVAL, an operator should install the OVAL definition interpreter and use the specific OVAL schema that is defined for her platform.

2.3 The Common Vulnerability Scoring System (CVSS)

The CVSS [4] is designed to provide a composite score representing the overall security and risk a vulnerability represents. Using CVSS, the security personnel will have the basis for a common language with witch to discuss vulnerability severity. It is a modular system with three distinct groups that combine the characteristics of vulnerability. Each of these qualities or "metrics" has a specific way of being measured and each group has a unique formula for combining and weighing each metric. The three groups are the base, the temporal and the environmental group. The base group contains all of the qualities that are intrinsic to any given vulnerability that does not change over time or in different environments. The temporal group contains the characteristics of vulnerabilities that are time-dependant and change as the vulnerability ages. Finally, the environmental group contains the characteristics of vulnerabilities that are tied to implementation and are specific to a user's environment.

2.4   Extensible Configuration Checklist description Format (XCCDF)

The XCCDF specification [5] defines a data model and format for storing results of benchmark compliance testing. An XCCDF document is a structured collection of security configuration rules for a specific set of target systems. The model and its XML representation are intended to be platform-independent and portable, to foster broad adoption and sharing of rules and support information interchange, document generation, environmental tailoring, compliance testing and scoring.

2.5   Open Security Organization Advisory and Notification Markup Language (ANML)

The Open Security Organization (OpenSec) [6] is developing a framework of XML-based technologies to aid system management. The technologies planned for development include:
- Advisory and Notification Markup Language (ANML) to describe security advisories and other types of notifications in consistent and machine-readable way.
- System Information Markup Language (SIML), for describing a system's properties and providing a detailed inventory of software, hardware, and configuration information that will allow management software to assess the status of a system.
- Software Description Markup Language (SDML), for describing the properties of software and its environment.

3.   VULNERABILITY ASSESSMENT REPORT FORMAT DATA MODEL (VARF)

The Vulnerability Assessment Report Format data model is designed, based on the emerging standardization efforts of Intrusion Detection Working Group [7] and Incident Handling Working Group [8], to provide a standard representation of vulnerability assessment report in an unambiguous fashion. This could permit the association between reports generated by vulnerability assessment tools that address system and network level vulnerabilities.

The top-level class for all VARF messages is *VulnerabilityReport*; each type of message is a subclass of this top-level class. There are presently two types of messages defined; *Reports* and *ScanAlerts*. Within each message, subclasses of the message class are used to provide the detailed information carried in the VARF message. It is important to note that the data model does not specify how vulnerabilities in system and network level should be classified or identified. However, once a vulnerability assessment tool has determined the type of vulnerability that exists, the model dictates how that vulnerability information could be formatted. VARF does not deal with the formatting of application level vulnerabilities (like the schemas presented in section 2).

In this section, the individual components of the VARF data model are explained in detail. Some UML diagrams of the model are provided to present how the components are related to each other, and the relevant sections of the XML DTD are presented to indicate how the model is translated into XML. Figure 1 depicts the relationship between the principal components of the data model (due to limited space occurrence indicators and attributes are omitted).

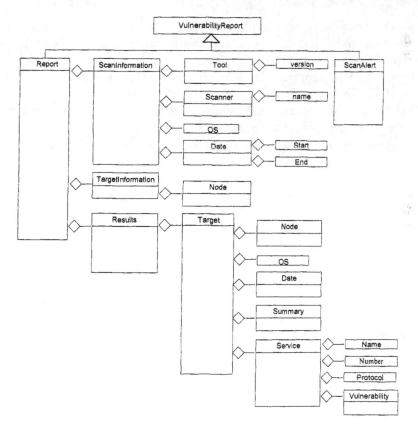

Figure 1. Data model overview.

The VulnerabilityReport Class: All VARF reports are instances of the VulnerabilityReport class; it is the top-level class of the VARF data model, as well as the VARF DTD. There are currently two types (subclasses) of *VulnerabilityReport* the *Report* and the *ScanAlert*. Because DTDs do not support sub classing, the inheritance relationship between *VulnerabilityReport* and the *Report* and *ScanAlert* subclasses have been replaced with an aggregate relationship. This is declared in the VARF DTD as follows:

```
<!ENTITY % attlist.varf "version CDATA #FIXED
'1.0' ">

<!ELEMENT VulnerabilityReport ( Report , ScanAlert
)>

<!ATTLIST VulnerabilityReport %attlist.varf;>
```

The *VulnerabilityReport* class has the single attribute Version, which is the version of the *VulnerabilityReport* specification this message conforms to.

Report class: The *Report* is generated every time a vulnerability assessment tool is deployed. The *Report* is composed of three aggregate classes which are:

- *ScanInformation* (exactly one), which contains identification information for the vulnerability tool that generated the report.
- *TargetInformation* (exactly one), that contains identification information for the target of evaluation.
- *Results* (exactly one) that contains all the useful assessment results.

ScanAlert class (Figure 2): The *ScanAlert* (exactly one) is modeled on the IODEF *IncidentAlert*, but it provides a different type of functionality. In the same manner, that the *IncidentAlert* is used to simply alert the occurrence of an incident and provide relevant information (such as raw IDMEF messages), the *ScanAlert* may alert an intrusion detection management system that a scan is going to be performed against the hosts specified in the *ScanAlert*. By taking this information into account, false positives could be suppressed by a correlation engine. As part of this alert, the scanner would provide *ScanInformation* and *TargetInformation*.

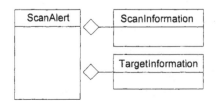

Figure 2. The ScanAlert Class.

The *ScanInformation* class carries additional information related to the conducted vulnerability assessment. The aggregate classes that make up *ScanInformation* are the *Tool*, *Scanner*, *OS* and *Date*:

- The *Tool* class (exactly one) includes the name attribute, which is the name of the tool that performed the assessment and the *Version* class (zero or one), which is the version of the deployed VA tool.
- *Scanner* class (exactly one): The aggregate class that makes up Scanner is Name, which is the host name of the machine where the VA tool is installed.
- *OS* (zero or one): The name of the OS of the host where the VA tool is installed, e.g. Linux.
- *Date*: (exactly one): Information about the time that the assessment occurred.

The aggregate classes that make up *Date* are *Start* (exactly one) and *End* (exactly one). *Start* and *End* are date time strings that identify the particular instant in time that the vulnerability assessment session was started and ended respectively.

The *TargetInformation* Class provides basic information about the assessed nodes. The aggregate class that make up *TargetInformation* class is *Node*. The *Node* class is composed by the *Name* (exactly one), which provides the host name of the target of evaluation and *Address* (exactly one), which is the IP address of the node that is the target of evaluation.

The *Results* Class: The *Results* element is meant to take the place of SARA vulnerability assessment tool [9] *Details* and Nessus [10] *Results*. It is closely tied to the IODEF *Attack* class, which in turn shares a great deal of structure with IDMEF *Alerts*. The aggregate class that makes up *Results* class is *Target* (figure 3).

Target (one or more): It includes the full assessment information discovered by the tool. The aggregate class that make up Target class are:

- *Node* (exactly one): It includes basic information about the node.
- *OS* (zero or one): It includes information about the operating system.
- *Date* (exactly one): It includes information about the time that the assessment occurred of the specific target.
- TargetSummary (zero or one): The elements that are included are the Number of services, Number of security holes, Number of security warnings, Number of security notes.
- *Service* class (zero or more), which is made up by the classes *Name* (zero or one), Number (zero or one), Protocol (exactly one), Vulnerability (zero or more).

By using the IDMEF/IODEF *Target* class, a related format for representing the 'host' specific information is achieved. This includes support for the standard types of address that Nessus and SARA vulnerability assessment tools support. Other different types of addresses and names, as defined in the IDMEF draft could be included. By using the IODEF version, it is also possible to accommodate the type of operating system for a target, useful for tools make use of stack fingerprinting and other OS detection techniques.

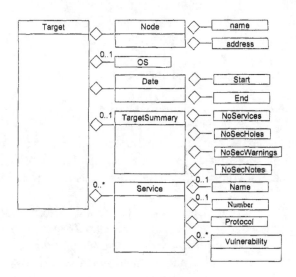

Figure 3. The Target class.

This is declared in the VARF DTD as follows:

```
<!ELEMENT Results (Target+)>
<!ELEMENT Target (
  Node, OS?, Date, Summary?, Service*)>
<!ELEMENT Service (
  Name?, Number?, Protocol, Vulnerability*)>
```

The aggregate classes that make up *Vulnerability* class (Figure 4) are *Name* (exactly one), *Family* (zero or one), *Summary* (zero or one), *Category* (zero or one), *Classification* (zero or more), *Assessment* (zero or more), *Data* (zero or one).

The *Data* element contains additional textual information related to the reported vulnerability and provides a catchall rule to accommodate items that have not been directly addressed by the data model.

The *Classification* class provides the name of vulnerability, or other information allowing the analyst to determine what it is. The purpose of the *Classification* element is to allow the analyst who receives the Vulnerability message to be able to obtain additional information. To accommodate this, a name and an URL are included. The current list of valid source values includes "unknown", "vendor-specific", and CVE. The Classification class is composed of two aggregate classes. The aggregate classes that make up *Classification* are:

- *Name* (exactly one): The name of the vulnerability (e.g. CAN-2002-1165), from one of the origins listed below.
- *URL* (exactly one): A URL (string) at which the risk analyst may find additional information about the vulnerability.

The document pointed to by the URL may include an in-depth description of the vulnerability, appropriate countermeasures, or other information deemed relevant by the vendor.

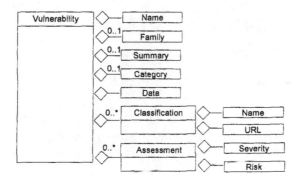

Figure 4. The Vulnerability class.

This is declared in the VARF DTD as follows.

```
<!ELEMENT Vulnerability (
    Name, Family?, Summary?, Category?, Data?,
    Classification*, Assessment*)>
```

Table 1. The values of the Origin attribute

Origin attribute	Explanation
Unknown	Origin of the name is not known
Bugtraqid	The Security Focus vulnerability database identifier [11]
CVE	The common Vulnerabilities and Exposures name
Vendor-specific	A vendor-specific name and hence, URL; it can be used to provide product specific information

The *Classification* class has the attribute *Origin* (required), which provides the source from which the name of the alert originates. The attribute's values and their explanations are given in table 1. The default value is "unknown".

The *Assessment* class provides information related to the VA tool's assessment of a discovered vulnerability, its severity and the related risk. The *Assessment* class is composed of two aggregate classes:

Severity (exactly one): The VA tool's assessment of the impact that the vulnerability might have.

Risk (exactly one): The level of risk that the discovered vulnerability poses. This is declared in the VARF DTD as follows.

```
<!ENTITY % attvals.origin "

( unknown | bugtraqid | cve | vendor-specific )">

<!ELEMENT Classification ( name, url )>

<!ATTLIST Classification %attvals.origin;
'unknown'>

<!ELEMENT Assessment ( Severity, Risk )>
```

By introducing the VARF model, an end user of vulnerability assessment tools would have an extended ability to process vulnerability information. The next section tries to demonstrate this enhancement.

4.   PROOF OF CONCEPT

The previous section detailed an approach to represent infrastructure level vulnerability data as XLM documents. In this section we will discuss some applications that could use these representations.

4.1   Vulnerability reports

The most obvious place to implement VARF is in the data path between a vulnerability assessment tool and the database that collects all the risk analysis information. A set of scripts was built in order to transform the output of Nessus open source vulnerability assessment tool to a VARF compliant report (Figure 5). The outcome of the transformation extracts the asset information and groups together the associated vulnerabilities.

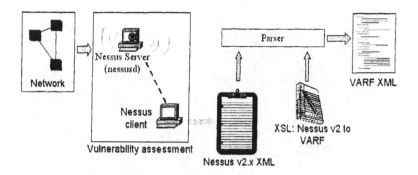

Figure 5. Nessus to VAFR tranformation.

By transforming Nessus data in VARF format, the data are better structured and further transformations to other formats (e.g. HTML) that integrate to the IT needs of an organization become feasible. This enhanced structure allows for further transformations to be delivered in order to satisfy organization needs for other data formats (for example to transform a VARF report to an HTML page is quite trivial).

4.2   Vulnerability diagrams

A visualisation of the reported vulnerabilities can be achieved by producing a tree-structured diagram. Figure 6 depicts the direct association between network assets and vulnerabilities. This diagram could increase the readability of the results and help to ensure that fewer discovered vulnerabilities go unnoticed. Figure 7 shows a process that enables us to generate vulnerability diagrams. VARF based vulnerability reports, obtained with the method explained in the previous paragraph, were feed to the Graphviz open source graph drawing software [12] that produced the diagrams in image format (GIF, JPEG, etc). Since Graphviz only accepts input complied with a particular format, the VARF based reports need to be processed by additional XSLT transformation before presented to the drawing software. Being in XML format this in not complicated.

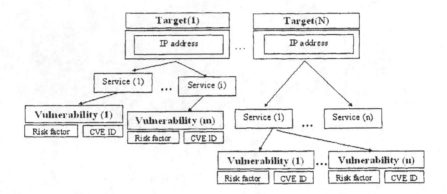

Figure 6. Vulnerability diagram.

Also, by deploying the Graphotron open source tool [13] the development of the Graphviz XSLT transformation can be further simplified.

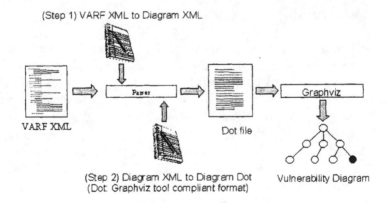

Figure 7. Producing a vulnerability diagram

We actually perform vulnerability assessment on a number of segments of our campus switched network. By processing the results using our VARF based transformations their visibility was increased and the administration task was simplified.

Other places where the VARF could be useful is an event correlation system that would accept vulnerability assessment reports and IDS alerts from a variety of vulnerability assessment and intrusion detection tools and perform cross-correlation and cross-confirmation computations in order to provide more focused assessments of high-priority threats. The *Report(s)* will detail vulnerable systems and have the potential to be easily used for automatic validation of perimeter defenses, by comparing *Results* and IDMEF's *Alerts* since both are XML based datasets.

5.   CONCLUSIONS

The increasing complexity of today's IT dependent systems urges the improvement of existing methods for analysing systems in order to increase the likelihood that all possible threats and vulnerabilities are taken into consideration. Many current tools address vulnerabilities in the context of a single host. However, due to their proprietary nature and lack of standardisation, the effectiveness of their large reports, is constrained. In order to reduce the window of exposure, the security personnel need a way to set priorities and reduce the volume of vulnerabilities generated by the tools down to the few critical risks that matters. A short overview of the standardisation efforts that focus on the information systems security was given on the section 2.

An area of potential improvement, which could enhance communication between existing security tools, products and groups, has been identified and the Vulnerability Assessment Report Format XML data model, based on the IDMEF work, was proposed in sections 3.

By introducing the VARF model, an end user of vulnerability assessment tools would have a standards based format to describe vulnerabilities that would allow sharing information easier and combining it with other data sets from a variety of compliant tools and systems. If XML is chosen as an implementation it is possible to immediately combine the assessment information with intrusion detection information (assuming that the latter is IDMEF compliant). For example, local statistics, from the intrusion alerts, could be used to perform focused assessments of high-priority threats.

In addition, if there were reasons for sharing assessment information in a manner similar to the sharing of IDMEF messages via IODEF in order to gather statistics, the suggested data format would simplify this exchange of information. It is established that having a common format or framework encourages vendors to invest in new or improved products, services and approaches.

As proof of concept XML technologies like XPath and XSLT were deployed to process vulnerability assessment data reported by Nessus open source vulnerability assessment tool and produce vulnerability diagrams, in order to indicate how VARF data model may contribute to the optimisation of the vulnerability management effort. We plan to scale up the vulnerability assessments on our campus network including more segments and increasing the number of the assessed hosts. Finally, it is our intention to extend the assessment operations to web services by deploying WSDL and SOAP [14].

6.   REFERENCES

1. CERT Coordination Centre, Overview of Attack Trends, (June 4, 2004); http://www.cert.org/archive/pdf/attack_trends.pdf
2. D.Mann and S.Christey, Towards a Common Enumeration of Vulnerabilities, (January 8, 1999); http://www.cve.mitre.org/docs/cerias.html
3. Open Vulnerability Assessment Language XML specification page, (June 4, 2004); http://oval.mitre.org/oval/xml_specification.html
4. Common Vulnerability Scoring System (CVSS), (April 14, 2005); http://www.first.org/cvss/
5. Extensible Configuration Checklist Description Format (XCCDF) specification, (April 18, 2005); http://csrc.nist.gov/checklists/xccdf.html
6. OpenSec, The Open Security Project, (January 7, 2005); http://www.opensec.org
7. IETF Intrusion Detection Working Group, (January 7, 2005); http://www.ietf.org/html.charters/idwg-charter.html
8. Incident Object Description and Exchange Format Working Group (IODEF WG), (January 7, 2005); http://www.terena.nl/tech/task-forces/tf-csirt/iodef
9. The Security Auditor's Research Assistant (SARA), (March 7, 2005); http://www-arc.com/sara
10. Nessus vulnerability assessment tool, (March 7, 2005); http://www.nessus.org
11. SecurityFocus Bugtraq Searchable Database by Keyword. (January 12, 2004); http://www.securityfocus.com/bid/keyword
12. Graphviz, an Open source graph drawing software, (September 20, 2004); http://www.research.att.com/sw/tools/graphviz
13. Graphotron (September 20, 2004); http://www.zvon.org/ZvonSW/ZvonGraphotron
14. F. Curbera, M. Duftler, R. Khalaf, W. Nagy, N. Mukhi, and S.Weerawarana, Unraveling the Web Services Web: An Introduction to SOAP, WSDL, and UDDI, *IEEE Internet Computing*, Vol. 6, No. 2, Mar.-Apr. 2002, pp.86-93.

ADMISSION CONTROL FOR THE CUSTOMERS OVER THE VENDOR'S VPN

G. Narendra Kumar[1]
ECE Dept.
UVCE, Bangalore
gnarenk@yahoo.com

P. Venkataram *
PET-UNIT,ECE Dept.
Indian Institute of Science,Bangalore
pallapa@ece.iisc.ernet.in

V.S.N. Kumar
ECE Dept.
UVCE, Bangalore

Abstract

There is considerable interest for electronic merchants with limited resources but a limitless ambition for profits, providing quality of service to customers in proportion to their buying potential or finds a legal way of maximizing their profits. The on-line customers always demand fast response and secure transactions, at the same time the electronic merchants are relentless in managing their finite resources to maximize their profits.

We propose a Genetic Algorithm(GA) based call admission control(CAC) scheme for all the customers of a vendor on the vendor's VPN. The algorithm prioritizes the customers based on their past purchase history so that the vendors can select the genuine customer to boost their profits.

Customer Behavior Transition Diagram(CBTD) is used to compute the customer based priority of the vendor. Priorities keep changing dynamically as a function of the status of the customer based on the past purchase history at the e-commerce site. The designed method has been tested analytically and simulated in a real time Internet environment on an e-commerce site consisting of multiple servers distributed on LANs and WANs. This mechanism of admitting clients(customers) on requests among the servers(vendors) at the e-commerce

*Corresponding Author

site will improve its revenue at peak times. There is a fervent growth in the business through Internet. Virtual Private Network(VPN) is a must for virtual walk way to make it less vulnerable. Vendor controlled virtual path group(VPG) based VPN is adopted as an appropriate security policy on e-commerce by an architecture dedicated to host and serve the e-commerce site. The results are encouraging in admitting the potential customers and given the optimal service.

Keywords: e-commerce; genetic algorithm; call admission control; prioritized requests; Quality of service; customer behavior transition diagram; virtual private network.

Introduction

E-commerce services is an important branch of the Internet. With increasing number of Internet users and rapid growth of network technologies, electronic commerce(E-commerce) is perceived as one of the killer applications of the computer and communication technologies. E-commerce can be defined as "buying and selling of information, products and services through Computer networks. The consequence of the popularity is that some e-commerce sites receive more traffic than predicted and congestion occurs due to overload during peak business hours.
A customer who connects to an e-commerce site starts a session that will last some time before the customer has finished the transactions which consists of several requests for varying data and hopefully ends with an order to buy some product. During the whole session the customer expects short response time while requesting new data. If the response time is too long , the customer ends the session and the site will loose its profit from the potential customer. Problems that have been recognized for e-commerce sites are related to site performance and there is a tendency that customers leave and never come back to sites that perform poorly.

The behavior of the customer is also considered during the past visits to the e-commerce site to update the past history and explained using the transition diagram.
Today's VPN solutions overcome the security factor. Using special tunneling protocols and complex encryption procedures, data integrity and privacy is achieved in what seems, for most part like a dedicated point-to-point connection. Using the Internet, companies can connect their remote branch offices, project teams, business partners and e-customers into the main corporate network. Mobile workers and telecommuters can get some connectivity by dialing into the point-of presence(POP)of the load ISP. In this paper we discuss the call admission control for the customers visiting th e-commerce site on priority based on their past purchase history, provide security during transactions by adopting VPG based VPN services for resource allocation and at the same

time boost the profit of the vendors without compromising QoS.

Call Admission Control to E-Commerce Vendor's Site

E-commerce sites have limited network resources such as bandwidth and buffers. Hence, it becomes necessary to have some kind of admission control mechanism during congestion occurring at E-commerce site. Further, customers believe that if the site is heavily loaded it is important to receive information about this rather than waiting. If a customer must be rejected, a discount or some kind of 'coupon' should be offered as an incentive to go back to the site. A proper CAC algorithm will ensure prevention of congestion at the sites based on the available resources and prioritized users. Cherkasova and phaal [1] developed a session based admission control, that rejected new customers during congestion.

Introduction to Genetic Algorithms

Genetic algorithms(GAs), which were introduced by Holland[16], are iterative search techniques based on the the spirit of natural selection. By emulating biological selection and reproduction, GAs can efficiently search through the solution space of complex problems. Genetic algorithms operates on a population of candidate solutions called *chromosomes*. A chromosome, which is composed of numerous genes, represents encoding of the problem and associates it with a fitness value evaluated by the fitness function. This fitness value determines the goodness and the survival ability of the chromosome. In fact genetic algorithms include; an individual, or a possible solution to the problem; a chromosome, or the parameters that define a solution; a gene, or a parameter; fitness, or how similar a solution is to the desired solution. Gentic algorithm uses the following operators;

Crossover. Crossover [5], selects random genes from parent chromosomes and creates a new offspring.Chromosomes of the two parents are split into two (equal or unequal) halves each. The halves are interchanged and combined to form the child chromosome.

Mutation & Elitism. After a crossover is performed, the resulting solution might fall into a local optimum - hence some genes of the child chromosome are randomly changed.

However, when creating a new population by crossover & mutation, the best chromosome might be lost. Hence, Elitism is a method which first copies the best chromosome(s) to the new population. Elitism rapidly increases the performance of the GA, by preventing loss of the best-found solution.

After the crossover and mutation process is over the offspring is used for replacing some chromosomes in the population with the probability consistent with their fitness values. In other words, GA could construct better and better chromosomes from the best partial genes of past samplings.

In summary, GA is composed of a fitness function, a population of chromosomes and three operators - selection, crossover and mutation. The parameter settings of the operators can be chosen depending on the applications or remain unchanged even when the applications are varied. However, the fitness function and the encoding method are required to be specially designed for each problem.

Genetic algorithm starts initializing the population and evaluating its corresponding fitness values and produces newer generations iteratively. At each generation, a portion of the chromosome is selected according to the survival ability for reproducing offspring. A genetic algorithm operates by the following steps:

1   randomly generating an initial population of solutions, for example numbers, that can be represented in bit-strings,

2   evaluating each individual's fitness via an appropriate fitness function,

3   creating new individuals by mating the current ones by mixing their bit strings together,

4   deleting some or all of the population to make room for new members,

5   repeating all but step (1) for the desired number of generations.

This algorithm is straight forward but involves many variable parameters to be resolved, including:

1   fitness evaluation method, how the mating parents are chosen;

2   mating techniques, how each parent's representative bit string is mixed with others to create new individuals;

3   mutation rate, the probability any bit may change value;

4   population size; and the number of generations.

Proposed Work

In this paper we present a Call Admission Control mechanism, using Genetic Algorithm, of customers request over the Vendor's Virtual Private Network.

Rest of the paper organization

The rest of the paper is organized as follows; Vendor Controlled Virtual Path Group based VPN establishment is described in section 1. Section 2 describes the proposed call admission control for the customers over the vendor's VPN. Simulations and its observations are discussed in section 3. Finally we conclude in section 4.

1. Vendor controlled Virtual Private Network for E-Commerce

The potential customer is selected and resources are allocated by employing the Virtual Path Group(VPG) based VPN which enhances the vendor's capability for Virtual Path(VP) capacity control. It allows transparent signaling and dynamic VP bandwidth allocation within the vendor domain. A vendor can change the VP capacities, within the limits of the VPG capacities without interacting with the provider, Fig.1. Further, the VPG bandwidth can be shared by VPs with different source destination pairs and vendors can independently achieve the optimum balance between the resources needed for VP control to handle the traffic load. In our client-server relation model we have incorporated the Virtual Path Group based VPN as the appropriate security policy dedicated to serve the e-commerce site. VPG is defined as a logical link with in the public network provider's ATM network. A VPG is permanently set up between virtual path(VP) cross connect node and a Vendor Private Network(VDPN) switch that acts as a customer access point for the VPN service. The VPN provider allocates bandwidth to a VPG, which defines the maximum total capacity for all VPs within the VPG.

- Encrypting is made through public key;
- Uses two keys of different type, one public and the other private;
- Owner of the key can encrypt data but can't decrypt;
- Private key is used to decrypt data which is encrypted using public key.

The vendor control contains three controllers: VP admission controller, VPG controller and the VPN controller, all operating on different time-scales to run asynchronously. Assume that one of the VPs experiences a sudden increase in traffic load, the VP admission controller associated with admits all the calls as long as there is sufficient capacity but blocks the calls when overloaded. The VPG controller detects the congestion in that particular VP and attempts to allocate additional bandwidth. If the traffic load is transient the demand for bandwidth drops and the interaction is terminated and if the congestion still persists the VPN controller will request additional VPN capacity from the provider.

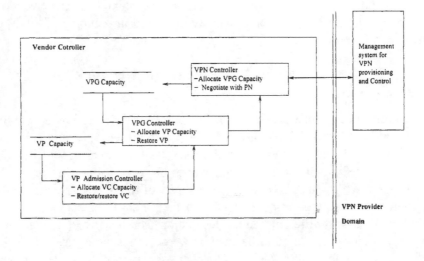

Figure 1. Event Diagram for Vendor control

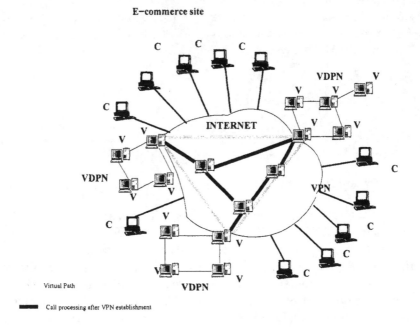

Figure 2. Call Processing after VPN establishment

The VP admission controller decides whether a call can be admitted into the VPN based on the VP capacity, its current utilization and the admission control policy, Fig.2. The VP admission controller always ensures that enough capacity is available, such that cell-level QoS can be guaranteed for all calls that are accepted which runs on the timescale of the call arrival and departure rates. Depending on the state of the VPs and the control objectives the VPG controller dynamically changes the amount of bandwidth allocated to associated VPs, enables the customers to exploit variations in utilization among VPs that traverse the same VPG allowing bandwidth between VPs of different source destination pairs to be shared without interacting with the provider. To maintain the QoS, the sum of the VP capacities must be less than or equal to the capacity of the VPG link. The VPN controller dynamically negotiates the bandwidth of the VPG links with the provider, based on traffic statistics and control objectives while observing the customer's QoS requirements.

2. Proposed Call Admission Control

In this section we describe a call admission control scheme that may be used in a distributed commercial web site. The control scheme uses the past purchase history of the customers as variables to determine the customer's priority and the vendor's priority to admit the customers. More revenue is generated and at the same time a good quality of service is maintained. The proposed CAC Algorithm admits the clients of the vendor for optimally allocating bandwidth among the E-commerce users. We have designed a Call admission control algorithm using genetic algorithms for e-commerce merchants to increase/maximize the profits obtained from the users/customers by transacting through Internet.

Clients-Vendors relation model

We have proposed a clients-vendors model in Fig.3 for implementation of priority based CAC using GA at the router. It represents how the customers are given access to the e-commerce site and allocate the resources available on the vendors secured VPN(virtual private network). The customer requests for entry into the site with a predetermined priority i.e. the customer priority C_p. The customer priority C_p is evaluated based on the past purchase activities at the e-commerce site stored in the database available at the router. Each customer is also given a priority from the vendor's side based on the revenue generated which is termed as vendor's priority V_p. The client-vendor model discussed aims at finding the genuine customers with good C_p and V_p to give higher order of preference.

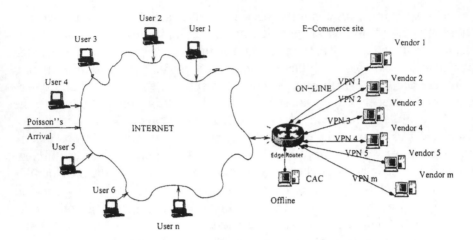

Figure 3.   Clients-Vendors Model.

Salient features of the client-vendor relation model

- Learns the customer behavior and computes the customer buying probability.

- Plans multimedia presentation of the queried information for the customer based on the customer buying behavior.

- Presentation access to the customer is based on resource availability and the customer's past purchase history.

- Admission policy is based on past purchase history of the customers at the e-commerce site.

- Vendors policy is to generate more revenue without compromising with the QoS.

Customer Behavior Transition Diagram

In a commercial environments, it has been observed that 5% of the customers stay at home and place orders for necessary goods from the vendor. Evaluation regarding the potential of the customer in terms of profit to the vendor at the e-commerce site is done from the profile of the customer.

We have considered small and heavy buyers as occasional buyers we have built a Customer Behavior Transition Diagram (CBTD)(see Fig.4). The Poisson process is used to model user initiated session arrivals in the Internet to find the transition probabilities in the state diagram. The exit state is reached when ever the customer finishes his transactions or when the customer is no more interested at the e-commerce site due to unfriendly navigation, poor contents, a unattractive prices, poor performance and consumes more time to correspond.

The mean time taken by the customer at each state is the 'thinking time' of the potential customers. When a customer has sent a request to the site, he/she waits for the reply. When the reply has arrived, the customer either sends a new request to go to other state or decides to leave the site.

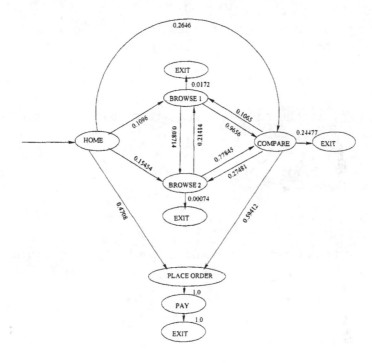

Figure 4. Customer Behavior Transition Diagram

In the CBTD the session length is geometrically distributed. After sending a request of type y the customer will wait for a S_y seconds. If the reply does not arrive with in the time the customer becomes impatient and abandons the site by pressing the exit button. The customer visits to the vendor on several occasions and also, at each occasion in which state he/she discontinued the transaction would be taken for the weight-age calculation.

Required Bandwidth Establishment

For the link the expected OD(origin-destination) traffic and the link capacity we find the optimal bandwidth assignment which maximizes the total expected throughput and the profit for the vendor. We consider all the customers in the queue at the entry point which is defined as the deviation of assigned capacity from the capacity required to give 95% satisfaction of utility function.

Let 'C' be the bandwidth available on the particular link 'i' through which the vendor serves all his 'n' clients.

We define,

C_i^{link} -Available bandwidth of link i,

N_p -Number of unidirectional OD pair j,

U_j -Bandwidth assigned to the OD pair j,

P_j -Number of predetermined possible paths connecting the OD pair,

T_j^{min} & T_j^{max} -are the minimal and maximal bandwidth assigned to the OD pair j,

δ_j^i -a indicator variable which takes the value 1 if the OD pair utilizes the link i,

$F_j(U_j)$ and $f_j(u)$ are the probability function and probability density function for the bandwidth demand.

Then,

$$\sum_{j=1}^{N_p} \delta_j^i \times U_j \leq C_i^{link}$$

$$T_j^{min} \geq U_j$$

Analyzing the throughput to be like liquid flow the objective function, $D_j(U_j)$

$$= \int_0^{u_j} u f_j(u)du + U_j \int_{u_j}^{\infty} f_j(u)du$$
$$= \int_0^{u_j} u f_j(u)du + U_j[1 - F_j(u_j)]$$

we employ M/M/1 queuing mechanism for Poisson arrivals,

$$F_j(U_j) = \frac{\lambda t^n}{n!} e^{-\lambda t}$$
$$F_j(u)du = \lambda e^{-u\lambda}du$$

where,

λ-Mean arrival rate;

n-Number of customers in queue over a interval of time t.

- **Fitness function evaluation**

Evaluation regarding the potential of the customer in terms of profit to the vendor at the e-commerce site is done from the profile of the customer.

Fitness function

$= [\int_0^{u_j} u f_j(u)du + U_j[1 - F_j(u_j)]]*C_{p_i} *V_{p_j} *CS_{w_{ij}}$

where, $C_p = \frac{(a+2b+3c)yz}{10^5}$,

$$CS_{w_{ij}} = \frac{\Psi}{\tau^2}$$

and

$$V_p = \frac{1}{\sqrt{2\pi\sigma^2}} \int_0^{V_p'} exp - \frac{1}{2}\left(\frac{V_p'-\mu}{\sigma}^2\right) dV_p'$$

The total weight-age of the ith customer with the jth vendor is $CS_{w_{ij}}$ with Ψ is the total time spent at the site and τ is the sum of time allocated for each state transition.

Now a call admission control program is run off-line using GA which gives a list of the priorities of all the customers from the database during congestion of customers at the E-commerce site . The list is compared with all the on-line users and gives access to the customers with the greatest priority. As more customers come on-line the CAC will check the priority and grant/deny access accordingly. After the customer is granted access the vendor controller decides the dynamic allocation of bandwidth and maintain QoS.

CAC Algorithm. The proposed call admission control algorithm works on taking the several customer's requests to one or several. It is based on many to one and/or to many relationships among the customers and vendors.

Admission policy

We have adopted following policy in admitting the customers based on the past purchase history with the vendors.

- Customers should be prioritized according to their previous buying patterns and likely wood of buying.

- Infrastructure resources should be assigned to customers according to their priorities.

- CAC is implemented off-line at the router depending on the past history of the customer stored in the database at the vendor.

- History of the customer is available at CAC from all the vendors through user log file whenever a customer logs on during congestion.

- Every time a customer logs in, a new log file containing the details of number of customers on line and their respective histories from all the vendors is created in a log file.

- Log file is sent to CAC which seeks a new log file every time it is up-dated.

- CAC utilizes the history to create priorities to admit customers on prior-ity.

- Every time the CAC receives a updated log file it creates a new priority list.

Customer request for entry into e-commerce site. The customers priority with the e-commerce site, i.e., Cp is evaluated. The vendors priority for the customers from the vendors, i.e., Vp is evaluated. The GA program is run based on the fitness function to find the priority of the customer seeking access to the e-commerce site. The outcome of the GA program evaluates customer for the allocation of the resources and gives admission.

```
CAC- algorithm()
{
  if (customer_request==TRUE)
  {
customer_id = get request(customer_request);
find_customer_priority(customer_id);
for (i=0; i<m;i++)
find_vendor_priority(customer_id, i);
grant_permission = determine_permission();
if(grant_permission)
allocate_resources(customer_id);
  }
}
```

3.   Simulation

We have carried out the simulation of the customer behavior for customer priority for the e-commerce services on wired and wireless networks resulting in the best solution for maximum profit.

In the simulation we have considered several products and their information at several vendors. We have also considered a case of one product distributed among many vendors based on the information level (surface level, brief note, detailed level, etc). We have tested for several customers needing information and buying the product/s from the vendor/s.

We have simulated this environment at the router and the server of a vendor as a OD pair having 2MB maximum bandwidth capacity. The mating tech-nique used for all trials was uniform crossover with probability retained at 50% since there is a balance maintained between exploration and exploitation of the population upto 600 generations with population converging after approximately 60 generations and the results were not taken beyond this point. Mutation rate is also important for the mating process which is investigated between 0.2% and 30.0% and good results were obtained. This way a list of the fittest strings is obtained and then the CAC checks the on-line customers against this list if the resources are oversubscribed.

```
Algorithm:CAC using Genetic Algorithm()
{
    Initialize the population_n ;
    Calculate fitness function
    While(Fitness Value !=Optimal Value)
    {
        Selection ;
        Crossover ;
        Mutation ;
        Calculate Fitness Function ;
    }
}
```

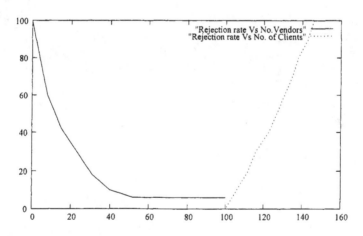

Figure 5. Rejection rate Vs No. of Clients and No. of Vendors

Results

The results are encouraging in selecting a genuine customer who are the potential customers and given optimal service. In the graph the initial convergence of GA is much faster but at the later stages saturates when run for more than 60 generations. The trend indicates that high mutation rates will approach an optimal value quickly and lower rate will nearly approach the optimal value when the fitness reaches a certain value.

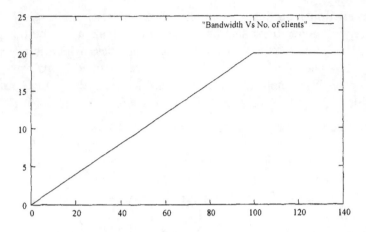

Figure 6.   Bandwidth allocation Vs No. of Clients

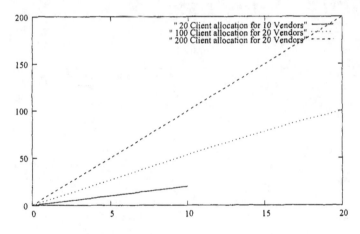

Figure 7.   Client allocation Vs No. of Vendors

4.   Conclusion

The results show that GA is suitable as the complexity of the database at the E-commerce site increases. Working on real time analysis would also lead to better results. The use of combination of the past purchase history of the customer and the behavior of the customer would avoid frustrating potential customers who have been very good buyers there by increasing the revenue throughput of the vendor at the e-commerce site. Further, the VPG based VPN enhances and effectively maximizes the profits of electronic merchants given the physical limits of their infrastructure resources.

References

1 L. Cherkasova and P. Phaal, "Predictive admission control strategy for overload commercial web server", Pro. of 8th International Symposium on Modeling Analysis and Simulation of Computer and Telecommunication Systems, 2000, pp 500-507.

2 Davi. E. Goldberg, "Genetic Algorithms in Search, Optimization & Machine-Learning", Addison Wesley, 1989.

   ivalent Capacity and its Applications to Bandwidth Allocation in High Speed Networks", IEEE, JSAC, Vol 9, No.7, Sept 1991.

3 Zhu. L, Wainwright. R. L and Schoenefeld. D. A, "A Genetic Algorithm for the Point to Multipoint Routing Problem with Varying Number of Requests". Proceedings IEEE Intl Conference on EC (ICEC 98), USA, 1998.

4 G.Narendra Kumar, P. Venkataram and V.S.N. Kumar, "A Call Admission Control For E-Commerce Users By Using GA's ",Pro. of International Conference, CIRAS'2003, Singapore, Dec 2003.

5 Stallings, W. "Network and Internet Security: Principals and Practice. "Prentice Hall, 1995.

6 Wasim E. "E-Commerce Systems Architecture and Applications." Artech House, 2000.

7 M.C.Chan, A.A.Lazer and R.Stadler, "Customer Management and Control of Broadband VPN Services", Centre for Telecommunications Research, New York.

ROLE OF THE CUSTOMER VALUE IN THE SOFTWARE AS A SERVICE CONCEPT
Empirical evaluation of the factors affecting the customer lock-in of the online newspapers

Markku Sääksjärvi, Aki Lassila
Department of Business Technology, Helsinki School of Economics, P.O. Box 1210, FIN-00101, Helsinki, Finland; E-mail: saaks@hkkk.fi, aki.lassila@iki.fi

Abstract: According to evolving literature on the Software as a Service (SaaS) concept, the benefits proposed for the customer and the provider are controversial as many of the customer benefits are also serious risks for the service provider. A sustainable service in the proposed one-to-many SaaS-mode will therefore require an effective business model capable to lock-in customers. For this purpose we propose applying general e-commerce business models. To tailor these for SaaS, we need to develop new instruments in order to study the customer benefits and value creation. For our explorative empirical study we propose that ease of use and usefulness from the Technology Acceptance Model (TAM) should be combined with content, context, and infrastructure from Rayport and Sviokla's model in order to study the evolution of the lock-in of the customers of online services. Our empirical data on 251 online newspaper readers showed that the above-mentioned predictors appeared in new factorial combinations of navigational characteristics, usefulness, novelty of the content, complementarities, and the context of the service. These combinations were significant predictors of the customer lock-in, many of them being competitive. For the experienced customers, personally relevant and useful content and effective infrastructure explained over 40 percent of the variance in the lock-in. For the non-experienced users the novelty of the services was the most significant predictor of the lock-in. We discuss the role of the customer value sources (novelty, effectiveness, and complementarities) for practical development of the online Software as a Service offering.

Key words: Software as a Service; online newspapers; e-commerce; value creation; customer lock-in.

1.   INTRODUCTION: WHAT CONSTITUTES SAAS?

The Software as a Service (SaaS) is a rather new and still somewhat ambiguous concept. Origins of the SaaS model can be traced back to the time-sharing services and one of the latest manifestations of the SaaS is the Application Service Provisioning (ASP) model. Originally, an IDC White paper (IDC, 1999) defined the following criteria for the ASP: it is 1) application centric, 2) only application access (not ownership) providing, 3) centrally managed, and 4) one-to-many service, that 5) is delivered on the contract. In this original ASP concept the customer could, besides remote usage of application software, purchase application support, and also rent the required data center infrastructure capacity. The ASP concept was offered as a new and competitive form of remotely hosted and outsourced application service for the customers.

In the late 1990s, many industry analysts forecasted explosive growth for the ASP market. So far, early studies on the success of ASP companies have shown only a modest rate of success (e.g. Desai and Currie 2003; Cherry Tree 2000). More recently, both significant ICT market analysts and software industry organizations have presented an improved and extended version of the ASP model, called "Software as a Service" (Cherry Tree, 2000; SIIA, 2001; Hoch F. et al., 2001; Mizoras and Goepfert, 2003).

A white paper of the Software & Information Industry Association eBusiness Division (SIIA, 2001) proposed a service initiative as well as introduced the term "Software as a Service". The aim of the paper was to change the perspective from outsourcing to network-based service point-of-view. The general assumption seemed to be that if the customers will get an easy access to valuable software service and the payment is not directly related to the real costs of development, the market will grow and thus the vendor will also benefit. What constituted a "service" was not defined explicitly, but it seemed that one should count the ex-ante application development and implementation plus integration of all the components of the online service infrastructure to accomplish the SaaS offering. This differs from the marketing definition of service, e.g. according to Grönroos et al. (2000) the main characteristic of services is their process nature. Grönroos et al. stated that" from this core characteristic of services follow other characteristics: the consumption of a service takes place simultaneously with the service process and customers participate more or less actively in the service process and by their behavior influence the progress and outcome of the process".

On the basis of our literature study (Sääksjärvi et al., 2005) we propose that the ASP/SaaS literature does not yet react to the fact that the SaaS model, which changes one-to-one (business-to-business) relationships into one-to-many relationships, will also transform the market relations and the traditional software licensing model to the one-to-many utility e-commerce model. This will require the creation of a strong brand, either enabling hybrid revenue logic where low priced software offering is still possible or requiring customization and lock-in to justify higher prices for the service. Apparently critical to the success of the SaaS model will be the types of new application and service innovations made. Not much is yet known of the factors that affect SaaS users' interest to begin and continue using these online services.

1.1   Objectives of the paper

The purpose of this paper is to apply the four value creation sources of Amit and Zott's e-commerce model (2001) and to carry out an empirical survey of the customer lock-in and its predictors in one special application domain area, the online newspapers. The online papers typically combine free content, special applications, and a variety of complementary services to attract new and retain their old online readers. Our objective is to apply the key factors, ease of use and usefulness, of the well-known Technology Acceptance Model (Davis, 1986), which was originally proposed for the evaluation of behavioral intention to use an IS application in the organizational context. We will combine these factors with a more recent conceptual Rayport and Sviokla's model's factors (1994). The main ingredient of our research is to integrate the items of the above-mentioned two models to improve their predicting power regarding the customer lock-in. We think that this is a novel and relevant approach as most of the online newspapers are portals offering content, interactive web-based services, and applications of digital products and services and therefore we can get valuable information of the factors affecting the customer value and behavior.

Earlier explorative work of Lu and Lin (2002) combined the very general Theory of Reasoned Action (TRA) model (Ajzen and Fishbein, 1980) with the Rayport and Sviokla's model and used students as respondents. Since Lu and Lin's work was based on the TRA model and did not integrate e.g. business model or e-commerce aspects into their study, we think that our research study provides more extensive and detailed view on the subject matter.

This paper is structured as follows. In chapter 2, we discuss briefly the problems that online application services are facing and lay ground for the need to integrate new online marketspace oriented instruments to measure customer value and behavior. In chapter 3, we describe the research methodology and present our research framework. In chapter 4, we describe our data collection and in chapter 5 we review the results. In the final chapter we conclude our observations and review the main findings and recommendations.

2. ONLINE NEWSPAPERS AS A TYPE OF SOFTWARE AS A SERVICE

As the SaaS provider can be a distributor for software applications, it can also be seen as a distributor for data (news, information) by providing access or an interface for the online papers' readers to content. In the Software as a Service model, the service is no longer only just an application provisioning service but integration of valuable application software into the online service infrastructure. We think that the SaaS model should be understood as a typical e-commerce arrangement dealing with digital products. Therefore also the problems associated with digital products e.g. durability, easy copying, experience product characteristics, and difficult price setting (Shapiro and Varian, 1999) should be taken into account. We define the SaaS model as follows (see Sääksjärvi et al., 2005): "Software as a Service is time and location independent online access to a remotely managed server application, that permits concurrent utilization of the same application installation by a large number of independent users (customers, subscribers), offers attractive payment logic compared to the customer value received, and makes a continuous flow of new and innovative software possible".

All in all, these observations make the SaaS model problematic since the entry barrier can be high. The SaaS concept seems realistic only if the online paper (i.e. the SaaS provider) is able to offer immediate and continuous customer value e.g. novelty and efficiency. Even then also customization and/or lock-in is required to make the business sustainable. It is important to note that many of the SaaS benefits are only efficiency based (Amit and Zott, 2001) and conditional, based on the pre-condition that the SaaS provider could overcome the above-mentioned significant risk issues.

2.1 The e-commerce view

Amit and Zott's value creation model (2001) is based on the virtual markets "in which business transactions are conducted via open networks based on the fixed and wireless Internet infrastructure". The underlying theoretical models of Amit and Zott's model are the value chain framework (Porter, 1985), Schumpeterian innovation (Schumpeter, 1942), the resource-based view of the firm (e.g. Wernerfelt, 1984; Barney, 1991), strategic network theory (e.g. Dyer and Singh, 1998; Gulati et al., 2000) and transaction cost economics (Williamson, 1975). Amit and Zott's model enables the evaluation of the value creation potential of different business models through four value drivers: efficiency, complementaries, lock-in, and novelty. Amit and Zott (2001) also emphasize the distinction between a business model and a revenue model: the business model primarily refers to value creation whereas the revenue model is centered on value appropriation. By the term "value" they refer to the total value created for all parties involved in the value network that a certain firm's business model compasses.

In the Amit and Zott's model (2001) the most important value driver is efficiency: the greater the transaction efficiency gains are i.e. when the costs per transaction decrease, the more valuable the e-business will be. Efficiency enhancements include e.g. streamlining the virtual value chain (Rayport and Sviokla, 1995) and enabling faster access to a wider range of real-time news. Another source of value creation are complementaries, such as providing online discussion rooms for readers or offering links to related information or news. Online newspapers can also create value by capitalizing on complementaries among activities e.g. when an online paper and a travel agency co-operate and offer discounts on vacation packages for the paper's subscribers.

According to Amit and Zott (2001) the value-creating potential of an online paper's business model also depends on the value driver called lock-in, which refers to the online paper's ability to e.g. get readers to renew their subscriptions. Lock-in usually refers to switching costs but in this case it refers to the online paper's readers' loyalty to remain as subscribers. Lock-in includes e.g. loyalty programs (discounts on longer subscriptions), personalization, customized news etc. The fourth value driver, novelty, consists of new ways e.g. of conducting the online business, offering news and articles (read sports news with your mobile phone) or new ways of combining products and services (subscribers of the "offline" paper gain access to the online version of the paper). Usually the four value drivers and their effects are interrelated with one another.

If we compare the value sources of Amit and Zott's general e-commerce model (2001) with the structure of the well-known TAM model, which is used to predict the intention to use an IS, we can see that there are a few interesting similarities from the customer point of view. First of all, the dependent variable of the TAM model, the behavioral intention of the customer to use the system, is one measure of the (mental) lock-in of the customer. The two major predictors of the user lock-in in the TAM model are ease of use and usefulness of the IS in question. When we think about online newspapers as a SaaS offering, both ease of use and efficiency are related to the infrastructure technology. In a typical web-based environment ease of use may loose part of its original importance and move closer to the efficiency dimension of the Amit and Zott's model (2001). Usefulness is also related to the novelty of the received content or infrastructure technology, partly due to the fact that usefulness and the value of the content of the online newspaper may be related. Other important sources of the customer value may be found in complementarities such as competitions, archival services, free e-mail etc.

2.2 The marketspace view

Rayport and Sviokla (1994) have examined and explained the differences between the physical, real-world marketplace and the virtual marketspace of the Internet. To illustrate their point of how value creation in the marketplace and marketspace differ they proposed a model, which consisted of three elements: content, or what companies are offering; context, or how they are offering it; and infrastructure, what enables the transaction to occur. Rayport and Sviokla emphasized that content in the marketspace may not automatically mean product and that distribution may not automatically refer to physical location. To outline an example of their model, Rayport and Sviokla used an online newspaper to show how content, context and infrastructure could be disaggregated in the marketspace. In the marketspace the content (news, business, sports, weather etc. pieces of information) can be separated from the context (online newspaper) and the infrastructure (network), which cannot be done with an offline newspaper that has its stories (content) printed on paper (context) in a printing press and is available to customers e.g. from newsstands or via postal delivery (infrastructure). This disaggregation of content, context, and infrastructure meant that in the marketspace new ways of adding value, lowering costs, forging relationships with non-traditional partners, and rethinking ownership issues was possible. Rayport and Sviokla also predicted that most newspaper publishers would find themselves competing in a service-focused, rather than product-focused, business. According to them, since managing in the marketspace means combining content, context and infrastructure in new and creative ways it also means that the interaction, or in this case the interface, between the customer and the companies has also changed. This means that the customer loyalty (lock-in) in the marketspace differs from that in the marketplace. The companies can now manage directly their interface and interaction with the customers at different levels. Now the companies can e.g. achieve brand differentiation and increase customer loyalty at different levels.

2.3 Research questions

In order to empirically study the factors that affect the online newspaper's customers' loyalty we formulated a research question following the idea of comparison and integration of the TAM (Davis, 1986) and Rayport and Sviokla's (1994) models for this research study about the online newspapers.

RQ: What are the roles of ease of use, usability, content, context, and infrastructure in predicting the customer lock-in (loyalty) in the case of online newspapers? Are the general e-commerce based value sources (novelty, effectiveness, and complementarities) relevant compared to them?

Our assumption, based on the theories, was that in the case of an online application service the users (at least the more experienced users) are no longer capable to separate the impact of ease of use and usefulness, because they have become parts of the standard Internet infrastructure. This should be seen in the resulting structure of the explorative factor analysis as integrating the single measures of the above models together and also when comparing the predicting power of the regression analyses.

Our empirical survey was carried out in the Finnish newspaper industry setting, which is an interesting market. Finland is one of the globally leading countries regarding the national IT infrastructure available for online services and their usage. Also the population's motivation and possibility to read newspapers on a daily basis are the highest globally (Statistics Finland/Tilastokeskus, 2002).

3. RESEARCH METHODOLOGY

We created and pre-tested an online survey questionnaire in cooperation with one of the leading newspaper companies in Finland in order to empirically study the customer value processes and the lock-in (loyalty) of their online newspaper's readers. In the survey instrument, we included the original items used in the earlier TAM studies for usefulness and ease of use, and we also included new items to cope with the content, context, and infrastructure items of the Rayport and Sviokla's model.

Several empirical studies have been published about the TAM model proving the original and modified items of the model to be quite reliable instruments in predicting user behavior (Legris et al., 2003). Originally, Davis (1986) proposed that the mediating role of user (behavioral) attitude was critical as a reliable predictor of the (Behavioral) Intention to use the system (BI). He proposed that two variables have an affect on Attitude (A): perceived Ease Of Use (EOU) and perceived Usefulness (U). In the later version of the model, Davis et al. (1989) leaved the attitude (A) item out and applied only intention (BI) as the success measure. We selected both of these measures into our survey to create a new dimension for measuring the mental lock-in (loyalty) of the SaaS customers.

Rayport and Sviokla's model (1994) is a conceptual one, proposing that online service providers should benefit from the new possibilities of both disaggregating content, context and infrastructure and from the renewal of the old value chain. We created new items for measuring the various aspects of the online newspaper's content, context (visual and structural characteristics of a web-site), and infrastructure (technical efficiency).

We finalized and pre-tested the survey questionnaire, which consisted of the above-mentioned items. As external variables we included items identifying the usage of complementary services and the exact demographics of the respondents including their age, gender, education, experience of using online newspapers, number of newspapers they frequently used, and self-evaluation of their level of Internet usage skills.

We did an exploratory factor analysis, which can be seen as a technique to aid in theory building (Sharma, 1996), in order to verify the constructs' reliability for the factor dimensions. To compare the predicting power of the new combined model to the other models, we also factored their items in order to get valid results. These constructs served as independent variables in a series of regression analyses, which were done in order to compare the predicting power of the different combinations of the factor dimensions.

4.   DATA COLLECTION

4.1   Sample selection and data collection

The survey questionnaire was pre-tested and improved in a few interviews with experienced online newspaper readers. We wanted to make sure that all questions were semantically precise and understandable. The names and e-mail addresses of the online newspaper's subscribers were picked out as a random sample of ca. 2500 names from the customer register of the newspaper company. An invitation letter was sent via e-mail to the respondents. The respondents were asked to participate in our study and fill in the questionnaire that was available on the web. After one reminder e-mail message we had received a total of 251 answers. We eliminated the possibility of getting double answers from one respondent by e.g. checking the IP addresses on the received responses. All in all, the response rate was ca. 10 percent. This is quite typical and acceptable in most web-based surveys, provided that all measures will be confirmed by factor analyses and also by splitting the data. In addition, the demographics of the respondents did not differ from the general profile of the registered customers and therefore the respondents represented well the selected newspaper's online customers.

4.2   Demographics of the respondents

The respondent sample was quite smoothly distributed among all age groups between 20 and 60 years. The respondents represented many different professions; typically they (over 40 percent) were white-collar office workers, one third of the whole population having a higher academic degree. However, there were a lot less female than male online readers among the respondents: only 26 percent of the answerers were women. As many as 78 percent of the respondents classified themselves as experienced Internet users, ca. 60 percent of all respondents having over four year experience of reading online newspapers. These online readers also had experience from several other online newspaper services as well: typically, the respondents were reading several (maximum of seven) online newspapers and were using a variety of complementary services. The number of complementary services used seemed to be related with the reader's experience of using the online newspaper. The typical palette of complementary services consisted of the news services, special theme pages, archival services, and the weather forecast service. These were all used at least by one third of all the readers of the online newspaper.

5.   RESULTS

5.1   Factor Analysis

The dimensions representing the new structural combinations of the factors perceived by the online readers are shown below (see details in Table 1). We named these six factor dimensions as follows (they are listed in the order of their eigenvalues, which are in parenthesis):
1. Navigational characteristics, F1-EASYNAVI (9.115)
2. Personal relevancy of content, F2-CONTVALUE (2.287)
3. Attractiveness of context, F3-CONTEXT (1.445)
4. Usefulness of complementarities, F4-COMPLEM (1.109)
5. Playfulness, F5-PLAY (1.106)
6. Free offerings, F6-FREE (1.011)

These six factors together explained 73 percent of the total variance. Interestingly, the strongest factor, Navigational characteristic (F1), was composed of the typical TAM-based usability items, and also Attractiveness of content (F3) was related with the structural part of the usability. The second factor (F2-CONTVALUE) was composed of three content based, two usefulness related and two infrastructure items. This combination was a good example of the fusion of usefulness (meaningful for me), content (good, broad coverage of the topics), and efficiency (website that was fast and effective to use). Factor F3 could be seen as structural and visual usability oriented dimension presenting issues, which are important in the new context of an online newspaper. Therefore, we named it as "Attractiveness of context".

The rest of the factors were weaker, not as stable as the first three when the data was split into two parts e.g. on the basis of the experience of the users. Interestingly, the Usefulness of complementarities factor (F4) integrated usability, content, and coverage items regarding complementary services. The last two factors, Playfulness (F5) and Free offerings (F6), were statistically weak. Leaving them out from the analysis did not change the remaining factor structure.

When we took only the less-experienced users (half of the sample) into the analysis, the factor structure slightly changed as one additional factor appeared in the structure. Three vague usefulness items that had to be dropped from the earlier factor structure formed a new factor called Novelty (F7), which consisted of characteristics such as "unique, up-to-date, and freshness" of the services.

Figure 1. The combined factor structure of the customer lock-in (N=251)

Factor	Factor loadings	Mean	Std. Dev.	Items correlation with total score	Eigenval % of var
CUSTOMER LOCK-IN					**4.072 (58.2%)**
A-01 Likes to use	0.729	4.63	1.000	0.688**	
A-02 Positive attitude toward usage	0.678	4.97	0.870	0.635**	
A-04 Favourite web-site	0.790	3.02	1.600	0.800**	
BI-01 Intention to continue usage	0.830	4.11	1.350	0.832**	
BI-02 Intention to recommend	0.831	4.22	1.230	0.814**	
BI-03 Intention to use frequently	0.784	3.78	1.550	0.794**	
BI-04 Intention to bookmark	0.679	4.25	1.840	0.734**	

** Correlation is significant at the 0.01 level

The dependent variable of our study, the customer lock-in, is described in Figure 1. We combined items representing the attitude (current satisfaction and positive attitude towards the online usage) and intention (motivation to continue the usage) to result in only one factor representing the (mental) lock-in of the readers. This variable, the Customer lock-in (loyalty), was used as the dependent variable in the following regression analyses.

Figure 2. Correlation coefficients between the key variables

Independent variables/models	Combined lock-in (Attitude and Behavioral Intention)
F1-EASYNAVI	0.455**
F2-CONTVALUE	0.650**
F3-CONTEXT	0.459**
F4-COMPLEM	0.489**
F5-PLAY	0.154*
F6-FREE	0.298**
(F7 NOVELTY)	(0.612**)
TAM-Usefulness U	0.686**
TAM-Structural EOU (F3)	0.459**
R-S-Content&Infra	0.604**
R-S-Context	0.459**

** Correlation is significant at the 0.01 level
* Correlation is significant at the 0.05 level

5.2 Results from the regression analyses

The correlation coefficients in Figure 2 demonstrate that the new integrated factor construct F2 (Personal relevancy of content) and the TAM-based usefulness (U) factor had somewhat higher correlation with the lock-in than the other factors. Accordingly, these two were the most significant single predictors of the lock-in. However, also the marketspace oriented factor Rayport and Sviokla's Content&Infra and the interesting Novelty (F7) factor had high (over 0.6) correlations. In addition, both usability measures (F1 and F3) were important predictors of the lock-in; however they had lower correlation with the lock-in (level 0.4). When determining the best combined regression models it turned out that the co-correlations between the factors typically eliminated the effects of the second and third predictors. We could conclude that the new combined measures were competitors (mediators, not moderators) of the two models used.

Furthermore, Playfulness (F6) explained less than 10% of the variance in the dependent variable. This is not surprising since the playfulness consisted of light entertainment and gossip columns, neither of which seemed to be high on the online newspapers' readers list of topics of interest.

From Figure 3, we can see the results of our comparison between the best three regression models, based on the three sets of the best predictors. The results show that the new combined constructs F2, F7, and F4 explained 48.7

percent of the variance of the lock-in. The other two sets of predictors also achieved a good R^2 values: TAM 43% and Rayport-Sviokla 38%.

Figure 3. Comparison of the regression models

Model (dependent variable in parenthesis)	R^2	Beta	Significance
TAM model (Behavioural Intention, BI)			
Usefulness (U)	41.6%	0.647	0.000
Usefulness (U) + F1-EASYNAVI	43.0%	0.145	0.009
Rayport-Sviokla model (Customer Lock-in)			
Content (CON) + Infra (INF)	36.3%	0.604	0.000
Content + Infra + Context (F3)	38.0%	0.169	0.006
Combined model (Customer Lock-in)			
F2-CONTVALUE	42.4%	0.650	0.000
F2 + F7-NOVELTY	48.0%	0.306	0.000
F2 + F7 + F4-COMPLEM	48.7%	0.118	0.037

When the data was split into subsets of readers according to the primary complementary services they used (whether it was archival, weather forecast, ice-hockey fun club etc.) we noticed some interesting development trends. According to the theory presented, the more experienced readers seemed to increase their palette of services. Broader service palette and more frequent usage of services seemed to improve the customer lock-in, at least to a certain limit (until 5 to 7 different services used).

The practical conclusions from the above results are that the online newspapers' readers seem to be interested not just in reading the news but also in the other additional services that the newspapers are offering. Together these two affect the continued usage of the online service. In order to increase the number of readers (i.e. to attract new readers) the online newspapers should concentrate more on novelty and complementarities and on useful content and effective infrastructure in order to maintain the lock-in of the existing customers.

6.   CONCLUSIONS

According to the evolving literature on the concept of "Software as a Service" (SaaS), the benefits proposed for the customer and the provider are controversial as many of the customer benefits are also listed as serious risks for the service provider. A sustainable service in the proposed one-to-many SaaS mode will therefore require an effective business model capable to create and maintain the lock-in of the customers. For this purpose we propose the usage of the Amit and Zott's e-commerce model, which is based on four value drivers one of them being the customer lock-in.

Our empirical data on 251 online newspaper readers showed that the predictors of the lock-in proposed in the earlier studies appeared in new factor constructs of navigational characteristics, personal relevancy of content, attractiveness of context, and usefulness of complementarities. The navigational and structural usability of the services were significant factors but they were not as good predictors of the customer lock-in as the new integrated constructs. This indicates that in the SaaS context the web-based interface will make the usability less critical as a separate predictor of lock-in. In the online context, customers seem to integrate the effects of infrastructure, content, and usefulness in a new way, and the customer value sources seem to be more complex than in the case of the typical organizational IS.

Based on the above-mentioned observations we argue that the evaluation of the Software as a Service offering could benefit from instruments that combine usability, usefulness, and customer value dimensions. Compared to the application centered TAM model, the typical SaaS context integrates application functionality with the content and the infrastructure efficiency. The e-commerce based value drivers of Amit and Zott's model (2001) seem to be relevant in building customer value attributes that explain the customer lock-in. Our results encourage further research and development of new instruments in order to evaluate the customer lock-in in a more reliable way, taking also the customer value creation sources (efficiency, novelty, and complementarities) into the analysis.

On the basis of our research we propose that a Software as a Service providers should also take into account the typical customer life cycle. Novelty seemed to be important to get the customers involved, however it was not sufficient for maintaining a sustainable lock-in. Usefulness (just for me content in an effective format) and a useful set of complementarities were the best predictors in explaining the continued usage of the online services.

7. REFERENCES

Amit, R., and Zott, C., 2001, Value creation in e-business, Strat. Management J. **22**:493-520.

Ajzen, I., and Fishbein, M., 1980, Understanding attitudes and predicting social behavior, Prentice-Hill, Englewood Cliffs, NJ.

Barney, J. B., 1991, Firm resources and sustained competitive advantage, J. of Management **17**:99-120.

Cherry Tree & Co., 2000, Framing the IT services industry: 2nd generation ASPs, Spotlight Report (September, 2000); www.cherrytreeco.com.

Davis, F. D., 1986, A technology acceptance model for empirically testing new end-user information systems: Theory and results, Doctoral dissertation, Sloan School of Management, MIT.

Davis, F. D., Bagozzi, R. P., and Warshaw, P. R., 1989, User acceptance of computer technology: A comparison of two theoretical models, Management Science **15**(8):982-1003.

Desai, B., and Currie, W., 2003, Application service providers: A model in evolution, 5th Intl Conference on E-Commerce (ICEC), Sep 30 - Oct 3, 2003, Pittsburgh, PA, pp. 174-180.

Dyer, J., and Singh, H., 1998, The relational view: Cooperative strategy and sources of interorganizational competitive advantage, Academy of Management Review **23**:660-679.

Grönroos, C., Heinonen, F., Isoniemi, K., and Lindholm, M., 2000, The NetOffer model: A case example from the virtual marketspace, Management Decision **38**(4):242-252.

Gulati, R., Nohria, N., and Zaheer, A., 2000, Strategic networks, Strat. Mgmt J. **21**:203-215.

Hoch, F. et al., 2001, Software as a service: "A to Z" for ISVs, Software & Information Industry Association (SIIA), Washington, D.C.; http://www.siia.com.

IDC, 1999, The ASPs' impact on the IT industry: An IDC-wide opinion, IDC Bulletin No. 20323.

Legris, P., Ingham, J., and Collerette, P., 2003, Why do people use information technology? A critical review of the technology acceptance model, Information and Management **40**:191-204.

Lu, H. and Lin, J.C-C., 2002, Predicting customer behaviour in the marketspace: A study of Rayport and Sviokla's framework, Information and Management **40**:1-10.

Mizoras, A., and Goepfert, J., 2003, 2003 AppSourcing taxonomy and research guide, IDC – Industry Developments and Models (February, 2003) IDC No. 28473.

Porter, M., 1985, Competitive advantage: Creating and sustaining superior performance, Free Press, New York, NY.

Rayport, J. F., and Sviokla, J., 1994, Managing in the marketspace, Harvard Business Review (November-December, 1994), pp. 141-150.

Rayport, J. F., and Sviokla, J., 1995, Exploiting the virtual value chain, Harvard Business Review (November-December, 1995), pp. 75-85.

Schumpeter, J. A., 1942, Capitalism, socialism and democracy, Harper, New York, NY.

Shapiro, C., and Varian, H., 1999, Information rules: A strategic guide to the network economy, Harvard Business School Press, Boston, MA.

Sharma, S., 1996, Applied multivariate results, John Wiley & Sons, New York, NY.

SIIA, 2001, Software as a service: Strategic backgrounder, Software & Information Industry Association (SIIA), Washington, D.C. (February, 2001); http://www.siia.com.

Statistics Finland/Tilastokeskus 2002, http://statfin.stat.fi/statweb, Päivälehtien levikki 1000 asukasta kohden 1990-1998, Joukkoviestintä markkinat Suomessa ja Euroopassa 1996, Tietotekniikka kotitalouksissa 1990-1999, Tietotekniikan käyttö Suomessa ja EU-maissa 1997 ja 1999, Uusien viestimien käyttö Kevät 1999.

Sääksjärvi, M., Lassila, A., and Nordström, H., 2005, Evaluating the software as a service business model: From CPU time-sharing to online innovation sharing, IADIS International Conference e-Society, Malta (June 27-30, 2005), pp. 177-186.

Wernerfelt, B., 1984, A resource-based view of the firm, Strat. Management J. **5**:171-180.

Williamson, O. E., 1975, Markets and hierarchies, analysis and antitrust implications: A study in the economics of internal organization, Free Press, New York, NY.

Appendix 1

Table 1. Combined Factor Structure (N=251)

Factor	Factor loadings	Mean	Std. Dev.	Items correlation with total score	Eigenval % of var
F1-EASYNAVI Navigational characteristics					**9.115** **(41.4%)**
EOU-05 Easy to locate oneself	0.758	4.19	1.230	0.832**	
EOU-06 Not getting easily lost	0.844	4.40	1.180	0.883**	
EOU-07 Easy to navigate	0.748	4.43	1.238	0.873**	
EOU-08 Quick and easy to learn	0.814	4.94	1.101	0.861**	
EOU-09 Easy to relearn usage	0.802	4.62	1.286	0.841**	
F2-CONTVALUE Personal relevancy of content					**2.287** **(10.4%)**
U-01 Personally interesting	0.588	4.50	1.122	0.672**	
U-09 Matches my personal needs	0.639	4.31	1.193	0.802**	
CON-01 Sufficient number of news	0.840	4.26	1.322	0.830**	
CON-02 News are well composed	0.804	4.18	1.352	0.835**	
CON-05 Sufficient coverage of news	0.763	4.32	1.104	0.818**	
INF-01 Services are fast to use	0.581	4.59	1.021	0.790**	
INF-02 Services are effortless to use	0.606	4.45	1.128	0.816**	
F3-CONTEXT Attractive context					**1,445** **(6.6%)**
EOU-01 Visually attractive design	0.811	4.38	1.154	0.845**	
EOU-02 Easy perceivable structure	0.726	4.48	1.154	0.909**	
EOU-03 Clear and logical structure	0.708	4.45	1.121	0.898**	
F4-COMPLEM Usefulness of complementarities					**1,109** **(5.04%)**
EOU-10 Usability of complements	0.548	4.16	1.199	0.805**	
U-06 Importance of complements	0.721	4.35	1.496	0.819**	
CON-03 Broad scale of complements	0.873	2.02	1.711	0.822**	
F5-PLAY Playfulness					**1,106** **(5.0%)**
U-08 Entertainment important	0.817	2.34	1.640	0.864**	
CON-04 More gossip columns	0.873	2.02	1.711	0.876**	
F6-FREE Free offerings					**1,011** **(4.6%)**
U-05 Free news service	0.845	4.04	1.753	0.863**	
U-07 Interesting headlines available	0.707	3.69	1.714	0.856**	

** Correlation is significant at the 0.01 level

ROBALO: A RISK-ORIENTED JOB DISPATCHING MECHANISM FOR WORKFORCE MANAGEMENT SYSTEM

Shi-Cho Cha, csc@mba.ntu.edu.tw
Hung-Wen Tung, hwtung@iii.org.tw
Han-Chao Lee, garry@iii.org.tw
Tse-Ming Tsai, eric@iii.org.tw
Raymund Lin, raymund@iii.org.tw
and Chih-Hao Hsu, eden@iii.org.tw
Advanced e-Commerce Institute, Institute for Information Industry, Taipei, Taiwan

Abstract   We proposed a framework, called *Risk-Oriented joB dispAtching for mobiLe workfOrce management system* (ROBALO), to ease the tension between (a) the reliability requirement to serve a job request, and (b) the cost of the job's assignment. In ROBALO, the risks for workers to execute a job are taken into consideration. Such consideration is especially useful in the scenario of mobile workforce management because mobile workers usually meet unexpected situations in the field. Therefore, we can find the job assignment with the minimum cost under a certain degree of risk. Therefore, the job dispatcher can reserve enough resources and make enough preparations for a incident. In tradition, job dispatching mechanism usually take exception handling processes to deal with the failure of job execution. Compared to this approach, the time to discover the failure can be saved because we try to do things right at the first time.

Keywords: Mobile Workforce Management System, Online Job Dispatching, Risk Management

1.   Introduction

As the advances of wireless technologies and hand-held computers, organizations are willing and able to deploy their *Mobile Workforce Management Systems (MWMSs)*, especially when their workers, such as sales, maintenance technicians, house care doctors, ..., need to deliver services in the field. Generally speaking, MWMSs can help organizations increase productivity by eliminating paperwork, arming technicians with more information at the point of performance, and capturing work completion data for enhanced management functions, etc. Hamilton, 2003,Sairamesh et al., 2004.

The main features of MWMSs includes Guido et al., 1998,Appelbald and Lonn, 2004: (1)*Automatic job dispatching*: automatically plan and dispatch job to field technicians or workforce; (2)*Workforce forecasting*: find out what effect a change in future workload; (3)*Schedule optimization*: let the system optimize an already existing and planned schedule; (4)*GIS/GPS support*; (5) *Mobility support*: support the workforce and make the workforce system available via some sort of mobile device; (6) *Monitoring*: monitor the progress of assigned job; (7)*Exception handling*.

Among these features, we focus on the job dispatching (especially the on-line job dispatching model) in this article. The main goal of job dispatching in MWMSs is to assign right people to satisfy a job request in the field under the constraints of time. Traditional job dispatching schemes usually treat failure of job execution as exceptions and take actions after failure is discovered. Obviously, the time to discover the failure is wasted in this case.

In light of this, we propose the Risk-Oriented joB dispAtching for mobiLe workfOrce management system (ROBALO). Simply speaking, ROBALO predicts the risk (or the expected loss) for works to finish a job assignment successfully based on the workers' capacities, statuses, and historical work experiences. When a job request is received, the request will be dispatched to workers so that the risk for the assignment can be controlled under a certain degree. Such consideration is especially useful in the scenario of MWMS because mobile workers usually meet unexpected situations in the field. In addition, while the cost for a person to execute a job is considered, our algorithm can find the assignment with the minimum cost under the degree of risk.

While we take risk into consideration, the following benefits can be achieved:

- The time to discover the failure can be saved because we try to do things right at the first time. It is especially important in the situation that time is critical.

- We provide a systematic approach to ease the tension between reliability and cost. Intuitively, the more number of workers are assigned to execute a job, the lower probability of failure. However, the more number of workers usually means the higher cost. While our approach finds the assignment with the minimum cost under a certain degree of risk, the requirement of reliability and cost can be balanced.

- With the risk information, job dispatcher can reserve some resources and make some preparations for the incident. For example, a dispatching center can have some insurance and transfer the risk to others.

- While we use the workers' experience and other historical data to calculate the risk, our approach can be self-adaptive to the real world. Obviously, the estimation of risk can become more precise while more historical data can be obtained.

The rest of the paper is organized as follows: Section 2 surveys related work on job dispatching on mobile workforce management. Section 3 gives an overview of the framework. Sections 4-6 discuss key components in the framework. Conclusions and future work are offered in Section 7.

2. Related Work

Traditional job dispatching methodologies can be classified into the following two categories: (1) the batch model and (2) the online model.

The batch model assumes that the job requests and available workers are known in advanced. Then the available workers are assigned to deal with these given jobs. For example, the classical job assignment problem in operation research domain tries to find a optimal solution of assigning n jobs to n workers with minimum cost while the cost of assigning worker i to job j is known Taha, 2003.

The batch model is useful for assigning the routine or scheduled jobs. However, in some cases, we cannot know every job requests in priori. For example, an emergency center may receive an emergency call from a injured person and need to dispatch an ambulance to take him/her to a nearby hospital. At this point, we can use online model to assign one or more workers to serve the incoming request.

We focus on the online model in this article (applying our system to the batch model is left to our future work). Current online job dispatching schemes usually assign workers to serve a incoming job request based on the workers' cost, capabilities, or current statuses. For example, HAMS (Healthcare Alert Management System)Chiu et al., 2004,Aydin et al., 2004 classifies staffs in a hospital into different roles based on their capacities. And each kind of tasks (or alerts) can only be assigned to the staffs with appropriate roles. When a alert is triggered, HAMS select a person from the available staff members who can play the roles required for the alert and dispatches the alert to the him/her. The SOS Alarm Normark, 2002 dispatch ambulances for emergency calls based on the proximity to the ambulance stations and the status of each ambulance.

Besides workers' capacities and statuses, we propose to take the probability that a person may fail to finish a job into consideration and use risks as a factor for job assignment in this article. Our ROBALO system assigns just enough workers so that a job can be finished within a specified level of risk. At the point of dealing with the failure of job execution, traditional online job dispatching systems usually initiate their exception handling processes while assigned workers fail to finish a job. For example, HAMS Chiu et al., 2004, Aydin et al., 2004 sends messages to all staffs with the same role as it finds that a staff does not confirm a job assignment. Intuitively, in comparison with traditional exception handling approach, the time to discover the failure can be saved because we can make some "preparation" (e.g., we can assign another person as backup) while the job is dispatching.

3.   System Overview

The architecture of ROBALO can be depicted in Figure 1. First of all, we maintain the following information for job dispatching:

- The *profiles of workforce* contains workers' basic information, capacities, and other demographic information.

- The *current statuses of the workforce* include workers' current location, availability information, etc. tracked by the *status monitor* (How to monitor the statuses is beyond the scope of this article).

- The *cost matrix* contains the cost for a person to execute a job.

- The *job execution historical logs* record the results for a worker or a working group to execute a job.

- The *past impact* logs the loss when a job is failed to execute.

Figure 2 shows the process of job dispatching. When a job request is received, the *Request Handler* parses the request to extract the context information from the request and generate constraints of the job. The *Candidate Filter* then uses these constraints to filter out unqualified workers and obtains a candidate list for this job.

In this article, we treat a risk as the expected loss when a job fails. And it can be calculated from a combinational function of loss expectancy and the probability of failure (the formal definition is shown in Section 6). Therefore, after the request context and candidate list are obtained from the above steps, the *Impact Evaluator* predicts the loss if the job cannot be finished on time based on the context of request and past impact history. On the other hand, the *Failure Probability Evaluator* predicts the probability of failure from the request context, the profiles of workforce, the workforce's current statuses and job execution historical logs.

With the predicted impacts and failure probability, the *Worker Selection* then calculates the risk for a worker or working group to execute and select the workers to execute the job. Finally, the *Job Dispatcher* dispatches the result of job assignment to the selected workers.

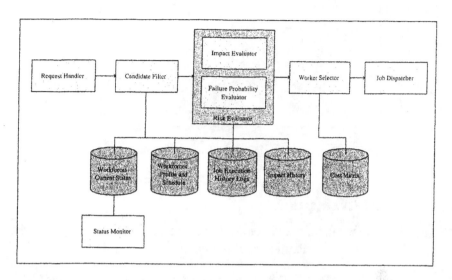

Figure 1. ROBALO Architecture

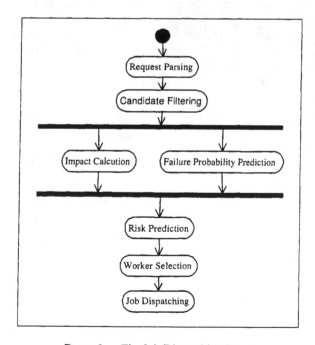

Figure 2. The Job Dispatching Process

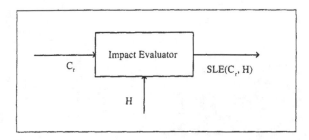

Figure 3.   The I/O of the Impact Evaluator

4.   Impact Evaluation

Figure 3 shows the input and output of the Impact Evaluator. First of all, the context of a request can be defined as follows:

DEFINITION 1 (CONTEXT) *The context of a request r (we denote it as C_r) is represented by a m-ary tuple: $(c_1, c_2, ..., c_m)$. Each c_i represents an attribute or a feature of the context.*

With the definition of context, we can further define the impact history:

DEFINITION 2 (IMPACT HISTORY) *The impact history H can be defined as a set of tuple (C_i, I_i). For a past failure request R_i, C_i is the context of this request. And I_i is the loss incurred from the failure execution of the job request.*

The output of the Impact Evaluator is the prediction of the loss when the request r cannot be finished on time (we denote it as $SLE(C_r, H)$). The traditional linear discriminant analysis methodology Fisher, 1936,Devijver and Kittler, 1982 can be used as follows:

- First, we classify the amount of loss into several classes. For example, we can divide the amount of loss into five classes as Table 1. For each value in $Class_i$ and $Class_j$, the value in $Class_i$ is less than the value in $Class_j$ if i is less than j.

- Secondly, for each adjacent class, find the linear discriminant function $g_{i,i+1}$ with the impact history H, where $g_{i,i+1}(X) = \sum_{1 \le k \le m}(v_k \times x_k + v_0)$ and X is a m-ary tuple: $(x_1, x_2, ..., x_m)$. These linear discriminant functions are re-calculated every some period of time so that these functions can reflect the up-to-date scenarios. For a tuple X, if $g_{i,i+1}(X) \le 0$, X belongs to $Class_k$ where $k \le i$. Otherwise, X belongs to $Class_l$ where $l > i$.

1.m = *the number of classes*
2.*for* $i=1$, $i \leq m-1$
3.   *if* $g_{i,i+1}(C_R) \leq 0$ *then* C_R *belongs to* $class_i$
4.*next i*
5.C_R *belongs to* $class_m$

Figure 4.   The Algorithm for Context Classification.

- Finally, when a context C_r is received, we calculate with class C_r as shown in Figure 4. And the ceiling of the range of the class is returned as $SLE(C_r, H)$.

Table 1.   Classification of Impacts

Class	Range
$Class_1$	$0 – $10K
$Class_2$	$10K – $1M
$Class_3$	$1M – $100M
$Class_4$	$100M – $10G
$Class_5$	$10G –

5.   Probability Evaluation

As shown in Figure 5, the Probability Evaluator predicts the probability that a working unit fails to finish a job under the context of the received request. Besides context, we have the following definitions:

DEFINITION 3 (WORKING UNIT) *A working unit W_r is the minimum set that can be assigned to serve a request r. Supposed that the universal set of workers is U (U = $\{u_i \mid u_i$ is a worker$\}$), $W_r \in U*$.*

DEFINITION 4 (JOB EXECUTION HISTORIES) *The job execution history EH can be defined as a set of tuple (C_i, W_i, S_i). For a past job request R_i, C_i is the context of this request, W_i is the work unit assigned to execute the job, and S_i is its result (either success or failure).*

DEFINITION 5 (PROFILES OF WORKFORCE) *The current profiles of workforce WP is represented by a set of x-ary tuple: ($wp_{i1}, wp_{i2}, ..., wp_{ix}$). Each wp_{ij} represents an attribute or a feature of the worker u_i's profile.*

DEFINITION 6 (WORKFORCE STATUSES) *Similar to the profiles of workforce, the current statuses of workers WS is represented by a set of y-ary tuple: $(ws_{i1}, ws_{i2}, ..., ws_{iy})$. Each ws_{ij} represents a kind of status of the worker u_i.*

To make it simple, we assume that the failure probabilities for each worker to execute a job is independent on another. This means that the failure probability of a work unit $P(W_r, C_r, EH, WP, WS)$ can be calculated from the product of $P(\{u_k\}, C_r, EH, WP, WS)$ where $u_k \in W_r$. Before computing $P(\{u_k\}, C_r, EH, WP, WS)$, a linear discriminant function d is found as follows:

- For each element (C_i, W_i, S_i) in EH, we extract the members of the working unit.

- For each worker u_k in the working unit W_i, we obtain the worker's profiles WP_{kt} and statuses WS_{kt} at that point of time t.

- We concatenate WP_{kt}, WS_{kt}, and C_i into a new $(x + y + m)$-ary tuple (we call it as a working features vector (wf_{kti})). And use the tuple to find out the linear discriminant function d.

- After the linear discriminant function d is found, we calculate wf_{kti} for each working features vector and generate a set D. In the set D, we have tuples of the value of $d(wf_{kti})$ and its related result, e.g., (0.12, success), (-1, failure), (0.01, failure), etc........ And we denote it as (d_{wf_i}, s_{wf_i})

Then, $P(\{u_k\}, C_r, EH, WP, WS)$ can be calculated as follows:

- First of all, we extract the user's profiles and statuses and concatenate them with C_r into a working features vector wf_k.

- Compute the value of $d(wf_k)$.

- Compare the value of each d_{wf_i} in D and find N-nearest tuples.

- Compute the number of tuples where the value of s_{wf_i} is failure. If the number is n, the probability of failure is predicted as n/N.

Finally, $P(W_r, C_r, EH, WP, WS)$ can be obtained from the product of $P(\{u_k\}, C_r, EH, WP, WS)$ (for each $u_k \in W_r$).

6. Worker Selection

As demonstrated in Figure 6, the Worker Selector select a set of disjointed work units S. That is, $S = \{W_i | W_i$ *is a working unit and* $\neg \exists W_j, W_j \in S, W_i \neq W_j,$ *and* $W_i \cup W_j \neq \phi\}$. Also, S satisfied the following constraints:

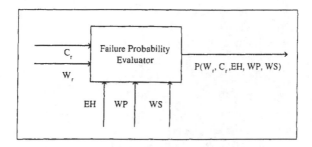

Figure 5. The I/O of the Probability Evaluator

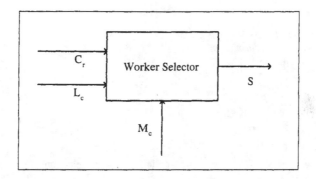

Figure 6. The I/O of the Worker Selector

If the acceptable risk is R_a, S is the assignment with the minimum cost among the possible assignments which risk are less than R_a. In this article, we adopt the risk definition in the domain of information security Tipton and Krause, 2004 and define risks as follows:

DEFINITION 7 (RISK) *The risk of a request R_r is the product of its loss expectancy ($SLE(C_r, H)$))(See Section 4) and the probability that a assignment S fails to serve the request ($P_r(S)$).*

Suppose that the failure probability for a working unit to execute a job is independent to others. We can calculate $P_r(S)$ from the product of $P(W_i, C_r, EH, WP, WS)$(See Section 5), for each $W_i \in S$.

With the candidate list L_c and cost matrix M_c, we can select S with the pseudo-code shown in Figure 7. Generally speaking, the algorithm wishes to find S with the minimized cost where $P_r(S) \times SLE(C_r, H) \leq R_a$ or $P_r(S) \times SLE(C_r, H) \leq R_a/SLE(C_r, H)$. Obviously, if $R_a/SLE(C_r, H)$ is greater or equal to 1, any job assignment can satisfy the constraint. Therefore, we can select the working unit W in L_c with the least cost. Otherwise, because $0 \leq P(W_i, C_r, EH, WP, WS) \leq 1$, we can apply the logarithmic function

1. *If $R_a/SLE(C_r, H) \geq 1$ then*
2.   *Select the working unit W in L_c with the least cost*
3. $S = \{W\}$
4.   *return S*
5. *Else*
6.   *current_risk = 0*
7. $W' = L_c$
8. $S = \{\}$
9.   *while current_risk > R_a and W' is not empty*
10.   *Find the work unit W_i in W' with the biggest $logP(W_i, C_r, EH, WP, WS)/C_{W_i}$,*
                      where W_i does not contain any workers in S
11. $W' = W' - W_i$
12. $S = S \cup W_i$
13.   *current_risk = $SLE(C_r, H) \times \Pi_{W_i \in S} P(W_i, C_r, EH, WP, WS)$*
14.   *End While*
15.   *If current_risk > R_a and W' is empty then*
16.   *The result cannot be found*
17.   *return ϕ*
18.   *End If*
19.   *return S*
20. *End If*

Figure 7.   The Pseudo-code for Worker Selection.

to the inequality $\Pi_{W_i \in S} P(W_i, C_r, EH, WP, WS) \leq R_a/SLE(C_r, H)$. The line 6–line 19 in Figure 7 try to find a solution to $\Sigma_{W_i \in S} log(P(W_i, C_r, EH, WP, WS)) \geq (log(R_a) - log(SLE(C_r, H)))$ with the minimized cost. The greedy algorithm is used here to choose the working unit with the biggest unit cost of $log(P(W_i, C_r, EH, WP, WS))$.

7.   Conclusions and Future Work

We proposed a framework, called *Risk-Oriented joB dispAtching for mobiLo workfOrce system* (ROBALO), to ease the tension between (a) the reliability requirement to service a job request, and (b) the cost of the job's assignment. In ROBALO, the risks for a worker or a working group to execute a job assignment are taken into consideration. Such consideration is especially useful in the scenario of mobile workforce management because mobile workers may usually meet unexpected situations in the field. Therefore, we can use a systematic approach to find the assignment with the minimum cost under a certain degree of risk. Therefore, job dispatcher can reserve enough resources and make enough preparations for a incident. In tradition, job dispatching mechanism usually take exception handling processes to deal with the failure of job execution. Compared to this approach, the time to discover the failure can be saved because we try to do things right at the first time.

Other than a concrete implementation of ROBALO, there are many interesting things left to be done. First, we observe that this paper focus on the online job dispatching scenarios. Similar methods may be used to develop a framework for batch scenarios. Secondly, current design in ROBALO assumes that the failure events are independent. The relationship between workers may be considered. Finally, our current system uses linear discriminant analysis to predict the risk from history data. More complicated approaches, such as non-linear programming technologies, may be included.

Acknowledgments

This research was supported by the Service Web Technology Research Project of Institute for Information Industry and sponsored by MOEA, ROC.

Appelbald, Agneta Soderpalm and Lonn, Stefan (2004). A study of workforce management. Master's thesis, IT University of Goteborg.

Aydin, Nizamettin, Marvasti, F., and Markus, H. S. (2004). Embolic doppler ultrasound signal detection using discrete wavelet transform. *IEEE Transactions on Information Technology in Biomedicine*, 8(2):182–190.

Chiu, Dickson K. W., Kwok, Benny W. C., Wong, Ray L. S., Cheung, Shing-Chi, and Kafeza, Eleanna (2004). Alert-driven e-service management. In *HICSS*.

Devijver, Pierre A. and Kittler, Josef (1982). *Pattern Recogintion: A Stastical Approach*. Prentice Hall. ISBN 0-13-654236-0.

Fisher, R. A. (1936). The use of multiple measurements in taxonomic problems. *Annal of Eugenics*, 7:179–188.

Guido, Bruno, Roberto, Gavazzi, Tria, Paolo Di, and Bisio, Rossella (1998). Workforce management (wfm) issues. In *Network Operations and Management Symposium*, pages 473–482.

Hamilton, Steve (2003). Workforce automation: Mobile computing for asset management. In *Proceedings of the 18th International Maintenance Conference (IMC2003)*.

Normark, Maria (2002). Sense-making of an emergency call: possibilities and constraints of a computerized case file. In *NordiCHI '02: Proceedings of the second Nordic conference on Human-computer interaction*, pages 81–90, New York, NY, USA. ACM Press.

Sairamesh, J., Goh, S., Stanoi, I., Padmanabhan, S., and Li, C. S. (2004). Disconnected processes, mechanisms and architecture for mobile e-business. *Mobile Networks and Applications*, 9(6):651–662.

Taha, Hamdy A. (2003). *Operations Research*. Prentice Hall. ISBN 0-13-048808-9.

Tipton, Harold F. and Krause, Micki (2004). *Information security management handbook 5-th ed.* CRC Press. ISBN 0-8493-1997-8.

DISCOVERY AND QUERY: TWO SEMANTIC PROCESSES FOR WEB SERVICES

Po Zhang[1], Juanzi Li[1] and Kehong Wang[1]
[1] Department of Computer Science of Tsinghua University, 100084, Beijing, China

Abstract: In this paper, we focuses on two process phases of web services, namely the web services discovery and web service query. Web services discovery is to locate the appropriate service, and web service query is to search the service data during execution of web service. When an end-user wants to book a ticket, he will discover the web service first, and then query this service to determine whether it can provide the satisfiable ticket. So the two process phases should work together, not only to discover possible satisfiable service, but to find the real satisfiable service data. It's a promising idea to adopt Semantic Web technology to implement the two processes. This paper first proposes the whole architecture for discovery and query, then gives four algorithms to discover web services and three algorithms to query web service based on the service data instance concept and similarity calculation. Accordingly, two frameworks separately for discovery and query are implemented. The result proves the approach of combination of two processes can really meet the personal requirements, so has certain application value.

Key words: Web Services Discovery; Query; Ontology; Similarity Computing.

1.   INTRODUCTION

Web services [1] are self-contained, self-describing, modular applications that can be published, located and invoked across the web. Once a web service is deployed, other applications or other web services can discover and invoke it. UDDI, WSDL and SOAP, which are three most important technologies of web services, provide limited support in mechanizing service recognition and discovery, service configuration and combination, service comparison and automated negotiation. Service discovery is currently done by name/key/category of the information model in UDDI which roughly defines attributes that describe the service provider, the relationships with other providers and how to access the service instance. The fixed set of attributes in UDDI limits the way queries can be composed. Although UDDI can find more service information in WSDL, the WSDL only describes the service in a low-level form of interface signature and communication protocol and can't provide enough semantic description for locating the service intelligently.

The semantic web [2] will make data on the web defined and linked in a way, that it can be used by machines - not just for display purposes, but also for using it in various applications. Bringing web services applications to their full potential requires their combination with semantic web technology.

Nowadays, lots of approaches for semantic web service discovery have been proposed. However, it's not enough for an end user only to find a web service interface. For example, which is from OpenTravel Alliance Message Users Guide [8] , "Bob is planning a trip for his wife and child to fly from London to Los Angeles. He would like to depart on August 13 and prefers a non-stop flight, but if he has to make a stopover, he prefers that there be a maximum of one stopover. He also would like to fly on a 757 and have his tickets mailed to him. He wants to fly economy class. Bob requests availability on flights from London to Los Angeles on August 13. And he wants to get the roundtrip tickets information." If Bob only find a web service interface which can provide a ticket, he still can not know whether the ticket can satisfy his concrete requirements such as the exact date or airplane type, even the logic expression of personal preferences.

So the approach proposed in this paper not only focused on semantic web service discovery, but adopts semantic web technology to support web service query. The combination with discovery and query can solve the above example case.

Section 2 proposes the whole architecture for combination of discovery and query. Upon this model and architecture, four algorithms for web service discovery and three algorithms for web service query is separately introduced in Section 3 and Section 4. Two frameworks for discovery and query are introduced in Section 5. Section 6 illustrates an example. Related works are discussed in section 7. Finally gives the conclusion and future work in section 8.

2. THE WHOLE ARCHITECTURE

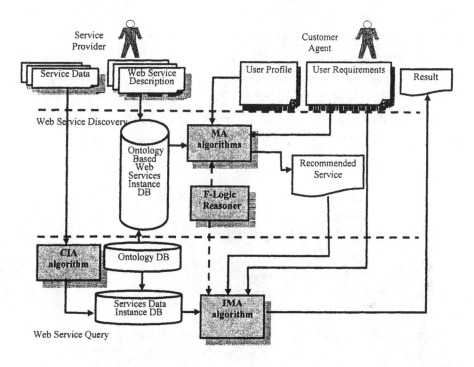

Figure 1. The whole architecture for web service discovery and query.

As illustrated in figure 1, Service Provider and Customer Agent are two important roles in this architecture. Service Provider provides web service description and service data for service discovery and query separately. Web service description will be stored in web services DB, and service data will be stored in service data instances DB through CIA (Create Instances Algorithm). MA is a general service match algorithm, which includes output/input match algorithm, precondition match algorithm and effect contentdegree algorithm. MA is used to fulfill the web services discovery and IMA (Instance Match Algorithm) is used to fulfill the web service query. F-Logic[7] Reasoner is to do the reasoning job during this two processes. Customer Agent provides the user profile which describes the user basic information and the user requirements which represents the service interface information and concrete service data requirements such as a specific ticket.

The ontologies in this architecture can be separated into two main categories, namely the domain ontology (DO) and service upper ontology

(SUO). The domain ontology used here is the travel domain ontology, which can be SchemaWeb[10], or from http://keg.cs.tsinghua.edu.cn/persons/zp/travel_onto_is.owl. And the service upper ontology adopts the OWL-S[11] Specification in order to align with current Web services Standards. OWL-S Specification is a OWL-based Web service ontology, and supplies Web service providers with a core set of markup language constructs for describing the properties and capabilities of their Web services in unambiguous, computer-interpretable form.

3.   DISCOVERY ALGORITHMS

3.1   General Match Algorithm

algorithm MA(S, cusProfile, reqSO, reqEff)
/* Input: candidate Services S, custom Profile cusProfile, required Service Operation reqSO, required Effect reqEff*/
/* Output: Services which satisfy user requirement Result*/

1)Result ← S

2)ServiceOperationF ← getCommonOper(S)

3)ServiceOperationS ← getSpecOper(S)

4)For each service[i] in Result

5)isMatched ← false

6)SOper ← accessSerivceOper(service[i])

7)SEff ← accessServiceEff(service[i])

8)If (reqEff ∈ SEff) ∧ PrecondtionMatch(service[i], cusProfile) goto 9)

           Else goto 19)

9)For each serviceoperation[i] in ServiceOperationF ∩ SOper

10)isMatched ← Output/InputMatch(serviceoperation[i], reqSO,

        Output|Input)

11)if (isMatched!=true) goto 19)

12)contentDegree ←queryOperEff(serviceoperation[i], reqEff)

13)remove serviceoperation[i] from ServiceOperationF
14)remove serviceoperation[i] from SOper

15)For each serviceoperation[i] in ServiceOperationS ∩ SOper Repeat

        10)-12)

16)remove serviceoperation[i] from ServiceOperationS
17)remove serviceoperation[i] from SOper
18)If (SOper!=NULL) For each serviceoperation[i] in SOper Repeat 10)-12)
19)If (isMatched!=true) remove service[i] from Result

20)Result ← Result.sort(contentDegree)

21)Return Result

This algorithm is the general match algorithm for web services discovery. Two operation sets for different purposes are defined. ServiceOperationF is the set of common operations in different services; ServiceOperationS is the set of specific operations in different services, complementing to ServiceOperationF. Because ServiceOperationF is more general than ServiceOperationS, ServiceOperationF will be matched before ServiceOperationS. If the common operation can not meet user requirements, then the match algorithm will remove the candidate service from result immediately. This optimized method will have better performance to discovery web services. accessServiceOper() is the method to get all the operations in a service instance; accessServiceEff() is the method to get all the effects in a service instance. Other algorithms such as Output/Input Match algorithm and queryOperEff algorithm will be introduced in the following sections.

3.2 Output/Input Match Algorithm

algorithm Output/InputMatch(SO, reqSO, direction)

/* Input: Service Operation SO, required Service Operation reqSO, Output or Input indicator direction*/
/* Output: true or false*/

1)isMatched ← false

2)If (direction==Output)   goto 3)   Else goto 9)

3)sCustomer ← accessOutput(reqSO)

4)If (sCustomer.size==0)   isMatched ← true, goto 14)

5)sOutput ← accessOutput(SO)

6)If (sOutput.size==0)   isMatched ← false, goto 14)

7)For each output[i] in sOutput

  isMatched ← isOntologySubsumeOrEqual(sCustomer, output[i])

8)goto 14)

9)sInput ← accessInput(SO)

10)If (sInput.size==0)   isMatched ← true, goto 14)

11)sCustomer ← accessInput(reqSO)

12)If (sCustomer.size==0)   isMatched ← false, goto 14)

13)For each input[i] in sInput

  isMatched ← isOntologySubsumeOrEqual(input[i], sCustomer)

14)Return isMatched

This algorithm is to match the output and input of an operation with user requirements. The main idea is that the outputs of service operation should meet the outputs of user requirements, while the inputs of user requirements should meet the inputs of service operation. For optimizing purpose, when the output of user requirements is empty or the input of service operation is empty, the match succeeds. accessOutput() is the method to get all the outputs of an operation; accessInput() is the method to get all the inputs of an operation; isOntologySubsumeOrEqual() is the method to use ontology relations to determine the subsume or equal relation between two output/input class.

3.3   Precondtion Match Algorithm

algorithm PreconditionMatch(Serv, cusProfile)
/* Input: a Service instance Serv, customer profile cusProfile*/
/* Output: true or false*/
1)isMatched ← false
2)SPre ← accessServicePre(Serv)
3)If (SPre.size==0)   isMacthed ← true, goto 14)

4)tempPre ← ϕ

5)For each precondition[i] in SPre
6)flogicFact ← cusProfile
7)flogicRule ← precondition[i]
8)If(flogic_engine(flogicFact+flogicRule)==true)
        tempPre.append(precondition[i])
9)If isEqual(tempPre, SPre) isMatched← true, goto 14)
10)SOper ← accessSerivceOper(Serv)
11)For each serviceoperation[i] in SOper
12)OPre ← accessOperPrecondtion(serviceoperation[i])
13)If (tempPre.contains(OPre)) isMatched← true, goto 14)
14)Return isMatched

This algorithm is to match the preconditions of a service instance with user profile. From the general match algorithm introduced in section 4.1, it can be inferred that precondition match algorithm should be done earlier than output/input match algorithm. It's also for optimizing purpose. This algorithm adopts flogic reasoning engine, which takes the user profile as flogicfact and the preconditions as flogicrule, to determine whether the user profile can match preconditions. It's obvious that if all the preconditions of a service instance are matched, the match algorithm will succeed. However, if not all the preconditions are matched, then to find one operation whose preconditions are all matched, if this operation exists, then the algorithm will also succeed. Otherwise, the algorithm fails. accessServicePre() is the method to get all the preconditions of a service instance; accessServiceOper() is the method to get all the operations in a service instance; accessOperPrecondtion() is the method to get all the preconditions of an operation.

3.4   Effect ContentDegree calculation Algorithm

algorithm queryOperEff(SO, reqEff)
/* Input: Service Operation SO, customer profile cusProfile*/
/* Output: contentDegree*/
1)If (reqEff.size==0) contentDegree ← 1, goto 7)
2) contentDegree ← 0
3)OEff ← accessOperEffect(SO)
4)If (OEff.size==0) goto 7)
5)contentDegree ← contentDegree + (reqEff∩OEff).size
6)contentDegree ← contentDegree/reqEff.size
7)Return contentDegree

This algorithm is to calculate the contentdegree to represent the effects match degree to user requirements. The contentdegree can be defined as the ratio of the cardinality of effects intersection set to the cardinality of requirement effects set. It's an important value for MA algorithm to sort the candidate services result.

4.   QUERY CALCULATIONS

4.1   Service Data Instance and Similarity calculation

Definition 4.1 Service Data Instance. The Ontology Instance constructed from service data based domain ontology is called Service Data Instance.

Definition 4.2 Category of Similarity. Assume a Service Data Instance I has N properties, in which p properties are plain text type, q properties are enumerated type, r properties are numerical type and k properties are boolean type, $N = p + q + r + k$. I can be represented as

$P(I) = \{(PT_1, PT_2,\ldots, PT_p), (PE_1, PE_2,\ldots, PE_q), (PN_1, PN_2,\ldots, PN_r), (PB_1, PB_2,\ldots, PB_k)\}$

PT stands for text property, PE stands for enumerated property, PN stands for numerical property, PB stands for boolean property.

Definition 4.3 Boolean Similarity. It's the simplest similarity, which is to compute the similarity of boolean type properties. The similarity function of PBs is as follows:

$$SimB(PB_i, PB_j) = \overline{XOR(value_1, value_2)}$$

Definition 4.4 Numerical Similarity. It is used to compute the similarity of numerical type properties. The similarity function of PNs is as follows:

$$SimN(PN_i, PN_j) = 1 - \frac{|value_i - value_j|}{MAX(value_i, value_j)}$$

Definition 4.5 Enumeration Similarity. It is used to compute the similarity between enumerated type properties. Set operation is used to define the similarity.

$$SimE(PE_i, PE_j) = \frac{|Set(PE_i) \cap Set(PE_j)|}{|Set(PE_i) \cup Set(PE_j)|}$$

Set(PE) represents the value set of PE, the calculation result is the ratio of the cardinality of intersection set to the cardinality of union set.

Definition 4.6 Text Similarity. It is used to compute the similarity of plain text type properties. With the cosine measure, the similarity function of FTs is as follows:

$$SimT(PT_i, PT_j) = \frac{\sum_{k=1}^{S} w_i^k w_j^k}{\sqrt{(\sum_{k=1}^{S} w_i^{k^2})(\sum_{k=1}^{S} w_j^{k^2})}}$$

w_i^k is the weight for kth value of feature vector of plain text, can be computed by frequency of features.

Definition 4.7 Single Layer Similarity. It's to compute different type of properties between two Ontology Instances, and then get the similarity between them. When encounter an objectproperty, the URI of this property referring to should be considered as plain text type and processed using Text Similarity.

Definition 4.8 Multi Layer Similarity. Different from Single Layer Similarity, when encounter an objectproperty, the URI of this property referring to should be considered as another Instance whose depth increases one, then assign the deeper layer instance similarity as this property similarity. This recursive calculation won't stop until all the properties are datatypeproperty or reach stop condition. The deepest layer similarity is the same as Single Layer Similarity. The calculated similarity is called Multi Layer Similarity.

4.2   Create Instances Algorithm

algorithm CIA(S, Onto)
/* Input: Web Service S, Ontology Model Onto*/
/* Output: The all service data instance InstanceList */

1) InstanceList ← ϕ

2) while (S has new output)
3) O1 ← the next output of S
4) Map O1 to Class C1 in Onto
5) for each property p of C1
7) if (p is DataTypeProperty) then goto 9)
8) else If (p is ObjectProperty) then goto 13)
9) Get the data value v of p from S, and erase v from S
10) if (the data value v is null) goto 5)
11) Store the data value v to p
12) goto 5)
13) if reach the stop condition goto 5)
14) for each range classes C of p
15) push C1
16) C1 ← C
17) goto 5)
18) pop C1
19) goto 14)

20) goto 5)

21) generate a new instance I1

22) append I1 to InstanceList

23) goto 2)

24) return InstanceList

This algorithm is to create instance from service data. Assuming service S has N outputs mapping to N classes in ontology DB, and one class averagely has M datatype properties and I object properties. When recursing k layers, the time complexity to create a service instance is equal to the time complexity to iterate all the properties and assign them: $N \times (M + I \times M + I^2 \times M + \cdots + I^{k-1}M + I^k)$, approximate $O(2NM^k)$ when $I \approx M$. This time complexity is exponential complexity to the number of properties of one class. Assuming the average length of one property value is L, the space complexity is $O(2NLM^k)$.

4.3   Multi Layer Similarity Calculation Algorithm

algorithm ComputeSimilarity(I1, I2, depth)

/* Input: ontology instance I1, ontology instance I2*/

/* Output: the similarity between I1 and I2*/

1) similarity ← 0, count ← 0

2) for each property of I1

3) if (p is DataTypeProperty) then goto 5)

4) else If (p is ObjectProperty) then goto 8)

5) similarity ← similarity + ComputeSimilarity(data value v1 of p in I1, data
            value v2 of p in I2)

6) count ← count + 1

7) goto 2)

8) if reach the stop condition goto 14)

9) for each range instances I1' of p in I1 and I2' of p in I2

10) similarity ← similarity + ComputeSimilarity(I1', I2', depth+1)

11) count ← count + 1

12) goto 9)

13) goto 2)

14) similarity ← similarity + ComputeSimilarity(uri1 of range instance of p
            in I1, uri2 of range instance of p in I2)

15) count ← count + 1

16) goto 2)

17) similarity ← similarity/count

18) return similarity

This algorithm is to calculate the multiple layer similarity between two ontology instances.   Assuming one class averagely has M properties. When recursing k layers, the time complexity to compute the two ontology instances is as twice as the time complexity to iterate all the properties and read them. From section 4.2, this time complexity is $O(4M^k)$, and the space complexity is $O(4LM^k)$.

4.4   Instance Match Algorithm

algorithm IMA(Req, S, Onto, Rules)
/* Input: User Reqirements Req, Web Service S, Ontology Model Onto, Logic Rules */
/* Output: The all satisfiable service data instances ResultList */

1) ResultList ← ϕ

2) InstanceList ← CIA(S, Onto)

3) for each instance I in InstanceList

4) for each rule R in Rules

5) flogicFact ← I

6) flogicRule ← R

7)If (flogic_engine(flogicFact+flogicRule)==true)
            then goto 9)

8) else goto 3)

9) goto 4)

10) similarity ← ComputeSimilarity(I, Req, 1)

11) assign similarity to instance I

12) append (I, similarity) to ResultList

13) goto 3)

14) ResultList.sort

15) return ResultList

This algorithm is to control CIA algorithm and similarity calculation algorithm. It also adopts flogic reasoning engine to do the logic comparison between the user preferences and service data instances, which takes the service data instances as flogic fact and the user preferences logic as flogic rule.

5. TWO FRAMEWORKS

5.1 The Web Services Discovery Framework

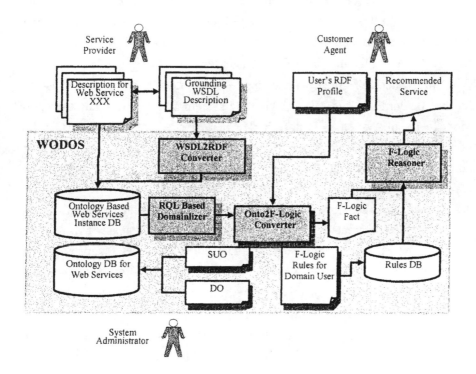

Figure 2. Web Services Intelligent Discovery System.

WSIDS (Web Services Intelligent Discovery System) is an intelligent web services discovery framework and consists of several components that cooperate in semantic Web Service discovery.

We use WODOS (Web Oriented Distributed Ontology System) to build the framework. The WODOS is a semantic web infrastructure system developed by us, something like Jena. The WSIDS will use these characteristics of WODOS:

1.   Store the ontology in the format of RDF/OWL-Lite into the relationship data base.

2.   Import/export the OWL-Lite/RDF file.

3.   Query ontology of base using RQL

4.   An embedded F-logic inference engine witch can import OWL-Lite/RDFS ontology as F-Logic's fact using a converter.

The key of the WODOS is that the platform is a "total solution" for the semantic web applications built on an expansible, flexible, scalable and open architecture. In this system, varied operations of ontology are added, updated and deleted dynamically. So we bring forward a WSDL2RDF converter and deploy it into WODOS. The WODOS is extended for the WSIDS.

As illustrated in figure 2, it is system administrator to create DO and SUO by the standard of OWL-Lite/RDFS. The system administrator can use some tools to do this, such as OntoEdit. He also need create F-Logic rules for domain users' references and constraints description. After the system administrator create the ontology and rules, WODOS can import the OWL-Lite files and F-Logic files into the database.

To discover web services, we need set up a services database based on the ontology system created by the administrator. The database will include semantic description of many services. The information need be provided by service provider. If the service provider need to insert a new service into the database, the WSDL file of this service and a service description OWL file grounded to the WSDL should be created. Then the WSDL2RDF converter will converter WSDL file to RDF file and import result file into database of WODOS together with the OWL file grounded to it.

The discovery procedure will begin if a customer agent gives a request. This request includes user's profile which includes the information about the customer such as country, sex, business trip or personal trip and so on. Then this profile will be translated to the F-Logic's fact by Onto2F-Logic converter. The Onto2F-Logic converter also translates all ontology of four layers into the F-Logic's fact. Before that, the RQL Based Domainlizer will "cut out" the ontology in the Web Services Instance DB into the same domain as the request of the customer agent. This is because of there are perhaps many domains of services ontology in the Instance DB and they need not be translated into F-Logic's fact. As getting the fact, the F-Logic reasoner also get the preferences and constraints rules from the rules DB, as the result of F-Logic reasoner, a list of services, which are recommended to customer and are not reject by the preferences and constraints rules, are brought forward to customer agent.

5.2 The Web Service Query Framework

WSDIM(Web Service Data Instances Matcher) is a framework to implement the Web Service query computation and algorithms. It not only supports the First-Order Logic such as F-Logic, but supports the Description Logic such as Racer [13]. The graphical user interface of this framework is illustrated in figure 3. This similarity result is the result of the example introduced in section 6.

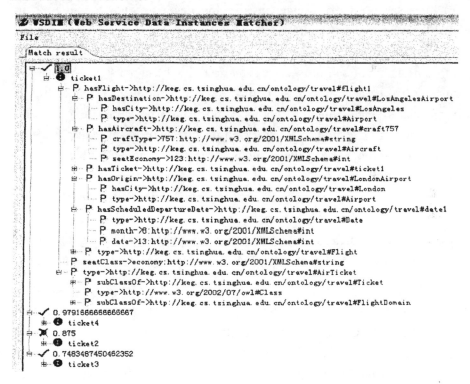

Figure 3. The similarity result computed by WSDIM.

6.   AN EXAMPLE

As the use case described in OpenTravel Alliance Message Users Guide [8], "Bob is planning a trip for his wife and child to fly from London to Los Angeles. He would like to depart on August 13 and prefers a non-stop flight, but if he has to make a stopover, he prefers that there be a maximum of one stopover. He also would like to fly on a 757 and have his tickets mailed to him. He wants to fly economy class. Bob requests availability on flights from London to Los Angeles on August 13. And he wants to get the roundtrip tickets information."

Assuming there are four different web services: AirChina_Service, CathayPacific_Service, ShanghaiAir_Service and NorthernAir_Service. AirChina_Service will provide an airchina ticket as output, while using ticket information and credit card information as inputs. The other three services also have ticket as output and the same inputs. According to Bob's requirements, all these four services can go through Output/Input Algorithm. However, the precondition of AirChina_Service requires the membership of airchia_zhiyin club which is not true for Bob whose profile gives the membership of POP and CSSS club. And the effects of ShanghaiAir_Service and CathayPacific_Service don't include the "ticketmailed" effect in user requirement, so the contentdegree of these two services are both 0 according to Effect ContentDegree calculation Algorithm, while NorthernAir_Service can provide this effect, gets contentdegree 1.   Then through the general MA algorithm, NorthernAir_Service which has the highest contentdegree will be recommended to Bob. Up to now, the discovery of web services has been finished.

Then Assuming NorthernAir_Service has some different service data, and we can pick four of them to delegate all the service data. The four service data (tickets) are: ticket1, ticket2, ticket3, ticket4. In which, ticket1, ticket2 and ticket4 is from London to LosAngeles, while ticket3 is from LosAngeles to London; the departure date of ticket1, ticket2 and ticket3 are all August 13, while ticket4 is October 15; ticket1 doesn't have a stopover, while ticket3 and ticket4 have one stopover NewYork airport, and ticket2 have two stopover NewYork airport and Washington airport; the airplane type of ticket1 and ticket4 is 757, while ticket3 is 747 and ticket2 is unknown; all these tickets provide economic class.

NorthernAir_Service description can be obtained from http://keg.cs.tsinghua.edu.cn/persons/zp/NorthernAir.owl, while the four service data instances can be obtained from http://keg.cs.tsinghua.edu.cn/persons/zp/NorthernAirInstances.owl. The similarity calculation algorithm is to get the similarity between two ontology instances. Now, the service data instances have been constructed, so the user requirements should also be constructed as ontology instance as illustrated in figure 4.

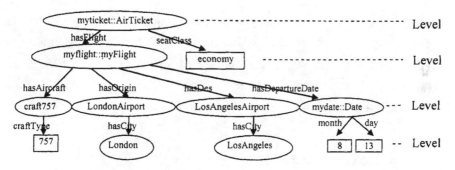

Figure 4. The ontology instance for end user requirements.

And the logic expression for user requirements can be written in f-logic format:

FORALL X,Y,X1,Y1,XO,XD isReturnTicket(X,Y) <-
  X["hasFlight"->>X1]
  AND Y["hasFlight"->>Y1]
  AND X1["hasOrigin"->>XO]
  AND X1["hasDestination"->>XD]
  AND Y1["hasOrigin"->>XD]
  AND Y1["hasDestination"->>XO].

This means the ticket X and ticket Y is roundtrip tickets whose origin airport is the other's destination airport and destination airport is the other's origin airport. This flogic result through F-Logic Engine can be obtained at http://keg.cs.tsinghua.edu.cn/persons/zp/result.txt.

Then through IMA algorithm, the sort of the four tickets is: tikcet1 1.0, ticket4 0.979, ticket2 0.875, ticket3 0.748. So the NorthernAir_Service not only provides the service interface to meet user requirements, but really provides the specific satisfiable ticket – ticket1.

After finishing the two processes, Bob eventually get the satisfiable ticket from NorthernAir_Service.

The meaning of myticket:AirTicket in figure 4 is that myticket is the instance of ontology class AirTicket, in order to represent the required ticket information. myflight:myFlight defines a new class myFlight, which is the subclass of class Flight, in order to extend the constraints for class Flight. Class myFlight adds owl:minCardinality and owl:maxCardinality constraints to the property hasStopover of class Flight, in which owl:minCardninality is 0 and owl:maxCardinality is 1, represents the user requirement for stopover constraints. The   user   request   can   be   obtained   from http://keg.cs.tsinghua.edu.cn/persons/zp/request.owl

7.   RELATED WORKS

Now semantic web service has become a hot research topic, which uses ontology concept to enhance service discovery. The work in [4] annotates the operation, input, and output description of a Web Service, described in WSDL format, with DAML+OIL-based ontological concepts. Precondition and effect of the service are also added to WSDL as additional information such as [9] [5], but they are not used for queries as only the matching of the operation, input, and output is considered. The work in [6] and [3] both consider behavioral aspects in their service models but those aspects are not fully considered or used as query constraints for service matching. The work in [3] enhances WSDL with DAML+OIL based ontological information and considers a web service by its behavioral aspects all rounds. It allows the operation, input, output, precondition, and effect to be used as query constraints, and additionally consider the case when output or effect of the service has some conditions placed on them - the case when we provide a rule-based reasoning to determine the output and effect for query matching. And METEOR-S project [12] also proposed a infrastructure for semantic publication and discovery of web services, which is called METEOR-S WSDI.

It seems that the research on web services discovery is more active than web service query. The technology used in web service query is still based on keyword search. Adopting semantic web technology to assist web service query, and then to combine web services discovery and query has more application value for meeting end user requirements.

8.   CONCLUSION AND THE FUTURE WORK

The new features in this paper comparing to other approaches are as follows:

The first is this paper use two kinds of ontologies for web services discovery and query. The domain ontology is a travel domain ontology, which constructed from Open Travel Alliance Guide which is a famous travel alliance including more than 150 travel industry companies. This ontology can be obtained from SchemaWeb[10], or from http://keg.cs.tsinghua.edu.cn/persons/zp/travel_onto_is.owl. And the service upper ontology adopts the OWL-S Specification in order to align with current Web services Standards.

The second is to propose a whole architecture for web services discovery and query, which is based on the service model above, and to represent end user requirements with flogic based user preferences and constraints.

Then various algorithms is given for the whole architecture proposed above, including the more detailed algorithms for web services discovery and the similarity calculation based algorithms for web service query. And two frameworks are implemented accordingly.

Finally the use case illustrated in this paper can be represented and solved easily in this architecture, and shows the application value for end user.

How to reduce the exponential complexity similarity algorithm to lower complexity is an important future study issue. And the automatic generation of preferences and constraints rules form learning of user choices is an important and interesting issue that will also be studied further.

9.   REFERENCES

1. Hugo Haas. Web Services activity statement. W3C, http://www.w3.org/2002/ws/Activity, 2001.
2. Tim Berners-Lee, James Hendler, Ora Lassila. The Semantic Web. Scientific American, 2001, 284(5):34-43.
3. Natenapa Sriharee and Twittie Senivongse, Department of Computer Engineering Chulalongkorn University, "Discovering Web Services Using Behavioral Constraints and Ontology", Distributed Applications and Interoperable Systems, 4th IFIP WG6.1 International Conference, DAIS 2003, Proceedings, Springer, Paris, France, November 17-21, 2003,   pp.248-259.
4. Kaarthik Sivashanmugam, Kunal Verma, Amit P. Sheth, John A. Miller, "Adding Semantics to Web Services Standards", Proceedings of the International Conference on Web Services, ICWS '03, Las Vegas, Nevada, USA. CSREA Press 2003, pp.395-401
5. Peer, J, "Bringing Together Semantic Web and Web Services", Proceedings of the 1st International Semantic Web Conference (ISWC 2002), Lecture Notes in Computer Science Vol. 2342. Springer Verlag, Sardinia (Italy), 2002, pp.279-291.
6. Paolucci, M. et al., "Semantic Matching of Web Services Capabilities", Proceedings of the 1st International Semantic Web Conference (ISWC 2002), Sardinia (Italy), Lecture Notes in Computer Science, Vol. 2342. Springer Verlag (2002).
7. Michael Kifer, Georg Lausen, and James Wu. Logical foundations of objectoriented and frame-based languages. Journal of the ACM, 42(4), 1995, pp. 741-843.
8. http://www.opentravel.org/
9. Uche Ogbuji. Supercharging WSDL with RDF - Managing structured Web Service metadata. IBM developerWorks article, 2000.
10. Po   Zhang.   Travel   Ontology. http://www.schemaweb.info/schema/SchemaDetails.aspx?id=236, 2005.2.
11. http://www.daml.org/services/owl-s/
12. METEOR   Project   on   Workflow   and   Semantic   Web   Process, http://lsdis.cs.uga.edu/proj/meteor/meteor.html
13. http://www.sts.tu-harburg.de/~r.f.moeller/racer/

DYNG: A MULTI-PROTOCOL COLLABORATIVE SYSTEM

Thomas Huriaux, Willy Picard
Department of Information Technology
The Poznań University of Economics
ul. Mansfelda 4, 60-854 Poznań, Poland
{thomas.huriaux, picard}@kti.ae.poznan.pl

Abstract   Existing systems supporting collaboration processes typically implement a single, fixed collaboration protocol, and collaboration process takes place inside a single group. In this paper, we present in details the *DynG* prototype which provides support for multiple collaboration protocols for non-monolithic collaboration processes, i.e. collaboration processes in which collaboration is spread among many groups. Collaboration protocols used by the *DynG* prototype includes communicative, "acting", and social aspects of collaboration processes, and the introduction of group actions provides support for group dynamics and helps to structure collaboration processes.

Keywords: CSCW, structured collaboration, non-monolithic collaboration, collaboration protocols, group dynamics, communication, social aspects, voting, electronic negotiations

1.   Introduction

From prehistoric tribes to trade unions, group structure has always been at the heart of human activities. Grouping their competences, humans are able to achieve great projects, from pyramids to railroad infrastructure construction. The keyword for group activities is *collaboration*. Collaboration is the process of sharing competences to achieve a common goal.

To a recent past, the collaboration process was limited by the requirement of a single location. People involved in a collaboration process needed to meet to exchange information. In reality, people are generally spread on large geographical area. Meetings are difficult to organize, because of schedule incompatibilities, and costly in terms of time and money.

Telecommunication networks provide a partial solution to the former problem. Telecommunication networks let collaborators be spread over various locations. The use of telephone allows collaborators to exchange information via voice communication. Documents can be exchanged via fax in a graphical format. Local area networks (LAN) are the basis of electronic information exchange inside enterprises, while wide area networks (WAN) – in between enterprises.

With the rise of telecommunication networks, collaboration models that rationalize the collaboration process have been developed. Most of them are document oriented, i.e. the fundamental object of the collaboration process is one or more documents. In enterprises' intranets, collaboration tools are currently widely used for sharing files, for group scheduling or for document collaborative writing.

Traditionally, research in electronic support for collaboration has concentrated on collaboration processes confined inside a single group. Few attention has been accorded to the case of non-monolithic collaboration processes, i.e. processes in which the collaborative activities are dynamically spread among potentially many groups. The term "non-monolithic" is taken from the negotiation vocabulary (see [Raiffa et al., 2002], pp. 4-5, 389-406), where a non-monolithic negotiation process is a negotiation process in which some parties do not behave as a unitary decision entity, i.e. a party consisting of many persons with various perceptions and goals.

In the field of computer support for collaborative work (CSCW), some works have addressed the issue of the group data organization in a dynamic way [Ettorre et al., 2003], the issue of non-monolithic collaborative document edition [Picard, 2004]. These works are usually poorly formalized and focus on very limited applications. In the field of electronic negotiations, some works addressed the issue of negotiation protocols [Benyoucef and Keller, 2000] [Cellary et al., 1998] [Hung and Mao, 2002] [Kersten and Lo, 2003] [Kim and Segev, 2003] [Schoop and Quix, 2001]. According to [Kersten et al., 2004], a negotiation protocol is "a formal model, often represented by a set of rules, which govern software processing, decision-making and communication tasks, and imposes restrictions on activities through the specification of permissible inputs and actions". One may consider a negotiation protocol as a collaboration protocol. Works in the field of electronic negotiations are usually limited to monolithic negotiations, or address a single user's point of view and do not provide support for group collaboration. To our best knowledge, the issue of support for both structured and non-monolithic collaboration processes has only been addressed in our previous work [Picard and Huriaux, 2005] [Picard, 2005]. In these two articles, a model for structured collaboration procotols has been presented. In this paper, the main focus is on a detailed presentation of the prototype implementing the model mentioned above.

In this paper, we present the *DynG* (for Dynamic Groups) prototype which provides support for multiple collaboration protocols for non-monolithic collaboration processes. In section 2, the theoretical background – i.e our previous work on a model for collaboration protocols integrating communicative, "acting", and social aspects – is presented. Next, the concept of action is refined with the introduction of a classification of types of actions. In section 4, both the overall architecture and implementation details of the *DynG* prototype are described. Next a complete example of the use of *DynG* to support a collaboration process is detailed. Section 6 concludes the paper.

2. Structuring Non-Monolithic Collaboration Processes

In non-monolithic collaborative processes, collaboration always occurs inside a group. Even when a single collaborator works alone, it may be considered as a group consisting of only herself/himself. Therefore, it may be stated that *a group is a non-empty set of collaborators*. An other aspect of this kind of collaboration is that collaborators are collaborating via message exchange. As we would like to structure non-monolithic collaboration processes, we have to address two issues: first, a mechanism to structure collaboration inside a given group has to be proposed, i.e. message exchange has to be structured, second, actions occuring inside a group have to be addressed.

Collaboration Protocols

Three elements may be distinguished in collaborative processes: a communicative aspect, an "acting" aspect, and a social aspect.

Communication is a major component of collaboration as collaborators need to exchange information to achieve their common goal [Weigand et al., 2003] [Schoop et al., 2003]. The acting aspect of collaboration concerns the fact that collaborators not only exchange information to reach their common goal, but also act to achieve it. Finally, the social aspect of collaborative processes concerns relationships among collaborators, the perceptions they have of others collaborators.

Let's take an example to illustrate the communicative, acting and social aspects of collaborative processes. Let's assume that a parent is reading a fairy tale to her/his child. They collaborate: their common goal being usually to spend some pleasant time together. They communicate: the child may ask why the wolf is so bad at the three little pigs, and the parent answers, or at least tries. They act: the child may point the wolf on a picture in the book, the parent turns pages. The parent and the child are obviously playing different social roles.

The concept of *behavioral unit* captures all three aspects – communicative, acting, and social – of collaborative processes.

Behavioral unit a behavioral unit is a triplet:

(UserRole, MessageType, Action)

- The *UserRole* addresses the social aspect. In the case of the former example, two *UserRoles* may be distinguished: *Parent* and *Child*.

- The *MessageType* addresses the communicative aspect. The introduction of message types allows to limit ambiguousness of communication [Schoop, 2001]. In the case of the former example, three *MessageTypes* may be distinguished: *Question, SureAnswer* or *PotentialAnswer*. Intentions of the collaborator can be clearer with an adapted message type. The message "the wolf is fundamentally bad" may be a *SureAnswer* or a *PotentialAnswer*, depending on the confidence of the person answering the question. In this case, the introduction of the adapted message type permits to evaluate the credibility/veracity of exchanged data.

- The *Action* addresses the acting aspect. In the case of the former example, two *Actions* may be distinguished: *PointingTheWolf* and *TurningPage*.

In the proposed model, collaboration processes result from exchange of behavioral units among collaborators. Collaborators are exchanging behavioral units, sending typed messages and acting, in a given role. Exchange of behavioral units causes the evolution of the group in which collaborators are working: each sent behavioral unit causes a transition of the group from a past state to a new state.

Transition A transition is a triplet:

(BehavioralUnit, SourceState, DestinationState)

In the case of the former example, let's define a transition that may occur after the child has asked a question, i.e. the group is in *WaitingForAnswer* state. The transition leads to the *Reading* state. The behavioral unit involved in the presented transition may be the following: *(Parent, SureAnswer, TurningPage)*.

It is now possible to define *collaboration protocols*, which may be used to structure collaboration processes.

Collaboration protocol A collaboration protocol consists of a set of transitions, a set of start states, and a set of terminating states.

One may notice that a protocol is a variant of finite state machines. A finite state machine (FSM) is usually defined as "a model of computation consisting of a set of states, a start state, an input alphabet, and a transition function that maps input symbols and current states to a next state". The set of states of the FSM can easily be deduced from the set of transitions of the protocol. The start state occurs in both the FSM and the protocol. The input alphabet of the FSM is the set of behavioral units which appear in all transitions of the protocols. Finally, the transition function of the FSM is defined by the set of transitions of the protocol. The only difference between FSMs and collaboration protocols is the existence of terminating states for protocols.

A collaboration protocol is a template definition for a set of collaboration processes. Using an analogy with object-oriented programming, one may say that a collaboration protocol is to a protocol instance what a class is to an object. In a given group, a given protocol instance regulates collaboration among group members.

Protocol instance A protocol instance is a triplet:

(Protocol, CurrentState, UserToRoleMapping)

The *UserToRoleMapping* is a function which associates a *UserRole* with a given user.

3. Refining the Concept of Action

Inside a group, many actions can occur, modifying the structure of this group, creating new groups, or having no real influence on the main structure of the collaboration. Three types of actions have been identified:

1 neutral actions;

2 actions modifying the structure of groups;

3 actions modifying the structure of collaboration processes.

Prior to a description of these three types of actions, let's define the concept of *structure of a group*. In the later, the structure of a group will refer to a pair that consists of the set of collaborators within the group and the mapping between users and roles.

By analogy, let's define the concept of *structure of a collaboration process*. In the later, the structure of a collaboration process will refer to a pair that consists of the set of groups within the collaboration process and the mapping between groups and protocols.

Neutral Actions

Neutral actions have no effect, neither on the structure of the collaboration, nor on the structure of the group in which the action is processed. Therefore,

different existing groups inside the collaboration process are not influenced
by these actions. Their structures remain the same, no new group is created.
Furthermore, the group inside which the action was processed keeps its own
structure unchanged, i.e. the same users with the same roles.

In the case of purely communicative behavioral units, i.e. behavioral units
which aim only at exchanging information, associated actions should be neutral ones. However, neutral actions should not be limited to the case of purely
communicative behavioral units: if a file is modified during the collaboration
process via an *edit* action, the *edit* action has no effect on the structure of neither the collaboration process nor the group.

Actions Modifying the Structure of a Group

As it has already been mentioned, a group is composed of one or more
users, each of them playing a given role. However, a user may have his/her
role changed during the collaboration process. Actions causing such changes
modify the structure of a group.

A user (1) with a role (2) is giving to a user (3) with a role (4) a new role
(5). Therefore, five parameters have to be taken in account:

1 the user executing the action;

2 the role of the user executing the action;

3 the user having his/her role changed;

4 the role of the user having his/her role changed;

5 the newly attributed role.

One may notice that the case in which a user changes his/her own role is just
a special case of the generic one presented above. Indeed, an action allowing a
user to change his/her role is just an action in which the values of the first and
the third parameters are the same.

Actions Modifying the Structure of a Collaboration Process

The structure of non-monolithic collaborative processes is usually highly
dynamic: groups are created and deleted in a dynamic way. Group dynamics
is the result of the execution of actions modifying the structure of the collaboration model: a collaborator may for instance decide to execute an action *cre-
ateANewGroup*. Two kind of actions may be distinguised modifying the structure of a collaboration process: actions may modify either the set of groups
– called *group actions* – or the mapping between groups and protocols – called
protocol dynamic actions.

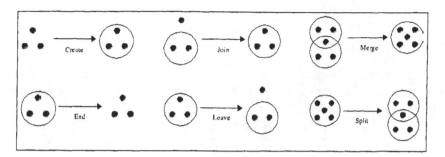

Figure 1.   Group actions

Group Actions.   The following group actions have been identified:

- *join* action: adds at least one collaborator to the set of collaborators of an existing group;

- *quit* action: removes at least one collaborator from the set of collaborators of an existing group;

- *split* action: splits an existing group in two or more new groups and the union of the sets of the collaborators of the created groups equals the set of collaborators of the existing group;

- *merge* action: creates a new group consisting of the union of the set of collaborators of at least two groups;

- *create* action: creates new group;

- *end* action: deletes an existing group.

These actions are illustrated on Figure 1. Dots represent collaborators while circles represent groups. One may notice that, as shown on Figure 1 for the *split* and *merge* actions, a given collaborator may participate at a given time in many groups.

Group actions may either modify only the group in which the action is processed – e.g. the *quit* action – or involve other groups – e.g. the *merge* action.

Protocol Dynamic Actions.   This type of action is required in two cases: to allow a group to change its protocol during the collaboration process, and to design and implement parameterized protocols.

A protocol is parameterized if it may have parameters whose values are specified during the collaboration process. An example of such a protocol could be a protocol in which an action is used to specify how many messages can be sent before going to the next step of the collaboration process.

4.   The *DynG* Prototype

Overall architecture

The *DynG* (for *Dynamic Groups*) prototype is an implementation of the formerly presented concepts: collaboration protocols and actions. It aims at being a platform supporting structured non-monolithic collaboration processes.

The *DynG* prototype consists of three parts: the *DynG* Core, the *DynG* Server, and the *DynG* Client (the term *DynG* will be omitted in the rest of the paper to improve readability).

The overall architecture is presented on Figure 2.

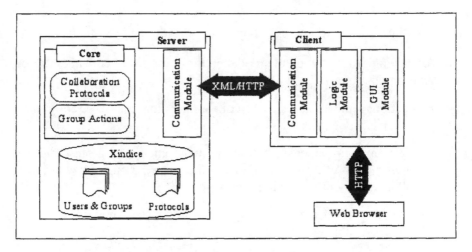

Figure 2.   Overall architecture of the *DynG* prototype

DynG Client

The Client is a Java Servlet aiming at providing an interface to the users. Each HTTP request coming from the users' web browser is passed to the logic module. The logic module may exchange information with the Server via the communication module. The communication module translates Java objects created by the user's request into XML messages to be sent to the server, and translates the responses from the server, which are also in XML format, into Java objects understandable by the Servlet. When the logic module has finished its work, it redirects to the GUI module which is responsible for generating dynamic HTML pages for the final user. The GUI module consists of a set of Java Server Pages (JSP).

During one request, many XML messages are exchanged between the Server and the Client. The user may require only information about the state of the collaboration, or may perform one action modifying the state of this collaboration. Each basic request requires one message. For example, three distinct requests between the Client and the Server are required to know in which groups the user belongs, to get the collaborators inside the group the user is working on and to get the potential actions the user may perform.

DynG Server

On the server side, three elements may be distinguished: the communication module, the Core, and a repository. The communication module is responsible for translating XML messages received via HTTP from the Client into calls to the Core, and to create response from Java objects into XML messages to send back to the Client.

The Core provides support for collaboration protocols and group actions and is responsible to maintain the state of the collaboration: existing users, protocols, groups, etc. The Core manages the collaboration processes according to protocols stored in the repository. In the current implementation of the *DynG* Server, the Xindice native XML database [Xindice, 2005] is used as a repository but it would be possible to use other storage mechanisms, such as file systems or relational databases. The repository is responsible for storing not only information concerning users and groups, but also protocols, exchanged messages, etc.

The *DynG* Administration

The introduction of protocols allows collaboration processes to be structured. At the implementation level, the introduction of protocol instances allows to restrict the set of possible behavioral units in a given state of a given group. As a consequence, the GUI module must be highly dynamic as it has to display to the user only behavioral units that are available at the current state and for his/her role. Therefore, depending both on the role of the user and the current state of the collaboration process, the graphical user interface (HTML pages) will be different, allowing him/her to perform different behavioral units.

First of all, the collaboration module has to be initialized to set the collaboration main protocol, i.e. the protocol that rules the collaboration process, to add concerned users, etc. The HTML page presented on the left side of Figure 3 shows how collaboration processes are administrated, and what is needed for a collaboration process to start. As a remark, collaboration processes take place in "workspaces" in the *DynG* prototype. A second HTML page, presented on the right side of Figure 3 provides an interface to assign roles to users inside the collaboration process, but only at the top level, i.e. at the workspace level.

Once a collaboration process is initialized, a collaborator can login and collaborate with other persons involved in the collaboration process.

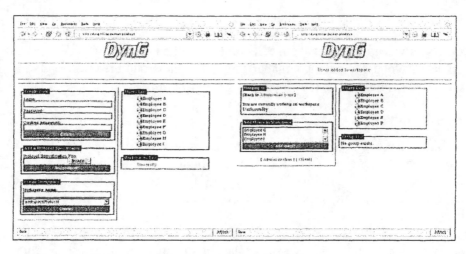

Figure 3.   DynG administration

5.   Example: Election of a University Rector

The goal of the current section is to present the potential use of *DynG* to support a real collaboration process. The collaboration process chosen for this example is the electoral process of the Rector of a university. The collaboration process is a slightly simplified version of the process existing in our university. To improve readability of this article, and because the communicative facet of this process is limited (except for the campain), the message types will be omitted.

Description of the Electoral Process

The pre-requisite is that candidates for the Rector position are known. Then, the electoral process is composed of three main phases: candidatures for the electoral chamber, votes for the electoral chamber, votes for the Rector. The two first steps will be fully described below. For the last step – the votes for the Rector – only elected members of the electoral chamber are concerned.

The process will be divided into two protocols: the candidatures and first votes steps grouped together, and the second votes in another protocol. In other words, the first protocol models the election of the electoral chamber, while the second one models the election of the Rector by the electoral chamber.

To assist the collaboration, an agent has been added. The software agent is considered as a normal user, i.e. it is sending behavioral units according to its role and the voting protocol.

The voting protocol is graphically represented on Figure 4, where rectangles are state, arrows are transition, and tabular are different behavorial units associated to a given transition.

Candidatures for the electoral chamber During this step, each employee of the university may be candidate. But the candidature must be proposed by somebody else, which is a candidate or not. Once somebody has been presented as a potential candidate, he/she can accept to be candidate or not. When the minimal number of candidates is reached, the agent will go through a transition going to a similar situation, except that now the commission manager can decide to stop the candidature period and to move to the vote for the members of the electoral chamber.

Votes for the electoral chamber During this procedure, each employee, candidate or not, may vote for up to the number of candidates to be elected. This "round" is finished either by the agent when everybody has voted, or when the commission manager decide it. If enough candidates have been elected, by reaching a pre-defined majority, then the vote ends. Otherwise a new "round" is started, after the removal of a pre-defined number of candidates.

The protocol is "tuned" by an action specifying how many members the electoral chamber consits of and how many candidates are removed after each round of the voting process. This action is a *protocol dynamic action*. This action is part of the behavioral unit denoted *Set vote specifications* in Figure 4.

During the last step of the vote, each member of the electoral chamber starts with the same default role, and can perform only one action: to vote. To be formally precise, this action is composed of two parts: one part changes the "default" role of the voter into a role "voted", while the second part adds one voice to the chosen Rector candidate.

Use of *DynG* to Support the Vote Process

The Main page displays to the collaborator the list of groups, the group she/he is working on, and the messages sent to this group. The situation at the beginning of the electoral processes is shown on the left side of Figure 5. In this situation, the only allowed action is to propose a candidate, as shown in the "Group Management" part of the interface. The messages present the different steps: the settings of the vote specification and the candidates already proposed, with their refusal or acceptance.

Once a candidate has been proposed, no action can be performed, except for the new potential candidate who can either accept or refuse his/her candidature. This situation is presented on the right part of Figure 5.

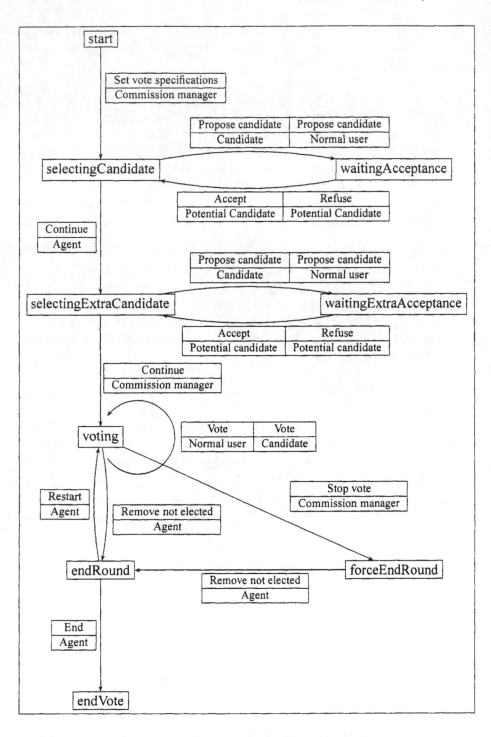

Figure 4.   Graph representing the electoral protocol

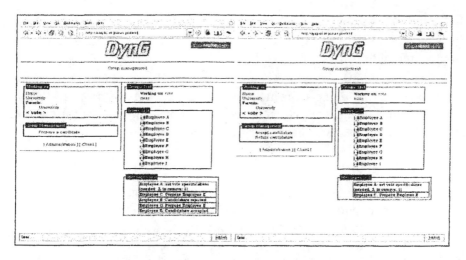

Figure 5. DynG client: the candidature period

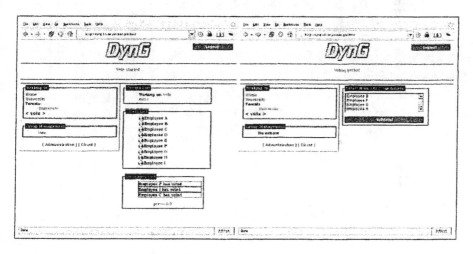

Figure 6. DynG client: the vote period

The same situation is repeated until the commission manager decides that there are enough candidates. The voting period then starts. As shown on the left part of Figure 6, the only action each user can now perform is to vote. Once a user decides to vote, she/he then has to choose for whom she/he will vote (right part of Figure 6) and then they cannot perform any action until the end of the vote.

It should be kept in mind that a given protocol rules a given group, and that various groups may be ruled by different protocols. Therefore, by clicking on the name of an other group in the group list, a user may get abilities to perform other behavioral units available in the new working group, depending on the protocol ruling the group and the role of the collaborator inside the group.

At last, the "Working on" component of GUI allows collaborators to get an overview of the group dynamics, by presenting both the parents and the children groups of the working group. The "Working on" component may be use to browse groups the collaborator belongs to.

6.   Conclusions

The introduction of collaboration protocols and group actions allows to provide computer support to non-monolithic collaboration processes. To our best knowledge, it is the first model for electronic support for non-monolithic collaborative processes.

It would be possible to build complex support systems for complex collaborative processes using the framework provided by the DynG prototype. The design of systems for non-monolithic collaboration processes may be resumed in the following steps: first, the roles involved in the collaboration process have to be identified. Next, the required actions have to be implemented. Then, message types should be defined. Therefore, behavioral units may be defined. Finally, collaboration protocol(s) may be specified.

The presented model could be used in a broad spectrum of potential applications. The presented model may for instance be applied to non-monolithic negotiations, such as international negotiations or business-to-business contract establishment. Another field of applications is the legislative process in which various political parties, potentially presenting various opinions, collaborate in order to establish laws in form of new or modified legal acts. The presented model could also be used to design support systems for collaborative documentation edition processes that often take place among business actors.

Among future works, it would be interesting to investigate the possibilities to embed a protocol instance into another protocol instance. This would allow to modularize protocols, to design protocols using smaller protocols, to develop "protocol libraries". In the example presented in this paper, one may notice that the candidature proposal phase can be seen as a "subprotocol" which could be reused in other protocols, or even many times within a single protocol.

Another field which could be the object of future works is the concept of role. The addition of relationships between various roles, such as inheritance or composition, would be an interesting work to be done.

References

[Benyoucef and Keller, 2000] Benyoucef, M. and Keller, R. K. (2000). An evaluation of formalisms for negotiations in e-commerce. In *DCW '00: Proceedings of the Third International Workshop on Distributed Communities on the Web*, pages 45–54. Springer-Verlag.

[Cellary et al., 1998] Cellary, W., Picard, W., and Wieczerzycki, W. (1998). Web-based business-to-business negotiation support. In *Int. Conference on Electronic Commerce EC-98*, Hamburg, Germany.

[Ettorre et al., 2003] Ettorre, M., Pontieri, L., Ruffolo, M., Rullo, P., and Sacca, D. (2003). A prototypal environment for collaborative work within a research organization. In *DEXA '03: Proceedings of the 14th International Workshop on Database and Expert Systems Applications*, pages 274–279. IEEE Computer Society.

[Hung and Mao, 2002] Hung, P. and Mao, J.-Y. (2002). Modeling of e-negotiation activities with petri nets. In *HICSS '02: Proceedings of the 35th Annual Hawaii International Conference on System Sciences (HICSS'02)-Volume 1*. IEEE Computer Society.

[Kersten and Lo, 2003] Kersten, G. E. and Lo, G. (2003). Aspire: an integrated negotiation support system and software agents for e-business negotiation. *International Journal of Internet and Enterprise Management*, 1(3).

[Kersten et al., 2004] Kersten, G. E., Strecker, S., and Law, K. P. (2004). Protocols for electronic negotiation systems: Theoretical foundations and design issues. In Bauknecht, K., Bichler, M., and Pröll, B., editors, *EC-Web*, volume 3182 of *Lecture Notes in Computer Science*, pages 106–115. Springer.

[Kim and Segev, 2003] Kim, J. B. and Segev, A. (2003). A framework for dynamic ebusiness negotiation processes. In *CEC*, pages 84–91. IEEE Computer Society.

[Picard, 2004] Picard, W. (2004). Towards support systems for non-monolithic collaborative document edition: The document-group-message model. In *DEXA Workshops*, pages 266–270. IEEE Computer Society.

[Picard, 2005] Picard, W. (2005). Towards support systems for non-monolithic electronic negotiations. *Special Issue of the Journal of Decision Systems on e-Negotiations*. To appear.

[Picard and Huriaux, 2005] Picard, W. and Huriaux, T. (2005). Dyng: Enabling structured non-monolithic electronic collaboration. In *The 9th International Conference on CSCW in Design*, Coventry, UK. To appear.

[Raiffa et al., 2002] Raiffa, H., Richardson, J., and Matcalfe, D. (2002). *Negotiation Analysis, The Science and Art of Collaborative Decision Making*. The Belknap Press of Harvard University Press.

[Schoop, 2001] Schoop, M. (2001). An introduction to the language-action perspective. *SIGGROUP Bull.*, 22(2):3–8.

[Schoop et al., 2003] Schoop, M., Jertila, A., and List, T. (2003). Negoisst: a negotiation support system for electronic business-to-business negotiations in e-commerce. *Data Knowl. Eng.*, 47(3):371–401.

[Schoop and Quix, 2001] Schoop, M. and Quix, C. (2001). Doc.com: a framework for effective negotiation support in electronic marketplaces. *Comput. Networks*, 37(2):153–170.

[Weigand et al., 2003] Weigand, H., Schoop, M., Moor, A. D., and Dignum, F. (2003). B2b negotiation support: The need for a communication perspective. In *Group Decision and Negotiation 12*, pages 3–29.

[Xindice, 2005] Xindice (2005). http://xml.apache.org/xindice/.

DEVELOPMENT CONCEPT FOR AND TRIAL APPLICATION OF A "MULUTIPLEX RISK COMMUNICATOR"

Ryoichi Sasaki*&, Saneyuki Ishii*,Yuu Hidaka*,Hiroshi Yajima*, Hiroshi Yoshiura+, Yuuko Murayama#

*Tokyo Denki University 2-2 Kandanishiki-cho Chiyoda-ku Tokyo, sasaki@im.dendai.ac.jp
Tel: +81-3-5280-3328   Fax: +81-3-5280-3592   + University of Electro-Communications,
Iwate Prefectual Univaersity, & Researcher at RISTEX of the Japan Science andTechnology Agency

Abstract: Risk has increased with the development of an Internet-oriented society, and to what extent that risk can be reduced has become a major issue. Thus, risk communication has become crucial for the formation of a consensus among decision-makers such as citizens.   Dealing with risk, however, requires the reduction of risks based on conflicting concepts such as security, privacy, and development costs; obtaining the consensus of individuals involved and determining optimal combinations of the measures are not easy.   A "multiplex risk communicator (MRC)" with (1) a simulator, (2) an optimization engine, and (3) displays for the formation of a consensus is needed in order to resolve such problems.   This paper describes the features an MRC should have, a simple prototype program to support it, and results of its trial application.

Key words: security, privacy, risk, risk communication, discrete optimization

1.   INTRODUCTION

Due to damage such as that from distributed denial of service (DDoS) attacks and various worms, interest with respect to security measures has heightened. In addition, circumstances have also called for greater interest in privacy measures such as those for personal information protection.

Many people assume that security measures are privacy measures. However, security measures and privacy measures are as clarified, (1) compatible or (2) conflicting[1]. Instances when they conflict in particular require the study of a combination of the most appropriate measures for security and privacy including cost and ease of use.

Recently, on the other hand, opinions regarding risk have been exchanged among people directly and indirectly involved, and interest regarding risk communication, the process of reaching a consensus, has also heightened[2)-6)].

In the past, risk was considered to be a single item, but in the above examples there is a risk of losing security and a risk of losing privacy. In addition, there are instances where ease of use is seen as an operational risk and development costs are seen as an economic risk. Thus, we must deal with multiple risks. Therefore, risk communication also requires being able to reach a consensus regarding the optimal combination of measures while considering multiple risks.

To achieve the above objectives, the development concepts of a multiplex risk communicator (denoted hereafter as MRC) were established. This paper describes the features an MRC should have, a simple prototype program to support it, and results of its trial application[7)].

2.   CONFLICTING RISKS AND NEED FOR AN MRC

Depicting the relationship between security and privacy with concepts, means, and technologies will yield a diagram like that shown in **Fig. 1**[1)].

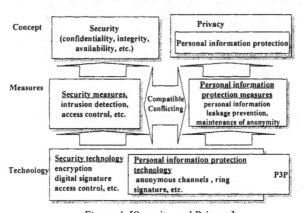

Figure 1. [Security and Privacy]

The relationship between security and privacy measures can roughly be classified into (1) compatible and (2) conflicting measures as follows.

An explanation of each has been provided below.

(1) Compatible: With measures to prevent the leakage of personal information, enacting security measures such as access control and data encryption is normally linked to protection of personal information. In this case, security measures are privacy measures.

(2) Conflicting: This is an instance where the implementation of security measures complicates the protection of personal information and was seldom examined in the past. As an example, (a) use of a public key certificate for a digital signature and encryption as a security measure has been linked to the outflow of personal information in the form of the address and date of birth written in the certificate. In addition, (b) permitting encrypted e-mail as a security measure against threats from a third party may also lead to the inability to monitor the outflow of personal information.

When there are multiple risks, i.e., a loss of security and a loss of privacy, technology as shown in **Fig. 2** can contribute significantly to resolving the conflict between these risks.

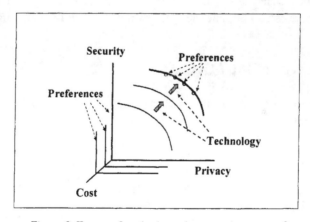

Figure 2. [Image of method to solve opposing concept]

As an example, if the leakage of personal information was caused by a public key certificate and privacy was to become a problem, then security and privacy can both be provided by handing over an attribute certificate that only describes attributes. As expected, however, security and usability will suffer compared to when a public key certificate is used. Therefore, whether emphasis is placed on indices such as security, privacy, or cost will become a problem in terms of selection by decision-makers.

Thus, tools are essential to obtaining and determining the consensus of decision-makers on an optimal combination of the measures for security and privacy including cost and ease of use.

3.   DELOPMENT CENCEPT FOR THE MRC

3.1   Requirements of the MRC

Based on reasons like those above, an MRC will be developed, but it must satisfy conditions like:

(Requirement 1) There are various conflicting risks, and measures must be considered while taking them into account.

(Requirement 2) Various measures are required for individual risks as well. Resolving every problem with one measure is not possible, and features to determine the most appropriate combination of numerous measures are essential.

(Requirement 3) For decision-making, numerous individuals involved (e.g. managers, citizens, customers, and employees) should be satisfied. Therefore, features to support risk communication among numerous individuals involved are essential.

3.2   Concept of the MRC

A structure like that shown in **Fig. 3** was developed as an MRC to satisfy those requirements.

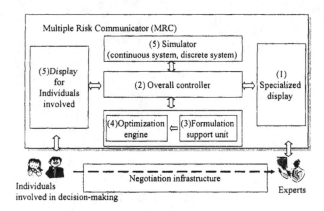

Figure 3. [Overview of Multiple Risk Communicator]

The MRC consists of the following 6 components:
   (1) Specialized display
   (2) Overall controller
   (3) Formulation support unit
   (4) Optimization engine
   (5) Simulator
   (6) Display for individuals involved

What provides the basic features to satisfy Requirement 1 and Requirement 2 are the (3) formulation support unit and (4) optimization engine. Here, a discrete optimization problem with various measures proposed as 0-1 variables (or a 0-1 programming problem)[9] is used for its formulation and obtaining its solution.

In addition, what satisfies Requirement 3 are the (1) specialized display, (5) simulator, and (6) display for individuals involved. The setup must be such that simulations are performed, results of measures are displayed in detail, and displays allow decisions to be easily made by experts and individuals involved.

In addition, what links the processing of these components is the (2) overall controller.

3.3   Envisioned usage of the MRC

(Step①) Experts furnish the MRC with the (a) objective function, (b) constraint function, (c) proposed measures, (d) coefficients, and (e) constraint values and formulate an optimization problem (using the (1) specialized display, (2) overall controller, and (3) formulation support unit).

Here, formulation of an optimization problem with various measures proposed as 0-1 variables is assumed. The reason for such a method is because formulation is easiest when determining the optimal combination of individual measures proposed.

Specific formulations differ depending on the target, but methods such as minimizing total social cost or maximizing total social benefit under risk constraints regarding cost, privacy, and security as shown in Fig. 4, for example, are acceptable.

In addition, the problem is formulated here so as not to determine only the first optimal solution but to determine the second, third, ·· the Lth optimal solutions as well. This is because, given factors that cannot possibly be quantified, it allows individuals involved to choose a satisfactory solution from the first to the Lth optimal solutions.

$$
\begin{aligned}
&\text{Min}(1-L) \quad T(x_i \,|i=1,2, \; n) \\
&\text{s.t. } P(x_i \,|i=1,2, \; n) \leqq P_t \\
&\quad\quad S(x_i \,|i=1,2, \; n) \leqq S_t \\
&\quad\quad C_k(x_i \,|i=1,2, \; n) \leqq C_{kt} \; (k=1,2, \; \cdots,K) \\
&\quad\quad x_i = 1 \text{ or } 0
\end{aligned}
$$

X_i :ith measure proposed

T : Total social cost

S : Security risk function

P : Privacy risk function

C_k : kth cost function for individuals involved

Min(1-L) means processing to determine optimal solutions from the first optimal solution to the Lth optimal solution

Figure 4. [Image of Formulated Result]

After a cost model was created and the cost of individual measures proposed was determined, the constraint equation regarding cost can be described by the following expression:

$$
\sum_{i=1}^{n} C_i X_i \leqq C_t \quad\text{------}\quad \text{Eq. 1}
$$

Here, C_i represents the cost of proposed measure i and C_t represents the constraint value of the total cost. In addition, X_i is a 0-1 variable; 1 represents adopting the proposed measure i and 0 represents not adopting it.

In addition, the security risk function and privacy risk function can, after individual proposed measures have been determined using fault tree analysis[8] or the like, be expressed as functions.

(Step②) The first-the Lth optimal combinations of proposed measures are determined using the (4) optimization engine (e.g.: a combination of proposed measures 1 and 3 is the first optimal solution, a combination of 1 and 4 is the second optimal solution, and so forth)

Here, the (4) optimization engine is the component that provides features to effectively determine the optimal solution for the formulated problem using the following techniques[9]:

(a) Exact method

Brute Force method: for when there is a small number of proposed measures

Effective method: for when there is a relatively large number of proposed measures. This method effectively searches for a solution by skipping instances where an optimal solution is clearly not possible in the process of searching for solutions based on the method of all possible combinations. The lexicographic enumeration method or the branch and bound method can be used.

(c) Approximate method: for when there is a large number of proposed measures. This method does not guarantee an optimal solution but it effectively determines approximate solutions without being limited to optimal solutions.

All of these methods were developed in the past to determine only the first optimal solution but with a little modification they can be used to determine the first-the Lth optimal solution.

(**Step③**) The results are displayed in an easy-to-understand format using the (5) simulator and (6) display for individuals involved.

After the optimal solution is determined, the simulator is used to predict the results of measures in detail and to display effects after the passage of time and regional changes for decision-makers.

There are plans to develop a program based on system dynamics[10], which is considered to be the easiest methodology to use to perform such simulations.

The (6) display for individuals involved expresses information required to reach a consensus by decision-makers such as citizens and employees in an easy-to-understand format.   Here, modifications are needed for (a) display details and display order to derive a satisfactory solution for each individual involved and for (b) a display order so consensus among individuals involved is easily reached.

(**Step④**) Opinions such as "constraint values are different" and other proposed measures should be considered" were voiced by individuals involved.

(**Step⑤**) The results were, using a negotiation infrastructure (with a tool for information exchange between two individuals as the base), conveyed to experts. Input modified by experts is furnished to the MRC and the results are displayed again.

Multiple risks are considered and opinions of multiple individuals involved are incorporated by repeating the above process, with increasing possibility that a mutually satisfactory solution will be reached.

3.4   Issues to be resolved

Application of the MRC to actual situations requires resolution of the following issues:

(1) For experts

(1-a) difficulty of formulation

(1-b) uncertainty of effects

(2) For decision-makers (average citizens)

(2-a) constraint ambiguity

(2-b) consideration of unquantified factors

(2-c) method of quickly reaching a solution that satisfies an individual involved

(2-d) resolution of disagreement between groups in terms of solutions

These are all difficult issues. However, they are major issues and must be resolved step by step through trial application.

4.   TRIAL APPLICATION AND DISCUSSION

4.1   Targets

There are, with regard to the MRC, few similar approaches, so the approach used was not to create a tidy program from scratch but to create a simple prototype program, apply it to multiple targets, improve the system itself, and create the next prototype program. First of all, we developed very simple prototype program based on the Excel.

The order of MRC application is as shown in Fig. 5; application was done by junior researchers. Here, preparations beforehand were preparatory work for formulation in an MRC as described in Step① of Sec. 3.3.

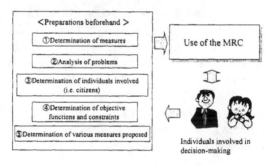

Figure 5. [Application of MRC to Personal Information Leakage Measures]

Here, "the problem of leakage of personal information" is dealt with, and application was done (corresponding to ① and ② in Fig. 5) with the following assumptions:

(1) Personal information from the firm possesses amounts to one million entries.

(2) The value of personal information is 10,000 yen per entry. In addition, when personal information is actually leaked the company pays compensation of 500 yen to each customer it has.

With regard to (4) personal information, there are three patterns of leakage of personal information via (a) internal crime 1 (employees let into segregated areas), (b) internal crime 2 (employees not let into segregated areas), and (c) external crime (an external third party that is not an employee and who is outside the corporate structure). The pattern of leakage caused by internal crime 1 (employees let into segregated areas) is shown in Figs. 6.

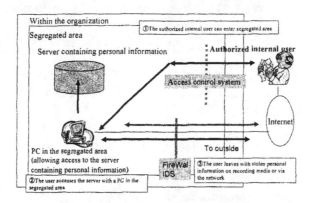

Figure 6. [Behavior Pattern of Internal Unjust Person(Type1)]

(5) Next, the risks for individuals involved when handling personal information are considered. The management risk that arises when handling personal information can be roughly classified into the following three types:

(a) First risk: risk of damage

First off is the risk of damage when personal information is leaked

(b) Second risk: cost of security measures

The cost of security measures to prevent the outflow of personal information must also be considered as a management risk when handling personal information.

(c) Third risk: burden on employees

The burden on employees produced by implementing measures must also be considered as a management risk from the perspective of work efficiency. The two types of burdens are as follows:

(a) Burden on privacy for employees accompanying measures

E-mail monitoring to prevent the leakage of personal information, for example, will lead to employee privacy not being protected and will place a burden on employees.

(b) Decline in employee convenience accompanying measures

4.2   Methods of application

In accordance with Fig. 5, application was done as indicated below. The ③ individuals involved were   (1) business manager,   (2) the firm's employees, and (3) customers.

The ④ objective function and results of constraint determination were as follows:

objective function: the sum of the risk of leakage of personal information and cost of measures satisfies constraints and is the smallest to next-to-smallest value.

Constraints:

(a) probability of leakage of personal information

(b) cost of measures

(c) burden on privacy for employees

(d) burden on convenience for employees

The proposed measures were listed up in Table 1 . In addition, values for costs for each of the proposed measures here were studied by individuals applying the MRC in consult with individuals involved, resulting in values shown in Table 1. The degree of a burden is a relative value indicated from 0 to 1 points and should use results of employee surveys.

Proposed measures	$\Delta P_{\alpha 1i}$ (Inside)	$\Delta P_{\alpha 2i}$ (Inside)	$\Delta P_{\beta i}$ (External)	Cost:Ci (M yen)	$D_1 i$	$D_2 i$
1:e-mail automatic monitoring	0.8	0.8	0.8	3.9	0.6	0
2:e-mail manual monitoring	0.95	0.95	0.95	30	1	0
3:firewall	0.9	0.9	0.9	0.75	0	0.4
4:IDS (intrusion detection system)	----	0.7	0.7	13	0	0
5: Vulnerability management	----	0.8	0.9	3.0	0	0.2
6:Prohibition of storing data in external memory	0.9	0.9	0.9	25	0	0.7
7:Entering and leaving management system	----	0.8	0.9	8	0.1	0.4
8: Check on belongings in the isolated area	0.8	0.8	0.9	30	0.8	0.6

Table 1. [List of Proposal measures]

Here is an explanation of the meaning of parameters in Table 1. Respective parameters depicted here are used for calculation of the subsequent probability of leakage, costs of measures, etc.

$\Delta P \alpha_1 i$: effects of measures on employees let into segregated areas.

$\Delta P \alpha_2 i$: effects of measures on employees not let into segregated areas.

$\Delta P \beta i$: effects of measures on external third parties who are not employees.

Cost Ci: cost of measures.

employee burden $D_1 i$: privacy burden on employees produced by implementing measures. employee burden $D_2 i$: convenience burden on employees produced by implementing measures.

A case where information leakage is caused by unauthorized internal users 1 is expressed using a fault tree[8] and is as shown in Fig. 7.

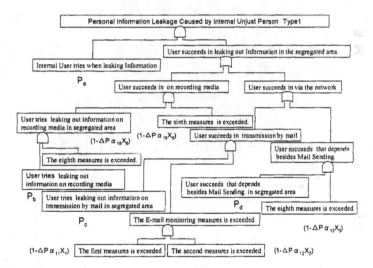

Figure 7. [Fault Tree for Personal Information Leakage Caused by Internal Unjust Person Type1]

sed on the above fault tree, the probability $P \alpha_1$ that personal information will be leaked by an internal (an employee let into a segregated area) unauthorized user can be formulated as

$$P_{\alpha_1} = P_a \left\{ \begin{array}{l} P_b \left(1 - \Delta P_{\alpha_1 8} X_8\right)\left(1 - P_{\alpha_1 6} X_6\right) + \\ P_c\left(1 - \Delta P_{\alpha_1 1} X_1\right)\left(1 - \Delta P_{\alpha_1 2} X_2\right) + P_d\left(1 - \Delta P_{\alpha_1 3} X_3\right) \end{array} \right\}$$

Similarly, the probability $P_{\alpha 2}$ and P_{β} can be formulated.

Here, we assume

Pa=0.05,Pb=0.01,Pc=0.04,Pd=0.05,Pe=0.004,,Pf=0.01,Pg=0.04,Ph=
0.05,Pi=0.01,Pj=0.5,Pk=0.01,Pl=0.1,Pm=0.4,Po=0.5,Pp=0.01.

Formulation results obtained are as shown in Fig. 8.

Minimization : $Min\{$Amount of damage $*(P_{\alpha 1}+P_{\alpha 2}+P_{\beta})+\sum_{i=1}^{8} Ci*Xi\}$

Subject to $\quad \sum_{i=1}^{8} C_i X_i \leq Ct \quad$ (Total cost of measures)

$$\sum_{i=1}^{8} D_{1i} X_i \leq D_1 \quad \text{(Degree of privacy burden)}$$

$$\sum_{i=1}^{8} D_{2i} X_i \leq D_2 \quad \text{(Degree of convenience burden)}$$

$$P_{\alpha 1} + P_{\alpha 2} + P_{\beta} \leq Pt \quad (X_i = 0,1)$$

(Probability of Information Leakage)

Figure 8. [Formulated Results]

4.3   Development of a simplified version of the MRC using Excel

Based on these formulation results, combinations with the smallest objective function, the second smallest objective function, and the third smallest objective function are determined by the method of all possible combinations while satisfying constraints using very simple prototype program based on Excel.

Excel has a feature to align values for an item (e.g. objective function value) in order of the smallest. Values not satisfying constraints can be filtered, so two or more optimal solutions can be easily determined using Excel. In this case, brute force method was used to obtain the optimal solutions, because the number of variables was small.

In addition, constraint values can be changed and easily recalculated, so optimal solutions can be determined in various cases and easily indicated to individuals involved. Furthermore, Excel is also replete with features for graphic representation, so solutions can be expressed in a relatively easy-to-understand form.

4.4 Results of application and Discussion

Next, constraints were specifically furnished and calculation performed. Here

the upper limit Ct of the cost of measures =80M yen, the upper limit Pt of the probability of leakage=0.15 (15% a year), D_1=0.3, and D_2=0.3
Results were:
The first optimal solution
Objective function value: **27,963,563**
Proposed measures adopted: 2,3,4,5,6,7
The second optimal solution
Objective function value: **39,813,235**
Proposed measures adopted: 1,3,4,5,6,7

Experiment to achieve consensus was done by role players as shown below.
Specialist :
researcher of MRC
Executive officer :
teacher at Tokyo Denki University
Employee :
student at Tokyo Denki University
Customer :
student at Tokyo Denki University

The process to obtain the consensus is as follows.
(1) The student who roles customer claimed that leakage probability should be fewer than 10% for the year. Then, the role player of the specialist calculated the optimum solution again, but first optimal solution was not changed.
(2) The student who roles employee claimed that degree of privacy burden should be under 0.15. Then, the role player of the specialist calculated the optimum solution again on the above condition. The first optimal solution was

Objective function value: **39,813,235**
Proposed measures adopted: 1,3,4,5,6,7

This first optimal solution is same as the second optimal solution of first calculation. Measure 1 "e-mail automatic monitoring" was added to the solution instead of measure 2 "e-mail manual monitoring" from the view point of employee's privacy.

This calculated result was also accepted by the role players of the executive officer and customer. Thus, consensus of all participants could be obtained.

Based on the above application and study results, the following statements regarding the MRC can be made:

(1) Handling the difficulty of formulation (Topic 1-a in Sec. 3.4): formulation is not easy, but the MRC appears applicable. Individuals applying the MRC gave the opinion that optimal solutions were sure to be obtained.

(2) Handling the uncertainty of effects (Topic 1-b) and constraint ambiguity (2-a): Of the various opinions voiced by individuals involved, individuals applying the MRC had the impression that problems of the uncertainty of effects of measures and constraint ambiguity could be resolved to some extent by changing values and determining new solutions, although this must also be confirmed through future testing.

(3) Handing of consideration of unquantified factors (2-b): individuals applying the MRC had the opinion that features to obtain not just the first optimal solution but the second - - the Lth optimal solution would be preferable since solutions could be selected from the first — the Lth optimum while considering factors that could not be formulated. This point must be confirmed through testing with a number of users.

(4) Handling the method of quickly reaching a solution that satisfies an individual involved (2-c) and resolution of disagreement between groups in terms of solutions (2-d): There were strong opinions that features allowing conditions to be changed and results immediately displayed would be effective in bundling satisfactory solutions, although the order in which they would be shown is currently being studied and is a topic for the future. In addition, individuals involved were curious about assumptions with which optimal solutions were determined, although how they can be shown effectively is also a topic for the future.

During the current trial application of the MRC, two specific settings where the MRC could be used were envisioned:

(a) When think tanks are commissioned by government bodies to make proposals to government bodies. This often leads to macro-models targeting the entire country of Japan.

(b) When an SI firm proposes systems accounting for risks to receive orders from a firm's system. This often leads to micro-models focusing on corporate environments.

5.   CONCLUSION

Preceding sections have described the features an MRC should have, a simple prototype program based on Excel to support it, and results of its trial application.

Development Concept for and trial application of a "mulutiplex risk 15
communicator"

There are plans to do the following work in the future:

(1) Apply the MRC in another 2-3 examples (for example, Illegal copy protection problem) and verify the features than an MRC should have.

(2) Improve the prototype program to make it possible to solve larger problems and to make it easy to use for risk communication.

Research themes for MRC are extremely difficult, but they are essential themes that must be dealt with in the future, so research will actively proceed.

The current research was conceived during work of the Safety and Security Working Group of the Application Security Forum (ASF) and is a deeper study of Mission Program II , Clarification and Resolution of Vulnerabilities of an Advanced Information Society, of the Japan Science and Technology Agency's Research Institute of Science and Technology for Society.

As research proceeds, the authors wish to thank individuals like Professor Norihisa Doi of Chuo University for their valued opinions.

References

1) R. Sasaki: Discussion regarding the relationship between security and personal information protection, Institute of Electronics, Information, and Communication Engineers, Technical Report SITE2003-14, pp1-6, Oct. 2003 (in Japanese)

2) J. Ross: The Polar Bear Strategy, Preceus Books Publishing, 1999

3)http://www.nrc.gov/reading-rm/doc-collections/nuregs/brochures/br0308/#chapter_1

4) http://web.sfc.keio.ac.jp/~hfukui/class/riskmg/risk.pdf (in Japanese)

5)http://www.riskworld.com/books/topics/riskcomm.htm

6) http://excellent.com.utk.edu/~mmmiller/bib.html

7) R. Sasaki: MRC development concepts, Institute of Electronics, Information, and Communication Engineers, SCIS2004 (in Japanese)

8) N.J. McCormick: Reliability and Risk Analysis, Academic Press Inc., (1981)

9) R.S. Garfinkel et al.: Integer Programming, Wiley and Sons, (1972)

10) Y. Kodama: Introductory system dynamics—Science to take on complex social systems, Kodansha Blue Back, (1984) (in Japanese)

Index of Authors

Adam, Otmar 63
Adams, Nicholas 265
Akahane, Yasuhiko 203
Apostolou, Dimitris 141
Askounis, Dimitrios 361

Baines, Susan 297
Balopoulos, Theodoros 187
Batini, Carlo 313
Bechini, Alessio 497
Braubach, Lars 235

Carlisle, George 251
Cha, Shi-Cho 559
Chikova, Pavlina 63
Cimino, Mario Giovanni C. A. 497

Damsgaard, Jan 435
De Santis, Luca 313
Dewan, Mohammed 1
Dritsas, Stelios 187

Gannon-Leary, Pat 297
Gao, Ping 435
Glassey, Olivier 125
Gordijn, Jaap 17, 449
Gritzalis, Stefanos 187
Gruhn, Volker 33
Gye, Hang Hong 49
Gymnopoulos, Lazaros 187

Hidaka, Yuu 607
Hofer, Anja 63
Hsu, Chin Chao 559
Huriaux, Thomas 591

Ishii, Saneyuki 607
Ito, Masumi 389
Ivanyukovich, Alexander 329

Johnston, Jim 265

Kaffai, Bettina 111
Kamada, Aqueo 157
Karyda, Maria 187
Kokalakis, S. 187
Kumar, Narendra 527
Kumar, Satyanaga 527

Lambrinoudakis, C. 187
Lamersdorf, Winfried 235
Lassila, Aki 543
Lee, Han-Chao 559
Li, Juanzi 571
Lin, Raymund 559
Lobo, Tomas Periente 141
Lupo, Caterina 313

Macintosh, Ann   265
Madeira, Edmundo   173
Marchese, Maurizio   329
Matheis, Thomas   111
Meier, Andreas   375
Mendes, Manuel   157
Milosevic, Zoran   235
Miro, Jofre Casas   141
Molina-Jimenez, Carlos   79
Morgan, Graham   79
Murakami, Yosuke   421
Murayama, Yuuku   607

Ndeti, Mkwana   251
Nieuwenhuis, Lambert J.M.   345

Oya, Makoto   389, 421
Ozaki, Masami   203

Paalvast, Edwin   17
Pankowski, Tadeusz   481
Papadakis, Andreas   141
Parhonyi, Robert   345
Parkin, Simon   79
Picard, Willy   591
Podgayetskaya, Tatyana   219
Pokahr, Alexander   235
Polemi, Despina   513
Pras, Aiko   345
Psarras, John   361

Raghavan, S.V.   281
Reddy, Annapareddy Vasudhara   281
Rigopoulos, George   361

Rykowski, Jarogniew 95, 405

Sasaki, Ryoichi 203, 607
Santos, Ivo 173
Sääksjärvi, Markku 543
Seel, Christian 111
Semoto, Koji 203
Skene, James 79
Soetendal, Jasper 17
Stojanovic, Ljiljana 141
Stormer, Henrik 375
Stucky, Wolffried 219
Sung, Ho Ha 49
Svobodova, Liba xxi

Tait, Bobby 465
Takada, Yusuke 421
Thomas, Olivier 111
Tomasi, Andrea 497
Tsai, Tse-Ming 559
Tschammer, Volker 173
Tung, Hung-Wen 559

Wang, Kehong 571
Weber, Thorsten 33
Weiss, Kurt xxiii
Werro, Nicolas 375
Wieringa, Roel 449
Wilson, Rob 297
Wu, Baolin 1

Vaccari, Lorenzino 329
Van Eck, Pascal 449
Vanderhaeghen, Dominik 63
Valvis, George 513

Index of Authors   627

Venkataram, Pallapa   527
Von Solms, Basie   465

Yajima, Hiroshi   607
Yamamoto, Rieko   449
Yang, Yun   1
Yasu, Kenji   203
Yoshiura, Hiroshi   607

Zhang, Po   571
Zang, Sven   63